21st Nordic Conference of Computational Linguistics (NODALIDA 2017)

NEALT Proceedings Series Volume 29

Gothenburg, Sweden
23 – 24 May 2017

Editor:

Jorg Tiedemann

ISBN: 978-1-5108-4170-3

NoDaLiDa 2017

**21st Nordic Conference of
Computational Linguistics**

Proceedings of the Conference

23 – 24 May 2017
Wallenberg Conference Center
Gothenburg, Sweden

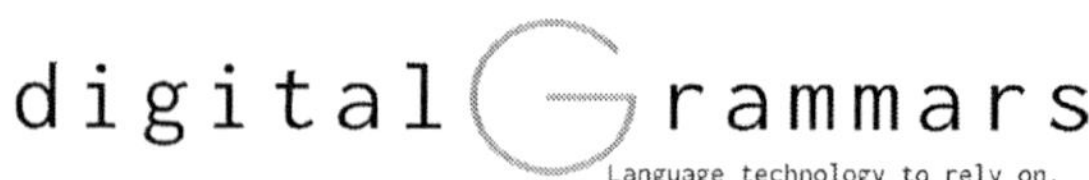

Introduction

On behalf of the program committee, I am pleased to welcome you to the 21st Nordic Conference on Computational Linguistics (NoDaLiDa 2017), held at the Wallenberg Conference Center in the beautiful city of Gothenburg in Sweden, on May 22–24, 2017. The proceedings are published as part of the NEALT Proceedings Series by Linköping University Electronic Press and they will also be available from the ACL Anthology together with the proceedings of the co-located workshops. The NoDaLiDa conference has been organized bi-annually since 1977 and returns to this anniversary event after 40 years back to Gothenburg, where it started as a friendly gathering to discuss on-going research in the field of computational linguistics in the Nordic countries. The Northern European Association for Language Technology (NEALT) was founded later in 2006, which is now responsible for organizing NoDaLiDa among other events in the Nordic countries, the Baltic states and Northwest Russia. Since the early days, NoDaLiDa has grown into a recognized international conference and the tradition continues with the program of this year's conference. It is a great honor for me to serve as the general chair of NoDaLiDa 2017 and I am grateful for all the support during the progress.

Before diving deeper into the acknowledgements, please, let me first briefly introduce the setup of the conference. Similar to the last edition, we included different paper categories to be presented: Regular long papers, student papers, short papers and system demonstration papers. Regular papers are presented orally during the conference and short papers received a slot in one of the two poster sessions. System demonstrations are given at the same time as the posters. We selected two student papers for an oral presentation and three student papers for poster presentations. In total, we received 78 submissions and accepted 49. The submissions included 32 regular papers (21 accepted, 65.6% acceptance rate), 8 student papers (5 accepted, 62.5% acceptance rate), 27 short papers (12 accepted, 44.4% acceptance rate) and 11 system demonstration papers (which we accepted all).

In addition to the submitted papers, NoDaLiDa 2017 also features invited keynote speakers – three distinguished international researchers: Kyunghyun Cho from New York University, Sharon Goldwater from the University of Edinburgh and Rada Mihalcea from the University of Michigan. We are excited about their contributions and grateful for their participation in the conference.

Furthermore, four workshops are connected to NoDaLiDa 2017: The First Workshop on Universal Dependencies (UDW 2017), the Joint 6th Workshop on NLP for CALL and 2nd Workshop on NLP for Research on Language Acquisition (NLP4CALL & LA), the Workshop on Processing Historical Language and the Workshop on Constraint Grammar - Methods, Tools, and Applications. We would like to thank the workshop organizers for their efforts in making these events happen enriching the whole conference and its scientific coverage.

Finally, I would also like to thank the entire team behind the conference. Organizing such an event is a complex process and would not be possible without the help of many people. I would like to thank all members of the program committee, especially Beáta Megyesi for a smooth transition from the previous NoDaLiDa and all her valuable input coming from the organization of that event, Inguna Skadiņa for taking care of the submission system EasyChair, Lilja Øvrelid for the publicity and calls that we need to send out. My greatest relieve from organisational pain came from the professional local committee in Gothenburg. It is a pleasure to work together with their team and without the hard work of the local organizers we could not run the event in any way. Thank you very much and especially thanks to Nina Tahmasebi for leading the local team. All names are properly listed below and I am grateful to all of you and your efforts. I would also like to acknowledge the large number of reviewers and sub-reviewers for their assessment of the submissions, NEALT for backing up the conference, Linköping University Press for publishing the proceedings as well as people behind the ACL Anthology for offering the space for storing our publications. And, last but not least, I would also thank our sponsors for all the financial support, which really helped us to organize a pleasant and affordable meeting.

With all of these acknowledgments, and with my apologies for forgetting to mention many names that should be listed here, I would like to wish you all, once again, a fruitful conference and a nice stay in Gothenburg. And I wish you a lot of pleasure with reading the contributions in this volume especially if you, for whatever reason, happen to read this welcome address after the conference has already ended.

Jörg Tiedemann (general chair of NoDaLiDa 2017)

Welcome Message by the Local Organizers

40 years ago, the first NoDaLiDa conference took place here in Gothenburg, arranged by what is now Språkbanken, the Swedish Language Bank. The aim of the conference was to bring together researchers from the five Nordic countries to discuss all aspects of language technology. Experiences and results with respect to the Nordic languages would benefit from being shared, compared and discussed. The community has grown and expanded since; today, NoDaLiDa brings together researchers and practitioners from 23 countries and a diverse field of studies. The first meeting attracted over 60 people and the current installment has more than doubled that amount. Though the field has developed, many of the topics raised in 1977 are still highly relevant and interesting today. For example, the creation of lexical resources, sense disambiguation and syntactic analysis, and analysis of large amounts of text. To celebrate the 40th anniversary of NoDaLiDa, we are happy to welcome you back to Gothenburg and this 21st edition of the conference. We hope that Gothenburg will show its most beautiful side, offering you sunshine, vast views of the sea and good food. We hope that you will enjoy interesting talks, posters and workshops during these three days of NoDaLiDa, which will provide inspiration in the 40 years to come. Welcome!

Nina Tahmasebi
Yvonne Adesam
Martin Kaså
on behalf of the local organizers

General Chair:

Jörg Tiedemann, University of Helsinki, Finland

Program Committee:

Jón Guðnason, Reykjavik University, Iceland
Beáta Megyesi, Uppsala University, Sweden
Kadri Muischnek, University of Tartu, Estonia
Inguna Skadiņa, University of Latvia, Latvia
Anders Søgaard, University of Copenhagen, Denmark
Andrius Utka, Vytautas Magnus University, Lithuania
Lilja Øvrelid, University of Oslo, Norway

Organizing Committee:

Nina Tahmasebi (chair), University of Gothenburg, Sweden
Yvonne Adesam (co-chair), University of Gothenburg, Sweden
Martin Kaså (co-chair), University of Gothenburg, Sweden
Sven Lindström (publication chair), University of Gothenburg, Sweden
Elena Volodina (sponsor chair), University of Gothenburg, Sweden
Lars Borin, University of Gothenburg, Sweden
Dana Dannélls, University of Gothenburg, Sweden
Ildikó Pilán, University of Gothenburg, Sweden

Invited Speaker:

Rada Mihalcea, University of Michigan
Kyunghyun Cho, New York University
Sharon Goldwater, University of Edinburgh

Reviewers:

Lars Ahrenberg, Linköping University
Tanel Alumäe, Tallinn University of Technology
Isabelle Augenstein, University College London
Ilze Auziņa, University of Latvia
Joachim Bingel, University of Copenhagen
Johannes Bjerva, University of Groningen
Bernd Bohnet, Google
Chloé Braud, University of Copenhagen
Lin Chen, UIC
Koenraad De Smedt, University of Bergen
Rodolfo Delmonte, Universita' Ca' Foscari
Leon Derczynski, University of Sheffield
Jens Edlund, Royal Technical Institute (KTH), Stockholm
Murhaf Fares, University of Oslo
Björn Gambäck, Norwegian University of Science and Technology
Filip Ginter, University of Turku
Gintarė Grigonytė, University of Stockholm
Normunds Grūzītis, University of Latvia
Angelina Ivanova, University of Oslo
Richard Johansson, University of Gothenburg
Sofie Johansson, Institutionen för svenska språket
Arne Jönsson, Linöping University
Heiki-Jaan Kaalep, University of Tartu
Jussi Karlgren, Gavagai & KTH Stockholm
Sigrid Klerke, University of Copenhagen
Mare Koit, University of Tartu
Andrey Kutuzov, University of Oslo
Ophélie Lacroix, University of Copenhagen
Emanuele Lapponi, University of Oslo
Krister Lindén, University of Helsinki
Pierre Lison, Norwegian Computing Center
Kaili Müürisep, University of Tartu
Costanza Navarretta, University of Copenhagen
Joakim Nivre, Uppsala University
Pierre Nugues, Lund University
Stephan Oepen, Universitetet i Oslo
Heili Orav, University of Tartu
Patrizia Paggio, University of Copenhagen
Eva Pettersson, Uppsala University
Mārcis Pinnis, Tilde
Tommi Pirinen, Universität Hamburg
Fabio Rinaldi, IFI, University of Zurich
Eiríkur Rögnvaldsson, University of Iceland
Marina Santini, SICS East ICT
Kairit Sirts, Tallinn University of Technology
Raivis Skadiņš, Tilde
Sara Stymne, Uppsala University
Torbjørn Svendsen, Norwegian University of Science and Technology
Andrius Utka, Vytautas Magnus University
Erik Velldal, University of Oslo

Sumithra Velupillai, KTH Royal Institute of Technology, Stockholm
Martin Volk, University of Zurich
Jürgen Wedekind, University of Copenhagen
Mats Wirén, Stockholm University
Roman Yangarber, University of Helsinki
Gustaf Öqvist Seimyr, Karolinska Institutet
Robert Östling, Stockholm University

Additional Reviewers:

Amrhein, Chantal
Fahlborg, Daniel
Klang, Marcus
Mascarell, Laura
Mitchell, Jeff
Pretkalniņa, Lauma
Vare, Kadri
Waseem, Zeerak

Table of Contents

Regular Papers

Student Papers

Short Papers

System Demonstration Papers

Conference Program

Tuesday, May 23, 2017

9:10–9:30   Opening Remarks

9:30–10:30   Invited Talk by Kyunghyun Cho

Session 1: Syntax

11:00–11:30   *Joint UD Parsing of Norwegian Bokmål and Nynorsk*
Erik Velldal, Lilja Øvrelid and Petter Hohle

11:30–12:00   *Replacing OOV Words For Dependency Parsing With Distributional Semantics*
Prasanth Kolachina, Martin Riedl and Chris Biemann

12:00–12:30   *Real-valued Syntactic Word Vectors (RSV) for Greedy Neural Dependency Parsing*
Ali Basirat and Joakim Nivre

Session 2: Semantics and Discourse

11:00–11:30   *Tagging Named Entities in 19th Century and Modern Finnish Newspaper Material with a Finnish Semantic Tagger*
Kimmo Kettunen and Laura Löfberg

11:30–12:00   *Machine Learning for Rhetorical Figure Detection: More Chiasmus with Less Annotation*
Marie Dubremetz and Joakim Nivre

12:00–12:30   *Coreference Resolution for Swedish and German using Distant Supervision*
Alexander Wallin and Pierre Nugues

Tuesday, May 23, 2017 (continued)

Session 6: Machine Translation

13:30–14:00   *North-Sámi to Finnish rule-based machine translation system*
Tommi Pirinen, Francis M. Tyers, Trond Trosterud, Ryan Johnson, Kevin Unhammer and
Tiina Puolakainen

14:00–14:30   *Machine translation with North Saami as a pivot language*
Lene Antonsen, Ciprian Gerstenberger, Maja Kappfjell, Sandra Nystø Ráhka, Marja-Liisa
Olthuis, Trond Trosterud and Francis M. Tyers

14:30–15:00   Lightning Talks

15:30–16:30   Posters and System Demonstrations

16:30–17:15   Tutorial on Swedish, Maia Andreasson

17:15–18:00   SIG Meetings

Wednesday, May 24, 2017

9:00–10:00   Invited Talk by Sharon Goldwater

10:00–10:30   Lightning Talks

10:30–11:30   Posters and System Demonstrations

11:30–12:30   NEALT Business Meeting

12:30–13:30   Lunch

Wednesday, May 24, 2017 (continued)

Session 7: Syntax

13:30–14:00   *SWEGRAM –A Web-Based Tool for Automatic Annotation and Analysis of Swedish Texts*
Jesper Näsman, Beáta Megyesi and Anne Palmér

14:00–14:30   *Optimizing a PoS Tagset for Norwegian Dependency Parsing*
Petter Hohle, Lilja Øvrelid and Erik Velldal

14:30–15:00   *Creating register sub-corpora for the Finnish Internet Parsebank*
Veronika Laippala, Juhani Luotolahti, Aki-Juhani Kyröläinen, Tapio Salakoski and Filip Ginter

Session 8: NLP Applications

13:30–14:00   *KILLE: a Framework for Situated Agents for Learning Language Through Interaction*
Simon Dobnik and Erik de Graaf

14:00–14:30   *Data Collection from Persons with Mild Forms of Cognitive Impairment and Healthy Controls - Infrastructure for Classification and Prediction of Dementia*
Dimitrios Kokkinakis, Kristina Lundholm Fors, Eva Björkner and Arto Nordlund

14:30–15:00   *Evaluation of language identification methods using 285 languages*
Tommi Jauhiainen, Krister Lindén and Heidi Jauhiainen

Session 9: NLP Applications

13:30–14:00   *Can We Create a Tool for General Domain Event Analysis?*
Siim Orasmaa and Heiki-Jaan Kaalep

14:00–14:30   *From Treebank to Propbank: A Semantic-Role and VerbNet Corpus for Danish*
Eckhard Bick

15:30–16:30   Invited Talk by Rada Mihalcea

16:30–17:00   Best Paper Awards and Closing Remarks

Tuesday, May 23, 2017

Poster Session 1

15:30–16:30   *Cross-lingual Learning of Semantic Textual Similarity with Multilingual Word Representations*
Johannes Bjerva and Robert Östling

15:30–16:30   *Will my auxiliary tagging task help? Estimating Auxiliary Tasks Effectivity in Multi-Task Learning*
Johannes Bjerva

15:30–16:30   *Iconic Locations in Swedish Sign Language: Mapping Form to Meaning with Lexical Databases*
Carl Börstell and Robert Östling

15:30–16:30   *Docforia: A Multilayer Document Model*
Marcus Klang and Pierre Nugues

15:30–16:30   *Finnish resources for evaluating language model semantics*
Viljami Venekoski and Jouko Vankka

15:30–16:30   *Málrómur: A Manually Verified Corpus of Recorded Icelandic Speech*
Steinþór Steingrímsson, Jón Guðnason, Sigrún Helgadóttir and Eiríkur Rögnvaldsson

15:30–16:30   *The Effect of Translationese on Tuning for Statistical Machine Translation*
Sara Stymne

System Demonstrations 1

15:30–16:30   *Multilingwis2 –Explore Your Parallel Corpus*
Johannes Graën, Dominique Sandoz and Martin Volk

15:30–16:30   *A modernised version of the Glossa corpus search system*
Anders Nøklestad, Kristin Hagen, Janne Bondi Johannessen, Michał Kosek and Joel Priestley

15:30–16:30   *Dep_search: Efficient Search Tool for Large Dependency Parsebanks*
Juhani Luotolahti, Jenna Kanerva and Filip Ginter

Tuesday, May 23, 2017 (continued)

15:30–16:30   *Proto-Indo-European Lexicon: The Generative Etymological Dictionary of Indo-European Languages*
Jouna Pyysalo

15:30–16:30   *Tilde MODEL - Multilingual Open Data for EU Languages*
Roberts Rozis and Raivis Skadiņš

Wednesday, May 24, 2017

Poster Session 2

10:30–11:30   *Mainstreaming August Strindberg with Text Normalization*
Adam Ek and Sofia Knuutinen

10:30–11:30   *Word vectors, reuse, and replicability: Towards a community repository of large-text resources*
Murhaf Fares, Andrey Kutuzov, Stephan Oepen and Erik Velldal

10:30–11:30   *Improving Optical Character Recognition of Finnish Historical Newspapers with a Combination of Fraktur & Antiqua Models and Image Preprocessing*
Mika Koistinen, Kimmo Kettunen and Tuula Pääkkönen

10:30–11:30   *Redefining Context Windows for Word Embedding Models: An Experimental Study*
Pierre Lison and Andrey Kutuzov

10:30–11:30   *The Effect of Excluding Out of Domain Training Data from Supervised Named-Entity Recognition*
Adam Persson

10:30–11:30   *Quote Extraction and Attribution from Norwegian Newspapers*
Andrew Salway, Paul Meurer, Knut Hofland and Øystein Reigem

10:30–11:30   *Wordnet extension via word embeddings: Experiments on the Norwegian Wordnet*
Heidi Sand, Erik Velldal and Lilja Øvrelid

10:30–11:30   *Universal Dependencies for Swedish Sign Language*
Robert Östling, Carl Börstell, Moa Gärdenfors and Mats Wirén

Joint UD Parsing of Norwegian Bokmål and Nynorsk

Erik Velldal and **Lilja Øvrelid** and **Petter Hohle**
University of Oslo
Department of Informatics
{erikve,liljao,pettehoh}@ifi.uio.no

Abstract

This paper investigates interactions in parser performance for the two official standards for written Norwegian: Bokmål and Nynorsk. We demonstrate that while applying models across standards yields poor performance, combining the training data for both standards yields better results than previously achieved for each of them in isolation. This has immediate practical value for processing Norwegian, as it means that a single parsing pipeline is sufficient to cover both varieties, with no loss in accuracy. Based on the Norwegian Universal Dependencies treebank we present results for multiple taggers and parsers, experimenting with different ways of varying the training data given to the learners, including the use of machine translation.

1 Introduction

There are two official written standards of the Norwegian language; Bokmål (literally 'book tongue') and Nynorsk (literally 'new Norwegian'). While Bokmål is the main variety, roughly 15% of the Norwegian population uses Nynorsk. However, language legislation specifies that minimally 25% of the written public service information should be in Nynorsk. The same minimum ratio applies to the programming of the Norwegian Public Broadcasting Corporation (NRK).

The two varieties are so closely related that they may in practice be regarded as 'written dialects'. However, lexically there can be relatively large differences. Figure 1 shows an example sentence in both Bokmål and Nynorsk. While the word order is identical and many of the words are clearly related, we see that only 2 out of 9 word forms are identical. When quantifying the degree of lexical overlap with respect to the treebank data we

will be using, (Section 3) we find that out of the 6741 non-punctuation word forms in the Nynorsk development set, 4152, or 61.6%, of these are unknown when measured against the Bokmål training set. For comparison, the corresponding proportion of unknown word forms in the Bokmål development set is 36.3%. These lexical differences are largely caused by differences in productive inflectional forms, as well as highly frequent functional words like pronouns and determiners.

In this paper we demonstrate that Bokmål and Nynorsk are different enough that parsers trained on data for a given standard alone can not be applied to the other standard without a vast drop in accuracy. At the same time, we demonstrate that they are similar enough that mixing the training data for both standards yields better performance. This also reduces the complexity required for parsing Norwegian, in that a single pipeline is enough. When processing mixed texts (as is typically the case in any real-world setting), the alternatives are to either (a) maintain two distinct pipelines and select the right one by applying an initial step of language identification (for each document, say), or (b) use a single-standard pipeline only and accept a substantial loss in accuracy (on the order of 20–25 percentage points in LAS and 15 points in tagger accuracy) whenever text of the non-matched standard is encountered.

In addition to simply combining the labeled training data as is, we also assess the feasibility of applying machine translation to increase the amount of available data for each variety. All final models and data sets used in this paper are made available online.[1]

2 Previous Work

Cross-lingual parsing has previously been proposed both for closely related source-target lan-

---

[1]https://github.com/erikve/bm-nn-parsing

Proceedings of the 21st Nordic Conference of Computational Linguistics, pages 1–10,
Gothenburg, Sweden, 23-24 May 2017. ©2017 Linköping University Electronic Press

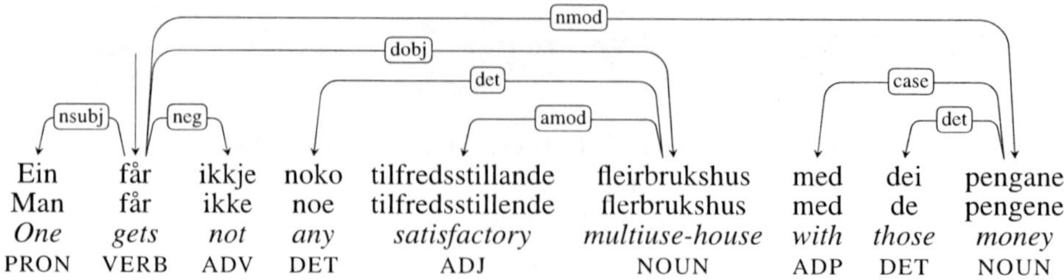

Figure 1: Example sentence in Nynorsk (top row) and Bokmål (second row) with corresponding English gloss, UD PoS and dependency analysis.

guage pairs and less related languages. This task has been approached via so-called 'annotation projection', where parallel data is used to induce structure from source to target language (Hwa et al., 2005; Spreyer et al., 2010; Agić et al., 2016) and as delexicalized model transfer (Zeman and Resnik, 2008; Søgaard, 2011; Täckström et al., 2012). The basic procedure in the latter work has relied on a simple conversion procedure to map part-of-speech tags of the source and target languages into a common tagset and subsequent training of a delexicalized parser on (a possibly filtered version of) the source treebank. Zeman and Resnik (2008) applied this approach to the highly related language pair of Swedish and Danish, and Skjærholt and Øvrelid (2012) extended the language inventory to also include Norwegian, and showed that parser lexicalization actually improved parsing results between these languages.

The release of universal representations for PoS tags (Petrov et al., 2012) and dependency syntax (Nivre et al., 2016) has enabled research in cross-lingual parsing that does not require a language-specific conversion procedure. Tiedemann et al. (2014) utilize statistical MT for treebank translation in order to train cross-lingual parsers for a range of language pairs. Ammar et al. (2016) employ a combination of cross-lingual word clusters and embeddings, language-specific features and typological information in a neural network architecture where one and the same parser is used to parse many languages.

In this work the focus is on cross-standard, rather than cross-lingual, parsing. The two standards of Norwegian can be viewed as two highly related languages, which share quite a few lexical items, hence we assume that parser lexicalization will be beneficial. Like Tiedemann et al. (2014), we experiment with machine translation of train-

ing data, albeit using a rule-based MT system with no word alignments. Our main goal is to arrive at the best joint model that may be applied to both Norwegian standards.

3 The Norwegian UD Treebank

Universal Dependencies (UD) (de Marneffe et al., 2014; Nivre, 2015) is a community-driven effort to create cross-linguistically consistent syntactic annotation. Our experiments are based on the Universal Dependency conversion (Øvrelid and Hohle, 2016) of the Norwegian Dependency Treebank (NDT) (Solberg et al., 2014).

NDT contains manually annotated syntactic and morphological information for both varieties of Norwegian; 311,000 tokens of Bokmål and 303,000 tokens of Nynorsk. The treebanked material mostly comprises newspaper text, but also includes government reports, parliament transcripts and blog excerpts. The UD version of NDT has until now been limited to the Bokmål sections of the treebank. For the purpose of the current work, the Nynorsk section has also been automatically converted to Universal Dependencies, making use of the conversion software described in Øvrelid and Hohle (2016) with minor modifications.[2]

UD conversion of NDT Nynorsk Figure 1 provides the UD graph for our Nynorsk example sentence. The NDT and UD schemes differ in terms of both PoS tagset and morphological features, as well as structural analyses. The conversion therefore requires non-trivial transformations of the dependency trees, in addition to mappings of tags and labels that make reference to a combination

____
[2]The data used for these experiments follows the UD v1.4 guidelines, but its first release as a UD treebank will be in v2.0. For replicability we therefore make our data available from the companion Git repository.

of various kinds of linguistic information. For instance, in terms of PoS tags, the UD scheme offers a dedicated tag for proper nouns (PROPN), where NDT contains information about noun type among its morphological features. UD further distinguishes auxiliary verbs (AUX) from main verbs (VERB). This distinction is not explicitly made in NDT, hence the conversion procedure makes use of the syntactic context of a verb; verbs that have a non-finite dependent are marked as auxiliaries.

Among the main tenets of UD is the primacy of content-words. This means that content words, as opposed to function words, are syntactic heads wherever possible, e.g., choosing main verbs as heads, instead of auxiliary verbs and promoting prepositional complements to head status instead of the preposition (which is annotated as a case marker, see Figure 1). The NDT annotation scheme, on the other hand, largely favors functional heads and in this respect differs structurally from the UD scheme in a number of important ways. The structural conversion is implemented as a cascade of rules that employ a small set of graph operations that reverse, reattach, delete and add arcs, followed by a relation conversion procedure over the modified graph structures (Øvrelid and Hohle, 2016). It involves the conversion of verbal groups, copula constructions, prepositions and their complements, predicative constructions and coordination, as well as the introduction of specialized dependency labels for passive arguments, particles and relative clauses.

Since the annotation found in the Bokmål and Nynorsk sections of NDT follow the same set of guidelines, the conversion requires only minor modifications of the conversion code described in Øvrelid and Hohle (2016). These modifications target (a) a small set of morphological features that have differing naming conventions, e.g., *ent* vs *eint* for singular number, and *be* vs *bu* for definiteness, and (b) rules that make reference to closed class lemmas, such as quantificational pronouns and possessive pronouns.

4 Experimental Setup

This section briefly outlines some key components of our experimental setup. We will be reporting results of two pipelines for tagging and parsing – one based on TnT and Mate and one based on UDPipe – described in the following.

TnT & Mate The widely used TnT tagger (Brants, 2000), implementing a 2nd order Markov model, achieves high accuracy as well as very high speed. TnT was used by Petrov et al. (2012) when evaluating the proposed universal tag set. Solberg et al. (2014) found the Mate dependency parser (Bohnet, 2010) to have the best performance for parsing of NDT, and recent dependency parser comparisons (Choi et al., 2015) have also found Mate to perform very well for English. The fast training time of Mate also facilitates rapid experimentation. Mate implements the second-order maximum spanning tree dependency parsing algorithm of Carreras (2007) with the passive-aggressive perceptron algorithm of Crammer et al. (2006) implemented with a hash kernel for faster processing times (Bohnet, 2010).

UDPipe UDPipe (Straka et al., 2016) provides an open-source C++ implementation of an entire end-to-end pipeline for dependency parsing. All components are trainable and default settings are provided based on tuning towards the UD treebanks. The two components of UDPipe used in our experiments comprise the MorphoDiTa tagger (Straková et al., 2014) and the Parsito parser (Straka et al., 2015).

MorphoDiTa implements an averaged perceptron algorithm (Collins, 2002) while Parsito is a greedy transition-based parser based on the neural network classifier described by Chen and Manning (2014). When training the components, we use the same parametrization as reported in Straka et al. (2016) after tuning the parser for version 1.2 of the Bokmål UD data. For the parser, this includes form embeddings of dimension 50, PoS tag, FEATS and arc label embeddings of dimension 20, and a 200-node hidden layer. For each experiment, we pre-train the form embeddings on the training data (i.e., the raw text of whatever portion of the labeled training data is used for a given experiment) using word2vec (Mikolov et al., 2013), again with the same parameters as reported by Straka et al. (2015) for a skipgram model with a window of ten context words.

Parser training on predicted tags All parsers evaluated in this paper are both tested *and* trained using PoS tags predicted by a tagger rather than gold tags. Training on predicted tags makes the training set-up correspond more closely to a realistic test setting and makes it possible for the parser to adapt to errors made by the tagger. While this is often achieved using jackknifing (n-fold training and tagging of the labeled training data), we here simply apply the taggers to the very same data they have been trained on, reflecting the 'training error' of the taggers. We have found that training on such 'silver-standard' tags improves parsing scores substantially compared to training on gold tags (Hohle et al., 2017). In fact, Straka et al. (2016) also found that this set-up actually yields higher parsing scores compared to 10-fold tagging of the training data. Of course, the test sets for which we evaluate the performance is still unseen data for the taggers.

Data split　For Bokmål we use the same split for training, development and testing as defined for NDT by Hohle et al. (2017). As no pre-defined split was established for Nynorsk we defined this ourselves, following the same 80-10-10 proportions and also taking care to preserve contiguous texts in the various sections while also keeping them balanced in terms of genre.

Evaluation　The taggers are evaluated in terms of tagging accuracy (*Acc* in the following tables) while the parsers are evaluated by labeled and unlabeled attachment score (*LAS* and *UAS*). For the TnT tagger, accuracy is computed with the `tnt-diff` script of the TnT-distribution, and scores are computed over the base PoS tags, disregarding morphological features. Mate is evaluated using the MaltEval tool (Nilsson and Nivre, 2008). For the second pipeline, we rely on UDPipe's built-in evaluation support, which also implements MaltEval.

5　Initial experiments

5.1　'Cross-standard' parsing

This section presents the initial results of tagging and parsing the two written standards for Norwegian – Bokmål (BM) and Nynorsk (NN). Table 1 shows the results for both TnT+Mate and UDPipe. In both cases, we also show the effect of 'cross-standard' training and testing, i.e., training models on the Bokmål data and testing them on the Nynorsk data, and *vice versa*.

Across all metrics and data configurations, we see that UDPipe performs slightly better than TnT+Mate, but in particular with respect to tagger accuracy. However, a direct comparison of the scores is not really meaningful, for several rea-

	Train	Test	Acc	LAS	UAS
TnT+Mate	BM	BM	96.67	84.13	87.34
		NN	81.02	59.96	67.26
	NN	NN	95.81	82.09	85.39
		BM	79.73	59.85	66.02
UDPipe	BM	BM	97.55	84.16	87.07
		NN	83.06	61.11	68.61
	NN	NN	97.11	82.63	85.56
		BM	82.17	62.04	68.67

Table 1: Results on the UD development data for tagging and parsing the two written standards for Norwegian, Bokmål (BM) and Nynorsk (NN), including 'cross-standard' training and testing.

sons. First, the UDPipe components make use of more of the information available in the training data than TnT+Mate. For example, the tagger uses information about lemmas, while both the tagger and parser use morphological features. In addition, UDPipe is trained with the development set as validation data, selecting models from the iterations with the best performance.

More interestingly, for both pipelines we see that performance suffers dramatically when a model trained for one variety is applied to the other. This means that one can not assume (as is sometimes done, often by necessity due to unavailable resources) that tools created for, say, Bokmål can be applied to Nynorsk without a substantial increase in errors.

5.2　The effect of data size

To gauge the effect that the size of the training set has on the performance of taggers and parsers applied to the Norwegian UD treebank, we computed learning curves where models are trained on partitions that are created by successively halving the training set (selecting every nth sentence). With data set size shown on a logarithmic scale, Figure 2 plots both tagger accuracy (left) and parser LAS (right) – where Mate and the UDPipe parser (Parsito) are applied to the tags predicted by TnT and the UDPipe tagger (MorphoDiTa) respectively. Note that the word embeddings used by Parsito are pre-trained on the corresponding subset of training data for each run.

A couple of interesting things can immediately be gleaned from these results: We see that while the TnT+Mate pipeline seems to be doing better than UDPipe when training on the smaller partitions, UDPipe outperforms TnT+Mate when train-

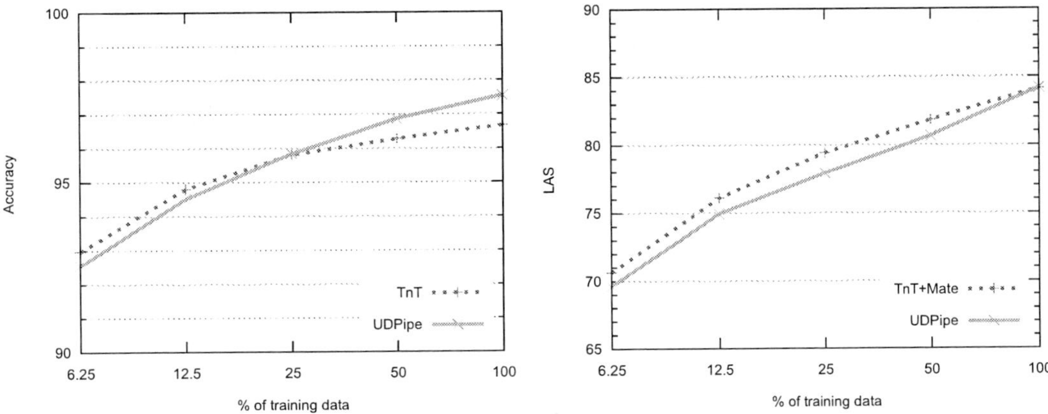

Figure 2: Learning curves when training the two pipelines TnT+Mate and UDPipe on successively halved partitions of the Norwegian Bokmål training set (using a log scale), while testing on the development set. UPoS tagging accuracy to the left; labeled attachment score to the right.

ing on the full training set. Moreover, in all cases, we observe a roughly log-linear trend where improvements are close to being constant for each n-fold increase of data. The trends also seem to indicate that having access to even more labeled data could improve performance further.

5.3 Motivating the further experiments

The 'cross-standard' experiments in Section 5.1 showed that models trained on labeled data for one of the two varieties of written Norwegian perform poorly when applied to the other. For all tested configurations, we observe a loss of between 20 and 25 percentage points in labeled attachment score compared to training and testing on one and the same variety. At the same time, it is important to realize that the results for 'within-standard' processing of either the Bokmål or Nynorsk treebank data in isolation, correspond to an idealized setting that is not representative of how written Norwegian is encountered 'in the wild'. In the news sources, blogs, government reports and parliament transcripts that form the basis for the treebank, both varieties of Norwegian will occur, intermixed. In practice, this means that the actual parsing results can be expected to lie somewhere in between the extremes reported in Table 1. Of course, a language identification module could be trained and applied as a pre-processing step for selecting the appropriate model, but in practice it would be much more convenient if we were able to have a single model that could process both varieties equally well.

In the next section, we look into various ways of mixing training data for the two written standards of Norwegian in order to create improved models for cross-standard joint processing. Moreover, given the empirical indications in Section 5.2 that more labeled training data could benefit the taggers and parsers, this strategy is also motivated by wanting to improve the absolute results for each standard in isolation.

6 Joint models

In this section we test the effects of combining the training data for Bokmål and Nynorsk, as well as extending it through machine translation.

6.1 Mixed training data

In a first round of experiments we simply concatenate the training sections for Bokmål and Nynorsk. The results can be seen in the row 'BM+NN' in Table 2. For both pipelines and both language varieties we observe the same trend: Despite a loss in tagging accuracy, parsing performance improves when compared to training on just a single variety (rows 'BM' or 'NN'). While effectively doubling the size of the training data, we do not see the same factor of improvement as for the learning curves in Figure 2, but we nonetheless see an increase in LAS of up to one additional percentage point. It is important to note that the results for 'BM+NN' represents using *joint* tagging and parsing pipelines across both written standards: For each set-up (TnT+Mate and UDPipe) we train a single pipeline, and then apply

	Bokmål				Nynorsk			
	Train	**Acc**	**LAS**	**UAS**	**Train**	**Acc**	**LAS**	**UAS**
Mate	BM	**96.67**	84.13	87.34	NN	**95.81**	82.09	85.39
	BM+NN	96.29	84.97	88.04	BM+NN	95.18	83.13	86.22
	BM+MT	96.32	**85.45**	**88.47**	NN+MT	94.98	**83.63**	**86.82**
	BM+NN+MT	96.30	85.05	88.12	BM+NN+MT	94.97	83.47	86.65
UDPipe	BM	**97.55**	84.16	87.07	NN	**97.11**	82.63	85.56
	BM+NN	97.01	84.65	87.42	BM+NN	96.43	82.81	85.84
	BM+MT	97.17	85.03	87.97	NN+MT	96.16	82.47	85.57
	BM+NN+MT	96.83	**85.10**	**88.01**	BM+NN+MT	96.15	**83.20**	**86.28**

Table 2: Development results for Bokmål and Nynorsk tagged and parsed with TnT+Mate and UDPipe, training on Bokmål or Nynorsk alone (rows BM or NN), mixed (BM+NN), or each combined with machine-translated data (BM+MT or NN+MT), or everything combined, i.e., the original and translated versions of both the Bokmål and Nynorsk training data (BM+NN+MT).

the same pipeline to both the Nynorsk and Bokmål development sets.

As a control experiment, to better understand to what extent the improvements are due only to larger training sets or also to the use of mixed data, we ran the same experiments after down-sampling the combined training set to the same size as the originals (simply discarding every second sentence). For TnT+Mate and UDPipe respectively, this gave a LAS of 82.81 and 82.77 for Bokmål, and 81.47 and 80.86 for Nynorsk. We see that while training joint models on the down-sampled mixed data gives slightly lower results than when using the full concatenation (or using dedicated single-standard models), it still provides a robust alternative for processing mixed data, given the dramatically lower results we observed for cross-standard testing in Section 5.1.

6.2 Machine-translated training data

The results above show that combining training data across standards can improve parsing performance. As mentioned in the introduction, though, there is a large degree of lexical divergence between the two standards. In our next suite of experiments, we therefore attempt to further improve the results by automatically machine-translating the training texts. Given the strong degree of structural equivalence between Norwegian Bokmål and Nynorsk, we can expect MT to yield relatively accurate translations. For this, we use the two-way Bokmål–Nynorsk MT system of Unhammer and Trosterud (2009), a rule-based shallow-transfer system built on the open-source MT platform Apertium (Forcada et al., 2011).

The raw text passed to Apertium is extracted from the full-form column of the UD CoNLL training data (translating the lemmas does not give adequate results). The only sanity-checking we perform on the result is ensuring that the number of tokens in the target translation matches that of the source. In cases where the token counts diverge – for example when the Bokmål form *fortsette* ('continue') is translated to Nynorsk as *halde fram* ('keep on') – the sentence is left in its original source form. For the NN→BM translation, this is the case for almost 4% of the sentences. The direction BM→NN appears to be slightly harder, where almost 13% of the sentences are left untranslated.

We tested the translated training data in two ways: 1) Training single-standard pipelines, for example training on the original Bokmål data and the Nynorsk data translated to Bokmål, and 2) training on all the available training data combined, i.e., both of the original versions and both of the translated versions, in effect increasing the amount of training data by a factor of four.

The results for the development data are shown in Table 2. Adding the MT data reinforces the trend observed for mixing the original training sets: Despite that PoS tagging accuracy typically (though not always) decreases when adding data, parsing accuracy improves. For the TnT+Mate pipeline, we see that the best parser performance is obtained with the single-standard models including the MT data, while UDPipe achieves the best results when using the maximal amount of training data. Coupled with the parser learning curves in Figure 2, this observation is in line with the expectation that neural network architectures both require and benefit more from larger training samples, but recall the caveat noted in Section 5.1

about how the scores are not directly comparable. Finally, note that this latter configuration, i.e., combining both of the original training sets with both of the translated versions, again corresponds to having a single joint model for both Bokmål and Nynorsk. Also for TnT+Mate, we see that this configuration yields better results than our previous joint model without the MT data.

6.3 Caveat on morphology

Although the development results demonstrate that the various ways of combining the training data lead to increased parser performance, we saw that the tagging accuracy was slightly reduced. However, the UDPipe tagging component, MorphoDiTa, performs additional morphological analysis beyond assigning UPoS tags. It also performs lemmatization and assigns morphological features, and in particular for the first of these tasks the drop in performance for the joint models is more pronounced. For example, when comparing the Bokmål development results for the UDPipe model trained on the original Bokmål data alone versus Bokmål and Nynorsk combined, the lemmatization accuracy drops from 97.29% to 95.18% (and the morphological feature accuracy drops from 96.03% to 95.39%). This is not surprising. Given the close similarities of Bokmål and Nynorsk, several words in the two variants will have identical inflected forms but different lemmas, introducing a lot of additional ambiguity for the lemmatizer. The drop in lemma accuracy is mostly due to a handful of high-frequent words having this effect, for example the verb forms *var* ('was') or *er* ('is') which should be lemmatized as *være* in Bokmål and *vere* in Nynorsk. However, for the taggers trained on the maximal training data where we include the machine-translated versions of both varieties, the lemma accuracy really plummets, dropping to 86.19% (and morphological feature accuracy dropping to 93.79%). Again, this is as expected, given that only the full-forms of training data were translated.

In our parsing pipeline, lemmas are not used and so this drop in accuracy does not affect downstream performance. However, for applications where lemmatization plays an important role, a joint tagger should either be trained without the use of the MT data (or an initial single-standard lemmatizer should be used to lemmatize this data after translation), and ideally should be made to take more context into consideration to be able to make more accurate predictions.

7 Held-out results

For the held-out results, we focus on testing the two joint models, i.e., (1) estimating models from the original training sets for Nynorsk and Bokmål combined, as well as (2) augmenting this further with the their MT versions (translating each variety into the other). We contrast the performance of these joint models with the results from training on either of the original single-standard training sets in isolation, including cross-standard testing. Table 3 summarizes the results for both pipelines – TnT+Mate and UDPipe – for the held-out sections of the treebanks for both of the Norwegian written varieties – Bokmål (BM) and Nynorsk (NN).

In terms of relative performance, the outcome is the same as for the development data: The joint models give better parsing performance across all configurations, compared to the dedicated single-standard models, despite reduced tagger accuracy. In terms of absolute figures, we see that UDPipe has the best performance.

It is also interesting to note that the UDPipe parser appears to be more robust to the noise introduced with MT data, and that this may even have had the effect of mitigating overfitting: While we observe a slight drop in performance for the single-variety models when moving from development to held-out results, the effect is the opposite for the joint model trained on the MT data. This effect is most pronounced for the Nynorsk data, which is also known to have the most translation errors in the training data.

Finally, note that while our parser scores are stronger than those previously reported for UDPipe on Norwegian (Bokmål only) (Straka et al., 2016), there are several reasons why the results are not directly comparable. First, we here use version 1.4 of the UD treebank as opposed to version 1.2 for the results of Straka et al. (2016), and secondly, the embeddings generated by word2vec are non-deterministic, meaning that strictly speaking, different UDPipe models for the same training data can only be directly compared if reusing the same embeddings.

8 Future work

Immediate follow-up work will include using a larger unlabeled corpus for pre-training the word

	Training	BM			NN		
		Acc	LAS	UAS	Acc	LAS	UAS
Mate	BM	**96.31**	83.80	87.04	81.66	60.51	67.55
	NN	80.32	60.64	67.13	**95.55**	81.51	85.06
	BM+NN	95.98	84.74	87.83	95.06	83.11	86.42
	BM+NN+MT	95.79	**84.88**	**87.89**	94.78	**83.87**	**87.16**
UDPipe	BM	**97.07**	83.42	86.28	83.35	60.95	68.15
	NN	82.92	62.85	69.66	**96.80**	82.40	85.38
	BM+NN	96.49	84.20	86.90	96.27	83.46	86.24
	BM+NN+MT	96.48	**85.31**	**88.04**	96.05	**84.17**	**87.18**

Table 3: Held-out test results for Norwegian Bokmål and Nynorsk tagged and parsed with TnT+Mate and UDPipe, using either the Bokmål or Nynorsk training data alone (rows BM or NN), Bokmål and Nynorsk mixed (BM+NN), or Bokmål and Nynorsk combined with machine-translated data, i.e., the original versions of both varieties as well as the translations of each into the other (BM+NN+MT).

embeddings used by UDPipe's Parsito parser. For this, we will use the Norwegian Newspaper Corpus which consists of texts collected from a range of major Norwegian news sources for the years 1998–2014, and importantly comprising both the Bokmål and the Nynorsk variety. Another direction for optimizing the performance of the pipelines is to use different training data for the different components. This is perhaps most important for the UDPipe model. While the parser benefits from including the machine-translated data in training, the tagger performs better when using the combination of the original training data. This is mostly noticeable when considering not just the accuracy of the UPoS tags but also the morphological features, which are also used by the parser. Finally, while the experimental results in this paper are based on the UD conversion of the Norwegian Dependency Treebank, there is of course no reason to expect that the effects will be different on the original NDT data. We plan to also replicate the experiments for NDT, and make available both pre-trained joint and single-standard models for this data set as well.

9 Conclusion

This paper has tackled the problem of creating a single pipeline for dependency parsing that gives accurate results across both of the official varieties for written Norwegian language – Bokmål and Nynorsk. Although the two varieties are very closely related and have few syntactic differences, they can be very different lexically. To the best of our knowledge, this is the first study to attempt to build a uniform tool-chain for both language standards, and also to quantify cross-standard perfor-

mance of Norwegian NLP tools in the first place.

The basis of our experiments is the Norwegian Dependency Treebank, converted to Universal Dependencies. For Bokmål, this treebank conversion was already in place (Øvrelid and Hohle, 2016), while for the Nynorsk data, the conversion has been done as part of the current study. To make our results more robust, we have evaluated and compared pipelines created with two distinct set of tools, each based on different learning schemes; one based on the TnT tagger and the Mate parser, and one based on UDPipe.

To date, the common practice has been to build dedicated models for a single language variant only. Quantifying the performance of models trained on labeled data for a single variety (e.g., the majority variety Bokmål) when applied to data from the other (Nynorsk), we found that parsing accuracy dramatically degrades, with LAS dropping by 20–25 percentage points. At the same time, we found that when combining the training data for both varieties, parsing performance in fact increases for both. Importantly, this also eliminates the issue of cross-standard performance, as only a single model is used. Finally, we have shown that the joint parsers can be improved even further by also including machine-translated versions of the training data for each variety.

In terms of relative differences, the trends for all observed results are consistent across both of our tool chains, TnT+Mate and UDPipe, although we find the latter to have the best absolute performance. Our results have immediate practical value for processing Norwegian, as it means that a single parsing pipeline is sufficient to cover both official written standards, with no loss in accuracy.

References

Željko Agić, Anders Johannsen, Barbara Plank, Héctor Alonso Martínez, Natalie Schluter, and Anders Søgaard. 2016. Multilingual projection for parsing truly low-resource languages. *Transactions of the Association for Computational Linguistics*, 4:301–312.

Waleed Ammar, George Mulcaire, Miguel Ballesteros, Chris Dyer, and Noah A. Smith. 2016. One parser, many languages. *arXiv preprint arXiv:1602.01595*.

Bernd Bohnet. 2010. Very High Accuracy and Fast Dependency Parsing is not a Contradiction. In *Proceedings of the 23rd International Conference on Computational Linguistics*, pages 89–97, Beijing, China.

Thorsten Brants. 2000. TnT - A Statistical Part-of-Speech Tagger. In *Proceedings of the Sixth Applied Natural Language Processing Conference*, Seattle, WA, USA.

Xavier Carreras. 2007. Experiments with a higher-order projective dependency parser. In *Proceedings of the Joint Conference on Empirical Methods in Natural Language Processing and Conference on Computational Natural Language Learning*, pages 957–961, Prague, Czech Republic.

Danqi Chen and Christopher Manning. 2014. A fast and accurate dependency parser using neural networks. In *Proceedings of the 2014 Conference on Empirical Methods in Natural Language Processing*, pages 740–750, Doha, Qatar.

Jinho D. Choi, Joel Tetreault, and Amanda Stent. 2015. It Depends: Dependency Parser Comparison Using A Web-Based Evaluation Tool. In *Proceedings of the 53rd Annual Meeting of the Association for Computational Linguistics*, pages 387–396, Beijing, China.

Michael Collins. 2002. Discriminative training methods for hidden markov models: Theory and experiments with perceptron algorithms. In *Proceedings of the 2002 Conference on Empirical Methods in Natural Language Processing*, pages 1–8, PA, USA.

Koby Crammer, Ofer Dekel, Joseph Keshet, Shai Shalev-Shwartz, and Yoram Singe. 2006. Online passive-aggressive algorithms. *Journal of Machine Learning Research*, 7:551–585.

Marie-Catherine de Marneffe, Timothy Dozat, Natalia Silveira, Katri Haverinen, Filip Ginter, Joakim Nivre, and Christopher D. Manning. 2014. Universal Stanford dependencies. A cross-linguistic typology. In *Proceedings of the International Conference on Language Resources and Evaluation*, pages 4585–4592, Reykjavik, Iceland.

Mikel L. Forcada, Mireia Ginestí-Rosell, Jacob Nordfalk, Jim O'Regan, Sergio Ortiz-Rojas, Juan Antonio Pérez-Ortiz, Felipe Sánchez-Martínez, Gema Ramírez-Sánchez, and Francis M. Tyers. 2011. Apertium: a free/open-source platform for rule-based machine translation. *Machine Translation*, 25(2):127–144.

Petter Hohle, Lilja Øvrelid, and Erik Velldal. 2017. Optimizing a PoS tagset for Norwegian dependency parsing. In *Proceedings of the 21st Nordic Conference of Computational Linguistics*, Gothenburg, Sweden.

Rebecca Hwa, Philip Resnik, Amy Weinberg, Clara Cabezas, and Okan Kolak. 2005. Bootstrapping parsers via syntactic projection across parallel texts. *Natural Language Engineering*, 11(3).

Tomas Mikolov, Kai Chen, Greg Corrado, and Jeffrey Dean. 2013. Efficient estimation of word representations in vector space. *arXiv preprint arXiv:1301.3781*.

Jens Nilsson and Joakim Nivre. 2008. MaltEval: An evaluation and visualization tool for dependency parsing. In *Proceedings of the Sixth International Conference on Language Resources and Evaluation*, pages 161–166, Marrakech, Morocco.

Joakim Nivre, Marie-Catherine de Marneffe, Filip Ginter, Yoav Goldberg, Jan Hajič, Christopher D. Manning, Ryan McDonald, Slav Petrov, Sampo Pyysalo, Natalia Silveira, Reut Tsarfaty, and Daniel Zeman. 2016. Universal dependencies v1: A multilingual treebank collection. In *Proceedings of the International Conference on Language Resources and Evaluation*, Portorož, Slovenia.

Joakim Nivre. 2015. Towards a Universal Grammar for Natural Language Processing. In *Computational Linguistics and Intelligent Text Processing*, volume 9041 of *Lecture Notes in Computer Science*, pages 3–16. Springer International Publishing.

Lilja Øvrelid and Petter Hohle. 2016. Universal Dependencies for Norwegian. In *Proceedings of the Tenth International Conference on Language Resources and Evaluation*, Portorož, Slovenia.

Slav Petrov, Dipanjan Das, and Ryan McDonald. 2012. A Universal Part-of-Speech Tagset. In *Proceedings of the Eighth International Conference on Language Resources and Evaluation*, pages 2089–2096, Istanbul, Turkey.

Arne Skjærholt and Lilja Øvrelid. 2012. Impact of treebank characteristics on cross-lingual parser adaptation. In *Proceedings of the Eleventh International Workshop on Treebanks and Linguistic Theories*, pages 187–198, Lisbon, Portugal.

Anders Søgaard. 2011. Data point selection for cross-language adaptation of dependency parsers. In *Proceedings of the 49th Annual Meeting of the Association for Computational Linguistics*, pages 682—686, Portland, Oregon.

Per Erik Solberg, Arne Skjærholt, Lilja Øvrelid, Kristin Hagen, and Janne Bondi Johannessen. 2014. The Norwegian Dependency Treebank. In *Proceedings of the Ninth International Conference on Language Resources and Evaluation*, pages 789–795, Reykjavik, Iceland.

Kathrin Spreyer, Lilja Øvrelid, and Jonas Kuhn. 2010. Training parsers on partial trees: A cross-language comparison. In *Proceedings of the International Conference on Language Resources and Evaluation (LREC)*.

Milan Straka, Jan Hajič, Jana Straková, and Jan Hajič jr. 2015. Parsing universal dependency treebanks using neural networks and search-based oracle. In *Proceedings of Fourteenth International Workshop on Treebanks and Linguistic Theories*, Warsaw, Poland.

Milan Straka, Jan Hajič, and Jana Straková. 2016. UD-Pipe: trainable pipeline for processing CoNLL-U files performing tokenization, morphological analysis, pos tagging and parsing. In *Proceedings of the Tenth International Conference on Language Resources and Evaluation*, Portorož, Slovenia.

Jana Straková, Milan Straka, and Jan Hajič. 2014. Open-Source Tools for Morphology, Lemmatization, POS Tagging and Named Entity Recognition. In *Proceedings of 52nd Annual Meeting of the Association for Computational Linguistics: System Demonstrations*, pages 13–18, Baltimore, Maryland.

Oscar Täckström, Ryan McDonald, and Jakob Uszkoreit. 2012. Cross-lingual word clusters for direct transfer of linguistic structure. In *Proceedings of the 2012 Conference of the North American Chapter of the Association for Computational Linguistics*, Montreal, Canada.

Jörg Tiedemann, Željko AgićZeljko, and Joakim Nivre. 2014. Treebank translation for cross-lingual parser induction. In *Proceedings of the Eighteenth Conference on Computational Natural Language Learning*, pages 130–140.

Kevin Brubeck Unhammer and Trond Trosterud. 2009. Reuse of Free Resources in Machine Translation between Nynorsk and Bokmål. In *Proceedings of the First International Workshop on Free/Open-Source Rule-Based Machine Translation*, pages 35–42, Alicante.

Dan Zeman and Philip Resnik. 2008. Cross-language parser adaptation between related languages. In *Proceedings of the IJCNLP-08 Workshop on NLP for Less Privileged Languages*, Hyderabad, India.

Replacing OOV Words For Dependency Parsing
With Distributional Semantics

Prasanth Kolachina [△] and **Martin Riedl** [◇] and **Chris Biemann** [◇]

[△] Department of Computer Science and Engineering, University of Gothenburg, Sweden

[◇] Language Technology Group, Universität Hamburg, Germany

prasanth.kolachina@gu.se

{riedl,biemann}@informatik.uni-hamburg.de

Abstract

Lexical information is an important feature in syntactic processing like part-of-speech (POS) tagging and dependency parsing. However, there is no such information available for out-of-vocabulary (OOV) words, which causes many classification errors. We propose to replace OOV words with in-vocabulary words that are semantically similar according to distributional similar words computed from a large background corpus, as well as morphologically similar according to common suffixes. We show performance differences both for count-based and dense neural vector-based semantic models. Further, we discuss the interplay of POS and lexical information for dependency parsing and provide a detailed analysis and a discussion of results: while we observe significant improvements for count-based methods, neural vectors do not increase the overall accuracy.

1 Introduction

Due to the high expense of creating treebanks, there is a notorious scarcity of training data for dependency parsing. The quality of dependency parsing crucially hinges on the quality of part-of-speech (POS) tagging as a preprocessing step; many dependency parsers also utilize lexicalized information, which is only available for the training vocabulary. Thus errors in dependency parsers often relate to OOV (out of vocabulary, i.e. not seen in the training data) words.

While there has been a considerable amount of work to address the OOV problem with continuous word representations (see Section 2), this requires a more complex model and hence, increases training and execution complexity.

In this paper, we present a very simple yet effective way of alleviating the OOV problem to some extent: we use two flavors of distributional similarity, computed on a large background corpus, to replace OOV words in the input with semantically or morphologically similar words that have been seen in the training, and project parse labels back to the original sequence. If we succeed in replacing OOV words with in-vocabulary words of the same syntactic behavior, we expect the tagging and parsing process to be less prone to errors caused by the absence of lexical information.

We show consistent significant improvements both for POS tagging accuracy as well as for Labeled Attachment Scores (LAS) for graph-based semantic similarities. The successful strategies mostly improve POS accuracy on open class words, which results in better dependency parses. Beyond improving POS tagging, the strategy also contributes to parsing accuracy. Through extensive experiments – we show results for seven different languages – we are able to recommend one particular strategy in the conclusion and show the impact of using different similarity sources.

Since our method manipulates the input data rather than the model, it can be used with any existing dependency parser without re-training, which makes it very applicable in existing environments.

2 Related Work

While part-of-speech (POS) tags play a major role in detecting syntactic structure, it is well known (Kaplan and Bresnan (1982) inter al.) that lexical information helps for parsing in general and for

Proceedings of the 21st Nordic Conference of Computational Linguistics, pages 11–19,
Gothenburg, Sweden, 23-24 May 2017. ©2017 Linköping University Electronic Press

dependency parsing in particular, see e.g. Wang et al. (2005).

In order to transfer lexical knowledge from the training data to unseen words in the test data, Koo et al. (2008) improve dependency parsing with features based on Brown Clusters (Brown et al., 1992), which are known to be drawing syntactic-semantic distinctions. Bansal et al. (2014) show slight improvements over Koo et al. (2008)'s method by tailoring word embeddings for dependency parsing by inducing them on syntactic contexts, which presupposes the existence of a dependency parser. In more principled fashion, Socher et al. (2013) directly operate on vector representations. Chen et al. (2014) address the lexical gap by generalizing over OOV and other words in a feature role via feature embeddings. Another approach for replacing OOV words by known ones using word embeddings is introduced by Andreas and Klein (2014).

All these approaches, however, require re-training the parser with these additional features and make the model more complex. We present a much simpler setup of replacing OOV words with similar words from the training set, which allows retrofitting any parser with our method.

This work is related to Biemann and Riedl (2013), where OOV performance of fine-grained POS tagging has been improved in a similar fashion. Another similar work to ours is proposed by Huang et al. (2014), who replace OOV named entities with named entities from the same (fine-grained) class for improving Chinese dependency parsing, which largely depends on the quality of the employed NER tagger and is restricted to named entities only. In contrast, we operate on all OOV words, and try to improve prediction on coarse universal POS classes and universal dependencies.

On a related note, examples for a successful application of OOV replacements is demonstrated for Machine Translation (Gangadharaiah et al., 2010; Zhang et al., 2012).

3   Methodology

For replacing OOV words we propose three strategies: replace OOV words by most similar ones using distributional semantic methods, replace OOV words with words with the most common suffix and replacing OOV words before or after POS tagging to observe the effect on dependency parsing.

The influence of all components is evaluated separately for POS tagging and dependency parsing in Section 5.

3.1   Semantic Similarities

In order to replace an OOV word by a similar in-vocabulary word, we use models that are based on the distributional hypothesis (Harris, 1951). For showing the impact of different models we use a graph-based approach that uses the left- and right-neighbored word as context, represented by the method proposed by Biemann and Riedl (2013), and is called distributional thesaurus (*DT*). Furthermore, we apply two dense numeric vector-space approaches, using the skip-gram model (*SKG*) and CBOW model of the `word2vec` implementation of Mikolov et al. (2013).

3.2   Suffix Source

In addition, we explore replacing OOVs with words from the similarity source that are contained in the training set and share the longest suffix. This might be beneficial as suffixes reflect morphological markers and carry word class information in many languages. The assumption here is that for syntactic dependencies, it is more crucial that the replacement comes from the same word class than its semantic similarity. This also serves as a comparison to gauge the benefits of the similarity source alone. Below, these experiments are marked with *suffix*, whereas the highest-ranked replacement from the similarity sources are marked as *sim*. As a *suffix-only* baseline, we replace OOVs with its most suffix-similar word from the training data, irrespective of its distributional similarity. This serves as a sanity check whether semantic similarities are helpful at all.

3.3   Replacement Strategies regarding POS

We explore two different settings for dependency parsing that differ in the use of POS tags:

(1) *oTAG*: POS-tag original sequence, then replace OOV words, retaining original tags for parsing;

(2) *reTAG*: replace OOV word, then POS-tag the new sequence and use the new tags for parsing.

The *oTAG* experiments primarily quantify the sensitivity of the parsing model to word forms, whereas *reTag* assess the potential improvements in the POS tagging.

3.4 Replacement Example

As an example, consider the automatically POS-tagged input sentence "We/P went/V to/P the/D aquatic/N park/N" where "aquatic" is an OOV word. Strategy *oTAG sim* replaces "aquatic" with "marine" since it is the most similar in-vocabulary word of "aquatic". Strategy *oTAG suffix* replaces it with "exotic" because of the suffix "tic" and its similarity with "aquatic". The *suffix-only* baseline would replace with "automatic" since it shares the longest suffix of all in-vocabulary words. The *re-TAG* strategy would then re-tag the sentence, so the parser will e.g. operate on "We/P went/V to/P the/D marine/ADJ park/N". Table 1 shows an example for different similarity-based strategies for English and German[1]. We observe that the *sim* strategy returns semantically similar words that do not necessarily have the same syntactic function as the OOV target.

	sim	**sim&suffix**
English OOV: upgraded		
Suffix-only	paraded	
CBOW	upgrade	downloaded
SKG	upgrade	expanded
DT	expanded	updated
German OOV: Nachtzeit		
Suffix-only	Pachtzeit	
CBOW	tagsüber	Ruhezeit
SKG	tagsüber	Echtzeit
DT	Jahreswende	Zeit

Table 1: Here we show replacements for different methods using different strategies.

4 Experimental Settings

Here we describe the methods, background corpora used for computing similarities and all further tools used for the experiments. With our experiments, we target to address the following research questions:

- Can syntactic processing benefit from OOV replacement, and if so, under what strategies and conditions?

- Is there a qualitative difference between similarity sources with respect to tagger/parser performance?

- Are there differences in the sensitivity of parsing inference methods to OOV replacement?

4.1 Similarity Computations

We are using two different approaches to determine semantic similarity: a symbolic, graph-based framework for distributional similarity and a neural language model that encodes words in a dense vector space.

Graph-based Semantic Similarity

The computation of a corpus-based distributional thesaurus (marked as *DT* below) is performed following the approach by Biemann and Riedl (2013) as implemented in the JoBimText[2] software. For computing similarities between words from large unlabeled corpora, we extract as word-context the left and right neighboring words, not using language-specific syntactic preprocessing. Words are more similar if they share more of their most salient 1000 context features, where salient context features are ranked by Lexicographer's Mutual Information (LMI), (Evert, 2005). Word similarity in the DT is defined as the count of overlapping salient context features. In addition we prune similar words[3] below a similarity threshold of 5.

In order to use such a DT to replace an OOV word, we look up the most similar terms for the OOV word and choose the highest-ranked word from the training data vocabulary, respectively the most similar word with the longest common suffix.

Neural Semantic Similarity

As an alternative similarity we run `word2vec` with default parameters (marked as *w2v* below) (Mikolov et al., 2013) on our background corpora, obtaining 200-dimensional dense vector embeddings for all words with a corpus frequency larger than 5. We conduct this for both flavors of *w2v*: skipgram, marked as *SKG* below (based on positional windows) and *CBOW* (based on bag of word sentential contexts).

Following the standard approach, we use the cosine between word vectors as a similarity measure: for each OOV, we compare vectors from all words in the training set and pick the word that correspond to the most similar vector as a replacement,

---

[1]Translations: Nachtzeit = night time; tagsüber = during the day; Pachtzeit = length of lease; Ruhezeit = downtime; Echtzeit = real time; Jahreswende = turn of the year

[3]we have tried a few thresholds in preliminary experiments and did not find results to be very sensitive in the range of 2 − 20

respectively the most similar word of those with the longest common suffix.

4.2 Corpora for Similarity Computation

As we perform the experiments on various languages, we will compute similarities for each language separately. The English similarities are computed based on 105M sentences from the Leipzig corpora collection (LCC) (Richter et al., 2006) and the Gigaword corpus (Parker et al., 2011). The German (70M) and the Hindi (2M) corpora are extracted from the LCC as well. We compute similarities on 19.7M sentences of Arabic, 259.7M sentences of French and 128.1M sentences of Spanish extracted from web corpora[4] provided by Schäfer and Bildhauer (2013). For the computation of the Swedish similarities we use a 60M-sentence news corpus from Spraakbanken.[5] In summary, all background corpora are in the order of about 1 Gigaword, except the Hindi corpus, which is considerably smaller.

4.3 Dependency Parser and POS Tagger

For the dependency parsing we use the implementation of the graph-based dependency parser provided in Mate-tools (Bohnet, 2010, version 3.6) and the transition-based Malt parser (Nivre, 2009, version 1.8.1). Graph-based parsers use global inference to construct the maximum spanning dependency tree for the input sequences. Contrary, the greedy algorithm in the transition-based parser uses local inference to predict the dependency tree. The parsing models for both parsers, Mate-tools and Malt parser, are optimized using cross-validation on the training section of the treebank[6]. We train the dependency parsers using POS tags (from the Mate-tools tagger) predicted using a 5-fold cross-validation. The evaluation of the parser accuracies is carried out using MaltEval. We report labeled attachment score (LAS) for both overall and on OOV token positions.

4.4 Treebanks

For training and testing we apply the treebanks (train/dev/test size in tokens in parentheses) from the Universal Dependencies project (Nivre et al.,

---

[4]http://corporafromtheweb.org/

[5]http://spraakbanken.gu.se

[6]Using Malt Optimizer (Ballesteros and Nivre, 2016) for the Malt parser; for Mate-tools, we tuned the parameter that represents the percentage of non-projective edges in a language, which matches the parameters suggested by Bohnet (2010).

2016, version 1.2 released November 15th, 2015) for Arabic, English, French, German, Hindi, Spanish and Swedish. Tagset definitions are available online.[7]

5 Results

In this section, we report experimental results and compare them to the baseline without OOV replacement. All statistical significance tests are done using McNemar's test. Significant improvements ($p < 0.05$) over the baseline without OOV replacement are marked with an asterisk ($*$), significant performance drops with a hashmark (#) and the best result per experiment is marked in bold.

5.1 Results for POS Tagging

In Table 2 we show overall and OOV-only POS tagging accuracies on the respective test set for seven languages using similarities extracted from the DT.

LANG	OOV %	baseline all	baseline OOV	suffix only all	suffix only OOV	DT sim all	DT sim OOV	DT suffix all	DT suffix OOV
Arabic	10.3	**98.53**	**94.01**	97.82#	87.44#	98.49#	93.67#	98.52	93.91
English	8.0	93.43	75.39	93.09#	72.03#	**93.82***	**78.67***	93.61*	76.75
French	5.3	95.47	83.29	95.17#	78.30#	95.68*	86.28*	**95.73***	**86.78***
German	11.5	**91.92**	85.63	90.88#	77.70#	91.84	85.32	**91.92**	**85.68**
Hindi	4.4	95.35	76.41	95.07#	71.27#	95.41	77.57	**95.44***	**78.00***
Spanish	6.9	94.82	79.62	95.00	81.17	95.45*	**86.36***	**95.49***	85.84*
Swedish	14.3	95.34	89.80	94.78#	86.04 #	95.57*	90.88*	**95.82***	**92.40***

Table 2: Test set overall OOV rates, POS accuracy in % for baseline, suffix-only baseline, DT similarity and suffix replacement strategies for seven languages.

Unsurprisingly, we observe consistent performance drops, mostly significant, for the *suffix-only* baseline. For all languages except German, the *DT*-based replacement strategies result in significant improvements of either overall accuracy, OOV accuracy or both. In most experiments, the *DT suffix* replacement strategy scores slightly higher than the *DT sim* strategy.

Table 3 lists POS accuracies for three languages for similarities from the *w2v* neural language model in its *SKG* and *CBOW* flavors using the cosine similarity. In contrast to the *DT*-based replacements, there are no improvements over the baseline, and some performance drops are even significant. Also replacing the cosine similarity with the Euclidian distance did not change this

---

[7]http://universaldependencies.org/

	SKG				CBOW			
LANG	sim		suffix		sim		suffix	
	all	OOV	all	OOV	all	OOV	all	OOV
Arabic	98.46#	93.39#	98.50#	93.73#	98.48#	93.60#	98.52	93.94
English	93.10#	72.29#	93.57	76.31	93.24#	73.91	93.52	75.70
German	90.99#	77.65#	91.62#	83.61#	91.78	83.92#	91.91	85.43

Table 3: Test set POS accuracies for *w2v*-based model's similarity and suffix replacement strategies for three languages.

observation. The suffix-based strategy seems to work better than the similarity-based strategy also for the *w2v*-based replacement.

It seems that count-based similarities perform better for the replacement. Thus, we did not extend the experiments with *w2v* to other languages.

5.2 Results for Dependency Parsing

As a general trend for all languages (see Table 4), we observe that the graph-based parser achieves higher LAS scores than the transition-based parser.

However, the optimal replacement strategy depends on the language for both parsers. Only for Swedish (*reTAG DT suffix*) and Spanish (*reTAG DT sim*), the same replacements yield the highest scores both on all words and OOV words for both parsers. Using the modified POS tags (*reTAG*) results in improvements for the transitions-based parser for 4 languages and for 5 languages using the graph-based parser. Whereas the results improve only marginal when using the *reTAG* strategy as can be observed from Table 4, most improvements are significant.

Using word embeddings for the *reTAG* strategy (see Table 5), we again observe performance drops, except for Arabic.

Following the *oTAG* strategy, we observe significant improvements on German and Arabic for the CBOW method. For German the best performance is obtained with the SKG model (74.47*) which is slightly higher then the *suffix only* replacement, which achieves high scores in the *oTAG* setting. Whereas for POS tagging the suffix-based DT replacement mostly results in the highest scores, there is no clear recommendation for a replacement strategy for parsing all languages. Looking at the average delta (Δ) values for all languages (see Tables 4 and 5) in comparison to the baseline, the picture is clearer: here, for both parser the *reTAG DT suffix* strategy yields the highest improvements and the CBOW and SKG methods only

result in consistent improvements for the oTAG strategy. Further average performance gains are observed for the CBOW suffix-based method using the reTAG strategy.

To sum up, we have noted that the *DT*-based strategies seem more advantageous than the *w2v*-strategies across languages. Comparing the different strategies for using *DTs*, we observe an advantage of *reTAG* over *oTAG* and a slight advantage over *suffix* vs. *sim*. Most notably, *DT reTAG suffix* is the only strategy that never resulted in a significant performance drop on all datasets for both parsers and yields the highest average Δ improvement of 1.50. Given its winning performance on the POS evaluation, we recommend to use this strategy.

6 Data Analysis

6.1 Analysis of POS Accuracy

Since POS quality has a direct influence on parser accuracy, we have analyzed the two *reTag* strategies *suffix* and *sim* for our three similarity sources (*DT*, *SKG*, *CBOW*) in more detail for German and English by comparing them to the *oTAG* baselines. In general, differences are mostly found for open word classes such as ADJ, ADV, NOUN, PROPN and VERB, which naturally have the highest OOV rates in the test data. In both languages, the DT-based strategies supply about 84% of the replacements of the *w2v* strategies.

For German, only the *DT suffix*-based replacements led to a slight overall POS improvement. All similarity sources improved the tagging of NOUN for *suffix*, but not for *sim*. All replacements led to some losses in VERBs, with *SKG* losing the most. Both *w2v* sources lost more on ADJ than the *DT*, which also showed the largest improvements on ADV. In addition, we analyzed the POS classification only for tokens that could be replaced both by the *DT* and the *w2v*-methods. For these tokens, the *SKG* method can not surpass the *oTAG* performance. Furthermore, for *DT* and *CBOW*, the *suffix* strategies achieve slightly lower scores than *sim* (0.18%-0.63%). On the tokens where all methods propose replacements, the *DT* results in better accuracy (86.00%) than *CBOW* (85.82%).

For English, the picture is similar but in general the improvement of the scores is larger: while the *DT sim* led to the largest and the *DT suffix* to the second-largest overall improvements, the *suffix*-based *w2v*-strategies can also improve POS

| | oTAG | | | | | | reTAG | | | | | |
| | baseline | | suffix only | | DT sim | | DT suffix | | suffix only | | DT sim | | DT suffix | |
Language	all	OOV	all	OOV	all	OOV	all	OOV	all	OOV	all	OOV	all	OOV
						Graph-based Parser								
Arabic	75.60	56.90	75.61	57.76*	75.74*	58.18*	75.71*	58.31*	74.54#	52.84#	**75.75***	58.18*	75.72*	58.31*
English	79.57	63.64	79.55	63.77	79.64	64.38*	79.54	64.20	79.24#	62.37	**79.95***	**66.17***	79.78*	65.30*
French	77.76	64.59	77.91	65.34	77.61	64.09	77.79	64.84	77.59	64.59	77.59	64.09	**77.97**	**65.84**
German	74.24	68.93	74.43*	**69.66***	74.27	69.14	74.21	69.24	72.26#	63.43#	74.13	68.10	74.22	69.09
Hindi	87.67	72.00	87.76*	72.74	**87.78***	72.80*	87.71	**72.86***	87.49#	70.60	87.67	72.62	87.69	72.74
Spanish	80.02	63.56	80.07	65.28*	80.32*	67.18*	80.30*	66.84*	79.38#	64.59	**80.41***	**68.91***	80.27	68.05*
Swedish	77.13	70.70	77.16	70.87	77.44*	71.07	77.31*	71.03	76.55#	69.12#	77.62*	71.96*	**77.65***	**72.05***
Δ all	0.00	0.00	0.10	0.72	0.10	0.89	0.08	0.93	-0.79	-1.89	0.02	0.95	**0.12**	**1.35**
						Transition-based Parser								
Arabic	72.63	52.81	72.71	53.67	72.79*	53.94*	72.75*	53.91*	71.75#	48.61#	72.77*	53.84*	72.74*	53.84*
English	77.26	61.84	77.15#	61.67	77.16	61.84	77.30	62.41	76.85#	60.14#	77.32	62.33	**77.53***	**63.29***
French	74.25	63.09	74.37	63.84	74.38	64.09	74.24	62.84	74.14	62.34	74.59*	**64.59**	**74.69***	64.09
German	70.29	63.02	70.24	62.97	70.22	62.76	70.29	63.07	67.97#	56.38#	70.21	62.19	70.16	62.34
Hindi	84.08	66.14	83.99#	65.16	**84.16***	**67.24***	84.14*	67.05*	83.78#	63.08#	84.10	66.99	84.14	66.99
Spanish	75.39	57.86	75.52	59.59*	75.67*	59.93*	75.38	59.07	75.19	60.10	**76.10***	**63.90***	75.68	62.52*
Swedish	73.45	66.59	73.48	66.46	73.52	66.66	73.60*	67.02	72.91#	64.61#	74.01*	68.27*	**74.09***	**68.53***
Δ all	0.00	0.00	0.02	0.36	0.11	0.70	0.02	0.53	-0.76	-2.10	0.12	1.01	**0.20**	**1.50**

Table 4: LAS scores for the parsing performance on the test sets when replacing OOV words with a DT. Additionally, we present Δ values for all languages.

	oTAG								reTAG							
	similarity				suffix				similarity				suffix			
	SKG		CBOW		SKG		CBOW		SKG		CBOW		SKG		CBOW	
Language	all	OOV	all	OOV	all	OOV	all	OOV	all	OOV	all	OOV	all	OOV	all	OOV
								Graph-based Parser								
Arabic	75.62	58.00*	75.71*	57.97*	75.67	**58.62***	75.73*	58.49*	75.54	57.66*	75.69	57.83*	75.65	58.42*	75.73*	58.49*
English	79.55	63.85	79.57	64.16	79.58	63.99	79.61	64.03	78.86#	59.97#	79.64	64.12	79.38	62.81	79.57	64.03
German	**74.47***	69.55*	74.39	69.29	74.39*	69.35	74.40*	69.24	72.82#	64.26#	73.70#	66.60#	74.06	67.95	74.14	68.41
Δ all	0.08	0.64	0.08	0.83	0.09	0.65	0.11	0.76	-0.73	-2.53	-0.11	-0.10	-0.13	-0.31	0.01	0.49
								Transition-based Parser								
Arabic	72.62	53.67*	72.65	53.60*	**72.88***	**54.80***	72.72	53.67*	72.60	53.46	72.64	53.49*	72.85*	54.53*	72.71	53.63*
English	77.10#	61.49	77.24	62.06	77.17	62.28	77.28	62.46*	76.54#	57.78#	77.22	61.84	77.07	60.58	77.24	62.37
German	70.19	63.07	70.22	63.38	70.17	**63.54**	**70.36**	63.49	68.90#	57.62#	69.48#	60.68#	69.98#	62.09	70.06	62.60
Δ all	-0.09	0.19	0.01	0.98	-0.02	0.46	0.06	0.65	-0.71	-2.94	-0.09	-0.16	-0.28	-0.55	0.06	0.31

Table 5: LAS scores for the parsing performance replacing OOV words with w2v and Δ values.

tagging quality, whereas the *sim w2v*-strategies decrease POS accuracy. Here, we see improvements for ADJ for all but the *sim*-based *w2v*-strategies, improvements on NOUN for all but *SKG suffix*, and for all *suffix* strategies for VERB. Inspecting again the words that can be replaced by all replacement strategies we observe the highest accuracy improvement using the *suffix* strategies: here the scores outperform the baseline (78.07%) up to 84.00% using the *DT* and up to 80.90% with *CBOW*.

The largest difference and the decisive factor for English and German happens on the PROPN tag: Whereas *DT sim* and *SKG suffix* only result in small positive changes, all other strategies frequently mis-tag PROPN as NOUN, increasing this error class by a relative 15% – 45%. These are mostly replacements of rare proper names with rare nouns, which are less found in *DT* replace-

ments due to the similarity threshold. Regarding the other languages, we found largest improvements in French for NOUN for the *DT sim* replacement, coupled with losses on PROPN. Both *DT* strategies improved VERB. For Spanish largest improvements were found in ADJ, NOUN and PRON for both *DT* strategies. Small but significant improvements for Hindi were distributed across parts of speech, and for Arabic, no sizeable improvements were observed.

Only for Arabic we observe a general performance drop when replacing OOV words. Inspecting the OOV words, we detect that around 97% of these words have been annotated as X (other). Overall, the test set contains 8.4% of such annotations, whereas X is rarely encountered in our other languages. Since the baseline performance for Arabic POS is very high, there is not much to improve with replacements.

6.2 Analysis of Parsing Accuracy by Relation Label

We have conducted a differential analysis comparing LAS F-scores on all our languages between the baseline and the different replacement options, specifically for understanding the effects of *DT reTAG* strategies. Focusing on frequent dependency labels (average occurrence: 4% – 14%), we gain improvements for the relations `conj`, `amod` and `case` across all test sets. Except for Hindi, the LAS F1 score increases up to 0.6% F1 for `case` relations, which is the relation between preposition (or post-positions) and the head noun of the prepositional phrase. For the `amod` relation that connects modifying adjectives to nouns, we observe a +0.5% – +1% improvement in F-score for all languages except Hindi and French, corresponding largely to the increased POS accuracy for nouns and adjectives.

For English, we found most improvements in the relations `compound` (about +1 F1) and `name` (+0.5 – +5.0 F1) for both parsers, while relations `cop` and `xcomp` were recognized less precisely (-0.2 – -0.9 F1). The graph-based parser also improves largely in `appos` (+3.5 – +4.2 F1) and `nmod:npmod` (+5.2 – +6.5 F1), while the transition-based parser sees improvements in `iobj` (+3.8 – +5.1 F1) and `neg` (+1.0 F1). For German, the `case` relation improves for both parsers with +0.2 – +0.6 F1. The graph-based parser improves on `auxpass` (+1.1 – 1.4 F1) and `conj` (+0.4 – +0.9 F1). Whereas pinpointing systematic differences between the two parsers is hardly possible, we often observe that the graph-based parser seems to perform better on rare relations, whereas the transition-based parser deals better with frequent relations.

As with the overall evaluation, there is no clear trend for the *suffix* vs. the *sim* strategy for single relations, except for graph-based German `dobj` and `iobj`, which stayed the same or performed worse for the *DT suffix reTAG* (0 – -0.9 F1), but improved greatly for *DT sim reTAG* (+0.9 – +2.4 F1).

In summary, OOV replacement seems to benefit dependency parsing mostly on relations that involve open class words, as well as relations that need semantic information for disambiguation, e.g. `case`, `dobj` and `iobj`.

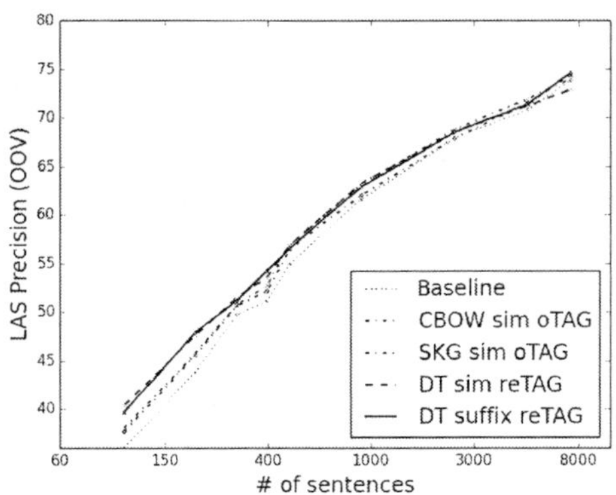

Figure 1: Learning curve of LAS for OOV words for English development set.

7 Discussion

In the following we want to discuss about selecting a recommendation for the OOV replacement and will highlight the differences we observed in our experiments between graph-based and dense-vector-based similarities.

7.1 Recommendations for OOV Replacement

Our experiments show that a simple OOV replacement strategy can lead to significant improvements for dependency parsing across typologically different languages. Improvements can be partially attributed to gains in the POS tagging quality especially with the *suffix*-based replacement strategy, and partially attributed to improved use of lexicalized information from semantic similarity.

Overall, the strategy of replacing OOV words first and POS-tagging the sequence on the basis of the replacements (*reTAG*) shows to be more effective than the other way around. While improvements are generally small yet significant, we still believe that OOV replacement is a viable strategy, especially given its simplicity. In learning curve experiments, as exemplified in Figure 1, we found the relative effect to be more pronounced for smaller amounts of training, despite having less in-vocabulary material to choose from. Thus, our approach seems especially suited for low-resource languages where labeled training material is notoriously scarce.

The question whether to use *DT suffix* or *DT sim* as replacement strategy for dependency parsing is not easily answered – while *DT suffix* shows the best overall improvements across the datasets, *DT sim* performs slightly better on Arabic and English graph-based parsing and English POS tagging.

7.2 On Differences between Graph-Based and Dense-Vector Similarity

What would be needed to fruitfully utilize the popular neural language model *w2v* as a similarity source, and why does the graph-based *DT* seems to be so much more suited for OOV replacement? From above analysis and from data inspection, we attribute the advantage of *DT* to its capability of NOT returning replacements when it has too low confidence, i.e. no in-vocabulary word is found with a similarity score of 5 or more. In contrast, vector spaces do not provide an interpretable notion of similarity/closeness that can be uniformly applied as a similarity threshold: we have compared cosine similarities of token replacements that lead to improvements, no changes and drops, and found no differences between their average values. A further difference is the structure of the vector space and the *DT* similarity rankings: Whereas the *DT* returns similar words with a frequency bias, i.e. rather frequent words are found in the most similar words per OOV target, the vector space does not have such frequency bias and, since there are more rare than frequent words in language, returns many rare words from the background corpus[8]. This effect can be alleviated to some extent when applying frequency thresholds, but is in turn aggravated when scaling up the background corpus. Thus, a condition that would only take the top-N most similar words from the background collection into account for expansions is also bound to fail for *w2v*. The only reasonable mechanism seems to be a background corpus frequency threshold on the in-vocabulary word. However, even when comparing only on the positions where both *DT* and *w2v* returned replacements, we still find *DT* replacements more advantageous. Inspection revealed that while many replacements are the same for the similarity sources, the *DT* replacements more often stay in the same word class (cf. Table 1), e.g. regarding conjugative forms of verbs and regarding the distinction between common and proper nouns.

---

[8]we have seen this effect repeatedly and consistently across corpora, languages and parameters

8 Conclusion

In this paper, we have shown that syntactic preprocessing, both POS tagging and dependency parsing, can benefit from OOV replacement. We have devised a simple yet effective strategy (*DT suffix reTAG*) to improve the quality of universal dependency parsing by replacing OOV words via semantically similar words that share a suffix, subsequently run the POS tagger and the dependency parser over the altered sequence, and projecting the labels back to the original sequence. In these experiments similar words from a count-based distributional thesaurus are more effective than the dense numeric w2v approach.

In future work, we will apply our method for other types of lexicalized parsers, such as constituency grammar and combinatory categorial grammar parsers, as well as examine the influence of OOVs on semantic tasks like semantic role labeling or frame-semantic parsing.

References

Jacob Andreas and Dan Klein. 2014. How much do word embeddings encode about syntax? In *Proceedings of the 52nd Annual Meeting of the Association for Computational Linguistics (Volume 2: Short Papers)*, pages 822–827, Baltimore, Maryland.

Miguel Ballesteros and Joakim Nivre. 2016. Maltoptimizer: Fast and effective parser optimization. *Natural Language Engineering*, 22:187–213, 3.

Mohit Bansal, Kevin Gimpel, and Karen Livescu. 2014. Tailoring Continuous Word Representations for Dependency Parsing. In *Proceedings of the 52nd Annual Meeting of the Association for Computational Linguistics*, ACL '14, pages 809–815, Baltimore, MA, USA.

Chris Biemann and Martin Riedl. 2013. Text: Now in 2D! A Framework for Lexical Expansion with Contextual Similarity. *Journal of Language Modelling*, 1(1):55–95.

Bernd Bohnet. 2010. Very High Accuracy and Fast Dependency Parsing is Not a Contradiction. In *Proceedings of the 23rd International Conference on Computational Linguistics*, COLING '10, pages 89–97, Beijing, China.

Peter F. Brown, Peter V. deSouza, Robert L. Mercer, Vincent J. Della Pietra, and Jenifer C. Lai. 1992. Class-based N-gram Models of Natural Language. *Computational Linguistics*, 18(4):467–479.

Wenliang Chen, Yue Zhang, and Min Zhang. 2014. Feature Embedding for Dependency Parsing. In *Proceedings of the 25th International Conference on*

Computational Linguistics, COLING 2014, pages 816–826, Dublin, Ireland.

Stefan Evert. 2005. *The Statistics of Word Cooccurrences: Word Pairs and Collocations*. Ph.D. thesis, Institut für maschinelle Sprachverarbeitung, University of Stuttgart.

Rashmi Gangadharaiah, Ralf D. Brown, and Jaime Carbonell. 2010. Monolingual Distributional Profiles for Word Substitution in Machine Translation. In *Proceedings of the 23rd International Conference on Computational Linguistics*, COLING 2010, pages 320–328, Beijing, China.

Zellig Sabbetai Harris. 1951. *Methods in Structural Linguistics*. University of Chicago Press, Chicago.

Hen-Hsen Huang, Huan-Yuan Chen, Chang-Sheng Yu, Hsin-Hsi Chen, Po-Ching Lee, and Chun-Hsun Chen. 2014. Sentence Rephrasing for Parsing Sentences with OOV Words. In *Proceedings of the Ninth International Conference on Language Resources and Evaluation (LREC'14)*, pages 26–31, Reykjavik, Iceland.

Ronald M. Kaplan and Joan Bresnan. 1982. Lexical-Functional Grammar: A Formal System for Grammatical Representation. In *The Mental Representation of Grammatical Relations*, pages 173–281. MIT Press, Cambridge, MA.

Terry Koo, Xavier Carreras, and Michael Collins. 2008. Simple Semi-supervised Dependency Parsing. In *Proceedings of the Annual Meeting of the Association for Computational Linguistics*, ACL '08, pages 595–603, Columbus, OH, USA.

Tomas Mikolov, Kai Chen, Greg Corrado, and Jeffrey Dean. 2013. Efficient Estimation of Word Representations in Vector Space. In *Proceedings of the International Conference on Machine Learning*, ICLR 2013, pages 1310–1318, Scottsdale, AZ, USA.

Joakim Nivre, Marie-Catherine de Marneffe, Filip Ginter, Yoav Goldberg, Jan Hajic, Christopher D. Manning, Ryan McDonald, Slav Petrov, Sampo Pyysalo, Natalia Silveira, Reut Tsarfaty, and Daniel Zeman. 2016. Universal dependencies v1: A multilingual treebank collection. In *Proceedings of the Tenth International Conference on Language Resources and Evaluation (LREC 2016)*, Portorož, Slovenia.

Joakim Nivre. 2009. Non-projective dependency parsing in expected linear time. In *Proceedings of the Joint Conference of the 47th Annual Meeting of the ACL and the 4th International Joint Conference on Natural Language Processing of the AFNLP*, ACL '09, pages 351–359, Suntec, Singapore.

Robert Parker, David Graff, Junbo Kong, Ke Chen, and Kazuaki Maeda. 2011. *English Gigaword Fifth Edition*. Linguistic Data Consortium, Philadelphia.

Matthias Richter, Uwe Quasthoff, Erla Hallsteinsdóttir, and Chris Biemann. 2006. Exploiting the Leipzig Corpora Collection. In *Proceedings of the IS-LTC 2006*, pages 68–73, Ljubljana, Slovenia.

Roland Schäfer and Felix Bildhauer. 2013. *Web Corpus Construction*. Synthesis Lectures on Human Language Technologies. Morgan and Claypool.

Richard Socher, John Bauer, Christopher D. Manning, and Andrew Y. Ng. 2013. Parsing with Compositional Vector Grammars. In *Proceedings of the 51st Annual Meeting of the Association for Computational Linguistics*, ACL '13, pages 455–465, Sofia, Bulgaria.

Qin Iris Wang, Dale Schuurmans, and Dekang Lin. 2005. Strictly Lexical Dependency Parsing. In *Proceedings of the Ninth International Workshop on Parsing Technology*, Parsing '05, pages 152–159, Vancouver, BC, Canada.

Jiajun Zhang, Feifei Zhai, and Chengqing Zong. 2012. Handling Unknown Words in Statistical Machine Translation from a New Perspective. In *Proceedings of the 1st Conference on Natural Language Processing and Chinese Computing*, NLP&CC '12, pages 176–187, Beijing, China.

Real-valued Syntactic Word Vectors (RSV) for Greedy Neural Dependency Parsing

Ali Basirat and Joakim Nivre
Department of Linguistics and Philology
Uppsala University
{ali.basirat,joakim.nivre}@lingfil.uu.se

Abstract

We show that a set of real-valued word vectors formed by right singular vectors of a transformed co-occurrence matrix are meaningful for determining different types of dependency relations between words. Our experimental results on the task of dependency parsing confirm the superiority of the word vectors to the other sets of word vectors generated by popular methods of word embedding. We also study the effect of using these vectors on the accuracy of dependency parsing in different languages versus using more complex parsing architectures.

1 Introduction

Greedy transition-based dependency parsing is appealing thanks to its efficiency, deriving a parse tree for a sentence in linear time using a discriminative classifier. Among different methods of classification used in a greedy dependency parser, neural network models capable of using real-valued vector representations of words, called *word vectors*, have shown significant improvements in both accuracy and speed of parsing. It was first proposed by Chen and Manning (2014) to use word vectors in a 3-layered feed-forward neural network as the core classifier in a transition-based dependency parser. The classifier is trained by the standard back-propagation algorithm. Using a limited number of features defined over a certain number of elements in a parser configuration, they could build an efficient and accurate parser, called the Stanford neural dependency parser. This architecture then was extended by Straka et al. (2015) and Straka et al. (2016). Parsito (Straka et al., 2015) adds a search-based oracle and a set of morphological features to the original architecture in order to make it capable of parsing the corpus of universal dependencies. UDPipe (Straka et al., 2016) adds a beam search decoding to Parsito in order to improve the parsing accuracy at the cost of decreasing the parsing speed.

We propose to improve the parsing accuracy in the architecture introduced by Chen and Manning (2014) through using more informative word vectors. The idea is based on the greedy nature of the back-propagation algorithm which makes it highly sensitive to the initial state of the algorithm. Thus, it is expected that more qualified word vectors positively affect the parsing accuracy. The word vectors in our approach are formed by right singular vectors of a matrix returned by a transformation function that takes a probability co-occurrence matrix as input and expand the data massed around zero. We show how the proposed method is related to HPCA (Lebret and Collobert, 2014) and GloVe (Pennington et al., 2014).

Using these word vectors with the Stanford parser we could obtain the parsing accuracy of 93.0% UAS and 91.7% LAS on Wall Street Journal (Marcus et al., 1993). The word vectors consistently improve the parsing models trained with different types of dependencies in different languages. Our experimental results show that parsing models trained with Stanford parser can be as accurate or in some cases more accurate than other parsers such as Parsito, and UDPipe.

2 Transition-Based Dependency Parsing

A greedy transition-based dependency parser derives a parse tree from a sentence by predicting a sequence of transitions between a set of configurations characterized by a triple $c = (\Sigma, B, A)$, where Σ is a stack that stores partially processed nodes, B is a buffer that stores unprocessed nodes in the input sentence, and A is a set of partial parse trees assigned to the processed nodes. Nodes are positive integers corresponding to linear positions of words in the input sentence. The process

Proceedings of the 21st Nordic Conference of Computational Linguistics, pages 20–28,
Gothenburg, Sweden, 23-24 May 2017. ©2017 Linköping University Electronic Press

of parsing starts from an initial configuration and ends with some terminal configuration. The transitions between configurations are controlled by a classifier trained on a history-based feature model which combines features of the partially built dependency tree and attributes of input tokens.

The arc-standard algorithm (Nivre, 2004) is among the many different algorithms proposed for moving between configurations. The algorithm starts with the initial configuration in which all words are in B, Σ is empty, and A holds an artificial node 0. It uses three actions *Shift*, *Right-Arc*, and *Left-Arc* to transition between the configurations and build the parse tree. Shift pushes the head node in the buffer into the stack unconditionally. The two actions Left-Arc and Right-Arc are used to build left and right dependencies, respectively, and are restricted by the fact that the final dependency tree has to be rooted at node 0.

3 Stanford Dependency Parser

The Stanford dependency parser can be considered as a turning point in the history of greedy transition-based dependency parsing. The parser could significantly improve both the accuracy and speed of dependency parsing. The key success of the parser can be summarized in two points: 1) accuracy is improved by using a neural network with pre-trained word vectors, and 2) efficiency is improved by pre-computation to keep the most frequent computations in the memory.

The parser is an arc-standard system with a feed-forward neural-network as its classifier. The neural network consists of three layers: An input layer connects the network to a configuration through 3 real-valued vectors representing words, POS tags, and dependency relations. The vectors that represent POS-tags and dependency relations are initialized randomly but those that represent words are initialized by word vectors systematically extracted from a corpus. Each of these vectors are independently connected to the hidden layer of the network through three distinct weight matrices. A cube activation function is used in the hidden layer to model the interactions between the elements of the vectors. The activation function resembles a third degree polynomial kernel that enables the network to take different combinations of vector elements into consideration. The output layer generates probabilities for decisions between different actions in the arc-standard sys-

tem. The network is trained by the standard back-propagation algorithm that updates both network weights and vectors used in the input layer.

4 Word Vectors

Dense vector representations of words, in this paper known as word vectors, have shown great improvements in natural language processing tasks. An advantage of this representation compared to the traditional one-hot representation is that the word vectors are enriched with information about the distribution of words in different contexts.

Following Lebret and Collobert (2014), we propose to extract word vectors from a co-occurrence matrix as follows: First we build a co-occurrence matrix $\mathbf{C}$ from a text. The element $\mathbf{C}_{i,j}$ is a maximum likelihood estimation of the probability of seeing word w_j in the context of word w_i, (i.e., $\mathbf{C}_{i,j} = p(w_j|w_i)$. It results in a sparse matrix whose data are massed around zero because of the disproportional contribution of the high frequency words in estimating the co-occurrence probabilities. Each column of $\mathbf{C}$ can be seen as a vector in a high-dimensional space whose dimensions correspond to the context words. In practice, we need to reduce the dimensionality of these vectors. This can be done by standard methods of dimensionality reduction such as principal component analysis. However, the high density of data around zero and the presence of a small number of data points far from the data mass can lead to some meaningless discrepancies between word vectors.

In order to have a better representation of the data we expand the probability values in $\mathbf{C}$ by skewing the data mass from zero toward one. This can be done by any monotonically increasing concave function that magnifies small numbers in its domain while preserving the given order. Commonly used transformation functions with these characteristics are the logarithm function, the hyperbolic tangent, the power transformation, and the Box-cox transformation with some specific parameters. Fig. 1 shows how a transformation function expands high-dimensional word vectors massed around zero.

After applying f on $\mathbf{C}$, we centre the column vectors in $f(\mathbf{C})$ around their mean and build the word vectors as below:

$$\Upsilon = \gamma \mathbf{V}_{n,k}^T \tag{1}$$

where Υ is a matrix of k dimensional word vectors associated with n words, $\mathbf{V}_{n,k}^T$ is the top k

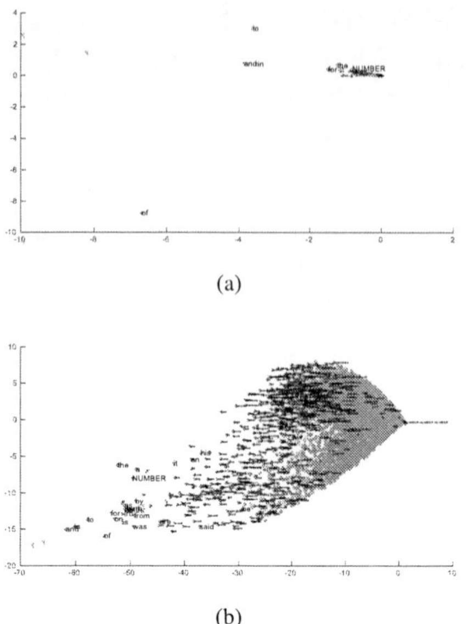

(a)

(b)

Figure 1: PCA visualization of the high-dimensional column-vectors of a co-occurrence matrix (a) before and (b) after applying the transformation function $\sqrt[10]{x}$

right singular vectors of $f(\mathbf{C})$, and $\gamma = \lambda\sqrt{n}$ is a constant factor to scale the unbounded data in the word vectors. In the following, we will refer to our model as RSV, standing for Right Singular word Vector or Real-valued Syntactic word Vectors as it is mentioned in the title of this paper.

5 Experimental Setting

We restrict our experiments to three languages, English, Swedish, and Persian. Our experiments on English are organized as follows: Using different types of transformation functions, we first extract a set of word vectors that gives the best parsing accuracy on our development set. Then we study the effect of dimensionality on parsing performance. Finally, we give a comparison between our best results and the results obtained from other sets of word vectors generated with popular methods of word embedding. Using the best transformation function obtained for English, we extract word vectors for Swedish and Persian. These word vectors are then used to train parsing models on the corpus of universal dependencies.

The English word vectors are extracted from a corpus consisting of raw sentences in Wall Street Journal (WSJ) (Marcus et al., 1993), English Wikicorpus,[1] Thomson Reuters Text Re-

search Collection (TRC2), English Wikipedia corpus,[2] and the Linguistic Data Consortium (LDC) corpus. We concatenate all the corpora and split the sentences by the OpenNLP sentence splitting tool.The Stanford tokenizer is used for tokenization. Word vectors for Persian are extracted from the Hamshahri Corpus (AleAhmad et al., 2009), Tehran Monolingual Corpus,[3] and Farsi Wikipedia download from Wikipedia Monolingual Corpora.[4] The Persian text normalizer tool (Seraji, 2015) is used for sentence splitting and tokenization.[5] Word vectors for Swedish are extracted from Swedish Wikipedia available at Wikipedia Monolingual Corpora, Swedish web news corpora (2001-2013) and Swedish Wikipedia corpus collected by Sprkbanken. [6] The OpenNLP sentence splitter and tokenizer are used for normalizing the corpora.

We replace all numbers with a special token NUMBER and convert uppercase letters to lowercase forms in English and Swedish. Word vectors are extracted only for the unique words appearing at least 100 times. We choose the cut-off word frequency of 100 because it is commonly used as a standard threshold in the other references. The 10 000 most frequent words are used as context words in the co-occurrence matrix. Table 1 represents some statistics of the corpora.

	#Tokens	#$W \geq 1$	#$W \geq 100$	#Sents
English	8×10^9	14 462 600	404 427	4×10^8
Persian	4×10^8	1 926 233	60 718	1×10^7
Swedish	6×10^8	5 437 176	174 538	5×10^7

Table 1: Size of the corpora from which word vectors are extracted; #Tokens: total number of tokens; #$W \geq k$: number of unique words appearing at least k times in the corpora; #Sents: number of sentences.

The word vectors are evaluated with respect to the accuracy of parsing models trained with them using the Stanford neural dependency parser (Chen and Manning, 2014). The English parsing models are trained and evaluated on the corpus of universal dependencies (Nivre et al., 2016) version 1.2 (UD) and Wall Street Journal (WSJ) (Marcus et al., 1993) annotated with Stanford typed dependencies (SD) (De Marneffe and Manning, 2010) and CoNLL syntactic dependencies (CD) (Johans-

---

[1] http://www.cs.upc.edu/~nlp/wikicorpus/

[2] https://dumps.wikimedia.org/enwiki/latest/ enwiki-latest-pages-articles.xml.bz2-rss.xml

[3] http://ece.ut.ac.ir/system/files/NLP/Resources/

[4] http://linguatools.org/tools/corpora/ wikipedia-monolingual-corpora

[5] http://stp.lingfil.uu.se/~mojgan

[6] https://spraakbanken.gu.se/eng/resources/corpus

son and Nugues, 2007). We split WSJ as follow: sections 02–21 for training, section 22 for development, and section 23 as test set. The Stanford conversion tool (De Marneffe et al., 2006) and the LTH conversion tool[7] are used for converting constituency trees in WSJ to SD and CD. The Swedish and Persian parsing models are trained on the corpus of universal dependencies. All the parsing models are trained with gold POS tags unless we clearly mention that predicted POS tags are used.

6 Results

In the following we study how word vectors generated by RSV influence parsing performance. RSV has four main tuning parameters: 1) the context window, 2) the transformation function f, 3) the parameter λ used in the normalization step, and 4) the number of dimensions. The context window can be symmetric or asymmetric with different length. We choose the asymmetric context window with length 1 i.e., the first preceding word, as it is suggested by Lebret and Collobert (2015) for syntactic tasks. λ is a task dependent parameter that controls the variance of word vectors. In order to find the best value of λ, we train the parser with different sets of word vectors generated randomly by Gaussian distributions with zero mean and isotropic covariance matrices λI with values of $\lambda \in (0, 1]$. Fig. 2a shows the parsing accuracies obtained from these word vectors. The best results are obtained from word vectors generated by $\lambda = 0.1$ and $\lambda = 0.01$. The variation in the results shows the importance of the variance of word vectors on the accuracy of parser. Regarding this argument, we set the normalization parameter λ in Eq. 1 equal to 0.1. The two remaining parameters are explored in the following subsections.

6.1 Transformation Function

We have tested four sets of transformation functions on the co-occurrence matrix:

- $f_1 = \tanh(nx)$

- $f_2 = \sqrt[n]{x}$

- $f_3 = n(\sqrt[n]{x} - 1)$

- $f_4 = \frac{\log(2^{n+1}x+1)}{\log(2^{n+1}+1)}$

where $x \in [0, 1]$ is an element of the matrix and n is a natural number that controls the degree of skewness, the higher the value of n is, the more

---

[7]http://nlp.cs.lth.se/software/treebank-converter/

the data will be skewed. Fig. 2b shows the effect of using these transformation functions on parsing accuracy. Best results are obtained from n^{th}-root and Box-cox transformation functions with $n = 7$, which are closely related to each other. Denoting the set of word vectors obtained from the transformation function f as $\Upsilon(f)$, it can be shown that $\Upsilon(f_3) = \Upsilon(f_2) - n$, since the effect of coefficient n in the first term of f_3 is cancelled out by the right singular vectors in Eq. 1.

Fig. 2c visualizes best transformation functions in each of the function sets. All the functions share the same property of having relatively high derivatives around 0 which allows of skewing data in the co-occurrence matrix to right (i.e., close to one) and making a clear gap between the syntactic structures that can happen (i.e., non-zeros probabilities in the co-occurrence matrix) and those that cannot happen (i.e., zero probabilities in the co-occurrence matrix. This movement from zero to one, however, can lead to disproportional expansions between the data close to zero and those that are close to one. It is because the limit of the ratio of the derivative of $f_i(x)$ $i = 1, 2, 3, 4$ to the derivative of $f_i(y)$ as x approaches to 0 and y approaches to 1 is infinity i.e., $\lim_{x \to 0, y \to 1} \frac{f_i'(x)}{f_i'(y)} = \infty$. The almost uniform behaviour of $f_1(x)$ for $x > 0.4$ results in a small variance in the generated data that will be ignored by the subsequent singular value decomposition step and consequently loses the information provided with the most probable context words. Our solution to these problems is to use the following piecewise transformation function f:

$$f = \begin{cases} \tanh(7x) & x \leq \theta \\ \sqrt[7]{x} & x > \theta \end{cases} \qquad (2)$$

where $\theta = 10^{-n}$ and $n \in \mathbb{N}$. This function expands the data in a more controlled manner (i.e., $\lim_{x \to 0, y \to 1} \frac{f'(x)}{f'(y)} = 49$) with less lost in information provided with the variance of data. Using this function with $\theta = 10^{-7}$, we could get UAS of 92.3 and LAS of 90.9 on WSJ development set annotated with Stanford typed dependencies, which is slightly better than other transformation functions (see Fig. 2b). We obtain UAS of **92.0** and LAS of **90.6** on the WSJ test set with the same setting.

6.2 Dimensionality

The dimensionality of word vectors is determined by the number of singular vectors used in Eq. 1.

23

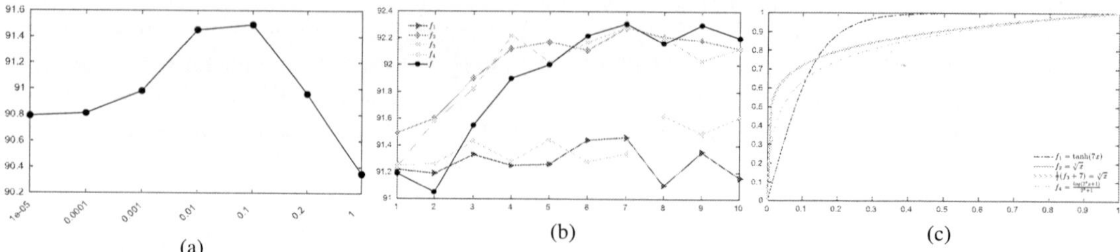

Figure 2: Unlabelled attachment score of parsing models trained with (**a**) the randomly generated word vectors, and (**b**) the systematically extracted word vectors using different transformation functions. The experiments are carried out with 50 dimensional word vectors. Parsing models are evaluated on the development set in Wall Street Journal annotated with Satnford typed dependencies (SD). f in (b) is the piecewise transformation function shown in Eq. 2. **c**: the transformation functions in each function set resulting in the best parsing models. The vertical axis shows the data in a probability co-occurrence matrix and the vertical axis shows their projection after transformation. For better visualization, the range of f_3 is scaled to $[0, 1]$.

High dimensional word vectors are expected to result in higher parsing accuracies. It is because they can capture more information from the original data, i.e., the Frobenius norm of the deference between the original matrix and its truncated estimation depends on the number of top singular vectors used for constructing the truncated matrix. This achievement, however, is at the cost of more computational resources a) to extract the word vectors, and b) to process the word vectors by parser. The most expensive step to extract the word vectors is the singular value decomposition of the transformed co-occurrence matrix. Using the randomized SVD method described by Tropp et al. (2009), the extraction of k top singular vectors of an $m \times n$ matrix requires $O(mn \log(k))$ floating point operations. It shows that the cost for having larger word vectors grows logarithmically with the number of dimensions.

The parsing performance is affected by the dimensionality of the word vectors, fed into the input layer of the neural network, in two ways: First, higher number of dimensions in the input layer lead to a larger weight matrix between the input layer and the hidden layer. Second, larger hidden layer is needed to capture the dependencies between the elements in the input layer. Given a set of word vectors with k dimensions connected to the hidden layer with h hidden units, the weight matrix between the input layer and the hidden layer grows with the scale of $O(kh)$, and the weight matrix between the hidden layer and the output layer grows with the scale of $O(h)$. For each input vector, the back-propagation algorithm passes the weight matrices three times per iteration 1) to forward each input vector through the net-

work, 2) to back propagate the errors, generated by the inputs, and 3) to update the network parameters. So, each input vector needs $O(3(kh + h)))$ time to be processed by the algorithm. Given the trained model, the output signals are generated through only one forward pass.

Table 2 shows how high dimensional word vectors affect the parsing performance. In general, increasing the number of hidden units leads to a more accurate parsing model at a linear cost of parsing speed. Increasing the dimensionality of word vectors to 200 dimensions consistently increases the parsing accuracy at again the linear time of parsing speed. However, increasing both the dimensionality of word vectors and the size of the hidden layer leads to a quadratic decrease in parsing speed. The best results are obtained from the parsing model trained with 100-dimensional word vectors and 400 hidden units, resulting in the parsing accuracy of **93.0** UAS and **91.7** LAS on our test set, $+1.0$ UAS and $+1.1$ LAS improvement over what we obtained with 50 dimensional word vectors. It is obtained at the cost of 47% reduction in the parsing speed.

6.3   Comparison and Consistency

We evaluate the RSV word vectors on different types of dependency representations and different languages. Table 3 gives a comparison between RSV and different methods of word embedding with respect to their contributions to dependency parsing and the time required to generate word vectors for English. All the parsing models are trained with 400 hidden units and 100-dimensional word vectors extracted from English raw corpus described in Sec. 5. The word vec-

$h\rightarrow$	200			300			400		
$\downarrow k$	UAS	LAS	P	UAS	LAS	P	UAS	LAS	P
50	92.3	90.9	392	92.9	91.5	307	93.0	91.6	237
100	92.6	91.2	365	92.9	91.5	263	**93.1**	**91.8**	206
150	92.6	91.2	321	92.9	91.5	236	93.1	91.8	186
200	**92.7**	**91.3**	310	**93.1**	**91.7**	212	93.1	91.8	165
250	92.7	91.2	286	92.9	91.5	201	93.0	91.7	146
300	92.6	91.2	265	92.9	91.6	180	92.9	91.5	119
350	92.7	91.2	238	92.8	91.4	174	92.9	91.5	111
400	92.6	91.2	235	92.8	91.3	141	93.0	91.5	97

Table 2: The performance of parsing models trained with k-dimensional word vectors and h hidden units. The parsing accuracies (UAS, LAS) are for the development set. P: parsing speed (sentence/second).

Model	Time	SD		CD		UD	
		UAS	LAS	UAS	LAS	UAS	LAS
		p-val	p-val	p-val	p-val	p-val	p-val
CBOW	8741	93.0	91.5	93.4	92.6	88.0	85.4
		0.00	0.00	0.02	0.00	0.00	0.00
SGram	11113	93.0	91.6	93.4	92.5	87.4	84.9
		0.06	0.02	0.00	0.00	0.00	0.00
GloVe	3150	92.9	91.6	93.5	92.6	**88.4**	85.8
		0.02	0.02	0.04	0.06	0.54	0.38
HPCA	**2749**	92.1	90.8	92.5	91.7	86.6	84.0
		0.00	0.00	0.00	0.00	0.00	0.00
RSV	2859	**93.1**	**91.8**	**93.6**	**92.8**	**88.4**	**85.9**

Table 3: Performance of word embedding methods: Quality of word vectors are measured with respect to parsing models trained with them. The efficiency of models is measured with respect to the time (seconds) required to extract a set of word vectors. Parsing models are evaluated on our English development set; SGram: SkipGram, SD: Stanford typed Dependencies, CD: CoNLL Dependencies, UD: Universal Dependencies, and p-val: p-value of the null hypothesis: *RSV is no better than the word embedding method corresponding to each cell of the table.*

tors are extracted by a Linux machine running on 12 CPU cores. The free parameters of the word embedding methods, i.e., context type and context size, have been tuned on the development set and the best settings, resulting in the highest parsing accuracies, were then chosen for comparison. It leads us to asymmetric window of length 1 for RSV, GloVe and HPCA, and symmetric window of length 1 for word2vec models, CBOW and SkipGram. The GloVe word vectors are extracted by available implementation of GloVe (Pennington et al., 2014) running for 50 iterations. The HPCA word vectors are extracted by our implementation of the method (Lebret and Collobert, 2014). CBOW and SkipGram word vectors are extracted by available implementation of word2vec (Mikolov et al., 2013) running for 10 iterations, and a negative sampling value of 5. In order to show the validity of the results, we perform a bootstrap statistical significance test (Berg-Kirkpatrick et al., 2012) on the results obtained from each parsing experiment and RSV with the null hypothesis H_0: *RSV is no better than the model B*, where B can be any of the word embedding methods. The resulting p-values are reported together with the parsing accuracies.

The empirical results show that HPCA, RSV, and GloVe are ranked as fastest methods of word embedding in order of time. The reason why these methods are faster than word2vec is because they scan the corpus only one time and then store it as a co-occurrence matrix in memory. The reason why HPCA is faster than RSV is because HPCA stores the co-occurrence matrix as a sparse matrix but RSV stores it as a full matrix. This expense makes RSV more qualified than HPCA when they are used in the task of dependency parsing.

The results obtained from RSV word vectors are comparable and slightly better than other sets of word vectors. The difference between RSV and other methods is more clear when one looks at the difference between the labelled attachment scores. Apart from the parsing experiment with GloVe on the universal dependencies, the relatively small p-values reject our null hypothesis and confirms that RSV can result in more qualified word vectors for the task of dependency parsing. In addition to this, the constant superiority of the results obtained from RSV on different dependency styles is an evidence that the results are statistically significant, i.e., the victory of RSV is not due merely to chance. Among the methods of word embedding, we see that the results obtained from GloVe are more close to RSV, especially when they come with universal dependencies. We show in Sec. 8 how these methods are connected to each other.

Table 4 shows the results obtained from Stanford parser trained with RSV vectors and two other *greedy* transition-based dependency parsers MaltParser (Nivre et al., 2006) and Parsito (Straka et al., 2015). All the parsing models are trained with the arc-standard system on the corpus of universal dependencies. Par-St and Par-Sr refer to the results reported for Parsito trained with static oracle and search-based oracle. As shown, in all cases, the parsing models trained with Stanford parser and RSV (St-RSV) are more accurate than other parsing models. The superiority of the results obtained from St-RSV to Par-Sr shows the importance of word vectors in dependency parsing in comparison with adding more features to the parser or performing the search-based oracle.

	Par-St	Par-Sr	Malt	St-RSV
	UAS	UAS	UAS	UAS
	LAS	LAS	LAS	LAS
English	86.7	87.4	86.3	**87.6**
	84.2	84.7	82.9	**84.9**
Persian	83.8	84.5	80.8	**85.4**
	80.2	81.1	77.2	**82.4**
Swedish	85.3	85.9	84.7	**86.2**
	81.4	82.3	80.3	**82.5**

Table 4: Accuracy of dependency parsing. Par-St and Par-Sr refer to the Parsito models trained with static oracle and search-based oracle. St-RSV refers to the Stanford parser trained with RSV vectors.

The results obtained from Stanford parser and UDPipe (Straka et al., 2016) are summarized in Table 5. The results are reported for both predicted and gold POS tags. UDPipe sacrifice the greedy nature of Parsito through adding a beam search decoder to it. In general, one can argue that UDPipe adds the following items to the Stanford parser: 1) a search-based oracle, 2) a set of morphological features, and 3) a beam search decoder. The almost similar results obtained from both parsers for English show that a set of informative word vectors can be as influential as the three extra items added by UDPipe. However, the higher accuracies obtained from UDPipe for Swedish and Persian, and the fact that the training data for these languages are considerably smaller than English, show the importance of these extra items on the accuracy of parsing model when enough training data is not provided.

	Predicted tags		Gold tags	
	UDPipe	St-RSV	UDPipe	St-RSV
	UAS	UAS	UAS	UAS
	LAS	LAS	LAS	LAS
English	84.0	**84.6**	87.5	**87.6**
	80.2	**80.9**	**85.0**	84.9
Swedish	**81.2**	80.4	**86.2**	86.2
	77.0	76.6	**83.2**	82.5
Persian	**84.1**	82.4	**86.3**	85.4
	79.7	78.1	**83.0**	82.4

Table 5: Accuracy of dependency parsing on the corpus of universal dependencies. St-RSV refers to the Stanford parser trained with RSV vectors.

7   Nature of Dimensions

In this section, we study the nature of dimensions formed by RSV. Starting from high-dimensional space formed by the transformed co-occurrence matrix $f(\mathbf{C})$, word similarities can be measured by a similarity matrix $K = f(\mathbf{C}^T)f(\mathbf{C})$ whose leading eigenvectors, corresponding to the leading right singular vectors of $f(\mathbf{C})$, form the RSV word vectors. It suggests that RSV dimensions measure a typical kind of word similarity on the basis of variability of word's contexts, since the eigenvectors of K account for the directions of largest variance in the word vectors defined by $f(\mathbf{C})$.

To assess the validity of this statement, we study the dimensions individually. For each dimension, we first project all unit-sized word vectors onto it and then sort the resulting data in ascending order to see if any syntactic or semantic regularities can be seen. Table 6 shows 10 words appearing in the head of ordered lists related to the first 10 dimensions. The dimensions are indexed according to their related singular vectors. The table shows that to some extent the dimensions match syntactic and semantic word categories discussed in linguistics. There is a direct relation between the indices and the variability of word's contexts. The regularities between the words appearing in highly variable contexts, mostly the high frequency words, are captured by the leading dimensions.

To a large extent, the first dimension accounts for the degree of variability of word's contexts. Lower numbers are given to words that appear in highly flexible contexts (i.e., high frequency words such as *as, but, in* and ...). Dimensions 2–5 are informative for determining syntactic categories such as adjectives, proper nouns, function words, and verbs. Dimensions 2 and 8 give lower numbers to proper names (interestingly, mostly last names in 2 and male first names in 8). Some kind of semantic regularity can also be seen in most dimensions. For example, adjectives in dimension 2 are mostly connected with society, nouns in dimension 6 denote humans, nouns in dimension 7 are abstract, and words in dimension 9 are mostly connected to affective emotions.

8   Related Work on Word Vectors

The two dominant approaches to creating word vectors (or word embeddings) are: 1) incremental methods that update a set of randomly initialized word vectors while scanning a corpus (Mikolov et al., 2013; Collobert et al., 2011), and 2) batch methods that extract a set of word vectors from a co-occurrence matrix (Pennington et al., 2014; Lebret and Collobert, 2014). Pennington et al. (2014) show that both approaches are closely related to

Dim	Top 10 words
1	. – , _ is as but in ... so
2	domestic religious civilian russian physical social iraqi japanese mexican scientific
3	mitchell reid evans allen lawrence palmer duncan russell bennett owen
4	. but in – the and or as at ,
5	's believes thinks asks wants replied tries says v. agrees
6	citizens politicians officials deputy businessmen lawmakers former elected lawyers politician
7	cooperation policy reforms policies funding reform approval compliance oversight assistance
8	geoff ron doug erik brendan kurt jeremy brad ronnie yuri
9	love feeling sense answer manner desire romantic emotional but ...
10	have were are but – _ . and may will

Table 6: Top 10 words projected on the top 10 dimensions

each other. Here, we elaborate the connections between RSV and HPCA (Lebret and Collobert, 2014) and GloVe (Pennington et al., 2014).

HPCA performs Hellinger transformation followed by principal component analysis on co-occurrence matrix $\mathbf{C}$ as below:

$$Y = SV^T \tag{3}$$

where Y is the matrix of word vecors, and S and V are matrices of top singular values and right singular vectors of $\sqrt[2]{\mathbf{C}}$. Since the word vectors are to be used by a neural network, Lebret and Collobert (2014) recommend to normalize them to avoid the saturation problem in the network weights (LeCun et al., 2012). Denoting $\tilde{Y}$ as the empirical mean of the column vectors in Y and $\sigma(Y)$ as their standard deviation, Eq. 4 suggested by Lebret and Collobert (2014) normalizes the elements of word vectors to have zero mean and a fixed standard deviation of $\lambda \leq 1$.

$$\Upsilon = \frac{\lambda(Y - \tilde{Y})}{\sigma(Y)} \tag{4}$$

$\tilde{Y}$ is $\mathbf{0}$ if one centres the column vectors in $\sqrt[2]{\mathbf{C}}$ around their mean *before* performing PCA. Substituting Eq. 3 into Eq. 4 and the facts that $\tilde{Y} = \mathbf{0}$ and $\sigma(Y) = \frac{1}{\sqrt{n-1}}S$, where n is the number of words, we reach Eq. 1.

In general, one can argue that RSV generalises the idea of Hellinger transformation used in HPCA through a set of more general transformation functions. Other differences between RSV and HPCA are in 1) how they form the co-occurrence matrix $\mathbf{C}$, and 2) when they centre the data. For each word w_i and each context word w_j, $\mathbf{C}_{i,j}$ in RSV is $p(w_j|w_i)$, but $p(w_i|w_j)$ in HPCA. In RSV, the

column vectors of $f(\mathbf{C})$ are centred around their means before performing SVD, but in HPCA, the data are centred after performing PCA. In Sec. 6, we showed that these changes result in significant improvement in the quality of word vectors.

The connections between RSV and GloVe is as follows. GloVe extracts word vectors from a co-occurrence matrix transformed by logarithm function. Using a global regression model, Pennington et al. (2014) argue that linear directions of meanings is captured by the matrix of word vectors $\Upsilon_{n,k}$ with following property:

$$\Upsilon^T \Upsilon = \log(\mathbf{C}) + \mathbf{b1} \tag{5}$$

where, $\mathbf{C}_{n,n}$ is the co-occurrence matrix, $\mathbf{b}_{n,1}$ is a bias vector, and $\mathbf{1}_{1,n}$ is a vector of ones. Denoting Υ_i as ith column of Υ and assuming $\|\Upsilon_i\| = 1$ for $i = 1 \ldots n$, the left-hand side of Eq. 5 measures the cosine similarity between unit-sized word vectors Υ_i in a kernel space and the right-hand side is the corresponding kernel matrix. Using kernel principal component analysis (Schölkopf et al., 1998), a k-dimensional estimation of Υ in Eq. 5 is

$$\Upsilon = \sqrt{S}V^T \tag{6}$$

where S and V are the matrices of top singular values and singular vectors of K. Replacing the kernel matrix in Eq. 5 with the second degree polynomial kernel $K = f(\mathbf{C}^T)f(\mathbf{C})$, which measures the similarities on the basis of the column vectors defined by the co-occurrence matrix, the word vectors generated by Eq. 6 and Eq. 1 are distributed in the same directions but with different variances. It shows that the main difference between RSV and GloVe is in the kernel matrices they are using.

9 Conclusion

In this paper, we have proposed to form a set of word vectors from the right singular vectors of a co-occurrence matrix that is transformed by a 7th-root transformation function. It has been shown that the proposed method is closely related to previous methods of word embedding such as HPCA and GloVe. Our experiments on the task of dependency parsing show that the parsing models trained with our word vectors are more accurate than the parsing models trained with other popular methods of word embedding.

References

Abolfazl AleAhmad, Hadi Amiri, Ehsan Darrudi, Masoud Rahgozar, and Farhad Oroumchian. 2009. Hamshahri: A standard persian text collection. *Knowledge-Based Systems*, 22(5):382–387.

Taylor Berg-Kirkpatrick, David Burkett, and Dan Klein. 2012. An empirical investigation of statistical significance in nlp. In *Proceedings of the 2012 Joint Conference on Empirical Methods in Natural Language Processing and Computational Natural Language Learning*, EMNLP-CoNLL '12, pages 995–1005, Stroudsburg, PA, USA. Association for Computational Linguistics.

Danqi Chen and Christopher Manning. 2014. A fast and accurate dependency parser using neural networks. In *Proceedings of the 2014 Conference on Empirical Methods in Natural Language Processing (EMNLP)*, pages 740–750.

Ronan Collobert, Jason Weston, Léon Bottou, Michael Karlen, Koray Kavukcuoglu, and Pavel Kuksa. 2011. Natural language processing (almost) from scratch. *The Journal of Machine Learning Research*, 12:2493–2537.

Marie-Catherine De Marneffe and Christopher D Manning. 2010. Stanford typed dependencies manual (2008). *URL: http://nlp.stanford.edu/ software/dependencies_manual.pdf*.

Marie-Catherine De Marneffe, Bill MacCartney, Christopher D Manning, et al. 2006. Generating typed dependency parses from phrase structure parses. In *Proceedings of LREC*, volume 6, pages 449–454.

Richard Johansson and Pierre Nugues. 2007. Extended constituent-to-dependency conversion for english. In *16th Nordic Conference of Computational Linguistics*, pages 105–112. University of Tartu.

Rémi Lebret and Ronan Collobert. 2014. Word embeddings through hellinger pca. In *Proceedings of the 14th Conference of the European Chapter of the Association for Computational Linguistics*, pages 482–490, Gothenburg, Sweden, April. Association for Computational Linguistics.

Rémi Lebret and Ronan Collobert. 2015. Rehabilitation of count-based models for word vector representations. In *Computational Linguistics and Intelligent Text Processing*, pages 417–429. Springer.

Yann A LeCun, Léon Bottou, Genevieve B Orr, and Klaus-Robert Müller. 2012. Efficient backprop. In *Neural networks: Tricks of the trade*, pages 9–48. Springer.

Mitchell P. Marcus, Beatrice Santorini, and Mary Ann Marcinkiewicz. 1993. Building a large annotated corpus of English: The Penn treebank. *Computational Linguistics - Special issue on using large corpora*, 19(2):313–330, June.

Tomas Mikolov, Kai Chen, Greg Corrado, and Jeffrey Dean. 2013. Efficient estimation of word representations in vector space. In *Proceedings of Workshop at ICLR*.

Joakim Nivre, Johan Hall, and Jens Nilsson. 2006. Maltparser: A data-driven parser-generator for dependency parsing. In *Proceedings of the 5th International Conference on Language Resources and Evaluation (LREC)*, pages 2216–2219.

Joakim Nivre, Marie-Catherine de Marneffe, Filip Ginter, Yoav Goldberg, Jan Hajic, Christopher D Manning, Ryan McDonald, Slav Petrov, Sampo Pyysalo, Natalia Silveira, et al. 2016. Universal dependencies v1: A multilingual treebank collection. In *Proceedings of the 10th International Conference on Language Resources and Evaluation (LREC 2016)*.

Joakim Nivre. 2004. Incrementality in deterministic dependency parsing. In *Proceedings of the Workshop on Incremental Parsing: Bringing Engineering and Cognition Together*, pages 50–57. Association for Computational Linguistics.

Jeffrey Pennington, Richard Socher, and Christopher D Manning. 2014. Glove: Global vectors for word representation. In *EMNLP*, volume 14, pages 1532–1543.

Bernhard Schölkopf, Alexander Smola, and Klaus-Robert Müller. 1998. Nonlinear component analysis as a kernel eigenvalue problem. *Neural computation*, 10(5):1299–1319.

Mojgan Seraji. 2015. *Morphosyntactic Corpora and Tools for Persian*. Ph.D. thesis, Uppsala University.

Milan Straka, Jan Hajic, Jana Straková, and Jan Hajic jr. 2015. Parsing universal dependency treebanks using neural networks and search-based oracle. In *International Workshop on Treebanks and Linguistic Theories (TLT14)*, pages 208–220.

Milan Straka, Jan Hajic, and Jana Strakov. 2016. Udpipe: Trainable pipeline for processing conll-u files performing tokenization, morphological analysis, pos tagging and parsing. In Nicoletta Calzolari (Conference Chair), Khalid Choukri, Thierry Declerck, Sara Goggi, Marko Grobelnik, Bente Maegaard, Joseph Mariani, Helene Mazo, Asuncion Moreno, Jan Odijk, and Stelios Piperidis, editors, *Proceedings of the Tenth International Conference on Language Resources and Evaluation (LREC 2016)*, Paris, France, may. European Language Resources Association (ELRA).

A Tropp, N Halko, and PG Martinsson. 2009. Finding structure with randomness: Stochastic algorithms for constructing approximate matrix decompositions. Technical report, Applied & Computational Mmathematics, California Institute of Technology.

Tagging Named Entities in 19th Century and Modern Finnish Newspaper Material with a Finnish Semantic Tagger

Kimmo Kettunen
The National Library of Finland
Saimaankatu 6, Mikkeli FI-50100
Kimmo.kettunen@helsinki.fi

Laura Löfberg
Department of Linguistics and English
Language, Lancaster University, UK
l.lofberg@lancaster.ac.uk

Abstract

Named Entity Recognition (NER), search, classification and tagging of names and name like informational elements in texts, has become a standard information extraction procedure for textual data during the last two decades. NER has been applied to many types of texts and different types of entities: newspapers, fiction, historical records, persons, locations, chemical compounds, protein families, animals etc. In general a NER system's performance is genre and domain dependent. Also used entity categories vary a lot (Nadeau and Sekine, 2007). The most general set of named entities is usually some version of three part categorization of locations, persons and corporations.

In this paper we report evaluation results of NER with two different data: digitized Finnish historical newspaper collection Digi and modern Finnish technology news, *Digitoday*. Historical newspaper collection Digi contains 1,960,921 pages of newspaper material from years 1771–1910 both in Finnish and Swedish. We use only material of Finnish documents in our evaluation. The OCRed newspaper collection has lots of OCR errors; its estimated word level correctness is about 70–75%, and its NER evaluation collection consists of 75 931 words (Kettunen and Pääkkönen, 2016; Kettunen et al., 2016). Digitoday's annotated collection consists of 240

articles in six different sections of the newspaper.

Our new evaluated tool for NER tagging is non-conventional: it is a rule-based Finnish Semantic Tagger, the FST (Löfberg et al., 2005), and its results are compared to those of a standard rule-based NE tagger, FiNER.

1 Introduction

Digital newspapers and journals, either OCRed or born digital, form a growing global network of data that is available 24/7, and as such they are an important source of information. As the amount of digitized journalistic data grows, also tools for harvesting the data are needed to gather information. Named Entity Recognition has become one of the basic techniques for information extraction of texts since the mid-1990s (Nadeau and Sekine, 2007). In its initial form NER was used to find and mark semantic entities like person, location and organization in texts to enable information extraction related to this kind of material. Later on other types of extractable entities, like time, artefact, event and measure/numerical, have been added to the repertoires of NER software (Nadeau and Sekine, 2007). In this paper we report evaluation results of NER for both historical 19th century Finnish and modern Finnish. Our historical data consists of an evaluation collection out of an OCRed Finnish historical newspaper collection 1771–1910 (Kettunen et al., 2016). Our present day

Proceedings of the 21st Nordic Conference of Computational Linguistics, pages 29–36,
Gothenburg, Sweden, 23-24 May 2017. ©2017 Linköping University Electronic Press

Finnish evaluation collection is from a Finnish technology newspaper Digitoday[1].

Kettunen et al. (2016) have reported NER evaluation results of the historical Finnish data with two tools, FiNER and ARPA (Mäkelä, 2014). Both tools achieved maximal F-scores of about 60 at best, but with many categories the results were much weaker. Word level accuracy of the evaluation collection was about 73%, and thus the data can be considered very noisy. Results for modern Finnish NER have not been reported extensively so far. Silfverberg (2015) mentions a few results in his description of transferring an older version of FiNER to a new version. With modern Finnish data F-scores round 90 are achieved. We use an older version of FiNER in this evaluation as a baseline NE tagger. FiNER is described more in Kettunen et al. (2016). Shortly described it is a rule-based NER tagger that uses morphological recognition, morphological disambiguation, gazetteers (name lists), as well as pattern and context rules for name tagging.

Along with FiNER we use a non-standard NER tool, a semantic tagger for Finnish, the FST (Löfberg et al., 2005). The FST is not a NER tool as such; it has first and foremost been developed for semantic analysis of full text. The FST assigns a semantic category to each word in text employing a comprehensive semantic category scheme (USAS Semantic Tagset, available in English[2] and also in Finnish[3]). The Finnish Semantic Tagger (the FST) has its origins in Benedict, the EU-funded language technology project from the early 2000s, the aim of which was to discover an optimal way of catering for the needs of dictionary users in modern electronic dictionaries by utilizing state-of-the-art language technology of the early 2000s.

The FST was developed using the English Semantic Tagger as a model. This semantic tagger was developed at the University Centre for Corpus Research on Language (UCREL) at Lancaster University as part of the UCREL Semantic Analysis System (USAS[4]) framework, and both these equivalent semantic taggers were utilized in the Benedict project in the creation of a context-sensitive search tool for a new intelligent dictionary. The overall architecture of the FST is described in Löfberg et al. (2005) and the intelligent dictionary application in Löfberg et al. (2004).

In different evaluations the FST has been shown to be capable of dealing with most general domains which appear in a modern standard Finnish text. Furthermore, although the semantic lexical resources of the tagger were originally developed for the analysis of general modern standard Finnish, evaluation results have shown that the lexical resources are also applicable to the analysis of both older Finnish text and the more informal type of writing found on the Web. In addition, the semantic lexical resources can be tailored for various domain-specific tasks thanks to the flexible USAS category system.

Lexical resources used by the FST consist of two separate lexicons: the semantically categorized single word lexicon contains 45,871 entries and the multiword expression lexicon contains 6,113 entries, representing all parts of speech.

Our aim in the paper is twofold: first we want to evaluate whether a general computational semantic tool like the FST is able to perform a limited semantic task like NER as well as dedicated NER taggers. Secondly, we try to establish the gap on NER performance of a modern Finnish tool with 19th century low quality OCRed text and good quality modern newspaper text. These two tasks will inform us about the adaptability of the FST to NER in general and also its adaptability to tagging of 19th century Finnish that has lots of errors.

2 Results for the Historical Data

Our historical Finnish evaluation data consists of 75 931 lines of manually annotated newspaper text. Most of the data is from the last decades of 19th century. Our earlier NER evaluations with this data have achieved at best F-scores of 50–60 in some name categories (Kettunen et al., 2016).

We evaluated performance of the FST and FiNER using the *conlleval*[5] script used in Conference on Computational Natural Language Learning (CONLL). *Conlleval* uses standard measures of precision, recall and F-score, the last one defined as 2PR/(R+P), where P is precision and R recall (Manning and Schütze, 1999). Its evaluation is based on "exact-match evaluation" (Nadeau and Sekine, 2007). In this type of evaluation NER system is evaluated based on the micro-averaged F-measure (MAF) where precision is the percentage of correct named entities found by the NER software; recall is the percentage of correct named entities present in the tagged evaluation corpus that are found by the NER system. In the strict version of evaluation named entity is considered correct only if it is an exact match of the corresponding entity in the tagged evaluation corpus: a result is considered correct only if the boundaries and classification are exactly as annotated (Poibeau and Kosseim, 2001). As the FST does not distinguish multipart names with their boundaries only loose evaluation without entity boundary detection was performed with the FST.

The FST tags three different types of names: personal names, geographical names and other proper names. These are tagged with tags Z1, Z2, and Z3, respectively (Löfberg et al., 2005). Their top level semantic category in the UCREL scheme is *Names & Grammatical Words (Z),* which are considered as closed class words (Hirst, 2009, Rayson et al., 2004). Z3 is a slightly vague category with mostly names of corporations, categories Z1 and Z2 are clearly cut.

Table 1 shows results of the FST's tagging of locations and persons in our evaluation data compared to those of FiNER. We performed two evaluations with the FST: one with the words as they are, and the other with $w \rightarrow v$ substitution. Variation of w and v is one of the most salient features of 19th century Finnish. Modern Finnish uses w mainly in foreign names like *Wagner*, but in 19th century Finnish w was used frequently instead of v in all words. In many other respects the Finnish of late 19th century does not differ too much from modern Finnish, and it can be analyzed reasonably well with computational tools that have been developed for modern Finnish (Kettunen and Pääkkönen, 2016).

Tag	F-score FST	F-score FiNER	Found tags FST	Found tags FiNER
Pers	51.1	58.1	1496	2681
Locs	56.7	57.5	1253	1541
Pers w/v	52.2	N/A	1566	N/A
Locs w/v	61.5	N/A	1446	N/A

Table 1. Evaluation of the FST and FiNER with loose criteria and two categories in the historical newspaper collection. W/v stands for w to v substitution in words.

Substitution of w with v decreased number of unknown words to FST with about 2% units and it has a noticeable effect on detection of locations and a small effect on persons. Overall FST recognizes locations better; their recognition with w/v substitution is almost 5 per cent points better than without substitution. FST's performance with locations outperforms that of FiNER's slightly, but FST's performance with person names is 7% points below that of FiNER. Performance of either tagger is not very good, which is expected as the data is very noisy.

It is evident that the main reason for low NER performance is the quality of the OCRed texts. If we analyze the tagged words with a morphological analyzer (Omorfi v. 0.3[6]), we can see that wrongly tagged words are recognized clearly worse by Omorfi than those that are tagged right. Figures are shown in Table 2.

	Locs	Pers
The FST: right tag, word unrec. rate	5.6	0.06
The FST: wrong tag, word unrec. rate	44.0	33.3

Table 2. Percentages of non-recognized words with correctly and wrongly tagged locations and persons – Omorfi 0.3

Another indication of the effect of textual quality to tagging is comparison of amount of

---

[5] http://www.cnts.ua.ac.be/conll2002/ner/bin/conlleval.txt, author Erik Tjong Kim Sang, version 2004-01-26

[6] https://github.com/flammie/omorfi. This release is from year 2016.

tags with equal texts of different quality. We made tests with three versions of a 100,000 word text material that is different from our historical NER evaluation material but derives from the 19th century newspaper collection as well. One text version was old OCR, another manually corrected OCR version and third a new OCRed version. Besides character level errors also word order errors have been corrected in the two new versions. For these texts we did not have a gold standard NE tagged version, and thus we could only count number of NER tags in different texts. Results are shown in Table 3.

	Locs	Gain	Pers	Gain
Old OCR	1866		2562	
Manually corrected OCR	1986	+6.4%	2694	+5.2%
New OCR	2011	+7.8%	2879	+12.4%

Table 3. Number of the FST tags in different quality OCR texts

As the figures show, there is a 5–12% unit increase in the number of tags, when the quality of the texts is better. Although all of the tags are obviously not right, the increase is still noticeable and suggests that improvement in text quality will also improve finding of NEs. Same kind of results were achieved in Kettunen et al. (2016) with FiNER and ARPA.

NER experiments with OCRed data in other languages show usually improvement of NER when the quality of the OCRed data has been improved from very poor to somehow better (Lopresti, 2009). Results of Alex and Burns (2014) imply that with lower level OCR quality (below 70% word level correctness) name recognition is harmed clearly. Packer et al. (2010) report partial correlation of Word Error Rate of the text and achieved NER result; their experiments imply that word order errors are more significant than character level errors. Miller et al. (2000) show that rate of achieved NER performance of a statistical trainable tagger degraded linearly as a function of word error rates. On the other hand, results of Rodriquez et al. (2012) show that manual correction of OCRed material that has 88–92% word accuracy does not increase performance of four different NER tools significantly.

As the word accuracy of the historical newspaper material is low, it would be expectable, that somehow better recognition results would be achieved, if the word accuracy was round 80–90% instead of 70–75%. Our informal tests with different quality texts suggest this, too, as do the distinctly different unrecognition rates with rightly and wrongly tagged words.

Ehrmann et al. (2016) suggest that application of NE tools on historical texts faces three challenges: i) noisy input texts, ii) lack of coverage in linguistic resources, and iii) dynamics of language. In our case the first obstacle is the most obvious, as was shown. Lack of coverage in linguistic resources e.g. in the form of missing old names in the lexicons of the NE tools is also a considerable source of errors in our case, as our tools are made for modern Finnish. With dynamics of language Ehrmann et al. refer to different rules and conventions for the use of written language in different times. In this respect late 19th century Finnish is not that different from current Finnish, but obviously also this can affect the results and should be studied more thoroughly.

3 Results of the FST and FiNER for the Digitoday Data

Our second evaluation data is modern Finnish, texts of a technology and business oriented web newspaper, *Digitoday*. NE tagged Digitoday data [7] has been classified to eight different content sections according to the web publication (http://www.digitoday.fi/). Two sections, *Opinion* and *Entertainment*, have been left out of the tagged data. Each content section has 15–40 tagged files (altogether 240 files) that comprise of articles, one article in each file. The content sections are *yhteiskunta* (Society), *bisnes* (Business), *tiede ja teknologia* (Science and technology), *data, mobiili* (Mobile), *tietoturva* (Data security), *työ ja ura* (Job and career) and *vimpaimet* (Gadgets) We included first 20 articles of each category's tagged data in the evaluation. *Vimpaimet* had only 15 files, which were all included in the data. Each evaluation data set includes about 2700–4100 lines of text,

---

[7]   https://github.com/mpsilfve/finer-data/tree/master/digitoday/ner_test_data_annotatated.
Data was collected on the first week of October and November 2016 in two parts.

altogether 31 100 lines with punctuation. About 64% of the evaluation data available in the Github repository was utilized in our evaluation – 155 files out of 240. Structure of the tagged files was simple; they contained one word per line and possibly a NER tag. Punctuation marks were tokenized on lines of their own. The resulting individual files had a few tags like <paragraph> and <headline>, which were removed. Also dates of publishing were removed.

Table 4 shows evaluation results of the eight sections of the Digitoday data with the FST and FiNER section-by-section. Table 5 shows combined results of the eight sections and Figure 1 shows combined results graphically.

	F-score FST	F-score FiNER	Diff. FiNER vs. the FST's F-scores	Found tags FST	Found Tags FiNER
Business					
Persons	50.00	58.93	+8,93	39	67
Locations	67.14	76.47	+9,33	82	78
Corporations	31.27	65.89	+34,62	69	214
Society					
Persons	50.00	59.86	+9,86	40	79
Locations	78.26	81.63	+3,37	146	138
Corporations	34.65	62.56	+27,91	57	166
Scitech					
Persons	56.67	43.96	-12,71	32	63
Locations	57.14	57.41	+0,27	41	51
Corporations	42.49	61.93	+19,44	88	167
Data					
Persons	56.00	32.26	-23,74	29	72
Locations	64.58	67.42	+2,84	58	51
Corporations	23.85	59.21	+35,36	60	119
Mobile					
Persons	40.00	52.78	+12,78	20	52
Locations	70.77	68.49	-2,28	38	46
Corporations	50.73	62.07	+11,34	139	231
Work and career					
Persons	71.00	72.65	+1,65	79	113
Locations	68.09	76.09	+8,00	51	49
Corporations	48.67	74.64	+25,97	71	151
Data security					
Persons	40.65	46.71	+6,06	47	91
Locations	83.05	83.93	+0,88	66	60
Corporations	29.70	39.08	+9,38	60	119
Gadgets					
Persons	84.62	50.00	-34,62	13	35
Locations	48.28	66.67	+18,39	19	20
Corporations	57.87	68.29	+10,42	90	142

Table 4. Results of FiNER and the FST with Digitoday's data section-by-section

Sections combined	F-score FST	F-score FiNER	Diff. FiNER vs. FST's F-scores	Found tags FST	Found tags FiNER
Persons	56.15	55.39	-0.76	299	572
Locations	70.77	74.58	+3.81	501	493
Corporations	40.11	62.56	+22.45	634	1309
Total for the eight sections				1434	2374

Table 5. Combined results of all Digitoday's sections

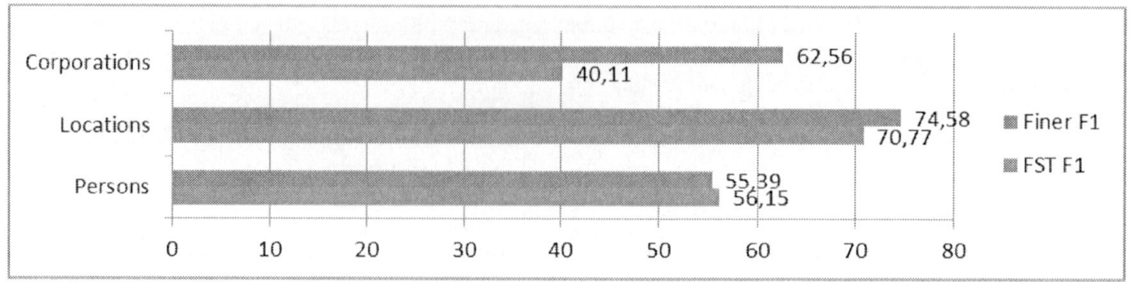

Figure 1. Combined results of all Digitoday's sections

FiNER achieves best F-scores in most of Digitoday's sections. Out of all the 24 cases, FiNER performs better in 20 cases and the FST in four. The FST performs worst with corporations, but differences with locations compared to FiNER are small. Performance differences with persons between FiNER and the FST are also not that great, and the FST performs better than FiNER in three of the sections.

Both taggers find locations best and quite evenly in all the Digitoday's sections. Persons are found varyingly by both taggers, and section wise performance is uneven. Especially bad they are found in the Data and Data security sections. One reason for FiNER's bad performance in this section is that many products are confused to persons. In Business and Society sections, persons are found more reliably. One reason for the FST's varying performance with persons is variance of section-by-section usage of Finnish and non-Finnish person names. In some sections mainly Finnish persons are discussed and in some sections mainly foreign persons. The FST recognizes Finnish names relatively well, but it does not cover foreign names as well. The morphological analyzer's components in the FST are also lexically quite old, which shows in some lacking name analyses, such as *Google, Facebook, Obama, Twitter,* if the words are in inflected forms.

4 Discussion

We have shown in this paper results of NE tagging of both historical OCRed Finnish and modern digital born Finnish with two tools, FiNER and a Finnish Semantic Tagger, the FST. FiNER is a dedicated rule-based NER tool for Finnish, but the FST is a general lexicon-based semantic tagger.

We set a twofold task for our evaluation. Firstly we wanted to compare a general computational semantics tool the FST to a dedicated NE tagger in named entity search. Secondly we wanted to see, what is the approximate decrease in NER performance of modern Finnish taggers, when they are used with noisy historical Finnish data. Answer to the first question is clear: the FST performs mostly as well as FiNER with persons and locations in modern data. With historical data FiNER outperforms the FST with persons; with locations both taggers perform equally. Corporations were not evaluated in the historical data. In Digitoday's data FiNER was clearly better than FST with corporations.

Answer to our second question is more ambiguous. With historical data both taggers achieve F-scores round 57 with locations, the FST 61.5 with w/v substitution. With Digitoday's data F-scores of 70–74.5 are achieved, and thus there is 9–16% point difference in the performance. With persons FiNER's score with both data are quite even in average. It would be expectable, that FiNER performed better with modern data. Some sections of Digitoday data (*Scitech, Data, Data Security*) are performing clearly worse than others, and FiNER's performance only in *Work and Career* is on expectable level. It is possible that section wise topical content has some effect in the results. The FST's performance with persons is worst with historical data, but with Digitoday's data it performs much better.

Technology behind FST is relatively old, but it has a sound basis and a long history. Since the beginning of the 1990s and within the framework of several different projects, the UCREL team has been developing an English semantic tagger, the EST, for the annotation of both spoken and written data with the emphasis on general language. The EST has also been redesigned to create a historical semantic tagger for English.

To show versatility of the UCREL semantic tagger approach, we list a few other computational analyses where the EST has been applied to:

- stylistic analysis of written and spoken English
- analysis and standardization of SMS spelling variation,
- analysis of the semantic content and persuasive composition of extremist media,
- corpus stylistics,
- discourse analysis,
- ontology learning,
- phraseology,
- political science research,
- sentiment analysis, and
- deception detection.

More applications are referenced on UCREL's web pages (http://ucrel.lancs.ac.uk/usas/; http://ucrel.lancs.ac.uk/wmatrix/#apps).

As can be seen from the list, the approach taken in UCREL that is also behind the FST is robust with regards to linguistic applications. Based on our results with both historical and modern Finnish data, we believe that the EST based FST is also a relevant tool for named entity recognition. It is not optimal for the task in its present form, as it lacks e.g. disambiguation of ambiguous name tags at this stage[8]. On the other hand, the FST's open and well documented semantic lexicons are adaptable to different tasks as they can be updated relatively easily. The FST would also benefit from an updated open source morphological analyzer. Omorfi[9], for example, would be suitable for use, as it has a comprehensive lexicon of over 400 000 base forms. With an up-to-date Finnish morphological analyzer and disambiguation tool the FST would yield better NER results and in the same time it would be a versatile multipurpose semantical analyzer of Finnish.

Overall our results show that a general semantic tool like the FST is able to perform in a restricted semantic task of name recognition almost as well as a dedicated NE tagger. As NER is a popular task in information extraction and retrieval, our results show that NE tagging does not need to be only a task of dedicated NE taggers, but it can be performed equally well with more general multipurpose semantic tools.

Acknowledgments

Work of the first author is funded by the EU Commission through its European Regional Development Fund, and the program Leverage from the EU 2014–2020.

References

Maud Ehrmann, Giovanni Colavizz, Yannick Rochat, and Frédéric Kaplan. 2016. Diachronic Evaluation of NER Systems on Old Newspapers. In Proceedings of the 13th Conference on Natural Language Processing (KONVENS 2016), 97–107. https://www.linguistics.rub.de/konvens16/pub/13_konvensproc.pdf

Graeme Hirst. 2009. Ontology and the Lexicon. ftp://ftp.cs.toronto.edu/pub/gh/Hirst-Ontol-2009.pdf

Kimmo Kettunen and Tuula Pääkkönen. 2016. Measuring Lexical Quality of a Historical Finnish Newspaper Collection – Analysis of Garbled OCR Data with Basic Language Technology Tools and Means. *LREC 2016, Tenth International Conference on Language Resources and Evaluation.* http://www.lrec-conf.org/proceedings/lrec2016/pdf/17_Paper.pdf.

Kimmo Kettunen, Eetu Mäkelä, Juha Kuokkala, Teemu Ruokolainen and Jyrki Niemi. 2016. Modern Tools for Old Content - in Search of Named Entities in a Finnish OCRed Historical Newspaper Collection 1771-1910. Krestel, R., Mottin, D. and Müller, E. (eds.), *Proceedings of Conference "Lernen, Wissen, Daten, Analysen", LWDA* 2016, http://ceur-ws.org/Vol-1670/

Laura Löfberg, Jukka-Pekka Juntunen, Asko Nykänen, Krista Varantola, Paul Rayson and Dawn Archer. 2004. Using a semantic tagger as dictionary search tool. In 11th EURALEX (European Association for Lexicography) International Congress Euralex 2004: 127–134.

---

[8] Many lexicon entries contain more senses than one, and these are arranged in perceived frequency order. For example, it is common in Finnish that a name of location is also a family name.

[9] https://github.com/flammie/omorfi

Laura Löfberg, Scott Piao, Paul Rayson, Jukka-Pekka Juntunen, Asko Nykänen and Krista Varantola. 2005. A semantic tagger for the Finnish language. `http://eprints.lancs.ac.uk/1268 5/1/cl2005_fst.pdf`

Daniel Lopresti. 2009. Optical character recognition errors and their effects on natural language processing. *International Journal on Document Analysis and Recognition,* 12(3): 141–151.

Eetu Mäkelä. 2014. Combining a REST Lexical Analysis Web Service with SPARQL for Mashup Semantic Annotation from Text. Presutti, V. et al. (Eds.), *The Semantic Web: ESWC 2014 Satellite Events.* Lecture Notes in Computer Science, vol. 8798, Springer: 424–428.

Christopher D. Manning and Hinrich Schütze. 1999. *Foundations of Statistical Language Processing.* The MIT Press, Cambridge, Massachusetts.

Mónica Marrero, Julián Urbano , Sonia Sánchez-Cuadrado , Jorge Morato and Juan Miguel Gómez-Berbís. 2013. Named Entity Recognition: Fallacies, challenges and opportunities. *Computer Standards & Interfaces* 35(5): 482–489.

David Miller, Sean Boisen, Richard Schwartz, Rebecca Stone and Ralph Weischedel. 2000. Named entity extraction from noisy input: Speech and OCR. *Proceedings of the 6th Applied Natural Language Processing Conference*: 316–324, Seattle, WA. `http://www.anthology.aclweb.org /A/A00/A00-1044.pdf`

David Nadeau and Satoshi Sekine. 2007. A Survey of Named Entity Recognition and Classification. *Linguisticae Investigationes* 30(1):3–26.

Thomas L. Packer, Joshua F. Lutes, Aaron P. Stewart, David W. Embley, Eric K. Ringger, Kevin D. Seppi   and Lee S. Jensen. 2010. Extracting Person Names from Diverse and Noisy OCR Tex. *Proceedings of the fourth workshop on Analytics for noisy unstructured text data. Toronto, ON, Canada*: ACM. `http://dl.acm.org/citation.cfm? id=1871845.`

Scott Piao, Paul Rayson, Dawn Archer, Francesca Bianchi, Carmen Dayrell,

Mahmoud El-Haj, Ricardo-María Jiménez, Dawn Knight, Michal Kren, Laura Löfberg, Rao Muhammad Adeel Nawab, Jawad Shafi, Phoey Lee Teh and Olga Mudraya. 2016. Lexical Coverage Evaluation of Large-scale Multilingual Semantic Lexicons for Twelve Languages. *Proceedings of LREC.* `http://www.lrec- conf.org/proceedings/lrec2016/p df/257_Paper.pdf.`

Thierry Poibeau and Leila Kosseim. 2001. Proper Name Extraction from Non-Journalistic Texts. *Language and Computers*, 37: 144–157.

Paul Rayson, Dawn Archer, Scott Piao and Tony McEnery. 2004. The UCREL semantic analysis system. *Proceedings of the workshop on Beyond Named Entity Recognition Semantic labelling for NLP tasks in association with 4th International Conference on Language Resources and Evaluation (LREC 2004)*: 7–12. `http://www.lancaster.ac.uk/staf f/rayson/publications/usas_lrec 04ws.pdf`

Kepa Joseba Rodriquez, Mike Bryant, Tobias Blanke and Magdalena Luszczynska. 2012. Comparison of Named Entity Recognition Tools for raw OCR text. *Proceedings of KONVENS 2012 (LThist 2012 wordshop), Vienna* September 21: 410–414.

Miikka Silfverberg. 2015. Reverse Engineering a Rule-Based Finnish Named Entity Recognizer. `https://kitwiki.csc.fi/twiki/pu b/FinCLARIN/KielipankkiEventNER Workshop2015/Silfverberg_presen tation.pdf.`

Machine Learning for Rhetorical Figure Detection:
More Chiasmus with Less Annotation

Marie Dubremetz
Uppsala University
Dept. of Linguistics and Philology
Uppsala, Sweden
marie.dubremetz@lingfil.uu.se

Joakim Nivre
Uppsala University
Dept. of Linguistics and Philology
Uppsala, Sweden
joakim.nivre@lingfil.uu.se

Abstract

Figurative language identification is a hard
problem for computers. In this paper we
handle a subproblem: chiasmus detection.
By chiasmus we understand a rhetorical
figure that consists in repeating two elements in reverse order: "**First** shall be
last, last shall be **first**". Chiasmus detection is a needle-in-the-haystack problem
with a couple of true positives for millions
of false positives. Due to a lack of annotated data, prior work on detecting chiasmus in running text has only considered
hand-tuned systems. In this paper, we explore the use of machine learning on a
partially annotated corpus. With only 31
positive instances and partial annotation of
negative instances, we manage to build a
system that improves both precision and
recall compared to a hand-tuned system
using the same features. Comparing the
feature weights learned by the machine
to those give by the human, we discover
common characteristics of chiasmus.

1 Introduction

Recent research shows a growing interest in the
computational analysis of style and rhetorics.
Works like Bendersky and Smith (2012) and
Booten and Hearst (2016) demonstrate that, with
sufficient amounts of data, one can even train a
system to recognize quotable sentences. Classical
machine learning techniques applied to text can
help discover much more than just linguistic structure or semantic content. The techniques applied
so far use a lot of data already annotated by internet users, for instance, tumblr sentences with
the label #quotation (Booten and Hearst, 2016). It
is a clever reuse of the web as an annotated corpus, but what happens if the stylistic phenomenon
we want to discover is not as popular on the web?
When there is no available corpus and when the
stylistic phenomenon is rare, collecting a substantial amount of annotated data seems unreachable
and the computational linguist faces the limits of
what is feasible.

This study is a contribution which aims at push-
ing this limit. We focus on the task of automatically identifying a playful and interesting study
case that is rather unknown in computational linguistics: the chiasmus. The chiasmus is a figure that consists in repeating a pair of identical
words in reverse order. The identity criterion for
words can be based on different linguistic properties, such as synonymy or morphological form.
Here we focus on chiasmi that have words with
identical lemmas, sometimes referred to as an-
timetabole, and illustrated in Example 1. From
now on, we will refer to this case as simply chiasmus.

(1) User services management: **changing** a
breed or **breeding** a **change**?

Chiasmus is named after the greek letter χ because
the pattern of repetition is often represented as an
'X' or a cross like in Figure 1.

There are several reasons why NLP should pay
attention to chiasmi. First it is a widespread linguistic phenomenon across culture and ages. Because of the Greek etymology of its name, one
might believe that chiasmus belongs only to the
rhetoricians of the classical period. It is actually
a much more ancient and universal figure. Welch
(1981) observes it in Talmudic, Ugaritic and even
Sumero-Akkadian literature. Contrary to what one

37

Proceedings of the 21st Nordic Conference of Computational Linguistics, pages 37–45,
Gothenburg, Sweden, 23-24 May 2017. ©2017 Linköping University Electronic Press

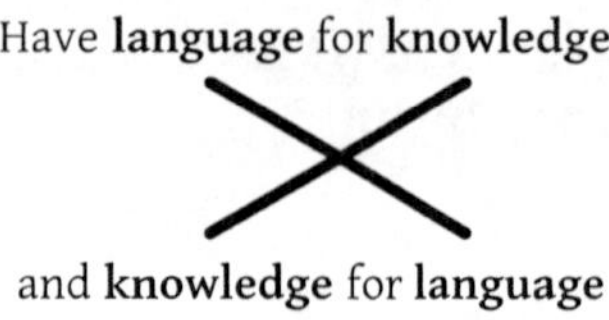

Figure 1: Schema of a chiasmus

may think, chiasmus is not an archaic ornament of language and it is used far beyond advertisement or political discourses. It is relevant for good writers of any century. Even scientists use it. For instance, currently, a small community of linguists gives a monthly 'Chiasmus Award' which each time reveals a new chiasmus produced recently by the scientific community.[1] Thus, we come to the same conclusion as Nordahl (1971). If the chiasmus has for a long time seemed to be dying, this is only true with respect to the interest devoted to it by linguists. In reality, the chiasmus, rhetorical or functional, is doing well (Nordahl, 1971). Such universality and modernity makes chiasmus detection a fruitful task to perform on many genres, on old text as on new texts.

Second, we can assume that the presence of chiasmus is a sign of writing quality because the author took the time to create it or to quote it. Nowadays the production of texts on the web is a huge industry where authors' compensation is often based on the number of words produced, which does not increase the quality. Thus, detecting such figures of speech is one clue (among others) that may help distinguish masterpieces from poorly written texts.

Finally, an additional reason for studying chiasmus, which is the focus of this paper, is its rarity. To see just how rare it is, consider Winston Churchill's *River War*, a historical narrative counting more than one hundred thousand words. Despite the author's well-known rhetorical skills, we could only find a single chiasmus in the book:

(2) **Ambition** stirs **imagination** nearly as much as **imagination** excites **ambition**.

Such rareness is a challenge for our discipline. It is well known that the statistical methods dominant in NLP work best for commonly occurring

linguistic phenomena and that accuracy often declines drastically for the long tail of low-frequency events typical of language. Detecting chiasmus is a needle-in-the-haystack problem where all the interesting instances are in the long tail. Simply identifying word pairs repeated in reverse order is trivial, but identifying the tiny fraction of these that have a rhetorical purpose is not.

Because of its rarity, the chiasmus is not well suited for large-scale annotation efforts. Previous efforts aimed at chiasmus detection have therefore not been able to use (supervised) machine learning for the simple reason that there has been no training data available. These efforts have therefore mainly been based on hand-crafted rules defining categorical distinctions and typically suffering from either low precision or low recall. Dubremetz and Nivre (2015; 2016) proposed a feature-based ranking approach instead, but because they had no annotated data to use for training, they had to resort to tuning feature weights by hand on the training set. However, an important side effect of their work was the release of a small annotated corpus of chiasmi, containing 31 positive instances, a few hundred (annotated) negative instances, and several million unannotated instances assumed to be negative.

This paper presents the first attempt to use machine learning to tune the weights of a model for chiasmus detection, using the corpus released by Dubremetz and Nivre (2016). To see whether it is possible to learn from this type of corpus at all, we train a log-linear model with the same features as Dubremetz and Nivre (2015) and Dubremetz and Nivre (2016). The results show that the machine-learned model, despite the small number of positive training instances, improves both precision and recall over the hand-tuned system, which is very encouraging. A comparison between the two types of systems reveals that they agree almost perfectly about which features are positive and negative, respectively, and that the difference in performance is therefore due simply to more well-calibrated weights. From a more general perspective, this shows that using a hand-tuned system to bootstrap a small seed corpus for machine learning may be a viable strategy for tackling needle-in-the-haystack problems like chiasmus detection.

---

[1] `http://specgram.com/psammeticuspress/chiasmus.html`

2 Related Work

When documenting chiasmus, the computational linguist ends up in a paradox: linguists have developed reflections on this rhetorical figure but those reflections are not the most helpful. Indeed, they never question the concept of criss-cross patterns as an insufficient condition for producing a rhetorical effect. Typically dictionaries and stylistic books (Fontanier, 1827; Dupriez, 2003) will explain why chiasmus should belong to the category of scheme and not of trope. Rabatel (2008) argues why chiasmus has different functions and should therefore be divided into subcategories. On the other side, Horvei (1985) demonstrates that chiasmus should not be considered as a simple subcategory of parallelism but rather as a figure on its own. All those reflections are interesting but they all focus on placing chiasmus into the vast family of rhetorical figures. Following this linguistics tradition, the first computational linguists (Gawryjolek, 2009; Hromada, 2011) working on chiasmus perform multiple figure detections. They focus on making detectors that can perform both the classification and detection of all kinds of repetitive figures such as epanaphora,[2] epiphora, [3] anadiplosis.[4] To some extent, their systems are a success in that they correctly distinguish figures from each other. Thus they prove that computers are excellent at extracting each repetition type with the right label (epiphora versus epanaphora versus chiasmus). However, they do not evaluate their systems on real corpora, using precision and recall, and therefore do not really confront the problem of false positives and accidental repetitions.

It is only a couple of years later that computational linguists dare to break with the pure linguistic tradition of handling all rhetorical figures together. With computational linguists like Strommer (2011; Dubremetz (2013) we observe the first of two important methodological shifts in how the problem is approached. For the first time computational linguists decide to focus on only one figure (epanaphora for Strommer (2011), chiasmus for Dubremetz (2013)) and provide some insight into precision/recall. By doing so, they come back to an essential question: When should we consider a repetition as accidental instead of rhetoric?

This question seems at first simpler than the question of categorising chiasmus against its alternative figures. But answering it leads to more universal and interesting answers for computational linguistics research. Indeed, repetition in language is extremely banal and viewing every repetition in a text as being rhetorical would be absurd. The very first problem in repetitive figure detection in general, in chiasmus detection in particular, is the disproportional number of false positives that the task generates. Dubremetz and Nivre (2015) point out that in 300 pages of historical tale the previous detector (Gawryjolek, 2009) extracts up to 66,000 of the criss-cross patterns (for only one true positive chiasmus to be found). At the opposite end, the more strict detector of Hromada (2011) ends up giving a completely empty output on the same book. The pattern that we have to work on, a pair of repetitions in reverse order, is so frequent and the true positive cases are so rare that it makes it impossible to annotate a corpus for a traditional classification task.

Dubremetz and Nivre (2015; 2016) introduce the second shift in the approach to chiasmus detection. Their observation is the same as the one made by Dunn (2013) on metaphora:

> One problem with the systems described [...] is that they are forced to draw an arbitrary line between two classes to represent a gradient phenomenon. (Dunn, 2013)

Like Dunn (2013) claims for metaphora, Dubremetz and Nivre (2015) claim that chiasmus detection is not a binary detection task. It is rather a ranking task similar to information retrieval. As documents are more or less relevant to a query, some chiasmi are more prototypical than others. There are extremely relevant cases like Sentence 3, some completely irrelevant repetitions like Sentence 4 and there are those in between or borderline cases like Sentence 5.

(3) How to talk so **business** will **listen** ... And **listen** so **business** will talk?

(4) Let me show you the **Disease** Ontology **update**: take a look at the expanded and **updated** database of human **diseases**, as we can see, it grew since 2014.

---

[2]"**We shall** not flag or fail. **We shall** go on to the end. **We shall fight** in France, we **shall** fight on the seas and oceans[...]"

[3]"When I was **a child**, I spoke as **a child**, I understood as **a child**, I thought as **a child**. "

[4]"Mutual recognition requires **trust, trust** requires common **standards**, and common **standards** requires solidarity."

(5) It is just as contrived to automatically allocate **Taiwan** to **China** as it was to allocate **China**'s territory to **Taiwan** in the past.

Consequently, they decide to convert the detection into a ranking task where prototypical chiasmi would be ranked at the top and less relevant instances would be gradually ranked lower. By doing so, they allow a new type of evaluation. Before evaluation was impossible due to the too big number of false instances to annotate (about 66,000 of them for only one true positive in 150,000 words). But instead of annotating the millions of instances in their training and test set, they decide to annotate only the top two hundred given by the machine. And by trying several systems and keeping trace of the previous annotations they gradually augment the number of true instances they can evaluate on (Clarke and Willett, 1997). Thus they make a needle-in-the-haystack problem a feasible task by reusing the data on which a system of detection is confident to improve evaluation and learning progressively. At the end of their study they show that chiasmi can be ranked using a combination of features like punctuation position, stopwords, similarity of n-gram context, conjunction detection, and syntax.

Because of lack of data, Dubremetz and Nivre (2015; 2016) tuned their features manually. They give average precision[5] results which is a good start. But they could not train a proper classifier. Thus, we have no idea if a computer can learn the patterns associated with rhetorical chiasmi and if a binary system would properly distinguish some true positives and not just throw all true instances in the overwhelming majority of false positives. This is the issue tackled in this paper. Using a partially annotated corpus we train a model automatically and compare the performance to the hand-tuned system. We evaluate the system using both average precision and F1-scores.

3 Corpus

We use the corpus from Dubremetz and Nivre (2015) as our training corpus (used to learn

weights for a fixed set of features) and a new corpus as our final test corpus. The training corpus consists of four million words from the Europarl corpus, containing about two million instances of criss-cross patterns. Through the previous efforts of Dubremetz and Nivre (2015; 2016), 3096 of these have been annotated by one annotator as True, False, Borderline or Duplicate.[6] The True, Borderline and Duplicate instances were then re-annotated by a second annotator. Only instances labeled True by both annotators will be considered as true positives in our experiments (at both training and test time). This makes sure that both training and evaluation is based on the most prototypical true examples. The test set is an unseen further extract of the Europarl corpus of 2 million words. For the test phase, two annotators were asked to annotate the top 200 instances of each system. In total, this produced 457 doubly annotated instances in our test set containing one million instances in total.

4 Features

Dubremetz and Nivre (2015) proposed a standard linear model to rank candidate instances:

$$f(r) = \sum_{i=1}^{n} x_i \cdot w_i$$

where r is a string containing a pair of inverted words, x_i is a set of feature values, and w_i is the weight associated with each features. Given two inversions r_1 and r_2, $f(r_1) > f(r_2)$ means that the inversion r_1 is more likely to be a chiasmus than r_2 according to the model.

The features used are listed in Table 1, using the notation defined in Figure 2. The feature groups **Basic**, **Size**, **Similarity** and **Lexical clues** come from Dubremetz and Nivre (2015), while the group **Syntactic features** was added in Dubremetz and Nivre (2016). We use the same features in our machine learning experiments but only train two systems, one corresponding to Dubremetz and Nivre (2015) (called Base) and one corresponding to Dubremetz and Nivre (2016) (called All features). This allows us to make a head-to-head comparison between the systems, where the only difference is whether feature weights have been tuned manually or using machine learning.

---

[5]Average precision is a common evaluation used in information retrieval. It considers the order in which each candidates is returned by making the average of the precision at each positive instance retrieved by the machine. Thus this measure gives more information on the performance of a ranking system than a single recall/precision value (Croft et al., 2010).

[6]For example, if the machine extracts both "**All for one, one** for **all**" and "**All for** one, one **for all**", the first is labeled True and the second Duplicate, even if both extracts cover a true chiasmus.

Figure 2: Schematic representation of chiasmus, C stands for context, W for word.

Feature	Description
Basic	
#punct	Number of hard punctuation marks and parentheses in C_{ab} and C_{ba}
#softPunct	Number of commas in C_{ab} and C_{ba}
#centralPunct	Number of hard punctuation marks and parentheses in C_{bb}
isInStopListA	W_a is a stopword
isInStopListB	W_b is a stopword
#mainRep	Number of additional repetitions of W_a or W_b
Size	
#diffSize	Difference in number of tokens between C_{ab} and C_{ba}
#toksInBC	Position of W'_a minus position of W_b
Similarity	
exactMatch	True if C_{ab} and C_{ba} are identical
#sameTok	Number of identical lemmatized tokens in C_{ab} and in C_{ba}
simScore	#sameTok but normalised
#sameBigram	Number of bigrams that are identical in C_{ab} and C_{ba}
#sameTrigram	Number of trigrams that are identical in C_{ab} and C_{ba}
#sameCont	Number of tokens that are identical in C_{Left} and C_{bb}
Lexical clues	
hasConj	True if C_{bb} contains one of the conjunctions 'and', 'as', 'because', 'for', 'yet', 'nor', 'so', 'or', 'but'
hasNeg	True if the chiasmus candidate contains one of the negative words 'no', 'not', 'never', 'nothing'
hasTo	True if the expression "from … to" appears in the chiasmus candidate or 'to' or 'into' are repeated in C_{ab} and C_{ba}
Syntactic Features	
sameTag	True if W_a W_b W_b' W_a' words have same PoS-Tag.
#sameDepW_a W_b'	Number of incoming dependency types shared by W_a and W_b'.
#sameDepW_b W_a'	Same but for W_b and W_a'
#sameDepW_a W_a'	Same but for W_a and W_a'
#sameDepW_b W_b'	Same but for W_b and W_b'

Table 1: The five groups of features used to rank chiasmus candidates

5 Learning

Training is performed on the same 4 million words corpus that was used by Dubremetz and Nivre (2015; 2016) for feature selection and manual tuning of weights. It contains more than two million instances of chiasmus candidates with 296 of them doubly annotated. We train a binary logistic regression classifier and use two fold cross-validation to set the parameters. To fit the system, we use the 31 instances labeled as True by both annotators as our positive examples. All other instances are labeled as False and thus considered as negative examples (even if most of them are actually unknown, because they were never encountered during the hand-tuning process).

We tried training on only annotated instances but the results were not satisfying. Normalizing features by the maximum values in order to get only 0 to 1 features deteriorated the result as well.

We tried over-sampling by giving a weight of 1000 to all true positive instances; this neither improved nor damaged the results. Finally, we tried support vector machines (SVM), with rbf and linear kernels, and obtained similar average precision scores as for logistic regression during training. When it comes to F-score, the SVM, unlike logistic regression, requires an over-sampling of true positives in order to perform as well as logistic regression. Otherwise, it converges to the majority baseline and classifies everything as false.

Based on these preliminary experiments, we decided to limit the final evaluation on the unseen test set to the logistic regression model, as its probability prediction allows us to rank chiasmi easily. In addition, its linear implementation allows us to observe the learned feature weights and compare them to those of the earlier hand-tuned systems. For the linear logistic regression implementation we used scikit-learn (Pedregosa et al., 2011).

Model		Avg Precision	Precision	Recall	F1-score
Machine	Base	57.1	80.0	30.8	44.4
Machine	All features	**70.8**	**90**	**69.2**	**78.3**
Human	Base	42.5	–	–	–
Human	All features	67.7	–	–	–

Table 2: Results for logistic regression model (Machine) with comparison to the hand-tuned models of Dubremetz and Nivre (2015; 2016) (Human). Inter annotator agreement $\kappa = 0.69$

6 Evaluation

Table 2 shows that the systems based on machine learning give better performance than the hand-tuned systems. With only base features, the average precision improves by as much as 15%. With syntactic features added, the difference is smaller but nevertheless 3%. The performance is measured on the 13 instances in the test set judged as True by both annotators. For the machine learning system, we also report precision, recall and F1-score. Again, we see that syntactic features help a lot, especially by improving recall from about 30% to over 69%. The F1-score of about 78% is surprisingly good given how imbalanced the classes are (13 positive instances to one million negative instances). The most impressive result is the precision score of 90% obtained by the machine when using all features. This means that 9 out of 10 instances classified as True were actually real positive instances.

7 Error Analysis

To cast further lights on the results, we performed an error analysis on the cross-validation experiments (run on the training set). In the all-features experiment, we encountered 4 false positives. Of these, 3 were actually annotated as Borderline by both annotators, and 1 was annotated as Borderline by one annotator and False by the other, which means that none of the false positives were considered False by both annotators. To illustrate some of the difficulties involved, we list 5 of the 31 positive instances in the training set (6–10), followed by the 3 borderline cases (11–13) and the 1 case of annotator disagreement (14).

Positive

(6) We do not believe that the **end** justifies the **means** but that the **means** prefigure the **end**.

(7) Do not **pick** the **winners** and let the **winners** **pick**.

(8) Europe has no problem converting **euros** into **research**, but has far greater difficulty converting **research** into **euros**.

(9) That it is not the **beginning** of the **end** but the **end** of the **beginning** for Parliament's rights.

(10) It is much better to bring **work** to **people** than to take **people** to **work**.

Borderline

(11) In parallel with the work on these practical aspects, a discussion is ongoing within the European Union on determining the mechanisms for participation both by EU Member **States** which are not members of **NATO** and by **NATO** countries which are not EU Member **States**.

(12) In that way, they of course become the **EU**'s representatives in the Member **States** instead of the Member **States**' representatives in the **EU**.

(13) If there is discrimination between a black person and a white person, or vice versa, for example if someone discriminates against a **white** Portuguese in favour of a **black** Portuguese, or against a **black** Portuguese in favour of a **white** Portuguese, this is clearly unlawful racism and should result in prosecution.

Disagreement

(14) European consciousness is that which must contribute to the development of mutual respect [...] and which must ensure that tolerance is not confused with laxity and an absence of **rules** and **laws** and that **laws** and **rules** are not made with the intention of protecting some and not others.

How can the classifier achieve such good results on both recall and precision with only 31 positive instances to learn from? We believe an important part of the explanation lies in the way the training set was constructed through repeated testing of hand-crafted features and weights. This process resulted in the annotation of more than 3 000 obvious false positive cases that were recurrently coming up in the hand-tuning experiments. The human started tuning and annotating with the most simple features like stop words to start filtering out false positives. This is in fact a necessary requirement. Without stop word filtering, the chance of finding a true positive in the top 200 instances is extremely small. Thus, if a false negative is hidden somewhere in the training set, it is likely to be one involving stop words. To the best of our knowledge, there is only one existing chiasmus ever reported in the history of rhetorics that relies exclusively on stopwords:

(15) **All** for **one**, **one** for **all**

Given this, we cannot guarantee that there are no false negatives in the training set, but we can definitely say that they are unlikely to be prototypical chiasmi. Thanks to this quality of the annotation, the machine had the maximum of information we could possibly give about false positives which is by far the most important class. In addition, the performance observed with only 31 positive training instances might be revealing something about chiasmus: the linguistic variation is limited. Thus, within 31 examples the patterns are repeated often enough so that a machine can learn to detect them.

8 Weights

Figure 3 shows the weights assigned to different features in the hand-tuning experiments of Dubremetz and Nivre (2015; 2016) and in the machine learning experiments reported in this paper. All weights have been normalized to the interval [0, 1] through division by the largest weight in each set.

The comparison gives rise to several interesting observations. The most striking one is that the machine and the human agree on which features are negative versus positive. The only exception is the **#sameTrigram** feature (cf. Table 1, group Similarity). This feature counts the number of trigrams that are identical in the two different parts of the

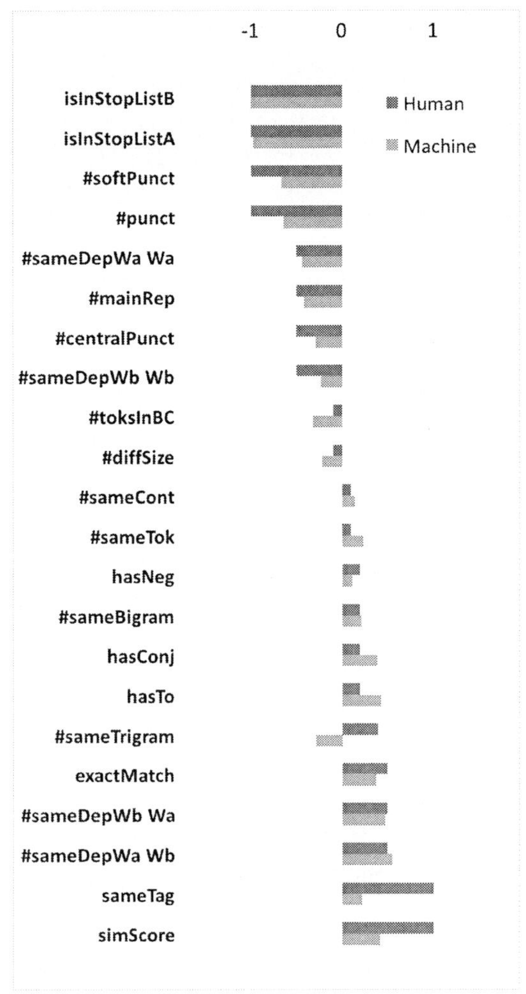

Figure 3: Feature weights from machine learning and hand-tuning, normalized to the interval [0, 1]

chiasmus. For instance, in the Kennedy quote (example 16), there is one identical trigram: *can do for*. However, we can easily explain this disagreement: this feature is one out of four that express the similarity between chiasmus propositions and may thus be redundant.

(16) Ask not what your **country** can do for **you**; ask what **you** can do for your **country**.

The machine assigned the largest weights to the stop word features, namely **isInStopListA** and **isInStopListB** (cf. Table 1), which agrees with human logic. Note, however, that the human gave the maximum weight to several other features as well, like features related to punctuation (negative) and part-of-speech tag identity (positive). Finally, we observe that the human gives the same absolute value to all the syntactic dependency features, while the machine tuned them slightly differently. It put a smaller weight on the negative feature **#sameDep$W_b W_b'$** but not on **#sameDep$W_a W_a'$**. These two negative features are of the same nature: they target the elimination of false positives based on enumerations. In prototypical chiasmi, like the one from Hippocrates (example 17), the two occurrences of a and b in the *abba* pattern have different syntactic roles because they switch positions in a repeated syntactic structure.

(17) Hippocrates said that **food** should be our **medicine** and **medicine** our **food**.

Therefore, both **#sameDep$W_a W_a'$** and **#sameDep$W_b W_b'$** penalize instances where the pairwise occurrences have the same role. To the human it was not obvious that they should be differentiated, but apparently this constraint is statistically stronger for the outermost a words.

9 Limitations and Future Work

An obvious limitation of our study is the small set of true positives on which we base the evaluation. As explained earlier, it is normal to have very few true examples even out of 2 million words of text. The Europarl corpus (Koehn, 2005), being large, consistent, but sometimes noisy, seemed to us convenient by its size and the robustness challenge it represented. Above all, it has a style that is not too specific, like poetry would be. Thus, we can hope that models tuned on this corpus would generalise to other genres (novels, for instance). A good follow-up experiment would therefore be to explore other genres and in this way test the generality of the system. This will be done in future research.

Another line of future research is to extend the approach to other (repetitive) rhetorical figures, such as *anadiplosis* (the repetition of the last word of one clause or sentence at the beginning of the next) or *anaphora* (the repetition of the same word or group of words at the beginning of successive clauses, sentences, or lines). It would be interesting to see, first, whether the same types of features would be useful and, secondly, how easy or difficult it is to discriminate between different figures.

10 Conclusion

In this paper, we target a task outside the NLP comfort zone: chiasmus detection. The challenge consists in training a model for an extremely rare stylistic phenomenon, with a corpus that is only very partially annotated. Previously, only hand tuned systems existed and we had no idea how many examples were needed to train an effective model. We trained a log-linear classifier on a four million word corpus of political debates. This corpus contained only 31 true examples, a few hundred instances explicitly annotated as false, and millions of unknown instances labeled as false by default. This method gives good recall and precision and even gives slightly higher accuracy than the hand-tuned system when it comes to ranking.

We observed strong similarities in the assignment of feature weights by human and machine, with almost total agreement on which features should be positive or not, although the machine could fine-tune the weights, for example, to account for differential syntactic patterns. An error analysis revealed that false positives were more likely than not to be cases that were considered borderline (or unclear) by human annotators. Taken together, these results indicate that we have created a system coherent with the human perception of rhetoric.

Our research is transforming a difficult needle-in-the-haystack problem into a feasible task and the only concession to do is to accept partial recall. As in old traditional methods (Blum and Mitchell, 1998; Yarowsky, 1995), we wielded the full potential of labeled and unlabeled data. We adapted it to the domain of style and creative language. Detecting chiasmus is a creative manipulation of texts that has potential applications in figurative language processing (Veale, 2011), where information retrieval becomes creative text retrieval.

References

Michael Bendersky and David Smith. 2012. A Dictionary of Wisdom and Wit: Learning to Extract Quotable Phrases. In *Proceedings of the NAACL-HLT 2012 Workshop on Computational Linguistics for Literature*, pages 69–77, Montréal, Canada. Association for Computational Linguistics.

Steven Bird, Ewan Klein, and Edward Loper. 2009. *Natural Language Processing with Python*. O'reilly edition.

Avrim Blum and Tom Mitchell. 1998. Combining Labeled and Unlabeled Data with Co-training. In *Proceedings of the Eleventh Annual Conference on Computational Learning Theory*, pages 92–100, New York, NY, USA. ACM.

Kyle Booten and Marti A Hearst. 2016. Patterns of Wisdom: Discourse-Level Style in Multi-Sentence Quotations. In *Proceedings of the 2016 Conference of the North American Chapter of the Association for Computational Linguistics: Human Language Technologies*, pages 1139–1144, San Diego, California, jun. Association for Computational Linguistics.

Sarah J. Clarke and Peter Willett. 1997. Estimating the recall performance of Web search engines. *Proceedings of Aslib*, 49(7):184–189.

Bruce Croft, Donald Metzler, and Trevor Strohman. 2010. *Search Engines: Information Retrieval in Practice: International Edition*, volume 54. Pearson Education.

Marie Dubremetz and Joakim Nivre. 2015. Rhetorical Figure Detection: the Case of Chiasmus. In *Proceedings of the Fourth Workshop on Computational Linguistics for Literature*, pages 23–31, Denver, Colorado, USA. Association for Computational Linguistics.

Marie Dubremetz and Joakim Nivre. 2016. Syntax Matters for Rhetorical Structure: The Case of Chiasmus. In *Proceedings of the Fifth Workshop on Computational Linguistics for Literature*, pages pages 47–53, San Diego, California,USA. Association for Computational Linguistics.

Marie Dubremetz. 2013. Vers une identification automatique du chiasme de mots. In *Actes de la 15e Rencontres des Étudiants Chercheurs en Informatique pour le Traitement Automatique des Langues (RECITAL'2013)*, pages 150–163, Les Sables d'Olonne, France.

Jonathan Dunn. 2013. What metaphor identification systems can tell us about metaphor-in-language. In *Proceedings of the First Workshop on Metaphor in NLP*, pages 1–10, Atlanta, Georgia. Association for Computational Linguistics.

Bernard Dupriez. 2003. *Gradus, les procédés littéraires*. Union Générale d'Éditions 10/18.

Pierre Fontanier. 1827. *Les Figures du discours*. Flammarion, 1977 edition.

Jakub J. Gawryjolek. 2009. *Automated Annotation and Visualization of Rhetorical Figures*. Master thesis, Universty of Waterloo.

Harald Horvei. 1985. *The Changing Fortunes of a Rhetorical Term: The History of the Chiasmus*. The Author.

Daniel Devatman Hromada. 2011. Initial Experiments with Multilingual Extraction of Rhetoric Figures by means of PERL-compatible Regular Expressions. In *Proceedings of the Second Student Research Workshop associated with RANLP 2011*, pages 85–90, Hissar, Bulgaria.

Philipp Koehn. 2005. Europarl: A Parallel Corpus for Statistical Machine Translation. In *The Tenth Machine Translation Summit*, pages 79–86, Phuket, Thailand.

Christopher D Manning, Mihai Surdeanu, John Bauer, Jenny Finkel, Steven J Bethard, and David McClosky. 2014. The Stanford CoreNLP Natural Language Processing Toolkit. In *Association for Computational Linguistics (ACL) System Demonstrations*, pages 55–60.

Helge Nordahl. 1971. Variantes chiasmiques. Essai de description formelle. *Revue Romane*, 6:219–232.

Fabian Pedregosa, Gaël Varoquaux, Alexandre Gramfort, Vincent Michel, Bertrand Thirion, Olivier Grisel, Mathieu Blondel, Peter Prettenhofer, Ron Weiss, Vincent Dubourg, Jake Vanderplas, Alexandre Passos, David Cournapeau, Matthieu Brucher, Matthieu Perrot, and Édouard Duchesnay. 2011. Scikit-learn: Machine Learning in Python. *Journal of Machine Learning Research*, 12:2825–2830.

Alain Rabatel. 2008. Points de vue en confrontation dans les antimétaboles PLUS et MOINS. *Langue française*, 160(4):21–36.

Claus Walter Strommer. 2011. *Using Rhetorical Figures and Shallow Attributes as a Metric of Intent in Text*. Ph.D. thesis, University of Waterloo.

Tony Veale. 2011. Creative Language Retrieval: A Robust Hybrid of Information Retrieval and Linguistic Creativity. In *The 49th Annual Meeting of the Association for Computational Linguistics: Human Language Technologies, Proceedings of the Conference, 19-24*, pages 278–287, Portland, Oregon, USA. Association for Computational Linguistics.

John Woodland Welch. 1981. *Chiasmus in Antiquity: Structures, Analyses, Exegesis*. Reprint Series. Research Press.

David Yarowsky. 1995. Unsupervised Word Sense Disambiguation Rivaling Supervised Methods. In *Proceedings of the 33rd Annual Meeting on Association for Computational Linguistics*, pages 189–196, Stroudsburg, PA, USA. Association for Computational Linguistics.

Coreference Resolution for Swedish and German using Distant Supervision

Alexander Wallin
Lund University
Department of Computer Science
Lund, Sweden
alexander@wallindevelopment.se

Pierre Nugues
Lund University
Department of Computer Science
Lund, Sweden
Pierre.Nugues@cs.lth.se

Abstract

Coreference resolution is the identification of phrases that refer to the same entity in a text. Current techniques to solve coreferences use machine-learning algorithms, which require large annotated data sets. Such annotated resources are not available for most languages today. In this paper, we describe a method for solving coreferences for Swedish and German using distant supervision that does not use manually annotated texts.

We generate a weakly labelled training set using parallel corpora, English-Swedish and English-German, where we solve the coreference for English using CoreNLP and transfer it to Swedish and German using word alignments. To carry this out, we identify mentions from dependency graphs in both target languages using hand-written rules. Finally, we evaluate the end-to-end results using the evaluation script from the CoNLL 2012 shared task for which we obtain a score of 34.98 for Swedish and 13.16 for German and, respectively, 46.73 and 36.98 using gold mentions.

1 Introduction

Coreference resolution is the process of determining whether two expressions refer to the same entity and linking them in a body of text. The referring words and phrases are generally called *mentions*. Coreference resolution is instrumental in many language processing applications such as information extraction, the construction of knowledge graphs, text summarizing, question answering, etc.

As most current high-performance coreference solvers use machine-learning techniques and su-

pervised training (Clark and Manning, 2016), building solvers requires large amounts of texts, hand-annotated with coreference chains. Unfortunately, such corpora are expensive to produce and are far from being available for all the languages, including the Nordic languages.

In the case of Swedish, there seems to be only one available corpus annotated with coreferences: SUC-Core (Nilsson Björkenstam, 2013), which consists of 20,000 words and 2,758 coreferring mentions. In comparison, the CoNLL 2012 shared task (Pradhan et al., 2012) uses a training set of more than a million word and 155,560 coreferring mentions for the English language alone.

Although models trained on large corpora do not automatically result in better solver accuracies, the two orders of magnitude difference between the English CoNLL 2012 corpus and SUC-Core has certainly consequences on the model quality for English. Pradhan et al. (2012) posited that larger and more consistent corpora as well as a standardized evaluation scenario would be a way to improve the results in coreference resolution. The same should apply to Swedish. Unfortunately, annotating 1,000,000 words by hand requires seems to be out of reach for this language for now.

In this paper, we describe a distant supervision technique to train a coreference solver for Swedish and other languages lacking large annotated corpora. Instead of using SUC-Core to train a model, we used it for evaluation.

2 Distant Supervision

Distant supervision is a form of supervised learning, though the term is sometimes used interchangeably with weak supervision and self training depending on the source (Mintz et al., 2009; Yao et al., 2010). The primary difference between distant supervision and supervised learning lies in the annotation procedure of the training data;

46

Proceedings of the 21st Nordic Conference of Computational Linguistics, pages 46–55,
Gothenburg, Sweden, 23-24 May 2017. ©2017 Linköping University Electronic Press

supervised learning uses labelled data, often obtained through a manual annotation, whereas in the case of distant supervision, the annotation is automatically generated from another source than the training data itself.

Training data can be generated using various methods, such as simple heuristics or from the output of another model. Distant supervision will often yield models that perform less well than models using other forms of supervised learning (Yao et al., 2010). The advantage of distant supervision is that the training set does not need an initial annotation. Distant supervision covers a wide range of methods. In this paper, we used an annotation projection, where the output of a coreference resolver is transferred across a parallel corpus, from English to Swedish and English to German, and used as input for training a solver in the target language (Martins, 2015; Exner et al., 2015).

3 Previous Work

Parallel corpora have been used to transfer syntactic annotation. Hwa et al. (2005) is an example of this. In the case of coreference, Rahman and Ng (2012) used statistical machine translation to align words and sentences and transfer annotated data and other entities from one language to another. They collected a large corpus of text in Spanish and Italian, translating each sentence using machine translation, applying a coreference solver on the generated text, and aligning the sentences using unsupervised machine translation methods.

Martins (2015) developed a coreference solver for Spanish and Portuguese using distant supervision, where he transferred entity mentions from English to a target language using machine-learning techniques.

In this paper, we describe a new projection method, where we use a parallel corpus similarly to Hwa et al. (2005) and, where we follow the methods and metrics described by Rahman and Ng (2012). We also reused the maximum span heuristic in Martins (2015) and the pruning of documents according to the ratio between correct and incorrect entity alignments.

4 Approach

4.1 Overview

Our goal was to create a coreference solver for Swedish and German with no labelled data to train the model. Swedish has no corpora of sufficient size to train a general coreference solver, whereas German has a large labelled corpus in the form of Tüba D/Z (Henrich and Hinrichs, 2014). Although we could have trained a solver from the Tüba D/Z dataset, we applied the same projection methods to German to determine if our method would generalize beyond Swedish.

We generated weakly labelled data using a parallel corpus consisting of sentence-aligned text with a sentence mapping from English to Swedish and English to German. We annotated the English text using a coreference solver for English and we transferred the coreference chains to the target language by word alignment. We then used the transferred coreference chains to train coreference solvers for the target languages.

4.2 Processing Pipelines

We used three language-dependent processing pipelines:

- We applied Stanford's CoreNLP (Manning et al., 2014) to annotate the English part. We used the parts of speech, dependency graphs, and coreference chains;

- Mate Tools (Björkelund et al., 2010) for German;

- For Swedish, we used Stagger (Östling, 2013) for the parts of speech and MaltParser for the dependencies (Nivre et al., 2007).

4.3 Evaluation

As annotation and evaluation framework, we followed the CoNLL 2011 and 2012 shared tasks (Pradhan et al., 2011; Pradhan et al., 2012). These tasks evaluated coreference resolution systems for three languages: English, Arabic, and Chinese. To score the systems, they defined a set of metrics as well as a script that serves as standard in the field.

We carried out the evaluation for both Swedish and German with this CoNLL script. For Swedish, we used SUC-Core (Nilsson Björkenstam, 2013) as a test set, while for German, we used the Tüba-D/Z corpus in the same manner as with SUC-Core (Henrich and Hinrichs, 2013; Henrich and Hinrichs, 2014).

5 Parallel Corpora

5.1 Europarl

As parallel corpora, we used the Europarl corpus (Koehn, 2005), consisting of protocols and articles from the EU parliament gathered from 1996 in 21 language pairs.

Europarl is a large sentence-aligned unannotated corpus consisting of both text documents and web data in the XML format. Each language pair has alignment files to map the respective sentences in the different languages. We only used the text documents in this study and we removed unaligned sentences.

Koehn (2005) evaluated the Europarl corpus using the BLEU metric (Papineni et al., 2002). High BLEU scores are preferable as they often result in better word alignments (Yarowsky et al., 2001).

The BLEU values for Europarl ranged from 10.3 to 40.2, with the English-to-Swedish at 24.8 and English-to-German at 17.6, where 0 means no alignment and 100 means a perfect alignment. Additionally, Ahrenberg (2010) notes that the English-Swedish alignment of Europarl contains a high share of structurally complex relations, which makes word alignment more difficult.

5.2 Word Alignment

To carry out the transfer of entity mentions, we aligned the sentences and the words of the parallel corpora, where English was the *source language* and Swedish and German, the *target languages*. Europarl aligns the documents and sentences using the Gale and Church algorithm. This introduces additional errors when aligning the words.

Instead, we used the precomputed word alignments from the open parallel corpus, OPUS, where improper word alignments are mitigated (Lee et al., 2010; Tiedemann, 2012). The word alignments in OPUS use the phrase-based grow-diag-final-and heuristic, which gave better results. Additionally, many of the challenges in aligning English to Swedish described by Ahrenberg (2010) appeared to be mitigated.

6 Bilingual Mention Alignment

From the word alignment, we carried out the mention transfer. We used a variation of the maximum span heuristic.

6.1 Maximal Span Heuristic

Bilingual word alignment is complicated even under ideal circumstances as modeling errors, language differences, and slight differences in meaning may all affect the word alignment negatively.

Figure 1 shows two examples of good and bad projections from Yarowsky et al. (2001). The figures describe two projection scenarios with varying levels of complexity from a source language on the top of the figures to a target language at the bottom. The solid lines correspond to word alignments while the dotted lines define the boundaries of their maximum span heuristic. Yarowsky et al. (2001) argue that even though individual word alignments are incorrect, a group of words corresponding to a noun phrase in the source language tends to be aligned with another group in the target language. The largest span of aligned words from a noun phrase in the target language usually corresponds to the original noun phrase in the source language.

Following Yarowsky et al. (2001), the maximal span heuristic is to discard any word alignment not mapped to the largest continuous span of the target language and discard overlapping alignments, where one mention is not bounded by the other mentions for each mention.

The heuristic is nontrivial to evaluate and we primarily selected it for its simplicity, as well as its efficiency with coreference solvers for Spanish and Portuguese using distant supervision (Martins, 2015).

6.2 Maximum Span Optimal Mention

The maximum span heuristic uses no syntactic knowledge other than tokenization for the target language.

We implemented a variation of the maximum span heuristic which utilizes syntactic knowledge of the target language. We selected the largest mention bounded by each maximum span instead of the maximum span itself. As result, the generated corpus would only consist of valid mentions rather than brackets of text without any relation to a mention. This has the additional benefit of simplifying overlapping spans as a mention has a unique head and the problem of overlapping is replaced with pruning mentions with identical bounds.

6.3 Document Pruning

We removed some documents in the corpus from the generated data set according to two metrics: The document length and alignment agreement as in Martins (2015).

The goal was to create a training set with comparable size to the CoNLL task, i.e. a million

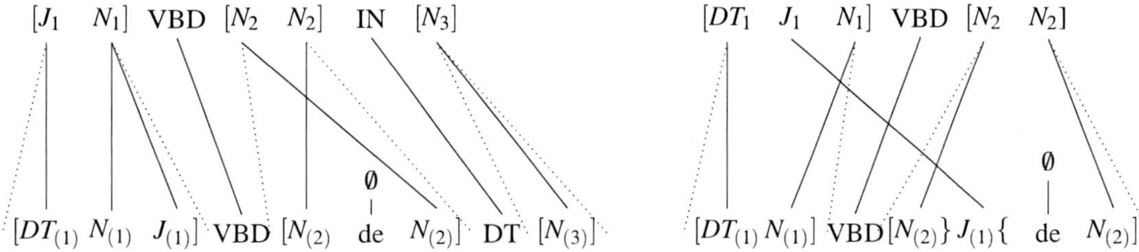

Figure 1: Left: Standard projection scenario according to Yarowsky et al. (2001); Right: Problematic projection scenario

words or more. To this effect, we aligned all the documents using the maximum span variant and we measured the alignment accuracy defined as the number of accepted alignments divided by the sum of all alignments.

We removed all the documents with lower than average alignment accuracy. Additionally, larger documents were removed until we could generate a total training set consisting of approximately a million words in total.

7 Evaluation

7.1 Metrics

There are multiple metrics to evaluate coreference resolution. We used the CoNLL 2012 score as it consists of a single value (Pradhan et al., 2012). This score is the mean of three other metrics: $MUC6$ (Vilain et al., 1995), B^3 (Bagga and Baldwin, 1998), and $CEAF_E$ (Luo, 2005). We also report the values we obtained with $CEAF_M$, and $BLANC$ (Recasens and Hovy, 2011).

7.2 Test Sets

Swedish: SUC-Core. The SUC-Core corpus (Nilsson Björkenstam, 2013) consists of 20,000 words and tokens in 10 documents with 2,758 coreferring mentions. The corpus is a subset of the SUC 2.0 corpus, annotated with noun phrase coreferential links (Gustafson-Capková and Hartmann, 2006).

The corpus is much too small to train a coreference solver, but it is more than sufficient to evaluate solvers trained on some different source material. As a preparatory step to evaluate coreference resolution in Swedish, the information from SUC-Core was merged with SUC 2.0 and SUC 3.0 to have a CoNLL 2012 compatible file format. Additionally, we removed the singletons from merged data files.

German: Tüba D/Z. The Tüba D/Z corpus (Henrich and Hinrichs, 2013; Henrich and Hinrichs, 2014) consists of 1,787,801 words and tokens organized in 3,644 files annotated with both part of speech and dependency graph information.

Although the corpus would be sufficient in size to train a coreference solver, we only used it for evaluation in this work. As with SUC-Core, we removed all the singletons. Due to time and memory constraints, we only used a subset of the Tüba D/Z corpus for evaluation.

7.3 End-to-End Evaluation

Similarly to the CoNLL 2011 and 2012 shared tasks, we evaluated our system using gold and predicted mention boundaries. When given the gold mentions, the solver knows the boundaries of all nonsingleton mentions in the test set, while with predicted mention boundaries, the solver has no prior knowledge about the test set. We also followed the shared tasks in only using machine-annotated parses as input.

The rationale for using gold mention boundaries is that they correspond to the use of an ideal method for mention identification, where the results are an upper bound for the solver as it does not consider singleton mentions (Pradhan et al., 2011).

8 Experimental Setup

8.1 Selection of Training Sets

For Swedish, we restricted the training set to the shortest documents containing at least one coreference chain. After selection and pruning, this set consisted of 4,366,897 words and 183,207 sentences in 1,717 documents.

For German, we extracted a training set consisting of randomly selected documents containing at least one coreference chain. After selection and pruning, the set consisted of 9,028,208 words and 342,852 sentences in 1,717 documents.

8.2 Mention Identification

Swedish. The mentions in SUC-Core correspond to noun phrases. We identified them automatically from the dependency graphs produced by Maltparser using a set of rules based on the mention headwords. Table 1 shows these rules that consist of a part of speech and an additional constraint. When a rule matches the part of speech of a word, we create the mention from its yield.

As SUC-Core does not explicitly define the mention bracketing rules, we had to further analyze this corpus to discern basic patterns and adjust the rules to better map the mention boundaries (Table 2).

German. The identification of noun phrases in German proved more complicated than in Swedish, especially due to the split antecedents linked by a coordinating conjunction. Consider the phrase *Anna and Paul. Anna, Paul,* as well as the whole phrase are mentions of entities. In Swedish, the corresponding phrase would be *Anna och Paul* with the conjunction *och* as the head word. The annotation scheme used for the TIGER corpus does not have the conjunction as head for coordinated noun phrases (Albert et al., 2003). In Swedish, the rule for identifying the same kind of split antecedents only needs to check whether a conjunction has children that were noun phrases, whereas in German the same rule required more analysis.

Table 3 shows the rules for the identification of noun phrases in German, and Table 4, the postprocessing rules.

9 Algorithms

9.1 Generating a Training Set

To solve coreference, we used a variation of the closest antecedent approach described in Soon et al. (2001). This approach models chains as a projected graph with mentions as vertices, where every mention has at most one antecedent and one anaphora. The modeling assumptions relaxes the complex relationship between coreferring mentions by only considering the relationship between a mention and its closest antecedent.

The problem is framed as a binary classification problem, where the system only needs to decide

POS	Additional rule	NP
UO	Dependency head has POS PM	No
	Otherwise	Yes
PM	Dependency head has POS PM but different grammatical case	Yes
	Dependency head has POS PM	No
	Otherwise	Yes
PS		Yes
PN		Yes
NN		Yes
KN	The head word is *och* and has at least one child who is a mention	Yes
	Otherwise	No
DT	The head word is *den*	Yes
	Otherwise	No
JJ	The head word is *själv*	Yes
	Otherwise	No

Table 1: Hand-written rules for noun phrase identification for Swedish based on SUC-Core. The rules are ordered by precedence from top to bottom

#	Description
1	Remove words from the beginning or the end of the phrase if they have the POS tags ET, EF or VB.
2	The first and last words closest to the mention head with the HP POS tag and all words further from the mention head is removed from the phrase.
3	Remove words from the beginning or the end of the phrase if they have the POS tags AB or MAD.
4	The first and last words closest to the mention head with the HP POS tag and with the dependency arch SS and all words further from the mention head is removed from the phrase.
5	Remove words from the end of the phrase if they have the POS tag PP.
6	Remove words from the beginning or the end of the phrase if they have the POS tag PAD.

Table 2: Additional hand-written rules for post processing the identified noun phrases

whether a mention and its closest antecedent corefer (Soon et al., 2001). When generating a training set, the negative examples are more frequent than

POS	Additional rule	NP
NN	Depend. head has POS NN	No
	Otherwise	Yes
NE	Depend. head has POS NE	No
	Otherwise	Yes
PRELS		Yes
PRF		Yes
PPOSAT		Yes
PRELAT		Yes
PIS		Yes
PDAT		Yes
PDS		Yes
FM		Yes
CARD		Yes

Table 3: Hand-written rules for noun phrase identification for German based on Tüba-D/Z

#	Rule
1	Remove words from the start or the end of the phrase if they have the POS tags $. $(PROP KON.
2	If there is a word with the POS tag VVPP after the head word the word prior to this word becomes the last word in the phrase.
3	If there is a dependant word with the POS tag KON and its string equals *und* create additional mentions from the phrases left and right of this word.
4	If there is a word with the POS tag APPRART after the head word the word prior to this word becomes the last word in the phrase.

Table 4: Additional hand-written rules for post processing the identified noun phrases in German

the positive ones, which may skew the model. We limited the ratio at somewhere between 4 and 5 % and randomizing which negative samples become part of the final training set.

9.2 Machine-Learning Algorithms

We used the C4.5, random forest, and logistic regression algorithms from the Weka Toolkit and LibLinear to train the models (Witten and Frank, 2005; Hall et al., 2009; Fan et al., 2008).

9.3 Features

Swedish. As features, we used a subset Stamborg et al. (2012) and Soon et al. (2001). Table 5 shows the complete list.

German. The feature set for German is described in Table 5. The primary difference between German and Swedish is the addition of gender classified names. We used the lists of names and job titles from IMS Hotcoref DE (Rösiger and Kuhn, 2016) to train the German model.

The morphological information from both CoreNLP and Mate Tools appeared to be limited when compared with Swedish, which is reflected in the feature set.

10 Results

10.1 Mention Alignment

Swedish. The Swedish EuroParl corpus consists of 8,445 documents. From these documents, we selected a subset consisting of 3,445 documents based on the size, where we preferred the smaller documents.

The selected documents contained in total 1,189,557 mentions that were successfully transferred and 541,608 rejected mentions.

We removed the documents with less than 70% successfully transferred mentions, which yielded a final tally of 515,777 successfully transferred mentions and 198,675 rejected mentions in 1,717 documents.

German. The German EuroParl corpus consists of 8,446 documents. From these documents, we randomly selected a subset consisting of 2,568 documents.

The selected documents contained in total 992,734 successfully transferred and 503,690 rejected mentions.

We removed the documents with less than 60% successfully transferred mentions, which yielded a final tally of 975,539 successfully transferred mentions and 491,009 rejected mentions in 964 documents.

10.2 Mention Identification

Swedish. Using the rules described in Table 1, we identified 91.35% of the mentions in SUC-Core. We could improve the results to 95.82% with the additional post processing rules described in Table 2.

Rule	Type	sv	de
Mentions are identical	Boolean	✓	✓
Mention head words are identical	Boolean	✓	✓
POS of anaphora head word is PN	Boolean	✓	
POS of antecedent head word is PN	Boolean	✓	
POS of anaphora head word is PM	Boolean	✓	
POS of antecedent head word is PM	Boolean	✓	
Anaphora head word has the morphological feat DT	Boolean	✓	
Antecedent head grammatical article	Enum	✓	
Anaphora head grammatical article	Enum	✓	
Antecedent grammatical number	Enum	✓	
Anaphora grammatical number	Enum	✓	
Checks if mention contains a word which is a male first name	Boolean		✓
Checks if mention contains a word which is a female first name	Boolean		✓
Checks if mention contains a word which is a job title	Boolean		✓
Checks if mention contains a word which is a male first name	Boolean		✓
Checks if mention contains a word which is a female first name	Boolean		✓
Checks if mention contains a word which is a job title	Boolean		✓
Number of intervening sentences between the two mentions. Max. 10.	Integer		✓
Grammatical gender of antecedent head word	Enum	✓	✓
Grammatical gender of anaphora head word	Enum	✓	✓
Anaphora head is subject	Enum		✓
Antecedent head is subject	Enum		✓
Anaphora has the morphological feature gen	Enum		✓
Antecedent has the morphological feature gen	Enum		✓
Anaphora has the morphological feature ind	Enum		✓
Antecedent has the morphological feature ind	Enum		✓
Anaphora has the morphological feature nom	Enum		✓
Antecedent has the morphological feature nom	Enum		✓
Anaphora has the morphological feature sg	Enum		✓
Antecedent has the morphological feature sg	Enum		✓

Table 5: The feature set used for Swedish (sv) and German (de)

German. Using the rules described in Table 3, we identified 65.90% of the mentions in Tüba D/Z. With the additional post processing rules described in Table 4, we reached a percentage of 82.08%.

10.3 Coreference Resolution

Table 6 shows the end-to-end results when using predicted mentions and Table 7 shows the results with the same pipeline with gold mentions. These latter results correspond to the upper bound figures we could obtain with this technique with a same

Language	Method	$MUC6$	B^3	$CEAF_E$	$CEAF_M$	$BLANC$	$MELA_{CoNLL}$
Swedish	J48	**46.72**	**29.11**	**28.32**	**32.67**	**29.94**	**34.98**
	Random forest	46.29	28.87	27.68	32.21	29.41	34.28
	Logistic regression	39.18	2.4	1.01	8.88	5.46	14.19
German	J48	**34.29**	**2.63**	**2.55**	**12.81**	4.67	**13.16**
	Random forest	33.51	2.54	2.4	11.82	**5.46**	12.81
	Logistic regression	33.97	2.36	1.35	12.5	4.58	12.56

Table 6: End-to-end results using predicted mentions

Language	Method	$MUC6$	B^3	$CEAF_E$	$CEAF_M$	$BLANC$	$MELA_{CoNLL}$
Swedish	J48	61.43	**37.78**	40.97	42.36	**41.51**	**46.73**
	Random forest	61.37	37.72	**41.03**	**42.46**	41.22	46.71
	Logistic regression	**84.77**	13.37	1.95	16.68	15.5	33.37
German	J48	82.69	19.74	5.86	26.75	19.56	36.1
	Random forest	77.24	**24.16**	**9.53**	**26.94**	**32.72**	**36.98**
	Logistic regression	**83.71**	17.6	4.5	25.58	16.61	35.27

Table 7: End-to-end results using gold mention boundaries

feature set.

11 Conclusion

In this paper, we have described end-to-end coreference solvers for Swedish and German that used no annotated data. We used feature sets limited to simple linguistic features easily extracted from the Swedish treebank and the German Tiger corpus, respectively. A large subset of the feature set of Stamborg et al. (2012) would very likely improve the results in this work.

The results in Tables 6 and 7 show that even though the dependency grammar based approach for identifying mentions yields a decent performance compared with CoNLL 2011 and 2012, a better identification and pruning procedure would probably significantly improve the results. This is manifest in German, where using the gold mentions results in a considerable increase of the scores: Table 7 shows a difference of more than 23 points compared with those in Table 6. This demonstrates that the large difference in scores between Swedish and German has its source in the methods used for mention identification rather than in the different feature sets or the correctness of the training set. This can be explained by the difficulty to predict mentions for German, possibly because of the differences in the dependency grammar format, as relatively few mentions were identified using their head elements.

The final results also show that classifiers based on J48 and random forests produced better scores than logistic regression.

Coreference resolution using weak labelled training data from distant supervision enabled us to create coreference solvers for Swedish and German, even though the mention alignment in the parallel corpora was far from perfect. It is difficult to compare results we obtained in this article with those presented in CoNLL, as the languages and test sets are different. Despite this, we observe that when using gold mention boundaries, we reach a $MELA_{CoNLL}$ score for Swedish that is comparable with results obtained for Arabic in the CoNLL-2012 shared task using the similar preconditions. We believe this shows the method we proposed is viable. Our results are, however, lower than those obtained for English and Chinese in the same task and could probably be improved with a better mention detection.

Acknowledgments

This research was supported by Vetenskapsrådet, the Swedish research council, under the *Det digitaliserade samhället* program.

References

Lars Ahrenberg. 2010. Alignment-based profiling of Europarl data in an English-Swedish parallel corpus. In Nicoletta Calzolari (Conference Chair), Khalid Choukri, Bente Maegaard, Joseph Mariani, Jan Odijk, Stelios Piperidis, Mike Rosner, and Daniel

Tapias, editors, *Proceedings of the Seventh International Conference on Language Resources and Evaluation (LREC'10)*, Valletta, Malta, may. European Language Resources Association (ELRA).

Stefanie Albert, Jan Anderssen, Regine Bader, Stephanie Becker, Tobias Bracht, Sabine Brants, Thorsten Brants, Vera Demberg, Stefanie Dipper, Peter Eisenberg, et al. 2003. Tiger annotationsschema. Technical report, Universität des Saarlandes.

Amit Bagga and Breck Baldwin. 1998. Entity-based cross-document coreferencing using the vector space model. In *Proceedings of the 36th Annual Meeting of the Association for Computational Linguistics and 17th International Conference on Computational Linguistics - Volume 1*, ACL '98, pages 79–85, Stroudsburg, PA, USA. Association for Computational Linguistics.

Anders Björkelund, Bernd Bohnet, Love Hafdell, and Pierre Nugues. 2010. A high-performance syntactic and semantic dependency parser. In *Proceedings of the 23rd International Conference on Computational Linguistics: Demonstrations*, pages 33–36. Association for Computational Linguistics.

Kevin Clark and Christopher D. Manning. 2016. Improving coreference resolution by learning entity-level distributed representations. In *Proceedings of the 54th Annual Meeting of the Association for Computational Linguistics (Volume 1: Long Papers)*, pages 643–653, Berlin, Germany, August. Association for Computational Linguistics.

Peter Exner, Marcus Klang, and Pierre Nugues. 2015. A distant supervision approach to semantic role labeling. In *Fourth Joint Conference on Lexical and Computational Semantics (* SEM 2015)*.

Rong-En Fan, Kai-Wei Chang, Cho-Jui Hsieh, Xiang-Rui Wang, and Chih-Jen Lin. 2008. LIBLINEAR: A library for large linear classification. *Journal of machine learning research*, 9(Aug):1871–1874.

Sofia Gustafson-Capková and Britt Hartmann. 2006. Manual of the Stockholm Umeå corpus version 2.0. Technical report, Stockholm University.

Mark Hall, Eibe Frank, Geoffrey Holmes, Bernhard Pfahringer, Peter Reutemann, and Ian H Witten. 2009. The WEKA data mining software: an update. *ACM SIGKDD explorations newsletter*, 11(1):10–18.

Verena Henrich and Erhard Hinrichs. 2013. Extending the TüBa-D/Z treebank with GermaNet sense annotation. In *Language Processing and Knowledge in the Web*, pages 89–96. Springer Berlin Heidelberg.

Verena Henrich and Erhard Hinrichs. 2014. Consistency of manual sense annotation and integration into the TüBa-D/Z treebank. In *Proceedings of the 13th International Workshop on Treebanks and Linguistic Theories (TLT13)*.

Rebecca Hwa, Philip Resnik, Amy Weinberg, Clara Cabezas, and Okan Kolak. 2005. Bootstrapping parsers via syntactic projection across parallel texts. *Natural language engineering*, 11(03):311–325.

Philipp Koehn. 2005. Europarl: A parallel corpus for statistical machine translation. In *MT summit*, volume 5, pages 79–86.

Jae-Hee Lee, Seung-Wook Lee, Gumwon Hong, Young-Sook Hwang, Sang-Bum Kim, and Hae-Chang Rim. 2010. A post-processing approach to statistical word alignment reflecting alignment tendency between part-of-speeches. In *Proceedings of the 23rd International Conference on Computational Linguistics: Posters*, pages 623–629. Association for Computational Linguistics.

Xiaoqiang Luo. 2005. On coreference resolution performance metrics. In *Proceedings of the conference on Human Language Technology and Empirical Methods in Natural Language Processing*, pages 25–32. Association for Computational Linguistics.

Christopher D. Manning, Mihai Surdeanu, John Bauer, Jenny Finkel, Steven J. Bethard, and David McClosky. 2014. The Stanford CoreNLP natural language processing toolkit. In *Association for Computational Linguistics (ACL) System Demonstrations*, pages 55–60.

André F. T. Martins. 2015. Transferring coreference resolvers with posterior regularization. In *Proceedings of the 53rd Annual Meeting of the Association for Computational Linguistics and the 7th International Joint Conference on Natural Language Processing (Volume 1: Long Papers)*, pages 1427–1437, Beijing, China, July. Association for Computational Linguistics.

Mike Mintz, Steven Bills, Rion Snow, and Dan Jurafsky. 2009. Distant supervision for relation extraction without labeled data. In *Proceedings of the Joint Conference of the 47th Annual Meeting of the ACL and the 4th International Joint Conference on Natural Language Processing of the AFNLP: Volume 2-Volume 2*, pages 1003–1011. Association for Computational Linguistics.

Kristina Nilsson Björkenstam. 2013. SUC-CORE: A balanced corpus annotated with noun phrase coreference. *Northern European Journal of Language Technology (NEJLT)*, 3:19–39.

Joakim Nivre, Johan Hall, Jens Nilsson, Atanas Chanev, Gülsen Eryigit, Sandra Kübler, Svetoslav Marinov, and Erwin Marsi. 2007. MaltParser: A language-independent system for data-driven dependency parsing. *Natural Language Engineering*, 13(02):95–135.

Robert Östling. 2013. Stagger: An open-source part of speech tagger for Swedish. *Northern European Journal of Language Technology (NEJLT)*, 3:1–18.

Kishore Papineni, Salim Roukos, Todd Ward, and Wei-Jing Zhu. 2002. BLEU: a method for automatic evaluation of machine translation. In *Proceedings of the 40th annual meeting on association for computational linguistics*, pages 311–318. Association for Computational Linguistics.

Sameer Pradhan, Lance Ramshaw, Mitchell Marcus, Martha Palmer, Ralph Weischedel, and Nianwen Xue. 2011. CoNLL-2011 shared task: Modeling unrestricted coreference in ontonotes. In *Proceedings of the Fifteenth Conference on Computational Natural Language Learning: Shared Task*, pages 1–27. Association for Computational Linguistics.

Sameer Pradhan, Alessandro Moschitti, Nianwen Xue, Olga Uryupina, and Yuchen Zhang. 2012. CoNLL-2012 shared task: Modeling multilingual unrestricted coreference in ontonotes. In *Joint Conference on EMNLP and CoNLL-Shared Task*, pages 1–40. Association for Computational Linguistics.

Altaf Rahman and Vincent Ng. 2012. Translation-based projection for multilingual coreference resolution. In *Proceedings of the 2012 Conference of the North American Chapter of the Association for Computational Linguistics: Human Language Technologies*, pages 720–730. Association for Computational Linguistics.

Marta Recasens and Eduard Hovy. 2011. BLANC: Implementing the rand index for coreference evaluation. *Natural Language Engineering*, 17(04):485–510.

Ina Rösiger and Jonas Kuhn. 2016. IMS HotCoref DE: A data-driven co-reference resolver for German. In *LREC*.

Wee Meng Soon, Hwee Tou Ng, and Daniel Chung Yong Lim. 2001. A machine learning approach to coreference resolution of noun phrases. *Computational linguistics*, 27(4):521–544.

Marcus Stamborg, Dennis Medved, Peter Exner, and Pierre Nugues. 2012. Using syntactic dependencies to solve coreferences. In *Joint Conference on EMNLP and CoNLL-Shared Task*, pages 64–70. Association for Computational Linguistics.

Jörg Tiedemann. 2012. Parallel data, tools and interfaces in OPUS. In Nicoletta Calzolari (Conference Chair), Khalid Choukri, Thierry Declerck, Mehmet Ugur Dogan, Bente Maegaard, Joseph Mariani, Jan Odijk, and Stelios Piperidis, editors, *Proceedings of the Eight International Conference on Language Resources and Evaluation (LREC'12)*, Istanbul, Turkey, may. European Language Resources Association (ELRA).

Marc Vilain, John Burger, John Aberdeen, Dennis Connolly, and Lynette Hirschman. 1995. A model-theoretic coreference scoring scheme. In *Proceedings of the 6th conference on Message understanding*, pages 45–52. Association for Computational Linguistics.

Ian H Witten and Eibe Frank. 2005. *Data Mining: Practical machine learning tools and techniques*. Morgan Kaufmann.

Limin Yao, Sebastian Riedel, and Andrew McCallum. 2010. Collective cross-document relation extraction without labelled data. In *Proceedings of the 2010 Conference on Empirical Methods in Natural Language Processing*, pages 1013–1023. Association for Computational Linguistics.

David Yarowsky, Grace Ngai, and Richard Wicentowski. 2001. Inducing multilingual text analysis tools via robust projection across aligned corpora. In *Proceedings of the first international conference on Human language technology research*, pages 1–8. Association for Computational Linguistics.

Aligning phonemes using finte-state methods

Kimmo Koskenniemi
University of Helsinki
Helsinki, Finland
`kimmo.koskenniemi@helsinki.fi`

Abstract

The paper presents two finite-state methods which can be used for aligning pairs of cognate words or sets of different allomorphs of stems. Both methods use weighted finite-state machines for choosing the best alternative. Individual letter or phoneme correspondences can be weighted according to various principles, e.g. using distinctive features. The comparison of just two forms at a time is simple, so that method is easier to refine to include context conditions. Both methods are language independent and could be tuned for and applied to several types of languages for producing gold standard data.

The algorithms were implemented using the HFST finite-state library from short Python programs. The paper demonstrates that the solving of some non-trivial problems has become easier and accessible for a wider range of scholars.

1 Background

In this paper, finite-state automata (FSA) and finite-state transducers (FST) are used as the basic tools. In particular, the utility of weighted finite-state transducers (WFST) and automata (WFSA) is demonstrated.

Finite-state toolboxes have been freely available for some time, e.g. OpenFST (Mohri et al., 2002), Xerox XFST (Beesley and Karttunen, 2003), HFST – Helsinki Finite-State Transducer Technology (Lindén et al., 2011), SFST (Schmid, 2005) and Foma (Hulden, 2009). These implementations have been accessible as libraries for C or C++ programmers, some also as command line programs which can be pipelined (HFST), and some as scripting languages (XFST, SFST, Foma,

HFST). Combining independent programs using shell commands is easy and suitable for many kinds of tasks, but certain combinations of operations are difficult or impossible to achieve this way. Even the XFST and SFST scripting languages have their restrictions, especially for looping, testing and input/output. It seems that none of the tasks discussed in this paper could be conveniently solved using the XFST or SFST scripting language.

More recently, most finite-state packages have been also available through Python in one way or the other. The HFST Python embedding was used here for a few reasons: it is implemented for Python 3 which uses Unicode as its native code, one could use weighted transducers, and HFST contained the kinds of functions that were needed.

2 Previous work on alignment

Automatic alignment of letters or phonemes is relevant in several areas, e.g. finding the pronunciation of unknown words or names in speech synthesis, see e.g. (Jiampojamarn et al., 2007), phonetically based spelling correction, see e.g. (Toutanova and Moore, 2002), in comparing cognate words in historical linguistics, see e.g. (Covington, 1998; Kondrak, 2000) , reconstructing proto-languages, e.g. (Bouchard-Côté et al., 2009) and in many other areas of linguistics. Character by character alignment can be approached as a machine learning problem, as in (Ciobanu and Dinu, 2014) or as a linguistic task as is done in this paper. The methods presented here make use of general properties of phonology. Still, more specific rules can be included where needed.

Covington (1998) used a special six step measure for phoneme distances and (Nerbonne and Heeringa, 1997) used phonetic features and the plain Levenshtein distance between sequences of features in order to estimate differences between Dutch dialects. (Somers, 1999) used distinctive

Proceedings of the 21st Nordic Conference of Computational Linguistics, pages 56–64,
Gothenburg, Sweden, 23-24 May 2017. ©2017 Linköping University Electronic Press

features in the comparison and his algorithm used the (manually marked) stressed vowels as the starting point whereas other approaches progressed from left to right. All these approaches were local in the sense that they measure each pair of phonemes separately and the sum of the measures was the measure of the whole alignment. Their methods appear to depend on this assumption and therefore exclude the inclusion of context dependent phenomena e.g. assimilation, metathesis, constraints of syllable structure etc.

The work presented here separates the definition of the measure from the algorithm for finding the best alignment. Measures are represented as WFSTs and they are built by producing weighted regular expressions using simple Python scripts. The algorithms used here utilize the efficient algorithms already available in the finite-state calculus for finding the best paths from weighted acyclic automata (Mohri, 2009).

3 Weighting the correspondences of phonemes

Simple phoneme by phoneme (or letter by letter) alignment is needed when relating cognate words of related languages or e.g. relating the written words in old texts with their present day forms. The process of alignment consists here of making phonetically similar phonemes correspond to each other and adding zeroes Ø where necessary (due to epenthesis or elision). E.g. Estonian *leem* and Finnish *liemi* would be aligned by adding one zero at the end of the Estonian form:

```
l e e m Ø
l i e m i
```

In general, consonants may not correspond to vowels or vice versa, except for glides, approximants or semivowels which may correspond to certain vowels and certain consonants. In this paper, many-to-one, and one-to-many correspondences are simply expressed by using combinations of phoneme to phoneme correspondences, phoneme to zero and zero to phoneme correspondences.

Vowels can be described by using distinctive features such as the height of the tongue, frontness/backness and rounding/unrounding, see Figure 1. Using such features, one may compute distances between different vowels. Similarly, consonants can be characterized by their place of articulation, voicing and the manner of articulation, see

Figure 2. The measure used here is not intended to be an absolute or universal measure, it is just an ad hoc approximation suitable for Estonian and Finnish.

```
vowels = {
    'i':('Close','Front','Unrounded'),
    'y':('Close','Front','Rounded'),
    'ü':('Close','Front','Rounded'),
    'u':('Close','Back','Rounded'),
    'e':('Mid','Front','Unrounded'),
    'ö':('Mid','Front','Rounded'),
    'õ':('Mid','Back','Unrounded'),
    'o':('Mid','Back','Rounded'),
    'ä':('Open','Front','Unrounded'),
    'a':('Open','Back','Unrounded')}
```

Figure 1: Description of some Finnish and Estonian orthographic vowels using distinctive features. IPA symbol for letters for which they are not the letter itself: ü = y, ö = ø, õ = ɤ, ä = æ, a = ɑ

The work described here permits different kinds of definitions for measuring the distances, including those used in (Covington, 1998; Kondrak, 2000; Nerbonne and Heeringa, 1997; Somers, 1999). Any measure which can reasonably be expressed as a WFST can be used by the algorithm presented in Section 4.

From the phoneme descriptions shown in Figure 1, one can compute simple distances between any two vowels or any two consonants. The formula chosen in this study was heuristic. Tongue height had three steps corresponding to values 1, 2, 3 and the distance was taken to be the difference of those values. The distance between front and back was taken to be 1 as was the distance between rounding and unrounding. The distance between any two vowels was defined to be the sum of these three numbers.[1]

A similar formula was used for consonants where the positions of articulation was numbered from 1 to 5 and their difference was the distance, see Figure 2. Different voicing counted as 1, and so did the manner of articulation. Again, the total distance was the sum of these three numbers.

A double loop through vowels and another through consonants produced a list of feasible combinations of phonemes and the computed measure for their difference. These triplets were then formatted as strings and glued together into a long regular expression, see some samples of it

---

[1]This is sometimes called Manhattan distance as opposed to the Euclidean distance which would be the square root of the sum of squares.

```
consonants = {
    'm':('Bilab','Voiced','Nasal'),
    'p':('Bilab','Unvoiced','Stop'),
    'b':('Bilab','Voiced','Stop'),
    'v':('Labdent','Voiced','Fricative'),
    'f':('Labdent','Unvoiced','Fricative'),
    'n':('Alveolar','Voiced','Nasal'),
    't':('Alveolar','Unvoiced','Stop'),
    'd':('Alveolar','Voiced','Stop'),
    's':('Alveolar','Unvoiced','Sibilant'),
    'l':('Alveolar','Voiced','Lateral'),
    'r':('Alveolar','Voiced','Tremulant'),
    'j':('Velar','Voiced','Approximant'),
    'k':('Velar','Unvoiced','Stop'),
    'g':('Velar','Voiced','Stop'),
    'h':('Glottal','Unvoiced','Fricative')}
```

Figure 2: Description of some Finnish an Estonian consonants

below:

```
...  | u:u::0 | u:y::1 | u:ä::4 | u:ö::2 ...
| k:g::1 | k:h::2 | k:j::2 | k:k::0 ...
```

Note that the weight is after a double colon according to the extended notation for weighted regular expressions used in HFST. Thus, in the above formula, u may correspond to u at null cost, and k may correspond to g at a cost of 1.

Any phoneme could be deleted or inserted at a cost. A simple loop produced the additional correspondences and their weights:

```
...  | o:∅::3 | p:∅::3 | r:∅::3 | ...
| ∅:o::3 | ∅:p::3 | ∅:r::3 | ...
```

In Finnish and in Estonian, long vowels are represented as two successive vowels. The default correspondences and weights clearly allow shortening of long vowels (or double consonants), but there would be two ways to express it with equal weights: one where the first of the two corresponds to zero, and the other where the second component corresponds to zero. In order to avoid this ambiguity, there was yet another loop which produced the necessary pieces of expressions which had a slightly smaller weight than the deletion alone. Note that e.g. $p{:}\emptyset\ p$ will remain acceptable, but the expression below gives a lower weight for the combination where the latter component corresponds to zero.

```
...  | o ∅:o::2 | p ∅:p::2 | r ∅:r::2 ...
| o o:∅::2 | p p:∅::2 | r r:∅::2 ...
```

One can use the same technique for handling orthographic conventions. One language might use *kk* and the other *ck* for a geminate *k*, similarly *ks* instead of *x* and *ts* instead of *z*. One can make such correspondences to have a zero distance by listing them with an explicit zero weight, e.g.:

```
k:c::0 k::0 | k:x s:∅::0 | t:z s:∅::0
```

One could use the same mechanism for giving some phoneme relations a lower weight. One could e.g. prefer assimilations over arbitrary combinations by imposing a lower weight for a variant if preceded or followed by phoneme which articulated in the same place. Local metathesis affecting two consecutive phonemes could also be expressed fairly neatly.

When all expressions are glued together, enclosed in brackets and followed by a Kleene star, the regular expression is ready to be compiled into a WFST. After compilation, the WFST which holds the distances as weights, can be stored as a file to be used later by the aligning algorithm.

4 Aligning pairs of words

Now, we are ready to write a small but general Python script which reads in the similarity WFST described in Section 3 and (1) reads in a pair of cognate words from the standard input and (2) converts them into FSTs W1 and W2, (3) adds explicit zero symbols freely to each, (4) compares the zero-filled expressions using the weighed distance transducer ALIGN and produces in this way all possible alignments and their total weights as a weighted transducer RES. Of these many possible alignments accepted by RES, (5) the best one is chosen and (6) printed, see Figure 3.

```
import sys, hfst
algfile = hfst.HfstInputStream("d.fst")
ALIGN = algfile.read()
for line in sys.stdin:              # (1)
    F1,F2 = line.strip().split(sep=":")  # (1)
    W1 = hfst.fst(F1)               # (2)
    W1.insert_freely(("∅","∅"))     # (3)
    W2 = hfst.fst(F2)               # (2)
    W2.insert_freely(("∅","∅"))     # (3)
    W1.compose(ALIGN)               # (4)
    W1.compose(W2)                  # (4)
    RES = W1.n_best(1).minimize()   # (5)
    paths =                         # (6)
        res.extract_paths(output='text') # (6)
    print(paths.strip())            # (6)
```

Figure 3: Python program for aligning pairs of cognate words

The algorithm in Figure 3 considers all possible ways to add zero symbols to the cognates. It even adds an indefinite number of zeros to each cognate word. For Estonian *leem* and Finnish *liemi* the adding of the zeros would result in strings covered by the following expressions.

```
W1:     0* 1 0* e 0* e 0* m 0*
W2:     0* 1 0* i 0* e 0* m 0* i 0*
```

The key idea is in the composition of these two FSAs so that the distance metric transducer *ALIGN* is in the middle:

```
W1 .o. ALIGN .o. W2
```

Transducers W1, W2 and the ALIGN are all epsilon-free, so the composition accepts only same length string pairs. Note that the distance metric ALIGN does not allow a zero to correspond to another zero, so the zero filled strings may only be at most twice so long as the longer cognate was. There would still be quite a few comparisons to do, if one would compare and evaluate them one pair at a time.

The HFST function *n_best(1)* finds the pair of strings which would have the least weight. This is one of the operations that are efficient for WF-STs. The operation produces a FST which accepts exactly the best string pair. Another function is needed for extracting the transition labels which constitute the strings themselves.

The aligner was used among other things, for relating word forms of Modern Finnish and Finnish of a Bible translation of year 1642. With slight tuning of the WFST, the aligner worked as the primary tool for aligning further pairs of old and new words which were used for writing and testing the rules which related the two forms of Finnish. The old orthography was less phonemic than the modern one and there was more orthographic variation in the old texts. After the initial adjusting to the orthography of the old texts, only a little tuning was needed to modify the computation of the similarities until the formula appeared to be stable.

As an informal check, the manually edited and checked set of 203 pairs of old and new word forms was cleaned from the added zeros and re-aligned using the aligner. Only one difference was observed in the result as compared with the original.[2]

5 Other uses for the distance WFSTs

The aligner was developed for aligning pairs of cognate words given to it. In this task, the aligner can and perhaps must be quite general. When we

_____

[2]The manually aligned *lepäØsivät:lewäisiØØt* was problematic because Old Finnish had a different morpheme for the third person past tense *-it* whereas the Modern Finnish has *-ivät*. Thus, no 'correct' alignment actually exists. The pair to be aligned ought to be *lepäisit:lewäisit.*

are studying the relation between two languages, we ought not commit ourselves to certain sound changes (or sound laws) when we start by preparing the source data for analyzing the relation itself.

One might speculate that the aligner could also be used as a predictor of the likely shapes of the missing half of a cognate pair. The WFST alone is, however, not useful for such because it generates too many candidates, not only those which would follow from the sound changes which govern the relation of the languages. The correct candidate would be buried under a heap of incorrect ones.

Instead of proposing the missing halves of cognate pairs from scratch, one can get useful results if one has a word list of the other language. Preparing for the processing, one first converts the word list into a FSA, say *words-et.fst*.

Then, one types in a known word from the first language. The script (1) converts it into a FSA, (2) shuffles it freely with zeros, (3) composes it with the distance WFST, (4) deletes all zeros from the result and then (5) composes it with a FSA containing the word list. From the result of this chain, (6) the best word pairs are retrieved and printed for the user. Using HFST command line tools, the chain of programs looks like:

```
$ hfst-strings2fst |
    hfst-shuffle -2 zeros.fst |
    hfst-compose -2 chardist.fst |
    hfst-compose -2 del-zeros.fst |
    hfst-compose -2 words-et.fst |
    hfst-fst2strings -N 5 -w
```

This is a pipeline of programs which expects the user to feed words of the first language. For each word typed in, the programs do the operations, and from the resulting WFST, the last program prints five best matches, e.g. for the Finnish word *ajo* ('driving', 'trip') it produces:

```
> ajo
ajo:aju 1
ajo:aje 2
ajo:aie 3
ajo:äiu 3
ajo:agu 3
```

The pipeline computes five best guesses as pairs of the Finnish and the Estonian words, and shows their weights. In this case, the first guess Estonian *aju* happens to be the correct one. In other cases, the correct one may not the best scored candidate, as for *vierastus*, the correct candidate *võõrastus* is the third in the list. Some short words may have many similar words in the word list. For them, the desired candidate is often too far down in the list of best ranking candidates and will not be found this way.

Using the aligner is of course less precise than building a realistic model of sound changes as was done in (Koskenniemi, 2013a) where two-level rules were used for this purpose.

6 Aligning a set of stems or other morphs

Comparing several words is needed when relating more than two historically connected languages but also when relating e.g. different stems of a word in order to build lexical entries which can be used in morphological analysis. The reason for relating stems is usually to construct one common morphophonemic representation for all stems of a word.

In a simplified version of the two-level morphological analysis, one does not postulate underlying forms which are plain sequences of phonemes. Instead, one uses alternations of phonemes (morphophonemes) when different phonemes alternate with each other, cf. (Koskenniemi, 2013b). The problem of aligning three or more different words is similar to the one discussed above but somewhat different methods are needed.

Let us look at the Estonian word *pagu* ('an escape') which inflects in forms like *pagu, paos, pakku*. Traditional generative phonology would prefer an underlying stem like *paku* and derive the other forms from that using a sequence of rewriting rules. In contrast to this, the linguist following the methods of the simplified two-level morphology, would first locate the boundaries between the stem morphs and the suffix morphs, i.e. *pagu+, pao+s* and *pakku+*, then take the stems *pagu, pao,* and *pakku*, then insert a few zeros in order to make the stem morphs same length, i.e. *pagØu, paØØo, pakku*. Thus, the linguist would arrive at the morphophonemic representation *p a {gØk} {ØØk} {uou}* by merging the corresponding letters of each stem morph.

Let us see, how an algorithm could simulate the linguist when it starts from the point where the boundaries have already been located. The task of the algorithm is (1) to produce all alignments, including lots of nonsense alignments, (2) filter out infeasible alignments, and (3) to evaluate the feasible alignments and choose the best among them.

In order to carry out the first task, the algorithm blindly inserts some (or no) zero symbols into each stem in order to make all stem candi-

dates same length. Thus, some stems are expanded to a number of alternatives where the zeros are at all different places. Assuming that five letters suffice for our example word, the first stem needs one zero, the second stem needs two zeros, and the third stem does not need any.[3] The insertion of the zeros to the first stem *pagu* would produce the strings *Øpagu, pØagu, paØgu, pagØu* and *paguØ*. Only one of these five will turn out to be useful but the algorithm does not know yet which. It does not actually produce the set of strings with zeros, but instead, it produces an automaton which accepts all of them.

The feasibility of an alignment is evaluated using the phoneme (or letter) correspondences which are caused by the insertion of zeros. Aligning *Øpagu, paØØo* and *pakku* would imply correspondences *Ø-p-p, p-a-a, a-Ø-k, g-Ø-k* and *u-o-u*. Such an alignment is infeasible, as it includes two forbidden correspondences: the second and the third phoneme correspondences *p-a-a* and *a-Ø-k* are both infeasible because they contain both a consonant and a vowel (the dashes of the correspondences will be omitted hereafter). Another alignment, e.g. *pagØu, paØØ* and *pakku* would imply the correspondences *ppp, aaa, gØk, ØØk* and *uou* which all seem phonologically feasible containing only identical or closely related sounds and zeros.

Each phoneme correspondence is evaluated separately and assigned a weight according to the similarity of the participating phonemes. The goodness of an alignment is computed as a sum of all weights for the phoneme correspondences in the alignment. In the same manner as when comparing two words, a correspondence consisting of identical phonemes e.g. *ppp* has a zero weight.

Two different distance measures were used. For vowels, the number of distinct vowels participating the correspondence was used as the measure. If the zero was also a member of the correspondence, 0.4 was added. For consonants, the differences of their features was counted. If there were both voiced and unvoiced, then 1 was added, if there were different manners of articulation, then one less than the number of manners was added. The positions of articulation were numbered from

---

[3]One may start with the shortest possible stems. If no results are produced (because one would have to match some consonant to a vowel), one may add one more zero and try again, and repeat this until the matching succeeds, and then still try with adding one more zero.

0 to 4 and they contributed so that 0.5 times the difference of values for the most back and most front position was added. One or more zeros in the correspondence added 2.6 to the total measure.

Semivowels were included both as consonants and vowels. Their combinations with vowels was restricted to those that are actually feasible, e.g. *j* was allowed to combine with *i* but not with other vowels.

All these measures are ad hoc. Readers are encouraged to experiment and improve the formulas of the measures. In particular, machine learning methods could be utilized for optimizing the parameters.

7 Algorithm for aligning multiple stems

The goal for the aligning of several words or stems were specified in the preceding section. The logic of the algorithm which implements them is shown in Figure 4 as a Python function extracted from the full implementation.

```
def multialign(stems, target_len, weighf):
    R = shuffle_w_zeros(stems[0], target_len)
    for string in stems[1:]:
        S = shuffle_w_zeros(string, target_len)
        R.cross_product(S)
        R.fst_to_fsa()
        T = remove_bad_transitions(R, weightf)
    return = set_weights(T, weighf)
```

Figure 4: Function which produces the set of all feasible alignments and their weights as a weighted FSA

Variables containing binary FSAs or FSTs as their values are in capital letters. The Python function *shuffle_w_zeros()* takes a stem as a string and returns an automaton accepting strings of the required length (by using a few HFST functions) so that exactly the correct amount of zeros are inserted freely.

The first goal of the algorithm (after inserting the necessary zeros) is to produce all combinations of the first and the second stem (with zeros inserted). The function *cross_product()* is a standard HFST function for the cross product of two FSAs. As a result, R is a transducer which maps any of the possible versions of the first stem into any of the versions of the second stem. Our example from Section 6, i.e. *paku pao pakko* would become mappings between two sets of strings:

{*Øpagu, pØagu, paØgu, pagØu, paguØ*}
and
{*ØØpao, ØpØao, ØpaØo, ØpaoØ, pØØao,*
pØaØo, pØaoØ, paØØo, paØoØ, paoØØ}

The transducer R maps any of the stings in the first set into any of the second set. The combination of the fourth in the first set and the eighth in the second is a good candidate for the alignment, i.e. *pakØu:paØØo* or equivalently as a sequence of corresponding character pairs (where identical pairs are abbreviated): *p a g:Ø Ø u:o*. At this stage of the algorithm, however, R accepts all 50 combinations.

Two problems arise here: First, we cannot continue immediately, because for the next cross product, we need a FSA instead of a FST. A transducer can be encoded to become an automaton by a standard function *fst_to_fsa()* which substitutes all label pairs *x:y* with label pairs *xy:xy* so that the result becomes a FSA again.

The other problem is, that there may be many unwanted correspondences in the result, letting consonants correspond to vowels or vice versa. Thus, a user-made function *remove_bad_transitions()* checks the encoded FSA for infeasible labels and removes the corresponding transitions.[4]

Now the product of the first two stem expressions is again a FSA, and not too large. So we can proceed by applying the process to the next stem expression and so on. When all stems have been processed, we have a FSA representing all feasible combinations of the zero-padded stems, i.e. all feasible alignments. All alignments are feasible in the sense that they do not contain forbidden combinations of vowels and consonants.

Consider first stems *laps*, *lapse* and *las* and some of their feasible alignments, the morphophonemic representation, the weights for each correspondence (i.e. morphophoneme) and the sum of weights:

```
lapsØ lapse lasØØ
l a pps ssØ ØeØ
0 1 2   2.6 1.4    = 7.0

lapsØ lapse laØsØ
l a ppØ s ØeØ
0 1 2.6 0 1.4      = 5.0
```

The former is not entirely impossible. It involves a stem final deletion of *e* which is common

---

[4]In principle, the cross product multiplies the size of the automaton fast if there would be several stems and several zeros involved.

to both alignments, and in addition the deletion of *s* and changing the *p* into *s* (which would be uncommon). Considering the weights, the second alignment is clearly better because there is no alternation of *s*, only a deletion of *p*.

Other cases may be more difficult to resolve. Consider the stems *litter*, *litri* and *litre* where we would have at least two competing alignments, the latter of which is one inserted zero longer than the former:

```
litter litriØ litreØ
l i t trr eie rØØ
0 1 0  2   2  2.6        = 7.6

litterØ litØØri litØØre
l i t tØØ eØØ  r  Øie
0 1 0 2.6 1.4  0  2.4        = 7.4
```

The linguist would probably choose the latter and reject the former. So does the formula for assigning weights to the morphophonemes. The example also shows that that the algorithm must not stop on the shortest feasible alignment.

The algorithm has a function *weightf()* which computes a weight for each candidate combination of phonemes according to the principles explained in Section 6. It is used first in excluding completely impossible transitions when building the intermediate results. It is used again in another function *set_weights()* which inserts appropriate weights into the transitions of the final result containing still all feasible alignments for the stems.

Once we have a weighted FSA which represents all alignments, it is easy to choose the best alignment with an HFST function *n_best*. Some sets of stems, such as *töö tö* would have two equally good alignments, *töö töØ* and *töö tØö*. Therefore, more than one of the top alignments are chosen first. Out of the equally good top candidates, the program selects the one in which the deletions are more to the right. Behind this choice is the observation that in suffixing languages, the deletions are more likely to occur near the affix morphemes. Using this criterion, *töö töØ* is chosen over the other alternative.

Anyway, the weighting is made in a transparent manner in the program, so it would be easy to experiment, modify and tune the weighting, if it turns out that other types of languages need different principles to resolve such ties.

8 Aligning Estonian noun stems

After the initial implementation of the algorithm it was tested against a language resource *tyvebaas.pmf* containing Estonian words with inflectional information and was freely available from the Institute of the Estonian Language (Eesti Keele Instituut). The file contained among other things, a base form, inflectional class, part of speech code and a list of all actual stem allomorphs of the lexeme. For this experiment the nouns were extracted, and furthermore, only those nouns which had more than one stem given. Out of these entries, only the stems were extracted and all other information was ignored. The original file contained entries like:

```
='aasima 28_V | at: 'aasi, an: aasi
='aasta 01_S | a0: 'aasta, a0r: 0
=aastak 02_S | a0: aastak, b0: aastaku, b0r:...
~'aastane 10_A | a0: 'aastane, b0: 'aastase,...
```

The first and the last entries were not nouns and they were discarded. The second entry was a noun but only with one stem. It was discarded as well. The third entry was a noun and had more than one stem, and it was chosen and produced an entry for the purposes of this study. The selected 15 934 sets of noun stem sets entries were like the following examples (after some cleaning):[5]

```
aastak aastaku
aatom aatomi aatome
abajas abaja
```

The whole test material was run through the aligner and the result studied using some sampling and some other checking. Some example alignments made by the algorithm are given in Figure 5.

At least for the author, the alignments in Figure 5 appeared to be acceptable. The whole material was then checked by sampling and by looking at infrequent or untypical letter combinations in a frequency list of all letter combinations. In the whole material, three alignments were found where the author disagrees with the result of the algorithm, see Figure 6. The remaining 15 931 alignments might be acceptable.[6]

---

[5]The goal was just to test the algorithm, at this time not to produce a lexicon to be accompanied with endings and morphophonological rules. Those other tasks would seem quite feasible to do at a later stage with some cooperation with suitable parties.

[6]One could have used a more phonemic representation for the words by representing long vowels by a single phoneme, e.g. *A* instead of *aa*. Such a representation could have made the task a bit simpler and maybe the mistakes could have been avoided altogether.

```
birmalane birmalase birmalas birmalasi
    b i r m a l a nsss eeØi
faktuur faktuuri faktuure
    f a k t u u r Øie
hämarik hämarikku hämariku hämarikke
                              hämarike
    h ä m a r i k ØkØkØ Øuuee
koger kogre kokre kogri kokri
    k o ggkgk eØØØØ r Øeeii
kuusk kuuske kuuse kuuski kuusi
    k u u s kkØkØ Øeeii
liud liuda liua liudu
    l i u ddØd Øaau
mutter mutri mutre
    m u t tØØ eØØ r Øie
pagu pao pakku
    p a gØk ØØk uou
pugu pukku
    p u gk Øk u
ruga roa ruge rukka
    r uouu gØgk ØØØk aaea
sugu soo sukku
    s uou gØk ØØk uou
toht tohtu tohu tohte tohe
    t o h ttØtØ Øuuee
vahk vahku vahu vahke vahe
    v a h kkØkØ Øuuee
äie äige
    ä i Øg e
```

Figure 5: Some example stem sets and their alignments

```
raag raagu rao raage
    raagØ raagu raoØØ raage
    r a aaoa ggØg ØuØe
saad saadu sao saade
    saadØ saadu saoØØ saade
    s a aaoa ddØd ØuØe
sae saaja saaju
    saeØØ saaja saaju
    s a eaa Øjj Øau
```

Figure 6: The three questionable alignments found in the Estonian word list of nouns

9 Tasks for the future

Distances between phonemes as described in Section 4 seems like a challenge for further research. In essence, the relation looks like a two-level rule relation with weights. No present compiler for two-level rules can directly assign weights to correspondences. It appears to be possible to include some form of weighting to the rule formalism and write a compiler.

A two-level compiler dedicated for alignment tasks could express the language specific patterns of phoneme alternations. A clear case for such rules would be the proper handling of vowel lengthening and gemination. Furthermore, one guiding the insertions and deletions could be made more transparent and robust using rules.

Writing dedicated compilers for two-level rules has now become much easier. It would be a reasonable project to write a compiler which is oriented towards alignment. In this way, one could implement suitable context constraints for the target language(s) and integrate it into the process of alignment.

The algorithm with the weights made for Estonian stems, was tested also for the alignment of Finnish noun stems. The result appeared to be fully clean, but only model words for different inflectional classes were tested. The same weights were also tested for some cognate word sets for Uralic languages found in en.wictionary.org as far as the symbols were available. The alignments for those seemed to be OK. Extensive tests are needed to evaluate the performance on those areas.

All programs made and the testing data used in this project is in the open source and has been made accessible to all[7]. Even without a nicer compiler, the modification of the weighting schemes is easy for anybody who has slight command of Python programming. In particular, researchers interested in statistical or machine learning methods are encouraged to apply their methods for finding optimal weightings for phoneme combinations or using the material as a gold standard for other types of solutions. Even linguists who have better command of Estonian than the author, are encouraged to report mistakes in the aligned material or critique on what the optimal alignment ought to be.

Using the Python programs with the finite state tools requires the availability of Python3, the HFST library and the SWIG interface for using the library from Python.[8]

10 Credits

The FIN-CLARIN language infrastructure project has developed and maintains the HFST software. The author is grateful for their technical support and assistance. Particular thanks are due to Erik Axelsson.

---

[7]See *https://github.com/koskenni/alignment* for the programs and for the test data

[8]See *https://hfst.github.io/* for the documentation and instructions for downloading, installing and using the Python HFST

References

Kenneth R. Beesley and Lauri Karttunen. 2003. *Finite State Morphology*. Studies in Computational Linguistics, 3. University of Chicago Press. Additional info, see: www.stanford.edu/~laurik/fsmbook/home.html.

Alexandre Bouchard-Côté, Thomas L. Griffiths, and Dan Klein. 2009. Improved reconstruction of protolanguage word forms. In *Proceedings of Human Language Technologies: The 2009 Annual Conference of the North American Chapter of the Association for Computational Linguistics*, pages 65–73, Boulder, Colorado, June. Association for Computational Linguistics.

Alina Maria Ciobanu and Liviu P. Dinu. 2014. Automatic detection of cognates using orthographic alignment. In *Proceedings of the 52nd Annual Meeting of the Association for Computational Linguistics (Volume 2: Short Papers)*, pages 99–105, Baltimore, Maryland, June. Association for Computational Linguistics.

Michael A. Covington. 1998. Alignment of multiple languages for historical comparison. In *Proceedings of the 36th Annual Meeting of the Association for Computational Linguistics and 17th International Conference on Computational Linguistics, Volume 1*, pages 275–279, Montreal, Quebec, Canada, August. Association for Computational Linguistics.

Mans Hulden. 2009. Foma: a finite-state compiler and library. In *Proceedings of the Demonstrations Session at EACL 2009*, pages 29–32, Stroudsburg, PA, USA, April. Association for Computational Linguistics.

Sittichai Jiampojamarn, Grzegorz Kondrak, and Tarek Sherif. 2007. Applying many-to-many alignments and hidden markov models to letter-to-phoneme conversion. In *Human Language Technologies 2007: The Conference of the North American Chapter of the Association for Computational Linguistics; Proceedings of the Main Conference*, pages 372–379, Stroudsburg, PA, USA, April. Association for Computational Linguistics.

Grzegorz Kondrak. 2000. A new algorithm for the alignment of phonetic sequences. In *1st Meeting of the North American Chapter of the Association for Computational Linguistics, Proceedings*. Association for Computational Linguistics.

Kimmo Koskenniemi. 2013a. Finite-state relations between two historically closely related languages. In *Proceedings of the workshop on computational historical linguistics at NODALIDA 2013; May 22-24; 2013; Oslo; Norway*, number 87 in NEALT Proceedings Series 18, pages 53–53. Linköping University Electronic Press; Linköpings universitet.

Kimmo Koskenniemi. 2013b. An informal discovery procedure for two-level rules. *Journal of Language Modelling*, 1(1):155–188.

Krister Lindén, Erik Axelson, Sam Hardwick, Tommi A. Pirinen, and Miikka Silfverberg. 2011. Hfst – framework for compiling and applying morphologies. In Cerstin Mahlow and Michael Piotrowski, editors, *Systems and Frameworks for Computational Morphology 2011 (SFCM-2011)*, volume 100 of *Communications in Computer and Information Science*, pages 67–85. Springer-Verlag.

Mehryar Mohri, Fernando C. N. Pereira, and Michael Riley. 2002. Weighted finite-state transducers in speech recognition. *Computer Speech and Language*, 16(1):69–88.

Mehryar Mohri. 2009. Weighted automata algorithms. In Manfred Droste, Werner Kuich, and Heiko Vogler, editors, *Handbook of Weighted Automata*. Springer.

John Nerbonne and Wilbert Heeringa. 1997. Measuring dialect distance phonetically. In *Computational Phonology: Third Meeting of the ACL Special Interest Group in Computational Phonology*, pages 11–18. SigPHON, Association for Computational Linguistics.

Helmut Schmid. 2005. A programming language for finite state transducers. In *Proceedings of the 5th International Workshop on Finite State Methods in Natural Language Processing (FSMNLP 2005), Helsinki, Finland*.

Harold L. Somers. 1999. Aligning phonetic segments for children's articulation assessment. *Computational Linguistics*, 25(2):267–275, June.

Kristina Toutanova and Robert Moore. 2002. Pronunciation modeling for improved spelling correction. In *Proceedings of 40th Annual Meeting of the Association for Computational Linguistics*, pages 144–151, Philadelphia, Pennsylvania, USA, July. Association for Computational Linguistics.

Acoustic Model Compression with MAP adaptation

Katri Leino and Mikko Kurimo
Department of Signal Processing and Acoustics
Aalto University, Finland
katri.k.leino@aalto.fi
mikko.kurimo@aalto.fi

Abstract

Speaker adaptation is an important step in optimization and personalization of the performance of automatic speech recognition (ASR) for individual users. While many applications target in rapid adaptation by various global transformations, slower adaptation to obtain a higher level of personalization would be useful for many active ASR users, especially for those whose speech is not recognized well. This paper studies the outcome of combinations of maximum a posterior (MAP) adaptation and compression of Gaussian mixture models. An important result that has not received much previous attention is how MAP adaptation can be utilized to radically decrease the size of the models as they get tuned to a particular speaker. This is particularly relevant for small personal devices which should provide accurate recognition in real-time despite a low memory, computation, and electricity consumption. With our method we are able to decrease the model complexity with MAP adaptation while increasing the accuracy.

1 Introduction

Speaker adaptation is one of the most important techniques to improve automatic speech recognition (ASR) performance. While today many out-of-the-box ASR systems work fairly well, in noisy real-world conditions the accuracy and speed are often insufficient for large-vocabulary open-domain dictation. This is particularly annoying for people who have temporary or permanent mobility limitations and cannot utilize other input modalities. A feasible solution to improve the recognition performance is to personalize the system by recording adaptation data.

Speech recognition systems require high computational capacity and the recognition is typically run in the cloud instead of locally in the device. Computation requirements are due to large speaker independent (SI) acoustic and language models which slow the recognition process. Transferring data between the user end device and the cloud causes latency, particularly, when fast network is unavailable, hence it would be better if models were small enough to run the recognition locally. Speech recognition is typically used on devices which have only a single user, hence a large SI model contains a lot of unnecessary information. Speaker dependent (SD) models require only a fraction of the SI model size and are more accurate (Huang and Lee, 1993), hence they would be an ideal solution for smaller systems. A SD model, however, needs several hours of transcribed training data from the user which is often not possible in practice. Therefore, the large SI models are more commonly used.

There are many compression methods for the acoustic models. Popular approaches are vector quantization (Bocchieri and Mak, 2001) and compression of Hidden Markov model (HMM) parameters. The HMM parameters can be clustered by sharing parameters between the states. Typical clustering methods are subspace compression (Bocchieri and Mak, 2001), tying (Hwang and Huang, 1993) and clustering the Gaussian mixture models (GMMs) (Crouse et al., 2011). The compression methods, however, do not aim to improve the accuracy, as they have been developed to save memory and boost the recognition speed.

The accuracy of the SI model can be improved by speaker adaptation. Adaptation is a common technique for adjusting parameters of a general acoustic model for a specific acoustic situation. It can significantly improve performance for speakers that are not well represented in the training data. However, the conventional adaptation meth-

Proceedings of the 21st Nordic Conference of Computational Linguistics, pages 65–69,
Gothenburg, Sweden, 23-24 May 2017. ©2017 Linköping University Electronic Press

ods do not resolve the issue with the model size. In this paper we introduce speaker adaptation for GMM-HMM ASR system which also reduces the model size.

MAP adaptation (Gauvain and Lee, 1994) is one of the most common supervised speaker adaptation methods. The MAP adaptation requires at least several minutes of adaptation data, but as the amount of data increases, the MAP estimation converges towards the ML estimation of a SD model. An advantage in MAP adaptation is that it can be applied along with the compression methods and even with other adaptation methods such as the maximum likelihood linear regression (MLLR) (Leggetter and Woodland, 1995).

In this paper we propose a modification to the MAP adaptation that also reduces the model complexity. The acoustic model is simplified by merging Gaussian components that are the least relevant in the adaptation and improved by adapting the means of the components. Merging preserves some of the information merged Gaussians had which would be lost if the least relevant Gaussian components were simply removed.

Recently, it has been shown that deep neural network (DNN) acoustic models can clearly outperform GMMs in ASR (Hinton et al., 2012). In theory, a corresponding adaptation procedure as in this work could also be applied to DNNs to cut off connections and units that are the least relevant in the adaptation data and re-train the remaining network. However, it is much more complicated to re-train and to analyze the modified DNN model than a GMM. This is the reason we started to develop this new version of the MAP adaptation combined with model reduction using first the simple GMMs. If it is successful, the next step is to see how much it can benefit the DNNs.

This paper introduces a modified MAP adaptation. In the following section the MAP adaptation and the Gaussian split and merge operations are described. Initial experimental results are presented in Section 3 to show effectiveness of the method in our Finnish large vocabulary continuous speech recognition (LVCSR) system. The results are discussed in Section 4, and the final conclusions are drawn in Section 5.

2 Methods

In the MAP adaptation of Gaussian mixture HMMs, the mean of a single mixture component is updated as following (Young et al., 1997)

$$\hat{\boldsymbol{\mu}}_{map} = \frac{\gamma}{\gamma + \tau}\boldsymbol{\mu}_{ml} + \frac{\tau}{\gamma + \tau}\boldsymbol{\mu}_{prior}, \qquad (1)$$

where $\boldsymbol{\mu}_{ml}$ is a maximum likelihood (ML)-estimate for the mean over the adaptation data and $\boldsymbol{\mu}_{prior}$ is the mean of the initial model. The weight of prior knowledge is adjusted empirically with the hyperparameter τ. The occupancy of likelihood γ is defined as

$$\gamma = \sum_{r=1}^{R}\sum_{t=1}^{T_r} L^r(t), \qquad (2)$$

where L defines the likelihood probability in the sentence r at the time instant t. Other HMM parameters can be updated with MAP as well, but in this paper only the mean update was used.

As can be seen from Equation (1), if the occupancy of the components is small, i.e. the triphone does not frequently occur in the adaptation data, the MAP estimate will remain close to the mean of the initial model. On the other hand, if the triphone is well presented in the data, thus the occupancy is large, the MAP estimate is shifted more towards the ML estimate over the adaptation data. The shifting can be constrained with a weight parameter τ. The optimal τ depends on the initial model and data, and there is no closed form solution of finding the optimal value. Hence τ has to be determined empirically for each adaptation instances.

Split and merge operations are a practical method to control the model complexity during the Baum-Welch based training procedure which is commonly used training algorithm in ML training of acoustic models. In the training, for each Gaussian mixture component, the occupancy, i.e. probability mass, is accumulated in each training iteration. When the occupancy of the mixture component reaches a certain pre-determined threshold, the Gaussian distribution is *split* into two Gaussian distributions, and the mixture gains another component. On the other hand, if any pair of Gaussians in the mixture remain below a minimum occupancy level, the Gaussians are *merged* into a single component. The resulting Gaussian will be given parameters which are the average of the two merged Gaussians. The split and merge operations during the training cause the size of the training data set to determine the complexity of the model. As each HMM model accumulate different amount of occupancy, the number of components also varies for each mixture. (Huang et al., 2001)

The conventional MAP adaptation tunes the parameters of the SI acoustic model to correspond better to the adaptation data. As only parameters are changed, the size of the model does not change during the adaptation. However, if there is no need to keep a large SI model in the background, e.g., available for other users, the complexity control similar to the split and merge operations in the ML training can be included to the MAP adaptation as well. Because the adaptation data is only from a single target speaker, a much lower complexity is usually sufficient to model the data.

With our method, the model shrinks during the MAP adaptation because the initial model has too many components compared to the size of the adaptation set, thus enough occupancy is not accumulated to all components. Components that do not accumulate occupancy over the minimum occupancy threshold are merged together with their nearest neighbor. Because pairs of Gaussians are always merged, the model can compress by half in each iteration at maximum. How much the model is actually compressed depends on how the occupancy is divided between the components. It is expected that the components are reduced rapidly as the adaptation set is small compared to the training data. After merging, the Gaussians are reestimated to maximize the fit to the new set of observations associated to them.

3 Experiments

The modified MAP adatation is evaluated in a speaker adaptation task. The corpus for the task included three Finnish audio books each recorded by a different speaker. In addition to the variable readers also the style of reading varied significantly between the books. For example, the task of the first reader "Speaker1" was to avoid any interpretation of the text, because the book was intended for the blind audience. The two other readers "Speaker2" and " Speaker3" described everyday matters in a very lively reading style.

The same value for the MAP hyperparameter τ was used for all speakers with no speaker-specific optimization. The length of the adaptation sets was 25 minutes for all speakers. The evaluation set was 90 minutes long for "Speaker1" and 30 minutes for "Speaker2" and "Speaker3". The training set for an SD reference model for "Speaker1" had

90 minutes of speech, and the resulting Gaussian mixture model had 4500 Gaussian components.

The baseline SI model with 40 032 Gaussians was ML trained with Finnish Speecon corpus (Iskra et al., 2002) including 90 hours of speech. This model was also used as the initial model to be adapted in the experiments. The language model used for all experiment was trained with Finnish news texts. Because Finnish is an agglutinative language, the n-gram language model was based on statistical morphs instead of words to avoid out-of-vocabulary words (Hirsimaki et al., 2009).

The experiments were conducted by the morph-based LVCSR system, AaltoASR (Hirsimaki et al., 2009) developed at Aalto University. The source codes of the recognizer were recently published as open source[1]. The acoustic features were 39 dimensional MFCCs normalized by cepstral mean subtraction. The Gaussians had diagonal covariances and a global diagonalising transform was used. The acoustic models were based on decision-tree-tied triphones with GMMs.

In this paper the recognition accuracy is measured by using the word error rate (WER). It is noteworthy that in agglutinative languages, such as Finnish, words are often quite long. It means that sometimes one misrecognized phoneme in a word such as "kahvinjuojallekin" leads to 100% WER, whereas the same mistake in English "also for a coffee drinker" gives only 20%. Thus, the WER numbers in Finnish are typically high and 10% WER means already very good ASR.

Because the adaptation set is much smaller than the training set for the initial SI model, the occupancy will not accumulate for every Gaussian component. Whenever a Gaussian does not gain sufficient occupancy, it is merged into another Gaussian distribution as explained in the previous section. In the experiments for "Speaker1", for example, this extended MAP adaptation reduced the model size from 40 032 to the 26 224 Gaussian components after one iteration.

The results in Figure 1 show that the MAP adaptation improves the SI model for "Speaker1", even if the model size is also reduced. The blue bars represent WER after the normal MAP adaptation when the model size remains unchanged. The red bars show WER when the model is compressed during the adaptation. The purple horizontal line represents the performance of the base-

---

[1] https://github.com/aalto-speech/AaltoASR

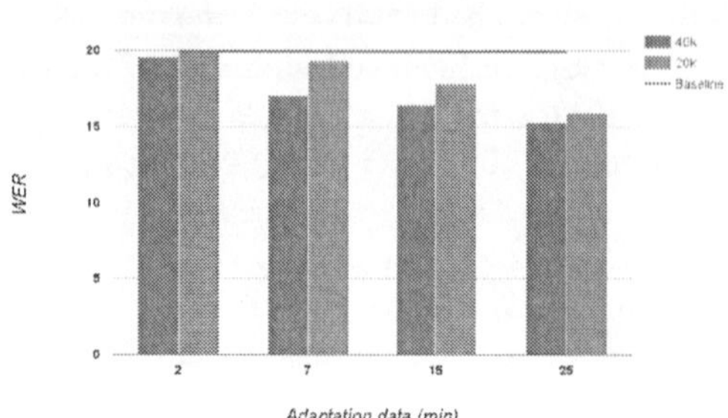

Figure 1: *WER comparison of the normally MAP adapted (40k) and compressed model (20k) for "Speaker 1", where the numbers indicate the number of Gaussian components.*

line SI model without any adaptations. The WER for the baseline was 19.93%. Figure 1 shows that as the adaptation set increases the accuracy improves with both methods and the difference in WER between the compressed and the uncompressed model reduces. The results were similar with the other speakers as well, as can be seen from the tables 1 and 2.

The improvement of the compressed models could be explained by the MAP estimates converging towards the SD model estimates as the adaptation data increases. The WER for "Speaker1" with the SD model was 10.02%. The results also imply that all the SI model components are not necessary for all users.

It was also experimented with the "Speaker1" if similar results could be achieved by using the ML estimates instead of the MAP estimates in compression. However, as can be seen from Table 3, the ML estimates do not improve the accuracy of the SI model, which had WER 19.93%, until the adaptation data has reached 25 minutes.

Table 1: *Uncompressed MAP (WER).*

		Adaption set			
	SI	2 min	7 min	15 min	25 min
Speaker1	19.93	19.58	17.00	16.42	15.28
Speaker2	27.40	23.30	22.80	23.30	22.20
Speaker3	29.7	30.20	28.90	28.00	27.30

Table 2: *Compressed MAP (WER).*

		Adaption set			
	SI	2 min	7 min	15 min	25 min
Speaker1	19.93	19.94	19.30	17.84	15.95
Speaker2	27.40	24.10	21.00	21.00	18.90
Speaker3	29.7	34.70	30.00	27.80	26.30

Table 3: *WER for "Speaker1" after adapting with ML estimates.*

			Adaption set			
	SI	SD	2 min	7 min	15 min	25 min
WER	19.93	10.02	25.19	21.40	20.55	19.76

4 Discussion

While the initial experiments were repeated for three quite different speakers and texts, trying even more speakers will be the obvious way to verify the conclusions. Non-standard test speakers, such as non-natives, elderly, children and those having speaking disorders will be particularly interesting to observe.

The initial acoustic model was a relatively large and robust SI model. With a smaller SI model, the behavior of the method could be different. Smaller models should compress more moderately than larger models, since the occupancy of the adaptation set is allocated to fewer model components and relatively more components achieve the minimum occupancy value.

The models were compressed by half in the experiments after a single iteration. It is however possible to use multiple iterations to reduce the size further. However, compressing the model too much without a sufficient amount of adaptation data could result a loss of important components and the accuracy would decrease. At the moment, the only way to control the amount of compression is to adjust the minimum occupancy threshold for merging. Unfortunately, this approach is limited as after the adaptation many components will have zero occupancy. The next step is to explore the optimal amount of compression and if different merging algorithms could provide better results.

The mean of each Gaussian has so far been the only parameter adapted in the experiments. The WER could be improved more rapidly by updating the other HMM parameters as well (Sharma and Hasegawa-Johnson, 2010).

The advantage in the MAP adaptation is that it

can be used in combination with other compression and adaptation methods, because it directly modifies the Gaussian parameters. We successfully adapted a discriminatively trained SI model with our method, as well. The results were similar with the ML SI model we presented in this paper. This implies that compressing MAP adaptation can be combined with a variety of techniques.

The usability of the speech recognition application depends on the accuracy and latency of the ASR system. Hence, the model size is crucial, since high complexity causes latency to the ASR system. Currently, large SI models dominate in the applications as they suit for many acoustic environments. However, it is easier to accomplish higher accuracy with an ASR system trained for a limited acoustic environment. With small personal devices there is no need for a large SI model, as they typically have a single user. If the models are small enough, it is possible to run the ASR system and store the model locally in the device. Utilizing the memory of the device would reduce the memory demand on the server. One possible application for our method would be to adapt and compress the SI model during the use and to move the models completely into the user's device, when the models are small enough.

5 Conclusions

The MAP adaptation was expanded with split and merge operations which are used in ML training. The initial results indicate that the method can compresses the SI model by a half while still improving the performance with the speaker adaptation. While the results are promising, more experiments are required to confirm that our method is suitable for the personalization of the acoustic model.

Acknowledgments

This work was supported by Academy of Finland with the grant 251170, Nokia Inc. and the Foundation for Aalto University Science and Technology with the post-graduate grant, and Aalto Science-IT project by providing the computational resources.

References

Enrico Bocchieri and Brian Kan-Wing Mak. 2001. Subspace Distribution Clustering Hidden Markov Model. *Speech and Audio Processing, IEEE Transactions on*, 9(3):264–275.

David F. Crouse, Peter Willett, Krishna Pattipati, and Lennart Svensson. 2011. A look at Gaussian mixture reduction algorithms. In *Information Fusion (FUSION), 2011 Proceedings of the 14th International Conference*.

Jean-Luc Gauvain and Chin-Hui Lee. 1994. Maximum a posteriori estimation for multivariate Gaussian mixture observations of Markov chains. *Speech and audio processing, ieee transactions on*, 2(2):291–298.

Geoffrey Hinton, Li Deng, Dong Yu, George E Dahl, Abdel-rahman Mohamed, Navdeep Jaitly, Andrew Senior, Vincent Vanhoucke, Patrick Nguyen, Tara N Sainath, et al. 2012. Deep Neural Networks for acoustic modeling in speech recognition: The shared views of four research groups. *Signal Processing Magazine, IEEE*, 29(6):82–97.

Teemu Hirsimaki, Janne Pylkkonen, and Mikko Kurimo. 2009. Importance of high-order n-gram models in morph-based speech recognition. *Audio, Speech, and Language Processing, IEEE Transactions on*, 17(4):724–732.

Xuedong Huang and Kai-Fu Lee. 1993. On speaker-independent, speaker-dependent, and speaker-adaptive speech recognition. *IEEE Transactions on Speech and Audio processing*, 1(2):150–157.

Xuedong Huang, Alex Acero, Hsiao-Wuen Hon, and Raj Foreword By-Reddy. 2001. *Spoken language processing: A guide to theory, algorithm, and system development*. Prentice Hall PTR.

Mei-Yuh Hwang and Xuedong Huang. 1993. Shared-distribution Hidden Markov Models for speech recognition. *Speech and Audio Processing, IEEE Transactions on*, 1(4):414–420.

Dorota J Iskra, Beate Grosskopf, Krzysztof Marasek, Henk van den Heuvel, Frank Diehl, and Andreas Kiessling. 2002. SPEECON-Speech databases for consumer devices: Database specification and validation. In *LREC*.

Christopher J Leggetter and Philip C Woodland. 1995. Maximum Likelihood Linear Regression for speaker adaptation of continuous density Hidden Markov Models. *Computer Speech & Language*, 9(2):171–185.

Harsh Vardhan Sharma and Mark Hasegawa-Johnson. 2010. State-transition interpolation and MAP adaptation for HMM-based dysarthric speech recognition. In *Proceedings of the NAACL HLT 2010 Workshop on Speech and Language Processing for Assistive Technologies*, pages 72–79. Association for Computational Linguistics.

Steve Young, Gunnar Evermann, Mark Gales, Thomas Hain, Dan Kershaw, Xunying Liu, Gareth Moore, Julian Odell, Dave Ollason, Dan Povey, et al. 1997. *The HTK book*, volume 2. Entropic Cambridge Research Laboratory Cambridge.

OCR and post-correction of historical Finnish texts

Senka Drobac and Pekka Kauppinen and Krister Lindén
University of Helsinki
Department of Modern Languages
{senka.drobac, pekka.kauppinen, krister.linden}@helsinki.fi

Abstract

This paper presents experiments on Optical character recognition (OCR) as a combination of Ocropy software and data-driven spelling correction that uses Weighted Finite-State Methods. Both model training and testing were done on Finnish corpora of historical newspaper text and the best combination of OCR and post-processing models give 95.21% character recognition accuracy.

1 Introduction

In recent years, optical character recognition of printed text has reached high accuracy rates for modern fonts. However, historical documents still pose a challenge for character recognition and OCR of those documents still does not yield satisfying results. This is a problem for all researchers who would like to use those documents as a part of their research.

The main reasons why historical documents still pose a challenge for OCR are: fonts differ in different materials, lack of orthographic standard (same words spelled differently), material quality (some documents can have deformations) and a lexicon of known historical spelling variants is not available (although if they were, they might not give any OCR advantage for morphologically rich languages as noted by Silfverberg and Rueter (2015), but they can be useful in the post-processing phase).

The leading software frameworks for OCR are commercial ABBYY FineReader[1] and two open source frameworks: Ocropy[2] (previously known as OCRopus) and Tesseract[3]. Springmann et al. (2014) experiment with these three and compare

their performance on five pages of historical printings of Latin texts. The mean character accuracy they achieve is 81.66% for Ocropy, 80.57% for ABBYY FineReader, and 78.77% for Tesseract.

However, Finnish historical documents are mainly written in Gothic (Fraktur) font, which is harder to recognize. The National Library of Finland has scanned, segmented and performed OCR on their historical newspaper corpus with ABBYY FineReader. On a test set that is representative of the bulk of the Finnish material, ABBYY FineReader's recognition accuracy is only 90.16%.

In this work we test how Ocropy performs optical character recognition on historical Finnish documents. We achieve a character accuracy of 93.50% with Ocropy when training with Finnish historical data. Additionally, we also wanted to find out whether any further improvement in the OCR quality could be achieved by performing OCR post-correction with an unstructured classifier and a lexicon on the Ocropy output.

Our experiments show that already with a relatively small training set (around 10,000 lines) we can get over 93% accuracy with Ocropy and with additional post-correction, the accuracy goes beyond 94%. With two training sets combined (around 60,000 lines), we get accuracy even over 95%.

1.1 Related work

In Springmann et al. (2014), they apply different OCR methods to historical printings of Latin text and get the highest accuracies when using Ocropy. Some work on Fraktur fonts has been reported in Breuel et al. (2013) where models were trained on artificial training data and got high accuracies when tested on scanned books with Fraktur text.

In Shafait (2009), alongside with the overview of different OCR methods, they present the architecture of Ocropy and explain different steps of a

---

[1] https://www.abbyy.com
[2] https://github.com/tmbdev/ocropy
[3] https://github.com/tesseract-ocr

Proceedings of the 21st Nordic Conference of Computational Linguistics, pages 70–76,
Gothenburg, Sweden, 23-24 May 2017. ©2017 Linköping University Electronic Press

typical OCR process.

Approaches to OCR post-processing are numerous and commonly rely on an error model for generating correction candidates. A language model may be incorporated to model output-level character dependencies. A lexicon can be used to determine which suggestions are valid words of the language – historical OCR may pose a challenge here if lexical resources are scarce. The post-processing method used in our work is described by Silfverberg et al. (2016) and can be described as an unstructured classifier. While the method is relatively simple from both a theoretical and computational points of view as it lacks a language model and a segmentation model found in many recently proposed approaches (see e.g. Eger et al. (2016), Llobet et al. (2010)) the classifier nevertheless captures the regularities of character-level errors occurring in OCR output and demonstrably improves the quality of the processed text. A more detailed comparison with other OCR-post processing methods can be found in Silfverberg et al. (2016).

2 Data and resources

2.1 Data

In our experiments, we use two data sets hereafter referred to as DIGI and NATLIB. Both are part of a larger corpus of historical newspapers and magazines that has been digitized by the National Library of Finland and consists of image files of individual lines of printed text as well the contents of said lines as plain text.

We created the DIGI data set as follows: first, a total of approximately 12,000 non-punctuational tokens were picked at random from the entire corpus. For each token, a random sentence containing said token was retrieved from the corpus together with information pertaining to the publication as well as as the page on which the sentence appears. The ABBYY METS/ALTO file and the corresponding image file of the scanned page on which the sentence appeared were retrieved from a repository, and the latter was subsequently cropped to only contain the line(s) on which the sentence occurred (i.e. the line segmentation was done by ABBYY FineReader). The contents of the lines were then manually written into a plain text file, which serves as the ground truth for training and testing our methods. Images whose contents could not be made out were ex-

cluded from the final data set, which consists of a total of over 12,000 image files and lines of manually edited ground truth data. This also gave us an fairly good idea of the overall quality of the corpus: we compared the ABBYY FineReader output with the manually edited ground truth and calculated a character error rate of 90.16%.

The NATLIB data set contains 54,087 line images and corresponding ground truth texts segmented from 225 pages of historical documents. The data was provided to us by the National Library of Finland.

2.2 Ocropy

Ocropy (previously known as OCRopus - Breuel (2008), Breuel (2009), Breuel et al. (2013)) is a leading open source software toolkit for training OCR models using long short term memory networks. In addition to character recognition, Ocropy offers tools for pre-processing documents (line segmentation, binzarization/normalization), tools for creation and correction of ground truth and evaluation tools.

2.3 Unstructured Classifier and Lexicon

We chose to perform OCR post-correction by using the unstructured classifier described by Silfverberg et al. (2016), as it was fast and easy to implement. The system is originally designed for correcting individual input strings and makes use of an error model that can be formulated as a series of weighted context-sensitive parallel replace rules implemented as a weighted finite-state transducer. Lexical lookup is used to validate or discard suggestions generated by the error model.

For validation, we used a modified version of the lexicon also used by Silfverberg et al. (2016), which in turn is a modified and extended version of a finite-state morphology of modern Finnish that has been specifically tailored to accept forms and spellings found in 19th century Finnish. We further modified this lexicon to accept strings with leading and trailing punctuation, as we found that punctuation often provides important clues for finding the correct substitution, which could be lost if the data was tokenized and the punctuation removed.

---

[3]https://github.com/tmbdev/ocropy

3   Method

In this section we describe the OCR process in its entirety. The method consists of three major parts: Data preparation, OCR and finally post-processing.

1. Preparing the data

   We divided the DIGI data set into three parts: 9,345 images and lines were allocated to training, 1,038 served as development data and the remaining 2,046 lines were reserved for testing. The motivation for splitting the data this way comes from practical reasons: we initially had separate sets of 10,383 and 2,046 lines, so we decided to take 10% from the bigger set as the development data, 90% as the training data and to use the smaller set for testing.

   The NATLIB data was on the other hand completely randomly split into three parts: 43,704 lines was used for training, 100 was used as development set and 5,308 as test set. In this case we used a very small development set because from our previous experience with DIGI data, we learned that recognition of large amount of lines can be quite slow. And since we had to do recognition for all saved models to find the best one, we decided to save time by reducing the size of the development set.

2. OCR

   (a) Since Ocropy works with black and white images files, the first step was to binarize our data. For this, we used the `ocropus-nlib` program with default settings, which alongside with binarization performs vertical normalization of the text. Example line images before and after binarization are shown in Figure 1.

   (b) Once the images were binarized, we used them together with ground truth texts to train neural network models. Training was performed with the `ocropus-rtrain` program which saved a model after every 1,000 iterations. We tested all those models on the development set and when the recognition accuracy stopped improving, we stopped the training. The model that achieved the

tivat tuota poloista, joka on jou-

osa säätyluokkaamme ruotsalaistunut.

(b)

tuntoasi. Tunne ja tunnusta Juma-

(c)

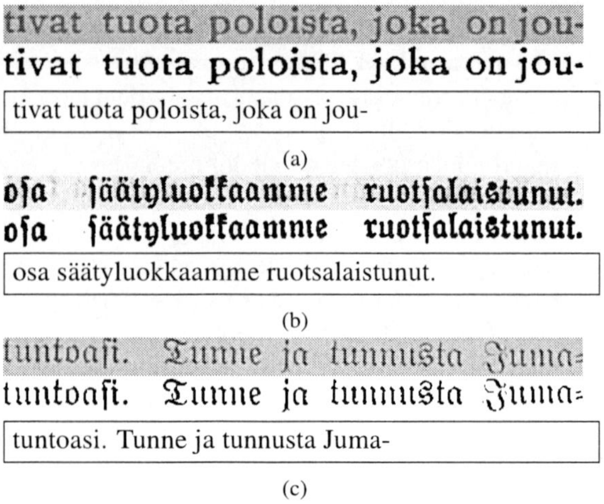

Figure 1: Example lines from DIGI test set. The first line shows the original scanned line, the second one is the binarized version, and the last one is the ground truth text.

highest accuracy on the development set was used for testing on the test sets.

   (c) Finally, prediction was done with the `ocropus-rpred` function. We tested the best model from both data sets on all test sets.

3. Post-processing

   (a) In order to train the error models used in post-correction, we ran the best OCR models on their respective training data sets and aligned the output with the corresponding ground truth data at the character level. The alignment was performed iteratively, with each iteration yielding a better alignment compared with the previous one.

   (b) The aligned data was then used to train a number of error models of varying sizes. The different models were obtained by varying the value of the threshold (T) i.e. the number of times a substitution must occur in a given context in the aligned training data in order to be included in the rule set and the final model. The resulting models were then tested on the development data set in order to determine the optimal value of T.

   (c) Finally, the training data sets and the development data sets were combined.

The final error model was trained on this data with the threshold set at its optimal value. The resulting model was applied to the test data processed by Ocropy.

Due to the technical limitations of the post-correction method using lexical lookup, the input data was automatically split into strings which were post-processed individually. The input lines were split into tokens at blanks, and the output yielded by the post-correction system was then joined back into lines before calculating the character accuracy rate (see below).

4. Evaluation

During both the prediction and evaluation phases, we measured the performance of the system by using character accuracy rate (CAR), which is essentially the percentage of correct characters in the system output and is a common metric in OCR-related tasks. It is the number of correct characters divided by the sum of correct characters and errors in the system output:

$$CAR = 100\% \times \frac{correct}{correct + errors} \quad (1)$$

The number of errors is the overall Levenshtein distance (Levenshtein, 1966) between the system output and the ground truth and includes deletions and insertions.

For languages with relatively long words such as Finnish, character accuracy rates and character error rates are arguably better indicators of the overall quality of the text than, for instance, word error rate, since longer words are more likely to contain multiple errors and are thus more difficult to correct. The legibility of a text may actually improve considerably without any notable change in its word error rate.

4 Results

For testing purposes we initially used two OCR models: the DIGI model and the NATLIB model. Both models were trained on their respective training sets (the DIGI training set with 451,000 iterations and the NATLIB training set with 177,000 iterations).

Table 1: Character accuracy rates after OCR and post-correction: the DIGI model (first column) was trained on DIGI training data with 451 000 iterations while the NATLIB model (second column) was trained on NATLIB training data with 177 000 iterations. The first two rows (DIGI-dev and NATLIB-dev) show the model CAR on the respective development sets. The DIGI-test row shows CAR for each model on the DIGI test set, with the following two rows showing results after post correction. The NATLIB-test row shows CAR for each model on the NATLIB test set and the final two rows show CAR after post-correction.

	DIGI model	NATLIB model
DIGI-dev	94.16%	-
NATLIB-dev	-	**94.73%**
DIGI-test	93.50%	89.05%
Post corr. (DIGI)	**93.68%**	89.12%
Post corr. (NATLIB)	93.59%	89.13%
NATLIB-test	93.82%	93.59%
Post corr. (DIGI)	94.05%	93.81%
Post corr. (NATLIB)	**94.13%**	93.94%

Table 1 shows character accuracy rates (CAR) for different combinations of trained models and the two test sets (DIGI-test and NATLIB-test) as well as post-correction results.

Afterwards, we also tested three models trained on combined data from both training sets: one trained from scratch on all lines from DIGI and NATLIB training sets, another trained on NATLIB train set with the DIGI model as the starting point and the third one was trained on the DIGI train set with the NATLIB model as the starting point. We chose the best models by calculating average CAR on both development sets.

Table 2 shows CAR for those three models tested on DIGI and NATLIB test sets as well as post-correction results.

Since the OCR accuracy on DIGI-test differs substantially depending on the model, we performed further analysis of the results on this test set using the `ocropus-econf` program. This is one of the Ocropy's evaluation programs which performs different kinds of evaluation tasks.

Tables 3 and 4 show the ten most common recognition mistakes on the DIGI test set. The first column in the tables gives the frequency of

Table 2: Character accuracy rates after OCR and post-correction of models with combined training data: (1) the model was trained from the beginning on both training data combined, (2) model was trained on NATLIB data with the DIGI model as starting point, (3) model was trained on DIGI data with the NATLIB model as starting point. The first row show the average character accuracy rate that the models scored on the two development sets. The following two rows show CAR on the DIGI test set before and after post correction. The last two rows show CAR on the NATLIB test set before and after post correction.

	(1)	(2)	(3)
Dev (avg)	**94.47%**	93.62%	93.62%
DIGI-test	93%	91.88%	92.32%
Post corr.	**93.27%**	92%	92.57%
NATLIB-test	94.83%	94.25%	93.68%
Post corr.	**95.21%**	94.56%	94.01%

the mistakes, the second column the recognition result and the third one the ground truth. Deletions are marked with "_" in the OCR column while insertions with "_" in the ground truth column. The most common mistake the DIGI model makes on the DIGI test set is insertion of spaces, which happened 122 times. Similarly, the most frequent mistake the NATLIB model made on the same test was deleting a hyphen symbol "-", which happened 663 times. One example when the hyphen was not recognized and simply left out is shown in Figure 1c. To better understand the severity of the mistakes, it is good to know that the DIGI test set has in total 78,116 characters.

Table 5 shows the frequency of Ocropy recognition mistakes per line for each model. The test set in both cases was DIGI-test. The DIGI-model does 100% correct OCR on 758 lines (37%) and the NATLIB-model on 351 lines (17%).

The best post-correction results were, due to the sparsity of the data, achieved by error models that were trained with high thresholds. This was especially the case with the NATLIB dataset, with threshold values between 60 and 70 yielding the best results for the development and test data sets. The resulting models could easily correct the most obvious cases without corrupting strings that were correct to begin with.

Table 3: A confusion matrix for the DIGI test set after recognition with the DIGI model (before post-correction)

Freq.	OCR	Ground truth
122		_
99	_	i
87	_	
78	u	n
60	i	_
43	_	-
41	_	t
41	.	,
36	l	i
31	e	o

Table 4: A confusion matrix for the DIGI test set after recognition with the NATLIB model (before post-correction)

Freq.	OCR	Ground truth
663	_	-
324	_	
109	_	i
76	a	_
74	s	e
67	a	n
65	_	v
63	r	v
62	_	t
61	_	y

Table 5: Number of mistakes per line after recognition on DIGI test set (before post correction) with both models. The first column shows the number of mistakes per line, the second column the frequency of lines after recognition with the DIGI-model and the third column the frequency of lines after recognition with the NATLIB-model

Mistakes per line	DIGI-model n.° lines	NATLIB-model n.° lines
0	758 (37%)	351 (17%)
1	427 (21%)	509 (25%)
2	273 (13%)	292 (14%)
3	160 (8%)	180 (9%)
4	119 (6%)	162 (8%)
…	…	…

musta, nelisolkinen naisen nahkawyö

GT:	musta, nelisolkinen naisen nahkawyö
DIGI:	ew.O:
NATLIB:	e.":.:s'

(a)

Ruusua ja kaikellaista särkyä parantaa hie-

GT:	Ruusua ja kaikellaista särkyä parantaa hie-
DIGI:	,:
NATLIB:	::,:

(b)

GIN LEIPURI- & KONDIITORI

GT:	GIN LEIPURI- & KONDIITORI
DIGI:	.tt 1h110 Ml. t 00khron
NATLIB:	u 1.kL10Ml. K0tte4

(c)

Figure 2: Example lines with a large number of mistakes for both models

5 Discussion

A surprising result was that the NATLIB model performed poorly on the DIGI test set. Since the NATLIB model was trained on approximately five times more data than the DIGI model, we expected to get better results with this model. The main reason for the lower recognition rate was a large number of unrecognized hyphens, as shown in Table 4. Although both training sets were picked up from the same corpora, the reason for this phenomena could be that the NATLIB model represents 225 pages of consecutive text, while the DIGI model has a better distribution over the entire corpus.

After combining the two training data sets, we got significantly better results for the NATLIB test set, however the best results for the DIGI test set were still gained by the model trained on the DIGI data solely.

Since the models are trained on lines, a major problem for OCR is incorrect line segmentation. For example, Figure 2 shows three example lines on which both models performed extremely poorly. The first two images Figure 2a and Figure 2b have been incorrectly segmented - there is too much information from the following line caused by a large starting letter. Our future work is to put more focus on segmentation and preparation of representative data. We should use a neural network model that is trained on both artificial as well as real data to see if a bigger data set could incorporate correct artificial data for currently observed problems.

The other big problem are images with rare fonts (rare in the sense that they are not well represented in the training data). In the third image (Figure 2c), part of the text has been cut off by the incorrect segmentation, but since visible characters were not recognized, we believe that the main reason for the poor OCR result is the font. This kind of font is not very common in Finnish historical documents that the models have been trained on, so it is not recognized. This problem could be solved by adding more fonts to the training data.

The unstructured post-correction method gave a small improvement, which was interesting and by no means self-evident: it could have turned out that the remaining errors were so spurious that no further regularities could be extracted. This suggests that there is room for improving the neural network to incorporate the benefits provided by the post-correction method.

The biggest problem for our current post-correction is that it cannot influence spaces and word boundaries and they seem to be a major source of errors. A task for future work is therefore testing a structured post-correction method using more advanced line-oriented post correction.

6 Conclusions

Our experiments show that already with a relatively small but well-chosen training set (around 10,000 lines), we can get a character accuracy rate of more than 93% with Ocropy and with additional unstructured post-correction, the accuracy goes beyond 94%. With combination of the two training sets and with additional unstructured post-correction, the accuracy reaches 95.21%.

References

Thomas M Breuel, Adnan Ul-Hasan, Mayce Ali Al-Azawi, and Faisal Shafait. 2013. High-performance OCR for printed English and Fraktur using LSTM networks. In *2013 12th International Conference on Document Analysis and Recognition*, pages 683–687. IEEE.

Thomas M Breuel. 2008. The OCRopus open source OCR system. In *Electronic Imaging 2008*, pages 68150F–68150F. International Society for Optics and Photonics.

Thomas Breuel. 2009. Recent progress on the OCRopus OCR system. In *Proceedings of the International Workshop on Multilingual OCR*, page 2. ACM.

Steffen Eger, Tim vor der Brck, and Alexander Mehler. 2016. A comparison of four character-level string-to-string translation models for (OCR) spelling error correction. *The Prague Bulletin of Mathematical Linguistics*, 105:77–99.

Vladimir I. Levenshtein. 1966. Binary codes capable of correcting deletions, insertions and reversals. *Soviet Physics Doklady*, 10:707.

R. Llobet, J. R. Cerdan-Navarro, J. C. Perez-Cortes, and J. Arlandis. 2010. OCR post-processing using weighted finite-state transducers. In *2010 20th International Conference on Pattern Recognition*, pages 2021–2024, Aug.

Faisal Shafait. 2009. Document image analysis with OCRopus. In *Multitopic Conference, 2009. INMIC 2009. IEEE 13th International*, pages 1–6. IEEE.

Miikka Silfverberg and Jack Rueter. 2015. Can morphological analyzers improve the quality of optical character recognition? In *Septentrio Conference Series*, number 2, pages 45–56.

Miikka Silfverberg, Pekka Kauppinen, and Krister Lindén. 2016. Data-driven spelling correction using weighted finite-state methods. In *Proceedings of the SIGFSM Workshop on Statistical NLP and Weighted Automata*, pages 51–59, Berlin, Germany, August. Association for Computational Linguistics.

Uwe Springmann, Dietmar Najock, Hermann Morgenroth, Helmut Schmid, Annette Gotscharek, and Florian Fink. 2014. OCR of historical printings of latin texts: problems, prospects, progress. In *Proceedings of the First International Conference on Digital Access to Textual Cultural Heritage*, pages 71–75. ACM.

Twitter Topic Modeling by Tweet Aggregation

Asbjørn Ottesen Steinskog **Jonas Foyn Therkelsen** **Björn Gambäck**

Department of Computer Science
Norwegian University of Science and Technology
NO–7491 Trondheim, Norway

asbjorn@steinskog.me jonas.foyn@gmail.com gamback@ntnu.no

Abstract

Conventional topic modeling schemes, such as Latent Dirichlet Allocation, are known to perform inadequately when applied to tweets, due to the sparsity of short documents. To alleviate these disadvantages, we apply several pooling techniques, aggregating similar tweets into individual documents, and specifically study the aggregation of tweets sharing authors or hashtags. The results show that aggregating similar tweets into individual documents significantly increases topic coherence.

1 Introduction

Due to the tremendous amount of data broadcasted on microblog sites like Twitter, extracting information from microblogs has turned out to be useful for establishing the public opinion on different issues. O'Connor et al. (2010) found a correlation between word frequencies in Twitter and public opinion surveys in politics. Analyzing tweets (Twitter messages) over a timespan can give great insights into what happened during that time, as people tend to tweet about what concerns them and their surroundings. Many influential people post messages on Twitter, and investigating the relation between the underlying topics of different authors' messages could

yield interesting results about people's interests. One could for example compare the topics different politicians tend to talk about to obtain a greater understanding of their similarities and differences. Twitter has an abundance of messages, and the enormous amount of tweets posted every second makes Twitter suitable for such tasks. However, detecting topics in tweets can be a challenging task due to their informal type of language and since tweets usually are more incoherent than traditional documents. The community has also spawned user-generated metatags, like hashtags and mentions, that have analytical value for opinion mining.

The paper describes a system aimed at discovering trending topics and events in a corpus of tweets, as well as exploring the topics of different Twitter users and how they relate to each other. Utilizing Twitter metadata mitigates the disadvantages tweets typically have when using standard topic modeling methods; user information as well as hashtag co-occurrences can give a lot of insight into what topics are currently trending.

The rest of the text is outlined as follows: Section 2 describes the topic modeling task and some previous work in the field, while Section 3 outlines our topic modeling strategies, and Section 4 details a set of experiments using these. Section 5 then discusses and sums up the results, before pointing to some directions for future research.

Proceedings of the 21st Nordic Conference of Computational Linguistics, pages 77–86,
Gothenburg, Sweden, 23-24 May 2017. ©2017 Linköping University Electronic Press

2 Topic modeling

Topic models are statistical methods used to represent latent topics in document collections. These probabilistic models usually present topics as multinomial distributions over words, assuming that each document in a collection can be described as a mixture of topics. The language used in tweets is often informal, containing grammatically creative text, slang, emoticons and abbreviations, making it more difficult to extract topics from tweets than from more formal text.

The 2015 International Workshop on Semantic Evaluation (SemEval) presented a task on Topic-Based Message Polarity Classification, similar to the topic of this paper. The most successful systems used text preprocessing and standard methods: Boag et al. (2015) took a supervised learning approach using linear SVM (Support Vector Machines), heavily focused on feature engineering, to reach the best performance of all. Plotnikova et al. (2015) came in second utilizing another supervised method, Maximum Entropy, with lexicon and emoticon scores and trigrams, while essentially ignoring topics, which is interesting given the task. Zhang et al. (2015) differed from the other techniques by focusing on word embedding features, as well as the traditional textual features, but argued that to only extend the model with the word embeddings did not necessarily significantly improve results.

Although the informal language and sparse text make it difficult to retrieve the underlying topics in tweets, Weng et al. (2010) previously found that **Latent Dirichlet Allocation** (LDA) produced decent results on tweets. LDA (Blei et al., 2003) is an unsupervised probabilistic model which generates mixtures of latent topics from a collection of documents, where each mixture of topics produces words from the collection's vocabulary with certain probabilities. A distribution over topics is first sampled from a Dirichlet distribution, and a topic is chosen based on this distribution. Each document is modeled as a distribution over topics, with topics represented as distributions over words (Blei, 2012).

Koltsova and Koltcov (2013) used LDA mainly on topics regarding Russian presidential elections, but also on recreational and other topics, with a dataset of all posts by 2,000 LiveJournal bloggers. Despite the broad categories, LDA showed its robustness by correctly identifying 30–40% of the topics. Sotiropoulos et al. (2014) obtained similar results on targeted sentiment towards topics related to two US telecommunication firms, while Waila et al. (2013) identified socio-political events and entities during the Arab Spring, to find global sentiment towards these.

The **Author-topic model** (Rosen-Zvi et al., 2004) is an LDA extension taking information about an author into account: for each word in a document d, an author from the document's set of authors is chosen at random. A topic t is then chosen from a distribution over topics specific to the author, and the word is generated from that topic. The model gives information about the diversity of the topics covered by an author, and makes it possible to calculate the distance between the topics covered by different authors, to see how similar they are in their themes and topics.

Topic modeling algorithms have gained increased attention in modeling tweets. However, tweets pose some difficulties because of their sparseness, as the short documents might not contain sufficient data to establish satisfactory term co-occurrences. Therefore, pooling techniques (which involve aggregating related tweets into individual documents) might improve the results produced by standard topic model methods. Pooling techniques include, among others, aggregation of tweets that share hashtags and aggregation of tweets that share author. Hong and Davison (2010) compare the LDA topic model with an Author-topic model for tweets, finding that the topics learned from these methods differ from each other. By aggregating tweets written by an author into one individual document, they mitigate the disadvantages caused by the sparse nature of tweets. Moreover, Quan et al. (2015) present a solution for topic modeling for sparse documents, finding that automatic text aggregation during topic modeling is able to produce more interpretable topics from short texts than standard topic models.

3 Extracting topic models

Topic models can be extracted in several ways, in addition to the LDA-based methods and SemEval methods outlined above. Specifically, here three sources of information are singled out for this purpose: topic model scores, topic clustering, and hashtags.

3.1 Topic model scoring

The unsupervised nature of topic discovery makes the assessment of topic models challenging. Quantitative metrics do not necessarily provide accurate reflections of a human's perception of a topic model, and hence a variety of evaluation metrics have been proposed.

The **UMass coherence metric** (Mimno et al., 2011) measures *topic coherence*: $C = \sum_{m=2}^{M} \sum_{l=1}^{m-1} log \frac{D(w_m,w_l)+1}{D(w_l)}$ with $(w_1,...,w_M)$ being the M most probable words in the topic, $D(w)$ the number of documents that contain word w, and $D(w_m,w_l)$ the number of documents that contain both words w_m and w_l. The metric utilizes word co-occurrence statistics gathered from the corpus, which ideally already should be accounted for in the topic model. Mimno et al. (2011) achieved reasonable results when comparing the scores obtained by this measure with human scoring on a corpus of 300,000 health journal abstracts.

However, statistical methods cannot model a human's perception of the coherence in a topic model perfectly, so **human judgement** is commonly used to evaluate topic models. Chang et al. (2009) propose two tasks where humans can evaluate topic models: *Word intrusion* lets humans measure the coherence of the topics in a model by evaluating the latent space in the topics. The human subject is presented with six words, and the task is to find the *intruder*, which is the one word that does not belong with the others. The idea is that the subject should easily identify that word when the set of words minus the intruder makes sense together. In *topic intrusion*, subjects are shown a document's title along with the first few words of the document and four topics. Three of those are the highest probability topics assigned to the document, while the *intruder topic* is chosen randomly.

In addition to these methods, we introduce a way to evaluate author-topic models, specifically with the Twitter domain in mind. A topic mixture for each author is obtained from the model. The human subjects should know the authors in advance, and have a fair understanding of which topics the authors are generally interested in. The subjects are then presented a list of authors, along with topic distributions for each author (represented by the 10 most probable topics, with each topic given by its 10 most probable words). The task of the subject is to deduce which topic distribution belongs to which author. The idea is that coherent topics would make it easy to recognize authors from a topic mixture, as author interests would be reflected by topic probabilities.

3.2 Clustering tweets

An important task related to topic modeling is determining the number of clusters, k, to use for the model. There is usually not a single correct optimal value: too few clusters will produce topics that are overly broad and too many clusters will result in overlapping or too similar topics. The Elbow method can be used to estimate the optimal number of clusters, by running k-means clustering on the dataset for different values of k, and then calculating the sum of squared error (SSE $= \sum_{i=1}^{n}[y_i - f(x_i)]^2$) for each value.

For text datasets, Can and Ozkarahan (1990) propose that the number of clusters can be expressed by the formula $\frac{mn}{t}$, where m is the number of documents, n the number of terms, and t the number of non-zero entries in the document by term matrix. Greene et al. (2014) introduce a term-centric stability analysis strategy, assuming that a topic model with an optimal number of clusters is more robust to deviations in the dataset. However, they validated the method on news articles, that are much longer and usually more coherent than tweets. Greene et al. (2014) released a Python implementation[1] of the stability analysis approach, which we used to predict the optimal number of clusters for a Twitter dataset.

To estimate the number of topics in a tweet corpus, stability analysis was applied to 10,000 tweets posted on January 27, 2016, using a $[2, 10]$ k range for the number of topics. An initial topic model was generated from the whole dataset. Proceedingly, τ random subsets of the dataset were generated, with one topic model per k value for each subset $S_1, ..., S_\tau$. The stability score for a k value is generated by computing the mean agreement score between a reference set S_0 and a sample ranking set S_i for k: $\sum_{i=1}^{\tau} agree(S_0, S_i)$ (Greene et al., 2014). The number of terms to consider, t, also affects the agreement. A t value of 20 indicates that the top 10 terms for each topic were used. The stability scores were overall low, e.g., $t = 20$ ranging from 0.43 at $k = 2$ to 0.31 at $k = 10$. The low scores

---

[1] https://github.com/derekgreene/topic-stability

are likely caused by the sparse and noisy data in tweets, as this method was originally used for longer, more coherent documents. The method's estimation of number of topics is therefore not a good indication of the number of underlying topics in Twitter corpora.

Good results have been achieved by using a higher number of topics for tweets than what is needed for larger, more coherent corpora, since short messages and the diverse themes in tweets require more topics. Hong and Davison (2010) use a range of topics for tweets from 20 to 150, obtaining the best results for $t = 50$, although the chance of duplicate or overlapping topics increase with the amount of topics.

3.3   Hashtags

Tweets have user-generated metatags that can aid the topic and sentiment analysis. A hashtag is a term or an abbreviation preceded by the hash mark (#). Being labels that users tag their messages with, they serve as indicators of which underlying topics are contained in a tweet. Moreover, hashtags can help discover emerging events and breaking news, by looking at new or uncommon hashtags that suddenly rise in attention. We here present the usage of hashtag co-occurrences to divulge the hidden thematic structure in a corpus, using a collection of 3 million tweets retrieved during the Super Bowl game, February 7th, 2016.

Hashtag co-occurrences show how hashtags appear together in tweets. Since different hashtags appearing in the same tweet usually share the underlying topics, a hashtag co-occurence graph might give interesting information regarding the topics central to the tweet. Looking at which hashtags co-occur with the hashtag *#SuperBowl* gives us more information about other important themes and topics related to Super Bowl. Table 1 shows the 10 most popular hashtags from the Super Bowl corpus, about half of them being re-

Hashtag	Freq.
SB50	10,234
KCA	3,624
SuperBowl	2,985
FollowMeCameronDallas	1,899
Broncos	1,290
EsuranceSweepstakes	1,079
followmecaniff	995
FollowMeCarterReynolds	938
KeepPounding	794
SuperBowl50	783

Table 1: Hashtags during Super Bowl 2016

lated to the Super Bowl. Interestingly, (Denver) *Broncos*, the winning team of the match, was the 5th most mentioned hashtag, while the losing team (Carolina) *Panthers* only was the 17th most popular hashtag that day.

Some hashtags are related to a topic without it being apparent, since it requires further knowledge to understand how they are related: "Keep Pounding" is a quote by the late Carolina Panthers player and coach Sam Mills.

Hashtag co-occurrences help reveal such related hashtags, and hashtag-graph based topic models have been found to enhance the semantic relations displayed by standard topic model techniques (Wang et al., 2014). Figure 1 displays the 20 most co-occurring hashtags in a co-occurrence network for the Super Bowl corpus. Three clusters of hashtags emerge, with Super Bowl related hashtags forming the largest. Related topics and terms become more apparent when displayed in a co-occurrence graph like this, with *Keep-Pounding* and *SB50* being the 8th most co-occurring hashtag pair, and the artists *Beyonce* and *Coldplay* appearing in the Super Bowl cluster since they performed during the halftime show. The graph also indicates *EsuranceSweepstakes* to be related to Super Bowl, and indeed the company Esurance run an ad during the match, encouraging people to tweet using the hashtag *EsuranceSpeestakes*.

Another cluster consists of the three hash-

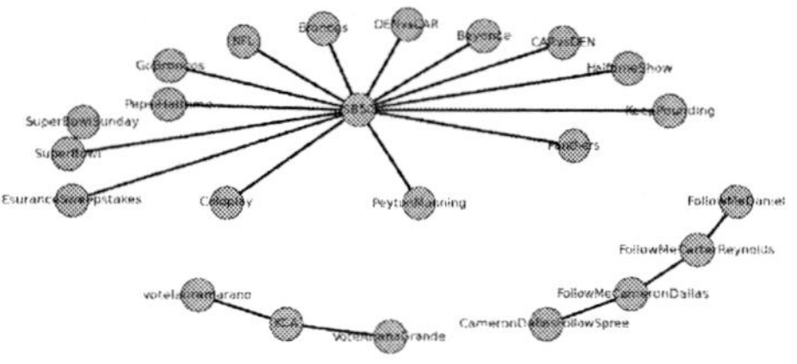

Figure 1: Hashtag co-occurrence network

tags *votelauramarano*, *KCA* and *VoteArianaGrande*. KCA is an abbreviation of *Kid's Choice Awards*, an annual award show where people can vote for their favorite television, movie and music acts, by tweeting the hashtag *KCA* with a specific nominee-specific voting hashtag (e.g., *VoteArianaGrande*).

4 Topic Modeling Experiments

Extending the studies of the previous section, a set of experiments related to topic modeling were conducted, comparing a standard LDA topic model to a hashtag-aggregated model, and comparing two author-topic models.

4.1 Hashtag-aggregated topic model

A pooling technique that involves aggregating tweets sharing hashtags was applied, the assumption being that tweets that share hashtags also share underlying topics. The main goal of this method is the same as for the Author-topic model and other pooling techniques; alleviating the disadvantages of short documents by aggregating documents that are likely to share latent topics. Some restrictions were introduced: only *single-hashtag* tweets were used, and only hashtags that appeared in at least 20 of the documents in the corpus.

Table 2 shows a sample of the resulting topics. They appear more coherent than the topics generated on tweets as individual documents, even though many of the less probable words in each topic might seem somewhat random. It is, however, easier to get an un-

Topic #7	Topic #21	Topic #24	Topic #34
revivaltour	new	purposetourboston	trump
selenagomez	soundcloud	justinbieber	hillary
whumun	news	boston	bernie
wtf	video	one	realdonaldtrump
getting	favorite	best	will
boyfriend	sounds	tonight	clinton
bitch	health	yet	greysanatomy
mad	blessed	shows	vote
resulted	efc	bitcoin	president
blend	mealamovie	redsox	people

Table 2: Four topics after hashtag aggregation

derstanding of the underlying topics conveyed in the tweets, and aggregating tweets sharing hashtags can produce more coherence than a topic model generated by single tweets as documents. The UMass coherence scores for the topics in this topic model are also much higher than for standard LDA, as shown in Figure 2.

4.2 Author-topic model experiments

Tweets from six popular Twitter users were obtained through the Twitter API, selecting users known for tweeting about different topics, so that the results would be distinguishable. Barack Obama would be expected to tweet mainly about topics related to politics, while the astrophysicist Neil deGrasse Tyson would assumingly tweet about science-related topics. The themes communicated by Obama and Donald Trump ought to be similar, both being politicians, while the inventor Elon Musk ought to show similarities with Tyson. Tweets from two pop artists, Justin Bieber and Taylor Swift, were also included and expected not to share many topics with the other users. To obtain tweets reflecting the author's interests and views, all retweets and quote tweets were discarded, as well as tweets containing media or URLs. Two approaches to author topic-modeling were compared, based on Rosen-Zvi et al. (2004) and on Hong and Davison (2010), respectively.

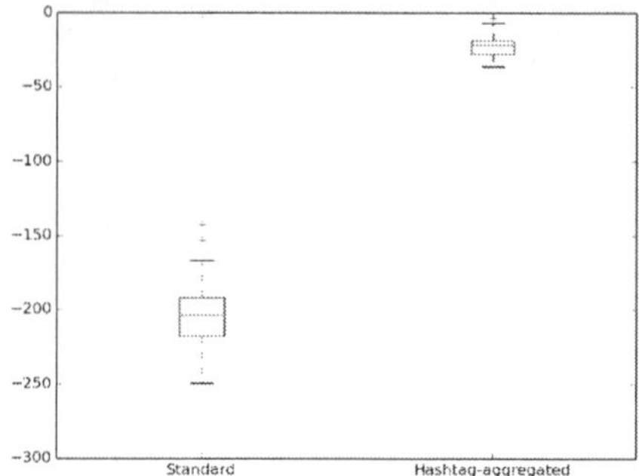

Figure 2: Coherence score of LDA topic model vs. hashtag-aggregated topic model

Ten topics were generated from the Rosen-Zvi et al. (2004) author-topic model, each topic being represented by the 10 most probable words. The resulting topics are reasonably coherent, and can be seen in Table 3. The quality of an author-topic model can be measured in its ability to accurately portray the user's interests. A person that has knowledge of which themes and topics a user usually talks about, should be able to recognize the user by their topic distribution. Eight persons were shown topic distributions such as the one in Figure 3 without knowing which user it belonged to, and asked to identify the users based on the topic distributions.

All participants managed to figure out which topic distribution belonged to which author for all author's, except the distributions of Taylor Swift and Justin Bieber, which were very similar, both having Topic 4 and 5 as most probable. The remaining author's had easily recognizable topic distributions, which was confirmed by the experiment.

The author-topic model proposed by Hong and Davison (2010) performs standard LDA on aggregated user profiles. To conduct the experiments, the model was thus first trained on a corpus where each document contains ag-

#1	#2	#3	#4	#5	#6	#7	#8	#9	#10
will	just	earth	night	tonight	just	people	great	president	don
new	like	moon	today	love	one	much	thank	obama	fyi
now	will	day	get	thank	know	time	trump2016	america	time
get	now	sun	new	thanks	orbit	won	will	sotu	tesla
america	good	world	happy	ts1989	two	tonight	cruz	actonclimate	first
make	think	ask	back	taylurking	might	way	hillary	economy	rocket
poll	also	universe	time	show	long	bad	makeamericagreatagain	work	science
many	around	full	see	got	planet	show	big	change	space
trump	live	space	one	crowd	star	morning	cnn	americans	launch
don	landing	year	good	tomorrow	instead	really	said	jobs	model

Table 3: The ten topics generated for the Rosen-Zvi et al. (2004) author-topic model

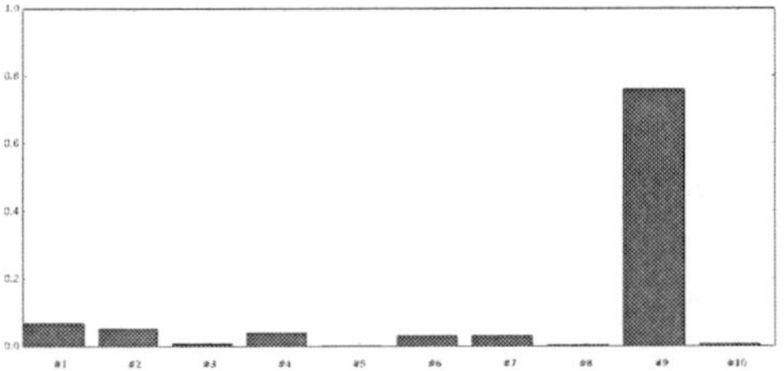

Figure 3: Topic distribution for Obama

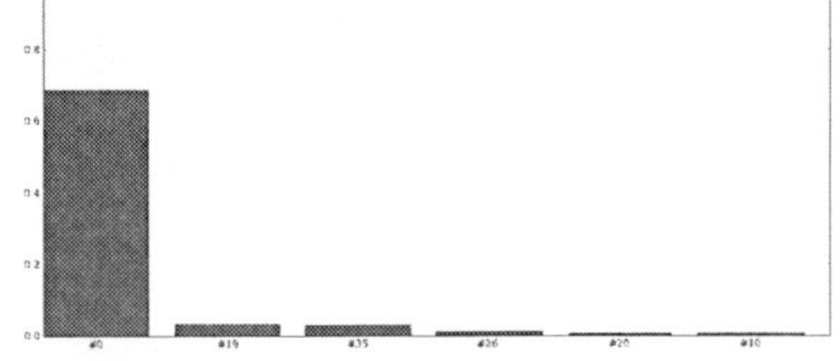

Figure 4: Obama's aggregated topics

gregated tweets for each user. Furthermore, new tweets for each author (which were not part of the training data) were downloaded, and the topic distribution inferred for each of the new tweets. Finally, the topic distribution for each user was calculated as the average topic distribution over all new tweets written by that user. Since a low number of topics produces too many topics containing the same popular words, 50 topics were used instead of the 10 in the previous experiments.

An example of the resulting topic mixtures for the authors can be seen in Figure 4, with the most probable topics for each of the authors tabulated in Table 4. As opposed to the previous topic mixtures, these topic mixtures generally had one topic that was much more probable than the remaining topics. Therefore, the diversity in the language by each author might not be captured as well by this model. On the other hand, the most probable topic for each author generally describes the author with a high precision. It is therefore easier to distinguish Justin Bieber from Taylor Swift than it was in the previous experiment.

5 Discussion and conclusion

A topic modeling system for modeling tweet corpora was created, utilizing pooling techniques to improve the coherence and interpretability of standard topic models. The results indicate that techniques such as author aggregating and hashtag aggregation generate more coherent topics.

Various methods for estimating the optimal number of topics for tweets were tested. The Elbow method almost exclusively suggested a k value between 3 and 5, no matter how large or diverse the corpus was. The stability score (Greene et al., 2014) also produced rather poor estimates for a number of topics when applied to a tweet corpus. The spar-

#0 (Obama)	#20 (Musk)	#26 (Tyson)	#35 (Trump)	#43 (Bieber)	#19 (Swift)
president	tesla	earth	will	thanks	tonight
obama	will	moon	great	love	ts1989
america	rocket	just	thank	whatdoyoumean	taylurking
sotu	just	day	trump2016	mean	just
actonclimate	model	one	just	purpose	love
time	launch	time	cruz	thank	thank
work	good	sun	hillary	lol	crowd
economy	dragon	people	new	good	night
americans	falcon	space	people	great	now
change	now	will	makeamericagreatagain	see	show

Table 4: The most probable topic for the six authors inferred from aggregated topic distribution

sity of tweets is likely the cause of this; the documents do not contain enough words to produce sufficient term co-occurrences. Hong and Davison (2010) found that 50 topics produced the optimal results for their author-topic model, although the optimal number of topics dependents on the diversity of the corpora. Thus k values of 10 and 50 were used in the experiments, with 50 for large corpora where a diverse collection of documents was expected.

Hashtag co-occurrences were used to divulge latent networks of topics and events in a collection of tweets. A hashtag aggregating technique was shown to mitigate the negative impacts sparse texts have on the coherence of a topic model. Hashtag aggregation technique is especially interesting, as it utilizes a specific metadata tag that is not present in standard documents. A hashtag aggregated topic model produced a much better coherence than the standard LDA variation for the same corpus; this is also consistent with recent research on topic models for microblogs. Two Author-topic models were used in our experiments, one using the Rosen-Zvi et al. (2004) topic model and the aggregated author-topic model proposed by Hong and Davison (2010), both seeming to produce interpretable topics. It is worth noting that there is no standardized methods for evaluating topic models, as most quantitative ways try to estimate human judgement. Moreover, there is no precise definition of a *gold standard* for topic models, which makes the task of comparing and ranking topic models difficult. A combination of a computational method and human judgement was therefore used in the evaluations.

One way to extend the topic modeling system would be to apply online analysis by implementing automatic updates of a topic model, continuously extended by new tweets retrieved from the Twitter Streaming API. This would help in detect emerging events, in a fashion similar to Lau et al. (2012). Moreover, Dynamic Topic Models could be considered to provide better temporal modeling of Twitter data. A limitation to topic modeling in general is the difficulties in evaluating the accuracy of the models. Computational methods try to simulate human judgement, which poses difficulties, as human judgement is not clearly defined. Further research could help provide better methods for evaluating topic models. In this paper, we aggregated tweets sharing authors and hashtags. Further work should look into other pooling schemes, and see how they compare to author and hashtag aggregation. One example would be to aggregate conversations on Twitter into individual documents. Tweets contain a lot of metadata that can aid the aggregation process.

References

David M Blei, Andrew Y Ng, and Michael I Jordan. 2003. Latent Dirichlet Allocation. In *the Journal of Machine Learning Research*, volume 3, pages 993–1022, MIT, Massachusetts, USA. JMLR. org.

David M. Blei. 2012. Probabilistic Topic Models. In *Communications of Association for Computer Machinery*, volume 55, New York, NY, USA, April. ACM.

William Boag, Peter Potash, and Anna Rumshisky. 2015. TwitterHawk: A Feature Bucket Based Approach to Sentiment Analysis. In *Proceedings of the 9th International Workshop on Semantic Evaluation (SemEval 2015)*, pages 640–646, Denver, Colorado, June. Association for Computational Linguistics.

Fazli Can and Esen A. Ozkarahan. 1990. Concepts and Effectiveness of the Cover-coefficient-based Clustering Methodology for Text Databases. In *ACM Transitional Database Systems*, volume 15, pages 483–517, New York, NY, USA, December. Association for Computer Machinery.

Jonathan Chang, Sean Gerrish, Chong Wang, Jordan L Boyd-Graber, and David M Blei. 2009. Reading tea leaves: How humans interpret topic models. In *Advances in neural information processing systems*, pages 288–296, Vancouver, British Columbia.

Derek Greene, Derek O'Callaghan, editor="Calders Toon Cunningham, Pádraig", Floriana Esposito, Eyke Hüllermeier, and Rosa Meo, 2014. *How Many Topics? Stability Analysis for Topic Models*, pages 498–513. Springer Berlin Heidelberg, Berlin, Heidelberg.

Liangjie Hong and Brian D. Davison. 2010. Empirical Study of Topic Modeling in Twitter. In *Proceedings of the First Workshop on Social Media Analytics*, SOMA '10, pages 80–88, New York, NY, USA. ACM.

Olessia Koltsova and Sergei Koltcov. 2013. Mapping the public agenda with topic modeling: The case of the Russian LiveJournal. In *Policy & Internet*, volume 5, pages 207–227, Russia.

Jey Han Lau, Nigel Collier, and Timothy Baldwin. 2012. On-line Trend Analysis with Topic Models:\# Twitter Trends Detection Topic Model Online. In *Proceedings of COLING 2012: Technical Papers, pages 1519–1534*, pages 1519–1534, Mumbai, India.

David Mimno, Hanna M. Wallach, Edmund Talley, Miriam Leenders, and Andrew McCallum. 2011. Optimizing semantic coherence in topic models. In *Proceedings of the Conference on Empirical Methods in Natural Language Processing*, EMNLP '11, pages 262–272, Stroudsburg, PA, USA. Association for Computational Linguistics.

Brendan O'Connor, Ramnath Balasubramanyan, Bryan R Routledge, and Noah A Smith. 2010. From Tweets to Polls: Linking Text Sentiment to Public Opinion Time Series. In *International Conference on Web and Social Media*, volume 11, pages 1–2, Washington DC, USA.

Nataliia Plotnikova, Micha Kohl, Kevin Volkert, Andreas Lerner, Natalie Dykes, Heiko Emer, and Stefan Evert. 2015. KLUEless: Polarity Classification and Association. In *Proceedings of the 9th International Workshop on Semantic Evaluation (SemEval 2015)*, Erlangen, Germany. Friedrich-Alexander-Universitat Erlangen-Nurnberg.

Xiaojun Quan, Chunyu Kit, Yong Ge, and Sinno Jialin Pan. 2015. Short and sparse text topic modeling via self-aggregation. In *Proceedings of the 24th International Conference on Artificial Intelligence*, IJCAI'15, pages 2270–2276. AAAI Press.

Michal Rosen-Zvi, Thomas Griffiths, Mark Steyvers, and Padhraic Smyth. 2004. The Author-topic Model for Authors and Documents. In *Proceedings of the 20th Conference on Uncertainty in Artificial Intelligence*, UAI '04, pages 487–494, Arlington, Virginia, United States. AUAI Press.

Dionisios N Sotiropoulos, Chris D Kounavis, Panos Kourouthanassis, and George M Giaglis. 2014. What drives social sentiment? An entropic measure-based clustering approach towards identifying factors that influence social sentiment polarity. In *Information, Intelligence, Systems and Applications, IISA 2014, The 5th International Conference*, pages 361–373, Chania Crete, Greece. IEEE.

Pranav Waila, VK Singh, and Manish K Singh. 2013. Blog text analysis using topic modeling, named entity recognition and sentiment classifier combine. In *Advances in Computing, Communications and Informatics (ICACCI), 2013 International Conference on*, pages 1166–1171, Mysore, India. IEEE.

Y. Wang, J. Liu, J. Qu, Y. Huang, J. Chen, and X. Feng. 2014. Hashtag Graph Based Topic Model for Tweet Mining. In *2014 IEEE International Conference on Data Mining*, pages 1025–1030, Shenzhen, China, Dec.

Jianshu Weng, Ee-Peng Lim, Jing Jiang, and Qi He. 2010. TwitterRank: Finding Topic-sensitive Influential Twitterers. In *Proceedings of the Third ACM International Conference on Web Search and Data Mining*, WSDM '10, pages 261–270, New York, NY, USA. ACM.

Zhihua Zhang, Guoshun Wu, and Man Lan. 2015. East China Normal University, ECNU: Multi-level Sentiment Analysis on Twitter Using Traditional Linguistic Features and Word Embedding Features. In *Proceedings of the 9th International Workshop on Semantic Evaluation (SemEval 2015)*, Shanghai, China. East China Normal University Shanghai.

A Multilingual Entity Linker Using PageRank and Semantic Graphs

Anton Södergren
Department of computer science
Lund University, Lund
karl.a.j.sodergren@gmail.com

Pierre Nugues
Department of computer science
Lund University, Lund
pierre.nugues@cs.lth.se

Abstract

This paper describes HERD, a multilingual named entity recognizer and linker. HERD is based on the links in Wikipedia to resolve mappings between the entities and their different names, and Wikidata as a language-agnostic reference of entity identifiers.

HERD extracts the mentions from text using a string matching engine and links them to entities with a combination of rules, PageRank, and feature vectors based on the Wikipedia categories. We evaluated HERD with the evaluation protocol of ERD'14 (Carmel et al., 2014) and we reached the competitive F1-score of 0.746 on the development set. HERD is designed to be multilingual and has versions in English, French, and Swedish.

1 Introduction

Named entity recognition (NER) refers to the process of finding mentions of persons, locations, and organizations in text, while entity linking (or disambiguation) associates these mentions with unique identifiers. Figure 1 shows an example of entity linking with the mention *Michael Jackson*, an ambiguous name that may refer to thousands of people and where 21 are famous enough to have a Wikipedia page (Wikipedia, 2016). In Fig. 1, the search engine selected the most popular entity (top) and used the cue word *footballer* (bottom) to link the phrase *Michael Jackson footballer* to the English defender born in 1973.

Entity recognition and linking has become a crucial component to many language processing applications: Search engines (Singhal, 2012), question answering (Ferrucci, 2012), or dialogue agents. This importance is reflected by a growing number of available systems; see TAC-KBP2015

(Ji et al., 2015), for instance, with 10 participating teams.

Although many applications include entity linkers, the diversity of the input texts, which can include tweets, search queries, news wires, or encyclopedic articles, makes their evaluation problematic. While some evaluations consider entity linking in isolation and mark the mentions in the input, end-to-end pipelines, where the input consists of raw text, need to combine entity recognition and linking. The ERD'14 challenge (Carmel et al., 2014) is an example of the latter.

2 Previous Work

Entity linking has spurred a considerable amount of work over the last 10 years. Bunescu and Pasca (2006), Mihalcea and Csomai (2007), and Cucerzan (2007) used Wikipedia as a knowledge source and its articles to define the entities, its hyperlinks to find the mentions, and semantic knowledge from redirect pages and categories, to carry out disambiguation. Milne and Witten (2008) used the likelihood of an entity given a mention M, $P(E|M)$, and a relatedness metric between two entities computed from the links to their corresponding pages to improve both recall and precision. Ferragina and Scaiella (2010) addressed shorter pieces of text with the idea to use a collective agreement between all the entities.

The Entity Recognition and Disambiguation Challenge (ERD'14) (Carmel et al., 2014) is a recent evaluation, where competitors were given a set of entities to recognize and link in a corpus of unlabelled text. This setting is closer to real world application than TAC (Ji et al., 2015), where participants have to link already bracketed mentions. The evaluation included two tracks: one with long documents of an average size of 600 words and a short track consisting of search query.

Finally, the CoNLL-2003 shared task (Tjong Kim Sang and De Meulder, 2003) is an influen-

Proceedings of the 21st Nordic Conference of Computational Linguistics, pages 87–95,
Gothenburg, Sweden, 23-24 May 2017. ©2017 Linköping University Electronic Press

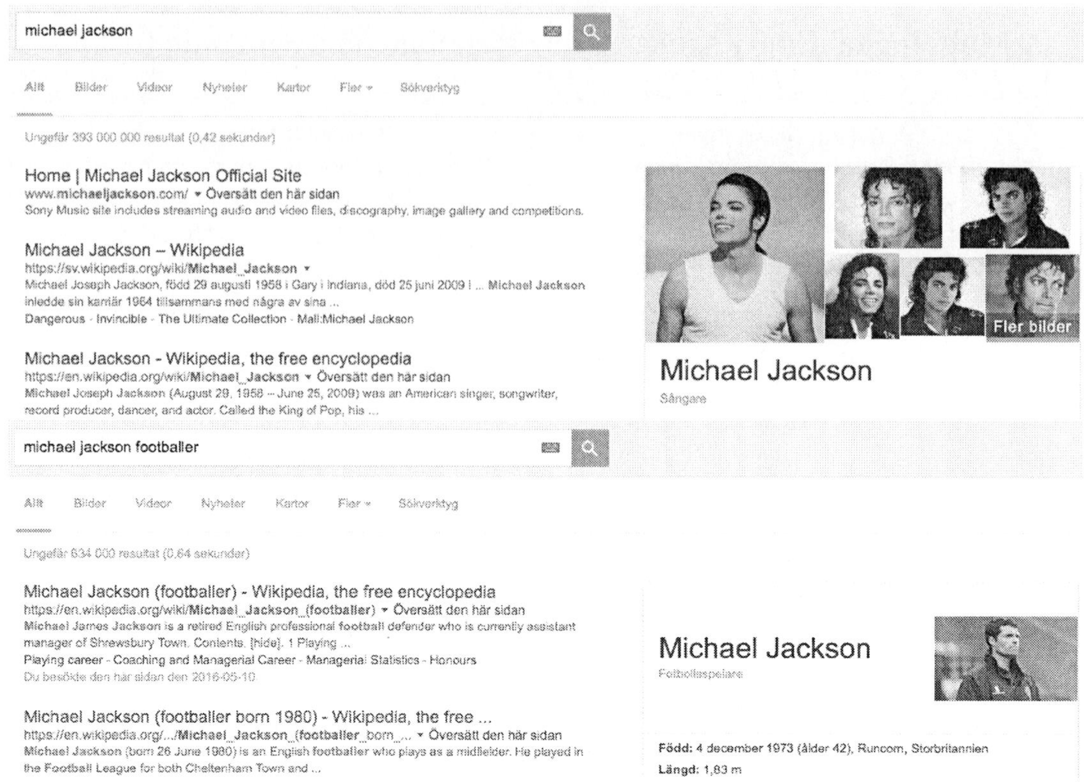

Figure 1: Search results for the queries *Michael Jackson* and *Michael Jackson footballer*. The engine returns the most popular entity (top) and uses the minimal context given in the query, *footballer*, to propose a less popular entity (bottom)

tial evaluation of language independent named entity recognition, with a focus on German and English. Hoffart et al. (2011) linked the names in the English corpus to Wikipedia pages making this dataset a useful corpus for entity linking.

In this paper, we used the ERD'14 development set as well as the CoNLL-2003 dataset with Wikidata links.

3 Building the Entity Knowledge Base

3.1 Mention-Entity Pairs

Following Mihalcea and Csomai (2007) and Bunescu and Pasca (2006), we collected the mention-entity pairs from the Wikipedia links (wikilinks). We built the entity base from the from three versions of Wikipedia: English, French, and Swedish, and the frequency of the wikilinks in each version. Figure 2 shows an example of a pair with the mention *Swedish Parliament*. This gives suggestions of how an entity is commonly referred to: i.e. its name or aliases.

Figure 2: The structure of wikilinks in Wikipedia.

3.2 Entity Nomenclature

As nomenclature for the entities, we used Wikidata, the linked database of Wikimedia. Wikidata connects the different language versions of each article in Wikipedia with a unique identifier called the Q-number. In addition to being a cross-lingual repository, Wikidata also links a large number of entities to structured information such as the dates of birth and death for persons.

In order to use a language-agnostic identifier, we translated the wikilinks into Q-numbers. We extracted the pairs of Q-numbers and article names from a Wikidata dump for each language. Since the dump does not contain any URL, the algo-

rithm must recreate the address from the titles. We
could reach a coverage of about 90%. The remaining 10% corresponds to *redirect pages* that
act as alternative names or to cover common mis-
spellings. We used the Wikipedia dump to identify
these redirects and we improved the coverage rate
to 99.1%.

3.3 Annotating the Mentions

We annotated the mention-entity pairs in our
knowledge base with a set of features that we used
in the subsequent processing:

1. The `Frequency` of the mention-entity pairs.
   Table 1 shows an example for the city of Honolulu.

2. We used dictionaries of common nouns, verb,
   and adjectives for each language. If a mention only consists of words in the dictionary,
   we mark it as `only-dictionary`. An example of this is the artist *Prince* in English and
   French.

3. We computed a list of the most frequent
   words (stop words) from Wikipedia for each
   language. They include *the*, *in*, *and*, and *a*, in
   English. If all the words in a mention are stop
   words, we mark it as `only-stop-words`.

4. The system marks the mentions with a high
   number of links as `highly-ambiguous`,
   such as *John* or *details* with almost 5,000 different entities linked to each.

5. Mentions without uppercase letters are
   marked as `lower-case`.

6. Family names and surnames. If the most
   common mention of a person has more than
   two words, we mark each mention of one
   word as `generic`, such as the mention *Bush*
   referring to the former president George W.
   Bush.

7. We also annotate the entities with their frequency (`total-frequency`). It corresponds
   to the sum of all their mentions frequencies.

3.4 Pruning the Knowledge Base

Although Wikipedia is reviewed by scores of volunteers, there are plenty of misleading mentions in
the collected knowledge base. We removed a part
of them using the following rules:

1. The mention is marked as `lower-case`
   and either `only-dictionary` or
   `only-stop-words`

2. The `frequency` of the entity-mention is exactly 1, while the `total-frequency` of that
   entity is above a threshold parameter that was
   empirically obtained.

3. The mention consists of two or more words,
   and starts with a lower-case stop word, that
   is not a definite article. This will filter out
   anchors of the type *a city in Sweden*.

We also clustered the mentions with a normalized Levenshtein distance (Levenshtein, 1966). If
the distance was less than 0.2 to any element, they
were considered to be in the same group. We applied the clustering to all the surface forms and we
discarded the mentions without a group.

4 System Components and Pipeline

The system consists of three main components: a
spotter that identifies the mentions, a set of rules
that prunes the results, and an improver that uses
contextual clues for entity recognition (Fig. 3).

The spotter outputs a match for every conceiv-
able mention of an entity, leaving us with a document where almost every word is tagged as an
entity. This output has a very high recall, but a
very low precision.

The filtering that comes after that tries to remove the most unlikely of the alternatives from the
spotter and raises the precision to a modest level
while trying to have a minimal impact on the recall. If the input data to the next step is completely
unfiltered the Contextual Improver is unable to affect the results in a positive way.

The Contextual Improver is the final step and
uses contextual clues, such as which categories the
entities belong to and which entities are commonly
seen together, to improve the result.

4.1 Mention Spotting

We use the mention-entity knowledge base to spot
the mentions in raw text and associate them with
all their possible entities. Following Lipczak et
al. (2014), we applied the Solr Text Tagger (Smiley, 2013) based on finite-state transducers and the
Lucene indexer. Solr Text Tagger was chosen as
it is a highly effective way of marking up possible
matches of a database in a text. It is based on the

Mention	Entity	Frequency	Mention	Entity	Frequency
Honolulu	Q18094	5117	Hawaii	Q18094	11
Honolulu, Hawaii	Q18094	2281	Honolulu, HI MSA	Q18094	7
Honolulu, HI	Q18094	600	HONOLULU	Q18094	7
Honolulu, Hawaii, USA	Q18094	67	city of Honolulu	Q18094	7
Honolulu, Hawai'i	Q18094	47	honolulu	Q18094	5
Honolulu, Hawai'i	Q18094	21	Honululu	Q18094	5
Honolulu CPD	Q18094	21			

Table 1: An example of the mention-entity counts for the entity Q18094, most commonly called Honolulu

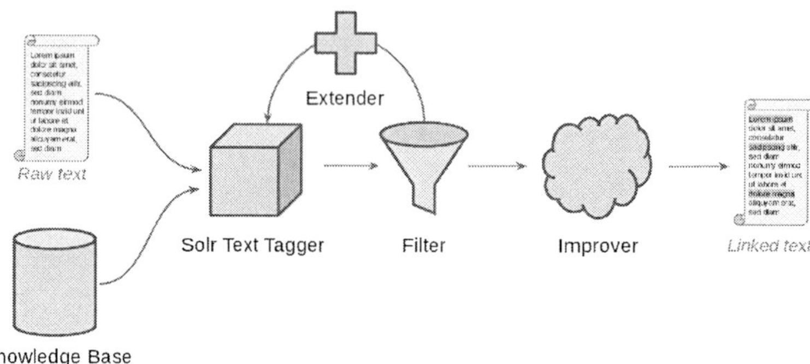

Figure 3: The system architecture, where the knowledge base contains the mention-entity pairs

Lucene open-source software and its implementation of finite-state transducers.

As a preprocessing step, Solr Text Tagger compiles all the mentions in the knowledge base, where the input labels are the letters and symbols of mentions and the output labels are the entity identifiers. Then, given an untagged text, the tagger marks all the occurrences, possibly overlapping, of all the names in the database. See Fig. 4.

4.2 Filtering and Expansion

The output of the Spotter is usually very noisy as most words can match some mention in the knowledge base. Examples include *It*, a novel by Stephen King, or *Is This It*, an album by The Strokes. The result is a high mention recall, but a low precision. We applied filters to remove some matches and improve the precision while preserving the recall.

The system uses a set of manually-written rules and empirically obtained hyper parameters to improve precision with a minimal effect on recall. We describe them in the sections below. The complete list of parameter values is provided in the

HERD source code available from GitHub[1].

4.2.1 Mention Probability

We computed the probability for a term or a phrase to be a link over the whole Wikipedia (Eckhardt et al., 2014) using the formula: Mention probability $= \frac{link(mention)}{freq(mention)}$. This gives a hint at whether a word sequence is more commonly used as a mention of entities or just as words.

Medical Center, for example, is linked 1.0% of the times used, while *Medical Center of Central Georgia* has a mention probability of 73.7%.

Any candidate that had less than 0.5% mention probability was immediately pruned.

4.2.2 Filters to Improve Precision

Filters are rules based on syntactical clues and the flags defined in Sect. 3.3. Each matching rule returns a suspicion score and we compute the sum of the scores. The most significant rules are:

1. Capitalization: Add suspicion to any mention that does not contain a capital letter. This loses some recall, but increases the precision

---

[1] https://github.com/AAAton/herd

dramatically. We improved it with a function that takes into consideration the number of capital letters, whether the mention is the start of a new sentence and whether the mention has the `only-dictionary` tag. Headlines also use capitalized words. We recognize fully capitalized sentences with regular expressions. Mentions in headlines with the `only-dictionary`, or `only-stop-words` tags, generate suspicion.

2. Generic names: We apply a two-pass analysis for `generic` mentions. We remove them from the first pass. In a second pass, the generic names are restored if a mention of the same entity that is not generic shows in the text i.e. the *Bush* mention is kept only when there is a full mention of *George W. Bush* in the text. This is to avoid the tagging of the mention *Bush* with every entity having this name as a generic name.

3. Colliding names: If two tags are immediate neighbors, with the exception of a space, they generate suspicion. The system considers all the candidate entities for a surface form, and only triggers suspicion if at least one of the entities is a generic name. This is a method to detect and avoid tagging a multiword name which does not exist in our knowledge base with multiple other candidates.

4.2.3 Extender to Improve Recall

We extended the detected mentions following the work of Eckhardt et al. (2014). Once we recognize a mention consisting of two words or more that passed the filter, we create new mentions with acronyms and generic version of the item by splitting it into multiple parts.

Given the text *a division of First Citizens Banc-Shares Inc. of Raleigh, N.C.*, where the system recognizes the mention *First Citizens BancShares Inc*, the extender creates possible acronyms, such as *FCBI* and *F.C.B.I.* It also looks for parentheses, immediately following a mention, giving a suggestion of how it is meant to be abbreviated.

The extender also splits the mention into parts of 1, 2, and 3 words. The mention above generates *First*, *Citizens*, *BankShares* and *Inc.*, as well as *First Citizens*, *Citizens BankShares*, *BankShares Inc*, and so forth. We associate the generated mentions with the set of entities of the original mention. The tagged extensions are filtered in the same manner as all the other tags.

4.3 Contextual Improver

For each document, the Improver uses PageRank to determine which candidates commonly occur together, and prunes the unseen combinations. This produces a result with a very high precision. We use this high precision output as the modelled context of the document. A weighted category graph is calculated for this modelled context. The named entity recognition is then widened by considering the similarity of all the candidates to the modelled context.

Once the improver has been applied, we carry out a final clean-up step, where we eliminate all the overlap and rank the remaining candidates for each mention.

4.3.1 PageRank

We apply a modified version of PageRank (Brin and Page, 1998) to the tagged mentions. Following Eckhardt et al. (2014), we create a node for every mention-entity pair that is detected in the text, and run three iterations of PageRank. We analyze the internal links of Wikipedia to determine which entities appear in the same context. Two entities are considered linked if the article of Entity A links to the article of Entity B or a link to both the article of Entity A and the article of Entity B occurs in the same paragraph.

The links calculated on Wikipedia are transferred to the tagged document and produce a graph of linked entities. Unlike the work of Eckhardt et al. (2014), we initialize each node with the standard value $1/N$, and the ratio between the initial value and the final value is used to modify the suspicion for a candidate.

After applying PageRank, some entities will be higher ranked than others which we take as an input to another round of filtering. The candidates with high suspicion are removed. This produces a high precision output, with a slight drop of the recall.

4.3.2 Weighted Category Graph

We use a weighted category graph (WCG) derived from the user-annotated categories of Wikipedia articles (Lipczak et al., 2014). For each article, we created this graph from all the languages in which the article is available. If an article has the same category in all the languages, this category is as-

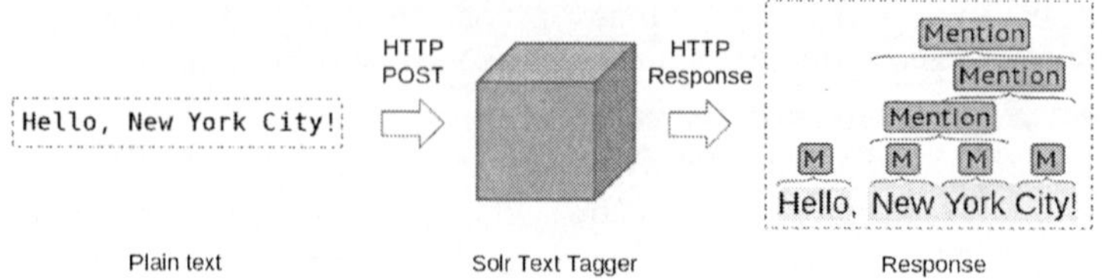

Figure 4: The Solr Text Tagger processing scheme, where the operations are carried out through POST requests.

signed the maximum weight of 1.0. The weight is then decreased as a linear function of the number of languages. The categories need to be weighted to avoid rare or incorrect categories assigned to articles.

Wikipedia categories are themselves categorized into parent categories. The category of *Sweden* has a parent category of *Countries in Europe* for example. A tree of categories is derived from each article by getting the top k categories of an article, and expanding those categories with the top k parents for each category. This process is repeated d times. This generalizes the categories of the article, which makes them easier to compare to adjacent articles.

The value k is set to 5, and the value d is set to 3, as proposed by Lipczak et al. (2014).

Table 2 shows an example of the categories we obtain from the article about *Sweden*.

The weighted category graph is used in the following way:

1. We input a set of core entities with high precision. The improver calculates a weighted category vector for each entity and creates a `topic centroid` as the linear combination of these vectors. This is meant to function as the general topic of the analyzed document.

2. We improve the precision of the core entities by comparing each of the high-precision entities to the topic centroid with a cosine similarity. If the score of an entity is under a threshold value of 0.6, it is removed. Finally, the topic centroid is recalculated.

3. We then compare each entity in the unfiltered output of Solr Text Tagger to the topic centroid with a cosine similarity. We keep the entities that are above a threshold value of 0.2.

Category	Ratio
Sweden	1.00
Countries in Europe	0.38
Member states of the European Union	0.30
Constitutional monarchies	0.20
Scandinavia	0.20

Table 2: Top 5 categories for Sweden, Q34

This procedure widens the scope of the entity selection and improves the recall in a context aware manner. Since the output of the weighted category graphs is similar to the input constraints of PageRank, and the output of PageRank is similar to the input requirements of the weighted category graph, we have set them into an iteration cycle in order to achieve higher results.

4.3.3 Clean-up

As a final step, we eliminate overlapping mentions: When two mentions overlap, we keep the longest. If the mentions are of equal length, we keep the rightmost.

The remaining candidates for each mention are then ranked by their wikilink frequency, and the most frequent candidate is selected as the correct disambiguation.

5 Experimental Setup and Results

We evaluated the system with two different data sets for English: ERD-51 and AIDA/YAGO and we used the evaluation metrics of ERD'14 Carmel et al. (2014). We did not have access to evaluation sets for the other languages.

ERD-51 is the development set of Carmel et al. (2014). It consists of 51 documents that have been scraped from a variety of sources with 1,169 human-annotated mentions. Each annotation has a start, an end, and a Freebase identifier (Bollacker et al., 2008). In the competition, a set of entities, slightly over 2 million, was given, and thus the problem of defining what a named entity actually is was avoided. We filtered our knowledge base to only contain mentions of entities from the given set.

AIDA/YAGO is derived from the CoNLL-2003 shared task (Tjong Kim Sang and De Meulder, 2003). It is a collection of 1393 news articles with 34,587 human-annotated names. 27,632 of those names have been disambiguated with a link to the corresponding Wikipedia site using a dump from 2010-08-17 (Hoffart et al., 2011).

Tables 4 and 3 show the results evolving over different versions of the system. The execution time is normalized to the time spent to process 5,000 characters. It should not be considered an absolute value, but can be used to compare the different algorithms.

Lipczak et al. (2014) and Eckhardt et al. (2014), respectively second and third of ERD'14, reported results of 0.735 and 0.72 on the test set. Our results are not exactly comparable as we used the development set. Nonetheless we believe our system competitive. The highest scoring participant (Cucerzan, 2014) with a score of 0.76 was one of the organizers and was not part of the competition. The reason for the difference in recognition score between the ERD-51 and the AIDA/YAGO dataset lies in the text genres. AIDA/YAGO is collected from well written news wires, mainly written by professionals with proper punctuation and capitalization, while ERD-51 is a collection of more poorly written texts collected from a wider variety of sources, spanning from blogs to eBay sales sites.

For the score of the linked systems, the results are the opposite. ERD-51 has been annotated and linked by humans from a predefined set of 2 million entities, while the linking in AIDA/YAGO has been done from an older dump of Wikipedia. The dump contains around 3 million different sites, unlike the dump we used that has around 5 million entities. Both the mismatch in the entities that are possible to use and the larger size of the knowledge base lead to a larger gap between recognition and linking.

With a latency of around 200 ms per 5,000 characters, the system should be able to tag the entire of the English Wikipedia under a day with a heavy duty computer. We estimate that the average length of a Wikipedia article is around 2,000 characters, that there are 5 million articles, 24 available

cores and 100% run time.

We implemented the entity linker as an interactive demonstration. The user can paste a text and visualize the results in the form of a text annotated with entity labels. Once the user hovers over the label, the ranked candidates are displayed with a link to the Wikidata page for that entity. Figure 5 shows an output of the system.

6 Conclusions and Future Work

We explored different methods to carry out language-independent entity linking from raw text and we presented evaluations on English. The version of the system that had the highest score used a 4-step pipeline, ending with an iteration cycle between a personalized version of PageRank and the usage of weighted category graphs. The system reached a weighted F1-score of 0.746 on the ERD-51 dataset.

The paper takes an unusual approach to named entity recognition and disambiguation as it does not separate the tasks, but treats every candidate to every mention as a separate possibility. The iteration between two context-aware algorithms with different precision/recall characteristics improved the results dramatically and is, to the best of our knowledge, a novel, language-independent approach to entity recognition and disambiguation. We also exposed a way of pruning unsatisfying links in a collected knowledge base by clustering.

The system and its approach can be improved in a number of ways. Firstly, the usage of manually written rules is suboptimal, as the rules may be dependent on the language. A method that only uses Wikipedia, or some other multilingual resource, and avoids syntactical clues altogether, would be a better solution. An approach like that would be more robust to the differences between languages.

We have also introduced a number of threshold values in different parts of the system, such as the suspicion cutoff in the manual rules and the similarity threshold in the WCG. These are difficult to optimize without an automated method. We think HERD would benefit from finding an alternative approach that avoids cutoff values or automates their optimization.

The approach would also benefit from a deeper evaluation on a wider variety of datasets, spanning over several languages, as well as the two English datasets used in this article.

Version	Exec. (ms)	Recognition			Linking		
		Precision	Recall	F	Precision	Recall	F
v0.1 Baseline	-	0.745	0.686	0.714	0.551	0.521	0.535
v0.2 With extender	-	0.673	0.762	0.715	0.520	0.581	0.549
v0.3 Remove colliding mentions	-	0.698	0.730	0.714	0.536	0.572	0.554
v0.4 Simplified filtering	-	0.723	0.720	0.721	0.613	0.610	0.611
v0.5 Relaxed filtering	-	0.642	**0.859**	0.734	0.522	0.720	0.605
v0.6 Part of headline	-	0.691	0.796	0.740	0.593	0.684	0.635
v0.7 Filter out candidates with low frequency	250	0.718	0.785	0.750	0.612	0.672	0.640
v0.8 PageRank	246	**0.865**	0.765	0.812	**0.747**	0.661	0.701
v1.0 PageRank & WCG	608	0.843	0.848	**0.845**	0.744	0.749	**0.746**

Table 3: Results on the ERD51 dataset

Version	Exec. (ms)	Recognition			Linking		
		Precision	Recall	F	Precision	Recall	F
v0.1 Baseline	-	0.940	0.630	0.755			
v0.2 With extender	-	0.889	0.684	0.773			
v0.3 Remove colliding nodes	-	0.923	0.678	0.782			
v0.4 Simplified filtering	-	**0.934**	0.705	0.803			
v0.5 Relaxed filtering	-	0.912	0.769	0.835			
v0.7 Filtered out candidates with low frequency	1088	0.888	0.789	0.835			
v0.8 PageRank	3325	0.935	0.819	0.873	0.732	0.631	0.678
v1.0 PageRank & WCG	4415	0.932	0.827	0.876	**0.740**	**0.647**	**0.690**

Table 4: Results on the AIDA/YAGO dataset

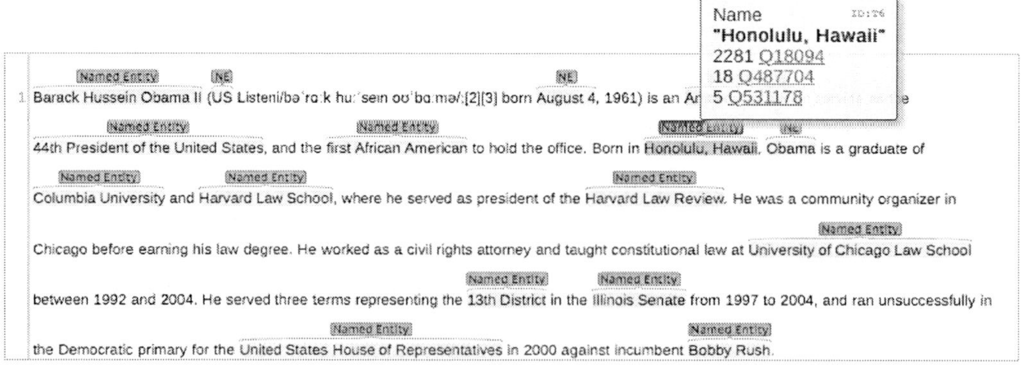

Figure 5: Visualizer

The HERD source code is available from GitHub at this repository: `https://github.com/AAAton/herd`. A demonstration of HERD as part of the Langforia processing pipelines (Klang and Nugues, 2016) is available at this location: `http://vilde.cs.lth.se:9000`.

Acknowledgements

This research was supported by Vetenskapsrådet, the Swedish research council, under the *Det digitaliserade samhället* program.

References

Kurt Bollacker, Colin Evans, Praveen Paritosh, Tim Sturge, and Jamie Taylor. 2008. Freebase: A collaboratively created graph database for structuring human knowledge. In *Proceedings of the 2008 ACM SIGMOD International Conference on Management of Data*, SIGMOD '08, pages 1247–1250, New York, NY, USA. ACM.

Sergey Brin and Lawrence Page. 1998. The anatomy of a large-scale hypertextual web search engine. *Computer Networks and ISDN Systems*, 30(1-7):107–117, April.

Razvan C Bunescu and Marius Pasca. 2006. Using encyclopedic knowledge for named entity disambiguation. In *European Chapter of the Association for Computational Linguistics*, volume 6, pages 9–16.

David Carmel, Ming-Wei Chang, Evgeniy Gabrilovich, Bo-June Paul Hsu, and Kuansan Wang. 2014. ERD'14: Entity recognition and disambiguation challenge. In *ACM SIGIR Forum*, volume 48, pages 63–77. ACM.

Silviu Cucerzan. 2007. Large-scale named entity disambiguation based on wikipedia data. In *Empirical Methods in Natural Language Processing and Computational Natural Language Learning*, volume 7, pages 708–716.

Silviu Cucerzan. 2014. Name Entities Made Obvious: The Participation in the ERD 2014 Evaluation. In *Proceedings of the First International Workshop on Entity Recognition & Disambiguation*, ERD '14, pages 95–100, New York, NY, USA. ACM.

Alan Eckhardt, Juraj Hreško, Jan Procházka, and Otakar Smri;. 2014. Entity linking based on the co-occurrence graph and entity probability. In *Proceedings of the First International Workshop on Entity Recognition & Disambiguation*, ERD '14, pages 37–44, New York, NY, USA. ACM.

Paolo Ferragina and Ugo Scaiella. 2010. Tagme: On-the-fly annotation of short text fragments (by wikipedia entities). In *Proceedings of the 19th ACM International Conference on Information and Knowledge Management*, CIKM '10, pages 1625–1628, New York, NY, USA. ACM.

David Angelo Ferrucci. 2012. Introduction to "This is Watson". *IBM Journal of Research and Development*, 56(3.4):1:1 –1:15, May-June.

Johannes Hoffart, Mohamed Amir Yosef, Ilaria Bordino, Hagen Fürstenau, Manfred Pinkal, Marc Spaniol, Bilyana Taneva, Stefan Thater, and Gerhard Weikum. 2011. Robust disambiguation of named entities in text. In *Proceedings of the 2011 Conference on Empirical Methods in Natural Language Processing*, pages 782–792, Edinburgh.

Heng Ji, Joel Nothman, Ben Hachey, and Radu Florian. 2015. Overview of tac-kbp2015 trilingual entity discovery and linking. In *Proceedings of the Eighth Text Analysis Conference (TAC2015)*.

Marcus Klang and Pierre Nugues. 2016. Langforia: Language pipelines for annotating large collections of documents. In *Proceedings of COLING 2016, the 26th International Conference on Computational Linguistics: System Demonstrations*, pages 74–78, Osaka, Japan, December. The COLING 2016 Organizing Committee.

V. I. Levenshtein. 1966. Binary Codes Capable of Correcting Deletions, Insertions and Reversals. *Soviet Physics Doklady*, 10:707, February.

Marek Lipczak, Arash Koushkestani, and Evangelos Milios. 2014. Tulip: Lightweight entity recognition and disambiguation using wikipedia-based topic centroids. In *Proceedings of the First International Workshop on Entity Recognition & Disambiguation*, ERD '14, pages 31–36, New York, NY, USA. ACM.

Rada Mihalcea and Andras Csomai. 2007. Wikify!: Linking documents to encyclopedic knowledge. In *Proceedings of the Sixteenth ACM Conference on Conference on Information and Knowledge Management*, CIKM '07, pages 233–242, New York, NY, USA. ACM.

David Milne and Ian H. Witten. 2008. Learning to link with wikipedia. In *Proceedings of the 17th ACM Conference on Information and Knowledge Management*, CIKM '08, pages 509–518, New York, NY, USA. ACM.

Amit Singhal. 2012. Introducing the knowledge graph: things, not strings. Official Google Blog. `http://googleblog.blogspot.com/2012/05/ introducing-knowledge-graph-things-not. html`. Retrieved 7 November 2013, May.

David Smiley. 2013. Solr text tagger, text tagging with finite state transducers. `https://github. com/OpenSextant/SolrTextTagger`.

Erik F. Tjong Kim Sang and Fien De Meulder. 2003. Introduction to the conll-2003 shared task: Language-independent named entity recognition. In *Proceedings of the Seventh Conference on Natural Language Learning at HLT-NAACL 2003 - Volume 4*, CONLL '03, pages 142–147, Stroudsburg, PA, USA. Association for Computational Linguistics.

Wikipedia. 2016. Michael Jackson (disambiguation) – Wikipedia, the free encyclopedia. `https://en.wikipedia.org/wiki/Michael_ Jackson_(disambiguation)`.

Linear Ensembles of Word Embedding Models

Avo Muromägi
University of Tartu
Tartu, Estonia
avom@ut.ee

Kairit Sirts
University of Tartu
Tartu, Estonia
kairit.sirts@ut.ee

Sven Laur
University of Tartu
Tartu, Estonia
swen@math.ut.ee

Abstract

This paper explores linear methods for combining several word embedding models into an ensemble. We construct the combined models using an iterative method based on either ordinary least squares regression or the solution to the orthogonal Procrustes problem.

We evaluate the proposed approaches on Estonian—a morphologically complex language, for which the available corpora for training word embeddings are relatively small. We compare both combined models with each other and with the input word embedding models using synonym and analogy tests. The results show that while using the ordinary least squares regression performs poorly in our experiments, using orthogonal Procrustes to combine several word embedding models into an ensemble model leads to 7-10% relative improvements over the mean result of the initial models in synonym tests and 19-47% in analogy tests.

1   Introduction

Word embeddings—dense low-dimensional vector representations of words—have become very popular in recent years in the field of natural language processing (NLP). Various methods have been proposed to train word embeddings from unannoted text corpora (Mikolov et al., 2013b; Pennington et al., 2014; Al-Rfou et al., 2013; Turian et al., 2010; Levy and Goldberg, 2014), most well-known of them being perhaps Word2Vec (Mikolov et al., 2013b). Embedding learning systems essentially train a model from a corpus of text and the word embeddings are the model parameters. These systems contain a randomized component and so the trained

models are not directly comparable, even when they have been trained on exactly the same data. This random behaviour provides an opportunity to combine several embedding models into an ensemble which, hopefully, results in a better set of word embeddings. Although model ensembles have been often used in various NLP systems to improve the overall accuracy, the idea of combining several word embedding models into an ensemble has not been explored before.

The main contribution of this paper is to show that word embeddings can benefit from ensemble learning, too. We study two methods for combining word embedding models into an ensemble. Both methods use a simple linear transformation. First of them is based on the standard ordinary least squares solution (OLS) for linear regression, the second uses the solution to the orthogonal Procrustes problem (OPP) (Schönemann, 1966), which essentially also solves the OLS but adds the orthogonality constraint that keeps the angles between vectors and their distances unchanged.

There are several reasons why using an ensemble of word embedding models could be useful. First is the typical ensemble learning argument— the ensemble simply is better because it enables to cancel out random noise of individual models and reinforce the useful patterns expressed by several input models. Secondly, word embedding systems require a lot of training data to learn reliable word representations. While there is a lot of textual data available for English, there are many smaller languages for which even obtaining enough plain unannotated text for training reliable embeddings is a problem. Thus, an ensemble approach that would enable to use the available data more effectively would be beneficial.

According to our knowledge, this is the first work that attempts to leverage the data by combining several word embedding models into a new improved model. Linear methods for combin-

Proceedings of the 21st Nordic Conference of Computational Linguistics, pages 96–104,
Gothenburg, Sweden, 23-24 May 2017. ©2017 Linköping University Electronic Press

ing two embedding models for some task-specific purpose have been used previously. Mikolov et al. (2013a) optimized the linear regression with stochastic gradient descent to learn linear transformations between the embeddings in two languages for machine translation. Mogadala and Rettinger (2016) used OPP to translate embeddings between two languages to perform cross-lingual document classification. Hamilton et al. (2016) aligned a series of embedding models with OPP to detect changes in word meanings over time. The same problem was addressed by Kulkarni et al. (2015) who aligned the embedding models using piecewise linear regression based on a set of nearest neighboring words for each word.

Recently, Yin and Schütze (2016) experimented with several methods to learn meta-embeddings by combining different word embedding sets. Our work differs from theirs in two important aspects. First, in their work each initial model is trained with a *different* word embedding system and on a *different* data set, while we propose to combine the models trained with the *same* system and on the *same* dataset, albeit using different random initialisation. Secondly, although the 1toN model proposed in (Yin and Schütze, 2016) is very similar to the linear models studied in this paper, it doesn't involve the orthogonality constraint included in the OPP method, which in our experiments, as shown later, proves to be crucial.

We conduct experiments on Estonian and construct ensembles from ten different embedding models trained with Word2Vec. We compare the initial and combined models in synonym and analogy tests and find that the ensemble embeddings combined with orthogonal Procrustes method indeed perform significantly better in both tests, leading to a relative improvement of 7-10% over the mean result of the initial models in synonym tests and 19-47% in analogy tests.

2 Combining word embedding models

A word embedding model is a matrix $W \in \mathbb{R}^{|V| \times d}$, where $|V|$ is the number of words in the model lexicon and d is the dimensionality of the vectors. Each row in the matrix W is the continuous representation of a word in a vector space.

Given r embedding models $W_1, \ldots, W_r$ we want to combine them into a target model Y. We define a linear objective function that is the sum of r linear regression optimization goals:

$$J = \sum_{i=1}^{r} \|Y - W_i P_i\|^2, \qquad (1)$$

where $P_1, \ldots, P_r$ are transformation matrices that translate $W_1, \ldots, W_r$, respectively, into the common vector space containing Y.

We use an iterative algorithm to find matrices $P_1, \ldots, P_r$ and Y. During each iteration the algorithm performs two steps:

1. Solve r linear regression problems with respect to the current target model Y, which results in updated values for matrices $P_1, \ldots P_r$;

2. Update Y to be the mean of the translations of all r models:

$$Y = \frac{1}{r} \sum_{i=1}^{r} W_i P_i. \qquad (2)$$

This procedure is continued until the change in the average normalised residual error, computed as

$$\frac{1}{r} \sum_{i=0}^{r} \frac{\|Y - W_i P_i\|}{\sqrt{|V| \cdot d}}, \qquad (3)$$

will become smaller than a predefined threshold value.

We experiment with two different methods for computing the translation matrices $P_1, \ldots, P_r$. The first is based on the standard least squares solution to the linear regression problem, the second method is known as solution to the Orthogonal Procrustes problem (Schönemann, 1966).

2.1 Solution with the ordinary least squares (SOLS)

The analytical solution for a linear regression problem $Y = PW$ for finding the transformation matrix P, given the input data matrix W and the result Y is:

$$P = (W^T W)^{-1} W^T Y \qquad (4)$$

We can use this formula to update all matrices P_i at each iteration. The problem with this approach is that because Y is also unknown and will be updated repeatedly in the second step of the iterative algorithm, the OLS might lead to solutions where both $W_i P_i$ and Y are optimized towards 0 which is not a useful solution. In order to counteract this effect we rescale Y at the start of each iteration. This is done by scaling the elements of Y so that the variance of each column of Y would be equal to 1.

	SOLS		SOPP	
Dim	**Error**	**# Iter**	**Error**	**# Iter**
50	0.162828	33	0.200994	5
100	0.168316	38	0.183933	5
150	0.169554	41	0.171266	4
200	0.172987	40	0.167554	4
250	0.175723	40	0.164493	4
300	0.177082	40	0.160988	4

Table 1: Final errors and the number of iterations until convergence for both SOLS and SOPP. The first column shows the embedding size.

Dim	**SOLS**	**SOPP**	**Mean** W
50	70098	**38998**	41933
100	68175	**32485**	35986
150	73182	**30249**	33564
200	73946	**29310**	32865
250	75884	**28469**	32194
300	77098	**28906**	32729
Avg	73064	**31403**	34879

Table 2: Average mean ranks of the synonym test, smaller values are better. The best result in each row is in bold. All differences are statistically significant: with $p < 2.2 \cdot 10^{-16}$ for all cases.

2.2 Solution to the Orthogonal Procrustes problem (SOPP)

Orthogonal Procrustes is a linear regression problem of transforming the input matrix W to the output matrix Y using an orthogonal transformation matrix P (Schönemann, 1966). The orthogonality constraint is specified as

$$PP^T = P^T P = I$$

The solution to the Orthogonal Procrustes can be computed analytically using singular value decomposition (SVD). First compute:

$$S = W^T Y$$

Then diagonalize using SVD:

$$S^T S = V D_S V^T$$
$$SS^T = U D_S U^T$$

Finally compute:

$$P = UV^T$$

This has to be done for each P_i during each iteration.

This approach is very similar to SOLS. The only difference is the additional orthogonality constraint that gives a potential advantage to this method as in the translated word embeddings $W_i P_i$ the lengths of the vectors and the angles between the vectors are preserved. Additionally, we no longer need to worry about the trivial solution where $P_1, \ldots, P_r$ and Y all converge towards $\mathbf{0}$.

3 Experiments

We tested both methods on a number of Word2Vec models (Mikolov et al., 2013b) trained on the Estonian Reference Corpus.[1] Estonian Reference

---

[1] http://www.cl.ut.ee/korpused/segakorpus

Corpus is the largest text corpus available for Estonian. Its size is approximately 240M word tokens, which may seem like a lot but compared to for instance English Gigaword corpus, which is often used to train word embeddings for English words and which contains more than 4B words, it is quite small. All models were trained using a window size 10 and the skip-gram architecture. We experimented with models of 6 different embedding sizes: 50, 100, 150, 200, 250 and 300. For each dimensionality we had 10 models available. The number of distinct words in each model is 816757.

During training the iterative algorithm was run until the convergence threshold $th = 0.001$ was reached. The number of iterations needed for convergence for both methods and for models with different embedding size are given in Table 1. It can be seen that the convergence with SOPP took significantly fewer iterations than with SOLS. This difference is probably due to two aspects: 1) SOPP has the additional orthogonality constraint which reduces the space of feasible solutions; 2) although SOLS uses the exact analytical solutions for the least squares problem, the final solution for Y does not move directly to the direction pointed to by the analytical solutions due to the variance rescaling.

4 Results

We evaluate the goodness of the combined models using synonym and analogy tests.

4.1 Synonym ranks

One of the common ways to evaluate word embeddings is to use relatedness datasets to measure the correlation between the human and model judge-

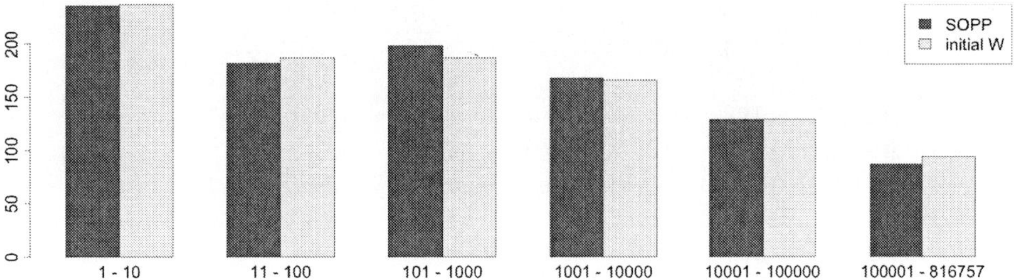

Figure 1: Histogram of the synonym ranks of the 100 dimensional vectors. Dark left columns show the rank frequencies of the SOPP model, light right columns present the rank frequencies of one of the initial models.

ments (Schnabel et al., 2015). In those datasets, there are word pairs and each pair is human annotated with a relatedness score. The evaluation is then performed by correlating the cosine similarities between word pairs with the relatedness scores. As there are no annotated relatedness datasets for Estonian, we opted to use a synonym test instead. We rely on the assumption that the relatedness between a pair of synonyms is high and thus we expect the cosine similarity between the synonymous words to be high as well.

We obtained the synonyms from the Estonian synonym dictionary.[2] We queried each word in our vocabulary and when the exact match for this word was found then we looked at the first synonym offered by the dictionary. If this synonym was present in our vocabulary then the synonym pair was stored. In this manner we obtained a total of 7579 synonym pairs. We ordered those pairs according to the frequency of the first word in the pair and chose the 1000 most frequent words with their synonyms for the synonym test.

For each first word in the synonym pair, we computed its cosine similarity with every other word in the vocabulary, ordered those similarities in the descending order and found the rank of the second word of the synonym pair in this resulting list. Then we computed the mean rank over all 1000 synonym pairs. We performed these steps on both types of combined models— Y_{SOLS} and Y_{SOPP}— and also on all input models W_i. Finally we also computed the mean of the mean ranks of all 10 input models.

The results as shown in Table 2 reveal that the

synonym similarities tend to be ranked lower in the combined model obtained with SOLS when compared to the input models. SOPP, on the other hand, produces a combined model where the synonym similarities are ranked higher than in initial models. This means that the SOPP combined models pull the synonymous words closer together than they were in the initial models. The differences in mean ranks were tested using paired Wilcoxon signed-rank test at 95% confidence level and the differences were statistically significant with p-value being less than $2.2 \cdot 10^{-16}$ in all cases. In overall, the SOPP ranks are on average 10% lower than the mean ranks of the initial models. The absolute improvement on average between SOPP and mean of W is 3476.

Although we assumed that the automatically extracted synonym pairs should be ranked closely together, looking at the average mean ranks in Table 2 reveals that it is not necessarily the case— the average rank of the best-performing SOPP model is over 31K. In order to understand those results better we looked at the rank histogram of the SOPP model and one of the initial models, shown on Figure 1. Although the first bin covering the rank range from 1 to 10 contains the most words for both models and the number of synonym pairs falling to further rank bins decreases the curve is not steep and close to 100 words (87 in case of SOPP and 94 in case of the initial model) belong to the last bin counting ranks higher than 100000. Looking at the farthest synonym pairs revealed that one word in these pairs is typically polysemous and its sense in the synonym pair is a relatively rarely used sense of this word, while there are other more common senses of this word with a

---

[2]The Institute of the Estonian Language, http://www.eki.ee/dict/sys/

	Hit@1					Hit@10				
Dim	SOLS	SOPP	Mean W	Min W	Max W	SOLS	SOPP	Mean W	Min W	Max W
50	0.058	**0.193**	0.144	0.124	0.170	0.158	**0.390**	0.329	0.305	0.347
100	0.116	**0.255**	0.185	0.170	0.197	0.239	**0.475**	0.388	0.371	0.409
150	0.085	**0.278**	0.198	0.170	0.228	0.224	**0.502**	0.398	0.378	0.417
200	0.066	**0.290**	0.197	0.178	0.224	0.205	**0.541**	0.408	0.390	0.425
250	0.093	**0.282**	0.200	0.181	0.224	0.193	**0.517**	0.406	0.394	0.421
300	0.069	**0.286**	0.197	0.162	0.228	0.212	**0.533**	0.401	0.359	0.440
Avg	0.081	**0.264**	0.187			0.205	**0.493**	0.388		

Table 3: Hit@1 and Hit@10 accuracies of the analogy test. SOLS and SOPP columns show the accuracies of the combined models. Mean W, Min W and Max W show the mean, minimum and maximum accuracies of the initial models W_i, respectively. The best accuracy among the combined models and the mean of the initial models is given in bold. The last row shows the average accuracies over all embedding sizes.

completely different meaning. We give some examples of such synonym pairs:

- **kaks** (*two*) - **puudulik** (*insufficient*): the sense of this pair is the insufficient grade in high school, while the most common sense of the word **kaks** is the number *two*;

- **ida** (*east*) - **ost** (loan word from German also meaning *east*): the most common sense of the word **ost** is *purchase*;

- **rubla** (*rouble*) - **kull** (*bank note in slang*): the most common sense of the word **kull** is *hawk*.

4.2 Analogy tests

Analogy tests are another common intrinsic method for evaluating word embeddings (Mikolov et al., 2013c). A famous and typical example of an analogy question is "a man is to a king like a woman is to a ___?". The correct answer to this question is "queen".

For an analogy tuple $a : b, x : y$ (a is to b as x is to y) the following is expected in an embedding space to hold:

$$\mathbf{w}_b - \mathbf{w}_a + \mathbf{w}_x \approx \mathbf{w}_y,$$

where the vectors $\mathbf{w}$ are word embeddings. For the above example with "man", "king", "woman" and "queen" this would be computed as:

$$\mathbf{w}_{king} - \mathbf{w}_{man} + \mathbf{w}_{woman} \approx \mathbf{w}_{queen}$$

Given the vector representations for the three words in the analogy question—$\mathbf{w}_a$, $\mathbf{w}_b$ and $\mathbf{w}_x$—the goal is to maximize (Mikolov et al., 2013b)

$$cos(\mathbf{w}_y, \mathbf{w}_b - \mathbf{w}_a + \mathbf{w}_x) \tag{5}$$

over all words y in the vocabulary.

We used an Estonian analogy data set with 259 word quartets. Each quartet contains two pairs of words. The word pairs in the data set belong into three different groups where the two pairs contain either:

- a positive and a comparative adjective form, e.g. *pime : pimedam, jõukas : jõukam* (in English *dark : darker, wealthy : wealthier*);

- the nominative singular and plural forms of a noun, e.g. *vajadus : vajadused, võistlus : võistlused* (in English *need : needs , competition : competitions*);

- The lemma and the 3rd person past form of a verb, e.g. *aitama : aitas, katsuma : katsus* (in English *help : helped, touch : touched*).

We evaluate the results of the analogy test using prediction accuracy. A prediction is considered correct if and only if the vector $\mathbf{w}_y$ that maximizes (5) represents the word expected by the test case. We call this accuracy Hit@1. Hit@1 can be quite a noisy measurement as there could be several word vectors in a very close range to each other competing for the highest rank. Therefore, we also compute Hit@10, which considers the prediction correct if the word expected by the test case is among the ten closest words. As a common practice, the question words represented by the vectors $\mathbf{w}_a$, $\mathbf{w}_b$ and $\mathbf{w}_x$ were excluded from the set of possible predictions.

The Hit@1 and Hit@10 results in Table 3 show similar dynamics: combining models with SOPP is much better than SOLS in all cases. The SOPP

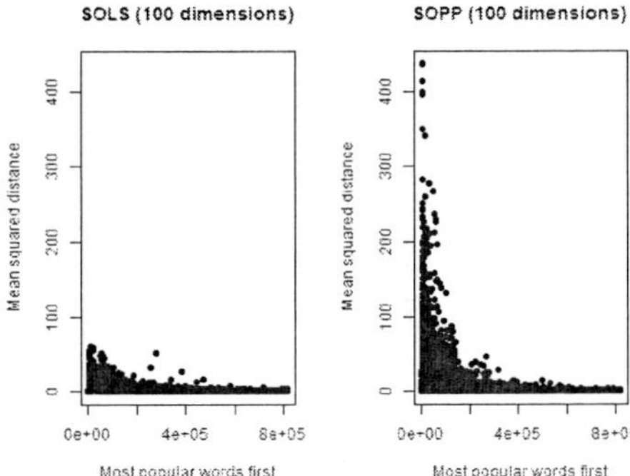

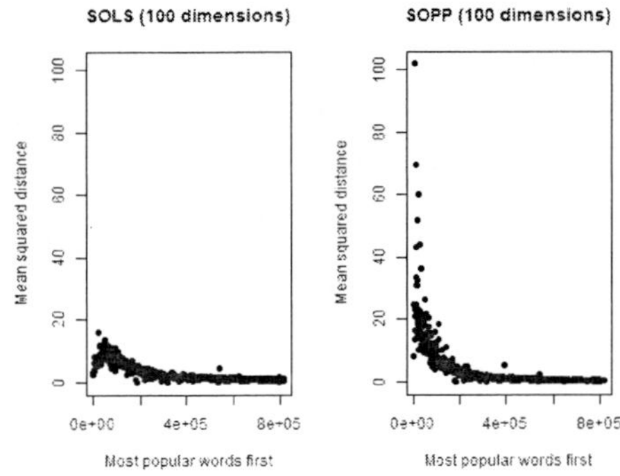

Figure 2: Mean squared distances describing the scattering of the translated word embeddings around the combined model embedding for every word in the vocabulary. The words in the horizontal axis are ordered by the frequency with most frequent words plotted first.

Figure 3: Mean squared distances describing the scattering of the translated word embeddings around the combined model embedding for a random sample of 1000 words. The words in the horizontal axis are ordered by the frequency with most frequent words plotted first.

combined model is better than the mean of the initial models in all six cases. Furthermore, it is consistently above the maximum of the best initial models. The average accuracy of SOPP is better than the average of the mean accuracies of initial models by 41%, relatively (7.7% in absolute) in terms of Hit@1 and 27% relatively (10.5% in absolute) in terms of Hit@10.

5   Analysis

In order to gain more understanding how the words are located in the combined model space in comparison to the initial models we performed two additional analyses. First, we computed the distribution of mean squared errors of the words to see how the translated embeddings scatter around the word embedding of the combined model. Secondly, we looked at how both of the methods affect the pairwise similarities of words.

5.1   Distribution of mean squared distances

We computed the squared Euclidean distance for each word in vocabulary between the combined model Y and all the input embedding models. The distance e_{ij} for a jth word and the ith input model is:

$$d_{ij} = \|Y_j - T_{ij}\|^2,$$

where $T_i = W_i P_i$ is the ith translated embedding model. Then we found the mean squared distance

for the jth word by calculating:

$$d_j = \frac{1}{r} \sum_{i=0}^{r} d_{ij}$$

These distances are plotted on Figure 2. The words on the horizontal axis are ordered by their frequency—the most frequent words coming first. We show these results for models with 100 dimensions but the results with other embedding sizes were similar.

Notice that the distances for less frequent words are similarly small for both SOLS and SOPP methods. However, the distribution of distances for frequent words is quite different—while the distances go up with both methods, the frequent words are much more scattered when using the SOPP approach.

Figure 3 shows the mean squared distances of a random sample of 1000 words. These plots reveal another difference between the SOLS and SOPP methods. While for SOPP, the distances tend to decrease monotonically with the increase in word frequency rank, with SOLS the distances first increase and only then they start to get smaller.

Our vocabulary also includes punctuation marks and function words, which are among the most frequent tokens and which occur in many different contexts. Thus, the individual models have a lot of freedom to position them in the word embedding space. The SOLS combined model is able to bring those words more close to each other

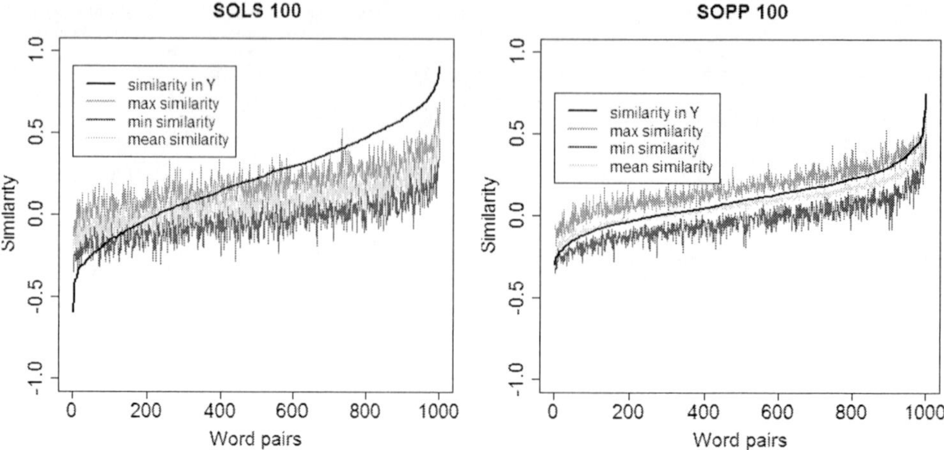

Figure 4: Cosine similarities of 1000 randomly chosen word pairs ordered by their similarity in the combined model Y. Red, blue and green bands represent the maximum, mean and minimum similarities in the initial models, respectively.

in the aligned space, while SOPP has less freedom to do that because of the orthogonality constraint. When looking at the words with largest distances under SOPP in the 1000 word random sample then we see that the word with the highest mean squared distance refers to the proper name of a well-known Estonian politician who has been probably mentioned often and in various contexts in the training corpus. Other words with a large distance in this sample include for instance a name of a month and a few quantifying modifiers.

5.2 Word pair similarities

In this analysis we looked at how the cosine similarities between pairs of words change in the combined model compared to their similarities in the input embedding models. For that, we chose a total of 1000 word pairs randomly from the vocabulary. For each pair we calculated the following values:

- cosine similarity under the combined model;

- maximum and minimum cosine similarity in the initial models W_i;

- mean cosine similarity over the initial models W_i.

The results are plotted in Figure 4. These results are obtained using the word embeddings with size 100, using different embedding sizes revealed the same patterns. In figures, the word pairs are ordered on the horizontal axis in the ascending order of their similarities in the combined model Y.

The plots reveal that 1) the words that are similar in initial models W_i are even more similar in the combined model Y; and 2) distant words in initial models become even more distant in the combined model. Although these trends are visible in cases of both SOLS and SOPP, this behaviour of the combined models to bring more similar words closer together and place less similar words farther away is more emphasized in the combined model obtained with SOLS.

In Figure 4, the red, green and blue "bands", representing the maximum, mean and minimum similarities of the initial models, respectively, are wider on the SOLS plot. This indicates that SOPP preserves more the original order of word pairs in terms of their similarities. However, some of this difference may be explained by the fact that SOPP has an overall smaller effect on the similarity compared to SOLS, which is due to the property of SOPP to preserve the angles and distances between the vectors during the transformation.

6 Discussion and future work

From the two linear methods used to combine the models, SOPP was performing consistently better in both synonym and analogy tests. Although, as shown in Figures 2 and 3, the word embeddings of the aligned initial models were more closely clustered around the embeddings of the SOLS combined model, this seemingly better fit is obtained at the cost of distorting the relations between the individual word embeddings. Thus, we have provided evidence that adding the orthogonality constraint to the linear transformation objective is important to retain the quality of the translated word embeddings. This observation is relevant both in the context of producing model ensembles as well as in other contexts where translating one embedding space to another could be relevant, such as when working with semantic time series or multilingual embeddings.

In addition to combining several models trained on the same dataset with the same configuration as demonstrated in this paper, there are other possible use cases for the model ensembles which could be explored in future work. For instance, currently all our input models had the same dimensionality and the same embedding size was also used in the combined model. In future it would be interesting to experiment with combining models with different dimensionality, in this way marginalising out the embedding size hyperparameter.

Our experiments showed that the SOPP approach performs well in both synonym and analogy tests when combining the models trained on the relatively small Estonian corpus. In future we plan to conduct similar experiments on more languages that, similar to Estonian, have limited resources for training reliable word embeddings.

Another idea would be to combine embeddings trained with different models. As all word embedding systems learn slightly different embeddings, combining for instance Word2Vec (Mikolov et al., 2013b), Glove (Pennington et al., 2014) and dependency based vectors (Levy and Goldberg, 2014) could lead to a model that combines the strengths of all the input models. Yin and Schütze (2016) demonstrated that the combination of different word embeddings can be useful. However, their results showed that the model combination is less beneficial when one of the input models (Glove vectors in their example) is trained on a huge text corpus. Thus, we predict that the ensemble of word embeddings constructed based on different embedding models also has the most effect in the setting of limited training resources.

Finally, it would be interesting to explore the domain adaptation approach by combining for instance the embeddings learned from the large general domain with the embeddings trained on a smaller domain specific corpus. This could be of interest because there are many pretrained word embedding sets available for English that can be freely downloaded from the internet, while the corpora they were trained on (English Gigaword, for instance) are not freely available. The model combination approach would enable to adapt those embeddings to the domain data by making use of the pretrained models.

7   Conclusions

Although model ensembles have been often used to improve the results of various natural language processing tasks, the ensembles of word embedding models have been rarely studied so far. Our main contribution in this paper was to combine several word embedding models trained on the same dataset via linear transformation into an ensemble and demonstrate the usefulness of this approach experimentally.

We experimented with two linear methods to combine the input embedding models—the ordinary least squares solution to the linear regression problem and the orthogonal Procrustes which adds an additional orthogonality constraint to the least squares objective function. Experiments on synonym and analogy tests on Estonian showed that the combination with orthogonal Procrustes was consistently better than the ordinary least squares, meaning that preserving the distances and angles between vectors with the orthogonality constraint is crucial for model combination. Also, the orthogonal Procrustes combined model performed better than the average of the individual initial models in all synonym tests and analogy tests suggesting that combining several embedding models is a simple and useful approach for improving the quality of the word embeddings.

Acknowledgments

We thank Alexander Tkachenko for providing the pretrained input models and the analogy test questions. We also thank the anonymous reviewers for their helpful suggestions and comments.

References

Rami Al-Rfou, Bryan Perozzi, and Steven Skiena. 2013. Polyglot: Distributed word representations for multilingual NLP. In *Proceedings of the Seven-*

teenth Conference on Computational Natural Language Learning, pages 183–192.

William L. Hamilton, Jure Leskovec, and Dan Jurafsky. 2016. Diachronic word embeddings reveal statistical laws of semantic change. In *Proceedings of the 54th Annual Meeting of the Association for Computational Linguistics (Volume 1: Long Papers)*, pages 1489–1501.

Vivek Kulkarni, Rami Al-Rfou, Bryan Perozzi, and Steven Skiena. 2015. Statistically significant detection of linguistic change. In *Proceedings of the 24th International Conference on World Wide Web*, pages 625–635.

Omer Levy and Yoav Goldberg. 2014. Dependency-based word embeddings. In *Proceedings of the 52nd Annual Meeting of the Association for Computational Linguistics (Volume 2: Short Papers)*, pages 302–308.

Tomas Mikolov, Quoc V. Le, and Ilya Sutskever. 2013a. Exploiting similarities among languages for machine translation. *CoRR*, abs/1309.4168.

Tomas Mikolov, Ilya Sutskever, Kai Chen, Greg S Corrado, and Jeff Dean. 2013b. Distributed representations of words and phrases and their compositionality. In *Advances in Neural Information Processing Systems 26*, pages 3111–3119.

Tomas Mikolov, Scott Wen-tau Yih, and Geoffrey Zweig. 2013c. Linguistic regularities in continuous space word representations. In *Proceedings of the 2013 Conference of the North American Chapter of the Association for Computational Linguistics: Human Language Technologies*, pages 746–751.

Aditya Mogadala and Achim Rettinger. 2016. Bilingual word embeddings from parallel and non-parallel corpora for cross-language text classification. In *Proceedings of the 2016 Conference of the North American Chapter of the Association for Computational Linguistics: Human Language Technologies*, pages 692–702.

Jeffrey Pennington, Richard Socher, and Christopher D. Manning. 2014. Glove: Global vectors for word representation. In *Proceedings of the 2014 Conference on Empirical Methods in Natural Language Processing*, pages 1532–1543.

Tobias Schnabel, Igor Labutov, David Mimno, and Thorsten Joachims. 2015. Evaluation methods for unsupervised word embeddings. In *Proceedings of the 2015 Conference on Empirical Methods in Natural Language Processing*, pages 298–307.

Peter H. Schönemann. 1966. A generalized solution of the orthogonal procrustes problem. *Psychometrika*, 31(1):1–10.

Joseph Turian, Lev Ratinov, and Yoshua Bengio. 2010. Word representations: A simple and general method for semi-supervised learning. In *Proceedings of the 48th Annual Meeting of the Association for Computational Linguistics*, pages 384–394.

Wenpeng Yin and Hinrich Schütze. 2016. Learning Word Meta-Embeddings. In *Proceedings of the 54th Annual Meeting of the Association for Computational Linguistics*, pages 1351–1360.

Using Pseudowords for Algorithm Comparison:
An Evaluation Framework for Graph-based Word Sense Induction

Flavio Massimiliano Cecchini
DISCo
Università degli Studi di Milano-Bicocca
`flavio.cecchini@disco.unimib.it`

Martin Riedl, Chris Biemann
Language Technology Group
Universität Hamburg
`riedl@informatik.uni-hamburg.de`
`biemann@informatik.uni-hamburg.de`

Abstract

In this paper we define two parallel data sets based on pseudowords, extracted from the same corpus. They both consist of word-centered graphs for each of 1225 different pseudowords, and use respectively first-order co-occurrences and second-order semantic similarities. We propose an evaluation framework on these data sets for graph-based Word Sense Induction (WSI) focused on the case of coarse-grained homonymy: We compare different WSI clustering algorithms by measuring how well their outputs agree with the *a priori* known ground-truth decomposition of a pseudoword. We perform this evaluation for four different clustering algorithms: the Markov cluster algorithm, Chinese Whispers, MaxMax and a gangplank-based clustering algorithm. To further improve the comparison between these algorithms and the analysis of their behaviours, we also define a new specific evaluation measure. As far as we know, this is the first large-scale systematic pseudoword evaluation dedicated to the induction of coarse-grained homonymous word senses.

1 Introduction and Related Work

Word Sense Induction (WSI) is the branch of Natural Language Processing (NLP) concerned with the unsupervised detection of all the possible senses that a term can assume in a text document. It could also be described as "unsupervised Word Sense Disambiguation" (Navigli, 2009). Since ambiguity and arbitrariness are constantly present in natural languages, WSI can help improve the analysis and understanding of text or speech (Martin and Jurafsky, 2000). At its core we find the notion of distributional semantics, exemplified by the state-

ment by Harris (1954): *"Difference of meaning correlates with difference of distribution."*

In this paper, we focus on graph-based methods. Graphs provide an intuitive mathematical representation of relations between words. A graph can be defined and built in a straightforward way, but allows for a very deep analysis of its structural properties. This and their discrete nature (contrary to the continuous generalizations represented by vector spaces of semantics, cf. Turney and Pantel (2010)) favour the identification of significative patterns and subregions, among other things allowing the final number of clusters to be left unpredetermined, an ideal condition for WSI.

The main contribution of this paper is threefold: We present two parallel word graph data sets based on the concept of pseudowords, both for the case of semantic similarities and co-occurrences; on them, we compare the performances of four WSI clustering algorithms; and we define a new *ad hoc* evaluation measure for this task, called TOP2.

Pseudowords were first proposed by Gale et al. (1992) and Schütze (1992) as a way to create artificial ambiguous words by merging two (or more) random words. A pseudoword simulates homonymy, i.e. a word which possesses two (or more) semantically and etymologically unrelated senses, such as *count* as "nobleman" as opposed to "the action of enumerating". The study of Nakov and Hearst (2003) shows that the performances of WSI algorithms on random pseudowords might represent an optimistic upper bound with respect to true polysemous words, as generic polysemy implies some kind of correlation between the categories and the distributions of the different senses of a word, which is absent from randomly generated ones. We are aware of the approaches proposed in (Otrusina and Smrž, 2010) and (Pilehvar and Navigli, 2013), used e.g. in (Başkaya

Proceedings of the 21st Nordic Conference of Computational Linguistics, pages 105–114,
Gothenburg, Sweden, 23-24 May 2017. ©2017 Linköping University Electronic Press

and Jurgens, 2016), for a pseudoword generation that better models polysemous words with an arbitrary degree of polysemy. Both works imply the emulation of existing polysemous words, following the semantic structure of WordNet (Miller, 1995): *pseudosenses* (the components of a pseudoword) corresponding to the *synsets* of a word are represented by the closest monosemous terms on the WordNet graph, according to Personalized PageRank (Haveliwala, 2002) applied to the WordNet graph. However, we want to remark the different nature of our paper. Here we compare the behaviours of different clustering algorithms on two data sets of pseudowords built to emulate homonymy, and relate these behaviours to the structure of the word graphs relative to these pseudowords. As homonymy is more clear-cut than generic polysemy, we deem that the efficacy of a WSI algorithm should be first measured in this case before being tested in a more fine-grained and ambiguous situation. Also, the task we defined does not depend on the arbitrary granularity of an external lexical resource[1], which might be too fine-grained for our purpose. Further, the sense distinctions e.g. in WordNet might not be mirrored in the corpus, and conversely, some unforeseen senses might be observed. Instead, our work can be seen as an expansion of the pseudoword evaluation presented in (Bordag, 2006), albeit more focused in its goal and implementation.

In our opinion, current WSI tasks present some shortcomings. A fundamental problem is the vagueness regarding the granularity (fine or coarse) of the senses that have to be determined. As a consequence, the definition of an adequate evaluation measure becomes difficult, as many of them have been showed to be biased towards few or many clusters[2]. Further, small data sets often do not allow obtaining significant results. Pseudoword evaluation, on the contrary, presents an objective and self-contained framework where the classification task is well characterized and gives the opportunity to define an *ad hoc* evaluation measure, at the same time automating the data set creation. Therefore, we tackle the following research questions: What are the limitations of a pseudoword evaluation for homonymy detection? How does the structure of a pseudoword's word graph depend on its components? How do different clustering strategies compare on the same data set, and what are the most suited measures to evaluate their performances?

The paper is structured as follows. In Section 2 we give a definition of the ego word graph of a word and present our starting corpus. Section 3 details our evaluation setting and describes our proposed measure TOP2. Section 4 introduces the four graph clustering algorithms chosen for evaluation. Lastly, Section 5 comments the results of the comparisons, and Section 6 concludes the paper.

2 Word Graphs and Data Set

For our evaluation we will use word graphs based both on semantic similarities (SSIM) and on co-occurrences. We define both as undirected, weighted graphs $G = (V, E)$ whose nodes correspond to a given subset V of the vocabulary of the considered corpus, and where two nodes v, w are connected by an edge if and only if v and w co-occur in the same sentence (co-occurrences) or share some kind of context (semantic similarities). In either case, we express the strength of the connection between two words through a weight mapping $p : E \longrightarrow \mathbb{R}^+$, for which we can take indicators such as raw frequency or pointwise mutual information. The higher the value on an edge, the more significant we deem their connection.

We will consider word-centered graphs, called *ego word graphs*. Both kinds of ego word graphs will be induced by the distributional thesauri computed on a corpus consisting of 105 million English newspaper sentences[3], using the JoBimText (Biemann and Riedl, 2013) implementation. In the case of co-occurrences, for a given word v we use a frequency-weighted version of pointwise mutual information called *lexicographer's mutual information* (LMI) (Kilgarriff et al., 2004; Evert, 2004) to rank all the terms co-occurring with v in a sentence and to select those that will appear in its ego word graph. Edge weights are defined by LMI and the possible edge between two nodes u and w will be determined by the presence of u in the distribu-

---

[1]As was also the case for task 13 of SemEval 2013, cf. (Jurgens and Klapaftis, 2013)

[2]See for example the results at task 14 of SemEval 2010 (Manandhar et al., 2010), where adjusted mutual information was introduced to correct the bias: https://www.cs.york.ac.uk/semeval2010_WSI/task_14_ranking.html.

[3]A combination of the Leipzig Corpora Collection (LCC), http://corpora.uni-leipzig.de (Richter et al., 2006) and the Gigaword corpus (Parker et al., 2011).

tional thesaurus of w, or viceversa.

The process is similar in the case of SSIMs, but here LMI is computed on term-context co-occurrences based on syntactic dependencies extracted from the corpus by means of the Stanford Parser (De Marneffe et al., 2006).

In both cases, the word v itself is removed from G, since we are interested just in the relations between the words more similar to it, following (Widdows and Dorow, 2002). The clusters in which the node set of G will be subdivided will represent the possible senses of v. We remark that co-occurrences are first-order relations (i.e. inferred directly by data), whereas SSIMs are of second order, as they are computed on the base of co-occurrences[4]. For this reason, two different kinds of distributional thesauri might have quite different entries even if they pertain to the same word. Further, the ensuing word graphs will show a complementary correlation: co-occurrences represent *syntagmatic* relations with the central word, while SSIMs *paradigmatic* ones[5], and this also determines different structures, as e.g. co-occurrences are denser than SSIMs.

3 Pseudoword Evaluation Framework

The method of *pseudoword evaluation* was first independently proposed in (Gale et al., 1992) and (Schütze, 1992). Given two words appearing in a corpus, e.g. *cat* and *window*, we replace all their occurrences therein with an artificial term formed by their combination (represented in our example as *cat_window*), a so-called *pseudoword* that merges the contexts of its components (also called *pseudosenses*). The original application of this evaluation assumes that all the components of a pseudoword are monosemous words, i.e. possess only one sense. Ideally, an algorithm trying to induce the senses of a monosemous word from the corresponding word graph should return only one cluster, and we would expect it to find exactly two clusters in the case of a pseudoword with two components. This makes evaluation more transparent, and we are restricting ourselves to monosemous words for this reason.

For the purpose of our evaluation, we extract monosemous nouns from the 105 million

sentences of the corpus described in Section 2, over which we compute all SSIM- and co-occurrence-based distributional thesauri. We divide all the nouns into 5 logarithmic frequency classes identified with respect to the frequency of the most common noun in the corpus. For each class, we extract random candidates: We retain only those that possess one single meaning, i.e. for which Chinese Whispers (see Section 4.2)[6] yields one single cluster, additionally checking that they have only one *synset* in WordNet (which is commonly accepted to be fine-grained). We repeat this process until we obtain 10 suitable candidates per frequency class. In the end, we obtain a total of 50 words whose combinations give rise to 1225 different pseudowords. We then proceed to create two kinds of pseudoword ego word graph data sets, as described in Section 2: one for co-occurrences and one for semantic similarities. In both cases we limit the graphs to the topmost 500 terms, ranked by LMI.

The evaluation consists in running the clustering algorithms on the ego word graphs: since we know the underlying (pseudo)senses of each pseudoword A_B, we also know for each node in its ego word graph if it belongs to the distributional thesaurus, and thus to the subgraph relative to A, B or both, and thus we already know our ground truth clustering $\mathcal{T} = (T_A, T_B)$. Clearly, the proportion between T_A and T_B might be very skewed, especially if A and B belong to very different frequency classes. Despite the criticism of the pseudoword evaluation for being too artificial and its senses not obeying the true sense distribution of a proper polysemic word, we note that this is a very realistic situation for homonymy, since sense distributions tend to be skewed and dominated by a most frequent sense (MFS). In coarse-grained Word Sense Disambiguation evaluations, the MFS baseline is often in the range of 70% - 80% (Navigli et al., 2007).

Our starting assumption for very skewed cases is that a clustering algorithm will be biased towards the more frequent term of the two, that is, it will tendentially erroneously find only one cluster. It could also be possible that all nodes relative to A at the same time also appear in the distributional thesaurus of B, so that the word A is overshadowed by B. We call this a *collapsed pseudoword*. We

---

[4]About relations of second and higher orders, cf. (Biemann and Quasthoff, 2009).

[5]A fundamental source on this topic is (De Saussure, 1995 1916).

[6]We use the implementation from `https://sourceforge.net/projects/jobimtext/` with parameters: `-n 200 -N 200`.

decided not to take collapsed pseudowords into account for evaluation, since in this case the initial purpose of simulating a polysemous does not hold: we are left with an actually monosemous pseudoword.

We measure the quality of the clustering of a pseudoword ego graph in terms of the F-score of the BCubed metric (Bagga and Baldwin, 1998; Amigó et al., 2009), alongside with normalized mutual information[7] (NMI) (Strehl, 2002) and a measure developed by us, TOP2, loosely inspired by NMI. We define TOP2 as the average of the harmonic means of homogeneity and completeness of the two clusters that better represent the two components of the pseudoword.

More formally, suppose that the pseudoword A_B is the combination of the words A and B. We denote the topmost 500 entries in the distributional thesauri of A and B respectively as D_A and D_B, and we write $D'_A = D_A \cap V$ and $D'_B = D_B \cap V$, where V is the node set of G_{AB}, the pseudoword's ego word graph. We can express V as

$$V = \alpha \cup \beta \cup \gamma \cup \delta, \qquad (1)$$

where $\alpha = D'_A \backslash D'_B$, $\beta = D'_B \backslash D'_A$, $\gamma = D'_A \cap D'_B$, $\delta = V \backslash (D'_A \cup D'_B)$. So, elements in α and β are nodes in V that relate respectively only to A or B, elements of γ are nodes of V that appear in both distributional thesauri and elements in δ are not among the topmost 500 entries in the distributional thesauri of either A or B, but happened to have a significant enough relation with the pseudoword to appear in V. We note that we will not consider nodes in δ, and we will neither consider nodes of γ, since they act as neutral terms. Consequently, we take $T_A = \alpha$, $T_B = \beta$ as the ground truth clusters of $V \backslash (\gamma \cup \delta)$, which we will compare with $C \backslash (\gamma \cup \delta) = \{C \backslash (\gamma \cup \delta) \mid C \in C\}$, where $C = \{C_1, \ldots, C_n\}$ is any clustering of V. It is possible that either $\alpha = \emptyset$ or $\beta = \emptyset$, which means that in G_{AB} the relation $D'_A \subset D'_B$ or $D'_B \subset D'_A$ holds. In this case one word is totally dominant over the other, and the pseudoword actually collapses onto one sense. As already mentioned, we decided to exclude collapsed pseudowords from evaluation. To compute the BCubed F-score and NMI, we compare the ground truth clustering $T = \{\alpha, \beta\}$ to the clustering $C \backslash (\gamma \cup \delta)$ that we obtain from any

---

[7]NMI is equivalent to V-measure, as shown by Remus and Biemann (2013).

algorithm under consideration. However, for the TOP2 score we want to look only at the two clusters C_A and C_B that better represent component A and B respectively. We define them as:

$$C_A = \underset{C \in C}{\arg\max} \, |C \cap \alpha|, \quad C_B = \underset{C \in C}{\arg\max} \, |C \cap \beta|.$$

For C_A (respectively C_B) we define its precision or purity p_A (p_B) and its recall or completeness c_A (c_B) with respect to α (β) as

$$p_A = \frac{|C_A \cap \alpha|}{|C_A|}, \quad c_A = \frac{|C_A \cap \alpha|}{|\alpha|}.$$

We take the respective harmonic means $h(p_A, c_A)$ and $h(p_B, c_B)$ and define the TOP2 score as their macro-average:

$$\text{TOP2} = \frac{h(p_A, c_A) + h(p_B, c_B)}{2}.$$

If it happens that $C_A = C_B$, we keep the best cluster for one component and take the second best for the other, according to which choice maximizes TOP2. If the clustering consists of only one cluster, we define either $C_A = \emptyset$ or $C_B = \emptyset$ and put the harmonic mean of its purity and completeness equal to 0. Therefore, in such case the TOP2 will never be greater than $\frac{1}{2}$. The motivation for the TOP2 score is that we know what we are looking for: namely, for two clusters that represent A and B. The TOP2 score then gives us a measure of how well the clustering algorithm succeeds in correctly concentrating all the information in exactly two clusters with the least dispersion; this can be generalized to the case of more than two pseudosenses.

4 The Algorithms

In our experimental setting we will compare four graph-based clustering algorithms commonly applied in, or especially developed for, the task of WSI. They are: the *Markov cluster algorithm* (MCL) (van Dongen, 2000); *Chinese Whispers* (CW) (Biemann, 2006); *MaxMax* (MM) (Hope and Keller, 2013); and the *gangplank clustering algorithm* (GP) (Cecchini and Fersini, 2015). They are detailed in the following subsections. We remark that none of these algorithms sets a predefined number of clusters to be found. This is a critical property of WSI algorithms, since it is not known *a priori* whether a word is ambiguous in the underlying data collection and how many senses it might have.

4.1 Markov Cluster Algorithm

The *Markov cluster algorithm* (van Dongen, 2000) uses the concept of random walk on a graph, or Markov chain: the more densely intra-connected a region in the graph, the higher the probability to remain inside it starting from one of its nodes and moving randomly to another one. The strategy of the algorithm is then to perform a given number n of steps of the random walk, equivalent to taking the n-th power of the graph's adjacency matrix. Subsequently, entries of the matrix are raised to a given power to further increase strong connections and weaken less significant ones. This cycle is repeated an arbitrary number of times, and, as weaker connections tend to disappear, the resulting matrix is interpretable as a graph clustering. Not rooted in the NLP community, MCL was used for the task of WSI on co-occurrence graphs in (Widdows and Dorow, 2002). Our implementation uses an expansion factor of 2 and an inflation factor of 1.4, which yielded the best results.

4.2 Chinese Whispers

The *Chinese Whispers* algorithm was first described in (Biemann, 2006). It is inspired by MCL as a simplified version of it and similarly simulates the flow of information in a graph. Initially, every node in the graph starts as a member of its own class; then, at each iteration every node assumes the prevalent class among those of its neighbours, measured by the weights on the edges incident to it. This algorithm is not deterministic and may not stabilize, as nodes are accessed in random order. However, it is extremely fast and quite successful at distinguishing denser subgraphs. The resulting clustering is generally relatively coarse. Besides its use for word sense induction, in (Biemann, 2006) CW was also used for the tasks of language separation and word class induction.

4.3 MaxMax

MaxMax was originally described in (Hope and Keller, 2013) and applied to the task of WSI on weighted word co-occurrence graphs. It is a soft-clustering algorithm that rewrites the word graph G as an unweighted, directed graph, where edges are oriented by the principle of *maximal affinity*: the node u dominates v if the weight of (u,v) is maximal among all edges departing from v. Clusters are then defined as all the maximal quasi-strongly connected subgraphs of G (Ruohonen,

2013), each of which is represented by its root. Clusters can overlap because a node could be the descendant of two roots at the same time. The algorithm's complexity is linear in the number of the edges and its results are uniquely determined.

4.4 Gangplanks

The *gangplank clustering algorithm* was introduced in (Cecchini and Fersini, 2015), where its use for the task of WSI on co-occurrence graphs is shown. There, the concept of *gangplank edges* is introduced: they are edges that can be seen as weak links between nodes belonging to different, highly intra-connected subgraphs of a graph, and thus help deduce a cluster partitioning of the node set. In its proposed implementation, the computation of gangplank edges and the subsequent clustering of G is actually performed on a second-order graph of G, a *distance graph* D_G which represents the distances between nodes of G according to a weighted version of Jaccard distance adapted to node neighbourhoods. The gangplank algorithm is deterministic and behaves stably also on very dense or scale-free graphs. The resulting clustering tends to be relatively fine-grained.

5 Results and Data Set Analysis

Table 2 summarizes the scores of BCubed F-measure (BC-F), NMI and TOP2 as mean scores over each possible pseudoword class, and Table 1 the overall mean scores per algorithm for the SSIM- and the co-occurrence-based data sets. The class of a pseudoword is the combination of the frequency classes of its two components, labelled from 1, comprising the least frequent words, to 5, comprising the most frequent words in the corpus. A total of 15 combinations are possible. Each has 45 pseudowords if the two words are of the same frequency class, and 100 otherwise. The case of having a collapsed pseudoword, discussed in Section 3, is more frequent for SSIMs than for co-occurrences. Formally, in the notation of (1), we say that one component of a pseudoword totally dominates the other one when either $\alpha = 0$ or $\beta = 0$. This happens 249 times for SSIM-based graphs and 143 times for co-occurrence-based ones. We excluded all such pseudowords from evaluation, since they actually possess only one sense and thus can not really be disambiguated. There is a clear and expected tendency for collapsed pseudowords to appear for very uneven

	BC-F		NMI		TOP2	
	SSIM	COOC	SSIM	COOC	SSIM	COOC
MCL	93.0±0.6	69.1±0.9	53.0±2.6	5.4±0.3	72.4±1.8	**39.3±0.7**
CW	**94.7±0.5**	88.7±0.5	**53.2±2.7**	4.1±0.4	**73.9±1.6**	25.6±1.1
MM	18.8±0.5	35.2±0.7	27.3±0.9	**11.1±0.4**	39.7±0.8	34.2±0.6
GP	55.0±1.2	58.2±2.0	30.4±1.4	4.2±0.4	58.6±1.2	35.4±0.5
BSL	85.1±0.7	**90.5±0.4**	0.0±0	0.0±0	41.1±0.4	38.8±0.5

Table 1: Mean scores in percentages over all pseudowords for each clustering algorithm and the baseline, for our three metrics and for both data sets. The 95% confidence interval is also reported for each mean value. The best values on each data set and for each measure are boldfaced.

combinations of frequency classes, like the extreme case 1-5, where out of 100 pseudowords this happens 72 times for similarities and 84 times for co-occurrences. On the contrary, when the components belong to the same frequency class, this phenomenon never arises. This can be explained by the fact that LMI (see Section 2) is proportional to the frequency of a particular context or co-occurrence, so that highly frequent words tend to develop stronger similarities in their distributional thesauri, relegating sparser similarities of less frequent words to a marginal role or outweighing them altogether. Especially in the two highest frequency classes 4 and 5, there are terms that always come to dominate the graphs of their related pseudowords (like *beer*).

Interestingly, we notice a drop of the NMI scores for similarities in the fields of Table 2a corresponding to the most skewed frequency class combinations, in particular 1-5, 2-5, 3-5, where some words tend to completely dominate their graphs, and clusterings tend to consist of a single big cluster, possibly accompanied by smaller, marginal ones. We also computed a most frequent score baseline (BSL), which yields just one single cluster for each ego word graph. Its NMI scores are always 0, as this measure heavily penalizes the asymmetry of having just one cluster in the output and two clusters in the ground truth. This, together with the fact that MaxMax, which is the most fine-grained among our examined algorithms, reaches NMI values that are on par with the other systems (or consistently better, in the case of co-occurrences) while regularly obtaining the lowest BC-F scores, leads us to claim that NMI is biased towards fine-grained clusterings[8]. On the opposite side of the spectrum, the more coarse-grained systems tend

to have very high BC-F scores close to the baseline, especially for the more skewed combinations. This depends on the fact that unbalanced graphs consist of nearly just one sense. Here the bias of BCubed measures becomes manifest: Due to their nature as averages over all single clustered elements, they stress the similarity between the *internal* structures of two clusterings, i.e. the distribution of elements inside each cluster, and disregard their *external* structures, i.e. their respective sizes and the distribution of cardinalities among clusters. The TOP2 measure, however, was defined so as to never assign a score greater than 0.5 in such occurrences. In fact, in the case of co-occurrences we see that the baseline achieves the best BC-F scores, but most of the time it is beaten by other systems in terms of TOP2 score. Overall, TOP2 seems to be the most suited measure for the evaluation of the task represented by our pseudoword data sets and is more in line with our expectations: higher scores when the ego word graph is more balanced, and much lower scores when the ego word graph is strongly skewed, without the excesses of NMI.

We remark that scores on the whole are usually worse for co-occurrences than for similarities, both globally and for each frequency class combination. For co-occurrences, TOP2 never goes over 0.5. This is a strong indication that the structure of co-occurrence ego word graphs is different than that of SSIM-based ones, as already discussed in Section 2; in particular, they are denser and noisier, but generally more balanced. Remarkably, a coarse-grained algorithm like Chinese Whispers obtains its worst scores on co-occurrences, according to TOP2, suffering from its very unbalanced, nearly-BSL clusterings. However, this very characteristic makes Chinese Whispers the best system overall on the less dense SSIMs (and the

---

[8]This bias is discussed more at length by Li et al. (2014).

The best values for each frequency class combination are highlighted.

(a) Scores on the SSIM-based data set.

Method	BC-F (1)	NMI (1)	TOP2 (1)	BC-F (2)	NMI (2)	TOP2 (2)	BC-F (3)	NMI (3)	TOP2 (3)	BC-F (4)	NMI (4)	TOP2 (4)	BC-F (5)	NMI (5)	TOP2 (5)	Comb.
MCL	92.6	71.9	79.7	89.7	67.6	81.1	87.4	64.0	83.4	**99.0**	**35.9**	**65.5**	98.0	26.3	55.0	1
CW	**94.7**	**79.6**	**85.6**	**94.2**	**78.4**	**87.0**	**91.8**	**73.0**	**86.8**	98.9	30.6	63.6	**99.4**	**29.7**	**61.4**	
MM	37.0	45.5	50.8	26.8	39.7	46.4	17.6	32.5	40.2	17.0	11.2	42.5	13.2	10.3	37.7	
GP	70.6	57.5	76.4	62.3	46.4	71.7	50.8	34.9	62.4	49.8	8.4	43.2	46.9	7.5	36.9	
BSL	72.5	0.0	35.5	75.8	0.0	38.2	81.5	0.0	41.6	98.4	0.0	47.9	98.3	0.0	44.1	
MCL				88.2	63.5	80.4	85.4	58.3	**79.0**	**98.2**	**43.2**	**68.4**	97.8	**12.9**	38.5	2
CW				**92.4**	**74.5**	**86.8**	**87.5**	**59.6**	78.8	98.2	27.2	60.9	**98.5**	10.9	**49.6**	
MM				22.7	38.9	40.8	16.3	33.6	34.8	16.9	13.1	45.3	12.5	9.0	28.6	
GP				60.4	47.3	72.7	55.5	40.4	67.0	51.6	9.7	45.2	48.1	6.8	35.7	
BSL				73.8	0.0	37.2	76.4	0.0	38.0	97.4	0.0	46.4	98.0	0.0	43.7	
MCL							83.5	**49.9**	**75.0**	**97.7**	**41.8**	**66.1**	97.3	**13.2**	44.1	3
CW							**84.3**	43.4	69.9	97.5	25.8	59.3	**97.7**	9.1	**49.4**	
MM							12.7	31.0	28.4	17.8	15.4	43.1	12.4	9.6	29.3	
GP							53.2	36.1	65.8	46.3	13.3	47.9	43.4	7.8	36.5	
BSL							76.6	0.0	38.1	96.5	0.0	45.4	97.5	0.0	43.3	
MCL										93.9	69.3	78.0	96.3	68.9	79.1	4
CW										**96.0**	**81.9**	**86.4**	**96.8**	**69.5**	**80.5**	
MM										21.4	40.0	41.7	18.2	33.1	39.6	
GP										69.2	48.2	69.5	59.8	37.8	64.3	
BSL										77.2	0.0	36.6	82.8	0.0	39.6	
MCL													96.6	**78.9**	**86.5**	5
CW													**96.9**	76.9	85.5	
MM													17.6	35.7	38.8	
GP													59.4	43.7	70.1	
BSL													81.0	0.0	40.2	

(b) Scores on the co-occurrence-based data set.

Method	BC-F (1)	NMI (1)	TOP2 (1)	BC-F (2)	NMI (2)	TOP2 (2)	BC-F (3)	NMI (3)	TOP2 (3)	BC-F (4)	NMI (4)	TOP2 (4)	BC-F (5)	NMI (5)	TOP2 (5)	Comb.
MCL	61.3	6.3	41.1	63.2	5.0	**45.8**	74.4	4.0	46.4	70.9	2.2	30.2	76.8	**5.1**	37.1	1
CW	69.9	7.1	38.3	80.5	4.4	34.4	92.5	3.2	25.9	95.8	0.3	7.3	98.7	0.1	12.8	
MM	49.6	**17.1**	**42.2**	40.7	**13.4**	39.7	38.3	**7.3**	39.2	34.7	**3.7**	28.0	36.9	3.7	32.7	
GP	48.1	5.3	40.9	45.0	5.0	37.1	27.7	4.5	28.0	57.3	2.5	34.7	73.7	0.7	37.9	
BSL	**71.9**	0.0	34.4	**83.5**	0.0	42.0	**94.4**	0.0	**46.7**	**98.9**	0.0	**47.9**	**99.7**	0.0	**48.9**	
MCL				60.5	4.8	**43.3**	67.5	5.0	**40.5**	65.8	4.6	38.8	77.6	4.6	34.0	2
CW				81.8	3.1	32.5	87.1	3.4	30.4	92.7	2.8	20.2	97.0	**5.7**	22.6	
MM				35.0	**13.8**	35.6	34.6	**11.8**	33.5	34.2	**8.7**	34.5	36.2	5.1	30.3	
GP				49.6	5.7	36.9	29.2	7.2	31.0	62.7	5.1	38.2	86.0	0.7	41.1	
BSL				**83.0**	0.0	38.2	**88.3**	0.0	36.8	**94.7**	0.0	**41.9**	**98.0**	0.0	**44.0**	
MCL							69.6	5.4	**34.0**	66.4	6.4	**37.1**	77.2	6.8	**43.1**	3
CW							85.6	3.3	25.1	88.4	3.3	23.2	94.6	5.7	24.4	
MM							32.7	**13.7**	27.9	31.7	**13.2**	30.6	33.4	**8.1**	34.5	
GP							38.5	5.8	28.5	63.5	6.2	36.6	88.3	0.9	39.9	
BSL							**86.7**	0.0	28.3	**89.6**	0.0	32.9	**95.8**	0.0	40.3	
MCL										59.2	8.5	**35.1**	71.9	7.7	**39.8**	4
CW										84.7	5.0	26.7	89.1	7.7	31.5	
MM										31.1	**18.5**	32.9	31.6	**14.3**	35.6	
GP										60.7	7.1	34.5	81.0	2.5	36.7	
BSL										**86.8**	0.0	27.3	**90.5**	0.0	35.5	
MCL													73.0	7.8	**33.7**	5
CW													85.1	4.3	27.2	
MM													30.5	**19.2**	32.4	
GP													81.9	1.4	29.5	
BSL													**86.8**	0.0	27.6	

Table 2: Mean scores per frequency class combination over both SSIM-based and the co-occurrence-based ego word graph data sets. The best values for each frequency class combination are highlighted.

other evaluation measures agree). At the same time, the more fine-grained GP and MCL seem to better adapt to the structure of co-occurrence graphs, while GP's performances clearly deteriorate on more unbalanced pseudowords for SSIMs. On the lower end of the spectrum, MaxMax shows a very constant but too divisive nature for our task of homonymy detection.

5.1 Example of Clusterings

We briefly want to show the differences between the clusterings of our four systems (CW, MCL, MaxMax, GP) on the SSIM ego word graph of a same pseudoword. We chose *catsup_bufflehead*: *catsup* (variant of *ketchup*) belongs to frequency class 2 and *bufflehead* (a kind of duck) to frequency class 1. Their graph has 488 nodes and a density of 0.548, above the global mean of 0.45. The node ratio is in favour of *catsup* at 3.05 : 1 against *bufflehead*, with respectively 111 against 339 exclusive terms, still being a quite balanced ego graph.

Chinese Whispers finds two clusters which seem to cover correctly the two senses of bird or animal on one side, {hummingbird, woodpecker, dove, merganser,...}, and food on the other side: {polenta, egg, baguette, squab,...}. Its scores are very high, respectively 0.95 for BC-F, 0.80 for NMI and 0.93 for TOP2.

The gangplank algorithm yields 5 clusters. One is clearly about the bird: {goldeneye, condor, peacock,...}. The other four have high precision, but lose recall for splitting the sense of food, e.g. in {puree, clove, dill,...} and {jelly, tablespoon, dripping,...}, and the distinction between them is not always clear. We obtain a BC-F of 0.66, a NMI of 0.51 and a TOP2 of 0.78.

The Markov cluster algorithm with an inflation factor of 1.4 fails to make a distinction and finds only one cluster: {raptor, Parmesan, coffee, stork,...}. Its scores are the same of our trivial baseline: BC-F 0.77, NMI 0.0 and TOP2 0.41 (< 0.5, see section 3).

MaxMax confirms its tendency of very fine-grained clusterings and produces 22 clusters. Each has a very high precision, but some consist of only two or three elements, such as {gin, rum, brandy} and {cashmere, denim} and in general they make very narrow distinctions.

The biggest cluster {chili, chily, ginger, shallot,...} has 89 elements. We also find a cluster with bird names, but the overall scores are low: BC-F 0.27, NMI 0.38 and TOP2 0.45.

6 Conclusions

The major contribution of this work is to present two new pseudoword ego word graph data sets for graph-based homonymy detection: one for context semantic similarities and one for co-occurrences. The data sets are modelled around 1225 pseudowords, each representing the combination of two monosemous words. We show that many ego word graphs are too skewed when the two components come from very different frequency classes, up to the point of actually collapsing on just one sense, but in general they represent a good approximation of homonymy. We evidence the biases of BCubed measures and NMI, respectively towards baseline-like clusterings (and BSL is the best performing system for co-occurrences in this sense) and finer clusterings. On the contrary, our proposed TOP2 metric seems to strike the right balance and to provide the most meaningful scores for interpretation. Chinese Whispers, which yields tendentially coarse clusterings, emerges as the best system overall for this task with regard to SSIM, and is closely followed by MCL, which is in turn the best system for co-occurrences, according to TOP2. The more fine-grained GP approach falls in-between. MaxMax systematically has the lowest scores, as its clusterings prove to be too fragmented for our task, and only achieves good NMI values, which are however biased.

These considerations lead us to identify Word Sense Discrimination[9] (WSD), commonly used as a synonym for Word Sense Induction, as an actually different, yet complementary task which necessitates different instruments, as exemplified by our double data set: whereas WSI is paradigmatic, WSD is syntagmatic. We deem that this distinction deserves further investigation. As a future work, beyond expanding our data sets we envision the implementation of consensus clustering (Ghaemi et al., 2009) and re-clustering techniques to improve results, and a more accurate analysis of the relation between creation of word graphs and algorithms' outputs.

---

[9]Defined as *"determining for any two occurrences [of a word] whether they belong to the same sense or not"*, after Schütze (1998).

References

Enrique Amigó, Julio Gonzalo, Javier Artiles, and Felisa Verdejo. 2009. A comparison of extrinsic clustering evaluation metrics based on formal constraints. *Information retrieval*, 12(4):461–486.

Amit Bagga and Breck Baldwin. 1998. Algorithms for scoring coreference chains. In *Proceedings of the first international Conference on Language Resources and Evaluation (LREC'98), workshop on linguistic coreference*, pages 563–566, Granada, Spain. European Language Resources Association.

Osman Başkaya and David Jurgens. 2016. Semi-supervised learning with induced word senses for state of the art word sense disambiguation. *Journal of Artificial Intelligence Research*, 55:1025–1058.

Chris Biemann and Uwe Quasthoff. 2009. Networks generated from natural language text. In *Dynamics on and of complex networks*, pages 167–185. Springer.

Chris Biemann and Martin Riedl. 2013. Text: Now in 2D! a framework for lexical expansion with contextual similarity. *Journal of Language Modelling*, 1(1):55–95.

Chris Biemann. 2006. Chinese whispers: an efficient graph clustering algorithm and its application to natural language processing problems. In *Proceedings of the first workshop on graph based methods for natural language processing*, pages 73–80, New York, New York, USA.

Stefan Bordag. 2006. Word sense induction: Triplet-based clustering and automatic evaluation. In *Proceedings of the 11th Conference of the European Chapter of the Association for Computational Linguistics*, pages 137–144, Trento, Italy. EACL.

Flavio Massimiliano Cecchini and Elisabetta Fersini. 2015. Word sense discrimination: A gangplank algorithm. In *Proceedings of the Second Italian Conference on Computational Linguistics CLiC-it 2015*, pages 77–81, Trento, Italy.

Marie-Catherine De Marneffe, Bill MacCartney, and Christopher Manning. 2006. Generating typed dependency parses from phrase structure parses. In *Proceedings of the fifth international Conference on Language Resources and Evaluation (LREC'06)*, pages 449–454, Genoa, Italy. European Language Resources Association.

Ferdinand De Saussure. 1995 [1916]. *Cours de linguistique générale*. Payot&Rivage, Paris, France. Critical edition of 1st 1916 edition.

Stefan Evert. 2004. *The statistics of word cooccurrences: word pairs and collocations*. Ph.D. thesis, Universität Stuttgart, August.

William Gale, Kenneth Church, and David Yarowsky. 1992. Work on statistical methods for word sense disambiguation. In *Technical Report of 1992 Fall Symposium - Probabilistic Approaches to Natural Language*, pages 54–60, Cambridge, Massachusetts, USA. AAAI.

Reza Ghaemi, Md Nasir Sulaiman, Hamidah Ibrahim, Norwati Mustapha, et al. 2009. A survey: clustering ensembles techniques. *World Academy of Science, Engineering and Technology*, 50:636–645.

Zellig Harris. 1954. Distributional structure. *Word*, 10(2-3):146–162.

Taher Haveliwala. 2002. Topic-sensitive pagerank. In *Proceedings of the 11th international conference on World Wide Web*, pages 517–526, Honolulu, Hawaii, USA. ACM.

David Hope and Bill Keller. 2013. MaxMax: a graph-based soft clustering algorithm applied to word sense induction. In *Proceedings of the 14th International Conference on Computational Linguistics and Intelligent Text Processing*, pages 368–381, Samos, Greece.

David Jurgens and Ioannis Klapaftis. 2013. SemEval-2013 task 13: Word sense induction for graded and non-graded senses. In **SEM 2013: The Second Joint Conference on Lexical and Computational Semantics*, volume 2, pages 290–299, Atlanta, Georgia, USA. ACL.

Adam Kilgarriff, Pavel Rychlý, Pavel Smrž, and David Tugwell. 2004. The sketch engine. In *Proceedings of the Eleventh Euralex Conference*, pages 105–116, Lorient, France.

Linlin Li, Ivan Titov, and Caroline Sporleder. 2014. Improved estimation of entropy for evaluation of word sense induction. *Computational Linguistics*, 40(3):671–685.

Suresh Manandhar, Ioannis Klapaftis, Dmitriy Dligach, and Sameer Pradhan. 2010. Semeval-2010 task 14: Word sense induction & disambiguation. In *Proceedings of the 5th international workshop on semantic evaluation*, pages 63–68, Los Angeles, California, USA. Association for Computational Linguistics.

James Martin and Daniel Jurafsky. 2000. *Speech and language processing*. Pearson, Upper Saddle River, New Jersey, USA.

George Miller. 1995. WordNet: a lexical database for English. *Communications of the ACM*, 38(11):39–41.

Preslav Nakov and Marti Hearst. 2003. Category-based pseudowords. In *Companion Volume of the Proceedings of the Human Language Technology Conference of the North American Chapter of the Association for Computational Linguistics (HTL-NAACL) 2003 - Short Papers*, pages 70–72, Edmonton, Alberta, Canada. Association for Computational Linguistics.

Roberto Navigli, Kenneth Litkowski, and Orin Hargraves. 2007. SemEval-2007 task 07: Coarse-grained English all-words task. In *Proceedings of the 4th International Workshop on Semantic Evaluations*, pages 30–35, Prague, Czech Republic. Association for Computational Linguistics.

Roberto Navigli. 2009. Word sense disambiguation: A survey. *ACM Computing Surveys (CSUR)*, 41(2):10.

Lubomír Otrusina and Pavel Smrž. 2010. A new approach to pseudoword generation. In *Proceedings of the seventh international Conference on Language Resources and Evaluation (LREC'10)*, pages 1195–1199. European Language Resources Association.

Robert Parker, David Graff, Junbo Kong, Ke Chen, and Kazuaki Maeda. 2011. *English Gigaword Fifth Edition*. Linguistic Data Consortium, Philadelphia, Pennsylvania, USA.

Mohammad Taher Pilehvar and Roberto Navigli. 2013. Paving the way to a large-scale pseudosense-annotated dataset. In *Proceedings of the 2013 Conference of the North American Chapter of the Association for Computational Linguistics: Human Language Technologies (HTL-NAACL)*, pages 1100–1109, Atlanta, Georgia, USA. Association for Computational Linguistics.

Steffen Remus and Chris Biemann. 2013. Three knowledge-free methods for automatic lexical chain extraction. In *Proceedings of the 2013 Conference of the North American Chapter of the Association for Computational Linguistics: Human Language Technologies (HTL-NAACL)*, pages 989–999, Atlanta, Georgia, USA. Association for Computational Linguistics.

Matthias Richter, Uwe Quasthoff, Erla Hallsteinsdóttir, and Chris Biemann. 2006. Exploiting the Leipzig Corpora Collection. In *Proceedings of the Fifth Slovenian and First International Language Technologies Conference*, IS-LTC '06, pages 68–73, Ljubljana, Slovenia. Slovenian Language Technologies Society.

Keijo Ruohonen. 2013. *Graph Theory*. Tampereen teknillinen yliopisto. Originally titled Graafiteoria, lecture notes translated by Tamminen, J., Lee, K.-C. and Piché, R.

Hinrich Schütze. 1992. Dimensions of meaning. In *Proceedings of Supercomputing'92*, pages 787–796, Minneapolis, Minnesota, USA. ACM/IEEE.

Hinrich Schütze. 1998. Automatic word sense discrimination. *Computational linguistics*, 24(1):97–123.

Alexander Strehl. 2002. *Relationship-based clustering and cluster ensembles for high-dimensional data mining*. Ph.D. thesis, The University of Texas at Austin, May.

Peter Turney and Patrick Pantel. 2010. From frequency to meaning: Vector space models of semantics. *Journal of artificial intelligence research*, 37(1):141–188.

Stijn van Dongen. 2000. *Graph clustering by flow simulation*. Ph.D. thesis, Universiteit Utrecht, May.

Dominic Widdows and Beate Dorow. 2002. A graph model for unsupervised lexical acquisition. In *Proceedings of the 19th international conference on Computational Linguistics*, volume 1, pages 1–7, Taipei, Taiwan. Association for Computational Linguistics.

North Sámi to Finnish rule-based machine translation system

Ryan Johnson[1] and **Tommi A Pirinen**[2] and **Tiina Puolakainen**[3]
Francis Tyers[1] and **Trond Trosterud**[1] and **Kevin Unhammer**[1]
[1] UiT Norgga Árktalaš universitehta, Giela ja kultuvrra instituhtta, Romssa, Norga
[2] Universität Hamburg, Hamburger Zentrum für Sprachkorpora, Deutschland
[3] Institute of the Estonian Language, Estonia
ryan.txanson@gmail.com, tommi.antero.pirinen@uni-hamburg.de,
tiina.puolakainen@eki.ee, {francis.tyers, trond.trosterud}@uit.no
kevin@unhammer.org

Abstract

This paper presents a machine translation system between Finnish and North Sámi, two Uralic languages. In this paper we concentrate on the translation direction to Finnish. As a background, the differences between the two languages is presented, followed by how the system was designed to handle some of these differences. We then provide an evaluation of the system's performance and directions for future work.

1 Introduction[0]

This paper presents a prototype shallow-transfer rule-based machine translation system between Finnish and North Sámi. The paper will be laid out as follows: Section 2 gives a short review of some previous work in the area of Uralic-Uralic language machine translation; Section 3 introduces Finnish and North Sámi and compares their grammar; Section 4 describes the system and the tools used to construct it; Section 5 gives a preliminary evaluation of the system; and finally Section 6 describes our aims for future work and some concluding remarks.

2 Previous work

Within the Apertium platform, work on several MT systems from North Sámi to Norwegian and to other Sámi languages have been developed (Tyers et al., 2009; Wiechetek et al., 2010; Trosterud and Unhammer, 2013; Antonsen et al., 2016)). Besides these systems, several previous works on making machine translation systems between Uralic languages exist, although to our knowledge none are publicly available, except for North Sámi

to Norwegian[1], and the translation between Estonian, Finnish and Hungarian being available via English as a pivot language in Google Translate.[2] For non-Uralic pairs there are also numerous similarly laid out systems e.g. in Apertium's Turkic pairs, e.g. (Salimzyanov et al., 2013), that can offer insights on how the pair is implemented, which are detailed later in the article but the main parts are the same.

3 The languages

North Sámi and Finnish belong to the Sámi and Finnic branches of the Uralic languages, respectively. The languages are mutually unintelligible, but grammatically quite similar. The orthographical conventions between Finnish and North Sámi written in Finland were quite similar until 1979, when an unified North Sámi orthography widened the distance to Finnish. Finnish is primarily spoken in Finland, where it is the national language, sharing status with Swedish as an official language. The total number of speakers is at least 6 million people. North Sámi is spoken in the Northern parts of Norway, Sweden and Finland by approximately 24.700 people, and it has, alongside the national language, some official status in the municipalities and counties where it is spoken. North Sámi speakers are bilingual in their mother tongue and in their respective national language, many also speak the neighbouring official language. An MT system between North Sámi and Finnish is potentially of great use to the language communities, although fulfilling different functions. In Finland, it may be used to understand Sámi text, and in Norway and Sweden, it may be used by North Sámi speakers to understand Finnish text. In principle, the system may also be used for North Sámi text production, although further de-

---

[0]Authors are listed here alphabetically

[1]https://gtweb.uit.no/jorgal
[2]https://translate.google.com

Proceedings of the 21st Nordic Conference of Computational Linguistics, pages 115–122,
Gothenburg, Sweden, 23-24 May 2017. ©2017 Linköping University Electronic Press

velopment will be needed to fulfil such a function.

3.1 Phonological differences

As related languages, Finnish and North Sámi share several phonological processes, the most important one being consonant gradation. However, North Sámi consonant gradation involves the vast majority of stem-internal consonant clusters, whereas the Finnish counterpart involves only the stops *p, t, k*. Vowel length has a more central role in Finnish than in North Sámi, Several instances of final vowel apocopy in North Sámi, as well as a neutralisation of *p, t, k* in word-final position, has also resulted in quite extensive morphological homonymy. A richer inventory of affricates and fricatives in North Sámi, as well as preaspiration, also add to the difference.

3.2 Orthographic differences

In the native vocabulary, neither Finnish nor North Sámi distinguish between voiced and unvoiced plosives, but whereas Finnish writes them as *p, t, k*, North Sámi writes *b, d, g*, as in *kirja : girji* "book". Finnish marks vowel length with double letter symbols. In North Sámi this distinction is marked for one vowel only, *a*, and with acute accent. Apart from this the orthographic principles of the two languages is quite similar, the almost total lack of free rides is a result of different phonology.

3.3 Morphological differences

There are a number of examples where the morphologies of Finnish and North Sámi are rather different.

North Sámi has a separate dual number, whereas Finnish has not. Otherwise the North Sámi and Finnish finite verb morphology is almost identical. The infinite verb conjugation is more different, though: Finnish has a rich array of infinitives that are inflected in different subsets of the case system.

Finnish has more than twice the number of cases as North Sámi has. Where North Sámi only has one case for the direct object (accusative), Finnish has two (accusative and partitive). The Finnish system of adverbial cases consist of a 2x3 matrix of inner/outer to/in/from cases, North Sámi has only one of these distinctions (to/in˜from), thus the 6 Finnish cases corresponds to 2 North Sámi ones. In principle, Finnish and North Sámi have the same system of possessive suffixes, but in North Sámi its use is far more restricted than in Finnish.

3.4 Syntactic differences

Syntactically speaking, there are two varieties of North Sámi, one used within and one outside of Finland. The Finnish variety is much closer to Finnish than the Scandinavian one. Comparing Finnish with the Scandinavian variety of North Sámi, the most striking difference is participle constructions vs. relative clauses. Where North Sámi uses subordinate clauses, written Finnish often use head-final participle constructions instead. Since both varieties are found in Finnish, at least to some degree, we at the moment let most "Scandinavian" varieties of North Sámi through, thereby giving North Sámi from Norway and Finland a different stylistic flavour in the Finnish output.

The North Sámi passive is a derivational process, whereas it for Finnish is an inflectional one, resulting in quite different syntactic patterns for passive. Finnish has a richer array of indefinite verb forms.

Finnish adjectives agree with their head noun in case and number, whereas North Sámi has an invariant *attribute* form for all but one adjective, the adjective *buorre* 'good', and partial agreement for determiners.

Existential and habitive clauses have the same structure in the two languages, *possessor.local-case copula possessed* and *adverbial copula e-subject* (*on me / in street is car* 'I have a car/There is a car in the street'). except that in Finnish, the possessed/e-subject behaves like objects, whereas it in North Sámi they behave like subjects. Thus, in North Sámi, the copula agrees with the possessed / e-subject, whereas in Finnish, it does not.

4 System

The system is based on the Apertium[3] machine translation platform (Forcada et al., 2011). The platform was originally aimed at the Romance languages of the Iberian peninsula, but has also been adapted for other, more distantly related, language pairs. The whole platform, both programs and data, are licensed under the Free Software Foundation's General Public Licence[4] (GPL) and all the software and data for the 30 released language pairs (and the other pairs being worked on) is available for download from the project website.

---

[3]http://apertium.sf.net
[4]https://www.gnu.org/licenses/gpl-3.0.en.html

4.1 Architecture of the system

The Apertium translation engine consists of a Unix-style pipeline or assembly line with the following modules (see Figure 1):

- A deformatter which encapsulates the format information in the input as *superblanks* that will then be seen as blanks between words by the other modules.

- A morphological analyser which segments the text in surface forms (SF) (words, or, where detected, multiword lexical units or MWLUs) and for each, delivers one or more lexical forms (LF) consisting of lemma, lexical category and morphological information.

- A morphological disambiguator (CG) which chooses, using linguistic rules the most adequate sequence of morphological analyses for an ambiguous sentence.

- A lexical transfer module which reads each SL LF and delivers the corresponding target-language (TL) LF by looking it up in a bilingual dictionary encoded as an FST compiled from the corresponding XML file. The lexical transfer module may return more than one TL LF for a single SL LF.

- A lexical selection module (Tyers et al., 2012b) which chooses, based on context rules, the most adequate translation of ambiguous source language LFs.

- A structural transfer module, which performs local syntactic operations, is compiled from XML files containing rules that associate an action to each defined LF pattern. Patterns are applied left-to-right, and the longest matching pattern is always selected.

- A morphological generator which delivers a TL SF for each TL LF, by suitably inflecting it.

- A reformatter which de-encapsulates any format information.

Table 1 provides an example of a single phrase as it moves through the pipeline.

4.2 Morphological transducers

The morphological transducers are compiled with the Helsinki Finite State Technology (Lindén et al., 2009),[5] a free/open-source reimplementation of the Xerox finite-state tool-chain, popular in the field of morphological analysis. It implements both the lexc morphology description language for defining lexicons, and the twol and xfst scripting languages for modeling morphophonological rules. This toolkit has been chosen as it—or the equivalent XFST—has been widely used for other Uralic languages (Koskenniemi, 1983; Pirinen, 2015; Moshagen et al., 2013), and is available under a free/open-source licence. The morphologies of both languages are implemented in lexc, and the morphophonologies of both languages are implemented in twolc.

The same morphological description is used for both analysis and generation. To avoid overgeneration, any alternative forms are marked with one of two marks, LR (only analyser) or RL (only generator). Instead of the usual compile/invert to compile the transducers, we compile twice, once the generator, without the LR paths, and then again the analyser without the RL paths.

4.3 Bilingual lexicon

The bilingual lexicon currently contains 19,415 stem-to-stem correspondences (of which 8044 proper nouns) and was built partly upon an available North Sámi—Finnish dictionary[6], and partly by hand (i.e., by translating North Sámi stems unrecognised by the morphological analyser into Finnish). The proper nouns were taken from existing lexical resources. Entries consist largely of one-to-one stem-to-stem correspondences with part of speech, but also include some entries with ambiguous translations (see e.g., Figure 2).

4.4 Disambiguation rules

The system has a morphological disambiguation module in the form of a Constraint Grammar (Karlsson et al., 1995). The version of the formalism used is vislcg3.[7] The output of each morphological analyser is highly ambiguous, measured at around 2.4 morphological analyses per form for Finnish and 2.6 for North Sámi[8]. The goal of

---

[5] https://hfst.github.io

[6] https://gtweb.uit.no/langtech/trunk/words/dicts/smefin/src/

[7] http://visl.cg.sdu.dk

[8] Cf. (Trosterud and Wiechetek, 2007)

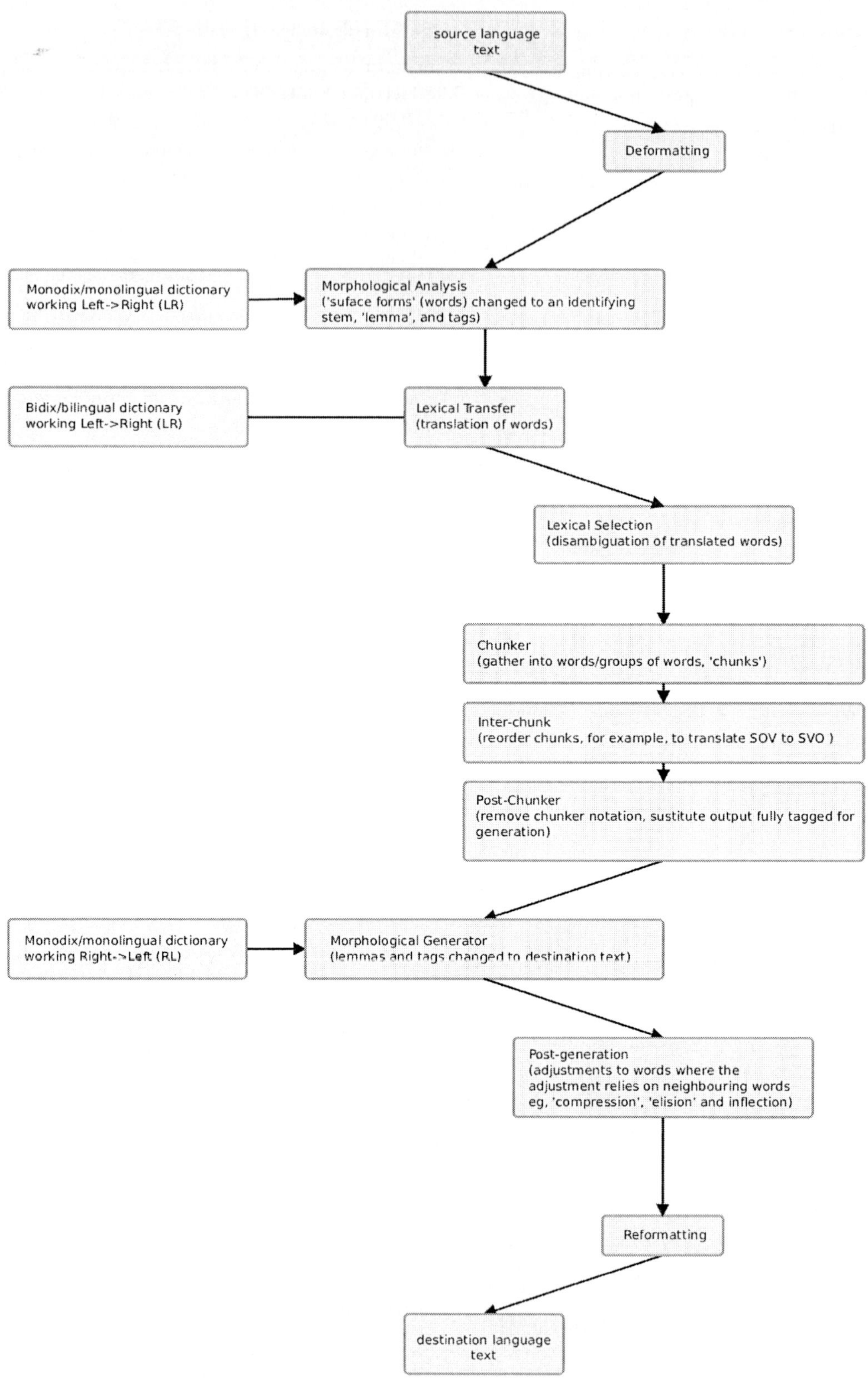

Figure 1: Apertium structure (Image from apertium wiki by user Rcrowther) http://wiki.apertium.org/wiki/Workflow_diagram

<table>
<tr><td>North Sámi input: Sámegielat leat gielat maid sámit hállet.</td></tr>
<tr><td>Morphological analysis:</td></tr>
<tr><td>^Sámegielat/ sámegielat<adj> <attr>/ sámegielat<adj> <sg><nom>/
sámegiella<n> <pl><nom>/ sámegiella<n> <sg><acc><px2sg>/
sámegiella<n> <sg><gen><px2sg>/ sámegiella<n> <sg><acc><px2sg>/
sámegiella<n> <sg><gen><px2sg>$

^leat/ leat<vblex><iv> <indic><pres><conneg>/
leat<vblex><iv> <indic><pres><p1><pl>/ leat<vblex><iv> <indic><pres><p2><sg>/
leat<vblex><iv> <indic><pres><p3><pl>/ leat<vblex><iv> <inf>$
^gielat/ giella<n> <pl><nom>/ giella<n> <sg><acc><px2sg>/

giella<n> <sg><gen><px2sg>/ giella<n> <sg><acc><px2sg>/
giella<n> <sg><gen><px2sg>$ ^maid/ maid<adv>/ mii<prn><itg> <pl><acc>/

mii<prn><itg> <pl><gen>/ mii<prn><itg> <sg><acc>/ mii<prn><rel> <pl><acc>/
mii<prn><rel> <pl><gen>/ mii<prn><rel> <sg><acc>$

^sámit/ sápmi<n> <pl><nom>/ sápmi<n> <pl><nom>$

^hállet/ hállat<vblex><tv> <imp><p2><pl>/
hállat<vblex><tv> <indic><pres><p3><pl>/ hállat<vblex><tv> <indic><pret><p2><sg>$
^./.<sent>$</td></tr>
<tr><td>Morphological disambiguation:</td></tr>
<tr><td>^Sámegielat/sámegiella<n> <pl><nom> <@SUBJ→>$
^leat/leat<vblex><iv> <indic><pres><p3><pl> <@+FMAINV>$
^gielat/giella<n> <pl><nom> <@←SPRED>$
^maid/mii<prn><rel> <pl><acc> <@OBJ→>$
^sámit/sápmi<n> <pl><nom> <@SUBJ→>$
^hállet/hállat<vblex><tv> <indic><pres><p3><pl> <@+FMAINV>$ ^./.<sent>$</td></tr>
<tr><td>Lexical translation:</td></tr>
<tr><td>^Sámegiella<n> <pl><nom> <@SUBJ→>/ Saamekieli<n> <pl><nom> <@SUBJ→>/
Saame<n> <pl><nom> <@SUBJ→>$

^leat<vblex><iv> <indic><pres><p3><pl> <@+FMAINV>/
olla<vblex> <actv><indic><pres><p3><pl> <@+FMAINV>/
sijaita<vblex> <actv><indic><pres><p3><pl> <@+FMAINV>$

^giella<n> <pl><nom> <@←SPRED>/ kieli<n> <pl><nom> <@←SPRED>/
ansa<n> <pl><nom> <@←SPRED>$

^mii<prn><rel> <pl><acc> <@OBJ→>/ mikä<prn><rel> <pl><acc> <@OBJ→>$

^sápmi<n> <pl><nom> <@SUBJ→>/ saame<n> <pl><nom> <@SUBJ→>$

^hállat<vblex><tv> <indic><pres><p3><pl> <@+FMAINV>/
puhua<vblex> <actv><indic><pres><p3><pl> <@+FMAINV>/
mekastaa<vblex> <actv><indic><pres><p3><pl> <@+FMAINV>$^.<sent>/.<sent>$</td></tr>
<tr><td>Structural transfer:</td></tr>
<tr><td>^Saamekieli<n> <pl><nom>$ ^olla<vblex> <actv><indic><pres><p3><pl>$
^kieli<n> <pl><nom>$ ^mikä<prn><rel> <pl><par>$
^saame<n> <pl><nom>$ ^puhua<vblex> <actv><indic><pres><p3><pl>$^.<sent>$</td></tr>
<tr><td>Finnish translation:</td></tr>
<tr><td>Saamekielet ovat kielet #mikä saamet puhuvat</td></tr>
</table>

Table 1: Translation process for the North Sámi phrase *Sámegielat leat gielat maid sámit hállet* (The Sámi languages are the languages that the Sámis speak)

```
<e><p><l>sálten<s n="n"/></l><r>suolaus<s n="n"/></r></p></e>
<e><p><l>sálti<s n="n"/></l><r>suola<s n="n"/></r></p></e>
<e><p><l>sámeduodji<s n="n"/></l><r>käsityö<s n="n"/></r></p></e>
<e><p><l>sámegiella<s n="n"/></l><r>saame<s n="n"/></r></p></e>
<e><p><l>sámegiella<s n="n"/></l><r>saamekieli<s n="n"/></r></p></e>
<e><p><l>sámi<s n="n"/></l><r>saame<s n="n"/></r></p></e>
<e><p><l>sámil<s n="n"/></l><r>sammal<s n="n"/></r></p></e>
```

Figure 2: Example entries from the bilingual transfer lexicon. Finnish is on the right, and North Sámi on the left.

the CG rules is to select the correct analysis when there are multiple analyses. Given the similarity of Finnish and North Sámi, ambiguity across parts of speech may often be passed from one language to the other and not lead to many translation errors. Disambiguating between forms within the inflectional paradigms in case of homonymy, on the other hand, are crucial for choosing the correct form of the target language, and there has been put much effort into developing CG rules to resolve such ambiguity for North Sámi. Currently, ambiguity is down to 1.08 for North Sámi (analysed with the disambigator used for MT on a 675534 word newspaper corpus[9]. The corresponding number for Finnish is 1.36, for a subcorpus of 770999 words of Wikipedia text. The Finnish CG rules are a conversion of Fred Karlsson's original CG1 rules for Finnish (Karlsson, 1990), and the poorer results for Finnish are due to conversion problems between the different CG version, and between CG1 and our Finnish FST.

5   Evaluation

All evaluation was tested against a specific version of Apertium SVN[10] and Giellatekno SVN[11]. The lexical coverage of the system was calculated over freely available corpora of North Sámi. We used a recent dump of Wikipedia [12] as well as a translation of the New Testament. The corpora were divided into 10 parts each; the coverage numbers given are the averages of the calculated percentages of number of words analysed for each of these parts, and the standard deviation presented is the

Corpus	Tokens	Cov.	std
se.wikipedia.org	190,894	76,81 %	±10
New Testament	162,718	92,45 %	±0.06

Table 2: Naïve coverage of sme-fin system

standard deviation of the coverage on each corpus. As shown in Table 2, the naïve coverage[13] of the North Sámi to Finnish MT system over the corpora approaches that of a broad-coverage MT system, with one word in ten unknown.

The coverage over the Wikipedia corpus is substantially worse, due to the fact that this corpus is "dirtier": it contains orthographical errors, wiki code [14], repetitions, lot of English texts, as well as quite a few proper nouns, this is easily seen in the large deviation between divided parts. The New Testament on the other hand is rather well covered and has practically uniformly distributed coverage throughout.

To measure the performance of the translator we used the Word Error Rate metric—an edit-distance metric based on Levenshtein distance (Levenshtein, 1966). We had three small North Sámi corpora along with their manually post-edited translations into Finnish to measure the WER. We have chosen not to measure the translation quality with automatic measures such as BLEU, as they are not the best suited to measure quality of translations for the use case, for further details see also Callison-Burch et al. (2006; Smith et al. (2016; Smith et al. (2014).

For translation post-edition we used three freely

---

[9]Cf. (Antonsen and Trosterud, forthcoming) for a presentation of the North Sámi CG.

[10]https//svn.code.sf.net/p/apertium/svn/ nursery/apertium-sme-fin: revision 76019

[11]https://victorio.uit.no/langtech/trunk/ langs/sme: revision 147464

[12]http://se.wikipedia.org

[13]A non-naïve coverage would require manual evaluation of correctness for the cases where word-forms are covered accidentally by e.g., morphological processes.

[14]While we have tried to clean the data from most of the Mediawiki codes and notations, there is always some left after the cleanup, due to new wiki codes after creation of the cleanup script or actual broken data

Corpus	Tokens	OOV	WER
Redigering.se	1,070	95	34.24
Samediggi.fi	570	33	36.32
The Story	361	0	19.94

Table 3: Word error rate over the corpora; OOV is the number of out-of-vocabulary (unknown) words.

available parallel texts from the internet: one from the Finnish Sámi parliament site[15], one from a Swedish regulation of minority people and languages and the story that is used with all Apertium language pairs as initial development set ("Where is James?"). Table 3 presents the WER for the corpora.

Analysing the changes in post-edition, a few classes of actual errors can be identified. One common example arises from the grammatical differences in the case system systems, in particular the remaining adpositions are often turned into a case suffix for the dependent noun phrase, e.g., the North Sámi "birra" has been turned into the Finnish adposition "ympäri" (around), where elative case is required, similarly for the translation "seassa" (among) instead of inessive case. Also visible, especially in the story text is the lack of possessive suffix agreement e.g. "heidän äiti" (their mother n sg nom) instead of "heidän äitinsä" (their mother n sp nom/gen pxsp3), while the former is perfectly acceptable in standard spoken Finnish it is not accepted as formal written language form. Another issue that appeared a number of times, maybe partially due to the genre of the texts selected, i.e. law texts, was the selection of adverb (form), e.g. the word-form "mukana" (with) was corrected to "mukaan" (according to). A large amount of simple lexical problems is due to the vocabulary of the selected texts as well: "hallintoalue" (governmental area), "seurantavastuu" (responsibility of surveillance), "itsehallinto" (autonomy), and their compounds, are all either missing or partially wrong due to lexical selections.

6   Concluding remarks

We have presented the first MT system from Finnish to North Sámi. With a WER of above 30%, it still is far from production-level performance, and it is also at the prototype-level in

terms of the number of rules. Although the impact of this relatively low number of rules on the quality of translation is extensive (cf., the difference in WER between the development and testing corpora), the outlook is promising and the current results suggest that a high quality translation between morphologically-rich agglutinative languages is possible. We plan to continue development on the pair; the coverage of the system is already quite high, although we intend to increase it to 95 % on the corpora we have we estimate that this will mean adding around 5,000 new stems and take 1–2 months. The remaining work will be improving the quality of translation by adding more rules, starting with the transfer component. The long-term plan is to integrate the data created with other open-source data for Uralic languages in order to make transfer systems between all the Uralic language pairs. Related work is currently ongoing from North Sámi to South, Lule and Inari Sámi, from North Sámi to Norwegian, and between Finnish and Estonian. The system presented here is available as free/open-source software under the GNU GPL and the whole system may be downloaded from Sourceforge and the open repository of Giellatekno.

Acknowledgements

The work on this North Sámi-Finnish machine translation system was partially funded by the Google Summer of Code and Google Code-In programmes, and partly by a Norsk forsingsråd grant (234299) on machine translation between Sámi languages.

References

Lene Antonsen and Trond Trosterud. forthcoming. Ord sett innafra og utafra – en datalingvistisk analyse av nordsamisk. Norsk Lingvistisk Tidsskrift.

Lene Antonsen, Trond Trosterud, and Francis Tyers. 2016. A North Saami to South Saami machine translation prototype. 4:11—27.

Chris Callison-Burch, Miles Osborne, and Philipp Koehn. 2006. Re-evaluation the role of bleu in machine translation research. In *EACL*, volume 6, pages 249–256.

Mikel L Forcada, Mireia Ginestí-Rosell, Jacob Nordfalk, Jim O'Regan, Sergio Ortiz-Rojas, Juan Antonio Pérez-Ortiz, Felipe Sánchez-Martínez, Gema Ramírez-Sánchez, and Francis M Tyers. 2011.

---

[15]http://samediggi.fi

Apertium: a free/open-source platform for rule-based machine translation. *Machine translation*, 25(2):127–144.

Fred Karlsson, Atro Voutilainen, Juha Heikkilae, and Arto Anttila. 1995. *Constraint Grammar: a language-independent system for parsing unrestricted text*, volume 4. Walter de Gruyter.

Fred Karlsson. 1990. Constraint grammar as a framework for parsing running text. In *Proceedings of the 13th conference on Computational linguistics-Volume 3*, pages 168–173. Association for Computational Linguistics.

Kimmo Koskenniemi. 1983. *Two-level morphology—A General Computational Model for Word-Form Recognition and Production*. Ph.D. thesis, Department of General Linguistics. University of Helsinki, Finland.

Vladimir I Levenshtein. 1966. Binary codes capable of correcting deletions, insertions, and reversals. In *Soviet physics doklady*, volume 10, pages 707–710.

Krister Lindén, Miikka Silfverberg, and Tommi Pirinen. 2009. Hfst tools for morphology–an efficient open-source package for construction of morphological analyzers. In *International Workshop on Systems and Frameworks for Computational Morphology*, pages 28–47. Springer.

Sjur N Moshagen, Tommi A Pirinen, and Trond Trosterud. 2013. Building an open-source development infrastructure for language technology projects. In *Proceedings of the 19th Nordic Conference of Computational Linguistics (NODALIDA 2013); May 22-24; 2013; Oslo University; Norway. NEALT Proceedings Series 16*, number 085, pages 343–352. Linköping University Electronic Press.

Tommi A Pirinen. 2015. Development and use of computational morphology of finnish in the open source and open science era: Notes on experiences with omorfi development. *SKY Journal of Linguistics*, 28:381–393.

Ilnar Salimzyanov, J Washington, and F Tyers. 2013. A free/open-source kazakh-tatar machine translation system. *Machine Translation Summit XIV*.

Aaron Smith, Christian Hardmeier, and Jörg Tiedemann. 2014. Bleu is not the colour: How optimising bleu reduces translation quality.

Aaron Smith, Christian Hardmeier, and Jörg Tiedemann. 2016. Climbing mount bleu: The strange world of reachable high-bleu translations. *Baltic Journal of Modern Computing*, 4(2):269.

Trond Trosterud and Kevin Brubeck Unhammer. 2013. Evaluating North Sámi to Norwegian assimilation RBMT. In *Proceedings of the Third International Workshop on Free/Open-Source Rule-Based Machine Translation (FreeRBMT 2012)*, volume 3 of

Technical report, pages 13–26. Department of Computer Science and Engineering, Chalmers University of Technology and University of Gothenburg.

Trond Trosterud and Linda Wiechetek. 2007. Disambiguering av homonymi i Nord- og Lulesamisk. *Suomalais-Ugrilaisen Seuran Toimituksia = Mémoires de la Société Fi nno-Ougrienne. Sámit, sánit, sátnehámit. Riepmočála Pekka Sammallahtii miessemánu 21. beaivve 2007*, 253:375–395.

Francis Tyers, Linda Wiechetek, and Trond Trosterud. 2009. Developing prototypes for machine translation between two Sámi languages. In *Proceedings of the 13th Annual Conference of the European Association for Machine Translation, EAMT09*, pages 120–128.

Linda Wiechetek, Francis Tyers, and Thomas Omma. 2010. Shooting at flies in the dark: Rule-based lexical selection for a minority language pair. *Lecture Notes in Artificial Intelligence*, 6233:418–429.

Machine translation with North Saami as a pivot language

Lene Antonsen and **Ciprian Gerstenberger** and **Maja Kappfjell**
Sandra Nystø Rahka and **Marja-Liisa Olthuis**
Trond Trosterud and **Francis M. Tyers**
Department of Language and Culture
UiT The Arctic University of Norway
`firstname.lastname@uit.no`

Abstract

Translating from a majority language into several minority languages implies duplicating both translation and terminology work. Our assumption is that a *manual* translation into one of the languages, and machine translation from this one into the other ones, will both cut translation time and be beneficial for work on terminology. We test the functionality of North Saami as a pivot language, with subsequent machine translation into South, Lule and Inari Saami.

1 Introduction

In this paper, we present a workflow with *manual* translation from the majority languages Finnish, Norwegian (and Swedish) into North Saami and subsequent rule-based machine translation (hereafter MT) into the target languages (hereafter TL) South, Lule and Inari Saami. Thus North Saami is source language (SL) for the MT system and pivot language for the overall evaluation[1]. The system is based upon grammatical analysis of sme transfer lexica, lexical-selection rules, and transfer rules for the syntactic differences between the languages. We deemed the rule-based approach a good fit for closely related languages with complex morphology and very few parallel texts.

In the remainder of the paper we delineate the linguistic and theoretical background of the project (Section 2), give an overview of the project (Section 3), describe the evaluation method of the systems (Section 4) and discuss different aspects of the evaluation method (Section 5). Finally, we point out the importance of such systems both for research and for society (Section 6).

2 Background

The Saami branch of the Uralic language family consists of 6 literary languages, 4 are included in the present article. sme is the largest one, it has 25,700 speakers in Norway, Sweden and Finland. The smaller languages, smn, sma and smj, each count 450–2000 speakers.[2] With the exception of sma, the neighbouring Saami languages are to some extent mutually intelligible.

All Saami languages are endangered minority languages, having a limited position as an official language in some domains in modern society. There is a continuous shortage of texts, and the lack of both writers and translators is a bottleneck to building full literacy. sme is in a better position than the other languages, especially in Norway, where the imbalance in speaker base is largest, i.e. the proportion of sme speakers to sma and smj speakers is the highest.

Our goal is to explore the use of MT between closely-related languages, for easing the translation bottleneck, by a setup with manual translation to one Saami language and then MT to other Saami languages, instead of manual translation from the three majority languages into several Saami languages (given the lack of MT systems into Saami).

2.1 Previous work

The literature on Saami MT includes several works. Relevant here is an article about an early version of an MT system sme → sma on a limited domain, where sme is used as pivot language for nob to sma translation (Antonsen et al., 2016)[3]. In a study on pivot translation for under-resourced languages, (Babych et al., 2007) a Ukrainian–English RBMT system performes better with the

---

[1] We will refer to the working languages by their language code: sma, sme, smj and smn for South, North, Lule and Inari Saami, as well as nob and fin for Norwegian Bokmål and Finnish.

[2] `http://www.ethnologue.com` and Pasanen (2015)

[3] The other works are (Tyers et al., 2009) on an early sme → smj system, comparing rule-based and statistical MT, (Wiechetek et al., 2010) on lexical selection rules for the same language pair, and (Trosterud and Unhammer, 2013) on an evaluation of a sme → nob system.

Proceedings of the 21st Nordic Conference of Computational Linguistics, pages 123–131,
Gothenburg, Sweden, 23-24 May 2017. ©2017 Linköping University Electronic Press

aid of Russian as a pivot language than one without.

Using Spanish as a pivot language between English and Brazilian Portuguese, (Masselot et al., 2010) shows translators only English original and Brazilian Portuguese MT output. This is a similar approach to ours: the evaluators were shown the fin or nob original and the target language MT output made by translating from the manually translated output in sme.

3 The project

The MT systems were implemented with Apertium (Forcada et al., 2011), which is a highly modular set of tools for building rule-based MT systems. For each language pair, the pipeline consists of the following modules[4]:

- morphological analysis of the SL by means of a Finite-State Transducer (hereafter FST)
- disambiguation and syntactic analysis with Constraint Grammar (hereafter CG)
- lexical transfer (word translation of the disambiguated source)
- lexical selection (choice of contextually appropriate lemma)
- one or more levels of FST-based structural transfer (reordering and changes to morphological features)
- generation of TL by means of FST

Figure 1 offers an overview of the modules and shows the output on each processing step.

3.1 Resource challenges

The backbone of the MT system is the lexical mapping, which is implemented as a dictionary between SL and TL. The described MT project deals with pairs of minority languages. As before the project there were no dictionaries between Saami languages, the resources had to be compiled in various ways.

Due to the proximity between sme and smj, it was possible to map the sme lexical entries into smj by means of a transliteration FST. The output was then post-edited by a native speaker of smj. This simple yet effective method ensured that the SL lexicon was congruent with the TL lexicon. However, this shallow lexical mapping is not possible for Saami languages that are by far more different than sme, as it is the case with sma and smn.

The dictionary between sme and sma was built by crossing the sme–nob with the nob–sma dictionary, both compiled at Giellatekno. The coverage of the resulting sme–sma dictionary has been incrementally extended during the system development work

The most difficult case was the compilation of the sme–smn lexical resource. The candidate word pairs were created by mapping sme–fin onto the fin–smn, and since the fin–smn dictionary gave several smn translations for each entry, the resulting sme–smn had about 3.62 translations for each smn. Since cognates were in most cases the best candidates, we calculated the Levenshtein distance (Levenshtein, 1965) between the sme form and a version of the smn candidate that was orthographically adjusted to sme, and sent the highest scoring candidate(s) to be manually corrected. As an illustration, for the sme entry *bahčit* 'to milk' there were two smn candidates: *pačĕeđ* 'to milk' and *cuskâdiđ* 'to stop a milk-feeding animal from giving milk'. After adjusting for regular sound changes, *pačĕeđ* gave a Levenshtein distance of 3, and *cuskâdiđ* of 6, and thus *pačĕeđ* was chosen. In the Saami languages, proper nouns are inflected for case, and heuristic recognition of names is thus not sufficient. Therefore, 80-90% of the bilingual dictionaries were devoted to proper noun pairs.

After a manual check, the sme–smn dictionary was ready for use in MT. All three dictionaries have been incrementally extended and refined during the system development.

3.2 Linguistic challenges

3.2.1 Linguistic differences

Generally, the grammatical differences between the Saami languages are minor. However, with only 7 cases, the pivot language, sme, is the one with the smallest case inventory. Of these, nouns and pronouns in accusative share forms with the genitive, and numerals in accusative share forms with the nominative. smn shares the system of grammatical and local cases with sme, but has two extra cases: partitive and abessive (corresponding to the sme postpositional phrase *N haga* ('without N')). smn also makes a distinction between accusative and genitive, most notably in the plural. sma and smj have a richer case system than sme: their genitive and accusative forms are always distinct from each other. Moreover, unlike the locative case syncretism in sme for in and from spatial relations, these languages encode the two different

---

[4]For a presentation of the grammatical analysers and generators, see Antonsen et al. (2010) and Antonsen and Trosterud (forthcoming).

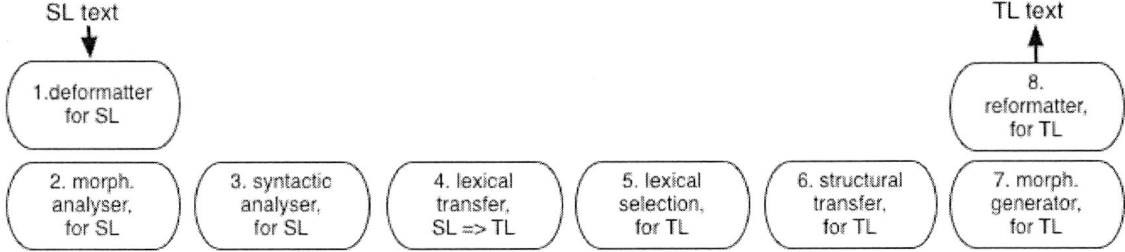

SL: Son bargá vuođđoealáhusas.

1–3. ^Son<prn><pers><p3><sg><nom><@SUBJ→>$ ^bargat<vblex><tv><indic><pres><p3><sg><@+FMAINV>$
^vuođđu<n><sem_semcon><cmp_sgnom><cmp>+ealáhus<n><sem_domain><sg><loc><@←ADVL-ine>$

4–5. ^Son<prn><pers><p3><sg><nom><@SUBJ→>/Dïhte<prn><pers><p3><sg><nom><@SUBJ→>$
^bargat <vblex><tv><indic><pres><p3><sg><@+FMAINV>/barkedh<v><iv><inf><@-FMAINV>$
^vuođđu <n><sem_semcon><cmp_sgnom><cmp>/våarome<n><sggencmp><cmp>$
^ealáhus<n><sem_domain><sg><loc><@←ADVL-ine>/jieliemasse<n><sem_domain><sg><loc><@←ADVL-ine>$

6. ^Dïhte<prn><pers><p3><sg><nom>$ ^våarome<n><cmp_sgnom><cmp>+jieliemasse<n><sg><ine>$
^barkedh<vblex><tv><indic><pres><p3><sg>$

7–8. TL: Dïhte våaromejieliemassesne barka.

Figure 1: Translation pipeline and processing example for *Son bargá vuođđoealáhusas* 'He works in-the-primary-sector' from sme to sma

relations by inessive and elative case, respectively. Hence, given the case syncretism of the SL, one of the challenges for the MT system is to make the contextually correct case distinction in the target language.

In NP-internal agreement in sme, the adjective does not agree with its head noun, but gets a separate *attributive* form, invariant in the different cases, but marking membership in the NP. In principle, all the other Saami languages have the same system, but there are some differences. smn, on the one hand, has a richer system of semi-agreement for large sub-parts of its adjectives, whereas sma often replaces adjective loanwords with genitive nouns. smj is here closer to sme.

As in fin, negation is expressed by a negation verb in the Saami languages. smn and sme have the same system as fin: in the present tense, the negation verb combines with a form identical to the imperative, while in past tense, it combines with a form identical to the perfect participle. In contrast, smj and sma have an older system, where the negation verb itself is inflected for tense while the main verb is identical to the imperative irrespective of tense.

Regarding syntax, sme and smn are quite similar, whereas in smj and especially in sma there is a strong tendency towards SOV word order, where sme and smn have SVO. With a verb complex *auxiliary + verb* (AV), the sme and smn may also have

SAOV in addition to SAVO, which is dependent upon the information structure of the sentence.

For NP structure and treatment of given and new information, sma also differs most from the rest. As for verbs, despite minor differences between SL and TL, the inventories of non-finite verbs are rather similar, which enabled a one-to-one mapping of verb forms.

3.2.2 Analysis of the pivot language

In order to cope with as many of the above-mentioned challenges, we enriched the input in the SL with pieces of information needed for the appropriate choice in the specific TL.

This has been realised partly by adding extra tags in the CG (the syntactic module), and partly by adding parallel paths to the FST (the morphological module). The sme accusative–genitive syncretism may exemplify this: this ambiguity is disambiguated in the syntactic analysis.

The issue of one-to-many mapping of the sme locative case, which should be translated either as inessive or elative into sma and smj, was solved by adding an extra tag to the adverbials in the syntactic analysis, marking the ambiguity between inessive and elative. This way eased the choice of the contextually appropriate case in the TL output.

Additionally, locative was also marked for *habitive*[5] in the syntactic module. Correct mark-

---

[5] The possessive construction as in 'I have a book.'

ing of habitive versus other adverbials is only relevant for sma, which uses genitive instead of the sme locative. In smj the habitive case is inessive, which is the default translation for the locative if it does not have a tag for elative in the syntactic analysis.

Adding extra tags was also the solution for the frequent sme particle *ge*, which is used for both negative and positive polarity. This extra marking eased the choice of the appropriate forms in smn and sma because these two TLs feature different clitics for polarity marking.

Other case assignment differences between SL and TLs such as **time** and **path** expressions were solved by enriching the SL analysis with tags indicating semantic category (e.g. *Sem/Time*). Semantic tags were used also for structural transfer of sme adposition phrases into sma.

3.2.3   Transfer rules

In a transfer-based MT system, the transfer module takes care not only of the simple lexical transfer but also of any structural discrepancy between source and target language by, e.g., changing morphological attributes, deleting or adding words, or changing word order. Table 1 shows some examples of structural mapping of grammatical patterns between source and target language.

The rules for transforming the word order, e.g., from VX in sme to XV in sma, have to cover all different syntactic constructions that VX is a part of, such as subject ellipsis, progressive constructions, complex objects, and verb phrases as complement to nouns or adjectives. By means of syntactic tags in the sme analysis, the transfer rules build chunks of syntactic phrases, and then the verb is moved past these chunks. Compared to earlier Apertium systems as described in (Antonsen et al., 2016), this is new, and a significant improvement. Unlike the MT systems for smn and smj that contain a similar amount of rules, the sma MT system has three times as many rules. This is due to the syntactic differences between sma and the other Saami languages.

4   Evaluation

We evaluated the output of the MT systems in three steps. First, we estimated the lexical coverage, then we analysed and evaluated the amount on editing on the the MT output text via the pivot language. Finally, the evaluators were asked to compare post-editing to translation of a similar text from the majority language, yet **without** access to

rule type	sme		
	→smn	→smj	→sma
modifying/ chunking	63	75	171
word order	7	24	37
macro rules	38	12	96
total	108	111	304

Table 1: Transfer rules for each of the language pairs. Macro rules modify morphological attributes, as a part of ordinary rules.

any MT output text.

4.1   Word coverage

To measure the system coverage, we used a corpus of 8.9 million words, consisting of texts on the Saami school system in Finland as well as administrative texts from the Saami Parliament of Norway. As Table 2 shows, the difference in coverage between the three language pairs is minimal[6].

	coverage	dynamic comp.	dynamic deriv.
sme–sma	0.938	0.557	15 types
sme–smj	0.940	0.558	22 types
sme–smn	0.944	0.822	26 types
Average	0.941	0.670	

Table 2: Coverage of text corpus (1.0 = 100%)

In Table 2, dynamic compounding means that the system translates any N + N compound. This makes up more than 8% points in coverage for smn and a little more than 5% for the other languages. Another significant difference is in how many dynamic derivations (= all stems are optionally directed to a set of derivational affixes) are transferred from SL to each TL: 26 dynamic derivation types to smn, 22 types to smj and only 15 types to sma.

As indicated by the amount of similarity in dynamic word formation, sme–smn is the most similar language pair both for compounding and derivations, while the largest differences are found between sme and sma.

---

[6]Note that for sme–sma, this is an improvement over the 87.4% reported in (Antonsen et al., 2016).

	sma	smj	smn	**Total**
WER	0.57	0.46	0.37	0.42
PER	0.45	0.39	0.32	0.35
PER/WER	0.79	0.85	0.86	0.83

Table 3: WER - all languages

	sma	smj	smn
Lexical selection	0.33	0.42	0.38
Word form correction	0.18	0.17	0.28
Word generation correction	0.01	0.11	0.03
Insert/delete/move word	0.43	0.26	0.26
Punctuation	0.04	0.04	0.03
Total	1.00	1.00	1.00

Table 4: Distribution of correction types

4.2 Word Error Rate

4.2.1 Evaluation setup

For the quantitative evaluation, we selected one text in nob and one in fin that had already been manually translated into sme. Since the coverage was measured in a separate test (see Section 4.1), we added the missing sme words into each of the systems. Using the MT systems, we translated the sme text with a nob original into sma and smj, and the sme text with a fin original into smn.

For each language pair, we had three evaluators, who were all professional translators. Each evaluator received both the nob or fin original and the MT output. The task was then to produce a good target language text, either by correcting the MT version or by translating the original. As two evaluators did not post-edit they are treated separately in Section 4.4.

For each evaluator, we calculated Word Error Rate and Position-independent Word Error Rate (hereafter WER and PER) of the MT version as compared to the post-edited text. WER is defined as the number of words being corrected, inserted, or deleted in the post-edited text. PER differs from WER in ignoring word-order changes. Thus, a WER of 10% means that every tenth word has been changed in one way or another in the post-edited text. Average WER and PER values for all evaluators for the different languages are shown in Table 3.

The best values were found for smn, which was also the language with the smallest WER/PER difference. sma had the highest values (i.e. worse results). sma is also the language with the largest WER/PER difference. Given the word order differences between sma and the other Saami languages, these values were as expected.

In order to get a better picture of the challenges, we looked at five different categories for each language pair. This gave the picture in Table 4.

sma stands out with word order being the largest category, for the two others lexical selection is largest, whereas word generation is problematic

for smj. We comment on the different types below.

4.2.2 Lexical selection

sme–sma had more lexical selection changes than the other pairs and there was also less consensus among the evaluators as to what to change to. In no instances did the every evaluator agree what to replace the MT suggestion with. Either they disagreed on whether to replace the MT suggestion, or they differed as to what to replace it with. An example of the former is where one evaluator accepted *evtiedimmienuepieh* for *utviklingsmuligheter* ('development possibilities'), where the other one wanted *evtiedimmiehille* (*nuepie, hille* meaning 'possibility', *nuepie* also 'offer'). An example of the latter type was *bærekraftig* 'sustainable', where the MT *gaarsje* was replaced, either with *nænnoes* 'solid' or with *jijtjeguedteldh* 'self carrying'. Similar examples were also found for sme–smn and sme–smj.

A closer investigation of lexical choice by the evaluators shows that usually the lexemes found in the MT output were retained, indicating that the bilingual dictionary is solid. In the cases where the correct lexeme was not chosen by the system, evaluators did not agree on which was most appropriate.

4.2.3 Word form correction

The choice of wrong forms in the TL output had several causes. Often, the correcting of word form was due to lexical selection, replacing a verb may, for instance, result in changing case for the adverbial as well.

Another reason was difficulties in the SL input analysis, i.e., mistakenly resolved ambiguities. sme features a series of systematic homonymies such as gen vs. acc, inf vs. prs.pl1 as well as sg.com vs. pl.loc. These homonymies can not be preserved into any of TLs: the one–to–many map-

nob	De siste **fem årene** ...
sme	Maŋimus **viđa jagis** ...
sma-mt	Minngebe **vïjhtene jaepesne**...
sma-e1	Minngemes **vïjhte jaepie** ...
sma-e2	Minngemes **vïjhte jaepesne**...
sma-e3	Daah minngemes **vïjhte jaepieh**...
smj-mt	Maŋemus **vidán jagen**...
smj-e1	Maŋemus **vidán jagen** ...
smj-e2	Maŋemus **vidá jage** ...
smj-e3	Maŋemus **vihtta jage** ...
	The last **five years**...

Table 5: Translation of the phrase *de siste fem årene* 'the last five years'

ping problem. As sme input, the nom–acc ambiguous form *dieđusge* 'of course' in the context of the gen–acc ambiguous form *bohccuid* 'reindeers' as in *Ailu lea maiddái oaidnán luonddus máŋggaid ealliid, bohccuid dieđusge* ('Ailu has also seen in-the-nature many animals, reindeers of course'), triggers the wrong gen form *poccui* in smn, instead of the correct acc form *poccuid*. Similar errors were found for the other language pairs as well.

An example of the amount of variation is the translation of the phrase *de siste fem årene* 'the last five years' into sma and smj. As presented in Table 5, all six evaluators gave different versions of the phrase, and only one of them agreed with the MT output (for smj) . This demonstrates that the languages involved have weak norms.

4.2.4 Word generation correction

Word form generation correction occurs when there is a correct analysis of the input, there is a correct mapping in the bilingual dictionary, but some word forms in the TL are not generated properly or the evaluator prefers another possible normative form. Generation corrections constituted the smallest type of the post-editing corrections. This indicates that each transducer is an accurate representation of the grammar of the language it models. The FST use for the proofing tools of the different Saami languages also supports this observation. smj stands out with the worst results here, this is partly due to different orthographic conventions for smj in Norway and Sweden.

4.2.5 Reordering, addition, and deletion

A common type of word addition is the addition of grammatical words. Thus, for the original

stimulere til etablering av nye næringer innenfor nye bransjer ('stimulate the establishing of new businesses within new industries') the sme *odđa surggiin* 'new industry.loc' (from nob *innenfor nye bransjer* ('within new industries') was rendered with inessive *orre suerkine* by the system. One of the evaluators accepted this, and the other one inserted a postposition instead (*orre suerkiej sistie* 'new industry.pl.gen within.po').

There is no norm for how to write year-numerals in sma and smj, and two of the evaluators for smj and one for sma had added the word 'year' for the case marking, e.g. inessive in front of postposition in smj: *jagen 2000 rájes* 'year-ine 2000 from' 'from 2000'.

In all three Saami languages pro-drop is common, but the pronouns tend to be kept in translations from languages without pro-drop. Both for sma and smj two of the evaluators deleted the third person singular pronominal subject in the same sentence in the MT text.

Word order change was an issue sma and smj. smn sentences, however, kept the sme word order. This was accepted by the evaluators, as expected, given the high degree of syntactic similarity between the two languages.

4.3 Qualitative evaluation

In addition to the text discussed in the previous section (Text B), the evaluators got another, equally-sized text (Text A) in the original language (nob/fin), without a machine-translated version. The level of difficulty of Text A was estimated to be similar to that of Text B. In addition to post-editing or translating Text B to the target language, the evaluators were asked to translate Text A. The second part of the evaluation consisted in comparing the two tasks: translation with and without the help of a pivot language. This step was carried out via a questionnaire[7] containing three multiple choice questions (cf. Table 6):

1. Compare the time you spent on the two texts, Text A (translating from scratch) and Text B (using the MT version).

2. How did you use the MT version?

3. Do you think that such an MT program will be useful for you as a translator?

In addition, there were two open questions: The evaluators were asked to comment upon the terms suggested by the MT system that cannot be found

---

[7]The URL to the original texts sent out will be provided after review.

Time spent	sma	smj	smn	Σ
more time on A than B	0	3	1	4
same amount of time on both	2	0	2	4
more time on B than A	0	0	0	0
How did you use the MT version?	sma	smj	smn	Σ
I used it for post-editing	2	2	3	7
I translated from scratch ...				
... but used it to find terms	0	1	0	1
... but it was of some help	1	0	0	1
It is so bad that I cannot use it	0	0	0	0
Is this MT program useful?	sma	smj	smn	Σ
Yes, ...				
even as it is now	3	3	3	9
only after much improvement	0	0	0	0
only when almost perfect	0	0	0	0
No, I do not think so	0	0	0	0

Table 6: Answers to multiple choice questions

in relevant term collections, and they were invited to comment freely upon their experience with using the MT program.

Both the sma and smj evaluators appreciated the new terms suggested by the MT system, although, in several instances, they would not have used the terms proposed.

Except for one smn evaluator, who had no comments, all others had positive overall comments to the program. It was of 'great help', it did the job of looking up all unknown words, and it was able to consistently give a good translation, where a human translator might get bored and fall back to just copying the nob syntax.

4.4 Translating from scratch

One sma and one smj evaluator did not post-edit, instead, they translated the text from scratch, yet using the MT output as a reference. Both had considerably higher WER results that the evaluators who have post-edited the MT output. It seems that MT output post-editing in itself gives rise to solutions closer to the MT output, thus closer to the pivot language sme.

A case in point is when the nob original writes about *en analyse som Telemarksforskning har gjennomført for Sametinget,* 'an analysis which T. has conducted for the Saami parliament'. Both the MT and the two evaluators post-editing the output write *mej Telemarksforskning tjïrrehtamme Saemiedigkien åvteste,* on a par with the sme *lea čađahan Sámedikki ovddas.* The third evaluator, writing from scratch, finds a drastically different solution. In this translation, Telemarksforsking

conducts an analysis which the Saami parliament supports (*maam Saemiedægkan dorjeme*). Again, for the wording choices of the translated text, there is a difference between post-editing an MT output and translating from scratch.

5 Using a pivot language

The first manual step in the translation process, from the original to the pivot language, has clearly had an influence on the result. To investigate the impact of this influence on the current translation process, we compare the WER results in Section 4.2 from a parallel evaluation from sme to smn, yet, this time measured not against the fin original, but against the MT source language itself. Where the two-step translation process gave WER and PER values of 0.37 and 0.32, respectively (cf. Table 3), the corresponding values for a similar translation from North Saami as SL were 0.11 and 0.11, more than three times as good.

In retrospect, we see the following as a weakness in the evaluation. In the first step, from nob and fin to sme, we deliberately chose actual translations, in order to make what we saw as a realistic setup. The next step, from sme to the target Saami language, we conducted as described in 4.2.1. The result was that the two translation steps served different functions: The first step made a sme text for a concrete set of readers in a concrete setting, whereas the last step was part of a decontextualised evaluation process. Rather than aiming at a realistic case only for the first step, we should have ensured the same function across the whole translation chain, either by having translators translate (accurately) from nob/fin to sme, or by correcting the sme translation ourselves.

The syntactic analysis of the pivot language is crucial for the generation or the correct target language sentence and the importance of a correct syntactic analysis increases with larger syntactic differences between pivot and target language. The smj and sma evaluation texts were the same, and nine bad suggestions in the sma MT output text were due to incorrect analysis: five because of incorrect or deficient disambiguation and four because of incorrect syntactic tag. Due to syntactic similarities between sme and smj, the same nine errors in the input analysis caused only three errors in the smj MT output text.

The target languages of this study are continuously suffering from the lack of adequate terminology, especially concerning the modern society and special fields. For example 'archery', fin *jou-*

siammunta, was translated into sme with *dávgebis-suin báhčin* 'shooting with bow gun', wherefrom it can be taken into smn with *tävgipissoin pääččim*.

Secondly, also some idiomatic expressions could be created using MT. The fin expression *toiminnallisilla rasteilla* 'at functional posts' (along the trail) can not be literally translated. The sme translator has chosen for *doaimmálaš bargob-ádji* 'functional workshop'. The same expression *toimâlâš pargopääji* can also be used for smn:

> fin toiminnallisilla rasteilla tutustutaan muun muassa riis-tanhoitoon.
> sme Doaimmalaš bargobájiid áigge mánát besset oahpás-muvvat fuođđodikšumii.
> mt Toimâli [pargopáájái ääigi] párnááh peesih uápásmuđ pivdoelleetipšomân.
> e12 Toimâlij pargopáájáin párnááh peesih uápásmuđ piv-doelleetipšomân.
> e3 Toimâlij pargopáájái ääigi párnááh peesih uápásmuđ pivdoelleetipšomân.
> tr During the workshops the children get to know how the wild animals are treated.

Offering literal translations, dynamic compounding and derivation from sme, the program successfully suggests adequate terms or other translation solutions. This is possible while a perfect equivalence at word level between the pivot language and the TL exists. This phenomenon was pointed out by several evaluators, especially the sma ones, as a positive experience with MT translations.

6 Conclusion

We have presented a project in which we built three rule-based MT systems to translate from sme to sma, smj and smn, respectively. Each of the systems was tested for coverage and three evaluators post-edited the MT translations and gave feeback on the system quality via a questionnaire.

All the MT systems were judged as useful by the evaluators, especially with respect to terminology. All but two evaluators used the MT output as a basis for post-editing, rather than writing from scratch. Half of the evaluators found post-editing time-saving, the rest found it equally fast as manual transtion.

A central problem was the lack of a stable norm in the target languages, both with respect to terminology, orthography and syntax, which made it hard to present a translation that could gather consensus among the evaluators. The lion's share of the errors still came from the pivot translation not following the original. With manual translations into the pivot language being closer to the original text, we anticipate the present setup to improve considerably.

Acknowledgments

This work was financed by Norsk forskingsråd (grant No. 234299), the Kone Foundation as well as our university. Thanks to Erika Sarivaara for work with the smn transducer.

References

Lene Antonsen and Trond Trosterud. forthcoming. Ord sett innafra og utafra – en datalingvistisk analyse av nordsamisk. *Norsk Lingvistisk Tidsskrift*.

Lene Antonsen, Trond Trosterud, and Linda Wiechetek. 2010. Reusing grammatical resources for new languages. In *Proceedings of LREC-2010*, Valetta, Malta. ELRA.

Lene Antonsen, Trond Trosterud, and Francis Tyers. 2016. A North Saami to South Saami machine translation prototype. *Northern Europe Journal of Language Technology*, 4.

Bogdan Babych, Tony Hartley, and Serge Sharoff. 2007. Translating from under-resourced languages: comparing direct transfer against pivot translation. In *Proceedings of the MT Summit XI*, pages 29–35.

Mikel L. Forcada, Mireia Ginestí-Rosell, Jacob Nordfalk, Jim O'Regan, Sergio Ortiz-Rojas, Juan Antonio Pérez-Ortiz, Felipe Sánchez-Martínez, Gema Ramírez-Sánchez, and Francis M. Tyers. 2011. Apertium: a free/open-source platform for rule-based machine translation. *Machine Translation*, 25(2):127–144.

V. I. Levenshtein. 1965. Binary codes capable of correcting deletions, insertions and reversals. *Soviet Physics Doklady 10, 707–710, trans. from Doklady Akademii Nauk SSSR*, 163:845–848.

Francois Masselot, Petra Ribiczey, and Gema Ramírez-Sánchez. 2010. Using the apertium spanish-brazilian portuguese machine translation system for localization. In *Proceedings of the 14th Annual Conference of the European Association for Machine Translation, EAMT10*.

Annika Pasanen. 2015. *Kuávsui já peeivičuová. 'Sarastus ja päivänvalo' : Inarinsaamen kielen revitalisaatio*. Uralica Helsingiensia, Helsinki.

Trond Trosterud and Kevin Brubeck Unhammer. 2013. Evaluating North Sámi to Norwegian assimilation RBMT. In *Proceedings of the Third International Workshop on Free/Open-Source Rule-Based Machine Translation (FreeRBMT 2012)*, volume 3 of *Technical report*, pages 13–26. Department of Computer Science and Engineering, Chalmers University of Technology and University of Gothenburg.

Francis Tyers, Linda Wiechetek, and Trond Trosterud.
2009. Developing prototypes for machine translation between two Sámi languages. In *Proceedings
of the 13th Annual Conference of the European Association for Machine Translation, EAMT09*, pages
120–128.

Linda Wiechetek, Francis Tyers, and Thomas Omma.
2010. Shooting at flies in the dark: Rule-based lexical selection for a minority language pair. *Lecture
Notes in Artificial Intelligence*, 6233:418–429.

SWEGRAM – A Web-Based Tool for Automatic Annotation and Analysis of Swedish Texts

Jesper Näsman
Linguistics and Philology
Uppsala University
jesper.nasman@lingfil.uu.se

Beáta Megyesi
Linguistics and Philology
Uppsala University
beata.megyesi@lingfil.uu.se

Anne Palmér
Scandinavian Languages
Uppsala University
anne.palmer@nordiska.uu.se

Abstract

We present SWEGRAM, a web-based tool for the automatic linguistic annotation and quantitative analysis of Swedish text, enabling researchers in the humanities and social sciences to annotate their own text and produce statistics on linguistic and other text-related features on the basis of this annotation. The tool allows users to upload one or several documents, which are automatically fed into a pipeline of tools for tokenization and sentence segmentation, spell checking, part-of-speech tagging and morpho-syntactic analysis as well as dependency parsing for syntactic annotation of sentences. The analyzer provides statistics on the number of tokens, words and sentences, the number of parts of speech (PoS), readability measures, the average length of various units, and frequency lists of tokens, lemmas, PoS, and spelling errors. SWEGRAM allows users to create their own corpus or compare texts on various linguistic levels.

1 Introduction

Although researchers in natural language processing have focused for decades on the development of tools for the automatic linguistic analysis of languages and state-of-the-art systems for linguistic analysis have achieved a high degree of accuracy today, these tools are still not widely used by scholars in the humanities and social sciences. The main reason is that many of the tools require programming skills to prepare and process texts. Furthermore, these tools are not linked in a straightforward way to allow the annotation and analysis on different linguistic levels that could be used easily in data-driven text research.

In this paper, we present SWEGRAM, a web-based tool for the automatic linguistic annotation and quantitative analysis of Swedish text, which allows researchers in the humanities and social sciences to annotate their own text or create their own corpus and produce statistics on linguistic and other text-related features based on the annotation. SWEGRAM requires no previous knowledge of text processing or any computer skills, and is available online for anyone to use.[1]

We start with a brief overview of some important infrastructural tools for processing language data. In Section 3 we give an introduction to SWEGRAM along with our goals and considerations in developing the web-based tool. Following this introductory section, we present the components used for the linguistic annotation on several levels, and the format of the data representation. We then give an overview of quantitative linguistic analysis, providing statistics on various linguistic features for text analysis. In Section 4 we describe a linguistic study of student essays to illustrate how SWEGRAM can be used by scholars in the humanities. Finally, in Section 5, we conclude the paper and identify some future challenges.

2 Background

To make language technology applications available and useful to scholars of all disciplines, in particular researchers in the humanities and social sciences has attracted great attention in the language technology community in the past years. One aim is to create language resources and tools that are readily available for automatic linguistic analysis and can help in quantitative text analysis. Important resources are corpora and lexicons of various kinds. Basic tools usually include a tokenizer for the automatic segmentation of tokens and sentences, a lemmatizer for finding the base form of words, a part-of-speech (PoS) tagger to annotate the words with their PoS and morpholog-

---

[1] http://stp.lingfil.uu.se/swegram/

Proceedings of the 21st Nordic Conference of Computational Linguistics, pages 132–141,
Gothenburg, Sweden, 23-24 May 2017. ©2017 Linköping University Electronic Press

ical features, and a syntactic parser to annotate the syntactic structure of the sentence.

Creating infrastructure for language analyis is not new and several projects have been focusing on developing on-line services for collection, annotation and/or analysis of language data with joint effort from the LT community. One of the important projects is the European Research Infrastructure for Language Resources and Technology CLARIN[2] with nodes in various countries, such as the Swedish SWE-CLARIN[3]. During the past years, we have seen a noticable increase in web-services allowing storage, annotation and/or analysis of data for various languages. Such example include LAP: The CLARINO Language Analysis Portal that was developed to allow large-scale processing service for many European languages (Kouylekov et al., 2014; Lapponi et al., 2014); WebLicht, a web-based tool for semi-annotation and visualization of language data (Hinrichs et al., 2010; CLARIN-D/SfS-Uni. Tübingen, 2012); The Australian project Alveo: Above and Beyond Speech, Language and Music infrastructure, a virtual lab for human communication science, for easy access to language resources that can be shared with workflow tools for data processing (Estival and Cassidy, 2016).

Many language technology tools are readily available as off-the-shelf packages and achieve a high degree of accuracy, including the analysis of Swedish text. A pipeline in which standard annotation tools can be run on-line was recently established through SPARV (Borin et al., 2016) at the Swedish Language Bank (Språkbanken),[4] for the linguistic analysis of uploaded text, including tokenization, lemmatization, word senses, compound analysis, named-entity recognition, PoS and syntactic analysis using dependency structures. Users can access the annotation directly online, or download the results as an XML document. The goal is to provide linguistic annotation and allow further analysis using Språkbanken's own corpus search tool, Korp (Borin et al., 2012).[5]

Many tools are available for various types of text analysis. These include search programs for analyzing specific resources or corpora. Examples include Xaira,[6] an open source software package that supports indexing and analysis of corpora using XML, which was originally developed for the British National Corpus; the BNCWeb (Hoffmann et al., 2008), a web-based interface for the British National Corpus; or Korp (Borin et al., 2012), for searches of Swedish corpora. Other popular tools are concordance programs, such as AntConc,[7] Webcorp[8] and ProtAnt (Anthony and Baker, 2015), which also displays other text related features such as frequencies, collocations and keywords. WordSmith Tools (Scott, 2016) is also commonly used for text analysis, allowing the creation of word lists with frequencies, concordance lists, clusters, collocations and keywords.

Next, we describe SWEGRAM, a publicly available on-line tool for corpus creation, annotation and data-driven analysis of Swedish text.

3 SWEGRAM

The main goal of SWEGRAM is to provide a simple web-based tool that allows linguistic annotation and quantitative analysis of Swedish text without any expert knowledge in natural language processing. SWEGRAM consists of two separate web-based applications: annotation and analysis. In the web-based interface, users can upload one or several text files of their choice and receive the annotated text(s), which can be sent for further text analysis, as specified by the user.

The annotation includes tokenization and sentence segmentation, normalization in terms of spelling correction, PoS tagging including morphological features, and dependency parsing to represent the syntactic structure of the sentence. The annotation tool can be used to annotate individual texts or create a large collection of annotated texts, a corpus.

Once the data set is uploaded and annotated, the analyzer provides information about the number of tokens, words, and sentences; the distribution of PoS and morphological features; various readability measures; average length of different units (such as words, tokens, sentences); frequency lists and spelling errors.

In developing SWEGRAM, we wanted to create a tool with open source components that was freely accessible, where users can upload any text without it being saved by the system. Another important goal was to build a modular system

[2]https://www.clarin.eu/
[3]https://sweclarin.se/eng/about
[4]https://spraakbanken.gu.se/sparv/
[5]https://spraakbanken.gu.se/korp/
[6]http://projects.oucs.ox.ac.uk/xaira/Doc/refman.xml

[7]http://www.laurenceanthony.net/software.html
[8]http://www.webcorp.org.uk/live/

in which the components involved can be easily changed as better models are developed, while individual components can be built on one another with a simple representation format that is easy to understand.

The pipeline handling linguistic annotation is written mainly in Python, and the user interface was developed using regular HTML, CSS and JavaScript. The backend of the web interface was developed using the Django web framework. Next, we will describe the components included for annotation and analysis in more detail.

3.1 Automatic Annotation

In order to automatically process and annotate texts, we use state-of-the-art natural language processing tools trained on Swedish standard texts with a documented high degree of performance. The annotation pipeline is illustrated in Figure 1. When a file is uploaded, the document is preprocessed by converting the file into a plain text format. The text is segmented into sentences and tokens by a tokenizer and misspelled tokens are corrected for spelling errors by a normalizer. The corrected text is run through a PoS tagger and lemmatizer to get the base form of the words and their correct PoS and morphological annotation given the context. Finally, the sentences are syntactically analyzed by a parsing module using dependency analysis. The following subsections contain descriptions of each of these modules.

3.1.1 Preprocessing

In many cases, SWEGRAM does not require any preprocessing of documents. Users can upload documents in formats such as DOC, DOCX and RTF and the document is automatically converted into a plain text file encoded in UTF-8, which is what the annotation pipeline requires as input. The text is converted using unoconv,[9] which can handle any format that LibreOffice is able to import.

3.1.2 Tokenization

Tokenization is used to separate the words from punctuation marks and segment the sentences. Two tokenizers were considered for SWEGRAM: the tokenizer written in Java and used in the PoS tagger Stagger (Östling, 2013) and the Svannotate tokenizer, originally developed for the Swedish Treebank (Nivre et al., 2008). A comparison was made between these tokenizers, and only a

___
[9]https://github.com/dagwieers/unoconv

few differences were found, since both tokenizers achieved similar results. However, while Svannotate is an independent, rule-based tokenizer written in Python, Stagger's tokenizer is built into the PoS tagger. We chose to include Svannotate for modularity and consistency in the pipeline since it is written in Python, like the rest of SWEGRAM.

In evaluating Svannotate to tokenize student writings (Megyesi et al., 2016), errors that occurred were due in part to the inconsistent use of punctuation marks – for example, when a sentence does not always end with an appropriate punctuation mark, either because abbreviations are not always spelled correctly or a new sentence does not always begin with a capital letter.

Since the annotation pipeline is modular, users have the option of tokenizing a text, manually correcting it and then using the corrected version for the remaining steps.

3.1.3 Normalization

After tokenization and sentence segmentation, normalization is carried out in the form of spelling correction, including correction of erroneously split compounds. Since there is no open source, state-of-the-art normalizer that is readily available for Swedish, we used a modified version of HistNorm (Pettersson et al., 2013) for spelling correction. HistNorm was originally developed to transform words in historical texts that had substantial variation in possible spellings of their modern variant using either Levenshtein-based normalization or normalization based on statistical machine translation (SMT). When used on historical data, HistNorm achieves accuracy of 92.9% on Swedish text, based on SMT. For texts written by students, however, we found that the Levenshtein-based normalization gave better results.

One type of spelling error that occurs frequently in Swedish is erroneously split compounds, that is, compounds that are split into two or more words instead of written as one word. If we consider the Swedish compound *kycklinglever* (chicken liver), erroneously splitting the words would form the two words *kyckling* (chicken) and *lever* (is alive). This significantly alters the meaning of the phrase and will affect the final output of the annotation, making the statistical analysis less accurate. Addressing these errors can lead to an improved annotation performance. This problem is addressed using a rule-based system as described by (Öhrman, 1998). Because of the PoS tags

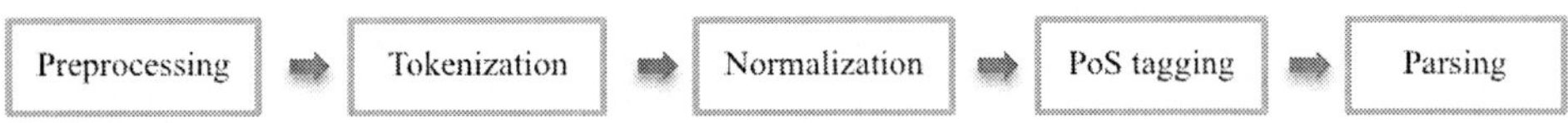

Figure 1: Screenshot of the web-based annotation interface.

rules for identifying split compounds for each token, PoS tagging has to be performed prior to correcting compounds. The text is then tagged again using the corrected compounds. We will return to how these types of corrections are represented while still keeping the original tokens in Section 3.1.6.

Further analysis and improvement are needed to adapt this normalization tool to texts written in less standard Swedish for a higher degree of accuracy.

3.1.4 Morpho-Syntactic Annotation

For the PoS and morphological annotation of the normalized texts, we use two types of annotation. One is based on the universal PoS tagset,[10] which consists of 17 main PoS categories: adjective, adposition, adverb, auxiliary, coordinating conjunction, determiner, interjection, noun, numeral, particle, pronoun, proper noun, punctuation, subordinating conjunction, symbol, verb and others with their morphological features. The other tagset used is the Stockholm-Umeå Corpus tagset (Gustafson-Capková and Hartmann, 2006), which contains 23 main PoS categories.

We compared two commonly used PoS taggers for Swedish, HunPos (Halácsy et al., 2007) and Stagger (Östling, 2013), and evaluated their performance on our test data. Both taggers used models trained on what is normally used as a standard corpus for Swedish, the Stockholm Umeå Corpus (Gustafson-Capková and Hartmann, 2006). The accuracy of these taggers when trained and evaluated on SUC 2.0 is very similar, 95.9% for HunPos (Megyesi, 2008) and 96.6% for Stagger (Östling, 2013). Testing these taggers on the Uppsala Corpus of Student Writings (Megyesi et al., 2016) using SUC models, Stagger performed slightly better. Another advantage of Stagger is that it can also perform lemmatization.

However, we ultimately decided to use a re-implementation of Stagger, the tagger called Efficient Sequence Labeler (efselab),[11] as the default tagger. This, like Stagger, uses an averaged perceptron learning algorithm, but Efselab has the ad-

vantage that it performs PoS tagging significantly faster (about one million tokens a second) while achieving similar performance results as Stagger.

3.1.5 Syntactic Annotation

The final step in the annotation pipeline is the syntactic annotation in terms of dependency structure. We apply universal dependencies (UD) (Nivre et al., 2016) to mark syntactic structures and relations where one word is the head of the sentence, attached to a ROOT, and all other words are dependent on another word in a sentence. Dependency relations are marked between content words while function words are direct dependents of the most closely related content word. Punctuation marks are attached to the head of the clause or phrase to which they belong. The UD taxonomy distinguishes between core arguments such as subjects, direct and indirect objects, clausal complements, and other non-core or nominal dependents. For a detailed description of the dependency structure and annotation, we refer readers to the UD website.[12]

To annotate the sentences with UD, we use MaltParser 1.8.1 (Nivre et al., 2006), along with a model trained on the Swedish data with Universal Dependencies (UD). Since parser input needs to be in the form of the universal tagset, the tags need to be converted. This conversion is carried out using a script that comes with efselab, which converts SUC to UD.

Since UD was developed in our field of natural language processing only recently, it has not been used widely by scholars outside our community. In the near future, we will experiment with various types of syntactic representation.

3.1.6 Format

In order to make it easy for scholars in the humanities to interpret the annotated texts, we chose the CoNLL-U tab-separated format[13] instead of an XML-based representation. Sentences consist of one or more lines of words where each line represents a single word/token with a series of 11 fields

---

[10]http://universaldependencies.org/u/pos/
[11]https://github.com/robertostling/efselab

[12]http://universaldependencies.org/
[13]http://universaldependencies.org/format.html

with separate tabs for various annotation types. Table 1 describes the fields that represent the analysis of each token. New sentences are preceded by a blank line, which marks sentence boundaries. Comment lines starting with hash (#) are also allowed and may be used for metadata information (such as sentence numbering) for the sentence following immediately. All annotations are encoded in plain text files in UTF-8.

In Table 2 an example is provided of an annotated text in the CoNLL-U format. In this example, the original text contains a spelling mistake, *vekan*, corrected as *veckan* in the column NORM, where the corrected form is analyzed. The example sentence also contains an erroneously split compound – *Syd Korea* which should be written as one word, *Sydkorea*. The corrected word is given the index numbers of the two original words, in this case 4-5, where the corrected version is analyzed linguistically while the original forms are left as they are without any further analysis.

Text containing metadata has been an important factor in the development of SWEGRAM. Metadata containing information about the text such as the author's age, gender, geographic area or type of text can be parsed and used during analysis, allowing users to filter their texts based on the metadata provided, and produce statistics on the features of the particular text(s). The metadata should be represented in the format <feature1, feature2 ... featureN>. Development is currently under way to allow metadata of any type (defined by the user) to be used in annotation and analysis.

3.1.7 Web-based Annotation Tool

The web-based annotation tool is illustrated in Figure 2. Users can upload one or several texts and annotate them.

Figure 2: Screenshot of the web-based annotation interface.

Modularity has been an important factor in developing the annotation tool. Any module can be deactivated, which enables users to exclude some part of the annotation if they wish and use their own annotation instead. For example, users can upload a text that is already tokenized in order to annotate it with PoS and syntactic features. After tokenization, normalization can also be carried out in the form of spell checking and correction of erroneously split compound words, or a text that is already corrected can be uploaded. Similarly, users could correct the PoS annotation given by the tool and run the syntactic analyzer on the corrected PoS tagged data. Users are thus free to decide which particular tools are needed, and the subsequent linguistic annotation is based on corrected, normalized forms, which could help improve the performance of subsequent steps since corrected data are used.

Each module may include several algorithms and models depending on the corpus data the models were trained on. We include the most frequently used models with the highest accuracy on standard Swedish, which were evaluated and published previously.

Moreover, the pipeline is built in such a way that new, better analyzers can be plugged into the system. It is also possible to select different models for the PoS tagger and the syntactic parser, but currently only one model is provided for each, both based on Stockholm-Umeå Corpus (SUC) 3.0 (Gustafson-Capková and Hartmann, 2006) and previously evaluated with a documented high degree of accuracy. However, one restriction in choosing syntactic annotation (the parser and parser model) is that only the PoS model that the parser was trained on may be run during the PoS tagging module to get consistent annotation.

Another important factor was that the format should be readable and easy to understand so that users can manually examine the data annotated. The results are made available to users in the form of a downloadable plain text file encoded in UTF-8 or shown directly on the web-page. In contrast to formats like SGML or XML, the CoNLL-U format, which is tab-separated with one token per line and has various linguistic fields represented in various columns, is well suited for our purposes. The format with fields separated by tabs allows users to import their file in Excel or another tool of their choice to carry out further quantitative analysis.

Since the corpus format allows several types of

FEATURE	Description
TEXT ID	Paragraph-sentence index, integer starting at 1 for each new paragraph and sentence
TOKEN ID	Token index, integer starting at 1 for each new sentence; may be a range for tokens with multiple words
FORM	Word form or punctuation symbol
NORM	Corrected/normalized token (e.g. in case of spelling error)
LEMMA	Lemma or stem of word form
UPOS	Part-of-speech tag based on universal part-of-speech tag
XPOS	Part-of-speech tag based on the Stockholm-Umeå Corpus; underscore if not available
XFEATS	List of morphological features for XPOS; underscore if not available
UFEATS	List of morphological features for UPOS; underscore if not available
HEAD	Head of the current token, which is either a value of ID or zero (0)
DEPREL	Dependency relation to the HEAD (root iff HEAD = 0) based on the Swedish Treebank annotation
DEPS	List of secondary dependencies (head-deprel pairs)
MISC	Any other annotation

Table 1: Annotation representation format for each token and field.

TEXT ID	ID	FORM	NORM	LEMMA	UPOS	XPOS	XFEATS	UFEATS	HEAD	DEPREL	DEPS	MISC
2.4	1	Jag	Jag	jag	PRON	PN	UTR |SIN |DEF |SUB	Case=Nom|Definite=Def|Gender=Com|Number=Sing	0	root	_	I
2.4	2	var	var	vara	VERB	VB	PRT |AKT	Mood=Ind|Tense=Past|VerbForm=Fin|Voice=Act	1	acl	_	was
2.4	3	i	i	i	ADP	PP	_	_	4-5	case	_	in
2.4	4-5		Sydkorea	Sydkorea	PROPN	PM	NOM	Case=Nom	2	nmod	_	South Korea
2.4	4	Syd	Syd									South
2.4	5	Korea	Korea									Korea
2.4	6	förra	förra	förra	ADJ	JJ	POS |UTR/NEU |SIN |DEF |NOM	Case=Nom|Definite=Def|Degree=Pos|Number=Sing	7	det	_	last
2.4	7	vekan	veckan	vecka	NOUN	NN	UTR |SIN |DEF |NOM	Case=Nom|Definite=Def|Gender=Com|Number=Sing	4-5	nmod	_	week
2.4	8	.	.	.	PUNCT	MAD	_	_	1	punct	_	.

Table 2: Example of the extended CoNLL-U shared task format for the sentence *Jag var i Syd Korea förra vekan* (I was in South Korea last week). It contains one misspelled word, *veckan*, and one erroneously split compound, *Syd Korea* – South Korea, which should be a single compound word in Swedish. Note that the *MISC* column here is used to provide English translations for this table.

annotation by including additional columns, users can easily choose between them based on their desires or choose to have all annotations available.

3.2 Automatic Quantitative Analysis

Users can upload one or several annotated texts for further quantitative analysis. Statistics are calculated and shown on several levels: for all texts, and if the text file is divided into several subtexts, for each of these. Figure 3 illustrates the start page of the quantitative analysis where information is given about the number of uploaded texts, words, tokens and sentences.

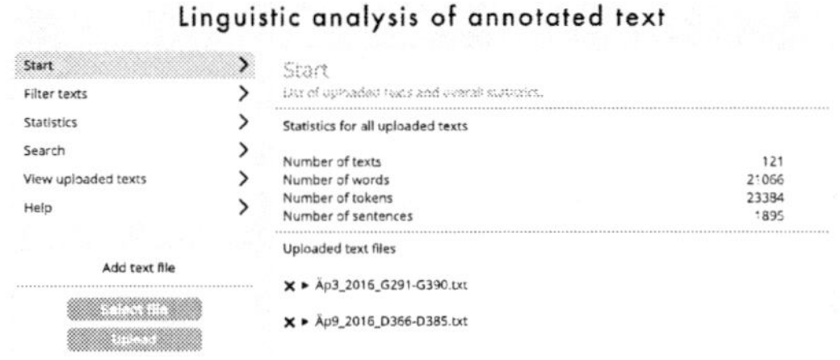

Figure 3: Automatic quantitative analysis.

The following features can be extracted automatically: number of tokens, words, sentences, texts and PoS; readability measures; average length of words, tokens, sentences, paragraphs and texts; frequency lists of tokens, lemmas and PoS; and spelling errors.

The statistical calculations are divided into three sections: general statistics, frequencies and spelling errors. General statistics provide users with the option of including statistics for all PoS or for specific ones, readability metrics in terms of LIX, OVIX and the nominal ratio, and frequencies of word length above, below or at a specific threshold value.

The frequencies section can provide users with frequency lists for all texts and for individual texts. These can be based on lemmas or tokens, with or without delimiters. In addition, the frequency lists can be sorted based on frequencies or words (lemmas or tokens) in alphabetical order. The frequency lists can also be limited to specific parts of speech.

The spelling errors section provides a list of spelling errors sorted by frequency, for all uploaded texts and for individual texts.

In addition, users can generate statistics by filtering the texts using metadata information. In order to do so, the uploaded texts have to be marked up with metadata as described in Section 3.1.6.

Given each field, the texts can be filtered based on the properties of the metadata. Examples of analyses are provided in the next section.

Users can also specify whether the output should be delivered as a downloadable file separated by tabs, which can be imported into other programs such as Excel for further analysis, or shown directly in the browser.

Separately from the statistics, users can also view the uploaded texts in their entirety and perform different types of searches in the annotated text. This includes searching for words, lemmas and PoS tags that either start with, end with, contain or exactly match a user-defined search query. The results are then printed and sorted according to what texts they appear in.

4   User Study

In this section we will demonstrate some of the possibilities of using SWEGRAM to analyze student writing as part of the national test carried out by school children in Sweden. We concentrate on two texts which are interesting to compare because they have some features in common but also differ in terms of the age of the writers, with the difference being three school years. Without making use of SWEGRAMs capacity to analyze extensive data, we simply want to demonstrate some features included in the tool and what they can show about the characteristics of the two texts.

Essay D245, from the last year of compulsory school, and essay C381, from the final year of upper secondary school, both represent the expository genre. Both essays have also been used as examples, benchmarks, of essays receiving the highest grade in the guide for assessing national tests. Therefore these two essays are both considered to be good writing for their respective school year. However, there is a three-year difference in age between the students, and the writing assignments given in the tests are different. Text D245 discusses a general subject, love. The introduction of the essay, translated into English, is: *Would you risk sacrificing your life for love, would you risk turning your entire existence upside down? The question is not easy to answer.* Text C381 is an expository essay on the fairytale *Sleeping Beauty*, which makes the subject more specific. The introduction to this essay is translated into English as: *Folk tales – anonymous stories that have been passed down from one generation to the next no matter where humans have lived /.../ Why is this old fairytale still widely read in society today?*.

We compare the documents in terms of different features that can give information relevant to text quality and writing development, such as lexical variation and specification, word frequencies, nominal ratio and distribution of parts-of speech.

Looking at the lexical variation, the two texts are about the same length; D245 has 790 words and C381 has 713 words. But the average word length of the text from upper secondary school is higher than that of the text from compulsory school, as shown in Table 3.

	D245	**C381**
Word length	4.70	5.66
Ovix	52.87	81.70
Nominal ratio	0.55	1.35
Sentence length	20.27	25.73

Table 3: Some measures from SWEGRAM.

These results indicate that C381 may be more specified and lexically varied than D245, since longer words correlate with specification and variation in a text (Hultman and Westman, 1977; Vagle, 2005). Lexical variation in a text can also be measured by Ovix, a word variation index (Hultman and Westman, 1977). This measure shows the same tendencies: more variation in the text from upper secondary school.

The lexicon can further be studied using SWEGRAMs word frequency lists. In the list of nouns we look for long, compound nouns, since this is considered one feature of Swedish academic language. We find a number of these long words, several with more than 12 letters, in C 381. In D 245 there are a few compound nouns but none as long as this, which makes the lexicon of this text less specified and dense.

Nominal ratio is used to measure the nominality of the text. A high nominal ratio indicates high information load, whereas a low nominal ratio indicates a less dense text (Magnusson and Johansson Kokkinakis, 2011). Texts with high nominality are often conceived as having more of a written style, whereas lower values tend to give the text a more colloquial character. The difference in the nominal ratio for the two texts is substantial, 0.55 in D245 and as high as 1.35 in C381, as shown in Table 3. As a result, the essay from upper secondary school is considerably more nominal, has a higher information load and presumably has more of a written style than the essay from compulsory school. The surprisingly high value of the nominal ratio in C381 could partly be explained by the fact that there are several references to other works in this text, and these include long nominal phrases.

D245	C381
VB (17.38%)	NN (19.82%)
NN (12.33%)	VB (13.34%)
PN (11.66%)	PP (11.27%)
AB (10.87%)	AB (7.12%)
PP (8.30%)	JJ (6.99%)

Table 4: The five most frequently occurring parts of speech.

A look at the parts of speech used most frequently shows that D245 is rich in verbs and pronouns, parts of speech that characterize a colloquial style; see Table 4. C381, on the other hand, has high proportions of nouns and prepositions, which are important words in forming nominal phrases.

Table 3 shows that there is a difference in the average sentence length in the two essays: 20.27 words in D245 and 25.73 in C381. Since longer sentences may contain more clauses than shorter ones, this result indicates that the syntax of the essay from upper secondary school may be more complex that in D 245. The hypothesis can be controlled by a frequency list of conjunctions and subjunctions, words that connect clauses. In D245 there are six different conjunctions and three different subjunctions, a total of nine connectives of this kind. In C381 there are eight different conjunctions and four subjunctions, a total of twelve different words. So the variation in connectives is more important in C381. The distribution of parts of speech also shows that conjunctions and subjunctions occur more frequently in C381 (KN + SN 7.12 %) than in D245 (KN + SN 5.54 %), which supports the hypothesis.

In summary, the analysis shows considerable differences between the two essays, as regards the lexicon, distribution of PoS and syntax. However, the result should not be interpreted in relation to the writing competence or writing development shown in the student texts. The purpose is to show the potential of analyses made with SWEGRAM without using the appropriate amount of data.

5   Conclusion

We presented a web-based interface for the automatic annotation and quantitative analysis of Swedish. The web-based tool enables users to upload a file, which is then automatically fed into a pipeline of tools for tokenization and sentence segmentation, spell checking, PoS tagging and morpho-syntactic analysis as well as dependency parsing for syntactic annotation of sentences. Users can then send the annotated file for further quantitative analysis of the linguistically annotated data. The analyzer provides statistics about the number of tokens, words, sentences, number of PoS, readability measures, average length of various units (such as words, tokens and sentences), frequency lists of tokens, lemmas and PoS, and spelling errors. Statistics can be also extracted based on metadata, given that metadata are defined by the user.

The tool can be easily used for the analysis of a single text, for the comparison of several texts, or for the creation of an entire corpus of the user's choice by uploading a number of text documents. The tool has been used succesfully in the creation of the Uppsala Corpus of Student Writings (Megyesi et al., 2016). Since SWEGRAM will be used to create corpora, the possibility of customizing the content and format of metadata is something that could be beneficial to users and will be implemented in the near future.

The tools are readily available and can be used by anyone who is interested in the linguistic annotation of Swedish text. As better models for standard Swedish are presented, our intention is to include them in the interface along with the old models to allow comparative studies. Our priority for further improvement is the normalization tool since there is no readily available open source tool for automatic spelling and grammar correction of Swedish. In addition, we would like to implement a visualization tool of the linguistic analysis, especially syntax, which will also facilitate syntactic searches.

Acknowledgments

This project was supported by SWE-CLARIN, a Swedish consortium in Common Language Resources and Technology Infrastructure (CLARIN) financed by the Swedish Research Council for the period 2014–2018.

References

Laurence Anthony and Paul Baker. 2015. ProtAnt: A tool for analysing the prototypicality of texts. *International Journal of Corpus Linguistics*, 20(3):273–292.

Lars Borin, Markus Forsberg, and Johan Roxendal. 2012. Korp – the corpus infrastructure of Språkbanken. In *Proceedings of the 8th International Conference on Language Resources and Evaluation*, LREC 2012, page 474478.

Lars Borin, Markus Forsberg, Martin Hammarstedt, Dan Rosén, Anne Schumacher, and Roland Schäfer. 2016. Sparv: Språkbanken's corpus annotation pipeline infrastructure. In *SLTC 2016*.

CLARIN-D/SfS-Uni. Tübingen. 2012. WebLicht: Web-Based Linguistic Chaining Tool. Online. Date Accessed: 28 Mar 2017. URL https://weblicht.sfs.uni-tuebingen.de/ .

Dominique Estival and Steve Cassidy. 2016. Alveo: Above and beyond speech, language and music, a virtual lab for human communication science. Online. Date Accessed: 28 Mar 2017. URL http://alveo.edu.au/about/.

Sofia Gustafson-Capková and Britt Hartmann, 2006. *Documentation of the Stockholm - Umeå Corpus*. Stockholm University: Department of Linguistics.

Péter Halácsy, András Kornai, and Csaba Oravecz. 2007. Hunpos: An open source trigram tagger. In *Proceedings of the 45th Annual Meeting of the ACL on Interactive Poster and Demonstration Sessions*, ACL '07, pages 209–212, Stroudsburg, PA, USA. Association for Computational Linguistics.

Erhard W. Hinrichs, Marie Hinrichs, and Thomas Zastrow. 2010. Weblicht: Web-based LRT services for German. In *Proceedings of the ACL 2010 System Demonstrations*, pages 25–29.

Sebastian Hoffmann, Stefan Evert, Nicholas Smith, David Lee, and Ylva Berglund Prytz. 2008. *Corpus Linguistics with BNCweb – A Practical Guide*. Frankfurt am Main: Peter Lang.

Tor G. Hultman and Margareta Westman. 1977. *Gymnasistsvenska*. LiberLäromedel, Lund.

Milen Kouylekov, Emanuele Lapponi, Stephan Oepen, Erik Velldal, and Nikolay Aleksandrov Vazov. 2014. LAP: The language analysis portal. Online. Date Accessed: 28 Mar 2017. URL http://www.mn.uio.no/ifi/english/research/projects/-clarino/.

Emanuele Lapponi, Erik Velldal, Stephan Oepen, and Rune Lain Knudsen. 2014. Off-road laf: Encoding and processing annotations in nlp workflows. In *9th edition of the Language Resources and Evaluation Conference (LREC)*.

Ulrika Magnusson and Sofie Johansson Kokkinakis. 2011. Computer-Based Quantitative Methods Applied to First and Second Language Student Writing. In Inger Källström and Inger Lindberg, editors, *Young Urban Swedish. Variation and change in multilingual settings*, pages 105–124. Göteborgsstudier i nordisk språkvetenskap 14. University of Gothenburg.

Beáta Megyesi, Jesper Näsman, and Anne Palmér. 2016. The Uppsala corpus of student writings: Corpus creation, annotation, and analysis. In Nicoletta Calzolari (Conference Chair), Khalid Choukri, Thierry Declerck, Sara Goggi, Marko Grobelnik, Bente Maegaard, Joseph Mariani, Helene Mazo, Asuncion Moreno, Jan Odijk, and Stelios Piperidis, editors, *Proceedings of the Tenth International Conference on Language Resources and Evaluation (LREC 2016)*, pages 3192–3199, Paris, France. European Language Resources Association (ELRA).

Beáta Megyesi. 2008. *The Open Source Tagger HunPoS for Swedish*. Uppsala University: Department of Linguistics and Philology.

Joakim Nivre, Johan Hall, and Jens Nilsson. 2006. Maltparser. In *Proceedings of the 5th International Conference on Language Resources and Evaluation*, LREC '06, pages 2216–2219.

Joakim Nivre, Beáta Megyesi, Sofia Gustafson-Capková, Filip Salomonsson, and Bengt Dahlqvist. 2008. Cultivating a Swedish treebank. In Joakim Nivre, Mats Dahllöf, and Beáta Megyesi, editors, *Resourceful Language Technology: A Festschrift in Honor of Anna Sågvall Hein*, pages 111–120.

Joakim Nivre, Željko Agić, Lars Ahrenberg, Maria Jesus Aranzabe, Masayuki Asahara, Aitziber Atutxa, Miguel Ballesteros, John Bauer, Kepa Bengoetxea, Yevgeni Berzak, Riyaz Ahmad Bhat, Eckhard Bick, Carl Börstell, Cristina Bosco, Gosse Bouma, Sam Bowman, Gülşen Cebirolu Eryiit, Giuseppe G. A. Celano, Fabrıcıo Chalub, Çar Çöltekin, Miriam Connor, Elizabeth Davidson, Marie-Catherine de Marneffe, Arantza Diaz de Ilarraza, Kaja Dobrovoljc, Timothy Dozat, Kira Droganova, Puneet Dwivedi, Marhaba Eli, Tomaž Erjavec, Richárd Farkas, Jennifer Foster, Claudia Freitas, Katarína Gajdošová, Daniel Galbraith, Marcos Garcia, Moa Gärdenfors, Sebastian Garza, Filip Ginter, Iakes Goenaga, Koldo Gojenola, Memduh Gökrmak, Yoav Goldberg, Xavier Gómez Guinovart, Berta Gonzáles Saavedra, Matias Grioni, Normunds Grūzītis, Bruno Guillaume, Jan Hajič, Linh Hà M, Dag Haug, Barbora Hladká, Radu Ion, Elena Irimia, Anders Johannsen, Fredrik Jørgensen, Hüner Kaşkara, Hiroshi Kanayama, Jenna Kanerva, Boris Katz, Jessica Kenney, Natalia Kotsyba, Simon Krek, Veronika Laippala, Lucia Lam, Phng Lê Hng, Alessandro Lenci, Nikola Ljubešić, Olga Lyashevskaya, Teresa Lynn, Aibek Makazhanov, Christopher Manning, Cătălina Mărănduc, David Mareček, Héctor Martínez Alonso, André Martins, Jan Mašek, Yuji Matsumoto, Ryan McDonald, Anna

Missilä, Verginica Mititelu, Yusuke Miyao, Simonetta Montemagni, Keiko Sophie Mori, Shunsuke Mori, Bohdan Moskalevskyi, Kadri Muischnek, Nina Mustafina, Kaili Müürisep, Lng Nguyn Th, Huyn Nguyn Th Minh, Vitaly Nikolaev, Hanna Nurmi, Petya Osenova, Robert Östling, Lilja Øvrelid, Valeria Paiva, Elena Pascual, Marco Passarotti, Cenel-Augusto Perez, Slav Petrov, Jussi Piitulainen, Barbara Plank, Martin Popel, Lauma Pretkalnia, Prokopis Prokopidis, Tiina Puolakainen, Sampo Pyysalo, Alexandre Rademaker, Loganathan Ramasamy, Livy Real, Laura Rituma, Rudolf Rosa, Shadi Saleh, Baiba Saulīte, Sebastian Schuster, Wolfgang Seeker, Mojgan Seraji, Lena Shakurova, Mo Shen, Natalia Silveira, Maria Simi, Radu Simionescu, Katalin Simkó, Mária Šimková, Kiril Simov, Aaron Smith, Carolyn Spadine, Alane Suhr, Umut Sulubacak, Zsolt Szántó, Takaaki Tanaka, Reut Tsarfaty, Francis Tyers, Sumire Uematsu, Larraitz Uria, Gertjan van Noord, Viktor Varga, Veronika Vincze, Lars Wallin, Jing Xian Wang, Jonathan North Washington, Mats Wirén, Zdeněk Žabokrtský, Amir Zeldes, Daniel Zeman, and Hanzhi Zhu. 2016. Universal dependencies 1.4. LINDAT/CLARIN digital library at the Institute of Formal and Applied Linguistics, Charles University in Prague.

Lena Öhrman, 1998. *Felaktigt särskrivna sammansättningar*. Stockholm University, Department of Linguistics.

Robert Östling. 2013. Stagger: An open-source part of speech tagger for Swedish. *Northern European Journal of Language Technology*, 3:1–18.

Eva Pettersson, Beáta Megyesi, and Joakim Nivre. 2013. Normalisation of historical text using context-sensitive weighted Levenshtein distance and compound splitting. In *Proceedings of the 19th Nordic Conference of Computational Linguistics*, NODALIDA '13.

Mike Scott, 2016. *WordSmith Tools Version 7*. Stroud: Lexical Analysis Software.

Wenche Vagle. 2005. Tekstlengde + ordlengdesnitt = kvalitet? Hva kvantitative kriterier forteller om avgangselevenas skriveprestasjoner. In Kjell Lars Berge, Siegfred Evensen, Frydis Hertzberg, and Wenche. Vagle, editors, *Ungdommers skrivekompetanse, Bind 2. Norskexamen som tekst*. Universitetsforlaget.

Optimizing a PoS Tagset for Norwegian Dependency Parsing

Petter Hohle and **Lilja Øvrelid** and **Erik Velldal**
University of Oslo
Department of Informatics
{pettehoh,liljao,erikve}@ifi.uio.no

Abstract

This paper reports on a suite of experiments that evaluates how the linguistic granularity of part-of-speech tagsets impacts the performance of tagging and syntactic dependency parsing. Our results show that parsing accuracy can be significantly improved by introducing more fine-grained morphological information in the tagset, even if tagger accuracy is compromised. Our taggers and parsers are trained and tested using the annotations of the Norwegian Dependency Treebank.

1 Introduction

Part-of-speech (PoS) tagging is an important pre-processing step for many NLP tasks, such as dependency parsing (Nivre et al., 2007; Hajič et al., 2009), named entity recognition (Sang and Meulder, 2003) and sentiment analysis (Wilson et al., 2009). Whereas much effort has gone into the development of PoS taggers – to the effect that this task is often considered more or less a solved task – considerably less effort has been devoted to the empirical evaluation of the PoS tagsets themselves. Error analysis of PoS taggers indicate that, whereas tagging improvement through means of learning algorithm or feature engineering seems to have reached something of a plateau, linguistic and empirical assessment of the distinctions made in the PoS tagsets may be an avenue worth investigating further (Manning, 2011). Clearly, the utility of a PoS tagset is tightly coupled with the downstream task for which it is performed. Even so, PoS tagsets are usually employed in a "one size fits all" fashion, regardless of the requirements posed by the task making use of this information.

It is well known that syntactic parsing often benefits from quite fine-grained morphological distinctions (Zhang and Nivre, 2011; Seeker and Kuhn, 2013; Seddah et al., 2013). Morphology interacts with syntax through phenomena such as agreement and case marking, and incorporating information on morphological properties of words can therefore often improve parsing performance. However, in a realistic setting where the aim is to automatically parse raw text, the generation of morphological information will often require a separate step of morphological analysis that can be quite costly.

In this paper, we optimize a PoS tagset for the task of dependency parsing of Norwegian Bokmål. We report on a set of experiments where PoS tags are extended with various morphological properties and evaluated in terms of both tagging accuracy and syntactic parsing accuracy. Our results show that the introduction of morphological distinctions not present in the original tagset, whilst compromising tagger accuracy, actually leads to significantly improved parsing accuracy. This optimization also allows us to bypass the additional step of morphological analysis, framing the whole pre-processing problem as a simple tagging task. The impact on parser performance is also more pronounced in this study than in similar previous work, as surveyed in Section 2 next.

For the remainder of the paper, Section 3 details the treebank that provides the basis for our experiments, while Section 4 describes the experimental setup. Section 5 goes on to provide the results from our tagset optimization, before we finally summarize our main findings and discuss some directions for future work in Section 6.

2 Previous Work

This section reviews some of the previous work documenting the impact that PoS tagsets has on the performance of taggers and parsers.

Megyesi (2002) trained and evaluated a range of PoS taggers on the Stockholm-Umeå Corpus (SUC) (Gustafson-Capková and Hartmann, 2006),

Proceedings of the 21st Nordic Conference of Computational Linguistics, pages 142–151,
Gothenburg, Sweden, 23-24 May 2017. ©2017 Linköping University Electronic Press

annotated with a tagset based on a Swedish version of PAROLE tags totaling 139 tags. Furthermore, the effects of tagset size on tagging was investigated by mapping the original tagset into smaller subsets designed for parsing. Megyesi (2002) argues that a tag set with complete morphological tags may not be necessary for all NLP applications, for instance syntactic parsing. The study found that the smallest tagset comprising 26 tags yields the lowest tagger error rate. However, for some of the taggers, augmenting the tagset with more linguistically informative tags may actually lead to a drop in error rate (Megyesi, 2002). Unfortunately, results for parsing with the various PoS tagsets are not reported.

In a similar study, MacKinlay (2005) investigated the effects of PoS tagsets on tagger performance in English, specifically the Wall Street Journal portion of the Penn Treebank (PTB) (Marcus et al., 1993). Based on linguistic considerations, MacKinlay (2005) mapped the 45 tags of the original PTB tagset to more fine-grained tagsets to investigate whether additional linguistic information could assist the tagger. Experimenting with both lexically and syntactically conditioned modifications, they did not find any statistically significant improvements, arguing that their results do not support the hypothesis that it is possible to achieve significant performance improvements in PoS tagging by utilizing a finer-grained tagset.

Moving beyond tagging, Seddah et al. (2009) focus on syntactic constituent parsing for French and show that extending the PoS tagset with information about mood and finiteness for verbs is indeed beneficial. Similarly, the recent shared tasks on parsing morphologically rich languages has seen quite a bit of work focused on evaluating the effect of various types of morphological information on syntactic parsing (both constituent-based and dependency-based) (Tsarfaty et al., 2010; Seddah et al., 2013). They find that the type of morphological information which is beneficial for parsing varies across languages and the quality of this information (i.e. whether it is gold standard or predicted) will also influence the results.

Rehbein and Hirschmann (2013) report on experiments for parsing German, demonstrating small but significant improvements when introducing more fine-grained and syntactically motivated distinctions in the tagset, based on the Stuttgard-Tübingen Tagset (STTS). However, the scope of the changes are limited to modifier distinctions and the new tagset only includes four new PoS tags, changing two of the original STTS categories. The setup also introduces some additional complexity in the parsing pipeline in that two taggers are used; a first pass of tagging with the original STTS tagset provides context features used in a second pass of tagging using the modified tagset. When training and testing on predicted tags using the Mate dependency parser (Bohnet, 2010), Rehbein and Hirschmann (2013) report a modest increase in LAS from 86.94 using STTS to 87.13 for the modified double-tagger setup. Using the Berkeley constituent parser, there is a corresponding increase in F-score from 75.45 to 75.55 (Rehbein and Hirschmann, 2013).

Maier et al. (2014) also experiment with applying the Berkeley constituency parser to German using tagsets of varying granularity; the 12 tags of the Universal Tagset (UTS) (Petrov et al., 2012), the 54 tags of STTS and an extended version of STTS including all the morphological information from the treebanks used for training, resulting in up to 783 tags. Maier et al. (2014) experimented with six different PoS taggers, but found TnT to have the most consistent performance across different tagsets and settings. Predictably, tagger accuracy drops as granularity increases, but the best parsing performance was observed for the medium-sized tagset, i.e., the original STTS.

Müller et al. (2014) attempt to improve dependency parsing with Mate by automatically defining a more fine-grained tagset using so-called split-merge training to create Hidden Markov models with latent annotations (HMM-LA). This entails iteratively splitting every tag into two subtags, but reverting to the original tag unless a certain improvement in the likelihood function is observed. Müller et al. (2014) argue that the resulting annotations "are to a considerable extent linguistically interpretable". Similarly to the setup of Rehbein and Hirschmann (2013), two layers of taggers are used. While the modifications of the tagset are optimized towards tagger performance rather than parsing performance, the parser's LAS on the test set improves from 90.34 to 90.57 for English (using a HMM-LA tagset of 115 tags) and from 87.92 to 88.24 for German (using 107 tags).

In the current paper, we introduce linguistically motivated modifications across a range of PoS tags in the Norwegian Dependency Treebank

Tag	Description
adj	Adjective
adv	Adverb
det	Determiner
inf-merke	Infinitive marker
interj	Interjection
konj	Conjunction
prep	Preposition
pron	Pronoun
sbu	Subordinate conjunction
subst	Noun
ukjent	Unknown (foreign word)
verb	Verb

Table 1: Overview of the original PoS tagset of NDT (excluding punctuation tags).

and demonstrate significant – and substantial – improvements in parser performance.

3 The Norwegian Dependency Treebank

Our experiments are based on the newly developed Norwegian Dependency Treebank (NDT) (Solberg et al., 2014), the first publicly available treebank for Norwegian. It was developed at the National Library of Norway in collaboration with the University of Oslo, and contains manually coded syntactic and morphological annotation for both *Bokmål* and *Nynorsk*, the two official written standards of the Norwegian language. This paper only reports results for Bokmål, the main variety. The treebanked material mostly comprises newspaper text, but also include government reports, parliament transcripts and blog excerpts, totaling 311 000 tokens for Norwegian Bokmål. The annotation process was supported by the rule-based Oslo-Bergen Tagger (Hagen et al., 2000) and then manually corrected by human annotators, also adding syntactic dependency analyses to the morphosyntactic annotation.

Morphological Annotation The morphological annotation and PoS tagset of NDT is based on the same inventory as used by the Oslo-Bergen Tagger (Hagen et al., 2000; Solberg, 2013), which in turn is largely based on the work of Faarlund et al. (1997). The tagset consists of 12 morphosyntactic PoS tags outlined in Table 1, with 7 additional tags for punctuation and symbols. The tagset is thus rather coarse-grained, with broad categories such as subst (noun) and verb (verb). The PoS tags are complemented by a large set of morphological features, providing information about morphological properties such as definiteness, number and

Head	Dependent
Preposition	Prepositional complement
Finite verb	Complementizer
First conjunct	Subsequent conjuncts
Finite auxiliary	Lexical/main verb
Noun	Determiner

Table 2: Central head-dependent annotation choices in NDT.

tense. Selected subsets of these features are used in our tagset modifications, where the coarse PoS tag of relevant tokens is concatenated with one or more features to include more linguistic information in the tags.

Syntactic Annotation The syntactic annotation choices in NDT are largely based on the Norwegian Reference Grammar (Faarlund et al., 1997). Some central annotation choices are outlined in Table 2, taken from Solberg et al. (2014), providing overview of the analyses of syntactic constructions that often distinguish dependency treebanks, such as coordination and the treatment of auxiliary and main verbs. The annotations comprise 29 dependency relations, including ADV (adverbial), SUBJ (subject) and KOORD (coordination).

4 Experimental Setup

This section briefly outlines some key components of our experimental setup.

Data Set Split As there was no existing standardized data set split of NDT due to its recent development, we first needed to define separate sections for training, development and testing.[1] Our proposed sectioning of the treebank follows a standard 80-10-10 split. In establishing the split, care has been taken to preserve contiguous texts in the various sections while also keeping them balanced in terms of genre.

Tagger As our experiments during development required many repeated cycles of training and testing for the various modified tagsets, we sought a PoS tagger that is both reasonably fast and accurate. There is often a considerable trade-off between the two factors, as the most accurate taggers tend to suffer in terms of speed due to their complexity. However, a widely used tagger that achieves both close to state-of-the-art accuracy as

---

[1] Our defined train/dev./test split is available for download at http://github.com/petterhh/ndt-tools and will be distributed with future releases of the treebank.

well as very high speed is TnT (Brants, 2000), and hence we adopt this for the current study.

Parser In choosing a syntactic parser for our experiments, we considered previous work on dependency parsing of Norwegian, specifically that of Solberg et al. (2014), who found the graph-based Mate parser (Bohnet, 2010) to have the best performance for NDT. Recent dependency parser comparisons (Choi et al., 2015) show very strong results for Mate also for English, outperforming a range of contemporary state-of-the-art parsers. We will be using Mate for gauging the effects of the tagset modifications in our experiments.

Evaluation To evaluate tagging and parsing with the various tagset modifications in our experiments, we employ a standard set of measures. Tagging is evaluated in terms of accuracy (computed by the TnT-included `tnt-diff` script; denoted *Acc* in the following tables), while parsing is evaluated in terms of labeled and unlabeled attachment score (LAS and UAS; computed by the `eval.pl`[2] script from the CoNLL shared tasks).

Tagging Baseline In addition to the tagging accuracy for the original unmodified tagset, we include the most-frequent-tag baseline (MFT), as another point of reference. This involves labeling each word with the tag it was assigned most frequently in the training data. All unknown words, i.e., words not seen in the training data, are assigned the tag most frequently observed for words seen only once. The MFT baseline will also serve to indicate the ambiguity imposed by the additional tags in a given tagset modification.

Predicted vs. Gold Tags Seeking to quantify the effects of PoS tagging on parsing, we choose to both evaluate *and* train the parser on automatically predicted PoS tags.[3] Training on predicted tags makes the training set-up correspond more closely to a realistic test setting and makes it possible for the parser to adapt to errors made by the tagger. While this is often achieved using jack-knifing (*n*-fold training and tagging of the labeled training data), we here simply apply the taggers to the very same data they have been trained on, reflecting the 'training error' of the taggers. In an initial experiment we also found that training on

---

[2]`http://ilk.uvt.nl/conll/software.html`
[3]Though some parsers also make use of morphological features, we removed all morphological features beyond the PoS tags in order to simulate a realistic setting.

Training	Testing	LAS	UAS
Gold	Gold	90.15	92.51
Gold	Auto	85.68	88.98
Auto	Auto	87.01	90.19

Table 3: Results of parsing with Mate using various configurations of PoS tag sources in training and testing. *Gold* denotes gold standard tags while *Auto* denotes tags automatically predicted by TnT.

such 'silver-standard' tags actually improves parsing scores substantially compared to training on gold tags, as shown in Table 3. In fact, Straka et al. (2016) also found that this set-up actually yields higher parsing scores compared to 10-fold tagging of the training data. Of course, the test set for which we evaluate the performance is still unseen data for the tagger.

5 Tagset Optimization

The modified tagsets used in the experiments reported in this section are defined as combinations of PoS tags and morphological features already available in the gold annotations of the treebank. In effect, we redefine the tags comprising the gold standard as provided by NDT. The best performing configuration can be seen as a tagset specifically optimized for dependency parsing. Note that the tag selection process itself can be seen as semi-automatic; while we for each introduced distinction empirically evaluate its impact on parsing performance – as to see whether it is worth including in the final configuration – the process is manually guided by linguistic considerations regarding which combinations to evaluate in the first place. Although our expressed goal is to identify a tagset optimized for the downstream task of dependency parsing, we will only consider tagset modifications we deem linguistically sensible.

The hope is that the introduction of more fine-grained distinctions in the tagset may assist the parser in recognizing and generalizing syntactic patterns. This will also increase the complexity of the tagging task, though, which can be expected to lead to a drop in tagger accuracy. However, the most accurate tagging, evaluated in isolation, does not necessarily lead to the best parse, and the aim of this section is to investigate how tagset modifications affect this interplay. In Section 5.1 we first report on a set of initial baseline experiments using the information in the treebank 'as is'. Sec-

Tagset	MFT	Acc	LAS	UAS
Original	**94.14**	**97.47**	87.01	90.19
Full	85.15	93.48	**87.15**	**90.39**

Table 4: Tagging and parsing our development section of NDT with the two initial tagsets. From left to right, we report the tagger accuracy of the most-frequent-tag baseline, the tagger accuracy of TnT, and the labeled and unlabeled attachment score for the Mate parser.

tion 5.2 then details the results of tuning the selection of tags for each word class in isolation, before finally discussing overall results for the complete optimized tagset in Section 5.3.

5.1 Baseline Experiments

In an initial round of experiments, we concatenated the tag of each token with its full set of morphological features, thereby mapping the original tagset to a new maximally fine-grained tagset, given the annotations available in the treebank. This resulted in a total of 368 tags, hereafter referred to as the *full* tagset. The two initial tagsets, i.e., the original tagset comprising 19 tags and the full tagset comprising 368 tags, thus represent two extremes in terms of granularity. To establish some initial points of reference for how tagset granularity affects the performance of tagging and parsing on NDT, we trained and tested a full pipeline with both of these initial tagsets. The results are reported in Table 4. Unsurprisingly, we see that the tagger accuracy plummets when we move from the original to the full tagset. While the MFT baseline for the original tagset is 94.14%, it drops by almost 9 percentage points to 85.15% for the full tagset. Correspondingly, TnT achieves 97.47% and 93.48% accuracy for the original and full tagset, respectively. These results confirm our hypothesis that the high level of linguistic information in the full, fine-grained tagset comes at the expense of reduced tagger performance. In spite of this drop, however, we see that the additional information in the full tagset still improves the parser performance. With the original tagset, Mate achieves 87.01% LAS and 90.19% UAS, which for the full tagset increases to 87.15% and 90.39%, respectively. These preliminary results are encouraging in indicating that the additional linguistic information assists the syntactic parser, motivating further optimization of the tagset.

5.2 Tagset Experiments

We modify the tags for nouns (subst), verbs (verb), adjectives (adj), determiners (det) and pronouns (pron) in NDT by appending selected sets of morphological features to each tag in order to increase the linguistic information expressed by the tags. For each tag, we in turn first experiment with each of the available features in isolation before testing various combinations. We base our choices of combinations on how promising the features are in isolation and what we deem worth investigating in terms of linguistic utility.

The morphological properties of the various parts-of-speech are reflected in the morphological features associated with the respective PoS tags. For instance, as nouns in Norwegian inflect for gender, definiteness and number, the treebank operates with additional features for these properties. In addition to morphological properties such as definiteness, tense and number, all classes except for verbs have a *type* feature that provides information about the subtype of the PoS, e.g., whether a noun is common or proper.

Nouns In Norwegian, nouns are assigned gender (feminine, masculine or neuter), definiteness (definite or indefinite) and number (singular or plural). There is agreement in gender, definiteness and number between nouns and their modifiers (i.e., adjectives and determiners). Additionally, NDT has a separate *case* feature for distinguishing nouns in genitive case. Genitive case marks possession, hence nouns marked with genitive case are quite different from other nouns, taking a noun phrase as complement. Distinguishing on type can be useful, as evident by the presence of separate tags for proper and common nouns in many tagsets, such as those of Penn Treebank and Stockholm-Umeå corpus.

The results for tagset modifications for nouns are shown in Table 5 and reveal that, apart from case, none of the tagset modifications improve tagging. However, they all result in increases in parser accuracy. The most informative features are definiteness, with an increase in LAS of 1.26 percentage points to 88.27%, and type, yielding an LAS of 88.07%. Turning to combinations of features, we found that the combination of type and case, as well as type and definiteness, were the most promising, which led us to combine type, case and definiteness in a final experiment, resulting in LAS of 88.81% and UAS of 91.73%. This

Feature(s)	Acc	LAS	UAS
—	97.47	87.01	90.19
Case	**97.48**	87.63	90.72
Definiteness	97.00	88.27	91.42
Gender	96.09	87.21	90.36
Number	96.37	87.97	91.00
Type	96.92	88.07	91.11
Case & definiteness	97.03	88.39	91.44
Type & case	96.92	88.46	91.51
Type & definiteness	96.99	88.44	91.48
Type, case & definiteness	97.05	**88.81**	**91.73**

Table 5: Tagging and parsing with modified PoS tags for nouns. The first row corresponds to using the original tagset unmodified.

constitutes an improvement of 1.80 percentage points and 1.54 percentage points, respectively.

Verbs Verbs are inflected for tense (infinitive, present, preterite or past perfect) in Norwegian and additionally exhibit mood (imperative or indicative) and voice (active or passive). Note that both voice and mood have only a single value in the treebank; pass (passive) and imp (imperative), respectively. Verbs which are not passive are implicitly active, and verbs which are not imperative are in indicative mood.

Table 6 presents the results from tagging and parsing with modified verb tags. Imperative clauses are fundamentally different from indicative clauses as they lack an overt subject, which is reflected in the fact that mood is the only feature leading to an increase in LAS, with a reported LAS of 87.04%. Although voice is a very distinguishing property for verbs, and passive clauses are very different from active clauses, introducing this distinction in the tagset leads to a drop in LAS of 0.05 percentage points, while distinguishing between the various tenses yields an LAS of 86.97%. Combining the two most promising features of mood and tense resulted in an LAS of 87.12% and UAS of 90.31%.

In an additional experiment, we mapped the verb tenses (and mood, in the case of imperative) to finiteness. All verbs have finiteness, hence this distinction has broad coverage. This mapping is syntactically grounded as finite verbs and nonfinite verbs appear in very different syntactic constructions, and proved to improve parsing with a 0.29 and 0.24 percentage points improvement over the baseline, for LAS and UAS, respectively. This coincides with the previous observations for

Feature(s)	Acc	LAS	UAS
—	**97.47**	87.01	90.19
Mood	97.43	87.04	90.19
Tense	97.30	86.97	90.18
Voice	97.45	86.96	90.09
Mood & tense	97.31	87.12	90.31
Voice & tense	97.28	86.99	90.15
Mood, tense & voice	97.27	86.83	90.05
Finiteness	97.35	**87.30**	**90.43**

Table 6: Tagging and parsing with modified PoS tags for verbs.

Feature(s)	Acc	LAS	UAS
—	**97.47**	87.01	90.19
Definiteness	96.84	87.14	90.29
Degree	97.41	**87.29**	**90.44**
Gender	96.89	87.10	90.25
Number	96.71	86.99	90.10
Type	97.40	87.11	90.25
Definiteness & degree	96.81	87.23	90.39
Definiteness & gender	96.31	87.18	90.39
Definiteness & number	96.78	87.27	**90.44**

Table 7: Tagging and parsing with modified PoS tags for adjectives.

Swedish in Øvrelid (2008), where finiteness was found to be a very beneficial feature for parsing.

Adjectives Adjectives agree with the noun they modify in terms of gender, number and definiteness. Furthermore, adjectives are inflected for degree (positive, comparative or superlative).

Table 7 shows the results of modifying the pron tag in NDT. All features except for number lead to increases in parser accuracy scores, the most successful of which is degree with a reported LAS of 87.29%, while distinguishing adjectives on definiteness yields an LAS of 87.14% and introducing the distinction of gender leads to LAS of 87.10%.

Turning to combinations of features, definiteness and number achieve the best parser accuracy scores, very close to those of degree. Adjectives agree with their head noun and determiner in definiteness and number, making this an expected improvement. The combination of definiteness and degree is also quite promising, obtaining LAS of 87.23% and UAS of 90.39%. It is interesting that none of the combinations surpass the experiment with degree in isolation, which indicates that degree does not interact with the other features in any syntactically significant way.

Determiners Like adjectives, determiners in Norwegian agree with the noun they modify in

Feature	Acc	LAS	UAS
—	97.47	87.01	90.19
Definiteness	97.49	**87.30**	**90.42**
Gender	97.28	87.09	90.31
Number	97.49	87.04	90.18
Type	**97.61**	87.00	90.11

Table 8: Tagging and parsing with modified PoS tags for determiners.

terms of gender, number and definiteness.

The results from the experiments with determiners are shown in Table 8. Introducing the distinction of type (demonstrative, amplifier, quantifier, possessive or interrogative) led to an increase in tagger accuracy of 0.14 percentage points to 97.61%, while marginally impacting the parsing, with LAS of 87.00%, 0.01 percentage points below that of the original tagset. The increase in tagger accuracy when introducing the distinction of type is noteworthy, as we expected the finer granularity to lead to a decrease in accuracy. This serves to indicate that more fine-grained distinctions for determiners, which is a quite disparate category in the treebank, may be quite useful for tagging.

Gender, on the other hand, improved parsing (87.09% LAS), but complicated tagging, as the various genders are often difficult to differentiate, in particular masculine and feminine, which share many of the same forms. The number of a determiner, i.e., singular or plural, led to a small increase in tagger accuracy and LAS, while marginally lower UAS. The introduction of definiteness gave the best parsing results, LAS of 87.30% and UAS of 90.42%, and additionally increased tagger accuracy slightly. The increase in LAS and UAS is rather interesting, as there are only 121 determiner tokens with marked definiteness in the development data. As this accounts for a very small number of tokens, we did not consider further fine-grained modifications with definiteness. This result further underlines the importance of definiteness for parsing of Norwegian.

Pronouns Pronouns in Norwegian include personal, reciprocal, reflexive and interrogative. They can furthermore exhibit gender, number and person, while personal pronouns can be distinguished by case (either accusative or nominative).

The results in Table 9 show that number, person and type are the most useful features for parsing, with LAS of 87.21%, 87.22% and 87.19%, respectively. However, when combining number

Feature(s)	Acc	LAS	UAS
—	97.47	87.01	90.19
Case	97.50	87.08	90.21
Gender	97.48	87.06	90.23
Number	97.49	87.21	90.33
Person	97.49	87.22	90.32
Type	97.48	87.19	90.40
Number & person	97.49	96.98	90.16
Type & case	97.51	**87.30**	**90.41**
Type & number	97.49	87.27	**90.41**
Type & person	97.49	87.00	90.14
Type, case & number	**97.52**	87.11	90.36

Table 9: Tagging and parsing with modified PoS tags for pronouns.

and person, we observe a drop of more than 0.2 percentage points, indicating that these features do not interact in any syntactically distinctive way. The most interesting observation is that all results exceed the tagging accuracy of the original tagset, with the most fine-grained distinction (type, case and number combined) provides the largest improvement (accuracy of 97.52%). This shows that the introduction of more fine-grained distinctions for pronouns aids the PoS tagger in disambiguating ambiguous words. While case alone yields an LAS of 87.08%, we found that the combination of type and case yields the second highest tagging accuracy of 97.51%. Pronouns of different type and personal pronouns of different case exhibit quite different properties and appear in different constructions. Pronouns in nominative case (i.e., subjects) primarily occur before the main verb, while pronouns in accusative case (i.e., objects) occur after the main verb, as Norwegian exhibits so-called V2 word order, requiring that the finite verb of a declarative clause appears in the second position.

5.3 Optimized Tagset

Category	Feature(s)	MFT	Acc	LAS
Original	—	94.14	97.47	87.01
Noun	Type, case, def.	89.61	97.05	88.81
Verb	Finiteness	93.72	97.35	87.30
Adjective	Degree	94.13	97.41	87.29
Determiner	Definiteness	94.13	97.49	87.30
Pronoun	Type, case	94.12	97.51	87.30

Table 10: Results of tagging and parsing with the best tagset modification for each category.

The most successful tagset modification for each PoS and the results from tagging and parsing with the respective modifications are seen in Table 10. Nouns benefit by far the most from

Tag	Description
adj|komp	Comparative adjective
adj|pos	Positive adjective
adj|sup	Superlative adjective
det|be	Definite determiner
det|ub	Indefinite determiner
pron|pers	Personal pronoun
pron|pers|akk	Personal pron., accusative
pron|pers|nom	Personal pron., nominative
pron|refl	Reflexive pronoun
pron|res	Reciprocal pronoun
pron|sp	Interrogative pronoun
subst|appell	Common noun
subst|appell|be	Common noun, def.
subst|appell|be|gen	Common noun, def., genitive
subst|appell|ub	Common noun, indef.
subst|appell|ub|gen	Common noun, indef., gen.
subst|prop	Proper noun
subst|prop|gen	Proper noun, genitive
verb|fin	Finite verb
verb|infin	Nonfinite verb

Table 11: Overview of the optimized tagset.

Data	Tagset	MFT	Acc	LAS	UAS
Dev	Original	**94.14**	**97.47**	87.01	90.19
	Optimized	85.15	96.85	**88.87**	**91.78**
Test	Original	**94.22**	**97.30**	86.64	90.07
	Optimized	88.08	96.35	**88.55**	**91.41**

Table 12: Results of tagging and parsing with the optimized tagset, compared to the original NDT coarse tagset. The parser is both trained and tested using automatically predicted tags from TnT.

the introduction of more fine-grained linguistically motivated distinctions, with an LAS of 88.81% and UAS of 91.73% when distinguishing on type, case and definiteness. We observe that the most promising tagset modifications for verbs, adjectives, determiners and pronouns all reach LAS of ~87.30% and UAS of ~90.40%. To investigate the overall effect of these tagset modifications, we tested each of the improvements in parser accuracy scores from those of the original tagset for statistical significance using Dan Bikel's randomized parsing evaluation comparator script[4], as used in the CoNLL shared tasks. For the most successful tagset modification for each of the categories seen in Table 10, the difference in LAS from the original tagset is statistically significant at significance level 0.05 (p-value < 0.05), as are all differences in UAS, except for verbs with finiteness (p=0.15) and pronouns with type and case (p=0.06).

An overview of the tags in the optimized tagset can be seen in Table 11, comprising three new tags for adjectives, two for determiners, six for pronouns, seven for nouns and two for verbs, totaling 20 tags. Appending these to the original tagset comprising 19 tags, we reach a total of 39 tags.

Final Evaluation In Table 12, we show the results of parsing with the optimized tagset on the held-out test data and the development data, compared to the results obtained with the original

tagset. We see significant improvements from the original tagset on both the development data and the held-out test data set. The improvement in LAS on the development data is 1.86 percentage points, while 1.91 percentage points on the held-out test data. These results indicate that the additional linguistic information in the tags of our optimized tagset benefits the task of syntactic parsing.

6 Summary

This paper has reported on a range of experiments with injecting more fine-grained morphological distinctions into an existing PoS tagset, and then empirically evaluating the effects both (intrinsically) in terms of tagging accuracy and (extrinsically) in terms of parsing accuracy. Our experimental results – based on the annotations of the Norwegian Dependency Treebank and using the TnT PoS tagger and the Mate dependency parser – show that the enriched tag set leads to significantly improved parsing accuracy, even though tagging accuracy in isolation is reduced. We also observe that the improvements are more pronounced than in related previous studies for other languages. The modified tagsets in our experiments are defined as combinations of PoS tags and morphological features, using only information that is already available in the gold annotations of the treebank. The best performing tag configuration is in effect a PoS tagset optimized for dependency parsing of Norwegian. While we expect that tags that prove informative for parsing will be useful for also other downstream applications, one can of course follow the same methodology to optimize a tagset specifically for other applications instead, by using another task for the extrinsic evaluation, such as sentiment analysis, named entity recognition or any other task making use of tagged data.

---

[4]Available as `compare.pl` at `http://ilk.uvt.nl/conll/software.html`

References

Bernd Bohnet. 2010. Very High Accuracy and Fast Dependency Parsing is not a Contradiction. In *Proceedings of the 23rd International Conference on Computational Linguistics*, pages 89–97, Beijing, China.

Thorsten Brants. 2000. TnT - A Statistical Part-of-Speech Tagger. In *Proceedings of the Sixth Applied Natural Language Processing Conference*, Seattle, WA, USA.

Jinho D. Choi, Joel Tetreault, and Amanda Stent. 2015. It Depends: Dependency Parser Comparison Using A Web-Based Evaluation Tool. In *Proceedings of the 53rd Annual Meeting of the Association for Computational Linguistics*, pages 387–396, Beijing, China.

Jan Terje Faarlund, Svein Lie, and Kjell Ivar Vannebo. 1997. *Norsk referansegrammatikk*. Universitetsforlaget, Oslo, Norway.

Sofia Gustafson-Capková and Britt Hartmann, 2006. *Manual of the Stockholm Umeå Corpus version 2.0*. Stockholm, Sweden.

Kristin Hagen, Janne Bondi Johannessen, and Anders Nøklestad. 2000. A Constraint-Based Tagger for Norwegian. In *Proceedings of the 17th Scandinavian Conference of Linguistics*, pages 31–48, Odense, Denmark.

Jan Hajič, Massimiliano Ciaramita, Richard Johansson, Daisuke Kawahara, Maria Antònia Martí, Lluís Màrquez, Adam Meyers, Joakim Nivre, Sebastian Padó, Jan Štěpanek, Pavel Straǎàk, Mihai Surdeanu, Nianwen Xue, and Yi Zhang. 2009. The CoNLL-2009 Shared Task: Syntactic and Semantic Dependencies in Multiple Languages. In *Proceedings of the Thirteenth Conference on Computational Natural Language Learning*, pages 1–18, Boulder, CO, USA.

Andrew MacKinlay. 2005. The Effects of Part-of-Speech Tagsets on Tagger Performance. Bachelor's thesis, University of Melbourne, Melbourne, Australia.

Wolfgang Maier, Sandra Kübler, Daniel Dakota, and Daniel Whyatt. 2014. Parsing German: How much morphology do we need? In *Proeceedings of the First Joint Workshop on Statistical Parsing of Morphologically Rich Languages and Syntactic Analysis of Non-Canonical Languages*, pages 1–14, Dublin, Ireland.

Christopher Manning. 2011. Part-of-Speech Tagging from 97% to 100%: Is It Time for Some Linguistics? In *Proceedings of the 12th International Conference on Computational Linguistics and Intelligent Text Processing*, pages 171–189.

Mitchell Marcus, Beatrice Santorino, and Mary Ann Marcinkiewicz. 1993. Building A Large Annotated Corpus of English: The Penn Treebank. Technical report, University of Philadelphia, Philadelphia, PA, USA.

Beáta Megyesi. 2002. *Data-Driven Syntactic Analysis: Methods and Applications for Swedish*. Ph.D. thesis, Royal Institute of Technology, Stockholm, Sweden.

Thomas Müller, Richard Farkas, Alex Judea, Helmut Schmid, and Hinrich Schütze. 2014. Dependency parsing with latent refinements of part-of-speech tags. In *Proceedings of the 2014 Conference on Empirical Methods in Natural Language Processing*, pages 963–967, Doha, Qatar.

Joakim Nivre, Johan Hall, Sandra Kübler, Ryan McDonald, Jens Nilsson, Sebastian Riedel, and Deniz Yuret. 2007. The CoNLL 2007 Shared Task on Dependency Parsing. In *Proceedings of the CoNLL Shared Task Session of EMNLP-CoNLL 2007*, pages 915–932, Prague, the Czech Republic.

Lilja Øvrelid. 2008. Finite Matters: Verbal Features in Data-Driven Parsing of Swedish. In *Proceedings of the Sixth International Conference on Natural Language Processing*, Gothenburg, Sweden.

Slav Petrov, Dipanjan Das, and Ryan McDonald. 2012. A Universal Part-of-Speech Tagset. In *Proceedings of the Eighth International Conference on Language Resources and Evaluation*, pages 2089–2096, Istanbul, Turkey.

Ines Rehbein and Hagen Hirschmann. 2013. POS tagset refinement for linguistic analysis and the impact on statistical parsing. In *Proceedings of the 13th International Workshop on Treebanks and Linguistic Theories*, pages 172–183, Tübingen, Germany.

Erik F. Tjong Kim Sang and Fien De Meulder. 2003. Introduction to the CoNLL-2003 Shared Task: Language-Independent Named Entity Recognition. In *Proceedings of the Seventh Conference on Natural Language Learning at HLT-NAACL 2003*, pages 142–147, Stroudsburg, PA, USA.

Djamé Seddah, Marie Candito, and Benoît Crabbé. 2009. Cross parser evaluation and tagset variation: A french treebank study. In *Proceedings of the 11th International Conference on Parsing Technologies*, IWPT '09, pages 150–161, Stroudsburg, PA, USA. Association for Computational Linguistics.

Djamé Seddah, Reut Tsarfaty, Sandra Kübler, Marie Candito, Jinho D. Choi, Richard Farkas, Jennifer Foster, Iakes Goenaga, Koldo Gojenola Galletebeitia, Yoav Goldberg, Spence Green, Nizar Habash, Marco Kuhlmann, Wolfgang Maier, Yuval Marton, Joakim Nivre, Adam Przepiorkowski, Ryan Roth, Wolfgang Seeker, Yannick Versley, Veronika Vincze, Marcin Wolinski, and Alina Wroblewska. 2013. Overview of the spmrl 2013 shared task: A cross-framework evaluation of parsing morphologically rich languages. In *Proceedings of the Fourth*

Workshop on Statistical Parsing of Morphologically Rich Languages, pages 146–182, Seattle, USA.

Wolfgang Seeker and Jonas Kuhn. 2013. Morphological and Syntactic Case in Statistical Dependency Parsing. *Computational Linguistics*, 39(1):23–55.

Per Erik Solberg, Arne Skjærholt, Lilja Øvrelid, Kristin Hagen, and Janne Bondi Johannessen. 2014. The Norwegian Dependency Treebank. In *Proceedings of the Ninth International Conference on Language Resources and Evaluation*, pages 789–795, Reykjavik, Iceland.

Per Erik Solberg. 2013. Building Gold-Standard Treebanks for Norwegian. In *Proceedings of the 19th Nordic Conference of Computational Linguistics*, pages 459–464, Oslo, Norway.

Milan Straka, Jan Hajič, and Jana Straková. 2016. UDPipe: trainable pipeline for processing CoNLL-U files performing tokenization, morphological analysis, pos tagging and parsing. In *Proceedings of the Tenth International Conference on Language Resources and Evaluation*, Portorož, Slovenia.

Reut Tsarfaty, Djamé Seddah, Yoav Goldberg, Sandra Kübler, Marie Candito, Jennifer Foster, Yannick Versley, Ines Rehbein, and Lamia Tounsi. 2010. Statistical parsing of morphologically rich languages (SPMRL): what, how and whither. In *Proceedings of the NAACL HLT 2010 First Workshop on Statistical Parsing of Morphologically-Rich Languages*.

Theresa Wilson, Janyce Wiebe, and Paul Hoffman. 2009. Recognizing Contextual Polarity: An Exploration of Features for Phrase-Level Sentiment Analysis. *Computational Linguistics*, 35(3):399–433.

Yue Zhang and Joakim Nivre. 2011. Transition-Based Dependency Parsing with Rich Non-Local Features. In *Proceedings of the 49th Annual Meeting of the Association for Computational Lingustics: Human Language Technologies*, pages 188–193, Portland, OR, USA.

Creating register sub-corpora for the Finnish Internet Parsebank

Veronika Laippala[1,2,3], Juhani Luotolahti[3],
Aki-Juhani Kyröläinen[2,3], Tapio Salakoski[3], Filip Ginter[3]
[1] Turku Institute for Advanced Studies, University of Turku, Finland
[2] School of Languages and Translation Studies, University of Turku, Finland
[3] Turku NLP Group, University of Turku, Finland
`first.last@utu.fi`

Abstract

This paper develops register sub-corpora for the Web-crawled Finnish Internet Parsebank. Currently, all the documents belonging to different registers, such as news and user manuals, have an equal status in this corpus. Detecting the text register would be useful for both NLP and linguistics (Giesbrecht and Evert, 2009) (Webber, 2009) (Sinclair, 1996) (Egbert et al., 2015). We assemble the sub-corpora by first naively deducing four register classes from the Parsebank document URLs and then developing a classifier based on these, to detect registers also for the rest of the documents. The results show that the naive method of deducing the register is efficient and that the classification can be done sufficiently reliably. The analysis of the prediction errors however indicates that texts sharing similar communicative purposes but belonging to different registers, such as news and blogs informing the reader, share similar linguistic characteristics. This attests of the well-known difficulty to define the notion of registers for practical uses. Finally, as a significant improvement to its usability, we release two sets of sub-corpus collections for the Parsebank. The A collection consists of two million documents classified to blogs, forum discussions, encyclopedia articles and news with a naive classification precision of >90%, and the B collection four million documents with a precision of >80%.

1 Introduction

The Internet offers a constantly growing source of information, not only in terms of size, but also in terms of languages and communication settings it includes. As a consequence, *Web corpora*, language resources developed by automatically crawling the Web, offer revolutionary potentials for fields using textual data, such as Natural Language Processing (NLP), linguistics and other humanities (Kilgariff and Grefenstette, 2003).

Despite their potentials, Web corpora are underused. One of the important reasons behind this is the fact that in the existing Web corpora, all of the different documents have an equal status. This complicates their use, as for many applications, knowing the composition of the corpus would be beneficial. In particular, it would be important to know what *registers*, i.e. text varieties such as a user manual or a blog post, the corpus consists of (see Section 2 for a definition). In NLP, detecting the register of a text has been noted to be useful for instance in POS tagging (Giesbrecht and Evert, 2009), discourse parsing (Webber, 2009) and information retrieval (Vidulin et al., 2007). In linguistics, the correct constitution of a corpus and the criteria used to assemble it have been subject to long discussions (Sinclair, 1996), and Egbert & al. (2015) note that without systematic classification, Web corpora cannot be fully benefited from.

In this paper, we explore the development of register sub-corpora for the Finnish Internet Parsebank[1], a Web-crawled corpus of Internet Finnish. We assemble the sub-corpora by first naively deducing four register classes from the Parsebank document URLs and then creating a classifier based on these classes to detect texts representing these registers from the rest of the Parsebank (see Section 4). The register classes we develop are news, blogs, forum discussions and encyclopedia articles. Instead of creating a full-coverage taxonomy of all the registers covered by the Parsebank, in this article our aim is to test this method in

---

[1] `http://bionlp.utu.fi`

Proceedings of the 21st Nordic Conference of Computational Linguistics, pages 152–161,
Gothenburg, Sweden, 23-24 May 2017. ©2017 Linköping University Electronic Press

the detection of these four registers. If the method works, the number of registers will be extended in future work.

In the register detection and analysis, we compare three methods: the traditional bag-of-words as a baseline, lexical trigrams as proposed by Gries & al. (2011), and Dependency Profiles (DP), co-occurrence patterns of the documents labelled in a specific class, assumed a register, and dependency syntax relations.

In addition to reporting the standard metrics to estimate the classifier performance, we evaluate the created sub-corpora by analysing the mismatches between the naively assumed register classes and the classifier predictions. In addition, we analyse the linguistic register characteristics estimated by the classifier. This validates the quality of the sub-corpora and is informative about the linguistic variation inside the registers (see Section 5).

Finally, we publish four register-specific sub-corpora for the Parsebank that we develop in this paper: blogs, forum discussions, encyclopedia articles and news (see Section 6). We release two sets of sub-corpora: the A collection consists of two million documents with register-specific labels. For these documents, we estimate the register prediction precision to be >90%. The collection B consists of four million documents. For these, the precision is >80%. These sub-corpora allow the users to focus on specific registers, which improves the Parsebank usability significantly (see discussions in (Egbert et al., 2015) and (Asheghi et al., 2016)).

2 Previous studies

Since the 1980s, linguistic variation has been studied in relation to the communicative situation, form and function of the piece of speech or writing under analysis (Biber, 1989; Biber, 1995; Biber et al., 1999; Miller, 1984; Swales, 1990). Depending on the study, these language varieties are usually defined as *registers* or *genres*, the definitions emphasising different aspects of the variation (see discussion in (Asheghi et al., 2016; Egbert et al., 2015). We adopt the term register and define it, following (Biber, 1989; Biber, 1995; Egbert et al., 2015), as a text variety with specific situational characteristics, communicative purpose and lexico-grammatical features.

Studies aiming at automatically identifying reg-

isters from the Web face several challenges. Although some studies reach a very high accuracy, their approaches are very difficult to apply in real-world applications. Other studies, adopting a more realistic approach, present a weaker performance. In particular, the challenges are related to the definition of registers in practice: how many of them should there be, and how to reliably identify them? In addition, it is not always clear whether registers have different linguistic properties (Schäfer and Bildhauer, 2016). Based on the situational characteristics of a register, a blog post discussing a news topic and a news article on the same topic should be analysed as different registers. But how does this difference show in the linguistic features of the documents, or does it?

For instance, Sharoff & al. (2010) achieve an accuracy of 97% using character tetragrams and single words with a stop list as classification features, while Lindemann & Littig (2011) report an F-score of 80% for many registers using both structural Web page features and topical characteristics based on the terms used in the documents. They, however, use as corpora only samples of the Web, which can represent only a limited portion of all the registers of the entire Web (Sharoff et al., 2010; Santini and Sharoff, 2009).

Another, more linguistically motivated perspective to study Web registers is adopted by Biber and his colleagues. Using typical end users of the Web to code a large number of nearly random Web documents (48 000) with hierarchical, situational characteristics, they apply a bottom-up method for creating a taxonomy of Web registers (Biber et al., 2015; Egbert et al., 2015). Then, applying a custom built tagger identifying 150+ lexico-grammatical features, they report an overall accuracy of 44.2% for unrestricted Web texts using a taxonomy of 20 registers (Biber and Egbert, 2015). In addition to the relatively weak register identification performance, their approach suffers from a low interannotator agreement for the register classes. Similar problems are also discussed in (Crowston et al., 2011; Essen and Stein, 2004), who note that both experts and end users have troubles identifying registers reliably. This leads to question, whether register identification can at all be possible, if even humans cannot agree on their labelling. This concern is expressed by Schäfer and Bildhauer (2016), who decide to focus on classifying their *COW Corpora*

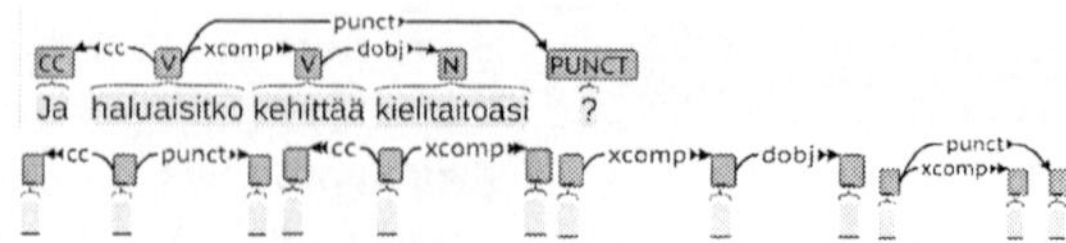

Figure 1: Unlexicalised syntactic biarcs from the sentence *Ja haluaisitko kehittää kielitaitoasi?* 'And would you like to improve your language skills?'

to topic domains, such as *medical* or *science* instead of registers. The recently presented Leeds Web Genre Corpus (Asheghi et al., 2016) shows, however, very reliable interannotator agreement scores. This proves that when the register taxonomy is well developed, the registers can as well be reliably identified.

3 Finnish Internet Parsebank

Finnish Internet Parsebank (Luotolahti et al., 2015) is a Web-crawled corpus on the Finnish Internet. The corpus is sampled from a Finnish Web-crawl data. The crawl itself is produced using SpiderLing Crawler, which is especially crafted for efficient gathering of unilingual corpora for linguistic purposes. The version we used is composed of 3.7 billion tokens, 6,635,960 documents and has morphological and dependency syntax annotations carried out with a state-of-the-art dependency parser by Bohnet (2010), with a labelled attachment score of 82.1% (Luotolahti et al., 2015). The Parsebank is distributed via a user interface at `bionlp-www.utu.fi/dep_search/` and as a downloadable, sentence-shuffled version at `bionlp.utu.fi`.

4 Detecting registers from the Parsebank

In this Section, we first discuss the development of the naive register corpora from the Parsebank. These will be used as training data for the system identifying the registers from the entire Parsebank. We then motivate our selection of features in the classifier development, and finally, we present the classification results.

4.1 Naive registers as training data

Our naive interpretation of the document registers was based on the presence of lexical cues in the Parsebank document URLs. For the purposes of this article, we used four well-motivated register classes: news, blogs, encyclopedia and forum discussions. These were identified by the presence of

Naive register	Entire PB	Training subset
Blogs	775,885	8,364
Forum discussions	307,797	3,076
Encyclopedia	127,884	1,580
News	771,058	13,197
All	**1,982,624**	**26,217**

Table 1: Total number of documents in the naively assembled register classes and in the subset used in SVM training

the following keywords in the URL: *lehti* 'newspaper', *uutis* 'news', *uutinen* 'news' or *news* for the news class; *wiki* for the encyclopedia class; *blog* for the blog class; and *discussion, forum* or *keskustelu* 'discussion' for the discussion class.

In deciding the registers to be searched for, we aimed at a simple, experimental solution that would be informative about the performance of the naive method and offer direct application potentials for the Parsebank to increase its usability. Therefore, instead of creating a full-coverage taxonomy of all registers possibly found online, our aim here was to experiment with a few generally acknowledged, broad-coverage terms for register classes. Once we can in this paper show that the naive method works, the number of the registers will be expanded in future work.

Table 1 presents the proportion of the naively assumed registers in the entire Parsebank and in the subset we use for the classifier training in Section 4.3. The sizes of the retrieved sub-corpora vary significantly. The most frequent, news and blogs, cover more than 10% of the Parsebank documents, respectively, while in particular the encyclopedia corpus remains smaller. Still, the sizes of these classes are relatively large, thanks to the size of the entire Parsebank.

The subset used for the classifier training is created by matching the document URLs of 100,000 first documents from the Parsebank. Of these, 26,216 had a URL that matched one of the keywords defined above. At this stage, all sentence-level duplicates were also removed from the training data to prevent the classifier from learning elements that are often repeated in Web pages, such as *Lue lisää* 'Read more' but should not be used as classifier features. This proved to be highly needed, as from the 3,421,568 sentences in the 100,000 documents, 497,449 were duplicates.

4.2 Lexical and syntactic approaches to model register variation

The work by Biber and colleagues on the variation of lexico-grammatical features across registers has been very influential in corpus linguistics over the years (Biber, 1995; Biber et al., 1999). Recently, they have extended their work to Web registers and applied the carefully tuned Biber tagger identifying both lexical and grammatical features to explore registers from the Web (Biber et al., 2015; Egbert et al., 2015). Gries & al. (2011) adopt an opposite approach by using simple word-trigrams. Sharoff and colleagues compare a number of different feature sets and conclude that bag-of-words and character n-grams achieve the best results (Sharoff et al., 2010). For detecting mostly thematic domains, Schäfer and Bildhauer (2016) apply lexical information attached to coarse-grained part-of-speech labels.

We compare three methods for detecting the four registers represented by our naively assembled sub-corpora. As a baseline method, we apply the standard bag-of-words, which, despite its simplicity, has often achieved a good performance (Sharoff et al., 2010). Second, we use word-trigrams similar to Gries & al. (2011), and finally, Dependency Profiles (DPs), which are co-occurrences of the register documents with unlexicalised syntactic biarcs, three-token subtrees of dependency syntax analysis with the lexical information deleted (Kanerva et al., 2014) (see Figure 1). As opposed to e.g. keyword analysis (Scott and Tribble, 2006) based on the document words, DPs do not restrict to the lexical or topical aspects of texts, and thus offer linguistically better motivated analysis tools. Many studies on register variation highlight the importance of syntactic and grammatical features (Biber, 1995; Biber et al., 1999; Gries, 2012). Therefore, we hypothesise that DPs would allow to generalise beyond individual topics to differentiate, e.g., between texts representing different registers but discussing similar topics, such as news and forum discussions on sports.

4.3 Classifier development and testing

To predict the registers for all the Parsebank documents, we trained a linear SVM. In the training and testing, we used a subset of the Parsebank described in Table 1. As features, we used the sets described in the previous Section. Specifically, the four register classes were modelled as a function of the feature sets, i.e. a co-occurence vector of the used features across the documents. These vectors were L2-normalised and then used to model the register class of a given document by fitting a linear SVM to the data, as implemented in the Scikit package[2] in Python. To validate the performance of the fitted model, we implemented a 10-fold cross-validation procedure with stratified random subsampling to keep the proportion of the register classes approximately equal between the training and test sets.

The results of the SVM performance are described in Table 2. First, the best results are achieved with the bag-of-words and lexical n-gram approaches with an F-score of 80 % and 81%. This already confirms that the registers can be identified and that our naive method of assuming the registers based on the URLs is justified.

Second, although the DPs consisting of syntactic biarcs would allow for detailed linguistic examinations of the registers, and even if they follow the influential work by Biber and colleagues on modelling registers, their classification performance is clearly lower than those of the lexical approaches. The average F-score for the biarcs is only 72%. Interestingly, combining biarcs and the bag-of-words results in a very similar F-score of 79% and does not improve the classifier performance at all. In other words, three of the four feature sets attest very similar performances. This can suggest that the remaining 20% of the data may be somehow unreachable with these feature sets and requires further data examination, which we will present in Section 5.1 and 5.2.

Third, it is noteworthy that the classifier performance varies clearly across the registers. News and blogs receive the best detection rates, rising to the very reliable 86% and 79% F-score, respectively, while the discussion and encyclopedia article detection rates are clearly lower, 70% and 73%. Naturally, the higher frequency of blogs and news in the training and test set explains some of these differences. Still, these differences merit fur-

---

[2]`http://scikit-kearn.org/stable/`

	Blog	Discussion	Encyclopedia	News	Avg.
Bag-of-words					
Precision	0.80	0.66	0.69	0.86	0.81
Recall	0.76	0.73	0.74	0.86	0.80
F-score	0.78	0.69	0.71	0.86	0.80
Biarcs					
Precision	0.70	0.50	0.43	0.83	0.73
Recall	0.66	0.47	0.60	0.83	0.72
F-score	0.68	0.48	0.51	0.82	0.72
Bag-of-words + biarcs					
Precision	0.78	0.63	0.65	0.86	0.80
Recall	0.75	0.69	0.73	0.85	0.79
F-score	0.76	0.66	0.69	0.85	0.79
Uni- bi - trigrams					
Precision	0.81	0.68	0.71	0.86	0.81
Recall	0.77	0.73	0.75	0.86	0.81
F-score	0.79	0.70	0.73	0.86	0.81

Table 2: The SVM results achieved with the four feature sets.

ther analyses in future work.

Finally, the variation between the precision and recall rates across the registers requires closer examination. While the precision and recall are very similar for the news class, for the blogs the precision is higher than the recall. This suggests that some features, words in this case, are very reliable indicators of the blog register, but that they do are not present in all the class documents. For the discussion and encyclopedia classes, the recall is higher than the precision, indicating that such reliable indicators are less frequent.

5 Validating the classifier quality

The classifier performance seems sufficiently reliable to be applied for identifying the registers from the Parsebank. Before classifying the entire corpus, we will, however, in this Section seek answers to questions raised by the SVM results. First, we analyse the classifier decisions to find possible explanations for the 20% of the data that the SVM does not detect. This will also ensure the validity our naive method for assuming the register classes. Second, we study the most important register class features, words in our case, estimated by the SVM. These can explain the variation between the precision and recall across the registers revealed, and also further clarify the classifier's choices and the classification quality.

5.1 Mismatches between the SVM predictions and the naively assumed registers

Mismatches between the SVM predictions and the naively assumed register labels are informative both about the SVM performance and about the coherence of the naive corpora: a mismatch can occur either because the classifier makes a mistake or because the document, in fact, does not represent the register its URL implies. This can also explain why the classifier results achieved with different feature sets were very similar.

We went manually through 60 wrongly classified Parsebank documents that did not belong to the subset on which the SVM was trained on. Although the number of documents was not high, the analysis revealed clear tendencies on the classification mismatches and the composition of the naively presumed registers.

Above all, the analysis proved the efficiency of our naive method of assuming the register. The blog, encyclopedia and discussion classes included only one document, respectively, where the URL did not refer to the document register. The news class included more variation, as in particular the documents with *lehti* 'magazine' in the URL included also other registers than actual news. Of the 15 analysed documents naively presumed news, nine were actual news, four columns or editorials and two discussions.

For the mismatches between the naive register labels and the SVM predictions, our analysis showed that many could be explained with significant linguistic variation within the registers, both in terms of the communicative aim of the document and its style. For instance, some of the blogs we analysed followed a very informal, narrative model, while others aimed at informing the reader on a current topic, and yet others resembled advertisements with an intention of promoting or selling. Also the distinction between news and encyclopedia articles that both can focus on informing the reader was for some documents vague in terms of linguistic features. Similarly, some shorter blog posts and forum discussion posts appeared very similar.

Similar communicative goals thus seem to result in similar linguistic text characteristics across registers. In addition to explaining the mismatches between the SVM predictions and the naively assumed registers, this linguistic variation inside registers clarifies the SVM results and the fact that the performances of three of the four feature sets were very similar. On one hand, this could also suggest that the registers should be defined differently than we have currently done, so that they would better correspond to the communicative aims and linguistic characteristics of the texts. For instance, the register taxonomy proposed by Biber and colleagues (Biber et al., 2015; Egbert et al., 2015) with registers such as *opinion* or *informational persuasion* follows better these communicative goals and could, perhaps, result in better classification results. On the other hand, such denominations are not commonly known and the registers can be difficult to identify, as noted by Asheghi & al. (2016). Also, they can result in very similar texts falling to different registers. For instance in the taxonomy presented by Biber & al; *personal blogs, travel blogs* and *opinion blogs* are all placed in different registers.

5.2   The most important register features

To obtain a better understanding of the classifier's decisions and the features it bases its decisions on, we analysed the most important words of each register class as estimated by the SVM classifier based on the training corpus. These words can be seen as the *keywords* of these classes. In corpus linguistics, keyword analysis (Scott and Tribble, 2006) is a standard corpus analysis method. These words are said to be informative about the corpus topic and style. (See, however, also Guyon and Elisseeff (2003) and Carpena & al. (2009).) To this end, we created a frequency list of the 20 words which were estimated as the most important in each register class across the ten validation rounds. Table 3 presents, for each class, five of the ten most frequent words on this list that we consider the most revealing.

The most important words for each register class listed in Table 3 reveal clear tendencies that the classifier seems to follow. Despite the extraction of sentence-level duplicates presented in Section 3, the blog and forum discussion classes include words coming from templates and other automatically inserted phrases, such as *Thursday, anonymous* and the English words. Although these do not reveal any linguistic characteristics of the registers, they thus allow the classifier to identify the classes, and also explain the higher precision than recall reported in Section 2. Interestingly, Asheghi & al. (2016) report similar keywords for both blogs and discussions in English, which demonstrates the similarity of these registers across languages. In our data, the encyclopedia and news classes include words reflecting topics, such as *20-tuumaiset* '20-inch', and for instance verbs denoting typical actions in the registers, such as *kommentoi* 'comments'. These are more informative also on the linguistic characteristics of the registers and their communicative purposes.

6   Finnish Internet Parsebank with register sub-corpora

The classifier performance results reported in Section 4.3 and the analysis described in Section 5 proved that the developed classifier is sufficiently reliable to improve the usability of the Parsebank. In this Section, we apply the model to classify the entire Parsebank.

6.1   Detecting five register classes with a four-class SVM

We classified all the Parsebank documents with the bag-of-words feature set and parameters reported in Section 4.3. The SVM was developed to detect the four classes for which we had the training data thanks to the naive labels present in the document URLs. The addition of a negative class to the training data, with none of the labels in the URLs, would have increased significantly its noisiness, as these documents could still, despite the absence of the naive label, belong to one of the positive classes. Therefore, we needed to take some additional steps in the Parsebank classification, as the final classification should still include a fifth, negative class.

First, we ran the four-class classifier on all the Parsebank documents. In addition to the register labels, we also collected the scores for each regis-

Blogs	Forum discussions	Encyclopedia	News
kirjoitettu 'written'	*keskustelualue* 'discussion area'	*20-tuumaiset* '20-inch'	*kertoo* 'tells'
ihana 'wonderful'	*wrote*	*opiskelu* 'studying'	*aikoo* 'will'
kl. 'o'clock'	*nimetön* 'anonymous'	*wikiin* 'to the wiki'	*tutkijat* 'researchers'
torstai 'Thursday'	*ketjussa* 'in the thread'	*perustettiin* 'was founded'	*huomauttaa* 'notes'
archives	*forum*	*liitetään* 'is attached'	*kommentoi* 'comments'

Table 3: The most important features for each register class as estimated by the classifier. The original words are italicised and the translations inside quotations. Note that some words are originally in English.

Register	Proportion
Narrative	31.2%
Informational description	24,5%
Opinion	11.2%
Interactive discussion	6.4%
Hybrid	29.2%

Table 4: Register frequencies in the English Web, as reported by Biber & al. (2015)

ter, as assigned by the SVM, and sorted the documents based on these scores. Then, we counted a naive precision rate for the predictions by counting the proportion of the correct SVM predictions that matched the naive register label gotten from the URL. This gave us a sorted list of the Parsebank documents, where, in addition to the scores assigned by the classifier, we also have an estimate of the prediction precisions. From this sorted list, we could then take the best ranking ones that are the most likely to be correctly classified.

These estimated precisions for the documents descend from 1 for the most reliably classified documents to 0.74 for the least reliable ones. The question is, where to set the threshold to distinguish the documents that we consider as correctly predicted and those that we do not. As we do not know the distribution of registers in the Finnish Web, this is difficult to approximate. The study by Biber & al. (2015) on a large sample of Web documents reports the most frequent registers in English. These are described in Table 4. Our news and encyclopedia registers would most likely belong to the *informational* category, blogs to the *narrative* and Forum discussions naturally to the *interactive discussion* category. Very likely many could also be classified as *hybrid*. Based on these, we can estimate that the registers we have can cover a large proportion of the Finnish Web and of the Parsebank, in particular if we consider them as relatively general categories that can include a number of subclasses, similar to (Biber et al., 2015).

6.2 Collections A and B

To improve the Parsebank usability to the maximum, we decided to release two sets of sub-corpora: the A collection includes all the Parsebank documents with best-ranking scores assigned by the SVM, where the naive match precision threshold was set to 90%, and the B corpora where the threshold was set to 80%[3] This allows the users to choose the precision with which the register labels are correct.

The sizes of the sub-corpus collections are presented in Tables 5 and 6. The A collection consists of altogether 2 million documents classified to four registers. Of these, the URLs of nearly 800,000 documents match the SVM prediction, and more than a million do not have a naive label deduced from the URL. The news sub-corpus is clearly the largest covering nearly 50% of the total, blogs including 0.5 million documents.

In the B collection, the total number of documents rises to four million, which presents nearly 60% of the Parsebank. Similarly to the A collection, News and Blogs are the largest register-specific classes. In this version, the number of documents with mismatches between the classifier predictions and the naively assumed registers is evidently higher than in the A, and also the number of documents without any naive label is higher. This naturally implies a lower register prediction quality. Despite this, the B collection offers novel possibilities for researchers. It is a very large corpus, where the registers should be seen as upper-level, coarse-grained classes. In addition to offering register-specific documents, this collection can be seen as a less noisy version of the Parsebank, which is useful also when the actual registers are not central.

---

[3]These corpora will be put publicly available on the acceptance of this article.

Register	Register total	URL match	W/o naive label	Mismatch
Blogs	521,777	274,447	224,630	22,700
Forum discussions	326,561	124,971	168,416	33,174
Encyclopedia	204,019	59,596	132,670	11,753
News	966,938	325,138	609,500	32,300
A collection total	**2,019,295**	**784,152**	**1,135,216**	**99,927**

Table 5: Sizes of the register classes in the A collection

Register	Register total	URL match	W/o naive label	Mismatch
Blogs	1,122,451	450,202	604,877	67,372
Forum discussions	673,678	189,441	394,501	89,736
Encyclopedia	483,425	74,679	376,586	32,160
News	2,425,261	542,970	1,735,926	146,365
B collection total	**4,704,815**	**1,257,292**	**3,111,890**	**335,633**

Table 6: Sizes of the register-specific classes in the B collection

7 Conclusion

The aim of this article was to explore the development of register sub-corpora for the Finnish Internet Parsebank by training a classifier based on documents for which we had naively deduced the register by the presence of keyword matches in the document URL. We also experimented with several feature sets in detecting these registers and evaluated the validity of the created sub-corpora by analysing their linguistic characteristics and classifier prediction mistakes.

First of all, the results showed that our naive method of assuming the document registers is valid. Only the news class proved to include some documents belonging to other, although related, registers. Of the four feature sets we experimented on, the best classification performance was achieved with the bag-of-words and lexical trigram sets. The average F-score of 81% proved that the registers can be relatively reliably identified. In addition, the analysis of the classifier mistakes showed that texts with similar communicative purposes, such as news articles and blog posts that both aim at informing the reader, share linguistic characteristics. This complicates their identification, and attests of the challenges related to defining registers in practice, as already discussed in previous studies.

After validating the classifier performance and the quality of the naively assembled sub-corpora, we classified the entire Parsebank using the four-class model developed with the naive registers. To create a fifth, negative class for the documents not belonging to any of the four known registers, we sorted the documents based on the scores estimated by the SVM and counted a naive classi-

fication precision based on the proportion of the documents with matching naive register labels deduced from the URL and classifier predictions. This allowed us to establish a precision threshold, above which we can assume the document labels to be sufficiently reliably predicted. To improve the Parsebank usability, we release to sets of sub-corpora: the A collection includes two million documents classified to four register-specific corpora with a precision above 90%, and the B collection four million documents with a precision above 80%.

Naturally, this first sub-corpus release leaves many perspectives and needs for future work. More precisely and reliably defined register classes would further increase the usability of the sub-corpora. Also the number of available registers should be increased, as the *none* class currently includes still many registers. The naming of the registers and their inner variation would also merit further analyses to decide how to deal with linguistically similar texts that at least in our current system belong to different registers, such as different texts aiming at informing the reader.

Acknowledgements

This work has been funded by the Kone Foundation. Computational resources were provided by CSC - It center for science.

References

Noushin Rezapour Asheghi, Serge Sharoff, and Katja Markert. 2016. Crowdsourcing for web genre annotation. *Language Resources and Evaluation*, 50(3):603–641.

Douglas Biber and Jesse Egbert. 2015. Using grammatical features for automatic regisgter identification in an unrestricted corpus of documents from the Open Web. *Journal of Research Design and Statistics in Linguistics and Communication Science*, 2(1).

Douglas Biber, S. Johansson, G. Leech, Susan Conrad, and E. Finegan. 1999. *The Longman Grammar of Spoken and Written English*. Longman, London.

Douglas Biber, Jesse Egbert, and Mark Davies. 2015. Exloring the composition of the searchable web: a corpus-based taxonomy of web registers. *Corpora*, 10(1):11–45.

Douglas Biber. 1989. *Variation across speech and writing*. Cambridge University Press, Cambridge.

Douglas Biber. 1995. *Dimensions of Register Variation: A Cross-linguistic Comparison*. Cambridge University Press, Cambridge.

Bernd Bohnet. 2010. Very high accuracy and fast dependency parsing is not a contradiction. In *Proceedings of the 23rd International Conference on Computational Linguistics*, COLING '10, pages 89–97, Stroudsburg, PA, USA. Association for Computational Linguistics.

Pedro. Carpena, Pedro. Bernaola-Galván, Michael Hackenberg, Ana. V. Coronado, and Jose L. Oliver. 2009. Level statistics of words: Finding keywords in literary texts and symbolic sequences. *Physical Review E (Statistical, Nonlinear, and Soft Matter Physics)*, 79(3):035102.

Kevin Crowston, Barbara Kwaśnik, and Joseph Rubleske, 2011. *Genres on the Web: Computational Models and Empirical Studies*, chapter Problems in the Use-Centered Development of a Taxonomy of Web Genres, pages 69–84. Springer Netherlands, Dordrecht.

Jesse Egbert, Douglas Biber, and Mark Davies. 2015. Developing a bottom-up, user-based method of web register classification. *Journal of the Association for Information Science and Technology*, 66(9):1817–1831.

S. Meyer Zu Essen and Barbara Stein. 2004. Genre classification of web pages: User study and feasibility analysis. *Proceedings of the 27th Annual German Conference on Artificial Intelligence*, pages 256–259.

Eugenie Giesbrecht and Stefan Evert. 2009. Is part-of-speech tagging a solved task? an evaluation of pos taggers for the german web as corpus. In *Web as Corpus Workshop (WAC5)*, pages 27–36.

Stephan Gries, John Newman, and Cyrus Shaoul. 2011. N-grams and the clustering of registers. *Empirical Language Research*.

Stephan Gries, 2012. *Methodological and analytic frontiers in lexical research*, chapter Behavioral Profiles: a fine-grained and quantitative approach in corpus-based lexical semantics. John Benjamins, Amsterdam and Philadelphia.

Isabelle M. Guyon and Andre Elisseeff. 2003. An introduction to variable and feature selection. *The journal of machine learning research*, 3:1157–1182.

Jenna Kanerva, Matti Luotolahti, Veronika Laippala, and Filip Ginter. 2014. Syntactic n-gram collection from a large-scale corpus of Internet Finnish. In *Proceedings of the Sixth International Conference Baltic HLT 2014*, pages 184–191. IOS Press.

Adam Kilgariff and Gregory Grefenstette. 2003. Introduction to the special issue on Web as Corpus. *Computational Linguistics*, 29(3).

Christoph Lindemann and Lars Littig, 2011. *Genres on the Web: Computational Models and Empirical Studies*, chapter Classification of Web Sites at Super-genre Level, pages 211–235. Springer Netherlands, Dordrecht.

Juhani Luotolahti, Jenna Kanerva, Veronika Laippala, Sampo Pyysalo, and Filip Ginter. 2015. Towards universal web parsebanks. In *Proceedings of the International Conference on Dependency Linguistics (Depling'15)*, pages 211–220. Uppsala University.

C.R. Miller. 1984. Genre as social action. *Quaterly journal of speech*, 70(2):151–167.

Marina Santini and Serge Sharoff. 2009. Web genre benchmark under construction. *JLCL*, 24(1):129–145.

Roland Schäfer and Felix Bildhauer, 2016. *Proceedings of the 10th Web as Corpus Workshop*, chapter Automatic Classification by Topic Domain for Meta Data Generation, Web Corpus Evaluation, and Corpus Comparison, pages 1–6. Association for Computational Linguistics.

Mike Scott and Chistopher Tribble. 2006. *Textual Patterns: keyword and corpus analysis in language education*. Benjamins, Amsterdam.

Serge Sharoff, Zhili Wu, and Katja Markert. 2010. The web library of Babel: evaluating genre collections.

John Sinclair. 1996. Preliminary recommendations on corpus typology.

John Swales. 1990. *Genre analysis: English in academic and research settings*. Cambridge University Press, Cambridge.

Vedrana Vidulin, Mitja Lustrek, and Matjax Gams. 2007. Using genres to improve search engines. In *Workshop "Towards genre-enabled Search Engines: The impact of NLP" at RANLP*, pages 45–51.

Bonnie Webber. 2009. Genre distinctions for discourse in the Penn treebank. In *Proceedings of the joint conference of the 47th annual meeting of the ACL and the 4th international joint conference on natural language processing of the AFNLP.*, pages 674–682. Association for Computational Linguistics.

KILLE: a Framework for Situated Agents for Learning Language Through Interaction

Simon Dobnik
CLASP
University of Gothenburg, Sweden
`simon.dobnik@gu.se`

Erik Wouter de Graaf
University of Gothenburg, Sweden
`kille@masx.nl`

Abstract

We present KILLE, a framework for situated agents for learning language through interaction with its environment (perception) and with a human tutor (dialogue). We provide proof-of-concept evaluations of the usability of the system in two domains: learning of object categories and learning of spatial relations.

1 Introduction

Situated conversational robots have to be capable of both linguistic interaction with humans and interaction with their environment through perception and action if we want them a part of our daily lives. Humans interact through language very efficiently and naturally and since most of them are not expert programmers, interaction with a robot in a natural language will be preferred. Secondly, by being part of the human environment containing everyday objects such as tables and chairs, robots too have to have knowledge how humans structure and organise their world which is again reflected in human language.

Connecting language with perception and action is commonly known as grounding (Harnad, 1990; Roy, 2002). The main challenge in grounding is that we are connecting two representation systems, (i) a perceptual which is commonly captured in physical sciences as continuous real-valued features and (ii) a symbolic conceptual system that makes up human language. There is no one-to-one correspondence between the two: linguistic descriptions such as "close to the table" and "red" correspond to some function predicting the degree of acceptability over physical or colour space (Logan and Sadler, 1996; Roy, 2002; Roy, 2005; Skočaj et al., 2010; Matuszek et al., 2012; Kennington and Schlangen, 2015; McMahan and Stone, 2015). The relations between concepts are not flat but are made increasingly more

abstract, structures are embedded and recursive (Fellbaum, 1998; Tenenbaum et al., 2011) and organised at several representational layers (Kruijff et al., 2007). It follows that several descriptions may be equally applicable for the same situation: the chair can be "close to the table" or "to the left of the table" which means *vagueness* is prevalent in grounding. This however, can be resolved through interaction by adopting appropriate interaction strategies (Kelleher et al., 2005; Skantze et al., 2014; Dobnik et al., 2015).

The meaning of words is not grounded just in perception and action but also grounded in particular linguistic interactions or conversations: participants continuously adapt and agree on the meaning of words as a part of their interaction (Clark, 1996; Fernández et al., 2011). This means that having a static model of grounded language which is learned offline from a corpus with a situated robot is not enough but this must be continuously adapted as the interaction unfolds (Skočaj et al., 2011; Matuszek et al., 2012). The idea of dynamic, continuously updated grounded language models is parallel to dynamic, continuously updated maps of the environment that have been commonly used in mobile robotics for a while (Dissanayake et al., 2001). Static models used in early robotics (Winograd, 1976) were just not able to deal with any changes in its environment and the uncertainty that these bring. We want to take the same view for language which is dynamically adjusted through interaction strategies.

In this paper we describe a framework for situated agents that learn grounded language incrementally and online called KILLE (Kinect Is Learning LanguagE) with the help of a human tutor in the fashion previously described. KILLE is a non-mobile table-top robot connecting Kinect sensors with image processing and classification and a spoken dialogue system. The system learns to recognise objects presented to it by a human tu-

162

tor from scratch. It can direct learning by asking for more objects of a particular category if it is not able to classify them with sufficient reliability. If more objects of a particular category are available in the scene and the system is able to recognise them, the system queries the user to describe spatial relations between them. Each of these kinds of descriptions focus on different perceptual features and represent two fundamental linguistic semantic categories: entities and entity relations. Overall, KILLE combines both passive and active learning which is incremental at the level of both kinds of linguistic categories.

The contributions of the KILLE framework are two-fold: (i) from the computational perspective it provides a platform for building models of situated language learning and answering questions how to integrate and test existing language technology tools (primarily intended for processing corpora) in an interactive tutoring framework; (ii) it also provides a platform for testing linguistic and psycho-linguistic theories, formalisms and applications on grounding language in interaction (Larsson, 2013; Dobnik et al., 2013) and implementing them computationally. This paper focuses on the construction of the Kille framework and its properties while it also provides a proof-of-concept evaluation of such learning of simple object and spatial relations representations. The paper is organised as follows. In Section 2 we describe the main components of the system. In Sections 3 and 4 we describe the perceptual representations and dialogue strategies that have been implemented so far. Section 5 describes proof-concept learning of objects and Section 5.2 learning of spatial descriptions that demonstrate the usability of the framework. We give conclusions and discussion of future work in Section 6.

2 The KILLE system

The system and the architecture that KILLE is using are similar to two existing systems for incremental interaction (Schlangen and Skantze, 2011) IrisTK (Skantze and Al Moubayed, 2012) and InproTK (Kennington et al., 2014). The difference is that instead of starting from the perspective of incremental language processing and dialogue management we focus on the mapping between language and robot's sensors and actuators and how to learn such mappings through particular dialogue and interactional strategies. Therefore, we

opt for a Robot Operating System (ROS) (Quigley et al., 2009) as our middle-ware which provides a common framework for building modules that communicate with each other (send and receive information) and runs on a variety of popular robotic hardware implementations which makes modules portable between them. We work with a very simple robotic hardware: a Microsoft Kinect sensor supported by the *libfreenect* library integrated in ROS.[1] The Kinect provides us with three sensors: an RGB camera of resolution 640x480, a depth sensor, which a structured-light 3D scanner that can perceive in a distance between 70 and 300 cm and gives a 3d representation of object, and a multi-array microphone (not used). The Kinect sensor is attached to a laptop computer running ROS and other software and together they represent our interactive robot. This robot does not have actuators which means it is not mobile and so it cannot turn gaze and focus on objects not in its vision field. Objects have to be brought into its attention field. We use glass pedestals as object support as to avoid the problem of object segmentation (e.g. object and hand) as glass is not detected by the depth sensor. Although simple, the platform satisfies well our requirements for incremental situated learning of perceptual language through dialogue. Through ROS the system can be ported to other, more sophisticated robotic platforms with very little modification.

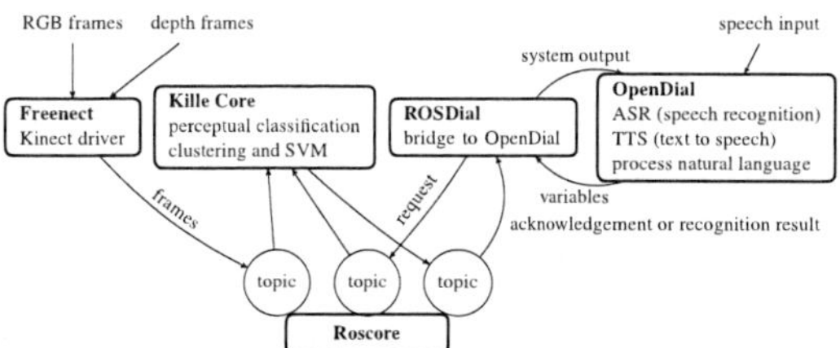

Figure 1: Kille modules

Figure 1 shows the main software modules that make up Kille and how they communicate with each other within the ROS framework. Each component (e.g. Kille, ROSDial, etc.) is a node which may have one or several topics. A node can publish to a topic or subscribe to a topic from another node. *Roscore* is a special node which is responsible for communication. As communication is per-

---

[1] See http://wiki.ros.org/freenect_stack We use an older version of Kinect hardware 1414 which is better supported by *libfreenect*.

formed over TCP/IP nodes can be distributed over several machines.

For dialogue management we use OpenDial[2] (Lison, 2013) which is a domain independent dialogue manager supporting probabilistic rules. It comes pre-packaged with several other popular NLP tools and interfaces to ASR and TTS systems. User utterances are ran through ASR and POS-tagged with the MaltParser. The output is then processed by a series of dialogue rules which define pre-conditions and post-conditions of their application. Since this is a perceptual dialogue system, dialogue rules involve both linguistic information and information received from the perceptual module of the system (Kille Core), for example the names of the objects detected and the certainty of detection, the spatial relation between them, etc. The dialogue rules can define further dialogue moves or actions for the perceptual system to take. In order to use OpenDial in our ROS configuration we had to build a bridge between the two which we call ROSDial. This sets up a ROS node and an instance of OpenDial. As OpenDial, ROSDial is written in Java. ROSDial translates the messages between OpenDial's information state and a ROS topic. It also ensures that Kille and OpenDial are synchronised. As the interaction is driven by OpenDIAL, sending requests to Kille is straightforward. However, it can also happen that a perceptual event is detected by Kille which the dialogue manager should act upon. ROSDial periodically instantiates a dialogue rule to interpret for any new information that has been pushed to its information state from Kille Core. Finally, Kille Core is written in Python and handles all perceptual representations and learning. The representations of objects and spatial relations can be saved and reloaded between sessions. Kille Core also sends and receives messages both to and from the Kinect library, e.g. scanned perceptual data, and ROSDial, e.g. linguistic data. Both ROSDial and Kille Core are available on Github.[3]

3 Perceptual representations

For visual representations we use OpenCV (Open Source Computer Vision)[4] which is a popular library for computer vision including machine learning applications. It is natively written in C

and C++, but has interfaces for other languages including Python (Bradski and Kaehler, 2008). It is also optimised for real-time applications. Through ROS we receive real-time frames from Kinect which include both data from the depth sensor and the visual RGB sensor. The frames are converted to the OpenCV format which is compatible with *NumPy* arrays and which allows for fast computational manipulation.

The visual processing is performed in two steps. In the first step the information from the depth sensor is used to detect the object in focus and remove irrelevant foreground and background in the RGB image. The depth sensor of Kinect cannot detect objects that are closer to it than 70 cm (Figure 2a). We define background as anything that is further away than 100 cm from the Kinect sensor and remove it (Figure 2b). This leaves us 30 centimetre of space that we can present objects in, which turns out to be sufficient and works well for our experiments.

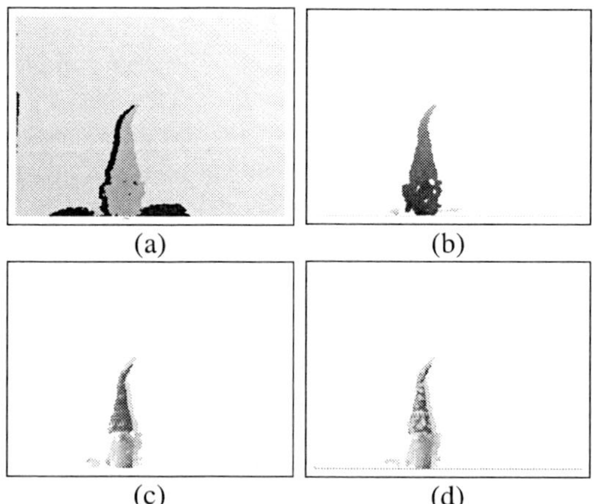

Figure 2: A perception of a plush gnome from the depth sensor (a) including the background, (b) with the background removed, (c) with the RGB image superimposed, and (d) with SIFT features detected in the image. The black border in (a) is a perceptual artefact arising from the interference of sensors.

In the next step, the RGB image is processed and only those pixels are preserved in the image that correspond to the remaining depth points (Figure 2c). These pixels, representing the object in focus, are processed with the SIFT (Scale-Invariant Feature Transform) algorithm (Lowe, 1999) which detects points of interest in a still image (Fig-

---

[2]https://github.com/plison/opendial
[3]https://github.com/masx/Kille
[4]http://opencv.org

ure 2c). Each point is represented as descriptor, a high dimensional vector which contains information about the visual properties surrounding each key-point, its orientation and location. SIFT is intended to be scale-invariant which means it is robust against changes that are introduced by scaling, can handle rotation and small changes in illumination. Note that objects (including those that are very similar and belong to the same category) will have different numbers of SIFT descriptors detected depending on their visual properties: some objects have a lot of visual details while others are smoother. In our interactive scenario this will also be the case each time when the same object will be re-introduced to the system as the captured frame will be slightly different from the previously captured one because of slight changes in location, lighting and camera noise.

4 Dialogue games

In the dialogue manager we implemented dialogue rules that act upon both linguistic and perceptual knowledge and allow us to have the following conversational games (Kowtko et al., 1992) with users.

1. **Direct instruction: objects**

   User: This is a cup.
   System: [Object is focused on and observed.]
   S: OK, I learned a cup.

2. **Direct instruction: spatial relations**

   U: The book is to the right of the mug.
   S: [Objects are focused on and observed.]
   S: OK. This relation is called "to the right of".
   S: [Objects are focused on and observed.]
   U: Where are the objects?
   S: The book is to the right of the mug.

3. **Describing objects and relations with (un)certainty**

   U: What is this?
   S: [Object is focused on and observed.]
   U: The object is thought to be a book, but it might also be a mug.

4. **Reinforcement from feedback**

   U: What is this?
   S: [Object is focused on and observed.]
   S: This is a cup.
   U: That is correct.
   S: [Observation is added to the models.]

5. **Self initiative: spatial relations**

   S: [Objects are focused on and observed.]
   S: One of the objects is book, the other one is box. Please tell me where things are.

U: The book is to the left of the box.
S: OK, this relation is called "to the left of".

6. **Unlearning immediately (e.g. after a mishearing)**

   U: This is a book.
   S: [Object is focused on and observed.]
   S: OK, this is a box.
   U: That is not what I said.
   S: OK, sorry. I will ignore it.

7. **Unlearning later**

   U: Forget a book.
   S: OK. I forgot a book.

8. **Renaming an object**

   U: This is a book.
   S: [Object is focused on and observed.]
   S: OK, this is a box.
   U: I said a book.
   S: OK, sorry. This is a book.

5 Interactive perceptional learning

In the following subsections we present a proof-of concept implementation and evaluation of perceptual learning through interaction which demonstrates the usability of the Kille framework.

5.1 Learning to recognise objects

As described in Section 3 every scan, even of the same scene, gives us a different set of SIFT descriptors which as data-structures are multidimensional vectors. One approach to use SIFT descriptors in classification is to pre-cluster them to bags of visual words (BoVW) (see (Bruni et al., 2014) for discussion) and then apply their occurrence counts as features in a classifier such as Linear Support Vector Machine (SVM). However, in the current implementation we chose a simple lazy-learning method based on SIFT clustering as it better fits with the incremental learning scenario. With the SVM method we would have to store and cluster instances and re-train the model on each instance update, thus doing far more computational work. Since the domain and the number of examples are small, lazy-learning is justified.

The SIFT descriptors of each object instance are stored in a database and then at each classification step the current SIFT descriptions are compared against objects stored in memory and the category of the best matching object is returned. The matching of SIFT descriptors as k-nearest neighbours has been implemented in the FLANN library (Muja and Lowe, 2009). This takes the longest list of descriptors (either from the current instance or a database instance) and matches each descriptor to k descriptors in the other list (in our case $k = 2$). The matched tuples (some of which will have zero or no similarity) have to be filtered. For this the ratio test of (Lowe, 2004) is used which calculates the Euclidean distance between two descriptors and those pairs that fall below the empirically defined threshold of 0.75 are discarded. Since different object representations contain a different number of SIFT features and there is a bias that representations with a small number of features match representations with a large number of features, we take the harmonic mean of the ratio $\frac{\#Matched}{\#Model}$ and the ratio $\frac{\#Matched}{\#Perceived}$ as the final matching score. In the evaluation 10 consecutive scans are taken and their recognition scores are averaged to a single score. This improves the performance as it makes observations more stable to noise but decreases the processing speed. The name of the item in the database with the closest match is returned. If there are several top-ranking candidates of the same category, their category is returned with their mean recognition score.

The location of the recognised object is estimated by taking the locations of the twenty matched descriptors with the shortest distance.

To evaluate the system's performance in an interactive tutoring scenario we chose typical household objects that could be detected in the perception field of the Kinect sensor and which fall into the following 10 categories: apple, banana, teddy bear, book, cap, car, cup, can of paint, shoe and shoe-box. A human tutor successively reintroduces the same 10 objects to the system in a pre-defined order over four rounds trying to keep the presentation identical as much as possible. In each round all objects are first learned and then queried. To avoid ASR errors both in learning and generation text input is used.

The average recognition scores over four rounds are shown in Table 1. We choose the name of the object with the highest recognition score. The highest values follow all but in one case the diagonal which means that on overall objects are recognised correctly. The only problematic object is the cap which has been consistently confused with a banana. SIFT features do not contain colour information according to which these two categories of objects could be distinguished. There were a few individual confusions which did not affect the overall mean score (not shown in Table 1): the

shoe-box was confused with a car in rounds 1 and 2, and with an apple in round 3. The apple was recognised as a banana in round 2. Otherwise, the system performed extremely accurately. The last column C-NI gives *Correct-NextIncorrect* score (a difference between the matching score of the target object with the object of the correct category and the matching score of the target object with the closest matching object not of the correct category) which shows on average how visually distinct the object is. The models of most objects preserve significant distinctiveness over presentations and learning across the 4 rounds. If we rank objects by this score, we get the following ranking (from more distinct to least distinct): book > car > shoe > cup > banana > bear > apple > paint > shoe-box > cap.

In the second experiment we evaluated re-recognition of objects at different degrees of rotation ($45°$, $90°$, $135°$, $180°$, $225°$, $270°$ and $315°$ in the clockwise direction) using the final model for objects built after the completion of round 4 in the previous experiment. Already at a rotation of $45°$ 6 out of 10 objects are mis-recognised. Objects are affected by rotation in different ways since their sides are visually distinct. For example shoe-box and to a large extent apple are correctly classified at most rotational angles. We observe similar classification scores at those angles at which symmetric sides of objects are exposed: $45°{:}315°$ and $90°{:}270°$, $135°{:}225°$ and $0°{:}180°$.

In the third experiment we tested the model from the end of the round 4 in the first experiment on 3 new objects of each category. The models for experiment one did not extend well to different objects for most categories. Only apples (2 out of 3 new objects) and shoe-boxes (all 3 new objects) were recognised correctly. Shoe-box is also the most common mis-classification which means it is similar to other objects.

Overall, the results and the discussion in this section show that our system is able to learn to recognise objects incrementally through interaction with a human tutor from just a few observations. The testing of our models in new contexts from the context in which they were learned (rotation and classification of different objects of the same category) demonstrate how sensitive our models are to the changes of contexts which are likely to arise in the interactive scenario. Of course, learning observations of objects in these

$\rightarrow$	apple	banana	bear	book	cap	car	cup	paint	shoe	shoe-box	C-NI
apple	**.343**	.227	.076	.046	.099	.058	.126	.074	.053	.166	.116
banana	.201	**.357**	.058	.035	.085	.087	.148	.066	.046	.124	.155
bear	.080	.121	**.260**	.074	.089	.091	.120	.099	.074	.136	.123
book	.142	.233	.074	**.496**	.114	.197	.246	.130	.085	.220	.250
cap	.122	**.208**	.076	.049	.146	.096	.103	.083	.061	.114	-.062
car	.104	.183	.053	.067	.077	**.414**	.119	.076	.069	.149	.231
cup	.099	.145	.063	.066	.091	.052	**.330**	.094	.054	.120	.185
paint	.119	.140	.075	.076	.083	.147	.121	**.221**	.062	.111	.075
shoe	.078	.123	.070	.056	.079	.116	.124	.076	**.319**	.103	.196
shoe-box	.190	.332	.099	.188	.145	.305	.313	.166	.111	**.376**	.044

Table 1: Average recognition scores over four rounds. The object tested are represented in rows. Columns indicate the categories that they were recognised as.

contexts specifically would increase the success of object recognition. Thus, the experiments also point to the complexity of the object recognition.

5.2 Learning to recognise spatial relations

Once the system learns to detect several objects in the scene it starts querying the user to describe spatial relations between them. The semantics of spatial relations requires at least three components of meaning: (i) knowledge about the geometrical arrangement of objects in the scene; (ii) world knowledge about the objects involved in particular how they interact with each other or what is our take on the scene; (iii) dialogue interaction between conversational partners, for example in coordinating and negotiation perspective or the origin of the frame of reference (FoR) used. We hope that Kille will provide us a platform for modelling and testing the interaction between all three components, some of which, for example (ii), are learned from a large corpus off-line. Here we mainly focus on interactive learning of the geometric component (i).

First, the system must recognise the target and the landmark objects ("the gnome/TARGET is to the left of the book/LANDMARK") both in the linguistic string and the perceptual scene. Twenty highest ranking SIFT features are taken for each object and their x (width), y (height) and z (depth) coordinates are averaged, thus giving us the centroid of the 20 most salient features of an object.[5] We chose the number 20 based on practical experience. Higher numbers of features are more demanding for processing in real time. The origin of the coordinate frame for spatial templates must be at the centre of the landmark ob-

ject which means that the coordinates of the target must be expressed as relative to the landmark's location. A further transformation of the coordinate frame could be made depending on the orientation of the viewpoint that sets the perspective. However, in our scenario the geometric coordinate frame was always relative to the orientation of Kille. Of course, in conversations with Kille humans could describe locations from a different perspective which means that this can lead (in an absence of a model of FoR assignment) to a more complicated/noisy and ambiguous model of geometric spatial template learned. For example the same region could be described as "to the left of" and "to the right of". The relativised location of the target to the landmark are fed to a Linear Support Vector Classifier (SVC) with descriptions as target classes.

A human tutor taught the system by presenting it the target object (a book) at 16 different locations in relation to the landmark (the car) as shown in Figure 3. The locations were arranged so that there were 8 locations separated at $45°$ at two different distances around and from the landmark. These objects were chosen because they have achieved a good recognition accuracy in the previous experiments. The book was shown to the system three times per location in a randomised order which gave us 48 presentations. The target was moved after each presentation. This ensured that there was no semantic influence on descriptions between the presentations.[6] The spatial descriptions that the human instructor used were *to the left of*, *to the right of*, *in front of*, *behind of*, *near* and *close to* (6). The first 4 descriptions are *projective descriptions* and require grounding of FoR, while the last two are *topological descrip-*

---

[5]This is a simplification as object shape is only partially expressed in the y variable. This way we distinguish between tall and short objects. Note also that the variables x and z describe object location while y describes object property.

[6]In a different evaluation setting we might want to explore such bias.

tions and do not require grounding of the FoR, only distance. The relativised spatial coordinates implicitly encode both of these features.

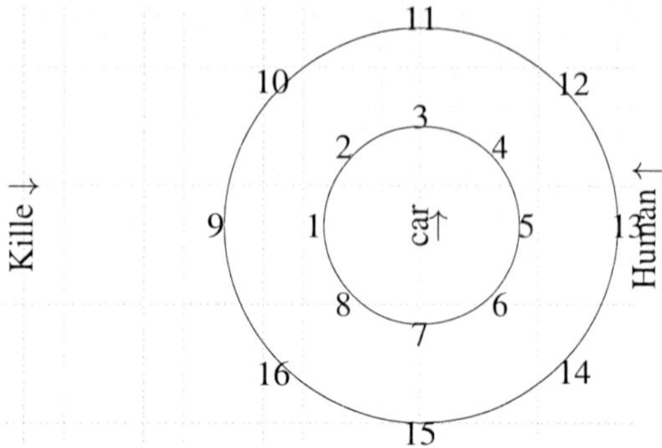

Figure 3: The locations of the target ("book"), the landmark ("car") and the conversational partners (Kille and the human). 1 and 9 have been slightly relaxed, as Kille would not be able to detect the car behind the book otherwise.

Note that spatial descriptions are not mutually exclusive: location 4 in Figure 3 could be described as "near", "close", "to the right of" and "in front of" (taking the human FoR) and "near", "close", "to the left of" and "behind" (taking Kille's FoR) which makes learning a difficult task. In the evaluation we are interested if the system would agree strictly with human observers on the most relevant description for that context, if this is not the case, would the system generate an alternative acceptable description. The agreement between annotators is highly informative as it tells us about the difficulty of the task.

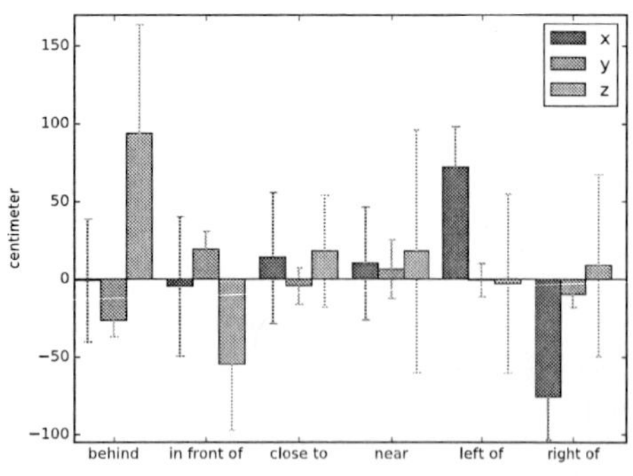

Figure 4: Average x, y and z values for spatial relations.

Figure 4 shows the average values of the x (width), y (height) and z (depth) features with the origin on the landmark object for the instances in our learning dataset. There is quite a clear opposition between "behind" and "in front of" as well as "to the left of" and "to the right of" which means that the instructor was consistent in the usage of the FoR. What is interesting is that different FoR is used for the front-and-back and the lateral dimensions. "behind" and "in front of" are grounded in an FoR relative to Kille (away from and towards Kille respectively) while "left" and "right" are grounded in an FoR relative to the conversational partner (e.g. "to the left of" corresponds to positive x values. Effectively, a split FoR is used. In this scenario, there is no effect of conversational roles on the assignment of FoR (information giver and information receiver) which has been reported by (Schober, 1995). The reason why the target is appears to be lower when it is described to be "behind" the landmark is due to the positioning of the sensor higher than the landmark at an angle looking down. This means that objects further away appear shorter. Finally both "close" and "near" show short distances from the landmark in each dimension as expected. However, there is, at least in this model, no clear difference between these two descriptions.

The performance of the system was independently evaluated by two human conversational partners, one of whom was also the tutor during the learning phase. As during learning, the target object was placed in one of the 16 locations and each location was used twice, which gave each human to evaluate a total of 32 situations which were presented in a random order. After each object placement, the evaluators first independently wrote down the description they would use to describe the scene. Then the system would be queried to describe the location of the target. The system's response was recorded and also whether the evaluators agreed with the generated description or not.

As mentioned earlier, several spatial descriptions may apply to the same location of the target and the landmark. The observed strict agreement between the evaluators independently choosing a description is 0.5313 (they independently choose the same description in just over 1/2 of cases). However, when we correct this value by agreement by chance in the form of the Kappa coefficient (κ), the estimated strict agreement between the evaluators is $\kappa = 0.4313$. Choosing a spatial description is thus quite a subjective task.

Match	Evaluator 1		Evaluator 2		Evaluator 1 + 2	
Independent	8	0.25	7	0.2188	15	0.2344
Secondary	11	0.3438	13	0.4063	24	0.375
Indep. + Second.	19	0.5938	20	0.6251	39	0.6094
Incorrect	13	0.4063	12	0.375	25	0.3906
Total	32	1	32	1	64	1

Table 2: Observed agreement between the evaluators and the system

The observed agreement between the evaluators and the system is shown in Table 2. The evaluators and the system independently chose the same description in 23.44% of cases which is a decrease from 53.13% where only evaluators are compared with each other. However, even if the description was not the one that evaluators chose in this situation, the evaluators thought that the generated description was nonetheless a good description in further 37.5% of situations. Overall, evaluators were satisfied with 60.94% of generations, while 39.06% were considered incorrect. Given the difficulty of the task and that the system on average had a chance to learn each description only from 8 trials (48/6 = 8), thus not observing each description at all possible 16 locations, the results are encouraging and are close to what has been reported for a similar task in the literature (Dobnik, 2009).

	behind	front	left	right	close	near	Total
behind	**4**	2	1	0	0	2	9
front	0	**5**	3	3	6	0	17
left	0	6	**1**	0	0	0	7
right	4	1	3	**3**	0	1	12
close	1	9	1	0	**1**	2	14
near	1	1	1	0	1	**1**	5
Total	10	24	10	6	8	6	64

Table 3: Agreement between two human evaluators (rows) and the system (columns)

Table 3 shows a confusion matrix for all 64 trials. The Kappa coefficient, thus the strict observed agreement of 0.2344 (Table 2) discounted by the agreement by chance is $\kappa = 0.0537$. If we examine Table 3 we can see, as also shown in Table 2, that non-agreements involve those descriptions that are appropriate alternatives. For example, we expect topological descriptions (e.g. "close") to partially overlap with projective descriptions (e.g. "front") or with other projective descriptions (e.g. "left" and "front"). The data also shows

that humans and evaluators have a slightly different preference for assigning descriptions. Humans assign descriptions with the following likelihoods (from the highest to the lowest): "front" (0.2656) > "close" (0.2188) > "right" (0.1875) > "behind" (0.1406) > "left" (0.1094) > "near" (0.0781) while the system has the following preference "front" (0.375) > "behind"/"left" (0.1563) > "close" (0.125) and > "right"/"near" (0.0938). The most important differences are thus in the usage of "close"/"right" *vs* "behind"/"left" and demonstrate the subjective nature of the task and possibly a usage of different FoRs.

6 Conclusion and future work

We presented Kille, a framework for situated agents for learning language through interaction. This is based on a Robotic Operating System (ROS) which simplifies the development of new applications and their communication, as well as allowing the system to be ported to a variety of more sophisticated popular robotic platforms. We focus on the linguistic interactional aspects with a situated agent in the context of learning through instruction and therefore our three main modules are the robotic perceptual system provided by the Kinect sensor, a dialogue system and a module for classification of grounded lexical meanings. We demonstrate and evaluate the usability of the system on two proof-of-concept applications: learning of object names and learning of spatial relations.

As stated in the introduction we hope that the framework will allow us to explore computational and linguistic questions related to situated learning. In particular, we are interested in how (i) different machine learning methods can be used with an interactive tutoring scenario including the application of image convolutions from deep learning to replace SIFT features. (ii) Integration of classifiers learned offline from a large corpus with the interactive learning and classification is also an open question. On the language side we are interested in (iii) what kind of interaction strategies or dialogue games are relevant in this scenario, (iv) how can these games be implemented in a situated dialogue system in terms of dialogue moves operating on linguistic and perceptual representations and linking to machine learning or classification, (v) and how effective individual dialogue games are in respect to the rate of learning.

References

Gary Bradski and Adrian Kaehler. 2008. *Learning OpenCV: Computer vision with the OpenCV library.* " O'Reilly Media, Inc.".

Elia Bruni, Nam-Khanh Tran, and Marco Baroni. 2014. Multimodal distributional semantics. *Journal of Artificial Intelligence Research (JAIR)*, 49(1-47).

Herbert H. Clark. 1996. *Using language.* Cambridge University Press, Cambridge.

M. W. M. G Dissanayake, P. M. Newman, H. F. Durrant-Whyte, S. Clark, and M. Csorba. 2001. A solution to the simultaneous localization and map building (SLAM) problem. *IEEE Transactions on Robotic and Automation*, 17(3):229–241.

Simon Dobnik, Robin Cooper, and Staffan Larsson. 2013. Modelling language, action, and perception in Type Theory with Records. In Denys Duchier and Yannick Parmentier, editors, *Constraint Solving and Language Processing: 7th International Workshop, CSLP 2012, Orléans, France, September 13–14, 2012, Revised Selected Papers*, volume 8114 of *Lecture Notes in Computer Science*, pages 70–91. Springer Berlin Heidelberg.

Simon Dobnik, Christine Howes, and John D. Kelleher. 2015. Changing perspective: Local alignment of reference frames in dialogue. In Christine Howes and Staffan Larsson, editors, *Proceedings of goDIAL - Semdial 2015: The 19th Workshop on the Semantics and Pragmatics of Dialogue*, pages 24–32, Gothenburg, Sweden, 24–26th August.

Simon Dobnik. 2009. *Teaching mobile robots to use spatial words.* Ph.D. thesis, University of Oxford: Faculty of Linguistics, Philology and Phonetics and The Queen's College, Oxford, United Kingdom, September 4.

Christiane Fellbaum. 1998. *WordNet: an electronic lexical database.* MIT Press, Cambridge, Mass.

Raquel Fernández, Staffan Larsson, Robin Cooper, Jonathan Ginzburg, and David Schlangen. 2011. Reciprocal learning via dialogue interaction: Challenges and prospects. In *Proceedings of the IJCAI 2011 Workshop on Agents Learning Interactively from Human Teachers (ALIHT)*, Barcelona, Catalonia, Spain.

Stevan Harnad. 1990. The symbol grounding problem. *Physica D*, 42(1–3):335–346, June.

J.D. Kelleher, F. Costello, and J. van Genabith. 2005. Dynamically structuring updating and interrelating representations of visual and linguistic discourse. *Artificial Intelligence*, 167:62–102.

Casey Kennington and David Schlangen. 2015. Simple learning and compositional application of perceptually grounded word meanings for incremental reference resolution. In *Proceedings of the 53rd Annual Meeting of the Association for Computational Linguistics and the 7th International Joint Conference on Natural Language Processing (Volume 1: Long Papers)*, pages 292–301, Beijing, China, July. Association for Computational Linguistics.

Casey Kennington, Spyros Kousidis, and David Schlangen. 2014. Inprotks: A toolkit for incremental situated processing. *Proceedings of SIGdial 2014: Short Papers.*

Jacqueline C Kowtko, Stephen D Isard, and Gwyneth M Doherty. 1992. Conversational games within dialogue. HCRC research paper RP-31, University of Edinburgh.

Geert-Jan M. Kruijff, Hendrik Zender, Patric Jensfelt, and Henrik I. Christensen. 2007. Situated dialogue and spatial organization: what, where... and why? *International Journal of Advanced Robotic Systems*, 4(1):125–138. Special issue on human and robot interactive communication.

Staffan Larsson. 2013. Formal semantics for perceptual classification. *Journal of Logic and Computation*, online:1–35, December 18.

Pierre Lison. 2013. *Structured Probabilistic Modelling for Dialogue Management.* Ph.D. thesis, Department of Informatics, Faculty of Mathematics and Natural Sciences, University of Oslo, 30th October.

Gordon D. Logan and Daniel D. Sadler. 1996. A computational analysis of the apprehension of spatial relations. In Paul Bloom, Mary A. Peterson, Lynn Nadel, and Merrill F. Garrett, editors, *Language and Space*, pages 493–530. MIT Press, Cambridge, MA.

David G Lowe. 1999. Object recognition from local scale-invariant features. In *Computer vision, 1999. The proceedings of the seventh IEEE international conference on*, volume 2, pages 1150–1157. IEEE.

David G Lowe. 2004. Distinctive image features from scale-invariant keypoints. *International journal of computer vision*, 60(2):91–110.

Cynthia Matuszek, Nicholas FitzGerald, Luke Zettlemoyer, Liefeng Bo, and Dieter Fox. 2012. A joint model of language and perception for grounded attribute learning. In John Langford and Joelle Pineau, editors, *Proceedings of the 29th International Conference on Machine Learning (ICML 2012)*, Edinburgh, Scotland, June 27th - July 3rd.

Brian McMahan and Matthew Stone. 2015. A bayesian model of grounded color semantics. *Transactions of the Association for Computational Linguistics*, 3:103–115.

Marius Muja and David G Lowe. 2009. Fast approximate nearest neighbors with automatic algorithm configuration. *VISAPP (1)*, 2(331–340):2.

Morgan Quigley, Ken Conley, Brian Gerkey, Josh Faust, Tully Foote, Jeremy Leibs, Rob Wheeler, and Andrew Y Ng. 2009. ROS: an open-source robot operating system. In *ICRA workshop on open source software*, volume 3, page 5.

Deb K. Roy. 2002. Learning visually-grounded words and syntax for a scene description task. *Computer speech and language*, 16(3):353–385.

Deb Roy. 2005. Semiotic schemas: a framework for grounding language in action and perception. *Artificial Intelligence*, 167(1-2):170–205, September.

David Schlangen and Gabriel Skantze. 2011. A general, abstract model of incremental dialogue processing. *Dialogue and discourse*, 2(1):83–111.

Michael F. Schober. 1995. Speakers, addressees, and frames of reference: Whose effort is minimized in conversations about locations? *Discourse Processes*, 20(2):219–247.

Gabriel Skantze and Samer Al Moubayed. 2012. IrisTK: a statechart-based toolkit for multi-party face-to-face interaction. In *Proceedings of the 14th ACM international conference on Multimodal interaction*, pages 69–76. ACM.

Gabriel Skantze, Anna Hjalmarsson, and Catharine Oertel. 2014. Turn-taking, feedback and joint attention in situated human-robot interaction. *Speech Communication*, 65:50–66.

Danijel Skočaj, Miroslav Janiček, Matej Kristan, Geert-Jan M. Kruijff, Aleš Leonardis, Pierre Lison, Alen Vrečko, and Michael Zillich. 2010. A basic cognitive system for interactive continuous learning of visual concepts. In *ICRA 2010 workshop ICAIR - Interactive Communication for Autonomous Intelligent Robots*, pages 30–36, Anchorage, AK, USA.

Danijel Skočaj, Matej Kristan, Alen Vrečko, Marko Mahnič, Miroslav Janíček, Geert-Jan M. Kruijff, Marc Hanheide, Nick Hawes, Thomas Keller, Michael Zillich, and Kai Zhou. 2011. A system for interactive learning in dialogue with a tutor. In *IEEE/RSJ International Conference on Intelligent Robots and Systems IROS 2011*, San Francisco, CA, USA, 25-30 September.

Joshua B. Tenenbaum, Charles Kemp, Thomas L. Griffiths, and Noah D. Goodman. 2011. How to grow a mind: Statistics, structure, and abstraction. *Science*, 331(6022):1279–1285.

Terry Winograd. 1976. *Understanding Natural Language*. Edinburgh University Press.

Data Collection from Persons with Mild Forms of Cognitive Impairment and Healthy Controls - Infrastructure for Classification and Prediction of Dementia

Dimitrios Kokkinakis, Kristina Lundholm Fors, Eva Björkner
Department of Swedish
University of Gothenburg
Sweden
`first.last@svenska.gu.se`

Arto Nordlund
Department of Psychiatry and Neurochemistry
Sahlgrenska Academy, University of Gothenburg
Sweden
`first.last@neuro.gu.se`

Abstract

Cognitive and mental deterioration, such as difficulties with memory and language, are some of the typical phenotypes for most neurodegenerative diseases including Alzheimer's disease and other dementia forms. This paper describes the first phases of a project that aims at collecting various types of cognitive data, acquired from human subjects in order to study relationships among linguistic and extra-linguistic observations. The project's aim is to identify, extract, process, correlate, evaluate, and disseminate various linguistic phenotypes and measurements and thus contribute with complementary knowledge in early diagnosis, monitor progression, or predict individuals at risk. In the near future, automatic analysis of these data will be used to extract various types of features for training, testing and evaluating automatic classifiers that could be used to differentiate individuals with mild symptoms of cognitive impairment from healthy, age-matched controls and identify possible indicators for the early detection of mild forms of cognitive impairment. Features will be extracted from audio recordings (speech signal), the transcription of the audio signals (text) and the raw eye-tracking data.

1   Introduction

Aiding the detection of very early cognitive impairment in Alzheimer's disease (AD) and assessing the disease progression are essential foundations for effective psychological assessment, diagnosis and planning; enabling patients to participate in new drug therapy research and design of new clinical trials; evaluating potential disease-modifying agents in suitable populations etc. Efficient tools for routine dementia screening in primary health care, and particularly non-invasive and cost-effective methods in routine dementia screening for the identification of subjects who could be administered for further cognitive evaluation and dementia diagnostics, could provide specialist centres the opportunity to engage in more demanding, advanced investigations, care and treatment. New paths of research for acquiring knowledge about Alzheimer's disease (AD) and its subtypes using Computational Linguistic/ Natural Language Processing (CL/NLP) techniques and tools based on the exploration of several complementary modalities, parameters and features, such as speech analysis and/or eye tracking could be integrated into established neuropsychological, memory and cognitive test batteries in order to explore potential (new) biomarkers for AD. This paper describes current efforts to acquire data from people with subjective (SCI) and mild cognitive impairment (MCI) and healthy, age-matched controls in order to analyse and evaluate potential useful linguistic and extra-linguistic features and build classifiers that could differentiate between benign and malignant forms of cognitive impairment. Non-invasive and cost-effective methods that could identify individuals at an early preclinical dementia stage remains a priority and a challenge for health care providers while language deficits have been reported early in the development of AD (Taler & Phillips, 2008). Moreover, NLP methods are applied more and more in various biomedical and clinical settings, while patient language samples and large datasets are used routinely in NLP research such as the Dementia Bank corpus (a part of the TalkBank project; MacWhinney et al., 2011) and the Cambridge Cookie-Theft Corpus (Williams et al., 2010). The SCI, the MCI, and the

Proceedings of the 21st Nordic Conference of Computational Linguistics, pages 172–182,
Gothenburg, Sweden, 23-24 May 2017. ©2017 Linköping University Electronic Press

Alzheimer's disease (AD) are on a spectrum of disease progression. Subjective cognitive impairment (SCI) is a common diagnosis in elderly people, sometimes suggested to be associated with e.g. depression, stress or anxiety, but also a risk factor for dementia (Jessen et al., 2010). On the other hand, mild cognitive impairment (MCI) is a prodromal state of dementia (Ritchie & Touchon, 2010), in which a human subject has minor problems with cognition (e.g., problems with memory or thinking) but these are not severe enough to warrant a diagnosis of dementia or interfere significantly with daily life, but still difficulties which are worse than would normally be expected for a healthy person of their age.

This paper describes some efforts underway to acquire, assess, analyze and evaluate linguistic and extra-linguistic data from people with subjective (SCI) and mild cognitive impairment (MCI) and healthy, age-matched controls, with focus on infrastructure (e.g., resource collection, envisaged analysis and feature acquisition and modeling).

2 Background

New findings aim to provide a comprehensive picture of cognitive status and some promising results have recently thrown more light on the importance of language and language (dis)abilities as an essential factor that can have a strong impact on specific measurable characteristics that can be extracted by automatic linguistic analysis of speech and text (Ferguson et al., 2013; Szatloczki et al., 2015). The work by Snowdon et al. (2000), "The Nun Study", was one of the earliest studies which showed a strong correlation between low linguistic ability early in life and cognitive impairment in later life by analyzing autobiographies of American nuns. Snowdon et al. could predict who could develop Alzheimer's by studying the degradation of the idea density (that is, the average number of ideas expressed in 10 words; Chand et al., 2010) and syntactic complexity on the nuns' autobiographical writings. Since then, the body of research and interest in CL/NLP in the area of processing data from subjects with mental, cognitive, neuropsychiatric, or neurode-generative impairments has grown rapidly. Automatic spoken language analysis and eye movement measurements are two of the newer complementary diagnostic tools with great potential for dementia diagnostics (Laske et al.,

2014). Furthermore, the identification of important linguistic and extra-linguistic features such as lexical and syntactic complexity, are becoming an established way to train and test supervised machine learning classifiers that can be used to differentiate between individuals with various forms of dementia and healthy controls or between individuals with different types of dementia (Lagun et al., 2011; Roark et al., 2011; Olubolu Orimaye et al., 2014; Rentoumi et al., 2014).

Although language is not the only diagnostic factor for cognitive impairment, several recent studies (Yancheva et al., 2015) have demonstrated that automatic linguistic analysis, primarily of connected speech samples, produced by people with mild or moderate cognitive impairment compared to healthy individuals can identify with good accuracy objective evidence and measurable (progressive) language disorders. Garrard & Elvevåg (2014) comment that computer-assisted analysis of large language datasets could contribute to the understanding of brain disorders. Although, none of the studies presented in the special issue of Cortex vol. 55 moved "beyond the representation of language as text" and therefore finding reliable ways of incorporating features, such as prosody and emotional connotation, into data representation remains a future challenge, the editors acknowledged that current research indicates that "the challenges of applying computational linguistics to the cognitive neuroscience field, as well as the power of these techniques to frame questions of theoretical interest and define clinical groups are of practical importance". Nevertheless, studies have shown that a steady change in the linguistic nature of the symptoms and the degree in speech and writing are early and could be identified by using language technology analysis (Mortimer et al., 2005; Le et al., 2011). New findings also show a great potential to increase our understanding of dementia and its impact on linguistic degradation such as loss of vocabulary, syntactic simplification, poor speech content and semantic generalization. Analysis of eye movement is also a relevant research technology to apply, and text reading by people with and without mild cognitive impairment may give a clear ruling on how reading strategies differ between these groups, an area that has so far not been researched to any significant extent in this particular domain (Fernández et al., 2013, 2014;

Molitor et al., 2015). With the help of eye-tracking technology the eye movements of participants are recorded while suitable stimuli is presented (e.g., a short text).

3 Ethical Issues and Patient Recruitment

The ongoing Gothenburg mild cognitive impairment study (Nordlund et al., 2005; Wallin et al., 2016) is an attempt to conduct longitudinal in-depth phenotyping of patients with different forms and degrees of cognitive impairment using neuropsychological, neuroimaging, and neurochemical tools. The study is clinically based and aims at identifying neurodegenerative, vascular and stress related disorders prior to the development of dementia. All patients in the study undergo baseline investigations, such as neurological examination, psychiatric evaluation, cognitive screening (e.g., memory and visuospatial disturbance, poverty of language and apraxia), magnetic resonance imaging of the brain and cerebrospinal fluid collection. At biannual follow-ups, most of these investigations are repeated. The overall Gothenburg MCI-study is approved by the local ethical committee review board (reference number: L091–99, 1999; T479-11, 2011); while the currently described study by the local ethical committee decision 206-16, 2016). The project aims at gathering a rather homogeneous group of participants with respect to age and education level (50 with SCI/MCI and 50 controls). All subjects have participated into a comprehensive battery of e.g. memory, language and other tests which have been described in Wallin et al. (2016). Recruitment of patients in the project was consecutive and took place over the course of several months, from July 2016 to January 2017. All participants gave informed written consent and were advised that no notations were made that could be related to their identity, while the exclusion and inclusion criteria are specified according to the following protocol.

Inclusion criteria:

- Age range 50-79 years
- Swedish as a first language and not speaking languages other than Swedish before the age of 5
- Comparable education length of the participants

- No apparent organic cause of symptoms (such as e.g. stroke or brain tumor)
- Research subjects have read information about the research project and approved voice recording and eye movement measurements
- Participants have conducted *recent* neuropsychological tests – participants should not have deteriorated significantly since the last testing

Exclusion criteria:

- Participants have comorbid conditions affecting reading (e.g. dyslexia or other reading difficulties)
- Participants have deep depression
- Participants have an ongoing abuse of any kind
- Participants suffer from serious psychiatric or neurological diseases such as Parkinson's, Amyotrophic lateral sclerosis or have/had a brain tumor
- Participants do not understand the question or the context in the selection process
- Participants have poor vision (that cannot be corrected by glasses or lenses), cataract, nystagmus, or cannot see and read on the computer screen
- Participants decline participation during telephone call or later at the recording site
- Participants decline signing the paper of informed consent
- Recordings or eye movement measurements are technically unusable.

4 Material and Experimental Design

4.1 Spoken signal/audio

For the acquisition of the audio signal we use the Cookie-theft picture [1] (see Figure 1) from the *Boston Diagnostic Aphasia Examination* (BDAE;

---

[1] Cookie-theft is a picture that has been a source of knowledge for various clinical and experimental research worldwide which enables even future cross-linguistic comparisons.

Goodglass & Kaplan, 1983) which is often used to elicit speech from people with various mental and cognitive impairments. During the presentation of the Cookie-theft stimuli (which illustrates an event taking place in a kitchen) the subjects are asked to tell a story about the picture and describe everything that can be observed while the story is recorded. For the task the original label of the cookie jar is translated and substituted from the English "COOKIE JAR" to the Swedish label "KAKBURK". The samples are recorded in an isolated environment and the whole task is designed to evoke a monologue by the participant. The instruction given to the subject was: "Tell me everything you see going on in this picture, describe objects and events. You can go on as long as you prefer and you will be not interrupted until you indicate that you do not have more to say".

Figure 1: The Cookie-theft picture.

We chose to use the Cookie Theft picture since it provides a standardized test that has been used in various studies in the past, and therefore comparisons can be made based on previous results, e.g. with research on the DementiaBank database or other collections (MacWhinney, 2007; Williams et al., 2010; Fraser & Hirst, 2016) and even Swedish studies (Tyche, 2001). The picture is considered an "ecologically valid approximation" to spontaneous discourse (Gilles et al., 1996). Moreover, in order to allow the construction of a comprehensive speech profile for each research participant, the speech task also includes reading aloud a short text from the *International Reading Speed Texts* collection (IReST; Trauzettel-Klosinski et al., 2012) presented on a computer screen. As a matter of fact, two texts are used from the IReST collection, in connection to the eye tracking experiment, but only one of those texts is read aloud and thus combined with eye-tracking recording; cf. Meilán et al., 2012 and 2014 for

similar "reading out" text passage experiments. IReST is a multilingual standardized text collection used to assess reading performance, for multiple equivalent texts for repeated measurements. Specifically in our project we use the Swedish IReST translations, namely texts "one" and "seven" (Öqvist Seimyr, 2010). For the audio capture of both we use a H2n Handy recorder while the audio files are saved and stored as uncompressed audio in .wav 44.1 kHz with 16-bit resolution. This recording is carried out in the same isolated environment in order to avoid noise.

4.2 Verbatim transcriptions

The textual part of the infrastructure consists of manually produced transcriptions of the two audio recordings previously described. The digitized speech waveform is semi-automatically aligned with the transcribed text. During speech transcription, special attention is also paid to non-speech acoustic events including speech dysfluencies consisting of filled pauses a.k.a. hesitation ("um"), false-starts, repetitions as well as other features, particularly non-verbal vocalizations such as laughing, sniffing and coughing. A basic transcription manual, with the various conventions to be used, is produced which helps the human transcribers accomplish a homogeneous transcription. For instance, all numerals should be written out as complete words, while symbols, such as square brackets, are used for the encoding of pauses or transcriber's comments. Furthermore, for the transcription the PRAAT application (Boersma & Weenink, 2013) is utilized; using a 2-tier text grid configuration, one for orthographic transcription (standardized spelling) and one with maintained spoken language phenomena, such as partial words, see Figure 2.

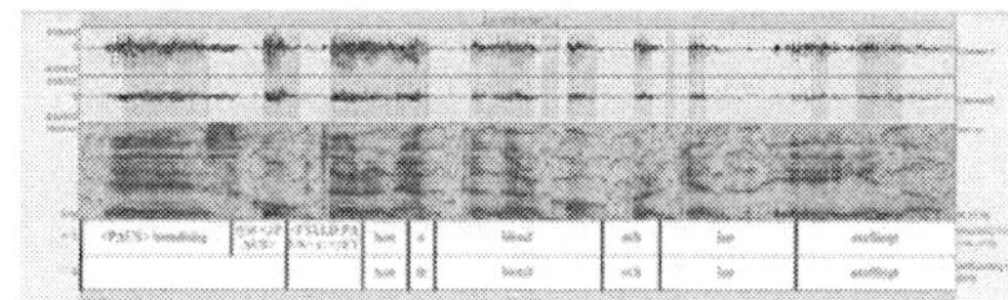

Figure 2: Transcription of the collected data.

4.3 Eye-tracking

The investigation of eye movement functions in SCI/MCI, and any differences or changes in eye movements that could be potentially detected for those patients is of great importance to clinical

AD research. However, until now, eye tracking has not been used to investigate reading for MCI-persons on a larger scale, possibly due to the number of procedural difficulties related to this kind of research. On the other hand, the technology has been applied in a growing body of various experiments related to other impairments such as autism (Yaneva et al., 2016; Au-Yeung et al., 2015), dyslexia (Rello & Ballesteros, 2015) and schizophrenia (Levy et al., 2010); for a thorough review see Anderson & MacAskill (2013). For the experiments we use EyeLink 1000 Desktop Mount with monocular eye tracking with head stabilization and a real-time sample access of 1000Hz. Head stabilization provides an increased eye tracking range performance. The participants are seated in front of the monitor at a distance of 60-70 cm. While reading, the eye movements of the participants are recorded with the eye-tracking device while interest areas around each word in the text are defined by taking advantage of the fact that there are spaces between each word in the text. The eye-tracking measurements are used for the detection and calculation of fixations, saccades and backtracks. Fixation analyses is conducted within predefined Areas of Interest (AOI); in our case each word is an AOI (see Figure 3).

Figure 3: A text from the IReST collection with marked fixations (top) and saccades (bottom).

4.4 Comparison over a two year period

The previously outlined experiments/audio recordings will be repeated two years after the first recording which took place during the second half of 2016. This way we want to analyze whether there are any differences between the two audio and eye-tracking recordings, and at which level and magnitude. We want to compare and examine whether there any observable, greater, differences/decline on some features and which these could be and therefore the nature and eventually progression of speech impairment or eye movement alterations observed over a two year period. We are aware that more longitudinal data samples over longer time periods would be desirable but at this stage only a single repetition is practically feasible to perform. Longitudinal experiments, e.g. in investigating the nature and progression of the spontaneous writing, patterns of impairment were observed in patients with Alzheimer's disease over a 12-month period, these were dominated by semantic errors (Forbes-McKay et al., 2014). Ahmed et al. (2013) reported changes that took place in spoken discourse over the course of three clinical stages. Measures of language function mirrored global progression through the successive clinical stages of the disease. In an individual case analysis, results showed that there were significant but heterogeneous changes in connected speech for 2/3 of the studied MCI-group.

5 Analysis and Features

The envisaged analysis and exploration intends to extract, evaluate and combine a number of features from the three modalities selected to be investigated. These are speech-related features, text/transcription-related features and eye tracking-related features.

5.1 Speech-related analysis

A large number of acoustic and prosodic features has been proposed in the literature which pinpoints the importance of distinguishing between vocal changes that occur with "normal" aging and those that are associated with MCI (and AD). Finding reliable and robust acoustic features that might differentiate spoken language of SCI/MCI and healthy controls remains an ongoing challenge but the technology develops rapidly. Based on related literature, we would expect that our spoken samples might show different qualities depending on whether they are produced spontaneously (when talking about the Cookie-theft picture) or they consist of a read aloud task.

Prosodic features have been found to be useful in distinguishing between subjects with cognitive impairment and healthy controls, and between groups with varying degrees of cognitive impairment. Pause frequency has been identified as a feature differentiating spontaneous speech in patients with AD from control groups (Gayraud et al., 2011), and may also be used to distinguish between mild, moderate and severe AD (Hoffman et al., 2010). Subjects with AD also tend to make more pauses and non-syntactic boundaries (Lee et al., 2011). Speech tempo, which is defined as phonemes per second (including hesitations) differs significantly between subjects with AD and controls. Speech tempo is also positively correlated with Mini Mental State Examination (MMSE) results (Hoffman et al., 2010), which suggests that people with less cognitive deficits will produce speech at a faster rate.

Speech-related features have been used successfully in machine learning experiments where the aim has been to identify subjects with AD. Roark et al. (2011) used 21 features in supervised machine learning experiments (using Support Vector Machines, SVM) from 37 MCI subjects and equally many controls (37/37). Features from both the audio and the transcripts included: pause frequency, filled pauses, total pause duration and linguistic variables such as Frazier and Yngve scores and idea density, while best accuracy with various feature configurations were 86.1% for the area under the ROC curve. Pause frequency has been identified as a feature differentiating spontaneous speech in patients with AD from control groups (Gayraud et al., 2011), and may also be used to distinguish between mild, moderate and severe AD (Hoffman et al., 2010). Meilán et al. (2014) used AD subjects and spoken data (read loud and clear sentences on a screen). They used acoustic measures such as pitch, volume and spectral noise measures. Their method was based on linear discriminant analysis and their results could characterize people with AD with an accuracy of 84.8%. Yancheva et al. (2015) used spoken and transcriptions features provided from the DementiaBank (Cookie-theft descriptions) using 393 speech samples (165/90). They extracted and investigated 477 different features both lexicosyntactic ones (such as syntactic complexity; word types, quality and frequency) and acoustic ones (such as Melfrequency cepstral coefficients – MFCC, including mean, variance, skewness, and kurtosis; pauses and fillers; pitch

and formants and aperiodicity measures) and semantic ones (such as concept mention) in order to predict MMSE scores with a mean absolute error of 3.83 while with individuals with more longitudinal samples the mean absolute error was improved to 2.91, which suggested that the longitudinal data collection plays an important role. König et al. (2015) looked also at MCI and AD subjects (23/26) and examined vocal features (silence, voice, periodic and aperiodic segment length; mean of durations) using Support Vector Machines. Their classification accuracy of automatic audio analysis was 79% between healthy controls and those with MCI; 87% between healthy controls and those with AD; and between those with MCI and those with AD, 80%. Tóth et al. (2015) used also SVM and achieved 85.3% F-score (32 MCI subjects and 19 controls) by starting with eight acoustic features extracted by applying automatic speech recognition (such as speech tempo i.e. phones per second) and extending them to 83. Finally, Fraser et al. (2016) also looked at the DementiaBank and using 240 samples from AD subjects and 233 from healthy controls, extracted 370 features, such as linguistic variables from transcripts (e.g., part-of-speech frequencies; syntactic complexity and grammatical constituents), psycholinguistic measures (e.g., vocabulary richness) and acoustic variables from the audio files (e.g., MFCC). Using logistic regression, Fraser et al. could obtain a classification accuracy of 81% in distinguishing individuals with AD from those without based on short samples of their language on the Cookie-theft picture description task.

In our analysis, we plan to extract prosodic features such as pitch variation, pause length and frequency, hesitation rate and speech rate, and use these both in stand-alone machine learning experiments, and combined with features extracted from voice analysis, eye-tracking and the transcriptions.

5.2 Voice acoustic-related analysis

Depression commonly occurs among patients diagnosed with MCI. Signs of depression are often expressed as an emotional feeling of sadness or "low mood". Johnson et al (2013) found that MCI participants with depression experienced greater deficits in cognitive functioning than their non-depressed counterparts, and "low mood" were shown by Caracciolo et al. (2011) to be particularly prominent in the very early stages of cognitive decline and strongly associated with amnestic mild cognitive impairment (aMCI), i.e. the pre-dementia stage of Alzheimer's, than with global cognitive impairment. Different emotions are accompanied by various adaptive responses in the autonomic and somatic nervous systems (Johnstone & Scherer, 2000). These responses are known to lead to changes in the functioning parts of the speech production system, such as respiration, vocal fold vibration and articulation. The vibrating vocal folds produce the voiced sound (voice source) and the articulation determines the position of the formant frequencies (Hz), determining the vowel and the sound quality of the voice.

The most commonly used parameters in speech acoustic analysis are fundamental frequency (F0) and formant frequency analysis, perturbation measurement such as jitter and shimmer (cycle-to-cycle variations in frequency and amplitude, respectively), and harmonic-to-noise ratios (HNR/NHR). Studying the role of voice production in emotional speech, Patel et al (2011) found significant emotion main effects for 11 of 12 acoustic parameters for five emotions (joy, relief, hot anger, panic fear, sadness) where sadness was characterized by low energy and a hypo-functioning voice quality. Further, Meilán et al. (2014) found voice perturbation parameters to distinguish people with AD from healthy controls with an accuracy of 84.8%.

The aim of the acoustic analysis in the present study is to see if voice parameters can be used to distinguish also between healthy controls and SCI/MCI-patients. Several vowel /a/ and /i/-samples from the read aloud text and the spontaneously spoken Cookie-theft picture will be analyzed for each subject, using the Praat software (Boersma and Weenink). The acoustic data will be compared and correlated according to age, gender, length of education, depression score and other parameters gained from the neuropsychological assessment (Wallin et al., 2016).

5.3 Transcribed speech analysis

Many of the previous studies combine both acoustic features and features from the transcriptions; cf. the supplementary material in Fraser et al. (2016). Some of the most common features and measures from transcribed text follow the lexicon-syntax-semantics continuum. These measures include (i) *lexical distribution measures* (such as type-token ratio, mean word length, long word counts, hapax legomena, hapax dislegomena, automated readability index and Coleman-Liau Index; also lexical and non-lexical fillers or disfluency markers, i.e. "um", "uh", "eh") and out-of-vocabulary rate (Pakhomov et al., 2010). (ii) *syntactic complexity markers* (such as frequency of occurrence of the most frequent words and deictic markers; [context free] production rules, i.e. the number of times a production rule is used divided by the total number of productions; dependency distance, i.e. the length of a dependency link between a dependent token and its head, calculated as the difference between their positions in a sentence; parse tree height, i.e. is the mean number of nodes from the root to the most distant leaf; depth of a syntactic tree, i.e. the proportion of subordinate and coordinate phrases to the total number of phrases and ratio of subordinate to coordinate phrases; noun phrase average length and noun phrase density, i.e. the number of noun phrases per sentence or clause; words per clause); and (iii) *semantic measures* (such as the idea or propositional density, i.e. the operationalization of conciseness – the average number of ideas expressed per words used; the number of expressed propositions divided by the number of words; a measure of the extent to which the speaker is making assertions, or asking questions, rather than just referring to entities etc.). Since some of the features to be extracted (e.g. part-of-speech and syntactic labels from the speech transcriptions) are language-dependent it requires the use of a language-specific infrastructure (in our case Swedish), for that reason we plan to use available resources; cf. Ahlberg et al. (2013); therefore testing and modifications to the transcribed language are also envisaged. Two wide-coverage parser systems will be used for parsing the speech transcripts. The Malt parser for Swedish (Nivre et al., 2006), that outputs grammatical dependency relations, and a constituent parser for the same language (Kokkinakis, 2001) that utilises a semi-automatically developed grammar. Although the transcribed corpus is describing spoken language and contains various spoken language phenomena, such as filled pauses, we chose to keep the verbatim transcriptions intact. Such phenomena are usually deleted prior to parsing for better performance (Lease & Johnson 2006; Geertzen, 2009). Moreover, since we apply a 2-tier text grid configuration during the transcription, we can easily experiment with both the orthographic transcription (standardized spelling) and the verbatim one.

5.4 Eye-tracking analysis

Eye tracking data has been used in machine learning methods in the near past. By taking advantage of biomarkers extracted from eye dynamics (Lagun et al; 2011) there is an indication that these could aid the automatic detection of cognitive impairment (i.e., distinguish healthy controls from MCI-patients). Several studies provide evidence and suggest that eye movements can be used to detect memory impairment and serve as a possible biomarker for MCI and, in turn, AD (Fernández et al., 2013). Basic features we intend to investigate in this study are *fixations* (that is the state the eye remains still over a period of time); *saccades* (that is the rapid motion of the eye from one fixation to another) and *backtracks* (that is the relationship between two subsequent saccades where the second goes in the opposite direction than the first); for a thorough description of possible eye-tracking related features cf. Holmqvist et al. (2015:262). Saccades are of particular interest because they are much related to attention and thus, they are likely to be disturbed by cognitive impairments associated with neurodegenerative disorders (Anderson & MacAskill, 2013). Note that there are many assumptions behind the use of eye tracking technology for experiments designed for people with MCI. For instance, the longer the eye gaze fixation is on a certain word, the more difficult the word could be for cognitive processing, therefore the durations of gaze fixations could be used as a proxy for measuring cognitive load (Just & Carpenter, 1980). Molitor et al. (2015) provide a recent review on the growing body of literature that investigates changes in eye movements as a result of AD and the alterations to oculomotor function and viewing behaviour.

5.5 Correlation analysis

We intend to further perform correlation analysis with the features previously outlined and the results of the various measures/scores on tasks from language-related tests performed in the Gothenburg MCI-study, applied for assessing possible dementia. Typically, clinicians use tests such as the MMSE, linguistic memory tests and language tests. Language tests include the token test, subtest V, which is a test of syntax comprehension; the Boston naming test, the semantic similarity test; the letter/word fluency FAS test (the generation of words beginning by the letters F, A, and S) and the category or semantic fluency test (the generation of words that fall into a given semantic category, such as animals). This investigation intends to identify whether there are language-related features, acquired from the range of available tests, which could be (highly negative or highly positive) correlated with i.e. the MCI class, yet uncorrelated with each other i.e. the healthy controls or SCI. We want to further investigate which scores correlate with which variables derived from the picture description. It has been argued, Kavé & Goral (2016), that the picture naming task *could* be a better predictor of word retrieval in context than the semantic fluency task for several reasons, for instance the speech elicitation method most likely involves cognitive demands that are similar to the ones required for the picture naming task, e.g., specific labelling.

6 Conclusions and Future Work

In this paper we have introduced work in progress towards the design and infrastructural development of reliable multi-modal data resources and a set of measures (features) to be used both for experimentation with feature engineering and evaluation of classification algorithms to be used for differentiating between SCI/MCI and healthy adults, and also as benchmark data for future research in the area. Evaluation practices are a crucial step towards the development of resources and useful for enhancing progress in the field, therefore we intend to evaluate both the relevance of features, compare standard algorithms such as Support Vector Machines and Bayesian classifiers and perform correlation analysis with the results of established neuropsychological, memory and cognitive tests. We also intend to repeat the experiments two years after (2018) the current acquisition of data in order to assess possible changes at each level of analysis. We believe that combining data from three modalities (a form of data fusion; Mitchel, 2007) could be useful, but at this point we do not provide any clinical evidence underlying these assumption since the analysis and experimentation studies are currently under way (year 2 of the project, 2017). Therefore, at this stage, the paper only provides a high-level review of the current stage of the work.

Acknowledgments

This work has received support from *Riksbankens Jubileumsfond* - The Swedish Foundation for Humanities and Social Sciences, through the grant agreement no: NHS 14-1761:1.

References

Malin Ahlberg et al. 2013. *Korp and Karp – a bestiary of language resources: the research infrastructure of Språkbanken.* 19th Nordic Conf of Computational Linguistics (NODALIDA). Linköping Electronic Conference Proceedings #85.

Samrah Ahmed, Anne-Marie Haigh, Celeste de Jager and Peter Garrard. 2013. Connected speech as a marker of disease progression in autopsy-proven Alzheimer's disease. *Brain.* 136(Pt 12):3727-37.

Tim J. Anderson and Michael R. MacAskill. 2013. Eye movements in patients with neurodegenerative disorders. *Nat Rev Neurology* 9: 74-85. doi:10.1038/nrneurol.2012.273.

Eiji Aramaki, Shuko Shikata, Mai Miyabe and Ayae Kinoshita. 2016. Vocabulary Size in Speech May Be an Early Indicator of Cognitive Impairment. *PLoS One.* 11(5):e0155195.

Sheena K. Au-Yeung, Johanna Kaakinen, Simon Liversedge and Valerie Benson. 2015. Processing of Written Irony in Autism Spectrum Disorder: An Eye-Movement Study. *Autism Res.* 8(6):749-60. doi: 10.1002/aur.1490.

Paul Boersma and David Weenink. 2013. *Praat: doing phonetics by computer* [Computer program]. Version 6.0.19, retrieved in Aug. 2016 from <http://www.praat.org/>.

Barbara Caracciolo et al. 2011. The symptom of low mood in the prodromal stage of mild cognitive impairment and dementia: a cohort study of a community dwelling elderly population. *J Neurol Neurosurg Psychiatry.* 82:788-793.

Vineeta Chand, Kathleen Baynes, Lisa M. Bonnici and Sarah Tomaszewski Farias. 2012. A Rubric for Extracting Idea Density from Oral Language Samples Analysis of Idea Density (AID): A Manual. *Curr Protoc Neurosci.* Ch. Unit10.5. doi:10.1002/0471142301.ns1005s58.

James W Dodd 2015. Lung disease as a determinant of cognitive decline and dementia. *Alzh Res & Therapy*, 7:32.

Alison Ferguson, Elizabeth Spencer, Hugh Craig and Kim Colyvas. 2014. Propositional Idea Density in women's written language over the lifespan: Computerized analysis. *Cortex* 55. 107-121.

Gerardo Fernández et al. 2013. Eye Movement Alterations during Reading in Patients with Early Alzheimer Disease. *Investigative Ophthalmology & Visual Science.* Vol.54, 8345-8352. doi:10.1167/iovs.13-12877.

Katrina Forbes-McKay, Mike Shanks and Annalena Venneria. 2014. Charting the decline in spontaneous writing in Alzheimer's disease: a longitudinal study. *Acta Neuropsychiatrica.* Vol. 26:04, pp 246-252.

Kathleen C. Fraser and Graeme Hirst. 2016. *Detecting semantic changes in Alzheimer's disease with vector space models.* LREC Workshop: Resources and ProcessIng of linguistic and extra-linguistic Data from people with various forms of cognitive/psychiatric impairments (RaPID). Pp. 1-8. Portorož Slovenia.

Peter Garrard and Brita Elvevåg. 2014. Special issue: Lang., computers and cognitive neuroscience. *Cortex* 55; 1-4.

Frederique Gayraud, Hye-Ran Lee and Melissa Barkat-Defradas. 2011. Syntactic & lexical context of pauses and hesitations in the discourse of Alzheimer patients and healthy elderly subjects. *Clin Ling&Phon.* 25(3):198-209.

Jeroen Geertzen. 2009. *Wide-coverage parsing of speech transcripts.* 11th Pars. Tech (IWPT). Pp 218–221. France.

Elaine Gilles, Karalyn Patterson and John Hodges. 1996. Performance on the Boston Cookie Theft picture description task in patients with early dementia of the Alzheimer's type: missing information. *Aphasiology.* 10:4:395-408.

Harald Goodglass and Edith Kaplan. 1983. *The Assessment of Aphasia and Related Disorders.* Lea&Febiger. USA.

Ildikó Hoffmann et al. 2010. Temporal parameters of spontaneous speech in Alzheimer's disease. *J of Speech-Language Pathology*, *12*(1), 29–34.

Kenneth Holmqvist, Richard Dewhurst, Marcus Nyström, Joost van de Weijer, Halszka Jarodzka and Richard Andersson. 2015. *Eye Tracking - A comprehensive guide to methods & measures.* OUP.

Frank Jessen et al. 2010. Prediction of dementia by subjective memory impairment: effects of severity and temporal association with cognitive impairment. *Arch. Gen. Psychiatry*, 67(4). Pp. 414–422.

Leigh A Johnson et al. 2013. Cognitive differences among depressed and non-depressed MCI participants. *J Geriatr Psychiatry.* 28(4):377-82.

Tom Johnstone and Klaus R. Scherer. 2000. Vocal communication of emotion. *The Handbook of Emotion.* Lewis & Haviland (eds). NY Guildford.

Marcel A. Just and Patricia A. Carpenter. 1980. A theory of reading: from eye fixations to comprehension. *Psychological review*, 87(4):329-354.

Gitit Kavé & Mira Goral. 2016. Word retrieval in picture descriptions produced by individuals with Alzheimer's disease. *J Clin Exp Neuropsychol.* 38(9):958-66.

Dimitrios Kokkinakis. 2001. *More than Surface-Based Parsing; Higher Level Evaluation of Cass-SWE.* 13th Nordic Computational Linguistics Conference (NODALIDA). Uppsala, Sweden.

Alexandra König et al. 2015. Automatic speech analysis for the assessment of patients with predementia and Alzheimer's disease. *Alzheimer's & Dementia: Diagnosis, Assessment & Disease Monitoring.* 1:112–124. Elsevier.

Dmitry Lagun et al. 2011. Detecting cognitive impairment by eye movement analysis using automatic classification algorithms. *J Neurosci Methods.* 201(1): 196–203. doi:10.1016/j.jneumeth. 2011.06.027.

Christoph Laske et al. 2014. Innovative diagnostic tools early detection of Alzheimer's disease. *Alzheimer's & Dementia.* 1-18.

Xuan Le, Ian Lancashire, Graeme Hirst, and Regina Jokel. 2011. Longitudinal Detection of Dementia through Lexical and Syntactic Changes in Writing: A Case Study of Three British Novelists. *JLLC* 26 (4): 435-461.

Matthew Lease and Mark Johnson. 2006. Early deletion of fillers in processing conversational speech. Proceedings of the Human Language Technology Conference of the North American Chapter of the ACL, pages 73–76.

Hyeran Lee, Frederique Gayraud, Fabrice Hirsh and Melissa Barkat-Defradas. 2011. Speech dysfluencies in normal and pathological aging: A comparison between Alzheimer patients and healthy elderly subjects. *ICPhS: proceedings of the 17th International Congress of Phonetic Sciences.* Pp. 1174–1177. Hong Kong.

Deborah L. Levy, Anne B. Sereno, Diane C. Gooding,and Gilllian A. O'Driscoll. 2010. Eye Tracking Dysfunction in Schizophrenia: Characterization and Pathophysiology. *Curr Top Behav Neurosci.* 4: 311–347.

Juan JG. Meilán, Francisco Martínez-Sánchez, Juan Carro, José A. Sánchez and Enrique Pérez. 2012. Acoustic Markers Associated with Impairment in Language Processing in AD. Spanish *J of Psych.* Vol. 15:2, 487-494.

Juan JG. Meilán et al. 2014. Speech in Alzheimer's Disease: Can Temporal and Acoustic Parameters Discriminate Dementia? *Dement Geriatr Cogn Disord* 2014;37:327–334. doi: 10.1159/000356726.

H. B. Mitchell. (2007). *Multi-Sensor Data Fusion: An Introduction.* Springer.

Robert J. Molitor, Philip C. Ko and Brandon A. Ally. 2015. Eye Movements in Alzheimer's Disease. *J of Alzheimer's Disease* 44, 1–12. IOS Press.

James A. Mortimer, Amy R. Borenstein, Karen M. Gosche and David A. Snowdon. 2005. Very Early Detection of Alzheimer Neuropathology and the Role of Brain Reserve in Modifying Its Clinical Expression. *J Geriatr Psychiatry Neurol.* 18(4): 218–223.

Joakim Nivre et al. 2007. MaltParser: A language-independent system for data-driven dependency parsing. *Natural Language Engineering.* 13(2):95-135.

Arto Nordlund, S. Rolstad, P. Hellström, M. Sjögren, S. Hansen and Anders Wallin. 2005. The Goteborg MCI study: mild cognitive impairment is a heterogeneous condition. *J Neurol Neurosurg Psychiatry.* 76(11):1485-90.

Sylvester Olubolu Orimaye, Jojo Sze-Meng Wong and Kren J. Golden. 2014. *Learning Predictive Linguistic Features for Alzheimer's Disease and related Dementias using Verbal Utterances.* Workshop on Computational Ling. & Clinical Psychology: From Linguistic Signal to Clinical Reality. 78–87. Maryland, USA.

Serguei VS Pakhomov et al. 2010. A co-mputerized technique to assess language use patterns in patients with frontotemporal dementia. *J Neuroling.* 23(2):127–144.

Sona Patel, Klaus R. Scherer, Eva Björkner, Johan Sundberg. 2011. Mapping emotions into acoustic space: The role of voice production. *Biological Psychology* 87. 93–98.

Sajidkhan S. Pathan et al. 2011. Association of lung function with cognitive decline and dementia: the Atherosclerosis Risk in Communities (ARIC) Study. *Eur J Neurol.* 18(6):888-9.

Luz Rello and Miguel Ballesteros. 2015. *Detecting Readers with Dyslexia Using Machine Learning with Eye Tracking Measures.* Proceedings of the 12th Web for All Conference W4A. Florence, Italy.

Vassiliki Rentoumi, Ladan Raoufian, Samrah Ahmed and Peter Garrard. 2014. Features and Machine Learning Classification of Connected Speech Samples from Patients with Autopsy Proven Alzheimer's Disease with and without Additional Vascular Pathology. *J of Alzheimer's Disease* 42. IOS Press. S3–S17.

Karen Ritchie and Jacques Touchon. 2010. Mild cognitive impairment: conceptual basis and current nosological status. *The Lancet.* Vol. 355:9199. Pp. 225–228. Doi:10.1016/S0140-6736(99)06155-3.

Brian Roark, Margaret Mitchell, John-Paul Hosom, Kristy Hollingshead, and Jeffrey Kaye. 2011. *Spoken Language Derived Measures for Detecting Mild Cognitive Impairment.* IEEE Trans Audio Speech Lang Processing. 19(7): 2081–2090.

David A. Snowdon, Lydia Greiner and William R. Markesbery. 2000. Linguistic ability in early life and the neuropathology of Alzheimer's disease and cerebrovascular disease. Findings from the Nun Study. *Annals of the NY Academy of Sciences.* 903:34-8.

Greta Szatloczki, Ildiko Hoffmann, Veronika Vincze, Janos Kalman and Magdolna Pakaski. 2015. Speaking in Alzheimer's disease, is that an early sign? Importance of changes in language abilities in Alzheimer's disease. *Frontiers in Aging Neuroscience.* Vol 7, article 195. doi: 10.3389/fnagi.2015.00195.

Vanessa Taler and Natalie Phillips. 2008. Language performance in Alzheimer's disease and mild cognitive impairment: A comparative review. *J Clin Exp Neuropsychol.* 30(5):501-56. doi: 10.1080/13803390701550128.

Susanne Trauzettel-Klosinski, Klaus Dietz & the IReST Study Group. 2012. Standardized Assessment of Reading Performance: The New International Reading Speed Texts IReST. *Investigative Ophthalmol&Visual Sc.* 53:9.

Laszló Tóth et al. 2015. *Automatic Detection of MCI from Spontaneous Speech using ASR.* Interspeech. Germany.

Anders Wallin et al. 2016. The Gothenburg MCI study: Design and distribution of Alzheimers disease and subcortical vascular disease diagnoses from baseline to 6-year follow-up. *J Cer Blood Flow Metab.* 36(1):114-31.

Olof Tyche. 2001. *Subtila språkstörningar hos patienter med diagnosen MCI.* Master's thesis. Karolinska institute, Sweden (In Swedish).

Brian MacWhinney, Davida Fromm, Margaret Forbes and Audrey Holland. 2011. AphasiaBank: Methods for studying discourse. *Aphasiology.* 25 (11), 1286-1307.

Caroline Williams et al. 2010. *The Cambridge Cookie-Theft Corpus: A Corpus of Directed and Spontaneous Speech of Brain-Damaged Patients and Healthy Individuals.* 7th Language Resources and Evaluation (LREC). Pp. 2824-2830. Malta.

Maria Yancheva, Kathleen Fraser and Frank Rudzicz. 2015. *Using linguistic features longitudinally to predict clinical scores for Alzheimer's disease and related dementias.* 6th SLPAT. Pp. 134–139, Dresden, Germany.

Victoria Yaneva, Irina Temnikova and Ruslan Mitkov. 2016. *Corpus of Text Data and Gaze Fixations from Autistic and Non-autistic Adults.* 10th Language Resources and Evaluation (LREC). Pp. 480-487. Slovenia.

Gustaf Öqvist Seimyr. 2010. *Swedish IReST translation.* The Bernadotte Laboratory, Karolinska institute, Sweden.

Evaluation of language identification methods using 285 languages

Tommi Jauhiainen
University of Helsinki
`@helsinki.fi`

Krister Lindén
University of Helsinki
`@helsinki.fi`

Heidi Jauhiainen
University of Helsinki
`@helsinki.fi`

Abstract

Language identification is the task of giving a language label to a text. It is an important preprocessing step in many automatic systems operating with written text. In this paper, we present the evaluation of seven language identification methods that was done in tests between 285 languages with an out-of-domain test set. The evaluated methods are, furthermore, described using unified notation. We show that a method performing well with a small number of languages does not necessarily scale to a large number of languages. The HeLI method performs best on test lengths of over 25 characters, obtaining an F_1-score of 99.5 already at 60 characters.

1 Introduction

Automatic language identification of text has been researched since the 1960s. Language identification is an important preprocessing step in many automatic systems operating with written text. State of the art language identifiers obtain high rates in both recall and precision. However, even the best language identifiers do not give perfect results when dealing with a large number of languages, out-of-domain texts, or short texts. In this paper seven language identification methods are evaluated in tests incorporating all three of these hard contexts. The evaluations were done as part of the Finno-Ugric Languages and The Internet project (Jauhiainen et al., 2015) funded by the Kone Foundation Language Programme (Kone Foundation, 2012). One of the major goals of the project is creating text corpora for the minority languages within the Uralic group.

In Section 2, we describe the methods chosen for this evaluation. In Section 3, we present the corpora used for training and testing the methods and in Section 4 we discuss and present the results of the evaluations of the methods using these corpora.

2 Previous work

There are not many previously published articles which provide language identification results for more than 100 languages. Results for such evaluations were provided by King and Dehdari (2008), Jauhiainen (2010), Vatanen et al. (2010), Rodrigues (2012), and Brown (2012). King and Dehdari (2008) achieved 99% accuracy with 500 bytes of input for over 300 languages. Vatanen et al. (2010) created a language identifier which included 281 languages and obtained an in-domain identification accuracy of 62.8% for extremely short samples (5-9 characters). Rodrigues (2012) presents a boosting method using the method of Vatanen et al. (2010) for language identification. His method could possibly also be used with other language identification methods and we leave the evaluation of the boosting method to future work. The language identifier created by Brown (2012), "whatlang", obtains 99.2% classification accuracy with smoothing for 65 character test strings when distinguishing between 1,100 languages (Brown, 2013; Brown, 2014).

The HeLI method described in Jauhiainen et al. (2016) was used successfully with 103 languages by Jauhiainen (2010). Some of the more detailed results concerning the Uralic languages for the evaluations presented in this paper were previously published by Jauhiainen et al. (2015).

In this section, we also include the original method of Cavnar and Trenkle (1994), as it is the most frequently used baseline in the language identification literature. As baselines, we have also included the methods presented by Tromp and Pechenizkiy (2011) and Vogel and Tresner-Kirsch (2012), which provided promising results when used with 6 languages.

Proceedings of the 21st Nordic Conference of Computational Linguistics, pages 183–191,
Gothenburg, Sweden, 23-24 May 2017. ©2017 Linköping University Electronic Press

2.1 On notation (Jauhiainen et al., 2016)

A corpus C consists of individual tokens u which may be words or characters. A corpus C is a finite sequence of individual tokens, $u_1, ..., u_l$. The total count of all individual tokens u in the corpus C is denoted by l_C. A set of unique tokens in a corpus C is denoted by $U(C)$. The number of unique tokens is referred to as $|U(C)|$. A feature f is some countable characteristic of the corpus C. When referring to all features F in a corpus C, we use C^F and the count of all features is denoted by l_{C^F}. The count of a feature f in the corpus C is referred to as $c(C, f)$. An n-gram is a feature which consists of a sequence of n individual tokens. An n-gram starting at position i in a corpus is denoted $u_{i,...,i-1+n}$. If $n = 1$, u is an individual token. When referring to all n-grams of length n in a corpus C, we use C^n and the count of all such n-grams is denoted by l_{C^n}. The count of an n-gram u in a corpus C is referred to as $c(C, u)$ and is defined by Equation 1.

$$c(C, u) = \sum_{i=1}^{l_C+1-n} \left\{ \begin{array}{ll} 1 & , \text{if } u = u_{i,...,i-1+n} \\ 0 & , \text{otherwise} \end{array} \right. \tag{1}$$

The set of languages is G, and l_G denotes the number of languages. A corpus C in language g is denoted by C_g. A language model O based on C_g is denoted by $O(C_g)$. The features given values by the model $O(C_g)$ are the domain $dom(O(C_g))$ of the model. In a language model, a value v for the feature f is denoted by $v_{C_g}(f)$. A corpus in an unknown language is referred to as a mystery text M. For each potential language g of a corpus M, a resulting score $R(g, M)$ is calculated.

2.2 N-Gram-Based Text Categorization

The method of Cavnar and Trenkle (1994) uses overlapping character n-grams of varying size calculated from words. The language models are created by tokenizing the training texts for each language g into words and then padding each word with spaces, one before and four after. Each padded word is then divided into overlapping character n-grams of sizes from 1 to 5 and the counts of every unique n-gram are calculated over the whole corpus. The n-grams are ordered by frequency and k of the most frequent n-grams, $u_1, ..., u_k$, are used as the domain of the language model $O(C_g)$ for the language g. The rank of an n-gram u in language g is determined by the n-gram frequency in the training corpus C_g and denoted $rank_{C_g}(u)$.

During language identification, the mystery text is treated in a similar way and a corresponding model $O(M)$ of the k most frequent n-grams is created. Then a distance score is calculated between the model of the mystery text and each of the language models. The value $v_{C_g}(u)$ is calculated as the difference in ranks between $rank_M(u)$ and $rank_{C_g}(u)$ of the n-gram u in the domain $dom(O(M))$ of the model of the mystery text. If an n-gram is not found in a language model, a special penalty value p is added to the total score of the language for each missing n-gram. The penalty value should be higher than the maximum possible distance between ranks. We use $p = k + 1$, as the penalty value.

$$v_{C_g}(u) = \left\{ \begin{array}{l} |rank_M(u) - rank_{C_g}(u)|, \text{if } u \in dom(O(C_g)) \\ p, \text{if } u \notin dom(O(C_g)) \end{array} \right.$$
$$\tag{2}$$

The score $R_{sum}(g, M)$ for each language g is the sum of values as in Equation 3.

$$R_{sum}(g, M) = \sum_{i=1}^{l_{M^F}} v_{C_g}(f_i) \tag{3}$$

The language having the lowest score $R_{sum}(g, M)$ is selected as the identified language.

2.3 LIGA-algorithm

The graph-based n-gram approach called LIGA was first described in (Tromp, 2011). The method is here reproduced as explained in (Vogel and Tresner-Kirsch, 2012). The language models consist of relative frequencies of character trigrams and the relative frequencies of two consecutive overlapping trigrams. The frequency of two consecutive overlapping trigrams is exactly the same as the 4-gram starting from the beginning of the first trigram. So the language models consist of the relative frequencies $v_{C_g}(u)$ of 3- and 4-grams as in Equation 4.

$$v_{C_g}(u) = \frac{c(C_g, u)}{l_{C_g^n}} \tag{4}$$

where $c(C_g, u)$, is the number of 3- or 4-grams u and $l_{C_g^n}$, is the total number of 3- and 4-grams in the training corpus.

The mystery text M is scanned for the 3- and 4-grams u. For each 3- and 4-gram found in the model of a language g, the relative frequencies are added to the score $R_{sum}(g, M)$ of the language g, as in Equation 3. The winner is the language with the highest score as opposed to the lowest score with the previous method.

In the logLIGA variation of the method, introduced by Vogel and Tresner-Kirsch (2012), the natural logarithm of the frequencies is used when calculating the relative frequencies, as in Equation 5.

$$v_{C_g}(u) = \frac{ln(c(C_g,u))}{ln(l_{C_g^n})} \qquad (5)$$

Otherwise the method is identical to the original LIGA algorithm.

2.4 The method of King and Dehdari (2008)

King and Dehdari (2008) tested the use of the relative frequencies of byte n-grams with Laplace and Lidstone smoothings in distinguishing between 312 languages. They separately tested overlapping 2-, 3-, and 4-grams with both smoothing techniques. They used the Universal Declaration of Human Rights corpus, which is accessible using NLTK (Bird, 2006), separating the testing material before training. The values for each n-gram are calculated as in Equation 6,

$$v_{C_g}(u) = \frac{c(C_g,u) + \lambda}{l_{C_g^n} + |U(C_g^n)|\lambda} \qquad (6)$$

where $v_{C_g}(u)$ is the probability estimate of n-gram u in the model and $c(C_g,u)$ its frequency in the training corpus. $l_{C_g^n}$ is the total number of n-grams of length n and $|U(C_g^n)|$ the number of distinct n-grams in the training corpus. λ is the Lidstone smoothing parameter. When using Laplace smoothing, the λ is equal to 1 and with Lidstone smoothing, the λ is usually set between 0 and 1. King and Dehdari (2008) found that Laplace smoothing with the bigram model turned out to be the most accurate on two of their longer test sets and that Lidstone smoothing (with λ set to 0.5) was better with the shortest test set. King and Dehdari (2008) used the *entropy(model, text)* function of NLTK, which evaluates the entropy between *text* and *model* by summing up the log probabilities of words found in the text.[1]

2.5 "Whatlang" program (Brown, 2013)

The "Whatlang" program uses variable length byte n-grams from 3 to 12 bytes as its language model. K of the most frequent n-grams are extracted from

training corpora for each language and their relative frequencies are calculated. In the tests reported in (Brown, 2013), K varied from 200 to 3,500 n-grams. After the initial models are generated, n-grams, which are substrings of longer n-grams in the same model, are filtered out, if the frequency of the longer n-gram is at least 62% of the shorter n-grams frequency. The value $v_{C_g}(u)$ of an n-gram u in the model of the corpus C_g is calculated as in Equation 7

$$v_{C_g}(u) = \left(\frac{c(C_g,u)}{l_{C_g^n}}\right)^{0.27} n^{0.09} \qquad (7)$$

where $c(C_g,u)$ is the frequency of the n-gram u and $l_{C_g^n}$ is the number of all n-grams of the length n in the training corpus C_g. The weights in the model are calculated so that the longer n-grams have greater weights than short ones with the same relative frequency. Baseline language models $O_{base}(C_g)$ are formed for each language g using the values $v_{C_g}(u)$.

For each language model $O_{base}(C_g)$, the cosine similarity between it and every other language model is calculated. A union of n-grams is formed by taking all of the models for which the similarity is higher than an empirically determined threshold. The corpus C_g is scanned for occurrences of the n-grams in the union. If some of the n-grams are not found at all, these n-grams are then appended with negative weights to the base model. The negative weight used for an n-gram u in the model $O(C_g)$ is the maximum cosine similarity between $O_{base}(C_g)$ and the models containing an n-gram u times the maximum $v_C(u)$ within those models. These negative weighted n-grams are called stop-grams. If the size of the training corpus for a certain model is less than 2 million bytes, the weights of the stop-grams are discounted as a function of the corpus size.

The score $R_{whatlang}(g,M)$ for the language g is calculated as in Equation 8

$$R_{whatlang}(g,M) = \frac{\sum_i v_{C_g}(u_i)}{l_{M^1}} \qquad (8)$$

where u_i are the n-grams found in the mystery text M. The score is also normalized by dividing it with the length (in characters) of the mystery text l_{M^1}. The language with the highest score is identified as the language of the mystery text.

Brown (2013) tested "Whatlang" with 1,100 languages as well as a smaller subset of 184 languages. The reported average of classification ac-

---

[1]Jon Dehdari recently uploaded the instructions to: https://github.com/jonsafari/witch-language

curacy with 1,100 languages for lines up to 65 characters is 98.68%, which is extremely good.

2.6 VariKN toolkit (Vatanen et al., 2010)

The problem with short text samples was considered by Vatanen et al. (2010). Several smoothing techniques with a naive Bayes classifier were compared in tests of 281 languages. Absolute discounting (Ney et al., 1994) smoothing with a maximum n-gram length of 5 turned out to be their best method. When calculating the Markovian probabilities in absolute discounting, a constant D is subtracted from the counts $c(C, u^n_{i-n+1})$ of all observed n-grams u^n_{i-n+1} and the left-out probability mass is distributed between the unseen n-grams in relation to the probabilities of lower order n-grams $P_g(u_i|u^{n-1}_{i-n+2})$, as in Equation 9.

$$P_g(u_i|u^{n-1}_{i-n+1}) = \frac{c(C, u^n_{i-n+1}) - D}{c(C, u^{n-1}_{i-n+1})} + \lambda_{u^{n-1}_{i-n+1}} P_g(u_i|u^{n-1}_{i-n+2}) \tag{9}$$

The language identification is performed using the "perplexity" program provided with the toolkit.[2] Perplexity is calculated from the Markovian probability $P(M|C_g) = \prod_i P_g(u_i|u^{n-1}_{i-n+1})$ for the mystery text M given the training data C_g as in Equations 10 and 11.

$$H_g(M) = -\frac{1}{c(M,u)} \prod_i log_2 P_g(u_i|u^{n-1}_{i-n+1}) \tag{10}$$

$$R_{perplexity}(g,M) = 2^{H_g(M)} \tag{11}$$

2.7 The HeLI method

The HeLI[3] method (Jauhiainen, 2010) is described in Jauhiainen et al. (2016) using the same notation as in this article. In the method, each language is represented by several different language models only one of which is used for every word found in the mystery text. The language models for each language are: a model based on words and one or more models based on character n-grams from one to n_{max}. When a word not included in the model based on words is encountered in the mystery text M, the method backs off to using the n-grams of the size n_{max}. If it is not possible to apply the n-grams of the size n_{max}, the method backs off to lower order n-grams and continues backing off until character unigrams, if needed. A development

set is used for finding the best values for the parameters of the method. The three parameters are the maximum length of the used character n-grams (n_{max}), the maximum number of features to be included in the language models (cut-off c), and the penalty value for those languages where the features being used are absent (penalty p). Because of the large differences between the sizes of the training corpora, we used a slightly modified implementation of the method, where we used relative frequencies as cut-offs c. The values in the models are 10-based logarithms of the relative frequencies of the features u, calculated using only the frequencies of the retained features, as in Equation 12

$$v_{C_g}(u) = \begin{cases} -log_{10}\left(\frac{c(C_g,u)}{l_{C_g}}\right) & \text{, if } c(C_g,u) > 0 \\ p & \text{, if } c(C_g,u) = 0 \end{cases} \tag{12}$$

where $c(C_g,u)$ is the number of features u and l_{C_g} is the total number of all features in language g. If $c(C_g,u)$ is zero, then $v_{C_g}(u)$ gets the penalty value p.

A score $v_g(t)$ is calculated for each word t in the mystery text for each language g, as shown in Equation 13.

$$v_g(t) = \begin{cases} v_{C_g}(t) & \text{, if } t \in dom(O(C_g)) \\ v_g(t, min(n_{max}, l_t + 2)) & \text{, if } t \notin dom(O(C_g)) \end{cases} \tag{13}$$

The whole mystery text M gets the score $R_{HeLI}(g,M)$ equal to the average of the scores of the words $v_g(t)$ for each language g, as in Equation 14

$$R_{HeLI}(g,M) = \frac{\sum_{i=1}^{l_{T(M)}} v_g(t_i)}{l_{T(M)}} \tag{14}$$

where $T(M)$ is the sequence of words and $l_{T(M)}$ is the number of words in the mystery text M. The language having the lowest score is assigned to the mystery text.

3 Test setting

In addition to the Uralic languages relevant to the project (Jauhiainen et al., 2015), the languages for the evaluation of the language identification methods were chosen so that we were able to train and test with texts from different sources, preferably also from different domains. We were able to gather suitable corpora for a set of 285 languages.[4]

---

[2] https://github.com/vsiivola/variKN
[3] https://github.com/tosaja/HeLI

[4] The list of all the languages and most of the sources can be found at http://suki.ling.helsinki.fi/LILanguages.html.

In our project we are interested in gathering as much of the very rare Uralic texts as possible, so we need a high recall. On the other hand, if our precision is bad, we end up with a high percentage of incorrect language labels for the rare languages. For these reasons we use the F_1-score as the main performance measure when evaluating the language identifiers. We calculate the language-level averages of recall, precision and the F_1-score. Language-level averages are referred to as *macro-averages* by Lui et al. (Lui et al., 2014). As the number of mystery texts for each language were identical, the macro-averaged recall equals the commonly used classification accuracy[5]. The F_β-score is based on the effectiveness measure introduced by van Rijsbergen (1979) and is calculated from the precision p and recall r, as in Equation 15

$$F_\beta = (1 + \beta^2)\left(\frac{pr}{(\beta^2 p) + r}\right) \qquad (15)$$

where $\beta = 1$ gives equal weight to precision and recall.

3.1 Training Corpora

The biggest bulk of the training corpora is formed from various Wikipedias.[6] The collection sizes range from a few articles for the very small languages to over a million articles in the English, German, French, Dutch and Italian collections. The sheer amount of linguistic material contained in the article collections makes using them as text corpora an appealing thought. The article collections had to be cleaned as they contained lots of non-lingual metadata and links as well as text in non-native languages. In addition to the text from Wikipedia, there is material from bible translations[7], other religious texts[8], the Leipzig Corpora Collection (Quasthoff et al., 2006), the AKU project[9], Sámi giellatekno[10], and generic web pages. Even with these additions, the amount

of training material differs greatly between languages.

Each language has one file including all the training texts for that language. Some of the texts are copyrighted, so they cannot be published as such. The amount of training material differs drastically between languages: they span from 2,710 words of Tahitian to 29 million words of English. Some of the corpora were manually examined to remove text obviously written in foreign languages. Even after all the cleaning, the training corpora must be considered rather unclean.

3.2 Testing Corpora

The test corpora are mostly derived from the translations of the universal declaration of human rights.[11] However, the test set includes languages for which no translation of the declaration is available and for these languages texts were collected from some of the same sources as for the training corpora, but also from Tatoeba.[12] Most of the test texts have been examined manually for purity, so that obvious inclusions of foreign languages were removed.

The aim was to have the mystery texts from different domains than the training texts. Wikipedia refers to the declaration of human rights in several languages and in many places. In order to deal with possible inclusion of test material in training corpora, every test corpus was divided into 30 character chunks and any lines including these chunks in the corresponding training corpus were removed. Also, if long sequences of numbers were noticed, they were removed from both corpora. There are still numbers in the test set and for example some of the 5 character or even 10 character sequences in the test set consist only or mostly of numbers.

The test set has been randomly generated from the test corpora. A test sample always begins at the beginning of a word, but it might end anywhere, including in the middle of a word. An extra blank was inserted in the beginning of each line when testing those language identifiers, which did not automatically expect the text to begin with a word. The test samples are of 19 different sizes ranging from 5 to 150 characters. Each language and size pair has 1,000 random (some can be identical) test samples. The full test set comprises of around 5.4

---

[5]The evaluation results for all the languages and identifiers can be found at `http://suki.ling.helsinki.fi/NodaEvalResults.xlsx`.

[6]`http://www.wikipedia.org`

[7]`http://gospelgo.com/biblespage.html`, `http://worldbibles.org`, `http://ibt.org.ru`, `http://gochristianhelps.com`

[8]`http://www.christusrex.org`, `https://www.lds.org`

[9]`http://www.ling.helsinki.fi/~rueter/aku-index.shtml`

[10]`http://giellatekno.uit.no`

[11]`http://www.unicode.org/udhr/`

[12]`http://tatoeba.org/eng/`

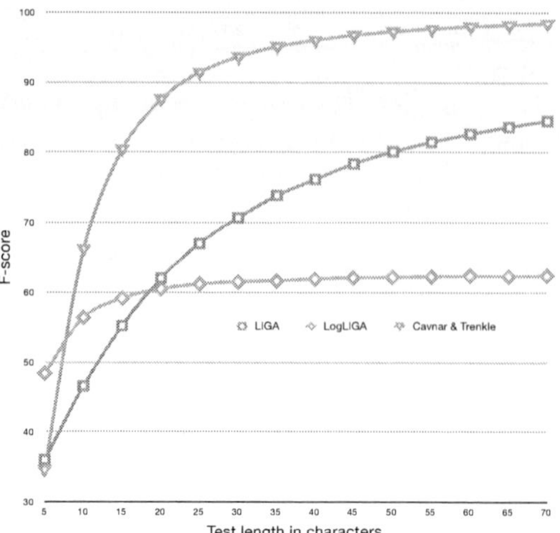

Figure 1: Comparison between the F_1-scores of the method of Cavnar and Trenkle (1994), LIGA, and logLIGA.

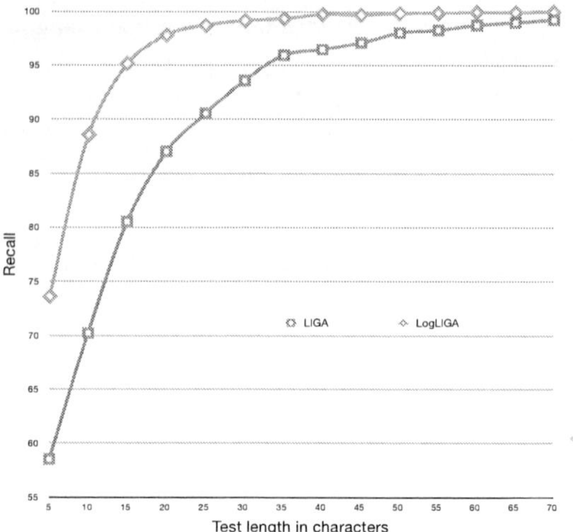

Figure 2: The recall of LIGA and logLIGA algorithms with 6 languages.

million samples to be identified.

4 The results and discussion

After training the aforementioned language identifiers with our own training corpora, we tested them against all the languages in our test suite.

4.1 The baselines

Cavnar and Trenkle (1994) included the 300 most frequent n-grams in the language models. In our tests the best results were attained using 20,000 n-grams with their method. From the LIGA variations introduced by Vogel and Tresner-Kirsch (2012), we chose to test the logLIGA as it performed the best in their evaluations in addition to the original LIGA algorithm. For these three methods, the averaged results of the evaluations for 285 languages can be seen in Figure 1.

The results of both the LIGA and logLIGA algorithms are clearly outperformed by the method of Cavnar and Trenkle (1994). Especially the poor results of logLIGA were surprising, as it was clearly better than the original LIGA algorithm in the tests presented by Vogel and Tresner-Kirsch (2012). To verify the performance of our implementations, we tested them with the same set of languages which were tested in (Vogel and Tresner-Kirsch, 2012), where the baseline LIGA had an average recall of 97.9% and logLIGA 99.8% over 6 languages. The tweets in their dataset average around 80 characters. The results

of our tests can be seen in Figure 2. The logLIGA clearly outperforms the LIGA algorithm and obtains 99.8% recall already at 50 characters even for our cross-domain test set. From these results we believe that especially the logLIGA algorithm does not scale to a situation with a large number of languages.

4.2 The evaluations

For the evaluation of the method of King and Dehdari (2008) we created Laplace and Lidstone smoothed language models from our training corpora and programmed a language identifier, which used the sum of log probabilities (we did not use NLTK) to measure the distance between the models and the mystery text. We tested n-grams from 1 to 6 with several different values of λ. King and Dehdari (2008) used byte n-grams, but as our corpus is completely UTF-8 encoded, we use n-grams of characters instead.

The best results (Figure 3) in our tests were achieved with 5-grams and a λ of 0.00000001. These findings are not exactly in line with those of King and Dehdari (2008). The number of languages used in both language identifiers is comparable, but the amount of training data in our corpus varies considerably between languages when compared with the corpus used by King and Dehdari (2008), where each language had about the same amount of material. The smallest test set they used was 2%, which corresponds to around 100 - 200 characters, which is comparable to the

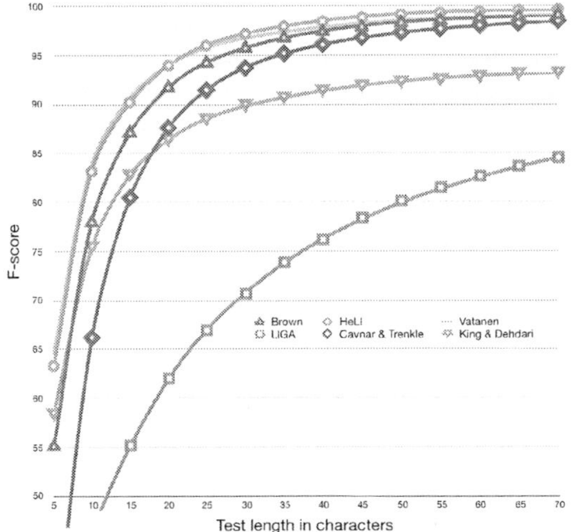 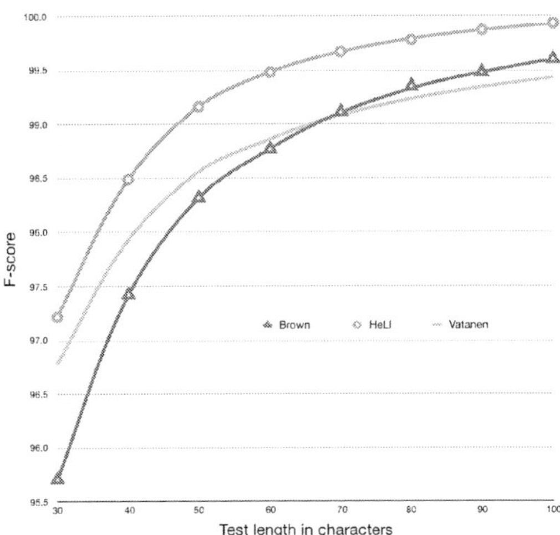

Figure 3: The F_1-scores of the six best evaluated methods.

Figure 4: The F_1-scores of the HeLI method compared with the methods of Brown (2012) and Vatanen et al. (2010).

longest test sequences used in this article. We believe that these two dissimilarities in test setting could be the reason for the differing results, but we decided that investigating this further was not within the scope of this article.

In the evaluation of the method of Brown (2013), we used the "mklangid" program provided with the Brown's package[13] to create new language models for the 285 languages of our test suite. The best results with the "whatlang" were obtained using up to 10-byte n-grams, 40,000 n-grams in the models, and 160 million bytes of training data as well as stop-grams. Stop-grams were calculated for languages with a similarity score of 0.4 or higher. The average recall obtained for 65 character samples was 98.9% with an F_1-score of 99.0%. Brown's method clearly outperforms the results of the algorithm of Cavnar and Trenkle (1994), as can be seen in Figure 3. One thing to note is also the running time. Running the tests using the algorithm of Cavnar and Trenkle (1994) with 20,000 n-grams took over two days, as opposed to the less than an hour with Brown's "Whatlang" program.

In order to evaluate the method used by Vatanen et al. (2010), we utilized the VariKN toolkit (Siivola et al., 2007) to create language models from our training data with the same settings: absolute discounting smoothing with a character n-gram length of 5. When compared with the Browns

identifier the results are clearly in favor of the VariKN toolkit for short test lengths and almost equal at test lengths of 70 characters, after which Brown's language identifier performs better.

For the evaluation of the HeLI method we used a slightly modified Python based implementation of the method. In our implementation, we used relative frequencies as cut-offs c instead of just the frequencies. In order to find the best possible parameters using the training corpora, we applied a simple form of the greedy algorithm using the last 10% of the training corpus for each language as a development set. We started with the same n-gram length n_{max} and the penalty value p, which were found to provide the best results in (Jauhiainen, 2010). Then we proceeded using the greedy algorithm and found at least a local optimum with the values $n_{max} = 6$, $c = 0.0000005$, and $p = 7$. The HeLI method obtains high recall and precision clearly sooner than the methods of Brown (2013) or Vatanen et al. (2010). The F_1-score of 99.5 is achieved at 60 characters, while Brown's method achieved it at 90 characters and the method of Vatanen et al. (2010) at more than 100 characters, which can be seen in Figure 4. The method of Vatanen et al. (2010) performs better than the HeLI method when the length of the mystery text is 20 characters or less.

The HeLI method was also tested without using the language models composed of words. It was found that in addition to obtaining slightly

---

[13]https://sourceforge.net/projects/la-strings/

Lang.	ISO	HL	LG	LL	VK	WL	CT	KG
N.-Aram.	aii	5	5	5	5	5	10	80
Amharic	amh	5	5	20	5	10	5	-
Tibetan	bod	5	10	10	5	5	25	20
Cherokee	chr	5	10	15	5	5	20	-
Greek	ell	5	5	5	5	5	10	40
Gujarati	guj	5	5	5	5	5	10	15
Armenian	hye	5	5	5	5	5	10	65
Inuktitut	iku	5	10	15	5	5	10	-
Kannada	kan	5	5	5	10	5	10	30
Korean	kor	5	5	5	5	5	15	70
Malayal.	mal	5	5	5	5	5	15	15
Thai	tha	5	5	5	20	5	15	25

Table 1: Some of the easiest languages to identify showing how many characters were needed for 100.0% recall by each method.

Lang.	ISO	HL	LG	LL	VK	WL	CT	KG
Achinese	ace	120	-	-	-	-	-	-
Bislama	bis	100	-	-	-	-	-	-
Chayah.	cbt	-	70	-	-	80	90	90
Danish	dan	150	-	-	-	-	100	-
T. Enets	enh	150	80	-	70	-	-	45
Evenki	evn	150	-	-	-	-	-	150
Erzya	myv	-	-	-	-	-	-	-
Newari	new	-	-	-	90	-	-	-
Tumbuka	tum	-	-	-	90	150	150	-
Votic	vot	-	-	-	150	-	100	-

Table 2: Some of the most difficult languages to identify showing how many characters were needed for 100.0% recall by each method.

lower F_1-scores, the language identifier was also much slower when the words were not used. We also tested using Lidstone smoothing instead of the penalty values. The best results were acquired with the Lidstone value of 0.0001, almost reaching the same F_1-scores as the language identifier with the penalty value p of 7. The largest differences in F_1-scores were at the lower mid-range of test lengths, being 0.5 with 25-character samples from the development set.

Some of the languages in the test set had such unique writing systems that their average recall was 100% already at 5 characters by many of the methods as can be seen in Table 1. Some of the most difficult languages can be seen in Table 2. In both of the Tables HL stands for HeLI, LG for LIGA, LL for LogLIGA, VK for VariKN, WL for Whatlang, CT for Cavnar and Trenkle, and KG for King and Dehdari.

5 Conclusions and Future Work

The purpose of the research was to test methods capable of producing good identification results in a general domain with a large number of languages. The methods of Vatanen et al. (2010) and Brown (2012) outperformed the other methods, even though the original method of Cavnar and Trenkle (1994) also obtained very good re-sults. The recently published HeLI method outperforms previous methods and considerably reduces the identification error rate for texts over 60 characters in length.

There still exists several interesting language identification methods and implementations that we have not evaluated using the test setting described in this article. These methods and implementations include, for example, those of Lui and Baldwin (2012), Majli[Pleaseinsertintopreamble] (2012), and Zampieri and Gebre (2014).

Acknowledgments

We would like to thank Kimmo Koskenniemi for many valuable discussions and comments. This research was made possible by funding from the Kone Foundation Language Programme.

References

Steven Bird. 2006. Nltk: the natural language toolkit. In *COLING-ACL '06 Proceedings of the COLING/ACL on Interactive presentation sessions*, pages 69–72, Sydney.

Ralf D. Brown. 2012. Finding and identifying text in 900+ languages. *Digital Investigation*, 9:S34–S43.

Ralf D. Brown. 2013. Selecting and weighting n-grams to identify 1100 languages. In *Text, Speech, and Dialogue 16th International Conference, TSD 2013 Pilsen, Czech Republic, September 2013 Proceedings*, pages 475–483, Pilsen.

Ralf D. Brown. 2014. Non-linear mapping for improved identification of 1300+ languages. In *Proceedings of the 2014 Conference on Empirical Methods in Natural Language Processing (EMNLP 2014)*, pages 627–632, Doha, Qatar.

William B. Cavnar and John M. Trenkle. 1994. N-gram-based text categorization. In *Proceedings of SDAIR-94, 3rd Annual Symposium on Document Analysis and Information Retrieval*, pages 161–175, Las Vegas.

Heidi Jauhiainen, Tommi Jauhiainen, and Krister Lindén. 2015. The finno-ugric languages and the internet project. *Septentrio Conference Series*, 0(2):87–98.

Tommi Jauhiainen, Krister Lindén, and Heidi Jauhiainen. 2016. Heli, a word-based backoff method for language identification. In *Proceedings of the 3rd Workshop on Language Technology for Closely Related Languages, Varieties and Dialects (VarDial)*, pages 153–162, Osaka, Japan.

Tommi Jauhiainen. 2010. Tekstin kielen automaattinen tunnistaminen. Master's thesis, University of Helsinki, Helsinki.

Josh King and Jon Dehdari. 2008. An n-gram based language identification system. The Ohio State University.

Kone Foundation. 2012. The language programme 2012-2016. http://www.koneensaatio.fi/en.

Marco Lui and Timothy Baldwin. 2012. langid.py: an off-the-shelf language identification tool. In *Proceedings of the 50th Annual Meeting of the Association for Computational Linguistics*, pages 25–30, Jeju.

Marco Lui, Jey Han Lau, and Timothy Baldwin. 2014. Automatic detection and language identification of multilingual documents. *Transactions of the Association for Computational Linguistics*, 2:27–40.

Martin Majliš. 2012. Yet another language identifier. In *Proceedings of the Student Research Workshop at the 13th Conference of the European Chapter of the Association for Computational Linguistics*, pages 46–54, Avignon.

Hermann Ney, Ute Essen, and Reinhard Kneser. 1994. On structuring probabilistic dependences in stochastic language modelling. *Computer Speech and Language*, 8(1):1–38.

Uwe Quasthoff, Matthias Richter, and Christian Biemann. 2006. Corpus portal for search in monolingual corpora. In *Proceedings of the fifth international conference on Language Resources and Evaluation, LREC 2006*, pages 1799–1802, Genoa.

Paul Rodrigues. 2012. *Processing Highly Variant Language Using Incremental Model Selection*. Ph.D. thesis, Indiana University.

Vesa Siivola, Teemu Hirsimäki, and Sami Virpioja. 2007. On growing and pruning kneser-ney smoothed n-gram models. *IEEE Transactions on Audio, Speech and Language Processing*, 15(5):1617–1624.

Erik Tromp and Mykola Pechenizkiy. 2011. Graph-based n-gram language identification on short texts. In *Benelearn 2011 - Proceedings of the Twentieth Belgian Dutch Conference on Machine Learning*, pages 27–34, The Hague.

Erik Tromp. 2011. Multilingual sentiment analysis on social media. Master's thesis, Eindhoven University of Technology, Eindhoven.

C. J. van Rijsbergen. 1979. *Information Retrieval*. Butterworths.

Tommi Vatanen, Jaakko J. Väyrynen, and Sami Virpioja. 2010. Language identification of short text segments with n-gram models. In *LREC 2010, Seventh International Conference on Language Resources and Evaluation*, pages 3423–3430, Malta.

John Vogel and David Tresner-Kirsch. 2012. Robust language identification in short, noisy texts: Improvements to liga. In *The Third International Workshop on Mining Ubiquitous and Social Environments*, pages 43–50, Bristol.

Marcos Zampieri and Binyam Gebrekidan Gebre. 2014. Varclass: An open source language identification tool for language varieties. In *Proceedings of Language Resources and Evaluation (LREC*.

Can We Create a Tool for General Domain Event Analysis?

Siim Orasmaa
Institute of Computer Science,
University of Tartu
siim.orasmaa@ut.ee

Heiki-Jaan Kaalep
Institute of Computer Science,
University of Tartu
heiki-jaan.kaalep@ut.ee

Abstract

This study outlines a question about the possibility of creation of a tool for general domain event analysis. We provide reasons for assuming that a TimeML-based event modelling could be a suitable basis for general domain event modelling. We revise and summarise Estonian efforts on TimeML analysis, both at automatic analysis and human analysis, and provide an overview of the current challenges/limitations of applying a TimeML model in an extensive corpus annotation. We conclude with a discussion on reducing complexity of the (TimeML-based) event model.

1 Introduction

It has been hypothesised in language comprehension research that human understanding of natural language involves a mental representation of events (situations) described in texts (Zwaan and Radvansky, 1998). As many texts can be interpreted as stories/narratives that are decomposable into events, the hypothesis gains further support from research in communication (Fisher, 1984) and in computer science (Winston, 2011), which emphasises the importance of the capability of understanding stories/narratives in natural language understanding. Following this, a creation of an automatic tool that analyses texts for events and their characteristics (e.g. participants and circumstances of events) can be seen as a prerequisite for applications involving text understanding, such as automatic question answering and summarisation. Furthermore, considering the vast amount of information created in online news media on daily basis, one can argue for a clear need of such tool, as it would help to provide a human intuitive overview (e.g. focusing on questions *who did what, when and where?*) on what is reported in online media (Vossen et al., 2014).

Since the Message Understanding Conferences (MUC) and the initiation of information extrac-tion (IE) research, numerous works have attacked the problem from a domain-specific side, focusing on automatic analysis of specific "events of interest". Following Cunningham (2005), this is due to automatic analysis of complex information (such as events) requires restricting focus to a specific domain (on specific events) to maintain an acceptable performance level. However, a thread of research, initiated by TimeML—a framework for time-oriented event analysis—(Pustejovsky et al., 2003a), suggests a possibility that event analysis (the annotation of events in texts) could be considered as an extensive automatic language analysis task approachable in a general domain manner, "not restricted to a specific domain" (Saurí et al., 2005). The TimeML-driven fine-grained (word- and phrase-level) event analysis has gained increasing research interest ever since, with the analysis being conducted for different languages (Bittar, 2010; Xue and Zhou, 2010; Caselli et al., 2011; Yaghoobzadeh et al., 2012), tested in several text domains (Pustejovsky et al., 2003b; Bethard et al., 2012; Galescu and Blaylock, 2012) and sub-domains (Bittar, 2010), and extended beyond time-oriented analysis and towards generic event analysis (Bejan and Harabagiu, 2008; Moens et al., 2011; Cybulska and Vossen, 2013; Fokkens et al., 2013). However, the question whether this thread of research should lead to a creation of *a tool for general-domain automatic event analysis*—a tool allowing similar extensive automatic analysis as grammatical level analysis tools (part-of-speech tagging, morphological analysis and syntactic parsing) allow—has not been outlined.

The current work outlines this question, revises and summarises the Estonian efforts on TimeML-based text annotation, both on automatic annotation (Orasmaa, 2012) and human annotation (Orasmaa, 2014a; Orasmaa, 2014b), and interprets the results in the context of creation of a tool for general domain event analysis (Orasmaa, 2016). As the human performance (interannotator agreement) on text analysis can be seen as an upper limit for what automatic analysis can

192

Proceedings of the 21st Nordic Conference of Computational Linguistics, pages 192–201,
Gothenburg, Sweden, 23-24 May 2017. ©2017 Linköping University Electronic Press

achieve, this provides an overview of current challenges/limitations of applying a TimeML model in an extensive corpus annotation. Observing these limitations, we also discuss a simplified model that could be explored in the future: a model that approximates event annotations to syntactic predicates, and focuses straightforwardly on the annotation of (temporal) relations, without the decomposition of the task.

This paper has the following structure. The next section gives a very general outline to the problem of event analysis, and also the motivation to pursue the problem from the perspective of time-oriented analysis. Section 3 introduces the TimeML model, and gives reasons why it could be considered as a suitable basis for general domain event model. Section 4 gives details on the basic assumptions in TimeML markup, and also revises the Estonian experience in contrast to these assumptions. Subsections of Section 4 focus on event mention, temporal relation and temporal expression annotation. Finally, Section 5 provides a discussion on reducing the complexity of (TimeML-based) event model, and a conclusion that attempts to put the time-oriented event modelling to a broader perspective.

2   The Problem of Event Analysis

Although not often emphasised, "the definition of an "event" is ill-defined" in Natural Language Processing (Bracewell, 2015), and the research progress on event analysis has been hindered by "linguistic and ontological complexity" of events (Nothman, 2013). The struggle with the definition of "event" can also be encountered in other fields, notably in philosophy, where "there is significant disagreement concerning the precise nature" of events (Casati and Varzi, 2014). In philosophy, important characteristics of events could be outlined, perhaps, only when contrasting events against "entities from other metaphysical categories", such as objects, facts, properties, and times (Casati and Varzi, 2014).

Despite the lack of common theoretical understanding on the concept of event, ever-growing volumes of digital and digitised natural language texts provide a motivation to pursue the research on event analysis. As our understanding of natural language texts can be seen as residing in understanding the "eventive" meanings encoded in texts (Zwaan and Radvansky, 1998), successes in au-

tomatic event analysis promise to open up more human-intuitive ways of automatically organising and summarising large volumes of texts, e.g. providing an overview about events described in on-line news media (Vossen et al., 2014).

While choosing a strong theoretical basis for a tool for automatic analysis of events is rather difficult, one could note that there seems to be an agreement among philosophers that events are generally related to time ("events /- - -/ have relatively vague spatial boundaries and crisp temporal boundaries") (Casati and Varzi, 2014). Verbs—a linguistic category most commonly associated with events—often convey markers of temporal meaning at the grammatical level, e.g. Estonian verb tenses provide a general distinction between past and present. Furthermore, some influential theoretical works have generalised from lexical and grammatical properties of verbs to models of time: Reichenbach argued that tenses of verbs can be abstracted to the level of temporal relations (Reichenbach, 1947), and Vendler proposed that verbs can be classified by their temporal properties (Vendler, 1957). This does suggest that it is reasonable to start out approaching general domain event analysis focusing on modelling temporal characteristics of events in natural language, and this is also the approach used in the TimeML framework (Pustejovsky et al., 2003a).

3   TimeML as a Base Model for General-domain Event Analysis

TimeML (and also its revised version: ISO-TimeML (Pustejovsky et al., 2010)) proposes a fine-grained (word- and phrase-level) approach to event analysis: firstly, event-denoting words, such as verbs (e.g. *meet*), nouns (e.g. *meeting*) and adjectives (e.g. *(be) successful*), and temporal expressions (such as *on 1st of February* or *from Monday morning*) are annotated in text, and then, temporal relations holding between events, and also between events and temporal expressions are marked. For example, a TimeML annotation would formalise that the sentence "*After the meeting, they had a lunch at a local gourmet restaurant*" expresses temporal precedence: the event of *meeting* happened before the event of *lunch*.

One can argue that TimeML's approach is a particularly suitable basis for a general-domain event analysis for the following reasons:

- TimeML's event is "simply something that can be related to another event or temporal expression", and, given this very generic definition, a TimeML-compliant event representation could be used for "different genres, styles, domains, and applications" (Pustejovsky et al., 2010);

- In TimeML, only a word that best represents the event is annotated in text (Xue and Zhou, 2010), without the full mark up / analysis of event's argument structure (except time-related arguments: temporal expressions). Following Cunningham (2005), there is a trade-off between an event model's complexity and its general applicability: an accurate automatic analysis of an event's complex argument structure requires focusing on a specific domain; however, TimeML's light-weight commitment to modelling argument structure does suggest a possibility that an accurate analysis could be extended beyond specific domains;

- TimeML follows a principle that in case of complex syntactic structures, only the head of a construction is annotated as an event mention (Saurí et al., 2009). As Robaldo et al. (2011) argue, this makes it particularily feasible to build TimeML annotations upon (dependency) syntactic structures. In case of a successful grounding of event annotations on syntactic structures, one could inherit the general domain analysis capabilities from a syntactic analysis;

- The extensions and derivations of TimeML event model indicate its potential as a generic event model. For instance, TimeML-based event models have been enriched with additional relations holding between events, such as subevent and causal relations (Bejan and Harabagiu, 2008) and spatial relations (Pustejovsky et al., 2011). A TimeML-derived model has been extended with other generic arguments, referring to participants and locations of events, resulting in a four component event model (expressing semantics: *who* did *what*, *when* and *where?*) (Fokkens et al., 2013; Cybulska and Vossen, 2013).

Considering the aforementioned reasons, we as-

sumed in this work that a TimeML model is a suitable basis for developing a general domain event analysis tool.

4 Estonian Experience

In the next subsections, we will discuss the Estonian experience on adapting the TimeML annotation framework. Data and experimental results we use as a basis are from Estonian TimeML-annotated corpus (Orasmaa, 2014b; Orasmaa, 2014a).[1] The corpus has the following characteristics important to our study:

- The corpus is fully annotated by three independent annotators (2 annotators per text), thus it can be used for retrospective inter-annotator agreement studies. Human agreements on analysis indicate the possible upper limits that automatic analysis could achieve;

- The corpus builds upon manually corrected morphological and dependency syntactic annotations of Estonian Dependency Treebank (Muischnek et al., 2014), thus it can be used for studying how well event annotations can be grounded on (gold standard) grammatical annotations;

- The corpus is compiled from news domain texts and covers different sub-genres of news, including local and foreign news, sports, and economy news. Given the heterogeneity of news texts, we assume the corpus is varied enough for using it as a testbed for a general domain event modelling;

In the current work, the inter-annotator agreement experiments on the corpus are revised, and the results are interpreted in the context of creation of a tool for general domain event analysis.

In addition, we also discuss Estonian experience on automatic temporal expression tagging: we contrast the Estonian results (Orasmaa, 2012) with the state-of-the-art results in English, and open up a discussion on the theoretical scope of TimeML's concept of temporal expression.

4.1 The Annotation of Event Mentions

Assumptions. TimeML assumes that before one can capture semantics of events in text, e.g. the temporal ordering of events and the placement

---

194

[1]The corpus is available at: `https://github.com/soras/EstTimeMLCorpus` (Last accessed: 2017-01-13)

on a timeline, one needs to establish a consistent **event mention** annotation, upon which semantic relation annotation can be built. At the linguistic level, the range of potential event-denoting units is assumed to be wide, covering "tensed or untensed verbs, nominalizations, adjectives, predicative clauses, or prepositional phrases" (Pustejovsky et al., 2003a).

When examining more closely, however, one could note that TimeML's modelling of events is leaning towards the verb category. Firstly, the guidelines (Saurí et al., 2009) instruct to mark up surface-grammatical attributes for characterising the event, and most of these attributes describe verb-related (or verb phrase related) properties (e.g. *tense, aspect*[2], *polarity*, or *modality*). For instance, the attribute *modality* indicates whether the event mention is in the scope of a modal auxiliary, such as *may, must, should*. Secondly, if we make a rough generalisation from English TimeML annotation guidelines (Saurí et al., 2006; Saurí et al., 2009) , with an admitted loss of some specific details, it appears that: 1) most of the annotation of non-verb event mentions focuses on nouns, adjectives and pre-positions; 2) out of the three parts-of-speech, only noun annotations cover a wide range of syntactic positions, as event mention annotations on adjectives and prepositions are limited to predicative complement positions.

Considering this rough outline of the TimeML event model, it is interesting to ask, how well does one extend the annotation of event mentions beyond the category of verbs, which could be considered as a "prototypical" category for event mentions. The Estonian TimeML-annotated corpus allows us to examine this question more closely.

Estonian experience. The Estonian TimeML annotation project aimed for a relatively extensive event mention annotation, attempting to maximise the coverage on syntactic contexts interpretable as "eventive". The corpus was created on top of a gold standard grammatical annotations, and it contains (independent) annotations of three different human annotators. Thus, the corpus allows to take out grammatically constrained subsets of event mention annotations, and to study the inter-annotator agreements on these subsets.

Table 1 shows how the inter-annotator agree-

ment and the coverage on event mention annotations changes when the annotations are extended beyond prototypically "eventive" syntactic contexts. The highest agreement, F1-score 0.982, was obtained in covering syntactic predicates with event mention annotations. The syntactic predicate consists of the root node of the syntactic tree (mostly a finite verb), and, in some cases, also its dependents: an auxiliary verb (in case of negation) or a finite verb (e.g. in case of modal verb constructions, where an infinite verb dominates the modal finite verb). The agreement remained relatively high (F1-score 0.943) if all verbs, regardless of their syntactic function, were allowed to be annotated as event mentions. However, including part-of-speech categories other than verbs in the event model caused decrease in agreements, and the largest decrease (F1-score falling to 0.832) was noted if nouns were included as event mentions. The high-agreement model (verbs as event mentions) covered only $\sim$65% of all event mentions annotated, and obtaining a high coverage (more than 90% of all event annotations) required the inclusion of the problematic noun category in the model.

4.2 Enriching Event Annotations: Providing Temporal Relation Annotations

Assumptions. Temporal semantics of events in text can be conveyed both by explicit and implicit means. Main **explicit** temporality indicators are verb tense, temporal relationship adverbials (e.g. *before, after* or *until*), and explicit time-referring expressions (e.g. *on Monday at 3 p.m.*). The interpretation of **implicit** temporal information usually requires world knowledge (e.g. knowledge about typical ordering of events), and/or applying temporal inference (inferring new relations based on existing ones).

It is stated that the ultimate goal of TimeML annotation is to capture/encode all temporal relations in text, "regardless of whether the relation is explicitly signaled or not" (Verhagen et al., 2009). The TempEval-1 and TempEval-2 evaluation campaigns (Verhagen et al., 2009; Verhagen et al., 2010) have approached this goal by dividing the task into smaller subtasks, and by providing systematic (relatively extensive in the coverage) annotations for these subtasks. Notably in

---

[2]Note that not all languages have the grammatical aspect as a property of the verb, and this is also the case with Estonian.

[3]In cases of counting EVENT coverage, each token with a unique position in text was counted once, regardless of how many different annotators had annotated it.

EVENT subset description	EVENT coverage[3]	IAA on EVENT extent
syntactic predicates	57.16%	0.982
verbs	65.18%	0.943
verbs and adjectives	70.18%	0.916
verbs and nouns	93.69%	0.832
verbs, adjectives and nouns	98.64%	0.815
all syntactic contexts	100.0%	0.809

Table 1: How the annotation coverage and inter-annotator agreement (F1-score) changed when extending EVENT annotations beyond (syntactic predicates and) verbs. Gold standard grammatical annotations were used as a guide in selecting subsets of EVENT annotations provided by three independent human annotators, and inter-annotator agreements and coverages (of all EVENT annotations provided by the annotators) were measured on these subsets. This is a revised version of the experiment firstly reported by Orasmaa (2014b).

TempEval-2, the relation annotations were guided by syntactic relations, e.g. one of the subtasks required the identification of temporal relations between two events in all contexts where one event mention syntactically governed another.

Estonian experience. Following the TempEval-2 (Verhagen et al., 2010) example, the Estonian TimeML annotation project split the temporal relation annotation into syntactically guided subtasks, and attempted to provide a relatively extensive/systematic annotation in these subtasks. However, the resulting inter-annotator agreements showed that approaching the task in this way is very difficult: on deciding the type of temporal relation, the observed agreement was 0.474, and the chance-corrected agreement (Cohen's kappa) was even lower: 0.355.

Still, the systematic coverage of the temporal annotations and the availability of gold standard syntactic annotations enabled us to investigate whether there existed grammatically constrained subsets of annotations exhibiting higher than average agreements. It was hypothesised that the human agreements were affected by explicit temporal cues: verb tenses encoded in morphology and temporal expressions syntactically governed by verb event mentions[4]. Table 2 shows how the quality of temporal relation annotation, measured in terms of the proportion of VAGUE relations used by annotators and the inter-annotator agreement, was affected by the presence of these

explicit temporal cues.

EVENT subset description	Proportion of VAGUE relations	Avg ACC	Avg κ
EVENTs in simple past tense	3.5%	**0.574**	**0.333**
EVENTs in present tense	28.5%	0.43	0.271
EVENTs governing TIMEX	**4.04%**	**0.607**	**0.476**
EVENTs not governing any TIMEX	21.1%	0.447	0.291

Table 2: How presence of explicit temporal cues affected the quality of manual temporal relation annotation. The quality was measured in terms of the proportion of VAGUE relations used by annotators, and the average inter-annotator agreement (accuracy and Cohen's kappa) on specifying temporal relation type. This is a revised version of the experiment firstly reported by Orasmaa (2014a).

The results showed that the presence of temporal expressions contributed most to the inter-annotator agreements: the observed agreement rose to 0.607 (kappa to 0.476), and the usage of VAGUE relations dropped to 4.04% (from 21.1%). The morphologically encoded verb tense, however, provided to be an ambiguous indicator of temporal semantics: simple past contributed to

---

[4]Important explicit cues would also be temporal relationship adverbials, such as *before* or *until*, however, these temporal signals were not annotated in the Estonian corpus.

making temporal relations more clearer for annotators, while the present tense contributed to increased temporal vagueness. This can be explained by the Estonian simple past serving mostly a single function—expressing what happened in the past—, while the present tense is conventionally used to express temporal semantics of present, future, recurrence, and genericity.

4.3 Annotation of Temporal Expressions

Assumptions. Temporal expressions are usually seen as an important part of event's structure, providing answers to questions such as when did the event happen (e.g. *on 2nd of February* or *on Monday morning*), how long did the event last (e.g. *six hours*), or how often did the event happened (e.g. *three times a week*)?

The research on temporal expression (TIMEX) annotation has a long tradition, starting along side with named entity recognition in the MUC competitions (Nadeau and Sekine, 2007), where the focus was mainly on mark-up of temporal expression phrases, and leading to the annotation schemes TIMEX2 (Ferro et al., 2005) and TimeML's TIMEX3 (Pustejovsky et al., 2003a), where, in addition to the mark-up, also expressions' semantics are represented in a uniform format. The representation of semantics (normalisation) in TIMEX2 and TIMEX3 builds upon a calendric time representation from the ISO 8601:1997 standard. It allows to encode meanings of common date and time expressions (such as *on 20th of May*, *last Wednesday*, or *12 minutes after midday*), as well as meanings of calendric expressions with fuzzy temporal boundaries (e.g. *in the summer of 2014*, or *at the end of May*), and generic references to past, present or future (e.g. *recently* or *now*). The TimeML scheme assumes a relatively clear separation between temporal expressions and event mentions, with the encoding of semantics of temporal expressions being considered as a straightforward task, while the encoding of semantics of event expressions being considered a complex task of involving mark-up of events, temporal expressions, and temporal relations connecting them.

From the practical point of view, the TimeML TIMEX3 scheme has proven to be relatively successful if one considers performance levels of automatic approaches. A recent evaluation of automatic temporal expression tagging in news domain, TempEval-3 evaluation exercise (UzZaman et al., 2013), reports 90.32% as the highest F1-score on detecting temporal expressions in English (82.71% as the highest F1-score for detection with *strict* phrase boundaries), and 77.61% as the highest F1-score on the task involving both detection and normalisation of expressions.

Estonian experience. A large-scale evaluation of an Estonian TimeML-based automatic temporal expression tagger was reported by Orasmaa (2012). We took the results on the news portion of that evaluation (a corpus in size of approximately 49,000 tokens and 1,300 temporal expressions), and recalculated precisions and recalls as TempEval-3 compatible F1-scores. The resulting scores are in the Table 3.

Subcorpus	F1	F1 (strict)	normalisation (F1)
Local news	89.38	84.19	80.98
Foreign news	91.83	88.44	85.68
Opinions	87.77	80.19	75.13
Sport	94.48	89.29	81.44
Economics	86.16	79.92	77.99
Culture	86.86	81.36	76.61
Total (macro-average)	89.41	83.90	79.64

Table 3: The state-of-the-art performance of Estonian automatic temporal expression tagging on different subgenres of news. The scores are based on precisions and recalls reported by Orasmaa (2012), recalculated as TempEval-3 (UzZaman et al., 2013) compatible F1-scores.

The results indicate that the performance levels on automatic temporal expression tagging in English (UzZaman et al., 2013) and Estonian compare rather well. Although the evaluation settings are not fully comparable, the initial comparison confirms the potential of the TimeML's TIMEX3 scheme in enabling high accuracy general domain automatic temporal expression tagging across different languages. From the theoretical point of view, however, we note that there is a room for a discussion on how well the information-extraction-oriented approach of TimeML scheme covers the language phenomenon.

The Grammar of Estonian (Erelt et al., 1993) describes a linguistic category similar to TimeML's temporal expressions: *temporal adverbials*. Temporal adverbials also express occurrence times, durations and recurrences. While

Marşic (2012) states that temporal expressions form "the largest subclass" of temporal adverbials, we note that in addition to the large overlap, the two categories also have notable differences. Temporal adverbials in The Grammar of Estonian are syntactically restricted to sentence constituents that modify the meaning of the main verb or the sentence. Temporal expressions, on the other hand, are not restricted to the syntactic role of an adverbial, e.g. they can also modify the meaning of a single constituent in the sentence, such as the expression *today* in the phrase *today's meeting*. Semantically, the class of temporal adverbials in The Grammar of Estonian is open: it also includes time expressions with no explicit calendric information (such as *in a stressful era*) and event-denoting time expressions (such as *since the congress*). This contrasts to TimeML's information extraction perspective that restricts the focus mainly on temporal expressions conveying calendric information.

5 Discussion

TimeML proposes a compositional approach to event analysis: first event mentions should be identified in text, and then, temporal semantics of the events should be encoded via markup of temporal relations.

It can be argued that temporal annotation in TimeML is inherently a very complex task, even for humans (Marşic, 2012), and that a high consistency in the process may not come from a single effort, but rather from an iterative annotation development process. An iteration in this process involves modelling the phenomenon, annotating texts manually according to the model, performing machine learning experiments on the annotations, and finally revising both the model and the machine learning algorithms before starting a new iteration (Pustejovsky and Moszkowicz, 2012; Pustejovsky and Stubbs, 2012). However, the aforementioned strategy may still not be sufficient to tackle the problem, as one could humbly remind that problems related to natural language understanding "have not been studied in linguistics nor anywhere else in the systematic way that is required to develop reliable annotation schemas" (Zaenen, 2006).

Reversing the compositional approach of TimeML, we can argue that a perceivable presence of explicit temporal information is actually one important indicator of "eventiveness": that one can interpret text units as "event mentions" with a high degree of certainty only in contexts that allow to place events reliably on a time-line or temporally order with respect to each other. However, the Estonian experience on manual annotation indicates these contexts are not pervasive in news texts, like the grammatically analysable contexts are. Rather, the evidence shows that higher than average consistency can be obtained only in certain syntactic contexts characterised by explicit temporal cues, such as temporal expressions and past-indicating verb tenses. This calls for a discussion for an alternative modeling of events, with the aim of reducing the complexity of the model.

Studies of narratology propose that the semantics of events have a lot to do with events' relations to other events. One could even go as far as to argue that events "become meaningful" only "in series", and "it is pointless to consider whether or not an isolated fact is an event" (Bal, 1997). This suggests that the perspective that considers a single event as an atomic unit for analysis could be revised, and events could be analysed in series from the beginning. A minimal unit to be annotated/detected would then be a pair of events connected by a relation, e.g. by a temporal or a causal relation. Note that while the ultimate aim of TimeML is capturing temporal relations, because of the decomposition of the task, someone employing the framework could easily get stuck with the problems of event mention annotation (e.g. how to reliably ground the concept of event at the grammatical level), and may be hindered from reaching temporal relation annotation.

A simpler annotation model could focus directly on annotation of relations between text units, without the decomposition of annotations into events and relations. Before the creation of TimeML, a similar idea was proposed by Katz and Arosio (2001), who did not use event annotation and simply marked temporal relations on verbs in their annotation project. The Estonian annotation experience also showed a high inter-annotator agreement on verbs as event mentions, and the highest agreement on syntactic predicates (main verbs). This suggests that syntactic predicates could be a reasonable (although, admittedly, very rough) approximation for event mentions, and the simple model involving mark-up of relations on syntactic predicates could be the first one to be developed and tested out in a general domain analysis, before developing more complex models, e.g. adding nouns as event mentions.

Lefeuvre-Halftermeyer et al. (2016) make a similar proposal to "characterize eventualities not at the text level, but on the syntactic structures of a treebank", i.e. to mark nodes in a syntactic tree as event mentions. The benefit would be that the syntactic structure would already approximate the event structure, and (to an extent) would provide an access to event's arguments without the need for an explicit markup of event-argument relations. However, the authors do not discuss reducing the complexity of the event model, which, in our view, would also be worth experimenting with. Focusing straightforwardly on the annotation of relations could enable more simple designs both for human annotation and machine learning experiments, which, in turn, could foster more experimentation and, hopefully, improvements on the current results.

In the markup of temporal relations, the Estonian experience showed increased agreements and also less vagueness in the contexts of temporal expressions. As the results of automatic temporal expression tagging in Estonian (reported in Table 3) were also rather encouraging, indicating that satisfactory practical performance levels (95% and above) may not be very far from the reach, one could argue for focusing future temporal relation annotation efforts on contexts with temporal expressions, taking advantage of their high accuracy pre-annotation.

However, contrasting TimeML-compatible temporal expressions with temporal adverbials distinguished in Estonian grammatical tradition revealed that the TIMEX (TIMEX2, TIMEX3) annotation standards have been, to a large extent, "optimised" for capturing "calendric" temporal expressions, i.e. expressions whose semantics can be modeled in the calendar system. A syntax-based view suggests that TimeML's temporal expressions do not cover non-calendric temporal references and also event mentions appearing in the syntactic positions of temporal adverbials. Instead, event mentions in TimeML are considered as markables clearly separable from temporal expressions.

If we are to step back, and attempt to put the problem in a broader philosophical context, we may note that historically, (calendric) temporal expressions also originate from event mentions. They refer to "major cyclic events of the human natural environment on earth", such as "the alternation of light and dark, changes in the shape of the moon, and changes in the path of the sun across the sky (accompanied by marked climatic differences)" (Haspelmath, 1997). One could say that (driven by the need for expressing time) the natural language has developed rather systematic and relatively unambiguous ways for expressing "calendric events".

This may also offer an explanation why the task of generic event analysis is so difficult to establish—compared to the task of analysing "calendric events" / temporal expressions. Temporal expression tagging builds on the part of human language usage that is already systematic, as it is based on a well-defined conventional system of time-keeping. Yet, it is still an open question whether there is a similar convention of expressing "events in general" in natural language, upon which a systematic general-domain event analyser can be built. While tending towards answering this question, we believe that it is also worthwhile to revise the existing event models for their complexity, and to test out simpler models building straightforwardly on the syntactic structure, and centring them on the explicit temporal cues available in texts.

Acknowledgments

This work was supported by Estonian Ministry of Education and Research (grant IUT 20-56 "Computational models for Estonian").

References

Mieke Bal. 1997. *Narratology: Introduction to the Theory of Narrative*. University of Toronto Press. https://archive.org/details/ BalNarratologyIntroductionToTheTheoryOfNarrative (Date accessed: 2017-01-10).

Cosmin Adrian Bejan and Sanda M Harabagiu. 2008. A Linguistic Resource for Discovering Event Structures and Resolving Event Coreference. In *LREC*.

Steven Bethard, Oleksandr Kolomiyets, and Marie-Francine Moens. 2012. Annotating Story Timelines as Temporal Dependency Structures. In *Proceedings of the Eight International Conference on Language Resources and Evaluation (LREC'12)*, Istanbul, Turkey, may. European Language Resources Association (ELRA).

André Bittar. 2010. *Building a TimeBank for French: a Reference Corpus Annotated According to the ISO-TimeML Standard.* Ph.D. thesis, Université Paris Diderot, Paris, France.

David B Bracewell. 2015. Long nights, rainy days, and misspent youth: Automatically extracting and categorizing occasions associated with consumer products. *SocialNLP 2015 @ NAACL*, pages 29–38.

Roberto Casati and Achille Varzi. 2014. Events. In Edward N. Zalta, editor, *The Stanford Encyclopedia of Philosophy.* Fall 2014 edition. http://plato.stanford.edu/archives/fall2014/entries/events/ (Date accessed: 2017-01-20).

Tommaso Caselli, Valentina Bartalesi Lenzi, Rachele Sprugnoli, Emanuele Pianta, and Irina Prodanof. 2011. Annotating Events, Temporal Expressions and Relations in Italian: the It-Timeml Experience for the Ita-TimeBank. In *Linguistic Annotation Workshop*, pages 143–151. The Association for Computer Linguistics.

Hamish Cunningham. 2005. Information Extraction, Automatic. *Encyclopedia of Language and Linguistics*, 5:665–677.

Agata Cybulska and Piek Vossen. 2013. Semantic Relations between Events and their Time, Locations and Participants for Event Coreference Resolution. In *RANLP*, pages 156–163.

Tiiu Erelt, Ülle Viks, Mati Erelt, Reet Kasik, Helle Metslang, Henno Rajandi, Kristiina Ross, Henn Saari, Kaja Tael, and Silvi Vare. 1993. *Eesti keele grammatika. 2., Süntaks (Grammar of Estonian: The syntax).* Tallinn: Eesti TA Keele ja Kirjanduse Instituut.

Lisa Ferro, Laurie Gerber, Inderjeet Mani, Beth Sundheim, and George Wilson. 2005. TIDES 2005 standard for the annotation of temporal expressions. https://www.ldc.upenn.edu/sites/www.ldc.upenn.edu/files/english-timex2-guidelines-v0.1.pdf (Date accessed: 2017-01-15).

Walter R Fisher. 1984. Narration as a human communication paradigm: The case of public moral argument. *Communications Monographs*, 51(1):1–22.

Antske Fokkens, Marieke Van Erp, Piek Vossen, Sara Tonelli, Willem Robert van Hage, Luciano Serafini, Rachele Sprugnoli, and Jesper Hoeksema. 2013. GAF: A grounded annotation framework for events. In *NAACL HLT*, volume 2013, pages 11–20. Citeseer.

Lucian Galescu and Nate Blaylock. 2012. A corpus of clinical narratives annotated with temporal information. In *Proceedings of the 2nd ACM SIGHIT International Health Informatics Symposium*, pages 715–720. ACM.

Martin Haspelmath. 1997. *From space to time: Temporal adverbials in the world's languages.* Lincom Europa.

Graham Katz and Fabrizio Arosio. 2001. The annotation of temporal information in natural language sentences. In *Proceedings of the Workshop on Temporal and Spatial Information Processing*, volume 13, pages 15–22. Association for Computational Linguistics.

Anaïs Lefeuvre-Halftermeyer, Jean-Yves Antoine, Alain Couillault, Emmanuel Schang, Lotfi Abouda, Agata Savary, Denis Maurel, Iris Eshkol-Taravella, and Delphine Battistelli. 2016. Covering various Needs in Temporal Annotation: a Proposal of Extension of ISO-TimeML that Preserves Upward Compatibility. In *LREC 2016*.

G. Marşic. 2012. Syntactically Motivated Task Definition for Temporal Relation Identification. *Special Issue of the TAL (Traitement Automatique des Langues) Journal on Processing of Temporal and Spatial Information in Language - Traitement automatique des informations temporelles et spatiales en langage naturel*, vol. 53, no. 2:23–55.

Marie-Francine Moens, Oleksandr Kolomiyets, Emanuele Pianta, Sara Tonelli, and Steven Bethard. 2011. D3. 1: State-of-the-art and design of novel annotation languages and technologies: Updated version. Technical report, TERENCE project–ICT FP7 Programme–ICT-2010-25410. http://www.terenceproject.eu/c/document_library/get_file?p_l_id=16136&folderId=12950&name=DLFE-1910.pdf (Date accessed: 2017-01-15).

Kadri Muischnek, Kaili Müürisep, Tiina Puolakainen, Eleri Aedmaa, Riin Kirt, and Dage Särg. 2014. Estonian Dependency Treebank and its annotation scheme. In *Proceedings of 13th Workshop on Treebanks and Linguistic Theories (TLT13)*, pages 285–291.

David Nadeau and Satoshi Sekine. 2007. A survey of named entity recognition and classification. *Lingvisticae Investigationes*, 30(1):3–26.

Joel Nothman. 2013. *Grounding event references in news.* Ph.D. thesis, The University of Sydney.

Siim Orasmaa. 2012. Automaatne ajaväljendite tuvastamine eestikeelsetes tekstides *(Automatic Recognition and Normalization of Temporal Expressions in Estonian Language Texts).* *Eesti Rakenduslingvistika Ühingu aastaraamat*, (8):153–169.

Siim Orasmaa. 2014a. How Availability of Explicit Temporal Cues Affects Manual Temporal Relation Annotation. In *Human Language Technologies— The Baltic Perspective: Proceedings of the Sixth International Conference Baltic HLT 2014*, volume 268, pages 215–218. IOS Press.

Siim Orasmaa. 2014b. Towards an Integration of Syntactic and Temporal Annotations in Estonian. In *LREC*, pages 1259–1266.

Siim Orasmaa. 2016. *Explorations of the Problem of Broad-coverage and General Domain Event Analysis: The Estonian Experience*. Ph.D. thesis, University of Tartu, Estonia.

James Pustejovsky and Jessica Moszkowicz. 2012. The Role of Model Testing in Standards Development: The Case of ISO-Space. In *LREC*, pages 3060–3063.

James Pustejovsky and Amber Stubbs. 2012. *Natural Language Annotation for Machine Learning*. O'Reilly Media, Inc.

James Pustejovsky, José Castaño, Robert Ingria, Roser Saurí, Robert Gaizauskas, Andrea Setzer, and Graham Katz. 2003a. TimeML: Robust specification of event and temporal expressions in text. In *Fifth International Workshop on Computational Semantics (IWCS-5)*.

James Pustejovsky, Patrick Hanks, Roser Sauri, Andrew See, Robert Gaizauskas, Andrea Setzer, Dragomir Radev, Beth Sundheim, David Day, Lisa Ferro, et al. 2003b. The TimeBank corpus. In *Corpus Linguistics*, volume 2003, pages 647–656.

James Pustejovsky, Kiyong Lee, Harry Bunt, and Laurent Romary. 2010. ISO-TimeML: An International Standard for Semantic Annotation. In *LREC*.

James Pustejovsky, Jessica L Moszkowicz, and Marc Verhagen. 2011. ISO-Space: The annotation of spatial information in language. In *Proceedings of the Sixth Joint ISO-ACL SIGSEM Workshop on Interoperable Semantic Annotation*, pages 1–9.

Hans Reichenbach. 1947. *Elements of symbolic logic*. Macmillan Co.

Livio Robaldo, Tommaso Caselli, Irene Russo, and Matteo Grella. 2011. From Italian text to TimeML document via dependency parsing. In *Computational Linguistics and Intelligent Text Processing*, pages 177–187. Springer.

Roser Saurí, Robert Knippen, Marc Verhagen, and James Pustejovsky. 2005. Evita: a robust event recognizer for QA systems. In *Proceedings of the conference on Human Language Technology and Empirical Methods in Natural Language Processing*, pages 700–707. Association for Computational Linguistics.

Roser Saurí, Jessica Littman, Robert Gaizauskas, Andrea Setzer, and James Pustejovsky. 2006. TimeML annotation guidelines, version 1.2.1. http://www.timeml.org/publications/timeMLdocs/annguide_1.2.1.pdf (Date accessed: 2017-01-20).

Roser Saurí, Lotus Goldberg, Marc Verhagen, and James Pustejovsky. 2009. *Annotating Events in English. TimeML Annotation Guidelines*. http://www.timeml.org/tempeval2/tempeval2-trial/guidelines/EventGuidelines-050409.pdf (Date accessed: 2017-01-15).

Naushad UzZaman, Hector Llorens, Leon Derczynski, Marc Verhagen, James Allen, and James Pustejovsky. 2013. SemEval-2013 Task 1: TEMPEVAL-3: Evaluating Time Expressions, Events, and Temporal Relations. http://derczynski.com/sheffield/papers/tempeval-3.pdf (Date accessed: 2017-01-15).

Zeno Vendler. 1957. Verbs and times. *The philosophical review*, pages 143–160.

Marc Verhagen, Robert Gaizauskas, Frank Schilder, Mark Hepple, Jessica Moszkowicz, and James Pustejovsky. 2009. The TempEval challenge: identifying temporal relations in text. *Language Resources and Evaluation*, 43(2):161–179.

Marc Verhagen, Roser Sauri, Tommaso Caselli, and James Pustejovsky. 2010. SemEval-2010 task 13: TempEval-2. In *Proceedings of the 5th international workshop on semantic evaluation*, pages 57–62. Association for Computational Linguistics.

Piek Vossen, German Rigau, Luciano Serafini, Pim Stouten, Francis Irving, and Willem Robert Van Hage. 2014. Newsreader: recording history from daily news streams. In *Proceedings of the 9th Language Resources and Evaluation Conference (LREC2014)*, Reykjavik, Iceland, May 26-31.

Patrick Henry Winston. 2011. The Strong Story Hypothesis and the Directed Perception Hypothesis. In Pat Langley, editor, *Technical Report FS-11-01, Papers from the AAAI Fall Symposium*, pages 345–352, Menlo Park, CA. AAAI Press.

Nianwen Xue and Yuping Zhou. 2010. Applying Syntactic, Semantic and Discourse Constraints in Chinese Temporal Annotation. In *Proceedings of the 23rd International Conference on Computational Linguistics*, COLING '10, pages 1363–1372, Stroudsburg, PA, USA. Association for Computational Linguistics.

Yadollah Yaghoobzadeh, Gholamreza Ghassem-Sani, Seyed Abolghasem Mirroshandel, and Mahbaneh Eshaghzadeh. 2012. ISO-TimeML Event Extraction in Persian Text. In *COLING*, pages 2931–2944.

Annie Zaenen. 2006. Mark-up barking up the wrong tree. *Computational Linguistics*, 32(4):577–580.

Rolf A Zwaan and Gabriel A Radvansky. 1998. Situation models in language comprehension and memory. *Psychological Bulletin*, 123(2):162.

From Treebank to Propbank:

A Semantic-Role and VerbNet Corpus for Danish

Eckhard Bick
Institute of Language and Communication
University of Southern Denmark
eckhard.bick@mail.dk

Abstract

This paper presents the first version of a Danish Propbank/VerbNet corpus, annotated at both the morphosyntactic, dependency and semantic levels. Both verbal and nominal predications were tagged with frames consisting of a VerbNet class and semantic role-labeled arguments and satellites. As a second semantic annotation layer, the corpus was tagged with both a noun ontology and NER classes. Drawing on mixed news, magazine, blog and forum data from DSL's Korpus2010, the 87,000 token corpus contains over 12,000 frames with 32,000 semantic role instances. We discuss both technical and linguistic aspects of the annotation process, evaluate coverage and provide a statistical break-down of frames and roles for both the corpus as a whole and across different text types.

1   Introduction

The syntactic potential and semantic structure of a language's lexicon can either be encoded explicitly in a dictionary or ontology, or implicitly through annotated data. Rule-based natural-language processing (NLP) will typically rely on the former, machine-learning (ML) systems on the latter. For the semantic annotation of predicate-argument structures, two well-known English ressources each addressing one of these two approaches are FrameNet (Baker et al. 1998, Johnson & Fillmore 2000, Ruppenhofer et al. 2010) and PropBank (Palmer et al. 2005),

respectively. While FrameNet categorizes verb senses into frames with semantically restricted "slot-filler" arguments, PropBank departs from syntactically annotated corpus data to assign both roles and argument structure to each verb consecutively. The data-driven approach of PropBank promises better coverage and statistical balance[1], and therefore better automatic ML tagging, but its semantic role inventory and numbered arguments are highly predicate-dependent, and do not support semantic generalization and interpretation as well as FrameNet. A third approach, VerbNet (Kipper et al. 2006), opts for less granularity and a more limited set of roles and predicate classes. In recent years, corpora with such medium-granularity semantic-role annotation have been published for various languages, e.g. German (Mújdricza-Maydt et al. 2009) and Dutch (Monachesi et al. 2007).

For Danish, a VerbNet-based FrameNet (Bick 2011), with similar granularity (35 roles, 200 predicate classes subdivided into 500), achieved reasonable coverage in automatic annotation, but so far no manually validated corpus has been published. The SemDaX corpus (Pedersen et al. 2016) does provide human-validated semantic annotation of a Danish corpus, but only for word senses, and (with the exception of 20 highly ambiguous nouns) only for WordNet super-senses (Fellbaum 1998), not for semantic roles and predicate frames. In this paper, we present a corpus of similar size and composition, but with

---

[1] Random or running text samples not only guarantees a real-life statistical representation of lexical items, but also forces annotators to confront - and resolve - unforeseen constructions and contexts.

Proceedings of the 21st Nordic Conference of Computational Linguistics, pages 202–210,
Gothenburg, Sweden, 23-24 May 2017. ©2017 Linköping University Electronic Press

the full structural Verbnet frame annotation proposed by (Bick 2011), and augmented with corresponding frames for nominal predications. For verbs, this implies full sense disambiguation. For nouns, senses were added in the form of semantic-prototype tags, but only fully disambiguated in the case of named entities.

2   The corpus

For our corpus, we use the term *PropBank* in a generic sense, agreeing with Merlo & Van der Plas (2009) that VerbNet-style generalizations are important in the face of new semantic role instances, and that they complement the structural constraints that can be learned from a PropBank. Our data source is Korpus2010 (Asmussen 2015), a sentence-randomized corpus of Danish around the year 2010, compiled and distributed by the Danish Society of Language and Literature (Det Danske Sprog- og Litteraturselskab). The 44.1 million token corpus has a fairly broad coverage and includes both printed, electronically published and non-standard sources:

Danish PropBank section	token percentage
Magazines (text files)	44.99%
Magazines (scanned)	12.97%
National newspapers	14.58%
Parliamentary speeches	10.51%
Chat fora, young adults	2.48%
Web sources (various)	5.9%
blogs	8.51%

Table 1: Corpus composition

Our subcorpus of ca. 87,000 tokens (4,924 sentences/utterances) was built using random id-based sentence extraction. Compared to Korpus2010 as a whole, the subcorpus has a higher percentage of blog and chat data, less news and more magazines. A few excerpts were discarded, mostly because the original automatic sentence separation was erroneously triggered by abbreviation dots resulting in incomplete fragments.

3   Annotation levels

While our research focus is on the semantic annotation of verb-argument structures, and - widening this scope - the semantic annotation of predications and roles in general, this higher-level annotation is built upon a skeleton of syntactic tags and dependency links, and the corpus can therefore also be used as an "ordinary" treebank. As such, it complements the bigger, but older Danish *Arboretum* treebank, that contains data from Korpus90 and Korpus2000[2]. Both resources are available in the ELRA catalogue (http://catalog.elra.info/).

3.1   Tokenization and morpho-syntax

We use functional units as tokens, rather than strictly space-separated strings, in order to facilitate assignment of higher-level syntactic and semantic tags. Thus, complex prepositions and conjunctions *(i=stedet=for [instead of], på=trods=af [despite], i=og=med [though], for=så=vidt [in so far as])* are used for syntactic perspicuity, and named entities are fused for semantic reasons. Non-adjacent parts of lexemes (verb particles) are marked, but only linked at the syntactic level.

Morphosyntactic annotation adopts an analytical scheme, with separate tags for POS, syntactic function and each morphological feature, rather than complex all-in-one tags. Due to the underlying automatic pre-annotation, native annotation uses Constraint Grammar (CG) abbreviations, but the corpus is available in a variety of treebank output formats, such as the cross-language analytical VISL standard (visl.sdu.dk), MALT xml, TIGER xml and Universal Dependencies in CoNLL format.

3.2   Valency and dependency relations

The corpus strives to make a connection between a verb's valency potential, dependency relations and semantic arguments. Thus, the latter can be viewed as fillers for valency slots projected by dependency links. We therefore mark both the instantiated valency (e.g. <v:vt> for monotransitive), syntactic dependency links and (separate) semantic argument links. This way, we support a triple representation of tree structure:

(a) a shallow, verb-marked lexical valency tag, chosen according to which arguments are actually present in a given sentence

(b) a traditional *syntactic* dependency tree, with prepositions and auxiliaries as heads of PP's and verb chains, respectively, and conjuncts chained onto each other

(c) a semantic (tectogrammatical) tree with only content words as nodes (i.e. main verbs and

---

[2]Like *Arboretum*, the new corpus will be distributed through the ELRA catalogue of Language Resources.

PP-nominals rather than auxiliaries and prepositions), and with conjuncts linked to the same head in parallel

This multi-layered approach is similar to the semantic role linking scheme used in the Prague Dependency Treebank (Böhmová et al. 2003), and different from the Universal Dependencies scheme (McDonald et al. 2003), which opts for a 1-layer approach by *replacing* syntactic links with semantic ones, while still maintaining "surface-near" non-semantic labels.

3.3 Semantic prototype annotation

Our annotation scheme maps a semantic ontology onto nouns, with around 200 so-called semantic prototype categories[3], organized in a shallow hierarchy. Thus, major categories like <H> (human), <V> (vehicle), <tool> etc. are further subdivided, e.g. <Hprof> (profession), <Vair> (planes), <tool-cut> etc. During treebank generation, these tags are used both for contextual disambiguation and as slot fillers for the identification of verb frames. Even in the face of polysemy, these tags are usually sufficient to pinpoint a given verb sense and frame, because the choice is further constrained by the syntactic function of a verb's arguments, as well as POS and morphological form.

Once frames and roles are established, these can be in turn used, to automatically discard non-appropriate noun senses, ideally leaving only one or at least non-conflicting sense tags[4]. In the current version of the Propbank, manual validation and disambiguation of sense tags has not yet been concluded. Once finished, another task will be to assign, where available, DanNet senses (Pedersen et al. 2008) in a semiautomatic way by mapping one ontology onto another.

3.4 NER annotation

Named entity recognition and classification (NER) of proper nouns and numerical expressions is needed to supplement semantic noun classification, and important for verb frame identification. In principle, the same ontology could be used, but the underlying parser already implements a separate scheme with around 20

NER categories, which can be seen as an extension of - and in some cases synonyms of - the semantic noun tags. Following the MUC conference standard, there are six main categories: person <hum>, organization <org>, place <top>, event <occ>, work of art <tit> and brand <brand>. Because some names have a cross-category potential, <civ> (civitas) was added for places that can act (e.g. build or go to war), <inst> for site-bound organizations or activities and <media> for names that can function as both titles and organizations (e.g. newspapers and certain websites). In these cases, the co-tagged semantic role label will functionally complete the NER categorization of a given name, for instance §AG (agent) vs. §LOC (location) for towns or countries. Tokenization is an important issue in NER, because many names (almost half in our corpus) are multi-word units (MWU) and need to be recognized before they can be classified. To do so, the input parser relies on both pattern matching/reprocessing, a gazetteer lexicon and contextual rules applied after the POS-tagging stage. In the published corpus, both NER tokenization and classification was manually revised. 3.6% of all non-punctuation words in the corpus are names, with a MWU proportion of 42%, and an average MWU length of 2.4 parts.

3.5 Syntactic function and dependency

Dependency links are the necessary backbone of a predicate-argument frame, and syntactic function tags (subject, different object types, subject and object complements, valency bound adverbials etc.) are useful as argument slot-filler conditions in the automatic assignment of frames. Annotation errors at the syntactic level will therefore often lead to frame and verb sense-errors. Because of this interdependency, inspection/revision of either annotation level helps identifying errors at the other one, too, effectively creating a traditional treebank and a propbank at the same time.

Structurally, however, syntactic trees and Propbank trees are not identical, because the latter propagate ordinary dependency links to meaning-carrying words. Thus, each argument in our corpus carries at least two head-id links, one for the immediate syntactic head (e.g. preposition, first conjunct, auxiliary), and one for the semantic relation (to a verbal or nominal predicator). Furthermore, while traditional dependency links only allow one head, semantic

---

[3] The category set adopted here is described at: http://visl.sdu.dk/semantic_prototypes_overview.pdf

[4] A non-conflict is a combination of a subset tag with its superset tag, or underspecified <sem-r> (readable) and <sem-l> (listenable) for "værk" (work of art).

relations may ask for multiple heads due to "transparent" arguments (e.g. relative pronouns) , unexpressed arguments (subjects of infinitive verbs) or coordination ellipsis. Thus, in Fig. 1, *Majbrit*, dependency-wise the subject of *sige* ("speak"), is not only role-linked to the latter as §SP (speaker), but also - as §EXP (experiencer) - to the predicate in a depending relative clause, *kan lide* ("likes"), and finally - as §AG (agent) - to an infinitive clause, *bo ...* ("live ..."), three levels further down in the dependency tree. In this case, ordinary treebank dependencies suffer from an argument overlap, impeding tasks like information extraction. Propbank annotation, on the other hand, clearly marks three different predications:

Majbrit	*siger* (says)	...	
§SP	<fn:say>	§SOA / §MES	
Majbrit	*kan lide* (likes)	*at bo ...* (to live)	
§EXP	<fn:like>	§TH	
Majbrit	*at bo* (to live)	*sammen med fire andre* (with four others) §AG-COM	
§AG	<fn:lodge>		

Table 2: Overlapping propositions

Word	Lex	Secondary, **Frame**	POS, morphology	Synt. funct.	Sem. role	Dep.
...						
siger	sige	<v:vq><fn:say>	V PR AKT	@FS-STA		#14->0
Majbrit	Majbrit	<fem>	PROP NOM	@<SUBJ	§SP:14 §EXP:20 §AG:24	#15-14
,	,		PU	@PU		#16->0
som	som	<clb> <rel> <H>	INDP nG nN	@SUBJ>		#17->19
godt	godt		ADV	@ADVL>		#18->20
kan	kunne	<auxmod> <aux>	V PR AKT	@FS-N<		#19->15
lide	lide	<v:vt><fn:like>	V INF AKT	@ICL-AUX<	§ATR:15	#20->19
hyggen	hygge		N UTR S IDF NOM	@<ACC	§TH:20	#21->20
ved	ved		PRP	@N<		#22->21
at	at		INFM	@INFM		#23->24
bo	bo	<v:vp><fn:lodge>	V INF AKT	@ICL-P<	§CIRC:21	#24->22
sammen =med	sammen =med		PRP	@<PIV		#25->24
fire	fire	<card> <value>	NUM P	@>N		#26->27
andre	anden	<diff>	DET nG P NOM	@P<	§AG-COM	#27->25

Fig.1: Multiple semantic heads
(*... **says** <u>Majbrit</u>, who **likes** the coziness in **living** together with four others*)

3.6 Verb frame annotation

Our annotation of proposition-argument

structures is based on the category set of the Danish FrameNet (Bick 2011), which uses ca. 500 classes based on the original VerbNet senses, albeit with a modified naming system[5] and additional subclassification. Thus, though syntactic alternations such as diathesis or word order are not considered frame-distinctors, the Danish FrameNet differs from both WordNet and VerbNet by introducing polarity antonyms like *increase - decrease, like - dislike*, and a self/other distinction (*move_self, move_other*). The scheme also avoids large underspecified classes, subdividing e.g. *change_of_state* into new classes like *heat - cool, activate - deactivate* and *open - close*.

A first-pass frame annotation was performed by running a frame-mapper program exploiting existing morphosyntactic and semantic class tags as well as argument-verb dependencies assigned by the DanGram parser. Action and event nouns with argument slots and a de-verbal morphology (in particular Danish *-else/-ing* verbs) were annotated with the corresponding verb frames. All verbs and deverbal nouns were then manually inspected together with their arguments, which led to corrections in 15-20% of all frames. About a quarter of these were due to syntactic annotation errors or, sometimes, faulty POS-tagging[6]. Given the high lexeme coverage of the Danish FrameNet, very few verbs were left completely frameless, so most of the errors were mistaggings due to frame patterns not foreseen in the Danish FrameNet lexicon, often involving phrasal constructions with incorporated adverbs

---

[5] We wanted the class names to on the one hand be real verbs, on the other to reflect hypernym meanings wherever possible. Therefore, we avoided both example-based names (common in VerbNet) and - mostly - abstrac concept names (common in FrameNet) that are not verbs themselves.

[6] The parser's error rate for POS is about 1%, and 5% for syntactic function.

and prepositions (e.g. *slå ned på* [hit down at] - "stop"-frame), or idiomatic expressions with non-literal nominal arguments (e.g. *bære frugt* [carry fruit] - "succeed"-frame). In these cases, the frame tagger defaults to the first frame listed for a given valency, or to a basic transitive or intransitive frame, if there is no valency match in the lexicon either.

In order to speed up manual revision work, missing frames were added to the FrameNet lexicon, and missing valencies to the parser lexicon, and automatic annotation was then repeated for the remaining, not-yet-revised part of the Propbank in steps of about 20%.

3.7 Semantic role annotation

Our Propbank assigns semantic roles to both predicate arguments and free (adverbial) satellites not valency-bound by their head. The former are automatically mapped onto syntactic predicate-argument "skeletons", together with the chosen verb sense, once a given frame is chosen. For a correct syntactic tree, errors in such roles will always manifest as frame/sense errors, too. Satellite roles, on the other hand, depend less on the verb, and have to be tagged from local clues alone, e.g. the preposition and semantic noun class of an adverbial PP. The annotation scheme distinguishes between 38 argument-capable semantic roles and an additional 14 roles that can only occur as satellites.

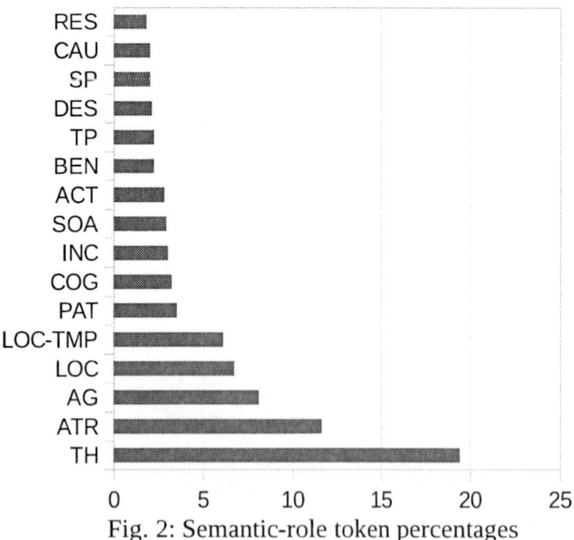

Fig. 2: Semantic-role token percentages

As can be seen from Fig. 2, the 5 main roles account for over 60% of all cases. Compared to the unrevised frame annotation of newspaper data reported in (Bick 2011), place and time locations (§LOC, §LOC-TMP) figure more prominently and there are more incorporates (§INC). The most likely explanation for this is not so much the difference in source genres, but rather the more complete coverage of satellite (free) adverbials and the exhaustive treatment of all verb particles and incorporated nouns in the corpus.

4   Annotation Procedure

The current annotation is a 1-annotator linguistic revision of an automatic annotation, with parallel improvements in the underlying DanGram parser[7] and Danish FrameNet lexicon[8] followed by intermittent re-annotation of not-yet-revised portions, in 20%-steps. The lack of multi-annotator cross-checks, while not standard procedure, has the advantage of reduced cost and more data per time unit. As a side effect, there is a certain consistency advantage compared to at least an *incomplete* multi-annotator setup where not *all* annotators revised *all* data, or where annotators could not agree.

The revision was performed twice - first with a focus on main verbs and valency-bound arguments, then with a focus on non-verbal predications and satellite roles. The first pass also resolved V/N part-of-speech errors, and consequently major tree structure errors, together with argument function errors. Unlike arguments and verbs, which warrant 100% semantic tagging, there is less linguistic consensus as to which tokens should be marked semantically, with satellite roles. Apart from lexically pre-marked material (in particular space, direction and time adverbs), nouns and names are the most likely semantic role carriers. For the latter, a complete, separate inspection pass was carried out, for the former, a mini Constraint Grammar was run on the already-annotated corpus to mark missing roles. The simplified marker rule below looks for nouns in the nominative without a §-marked role. Excluded are top-level nodes (ADVL [unattached adverbial] and NPHR [function-less NP]), plus transparent nouns (*slags/art* [kind of], quantifiers etc.). In order to ensure that only the main noun in an NP is addressed (e.g. *amerikaneren professor Pentland*), there are NEGATE checks for

---

[7] visl.sdu.dk/visl/da/parsing/automatic/parse.php

[8] http://framenet.dk

immediate parent or child nodes without interfering frame carriers (such as verbs).

```
MAP (§NOROLE) TARGET N + NOM - (/§.*/r)
   (NEGATE *p (/§.*/r) - (<fn:.*>r)
        BARRIER (<fn:.*>r))
   (NEGATE *c (/§.*/r @N<)
        BARRIER (<fn:.*>r))
   (NOT 0 @ADVL/NPHR OR <transparent>) ;
```

5 Evaluation and statistics

We evaluate our propbank statistically, in order to assess corpus parameters such as lexical spread, representativeness, frame and role type frequencies. In addition, the relative distribution of these semantic categories across text types, as well as their interdependence with other, lower-level linguistic categories is of interest, given that this is the first time a comprehensively annotated and revised Danish corpus is available for this level of annotation.

At the time of writing, the corpus contained 10,708 instances of main verbs, covering 1275 different lexemes, 100% of which were annotated with frames. By comparison, only 9.6% of the ca. 15,000 nouns were frame carriers, albeit with a much higher type/token ration (741 lexemes/1722 tokens) than for verbs. Frames for other word classes were only assigned to about 190 adjectives (65 lexeme types), a few direction adverbs and a single determiner:

- bange for [afraid of] + §CAU

- følsom over for [sensitive to] + §STI

- syd for [south of] + §LOC

- anden end [other than] + §COMP

In addition, 81 attributively used, prenominal participles (52 types), received "naked" verb frame senses, without arguments[9], mostly

---

[9] This is a gray zone - a number of Danish deverbal adjectives could arguably also be read as -ende/-et participles [-ing/ed], but for now we simply followed the choices made in the parser lexicon, assigning frames to attributive participles only where they were productively derived from verbs. Another decision was not to tag the heads of such attributive participles with argument roles referring back to their own modifiers (e.g. voksende [growing] + §PAT. Postnominal participles, on the other hand, are all argument/satellite-carriers in Danish, and hence assigned roles.

corresponding to the default sense of the underlying verb.

The corpus contains examples of 454 different frames, covering 91.9% of all frame types in the Danish Framenet, and 598 (or 44.7%) of the possible frame type combinations (e.g. "udgive sig for" - <fn: imitate && role_as>). Since frames are used to disambiguate the valency potential of a given verb and to define its senses, it is also possible to quantify verb polysemy in the corpus. All in all, we found different 2153 verb senses[10], amounting to an average of 1.69 senses per verb lexeme, albeit with huge differences between lemmas (table 3).

verb	senses	3 most frequent frame senses (number of instances)
gå	54	run 30, leave 14, reach&&participate 13
være	47	be_copula 1522, exist 260, be_place 217
komme	41	reach 69, appear 24, occur 17
tage	36	take 38, do 19, run 10
holde	27	run_obj 8, persist 8, defend_cog, endure, hold, keep, like, sustain 6
have	26	have 346, own 18, cope 13
stå	21	be_place 27, be_attribute 11, spatial_conf 8
sætte	21	put 12, start 6, decrease, change_body_position 4
lægge	20	put_spatial 14, suggest 5, create_semantic 3
slå	18	beat 6, confirm, deactivate, integrate, succeed 2
se	18	see 85, notice 22, be_attribute 16
gøre	18	do 78, turn_into 43, cause 11
få	18	get 165, cause 37, obtain 12

Table 3: Most polysemous verbs

In almost all cases, sense differences come with differences in argument structure or phrasal particles etc., but the inverse is not true - there may well be more than one syntactic realization of a given verb sense. Thus, there are 24.6% more valency-sense combinations for the verbs

---

[10] By comparison, the Danish FrameNet contains 11174 verb senses for 7033 lexemes, i.e. 1.59 senses per verb. Hence, our corpus data is slightly more ambiguous, even on a type basis, than the lexicon, probably because the corpus only covers the 18.1% most frequent verbs, and 19.7% of all senses in the FrameNet lexicon, lacking many rare, but unambiguous verbs.

in the corpus than just verb senses[11]. Interestingly, senses have a much more even frequency distribution for some verbs (e.g. "holde" [hold] and "slå" [hit]) than for others ("være" [be], "have" [have]).

Semantic role statistics are complicated due to the fact that one token may participate in several different frames across the sentence, and therefore carry multiple role tags. All in all, there were 20,437 semantic role tags for verb arguments, and 5252 role tags for verb satellites, corresponding to a 79.6% / 20.4% distribution. Arguments were more likely to share a token than satellites (with an average of 1.1 roles per token for the former, and 1.026 for the latter). For the rarer non-verbal frame-heads (mostly nouns), the argument-satellite balance was almost the opposite (29.7% / 70.3%), with 1303 argument roles and 3077 satellite roles, and a few multi-tag tokens (1.007 tag/token for arguments and 1.008 for satellites).

For classifying semantic roles as arguments or satellites, and to mark them for verbal or non-verbal head type, we used the same method described in ch. 4 for consistency checking, namely CG mark-up rules, exploiting syntactic function tags and frame relation links as context.

6 Linguistic text profiling

We also examined the distribution of both frames and semantic roles across different text types, hoping to identify text type- (or even genre-) specific traits in a semantically generalized fashion, different from - and arguably more linguistic and generalized than - standard techniques such as bag of words.

Role rank	News	Magazines	Blog	Forum	Parliament	Recipes
	4909	14898	1026	740	1412	317
1	**ORI**	**MES**	**DES**	**STI**	**FIN**	**CIRC**
2	**BEN**	**CAU**	**LOC-TMP**	**COG**	**TH-NIL**	**PAT**
3	**SP**	TH-NIL	COG	**EXP**	ACT	**EXT-TMP**
4	**ID**	TP	**INC**	ATR	**RES**	BEN
5	**EV**	ID	AG	TH	TP	DES
6	**COMP**	**SOA**	EXP	**COMP**	CAU	**LOC**
7	EXP	LOC	ATR	ID	SOA	**TH**
8	AG	RES		**REC**	ORI	ATR
9	SOA	SP			INC	ACT
10	LOC	REC			BEN	

Table 4: Relative role ranks across text types

The semantic role ranks in table 4 are computed by normalizing in-text relative frequencies according to all-corpus relative frequencies. Only roles more frequent than the corpus average are listed, and each role is bold-faced where it ranks highest in the table overall. By using normalized frequencies rather than absolute ranking, text differences are emphasized, and patterns become more salient.

Thus, the reporting style of news text rhymes with top ranks for §SP (speaker), §ID (typical of explaining name appositions) and §EV (events). The high rank for §ORI (origin) is symptomatic of quote sourcing ("according to .." etc.). Furthermore, the news texts evaluate facts by comparing them (§COMP) and by discussing who was affected, profited or suffered (§BEN, benefactive). Magazines, though a similar text type in other linguistic aspects, address more specific audiences and topics (§TP), and are - by comparison - more interested in bringing a message across (§MES) and making claims (§SOA, state-of-affairs).

Blogs and discussion fora are the most personal text types in our corpus, and are characterized by opinions and cognitiveness (§COG), relaying experiences (§EXP, §STI) and describing or judging things (§ATR, attribute). In addition, blogs, often written as a personal timeline or travel report, rank high for time markers (§LOC-TMP) and destinations (§DES). Interestingly, blog writers have high scores for non-literal language, with a lot of verb incorporations (§INC). While in theory also 1-person text types, parliamentary speeches are very different from blogs and fora, and more argumentative than the rest of the corpus, scoring high on intention/planning (§FIN), results (§RES) and discussed actions (§ACT). Also, these speeches rank higher than even news texts for impersonal constructions linked to formal subjects (§TH-NIL, "det er X der", "der + s-passive").

Finally, a small but "spicy" section of the corpus is dedicated to recipes, which are known to stand

[11] This count includes difference between transitive and ditransitive use and between NP and clausal objects, but not the difference between active and passive

out even in morphological ways (imperatives, uninflected nouns, unit numbers). In terms of semantic roles, recipe sentences are all about *changing* (e.g. frying) things (food, §PAT patient) in certain *circumstances* (§CIRC) for a certain *amount of time* (§EXT-TMP).

For frames, a text-wise break-down is informative, too, and provides a useful means of abstraction compared to simple lemma frequencies. Thus, frames help lump together both morphological and POS variation (*unhire* = fyring, massefyring, fyre) and lexical variation (*steal* = snuppe, nappe, stjæle). For the weighted ordering in table 5, relative in-text frequencies were used, with a weighting exponent of 1.5 for the numerator. Compound frames were split into atomic frames.

Text type	Weighted top-ranking frames (absolute numbers in parentheses)
News	be_copula (221); **unhire** (7); behave (8); **dispute** (5); **trade** (5); have (54); reach (30); succeed (13); **run_obj** (19); **tell** (22); lower (4)
Maga-zines	be_copula (712); **say** (137); have (163); **exist** (130); **assume** (69); **become** (97); affect (43); **get** (88); cause (68); relate (56); be_part (41)
Blog	**long** (5); serve_to (2); steal (3); be_copula (138); belong_to (3); **send** (10); **know** (25)
Forum	**like** (7); appear (9); be_copula (62); **hear** (3); add (3); **know** (10); **inquire** (3)
Parlia-ment	**compensate** (7), **exist** (61); **ensure** (17); **exempt** (2); adjust (16); **improve** (15); **unestablish** (4); be_copula (160); agree (15); suggest (16); exaggerate (3)
Recipes	**prepare_food** (23); supply (10); **combine** (7); **cover_ize** (4); add (5); pour (2); **put_spatial** (4); put_deposit (3)

Table 5: Frame ranking across text types

Frame analysis more or less supports the picture suggested by semantic role distribution, but is somewhat more concrete, and provides more insight into topics. Thus, news text is about firing people (unhire), disputes, trade and how to run things (run_obj). Parliamentary debates are about reform (ensure, improve, unestablish) and discussion (agree, suggest). The high rank for the *exist*-frame is a form-trait, and due to impersonal constructions *(der er)*. People in blogs and fora

are a bit more emotional (*long, like*), and information is essential (*know*, hear, *inquire*). The most concrete text type is recipes (*prepare_food*), where frames are about physically manipulating things (*combine, add, put, pour, cover_ize*).

7   Conclusions and outlook

We have presented a first proposition bank for Danish, with extensive annotation of both argument and satellite roles, for both verbal and nominal VerbNet frames. Offering both syntactic and semantic tree structures, and three levels of node annotation (syntactic function, semantic ontology and semantic role), the corpus aims to serve multiple ML and linguistic purposes. By way of example we have discussed frame- and role-based text profiling.

In terms of additional annotation, a useful next step would be to improve the semantic annotation of pronouns by adding anaphorical relations. The current, sentence-randomized corpus, however, will allow this only for in-sentence relations. The same is true for another type of relational annotation, discourse analysis, and a future version of the corpus should therefore include a running text section from a source, where this is not a copyright problem.

Also, using randomized sentences from a multi-source corpus, while providing a good statistical sample of a language, is not the best way to beat Zipf's law. Therefore, in order to extend per-type coverage for verb senses in the Danish FrameNet, future work should include a second propbank section, where sentences are extracted from an automatically pre-tagged Korpus2010 not randomly, but based on which verb senses they contain.

References

Asmussen, Jørg. 2015. Corpus Resources & Documentation. Det Danske Sprog- og Litteraturselskab, http://korpus.dsl.dk

Baker, Collin F.; J. Charles Fillmore; John B. Lowe. 1998. The Berkeley FrameNet project. In Proceedings of the COLING-ACL, Montreal, Canada

Bick, Eckhard. 2011. A FrameNet for Danish. In: Proceedings of NODALIDA 2011, May 11-13,

Riga, Latvia. NEALT Proceedings Series, Vol. 11, pp. 34-41. Tartu: Tartu University Library.

Böhmová, Alena ; Jan Hajič; Eva Hajji; Barbora Hladká. 2003. The Prague Dependency Treebank: A Three-Level Annotation Scenario. In: Anne Abeillé (ed.): Text, Speech and Language Technology Series. Vol. 20. pp 103-127. Springer

Ryan McDonald, Joakim Nivre, Yvonne Quirmbach-Brundage, Yoav Goldberg, Dipanjan Das, Kuzman Ganchev, Keith Hall, Slav Petrov, Hao Zhang, Oscar Täckström, Claudia Bedini, Núria Bertomeu Castelló, and Jungmee Lee. 2013. Universal dependency annotation for multilingual parsing. In Proceedings of ACL 2013

Fellbaum, Christiane (ed.). 1998. WordNet: An Electronic Lexical Database. Language, Speech and Communications. MIT Press: Cambridge, Massachusetts.

Johnson, Christopher R. & Charles J. Fillmore. 2000. The FrameNet tagset for frame-semantic and syntactic coding of predicate-argument structure. In: Proceedings of the 1st Meeting of the North American Chapter of the Association for Computational Linguistics (ANLP-NAACL 2000), April 29-May 4, 2000, Seattle WA, pp. 56-62.

Kipper, Karin & Anna Korhonen, Neville Ryant, and Martha Palmer. 2006. Extensive Classifications of English verbs. *Proceedings of the 12th EURALEX International Congress.* Turin, Italy. September, 2006.

Merlo, P. & Van Der Plas, L. (2009). Abstraction and generalisation in semantic role labels: Propbank, Verbnet or both? In: Proceedings of the Joint Conference of the 47th Annual Meeting of the ACL and the 4th International Joint Conference on Natural Language Processing of the AFNLP: Volume 1-Volume 1, pp 288–296. ACL

Monachesi, P.; G. Stevens; J. Trapman. 2007. Adding semantic role annotation to a corpus of written Dutch. In: Proceedings of the Linguistic Annotation Workshop. pp 77–84. ACL

Mújdricza-Maydt; Éva & Silvana Hartmann; Iryna Gurevych; Anette Frank. 2016. Combining Semantic Annotation of Word Sense & Semantic Roles: A Novel Annotation Scheme for VerbNet Roles on German Language Data. In: Calzolari et al. (eds). Proceedings of LREC 2016.

Palmer, Martha; Dan Gildea; Paul Kingsbury. 2005. The Proposition Bank: An Annotated Corpus of Semantic Roles. *Computational Linguistics, 31:1.,* pp. 71-105, March, 2005.

Pedersen, B.S.; S. Nimb; L. Trap-Jensen. 2008. DanNet: udvikling og anvendelse af det danske wordnet. In: Nordiske Studier i leksikografi Vol. 9, Skrifter published by Nordisk Forening for Leksikografi, pp. 353-370

Pedersen, Bolette Sandford; Braasch, Anna; Johannsen, Anders Trærup; Martinez Alonso, Hector; Nimb, Sanni; Olsen, Sussi; Søgaard, Anders; Sørensen, Nicolai. 2016. The SemDaX Corpus - sense annotations with scalable sense inventories. In: Proceedings of the 10th LREC (Slovenia, 2016).

Ruppenhofer, Josef; Michael Ellsworth; Miriam R. L. Petruck; Christopher R. Johnson; Jan Scheffczyk. 2010. FrameNet II: Extended Theory and Practice. http://framenet.icsi.berkeley.edu/ index.php? option=com_wrapper&Itemid=126

Cross-lingual Learning of Semantic Textual Similarity with Multilingual Word Representations

Johannes Bjerva
Center for Language and Cognition Groningen
University of Groningen
The Netherlands
j.bjerva@rug.nl

Robert Östling
Department of Linguistics
Stockholm University
Sweden
robert@ling.su.se

Abstract

Assessing the semantic similarity between sentences in different languages is challenging. We approach this problem by leveraging multilingual distributional word representations, where similar words in different languages are close to each other. The availability of parallel data allows us to train such representations on a large amount of languages. This allows us to leverage semantic similarity data for languages for which no such data exists. We train and evaluate on five language pairs, including English, Spanish, and Arabic. We are able to train well-performing systems for several language pairs, without any labelled data for that language pair.

1 Introduction

Semantic Textual Similarity (STS) is the task of assessing the degree to which two sentences are semantically similar. Within the SemEval STS shared tasks, this is measured on a scale ranging from 0 (no semantic similarity) to 5 (complete semantic similarity) (Agirre et al., 2016). Monolingual STS is an important task, for instance for evaluation of machine translation (MT) systems, where estimating the semantic similarity between a system's translation and the gold translation can aid both system evaluation and development. The task is already a challenging one in a monolingual setting, e.g., when estimating the similarity between two English sentences. In this paper, we tackle the more difficult case of cross-lingual STS, e.g., estimating the similarity between an English and an Arabic sentence.

Previous approaches to this problem have focussed on two main approaches. On the one hand, MT approaches have been attempted (e.g. Lo et al. (2016)), which allow for monolingual similarity assessment, but suffer from the fact that involving a fully-fledged MT system severely increases system complexity. Applying bilingual word representations, on the other hand, bypasses this issue without inducing such complexity (e.g. Aldarmaki and Diab (2016)). However, bilingual approaches do not allow for taking advantage of the increasing amount of STS data available for more than one language pair.

Currently, there are several methods available for obtaining high quality multilingual word representations. It is therefore interesting to investigate whether language can be ignored entirely in an STS system after mapping words to their respective representations. We investigate the utility of multilingual word representations in a cross-lingual STS setting. We approach this by combining multilingual word representations with a deep neural network, in which all parameters are shared, regardless of language combinations.

The contributions of this paper can be summed as follows: i) we show that multilingual input representations can be used to train an STS system without access to training data for a given language; ii) we show that access to data from other languages improves system performance for a given language.

2 Semantic Textual Similarity

Given two sentences, s_1 and s_2, the task in STS is to assess how semantically similar these are to each other. This is commonly measured using a scale ranging from 0–5, with 0 indicating no semantic overlap, and 5 indicating nearly identical content. In the SemEval STS shared tasks, the following descriptions are used:

0. The two sentences are completely dissimilar.

1. The two sentences are not equivalent, but are on the same topic.

211

Proceedings of the 21st Nordic Conference of Computational Linguistics, pages 211–215,
Gothenburg, Sweden, 23-24 May 2017. ©2017 Linköping University Electronic Press

2. The two sentences are not equivalent, but share some details.

3. The two sentences are roughly equivalent, but some important information differs/missing.

4. The two sentences are mostly equivalent, but some unimportant details differ.

5. The two sentences are completely equivalent, as they mean the same thing.

This manner of assessing semantic content of two sentences notably does not take important semantic features such as negation into account, and can therefore be seen as complimentary to textual entailment. Furthermore, the task is highly related to paraphrasing, as replacing an n-gram with a paraphrase thereof ought to alter the semantic similarity of two sentences to a very low degree. Successful monolingual approaches in the past have taken advantage of both of these facts (see, e.g., Beltagy et al. (2016)). Approaches similar to these can be applied in cross-lingual STS, if the sentence pair is translated to a language for which such resources exist. However, involving a fully-fledged MT system increases pipeline complexity, which increases the risk of errors in cases of, e.g., mistranslations. Using bilingual word representations, in order to create truly cross-lingual systems, was explored by several systems in SemEval 2016 (Agirre et al., 2016). However, such systems are one step short of truly taking advantage of the large amounts of multilingual parallel data, and STS data, available. This work contributes to previous work on STS by further exploring this aspect, by leveraging multilingual word representations.

3 Multilingual Word Representations

3.1 Multilingual Skip-gram

The skip-gram model has become one of the most popular manners of learning word representations in NLP (Mikolov et al., 2013). This is in part owed to its speed and simplicity, as well as the performance gains observed when incorporating the resulting word embeddings into almost any NLP system. The model takes a word w as its input, and predicts the surrounding context c. Formally, the probability distribution of c given w is defined as

$$p(c|w;\theta) = \frac{\exp(\vec{c}^T \vec{w})}{\Sigma_{c \in V} \exp(\vec{c}^T \vec{w})}, \qquad (1)$$

where V is the vocabulary, and θ the parameters of word emeddings ($\vec{w}$) and context embeddings ($\vec{c}$).

The parameters of this model can then be learned by maximising the log-likelihood over (w,c) pairs in the dataset D,

$$J(\theta) = \sum_{(w,c) \in D} \log p(c|w;\theta). \qquad (2)$$

Guo et al. (2016) provide a multilingual extension for the skip-gram model, by requiring the model to not only learn to predict English contexts, but also multilingual ones. This can be seen as a simple adaptation of Firth (1957, p.11), i.e., you shall judge a word by the *multilingual* company it keeps. Hence, the vectors for, e.g., *dog* and *perro* ought to be close to each other in such a model. This assumes access to multilingual parallel data, as word alignments are used in order to determine which words comprise the multilingual context of a word. Whereas Guo et al. (2016) only evaluate their approach on the relatively similar languages English, French and Spanish, we explore a more typological diverse case, as we apply this method to English, Spanish and Arabic. We use the same parameter settings as Guo et al. (2016).

3.2 Learning embeddings

We train multilingual embeddings on the Europarl and UN corpora. Word alignment is performed using the Efmaral word-alignment tool (Östling and Tiedemann, 2016). This allows us to extract a large amount of multilingual (w,c) pairs. We then learn multilingual embeddings by applying the *word2vecf* tool (Levy and Goldberg, 2014).

4 Method

4.1 System architecture

We use a relatively simple neural network architecture, consisting of an input layer with pre-trained word embeddings and a siamese network of fully connected layers with shared weights. In order to prevent any shift from occurring in the embeddings, we do not update these during training. The intuition here, is that we do not want the representation for, e.g., *dog* to be updated, which might push it further away from that of *perro*. We expect this to be especially important in cases where we train on a single language, and evaluate on another.

Given word representations for each word in our sentence, we take the simplistic approach of averaging the vectors across each sentence. The resulting sentence-level representation is then passed through a single fully connected layer, prior to the output layer. We apply dropout ($p = 0.5$) between each layer (Srivastava et al., 2014). All weights are initialised using the approach in Glorot and Bengio (2010). We use the Adam optimisation algorithm (Kingma and Ba, 2014), jointly monitoring the categorical cross entropy of a one-hot representation of the (rounded) sentence similarity score, as well as Pearson correlation using the actual scores. All systems are trained using a batch size of 40 sentence pairs, over a maximum of 50 epochs, using early stopping. Hyperparameters are kept constant in all conditions.

4.2 Data

We use all available data from all previous editions of the SemEval shared tasks on (cross-lingual) STS. An overview of the available data is shown in Table 1.

Table 1: Available data for (cross-lingual) STS from the SemEval shared task series.

Language pair	N sentences
English / English	3750
English / Spanish	1000
English / Arabic	2162
Spanish / Spanish	1620
Arabic / Arabic	1081

5 Experiments and Results

We aim to investigate whether using a multilingual input representation and shared weights allow us to ignore languages in STS. We first train and evaluate single-source trained systems (i.e. on a single language pair), and evaluate this both using the same language pair as target, and on all other target language pairs.[1] Secondly, we investigate the effect of bundling training data together, investigating which language pairings are helpful for each other. We measure performance between gold similarities and system output using the Pearson correlation measure, as this is standard in the SemEval STS shared tasks.

5.1 Single-source training

Results when training on a single source corpus are shown in Table 2. Training on the target language pair generally yields the highest

---

[1]This setting can be seen as a sort of model transfer.

results, except for one case. When evaluating on Arabic/Arabic sentence pairs, training on English/Arabic texts yields comparable, or slightly better, performance than when training on Arabic/Arabic.

Table 2: Single-source training results (Pearson correlations). Columns indicate training language pairs, and rows indicate testing language pairs. Bold numbers indicate best results per row.

Test \ Train	en/en	en/es	en/ar	es/es	ar/ar
en/en	**0.69**	0.07	-0.04	0.64	0.54
en/es	0.19	**0.27**	0.00	0.18	-0.04
en/ar	-0.44	0.37	**0.73**	-0.10	0.62
es/es	0.61	0.07	0.12	**0.65**	0.50
ar/ar	0.59	0.52	**0.73**	0.59	0.71

5.2 Multi-source training

We combine training corpora in order to investigate how this affects evaluation performance on the language pairs in question. In the first condition, we copy the single-source setup, except for that we also add in the data belonging to the source-pair at hand, e.g., training on both English/Arabic and Arabic/Arabic when evaluating on Arabic/Arabic (see Table 3).

Table 3: Training results with one source in addition to in-language data (Pearson correlations). Columns indicate added training language pairs, and rows indicate testing language pairs. Bold numbers indicate best results per row.

Test \ Train	en/en	en/es	en/ar	es/es	ar/ar
en/en	0.69	0.68	0.67	0.69	**0.71**
en/es	0.22	0.27	**0.30**	0.22	0.24
en/ar	0.72	0.72	**0.73**	0.71	0.72
es/es	0.63	0.60	0.63	0.65	**0.66**
ar/ar	0.71	0.72	**0.75**	0.70	0.71

We observe that the monolingual language pairings (en/en, es/es, ar/ar) appear to be beneficial for one another. We therefore run an ablation experiment, in which we train on two out of three of these language pairs, and evaluate on all three. Not including any Spanish training data yields comparable performance to including it (Table 4).

Table 4: Ablation results (Pearson correlations). Columns indicate ablated language pairs, and rows indicate testing language pairs. The *none* column indicates no ablation, i.e., training on all three monolingual pairs. Bold indicates results when not training on the language pair evaluated on.

Test \ Ablated	en/en	es/es	ar/ar	none
en/en	**0.60**	0.69	0.69	0.65
es/es	0.64	**0.64**	0.67	0.60
ar/ar	0.68	0.66	**0.58**	0.72

5.3 Comparison with Monolingual Representations

We compare multilingual embeddings with the performance obtained using the pre-trained monolingual Polyglot embeddings (Al-Rfou et al., 2013). Training and evaluating on the same language pair yields comparable results regardless of embeddings. However, when using monolingual embeddings, every multilingual language pair combination yields poor results.

6 Discussion

In all cases, training on the target language pair is beneficial. We also observe that using multilingual embeddings is crucial for multilingual approaches, as monolingual embeddings naturally only yield on-par results in monolingual settings. This is due to the fact that using the shared language-agnostic input representation allows us to take advantage of linguistic regularities across languages, which we obtain solely from observing distributions between languages in parallel text. Using monolingual word representations, however, there is no similarity between, e.g., *dog* and *perro* to rely on to guide learning.

For the single-source training, we in one case observe somewhat better performance using other training sets than the in-language one: training on English/Arabic outperforms training on Arabic/Arabic, when evaluating on Arabic/Arabic. We expected this to be due to differing data set sizes (English/Arabic is about twice as big). Controlling for this does, indeed, bring the performance of training on English/Arabic to the same level as training on Arabic/Arabic. However, combining these datasets increases performance further (Table 3).

In single-source training, we also observe that certain source languages do not offer any generalisation over certain target languages. Interestingly, certain combinations of training/testing language pairs yield very poor results. For instance, training on English/English yields very poor results when evaluating on English/Arabic, and vice versa. The same is observed for the combination Spanish/Spanish and English/Arabic. This may be explained by domain differences in training and evaluation data. A general trend appears to be that either monolingual training pairs and evaluation pairs, or cross-lingual pairs with overlap (e.g. English/Arabic and Arabic/Arabic) is beneficial.

The positive results on pairings without any language overlap are particularly promising. Training on English/English yields results not too far from training on the source language pairs, for Spanish/Spanish and Arabic/Arabic. Similar results are observed when training on Spanish/Spanish and evaluating on English/English and Arabic/Arabic, as well as when training on Arabic/Arabic and evaluating on English/English and Spanish/Spanish. This indicates that we can estimate STS relatively reliably, even without assuming any existing STS data for a given language.

7 Conclusions and Future Work

Multilingual word representations allow us to leverage more available data for multilingual learning of semantic textual similarity. We have shown that relatively high STS performance can be achieved for languages without assuming existing STS annotation, and relying solely on parallel texts. An interesting direction for future work is to investigate how multilingual character-level representations can be included, perhaps learning morpheme-level representations and mappings between these across languages. Leveraging approaches to learning multilingual word representations from smaller data sets would also be interesting. For instance, learning such representations from only the new testament, would allow for STS estimation for more than 1,000 of the languages in the world.

Acknowledgments

We would like to thank the Center for Information Technology of the University of Groningen for providing access to the Peregrine high performance computing cluster.

References

Eneko Agirre, Carmen Banea, Daniel Cer, Mona Diab, Aitor Gonzalez-Agirre, Rada Mihalcea, German Rigau, and Janyce Wiebe. 2016. Semeval-2016 task 1: Semantic textual similarity, monolingual and cross-lingual evaluation. In *Proceedings of SemEval*, pages 497–511.

Rami Al-Rfou, Bryan Perozzi, and Steven Skiena. 2013. Polyglot: Distributed word representations for multilingual nlp. *CoNLL-2013*.

Hanan Aldarmaki and Mona Diab. 2016. GWU NLP at SemEval-2016 Shared Task 1: Matrix factorization for crosslingual STS. In *Proceedings of SemEval 2016*, pages 663–667.

Islam Beltagy, Stephen Roller, Pengxiang Cheng, Katrin Erk, and Raymond J Mooney. 2016. Representing meaning with a combination of logical and distributional models. *Computational Linguistics*.

John R Firth. 1957. *A synopsis of linguistic theory, 1930-1955*. Blackwell.

Xavier Glorot and Yoshua Bengio. 2010. Understanding the difficulty of training deep feedforward neural networks. In *Aistats*, volume 9, pages 249–256.

Jiang Guo, Wanxiang Che, David Yarowsky, Haifeng Wang, and Ting Liu. 2016. A representation learning framework for multi-source transfer parsing. In *Proc. of AAAI*.

Diederik Kingma and Jimmy Ba. 2014. Adam: A method for stochastic optimization. *arXiv preprint arXiv:1412.6980*.

Omer Levy and Yoav Goldberg. 2014. Dependency-based word embeddings. In *ACL*, pages 302–308.

Chi-kiu Lo, Cyril Goutte, and Michel Simard. 2016. Cnrc at semeval-2016 task 1: Experiments in crosslingual semantic textual similarity. *Proceedings of SemEval*, pages 668–673.

Tomas Mikolov, Kai Chen, Greg Corrado, and Jeffrey Dean. 2013. Efficient estimation of word representations in vector space. *arXiv preprint arXiv:1301.3781*.

Robert Östling and Jörg Tiedemann. 2016. Efficient word alignment with markov chain monte carlo. *The Prague Bulletin of Mathematical Linguistics*, 106(1):125–146.

Nitish Srivastava, Geoffrey E Hinton, Alex Krizhevsky, Ilya Sutskever, and Ruslan Salakhutdinov. 2014. Dropout: a simple way to prevent neural networks from overfitting. *Journal of Machine Learning Research*, 15(1):1929–1958.

Will my auxiliary tagging task help?
Estimating Auxiliary Tasks Effectivity in Multi-Task Learning

Johannes Bjerva
University of Groningen
The Netherlands
j.bjerva@rug.nl

Abstract

Multitask learning often improves system performance for morphosyntactic and semantic tagging tasks. However, the question of *when* and *why* this is the case has yet to be answered satisfactorily. Although previous work has hypothesised that this is linked to the label distributions of the auxiliary task, we argue that this is not sufficient. We show that information-theoretic measures which consider the joint label distributions of the main and auxiliary tasks offer far more explanatory value. Our findings are empirically supported by experiments for morphosyntactic tasks on 39 languages, and are in line with findings in the literature for several semantic tasks.

1 Introduction

When attempting to solve a natural language processing (NLP) task, one can consider the fact that many such tasks are highly related to one another. A common way of taking advantage of this is to apply multitask learning (MTL, Caruana (1998)). MTL has been successfully applied to many linguistic sequence-prediction tasks, both syntactic and semantic in nature (Collobert and Weston, 2008; Cheng et al., 2015; Søgaard and Goldberg, 2016; Martínez Alonso and Plank, 2016; Bjerva et al., 2016; Ammar et al., 2016; Plank et al., 2016). It is, however, unclear *when* an auxiliary task is useful, although previous work has provided some insights (Caruana, 1998; Martínez Alonso and Plank, 2016).

Currently, considerable time and effort need to be employed in order to experimentally investigate the usefulness of any given main task / auxiliary task combination. In this paper we wish to alleviate this process by providing a means to investigating *when* an auxiliary task is helpful, thus also

shedding light on *why* this is the case. Concretely, we apply information-theoretic measures to a collection of data- and tag sets, investigate correlations between such measures and auxiliary task effectivity, and show that previous hypotheses do not sufficiently explain this interaction. We investigate this both experimentally on a collection of syntactically oriented tasks on 39 languages, and verify our findings by investigating results found in the literature on semantically oriented tasks.

2 Neural Multitask Learning

Recurrent Neural Networks (RNNs) are at the core of many current approaches to sequence prediction in NLP (Elman, 1990). A bidirectional RNN is an extension which incorporates both preceding and proceeding contexts in the learning process (Graves and Schmidhuber, 2005). Recent approaches frequently use either (bi-)LSTMs (Long Short-Term Memory) or (bi-)GRUs (Gated Recurrent Unit), which have the advantage that they can deal with longer input sequences (Hochreiter and Schmidhuber, 1997; Chung et al., 2014).

The intuition behind MTL is to improve performance by taking advantage of the fact that related tasks will benefit from similar internal representations (Caruana, 1998). MTL is commonly framed such that all hidden layers are shared, whereas there is one output layer per task. An RNN can thus be trained to solve one *main* task (e.g. parsing), while also learning some other *auxiliary* task (e.g. POS tagging).

3 Information-theoretic Measures

We wish to give an information-theoretic perspective on when an auxiliary task will be useful for a given main task. For this purpose, we introduce some common information-theoretic measures which will be used throughout this work.[1]

---

[1] See Cover and Thomas (2012) for an in-depth overview.

Proceedings of the 21st Nordic Conference of Computational Linguistics, pages 216–220,
Gothenburg, Sweden, 23-24 May 2017. ©2017 Linköping University Electronic Press

The **entropy** of a probability distribution is a measure of its unpredictability. That is to say, high entropy indicates a uniformly distributed tag set, while low entropy indicates a more skewed distribution. Formally, the entropy of a tag set can be defined as

$$H(X) = -\sum_{x \in X} p(x) \log p(x), \qquad (1)$$

where x is a given tag in tag set X.

It may be more informative to take the joint probabilities of the main and auxiliary tag sets in question into account, for instance using **conditional entropy**. Formally, the conditional entropy of a distribution Y given the distribution X is defined as

$$H(Y|X) = \sum_{x \in X} \sum_{y \in Y} p(x,y) \log \frac{p(x)}{p(x,y)}, \qquad (2)$$

where x and y are all variables in the given distributions, $p(x,y)$ is the joint probability of variable x cooccurring with variable y, and $p(x)$ is the probability of variable x occurring at all. That is to say, if the auxiliary tag of a word is known, this is highly informative when deciding what the main tag should be.

The **mutual information** (MI) of two tag sets is a measure of the amount of information that is obtained of one tag set, given the other tag set. MI can be defined as

$$I(X;Y) = \sum_{x \in X} \sum_{y \in Y} p(x,y) \log \frac{p(x,y)}{p(x)\,p(y)}, \qquad (3)$$

where x and y are all variables in the given distributions, $p(x,y)$ is the joint probability of variable x cooccurring with variable y, and $p(x)$ is the probability of variable x occurring at all. MI describes how much information is shared between X and Y, and can therefore be considered a measure of 'correlation' between tag sets.

3.1 Information Theory and MTL

Entropy has in the literature been hypothesised to be related to the usefulness of an auxiliary task (Martínez Alonso and Plank, 2016). We argue that this explanation is not entirely sufficient. Take, for instance, two tag sets X and X', applied to the same corpus and containing the same tags. Consider the case where the annotations differ in that the labels in every sentence using X' have been randomly reordered. The tag distributions in X and X' do not change as a result of this operation, hence their entropies will be the same. However, the tags in X' are now likely to have a very low

correspondence with any sort of natural language signal, hence X' is highly unlikely to be a useful auxiliary task for X. Measures taking joint probabilities into account will capture this lack of correlation between X and X'. In this work we show that measures such as conditional entropy and MI are much more informative for the effectivity of an auxiliary task than entropy.

4 Data

For our syntactic experiments, we use the Universal Dependencies (UD) treebanks on 39 out of the 40 languages found in version 1.3 (Nivre et al., 2016).[2] We experiment with POS tagging as a main task, and various dependency relation classification tasks as auxiliary tasks. We also investigate whether our hypothesis fits with recent results in the literature, by applying our information-theoretic measures to the semantically oriented tasks in Martínez Alonso and Plank (2016), as well as the semantic tagging task in Bjerva et al. (2016).

Although calculation of joint probabilities requires jointly labelled data, this issue can be bypassed without losing much accuracy. Assuming that (at least) one of the tasks under consideration can be completed automatically with high accuracy, we find that the estimates of joint probabilities are very close to actual joint probabilities on gold standard data. In this work, we estimate joint probabilities by tagging the auxiliary task data sets with a state-of-the-art POS tagger.

4.1 Morphosyntactic Tasks

Dependency Relation Classification is the task of predicting the dependency tag (and its direction) for a given token. This is a task that has not received much attention, although it has been shown to be a useful feature for parsing (Ouchi et al., 2014). We choose to look at several instantiations of this task, as it allows for a controlled setup under a number of conditions for MTL, and since data is available for a large number of typologically varied languages.

Previous work has suggested various possible instantiations of dependency relation classification labels (Ouchi et al., 2016). In this work, we use labels designed to range from highly complex and informative, to very basic ones.[3] The labelling schemes used are shown in Table 1.

---

[2] Japanese was excluded due to treebank unavailability.
[3] Labels are automatically derived from UD.

Category	Directionality	Example	H
Full	Full	nmod:poss/R_L	3.77
Full	Simple	nmod:poss/R	3.35
Simple	Full	nmod/R_L	3.00
Simple	None	nmod	2.03
None	Full	R_L	1.54
None	Simple	R	0.72

Table 1: Dependency relation labels used in this work, with entropy in bytes (H) measured on English. The labels differ in the granularity and/or inclusion of the category and/or directionality.

The systems in the syntactic experiments are trained on main task data ($\mathbb{D}_{main}$), and on auxiliary task data ($\mathbb{D}_{aux}$). Generally, the amount of overlap between such pairs of data sets differs, and can roughly be divided into three categories: i) identity; ii) overlap; and iii) disjoint (no overlap between data sets). To ensure that we cover several possible experimental situations, we experiment using all three categories. We generate ($\mathbb{D}_{main}$, $\mathbb{D}_{aux}$) pairs by splitting each UD training set into three portions. The first and second portions always contain POS labels. In the identity condition, the second portion contains dependency relations. In the overlap condition, the second and final portions contain dependency relations. In the disjoint condition, the final portion contains dependency relations.

4.2 Semantic Tasks

Martínez Alonso and Plank (2016) experiment with using, i.a., POS tagging as an auxiliary task, with main tasks based on several semantically oriented tasks: Frame detection/identification, NER, supersense annotation and MPQA. Bjerva et al. (2016) investigate using a semantic tagging task as an auxiliary task for POS tagging. We do not train systems for these data sets. Rather, we directly investigate whether changes in accuracy with the main/auxiliary tasks used in these papers are correctly predicted by any of the information-theoretic measures under consideration here.

5 Method

5.1 Architecture and Hyperparameters

We apply a deep neural network with the exact same settings in each syntactic experiment. Our system consists of a two layer deep bi-GRU (100 dimensions per layer), taking an embedded word representation (64 dimensions) as input. We ap-

ply dropout ($p = 0.4$) between each layer in our network (Srivastava et al., 2014). The output of the final bi-GRU layer, is connected to two output layers – one per task. Both tasks are always weighted equally. Optimisation is done using the Adam algorithm (Kingma and Ba, 2014), with the categorical cross-entropy loss function. We use a batch size of 100 sentences, training over a maximum of 50 epochs, using early stopping and monitoring validation loss on the main task.

We do not use pre-trained embeddings. We also do not use any task-specific features, similarly to Collobert et al. (2011), and we do not optimise any hyperparameters with regard to the task(s) at hand. Although these choices are likely to affect the overall accuracy of our systems negatively, the goal of our experiments is to investigate the effect in *change* in accuracy when adding an auxiliary task - not accuracy in itself.

5.2 Experimental Overview

In the syntactic experiments, we train one system per language, dependency label category, and split condition. For sentences where only one tag set is available, we do not update weights based on the loss for the absent task. Averaged results over all languages and dependency relation instantiations, per category, are shown in Table 2.

5.3 Replicability and Reproducibility

In order to facilitate the replicability and reproducibility of our results, we take two methodological steps. To ensure replicability, we run all experiments 10 times, in order to mitigate the effect of random processes on our results.[4] To ensure reproducibility, we release a collection including: i) A Docker file containing all code and dependencies required to obtain all data and run our experiments used in this work; and ii) a notebook containing all code for the statistical analyses performed in this work.[5]

6 Results and Analysis

6.1 Morphosyntactic Tasks

We use Spearman's ρ in order to calculate correlation between auxiliary task effectivity (as measured using Δ_{acc}) and the information-theoretic measures. Following the recommendations in Søgaard et al. (2014), we set our p cut-off value

---

[4]Approximately 10,000 runs using 400,000 CPU hours.
[5]https://github.com/bjerva/mtl-cond-entropy

Auxiliary task	$\rho(\Delta_{acc}, H(Y))$	$\rho(\Delta_{acc}, H(Y|X))$	$\rho(\Delta_{acc}, I(X;Y))$
Dependency Relations (Identity)	-0.06 (p=0.214)	0.12 (p=0.013)	0.08 (p=0.114)
Dependency Relations (Overlap)	0.07 (p=0.127)	0.27 (p<0.001)	**0.43 (p≪0.001)**
Dependency Relations (Disjoint)	0.08 (p=0.101)	0.25 (p<0.001)	**0.41 (p≪0.001)**

Table 2: Correlation scores and associated p-values, between change in accuracy (Δ_{acc}) and entropy ($H(Y)$), conditional entropy ($H(Y|X)$), and mutual information ($I(X;Y)$), calculated with Spearman's ρ, across all languages and label instantiations. Bold indicates the strongest significant correlations.

to $p < 0.0025$. Table 2 shows that MI correlates significantly with auxiliary task effectivity in the most commonly used settings (overlap and disjoint). As hypothesised, entropy has no significant correlation with auxiliary task effectivity, whereas conditional entropy offers some explanation. We further observe that these results hold for almost all languages, although the correlation is weaker for some languages, indicating that there are some other effects at play here. We also analyse whether significant differences can be found with respect to whether or not we have a positive Δ_{acc}, using a bootstrap sample test with 10,000 iterations. We observe a significant relationship ($p < 0.001$) for MI. We also observe a significant relationship for conditional entropy ($p < 0.001$), and again find no significant difference for entropy ($p \geq 0.07$).

Interestingly, no correlation is found in the identity condition between Δ_{acc} and any information-theoretic measure. This is not surprising, as the most effective auxiliary task is simply more data for a task with the highest possible MI. Hence, in the overlap/disjoint conditions, high MI is highly correlated with Δ_{acc}, while in the identity condition, there is no extra data. It is evident that tag set correlations in identical data is not helpful.

6.2 Semantic Tasks

Although we do not have access to sufficient data points to run statistical analyses on the results obtained by Martínez Alonso and Plank (2016), or by Bjerva et al. (2016), we do observe that the mean MI for the conditions in which an auxiliary task is helpful is higher than in the cases where an auxiliary task is not helpful.

7 Conclusions

We have examined the relation between auxiliary task effectivity and three information-theoretic measures. While previous research hypothesises that entropy plays a central role, we show experimentally that conditional entropy is a better predictor, and MI an even better predictor. This claim is corroborated when we correlate MI and change in accuracy with results found in the literature. It is especially interesting that MI is a better predictor than conditional entropy, since MI does not consider the order between main and auxiliary tasks. Our findings should prove helpful for researchers when considering which auxiliary tasks might be helpful for a given main task. Furthermore, it provides an explanation for the fact that there is no universally effective auxiliary task, as a purely entropy-based hypothesis would predict.

The fact that MI is informative when determining the effectivity of an auxiliary task can be explained by considering an auxiliary task to be similar to adding a feature. That is to say, useful features are likely to be useful auxiliary tasks. Interestingly, however, the gains of adding an auxiliary task are visible at test time for the main task, when no explicit auxiliary label information is available.

We tested our hypothesis on 39 languages, representing a wide typological range, as well as a wide range of data sizes. Our experiments were run on syntactically oriented tasks of various granularities. We also corroborated our findings with results from semantically oriented tasks in the literature. Hence our results generalise both across a range of languages, data sizes, and NLP tasks.

Acknowledgments

This work was funded by the NWO-VICI grant "Lost in Translation – Found in Meaning" (288-89-003). We would like to thank Barbara Plank, Robert Östling, Johan Sjons, and the anonymous reviewers for their comments on previous versions of this manuscript. We would also like to thank the Center for Information Technology of the University of Groningen for their support and for providing access to the Peregrine high performance computing cluster.

References

Waleed Ammar, George Mulcaire, Miguel Ballesteros, Chris Dyer, and Noah Smith. 2016. Many languages, one parser. *Transactions of the Association for Computational Linguistics*, 4:431–444.

Johannes Bjerva, Barbara Plank, and Johan Bos. 2016. Semantic tagging with deep residual networks. In *Proceedings of COLING 2016*, page 35313541, Osaka, Japan.

Rich Caruana. 1998. *Multitask learning*. Ph.D. thesis, Carnegie Mellon University.

Hao Cheng, Hao Fang, and Mari Ostendorf. 2015. Open-domain name error detection using a multitask rnn. In *EMNLP*.

Junyoung Chung, Caglar Gulcehre, KyungHyun Cho, and Yoshua Bengio. 2014. Empirical evaluation of gated recurrent neural networks on sequence modeling. *arXiv preprint arXiv:1412.3555*.

Ronan Collobert and Jason Weston. 2008. A unified architecture for natural language processing: Deep neural networks with multitask learning. In *Proceedings of the 25th international conference on Machine learning*, pages 160–167. ACM.

Ronan Collobert, Jason Weston, Léon Bottou, Michael Karlen, Koray Kavukcuoglu, and Pavel Kuksa. 2011. Natural language processing (almost) from scratch. *Journal of Machine Learning Research*, 12(Aug):2493–2537.

Thomas M Cover and Joy A Thomas. 2012. *Elements of information theory*. John Wiley & Sons.

Jeffrey L Elman. 1990. Finding structure in time. *Cognitive science*, 14(2):179–211.

Alex Graves and Jürgen Schmidhuber. 2005. Framewise phoneme classification with bidirectional lstm and other neural network architectures. *Neural Networks*, 18(5):602–610.

Sepp Hochreiter and Jürgen Schmidhuber. 1997. Long short-term memory. *Neural computation*, 9(8):1735–1780.

Diederik Kingma and Jimmy Ba. 2014. Adam: A method for stochastic optimization. *arXiv preprint arXiv:1412.6980*.

Héctor Martínez Alonso and Barbara Plank. 2016. Multitask learning for semantic sequence prediction under varying data conditions. In *arXiv preprint, to appear at EACL 2017 (long paper)*.

Joakim Nivre, Marie-Catherine de Marneffe, Filip Ginter, Yoav Goldberg, Jan Hajic, Christopher D Manning, Ryan McDonald, Slav Petrov, Sampo Pyysalo, Natalia Silveira, et al. 2016. Universal dependencies v1: A multilingual treebank collection. In *Proceedings of the 10th International Conference on Language Resources and Evaluation (LREC 2016)*.

Hiroki Ouchi, Kevin Duh, and Yuji Matsumoto. 2014. Improving dependency parsers with supertags. In *Proceedings of the 14th Conference of the European Chapter of the Association for Computational Linguistics, volume 2: Short Papers*, pages 154–158. Association for Computational Linguistics.

Hiroki Ouchi, Kevin Duh, Hiroyuki Shindo, and Yuji Matsumoto. 2016. Transition-Based Dependency Parsing Exploiting Supertags. In *IEEE/ACM Transactions on Audio, Speech and Language Processing*, volume 24.

Barbara Plank, Anders Søgaard, and Yoav Goldberg. 2016. Multilingual part-of-speech tagging with bidirectional long short-term memory models and auxiliary loss. In *Proceedings of ACL 2016*.

Anders Søgaard and Yoav Goldberg. 2016. Deep multi-task learning with low level tasks supervised at lower layers. In *Proceedings of the 54th Annual Meeting of the Association for Computational Linguistics*, volume 2, pages 231–235. Association for Computational Linguistics.

Anders Søgaard, Anders Johannsen, Barbara Plank, Dirk Hovy, and Hector Martinez. 2014. Whats in a p-value in NLP? In *CoNLL-2014*.

Nitish Srivastava, Geoffrey E Hinton, Alex Krizhevsky, Ilya Sutskever, and Ruslan Salakhutdinov. 2014. Dropout: a simple way to prevent neural networks from overfitting. *Journal of Machine Learning Research*, 15(1):1929–1958.

Iconic Locations in Swedish Sign Language:
Mapping Form to Meaning with Lexical Databases

Carl Börstell & Robert Östling
Department of Linguistics
Stockholm University
{calle,robert}@ling.su.se

Abstract

In this paper, we describe a method for mapping the phonological feature location of Swedish Sign Language (SSL) signs to the meanings in the Swedish semantic dictionary SALDO. By doing so, we observe clear differences in the distribution of meanings associated with different locations on the body. The prominence of certain locations for specific meanings clearly point to iconic mappings between form and meaning in the lexicon of SSL, which pinpoints modality-specific properties of the visual modality.

1 Introduction

1.1 Language and iconicity

The word forms of a language have traditionally been regarded as arbitrary, that is, there is no motivation for why a certain meaning is encoded by a specific form (de Saussure, 1916). The iconicity found in the word forms of spoken language is normally restricted to a few categories— e.g. onomatopoeia and ideophones (Perniss et al., 2010)—but also visible in so-called *phonaesthemes*, grouping certain meanings together— e.g. *tw-* in *twist* and *twirl* (Kwon and Round, 2015). Large-scale cross-linguistc comparisons of form and meaning have shown that there are some preferences for using and avoiding certain sounds for certain meanings (Blasi et al., 2016). However, since the extent of iconicity in spoken language is still quite limited, the general assumption is still that arbitrary word forms are the norm for any given language in that modality.

1.2 Signed language and iconic locations

Signed language uses the other of the two natural modalities of human language, being visual–gestural instead of auditive–oral. A key difference

Figure 1: The SSL sign THINK (Svenskt teckenspråkslexikon, 2016).

between signed and spoken language is that the former is widely regarded as more iconic (and consequently less arbitrary) than the latter, in terms of both lexically specified and morphologically modified depiction (Klima and Bellugi, 1979). The articulation of any sign is located in the physical space on or around the body of the signer. The location of the sign (a.k.a. *place of articulation*) can be iconic already in lexical signs (Taub, 2001), but sign locations may be altered to adhere to and syntax/discourse iconicity (Perniss, 2012; Meir et al., 2013).[1] In this study, we only focus on lexically specified locations of signs (see Section 2.1). Two examples of iconic locations in SSL signs are illustrated in Figure 1, in which the sign THINK is located at the forehead (representing brain activity), and Figure 2, in which the sign QUIET is located at the mouth (represented by a well-known gesture, depicting an obstacle in front of the lips).

The iconic relationship between form and meaning is well-attested for signed language, including location as one form feature. However, few studies that have investigated this link by quantitative means, and none for SSL.

---

[1] The co-speech gestures often accompanying spoken language may be similarly iconic, for instance with regard to the location of gesturing in the physical space (McNeill, 1992).

Proceedings of the 21st Nordic Conference of Computational Linguistics, pages 221–225,
Gothenburg, Sweden, 23-24 May 2017. ©2017 Linköping University Electronic Press

Figure 2: The SSL sign QUIET (Svenskt tecken-språkslexikon, 2016).

2 Data and Methodology

2.1 The SSL online dictionary

The SSL dictionary (SSLD) (Svenskt tecken-språkslexikon, 2016) is an online video dictionary of SSL. It is an ongoing language resource and documentation project, creating a lexical database constantly expanding in size (Mesch et al., 2012). The version used for this study included 15,874 sign entries. Each sign entry has one or more Swedish word translations, and also features a phonological transcription of the sign form, in which sign location is one value.

All sign data were exported from the SSLD database, and from this raw data, Swedish keywords and sign locations were extracted using a Python script. For the purposes of this study, complex signs with more than one location (e.g. compounds) were excluded.

For single location signs, we also excluded a) signs using the so-called *neutral space* as the location, and b) signs for which the other, non-dominant, hand was used as the location (Crasborn, 2011). The former were excluded since we were only interested in signs with body-specified locations.[2] The latter cases were excluded since the other hand is found to be iconic in terms of its shape and interaction with the dominant hand, rather than as a location *per se* (Lepic et al., 2016).

The finalized SSLD data consist of a list of 3,675 signs that met our criteria, their Swedish keywords, and location. In this list, 29 locations were present. These were collapsed into 20 locations, conflating near identical locations (e.g. eyes and eye). Table 1 shows a list of all locations and the number of signs per location.

Location	No. of signs
head	81
forehead	414
upper face	159
eyes	95
face	153
nose	214
ears	103
lower face	47
cheeks	210
mouth	398
chin	325
neck	196
shoulders	77
arm	36
upper arm	47
lower arm	110
chest	860
belly	101
hip	42
leg	7
Total	3,675

Table 1: Distribution of signs across locations (anatomically descending).

2.2 SALDO

SALDO (Borin and Forsberg, 2009) is a semantic lexicon of Swedish, in which each word sense is arranged into a hierarchy through its (unique) *primary descriptor* and its (one or more) *secondary descriptors*. Unlike the more familiar WordNet (Miller, 1995) style lexica, the precise semantic relationship indicated by SALDO's descriptors is not formally specified. While this makes some of the applications of WordNet difficult to reproduce with SALDO, generating a number of broad semantic categories is sufficient for our needs.

For the purposes of this work, we define the semantic category defined by a word sense to be the set of all primary or secondary descendants in SALDO. This implies that each sense in SALDO defines a category, possibly overlapping, and that the choice of which categories to investigate is very free. We selected categories that were large enough to provide a sensible analysis, as well as semantically tied to the human body. Because SSLD does not contain any mapping to SALDO's word senses, we approximate sense disambiguation by using the first SALDO sense of any SSLD entry. In practice, this amounts to looking up the

---

[2]This does not necessarily entail body contact.

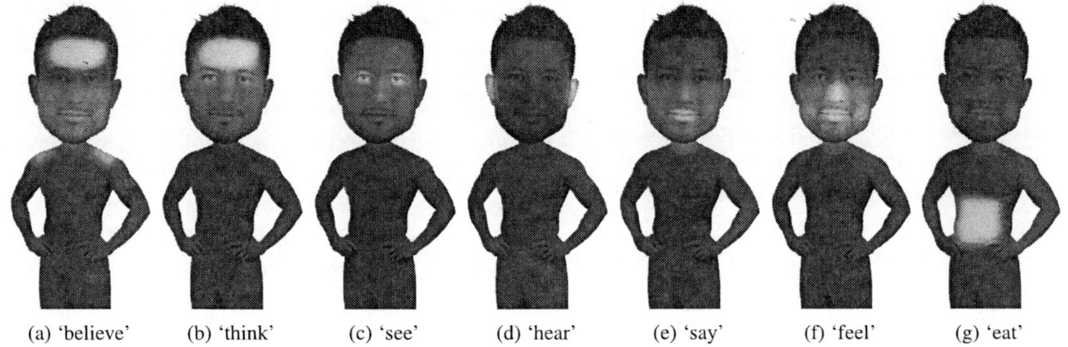

Figure 3: Location distributions for seven semantic categories. Brightness represents the degree to which a given body part is over-represented in the given semantic category, with respect to the distribution over locations for *all* signs in the lexicon.

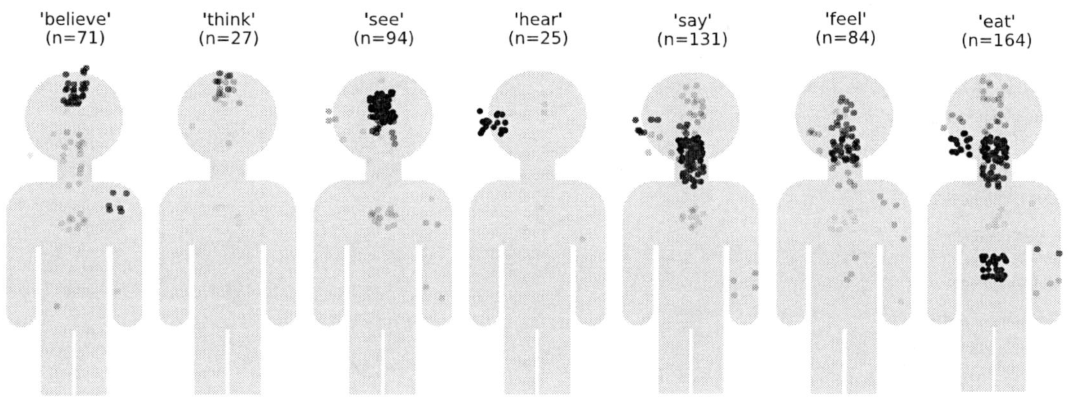

Figure 4: The distribution of locations for signs within seven semantic categories (with number of sign entries per semantic category in brackets).

Swedish translation available in each SSLD entry using SALDO, and choosing the first sense in case there are several. This is a surprisingly close approximation, because the first sense is generally the most common.[3]

To give a sense of how one of the semantic categories we study looks, we sample ten random signs in the category 'eat': *animal feed, appendix* (anatomy), *kiwi, gravy, foodstuff, lunch, belly ache, anorexia, full, oatmeal*. While many actual types of food are included, we also see terms such as *appendix* whose assocation to 'eat' is more indirect.

2.3 Visualization

We investigate the distribution of locations for a given semantic category by first looking up its members in SALDO as described above, then looking up the corresponding signs in SSLD through their Swedish translations. The locations of the resulting set of signs is then visualized in two ways:

- by varying the light level of body parts proportional to the (exponentiated) pointwise mutual information (PMI) of the given concept and that location (see Figure 3).

- by a jitter plot showing the number of signs within a concept with a certain location (see Figure 4).

---

[3]The exception to this among our concepts is 'feel', where we use the second SALDO sense of the corresponding Swedish word, 'känna'.

Pointwise mutual information is defined as

$$\text{PMI}(l,c) = \log \frac{p(l,c)}{p(l)p(c)}$$

where, as we use maximum-likelihood estimation, $p(l)$ is the proportion of signs articulated at location l, $p(c)$ is the proportion of signs that belong to category c, and $p(l,c)$ the proportion that are both of the above at the same time. Intuitively, this is a measure of how overrepresented a location is among the signs within a given concept, relative to the overall distribution of locations in the SSLD lexicon. In our visualization, high PMI is represented by brighter regions.

We have chosen to use two separate but similar visualization techniques for reasons of clarity, since the first gives an intuitive picture of where on the body a particular semantic category is focused in SSL vocabulary, whereas the second makes it easier to see the actual distribution of sign locations within a concept without comparison to the overall distribution.

3   Results

Figure 3 shows the location distributions for seven semantic categories: 'believe', 'think', 'see', 'hear', 'say', 'feel', and 'eat'.

The amount of iconicity in SSL is clearly visible in this figure, where signs in the categories 'believe' and 'think' are over-represented around the forehead (with specific meanings such as *suspect* and *ponder*), 'see' around the eyes (e.g. *stare*), 'hear' on the ears (e.g. *listen*), 'say' around the mouth (e.g. *speak*, *talk*) or neck (e.g. *voice*), 'feel' on several locations on the lower face related to sensory inputs (e.g. *smell*, *sweet*), and 'eat' around the mouth (e.g. *lunch*) or belly (e.g. *hungry*).

This iconicity is by no means absolute, as indicated by Figure 4. This shows that even in the most extreme cases, such as 'hear' and 'think', the bias in location is not absolute. Other categories, like 'say', are in fact distributed quite widely throughout the body although the mouth area is clearly over-represented.[4]

4   Conclusions

In this paper, we have showed clear examples of iconic patterning in the distribution of meanings across the lexically specified locations of SSL

---

[4]In Figure 4, the prominence of each location is shown by level of darkness in the plotted signs (i.e. darker means more prominent).

signs. This is done by quantitative means, using a novel method of matching Swedish word entries in the SSLD to the meanings in the semantic dictionary SALDO, followed by a visualization based on a prominence-ranking of locations to meaning domains. The results illustrate that some body locations are much more prominent than others within certain semantic domains. This is attributed to the iconic structure of signed language, with sign forms directly or metaphorically evoking salient properties of some referent. Since not all signs are necessarily iconic, and because iconic forms may choose from a range of features of its referent to depict, the distribution of meanings to locations is not absolute. Instead, locations are more or less prominent for certain meanings, and in many cases this is directly linked to iconicity.

Acknowledgments

We wish to thank the two anonymous reviewers for comments and suggestions on this paper.

References

Damián E. Blasi, Søren Wichmann, Harald Hammarström, Peter F. Stadler, and Morten H. Christiansen. 2016. Sound–meaning association biases evidenced across thousands of languages. *Proceedings of the National Academy of Sciences*, 113(39):10818–10823.

Lars Borin and Markus Forsberg. 2009. All in the family: A comparison of SALDO and WordNet. In *NODALIDA 2009 Workshop on WordNets and other Lexical Semantic Resources – between Lexical Semantics, Lexicography, Terminology and Formal Ontologies*, pages 7–12, Odense, Denmark.

Onno Crasborn. 2011. The other hand in sign language phonology. In Marc van Oostendorp, Colin J. Ewen, Elizabeth Hume, and Keren Rice, editors, *The Blackwell companion to phonology, vol. 1*, chapter 10, pages 223–240. Malden, MA & Oxford.

Ferdinand de Saussure. 1916. *Cours de linguistique générale*. Payot, Paris.

Edward S. Klima and Ursula Bellugi. 1979. Iconicity in signs and signing. In Edward S. Klima and Ursula Bellugi, editors, *The signs of language*, pages 9–34. Harvard University Press, Cambridge, MA.

Nahyun Kwon and Erich R. Round. 2015. Phonaesthemes in morphological theory. *Morphology*, 25(1):1–27.

Ryan Lepic, Carl Börstell, Gal Belsitzman, and Wendy Sandler. 2016. Taking meaning in hand: Iconic motivations for two-handed signs. *Sign Language & Linguistics*, 19(1):37–81.

David McNeill. 1992. *Hand and Mind: What Gestures Reveal about Thought*. University of Chicago Press, Chicago, IL.

Irit Meir, Carol Padden, Mark Aronoff, and Wendy Sandler. 2013. Competing iconicities in the structure of languages. *Cognitive Linguistics*, 24(2):309–343.

Johanna Mesch, Lars Wallin, and Thomas Björkstrand. 2012. Sign Language Resources in Sweden: Dictionary and Corpus. In Onno Crasborn, Eleni Efthimiou, Evita Fotinea, Thomas Hanke, Jette Kristoffersen, and Johanna Mesch, editors, *Proceedings of the 5th Workshop on the Representation and Processing of Sign Languages: Interactions between Corpus and Lexicon [LREC]*, pages 127–130, Paris. ELRA.

George A. Miller. 1995. WordNet: A lexical database for English. *Communications of the ACM*, 38(11):39–41.

Pamela Perniss, Robin L. Thompson, and Gabriella Vigliocco. 2010. Iconicity as a general property of language: evidence from spoken and signed languages. *Frontiers in Psychology*, 1(227).

Pamela Perniss. 2012. Use of sign space. In Roland Pfau, Markus Steinbach, and Bencie Woll, editors, *Sign language: An international handbook*, pages 412–431. De Gruyter Mouton, Berlin/Boston, MA.

Svenskt teckenspråkslexikon. 2016. Sign Language Section, Department of Linguistics, Stockholm University. http://teckensprakslexikon.ling.su.se/.

Sarah F. Taub. 2001. *Language from the body: Iconicity and metaphor in ASL*. Cambridge University Press, Cambridge.

Docforia: A Multilayer Document Model

Marcus Klang
Department of computer science
Lund University, Lund
`marcus.klang@cs.lth.se`

Pierre Nugues
Department of computer science
Lund University, Lund
`pierre.nugues@cs.lth.se`

Abstract

In this paper, we describe **Docforia**, a multilayer document model and application programming interface (API) to store formatting, lexical, syntactic, and semantic annotations on Wikipedia and other kinds of text and visualize them. While Wikipedia has become a major NLP resource, its scale and heterogeneity makes it relatively difficult to do experimentations on the whole corpus. These experimentations are rendered even more complex as, to the best of our knowledge, there is no available tool to visualize easily the results of a processing pipeline.

We designed Docforia so that it can store millions of documents and billions of tokens, annotated using different processing tools, that themselves use multiple formats, and compatible with cluster computing frameworks such as Hadoop or Spark. The annotation output, either partial or complete, can then be shared more easily. To validate Docforia, we processed six language versions of Wikipedia: English, French, German, Spanish, Russian, and Swedish, up to semantic role labeling, depending on the NLP tools available for a given language. We stored the results in our document model and we created a visualization tool to inspect the annotation results.

1   Introduction

Wikipedia is one of the largest freely available encyclopedic sources: It is comprehensive, multilingual, and continuously expanding. These unique properties make it a popular resource now used in scores of NLP projects such as translation (Smith et al., 2010), semantic networks (Navigli

and Ponzetto, 2010), named entity linking (Mihalcea and Csomai, 2007), information extraction, or question answering (Ferrucci, 2012).

Nonetheless, the Wikipedia size, where many language versions have now more that one million of articles makes it more difficult to handle than "classic" and older corpora such as the Penn treebank (Marcus et al., 1993). Processing the complete collection of Wikipedia articles, or a part of it, is a nontrivial task that requires dealing with multiple markup variants across the language versions, multiple tools and storage models. In addition, the application of a NLP pipeline to carry out the annotation (tokenization, POS tagging, dependency parsing, and so on) is a relatively costly operation that can take weeks on a single computer.

Docforia is a multilayer document model to store formatting, lexical, syntactic, and semantic annotations on Wikipedia and other kinds of text and visualize them. To deliver results in a reasonable time, Docforia is compatible with cluster programming frameworks such as Spark or Hadoop. Using the Langforia language processing pipelines (Klang and Nugues, 2016a), we processed six language versions of Wikipedia: English, French, German, Spanish, Russian, and Swedish, up to semantic role labeling, depending on the NLP tools available for a given language. We stored the results in the document model. We designed an interactive visualization tool, part of Langforia, so that a user can select languages, documents, and linguistic layers and examine the annotation output.

2   The Document Model

We created the Docforia multilayer document model library to store, query, and extract hypertextual information common to many NLP tasks such as part-of-speech tagging, coreference resolution, named entity recognition and linking, dependency parsing, semantic role labeling, etc., in

Proceedings of the 21st Nordic Conference of Computational Linguistics, pages 226–230,
Gothenburg, Sweden, 23-24 May 2017. ©2017 Linköping University Electronic Press

a standalone package.

This model is intended for large and heterogenous collection of text, including Wikipedia. We designed it so that we could store the original markup, as well as the the results of the subsequent linguistic processing. The model consists of multiple layers, where each layer is dedicated to a specific type of annotation. It is nondestructive and preserves the original white spaces.

The annotations are encoded in the form of graph nodes, where a node represents a piece of data: A token, a sentence, a named entity, etc., delimited by ranges. These nodes are possibly connected by edges as in dependency graphs. The data structure used is similar to a property graph and Fig. 1 shows the conversion pipeline from the Wikimedia dumps to the abstract syntactic trees (AST) and Docforia layers.

3 Previous Work

A few graph-based linguistic data models and serializations have structures that are similar to Docforia. They include HyGraphDB (Gleim et al., 2007), the Linguistic Framework Annotation (Ide and Suderman, 2014), Off-Road LAF (Lapponi et al., 2014), the D-SPIN Text Corpus Format (Heid et al., 2010), and the oft cited UIMA project (Ferrucci and Lally, 2004). Some tools also extend UIMA such as DKPro Core (Eckart de Castilho and Gurevych, 2014).

In contrast to the UIMA project (Ferrucci and Lally, 2004), which also provides an infrastructure to represent unstructured documents, the Docforia library by itself does not define an equivalent analysis infrastructure or rich type system. Docforia's main focus is data extraction and storage of informal heterogenous data, where the schema can change many times during a project.

The primary motivation of Docforia was a faster adaptability in research projects, where rigidity can adversely affect productivity. Docforia is semi-structured, contains a simplified static-type system for common types of layers and has support for a dynamic-type system. The static types are defined by convention, can be overridden, and are by no means enforced.

4 Use-case: Wikipedia

We convert Wikipedia from HTML dumps into Docforia records using an annotation pipeline. The first step converts the HTML documents into DOM trees using jsoup[1]. The second step extracts the original page structure, text styles, links, lists, and tables. We then resolve the links to unique Wikidata identifiers. These steps are common to all the language editions we process.

Wikidata is central to the multilingual nature of Docforia. Wikidata is an entity database, which assigns unique identifiers across all the language editions of Wikipedia. The University of Gothenburg, for instance, has the unique id: Q371522 that enables to retrieve the article pages in English, French, Swedish, or Russian.

In addition to the common processing steps and depending on the available tools, we can apply linguistic annotations that are language specific using Langforia. These annotations can range from a simple tokenization to semantic-role labels or coreference chains. We save all the results of the intermediate and final steps as files in the Parquet format; each record being a Docforia document as binary blob in addition to metadata such as Wikidata Q-number, title, and page-type. We selected this format because of its portability, efficiency, and ease of use with the Apache Spark data processing engine.

5 Application Programming Interface

The Docforia API builds on the concepts of document storage and document engine. The document storage consists of properties, layers (node or edge layers) to store typed annotations, token, sentence, relationship, where the nodes can have a range, and finally sublayer variants: gold, predicted, coreference chains. The document engine defines query primitives such as covers, for instance the tokens in a anchor, transactions, and partial lightweight documents called views.

The Docforia data structure is similar to a typed property graph. It consists of nodes (tokens, sentences, paragraphs, anchors, ...), edges (connections between e.g tokens to form a dependency tree), and properties per node and edge (Token: pos, lemma, ...).

The piece of code below shows how to create tokens from a string and assign a property to a range of tokens, here a named entity with the *Location* label:

```
Document doc = new MemoryDocument(
  "Greetings from Lund, Sweden!");
```

---

[1]http://jsoup.org/

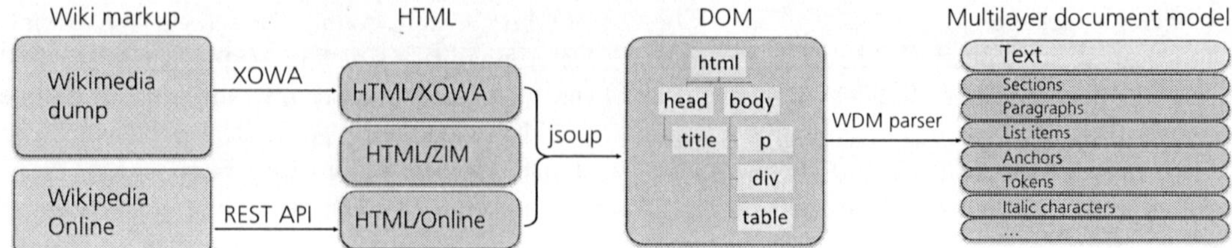

Figure 1: Conversion of Wikipedia dumps into abstract syntactic trees and the Docforia multilayer document model (Klang and Nugues, 2016b).

```
// 012345678901234567890012345678

Token Greetings    =
  new Token(doc).setRange(0,  9);
Token from         =
  new Token(doc).setRange(10, 14);
Token Lund         =
  new Token(doc).setRange(15, 19);
Token comma        =
  new Token(doc).setRange(19, 20);
Token Sweden       =
  new Token(doc).setRange(21, 27);
Token exclamation =
  new Token(doc).setRange(27, 28);


Sentence greetingsSentence =
  new Sentence(doc).setRange(0, 28);


NamedEntity lundSwedenEntity =
  new NamedEntity(doc)
    .setRange(Lund.getStart(),
      Sweden.getEnd())
        .setLabel("Location");
```

The API provides SQL-like query capabilities and the code below shows how to find the named entities in a document:

```
NodeTVar<Token> T = Token.var();
NodeTVar<NamedEntity> NE =
  NamedEntity.var();


List<Token> lundLocation =
  doc.select(T, NE)
    .where(T).coveredBy(NE)
    .stream()
    .sorted(StreamUtils.orderBy(T))
    .map(StreamUtils.toNode(T))
    .collect(Collectors.toList());
```

6 Visualization

We built a front-end application, part of Langforia, to enable the users to visualize the content of Docforia-based corpora. This application has the form of a web server that embeds the Docforia library and Lucene to index the documents. We created a Javascript component for the text visualization on the client. This client provides a user interface for searching and visualizing Docforia data in the index. The layers are selectable from a drop-down menu and the supported visualizations are the ranges and relationships between them.

Figure 2 shows the annotations of the parts of speech, named entities, and dependency relations of the sentence:

> Göteborgs universitet är ett svenskt statligt universitet med åtta fakulteter, 37 000 studenter, varav 25 000 helårsstudenter och 6000 anställda.

> 'The University of Gothenburg is a Swedish public university with eight faculties, 37,000 students, (25,000 full-time), and 6,000 staff members.'

The visualization tool is similar to the brat[2] components (Stenetorp et al., 2012), but includes a tooltip support and has a faster rendering. If we hover over the words, it shows the properties attached to a word in CoNLL-like format. In Fig. 3, the properties correspond to the word *Vasaparken*.

7 Conclusion and Future Work

We described Docforia, a multilayer document model, structured in the form of a graph. It enables a user to represent the results of large-scale multilingual annotations. Using it and the Langforia language processing pipelines, we annotated

---

[2]http://brat.nlplab.org/

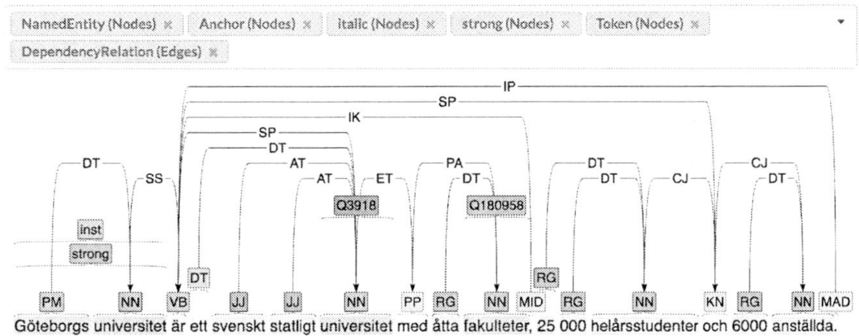

Figure 2: Visualization of six layers including: Tokens, named entities, and dependency relations

Figure 3: Visualization of properties

Wikipedia dump (Klang and Nugues, 2016a). When applied to Wikipedia, MLDM links the different versions through an extensive use of URI indices and Wikidata Q-numbers.

Together with Docforia, we used the Lucene library to index the records. The resulting system can run on a single laptop, even with multiple versions of Wikipedia.

Docforia is written in Java. In the future, we plan to develop a Python API, which will make it possible to combine Python and Java tools. This will enable the programmer to build prototypes more quickly as well as experiment more easily with machine learning algorithms.

Docforia is available from github at `https://github.com/marcusklang/docforia`.

Acknowledgements

This research was supported by Vetenskapsrådet, the Swedish research council, under the *Det digitaliserade samhället* program.

References

Richard Eckart de Castilho and Iryna Gurevych. 2014. A broad-coverage collection of portable nlp components for building shareable analysis pipelines. In *Proceedings of the Workshop on Open Infrastructures and Analysis Frameworks for HLT*, pages 1–11, Dublin, Ireland, August. Association for Computational Linguistics and Dublin City University.

David Ferrucci and Adam Lally. 2004. UIMA: an architectural approach to unstructured information processing in the corporate research environment. *Natural Language Engineering*, 10(3-4):327–348, September.

David Angelo Ferrucci. 2012. Introduction to "This is Watson". *IBM Journal of Research and Development*, 56(3.4):1:1 –1:15, May-June.

Rüdiger Gleim, Alexander Mehler, and Hans-Jürgen Eikmeyer. 2007. Representing and maintaining large corpora. In *Proceedings of the Corpus Linguistics 2007 Conference, Birmingham (UK)*.

Ulrich Heid, Helmut Schmid, Kerstin Eckart, and Erhard Hinrichs. 2010. A corpus representation format for linguistic web services: The D-SPIN text corpus format and its relationship with ISO standards. In *Proceedings of the Seventh International Conference on Language Resources and Evaluation (LREC'10)*, Valletta, Malta, may. European Language Resources Association (ELRA).

Nancy Ide and Keith Suderman. 2014. The Linguistic Annotation Framework: a standard for annotation interchange and merging. *Language Resources and Evaluation*, 48(3):395–418.

Marcus Klang and Pierre Nugues. 2016a. Langforia: Language pipelines for annotating large collections of documents. In *Proceedings of COLING 2016, the 26th International Conference on Computational Linguistics: System Demonstrations*, pages 74–78, Osaka, Japan, December. The COLING 2016 Organizing Committee.

Marcus Klang and Pierre Nugues. 2016b. WIKIPARQ: A tabulated Wikipedia resource using the Parquet format. In *Proceedings of the Ninth International Conference on Language Resources and Evaluation (LREC 2016)*, pages 4141–4148, Portorož, Slovenia, may.

Emanuele Lapponi, Erik Velldal, Stephan Oepen, and Rune Lain Knudsen. 2014. Off-Road LAF: Encoding and processing annotations in NLP workflows. In *Proceedings of the Ninth International Conference on Language Resources and Evaluation (LREC'14)*, Reykjavik, Iceland, may. European Language Resources Association (ELRA).

Mitchell Marcus, Mary Ann Marcinkiewicz, and Beatrice Santorini. 1993. Building a large annotated corpus of English: The Penn Treebank. *Computational Linguistics*, 19(2):313–330.

Rada Mihalcea and Andras Csomai. 2007. Wikify!: Linking documents to encyclopedic knowledge. In *Proceedings of the Sixteenth ACM Conference on CIKM*, CIKM '07, pages 233–242, Lisbon, Portugal.

Roberto Navigli and Simone Paolo Ponzetto. 2010. Babelnet: Building a very large multilingual semantic network. In *Proceedings of the 48th annual meeting of the ACL*, pages 216–225, Uppsala.

Jason R. Smith, Chris Quirk, and Kristina Toutanova. 2010. Extracting parallel sentences from comparable corpora using document level alignment. In *Human Language Technologies: The 2010 Annual Conference of the North American Chapter of the ACL*, pages 403–411.

Pontus Stenetorp, Sampo Pyysalo, Goran Topić, Tomoko Ohta, Sophia Ananiadou, and Jun'ichi Tsujii. 2012. brat: a web-based tool for nlp-assisted text annotation. In *Proceedings of the Demonstrations at the 13th Conference of the European Chapter of the Association for Computational Linguistics*, pages 102–107, Avignon, France, April. Association for Computational Linguistics.

Finnish resources for evaluating language model semantics

Viljami Venekoski
National Defence University
Helsinki, Finland
venekoski@gmail.com

Jouko Vankka
National Defence University
Helsinki, Finland
jouko.vankka@mil.fi

Abstract

Distributional language models have consistently been demonstrated to capture semantic properties of words. However, research into the methods for evaluating the accuracy of the modeled semantics has been limited, particularly for less-resourced languages. This research presents three resources for evaluating the semantic quality of Finnish language distributional models: (1) semantic similarity judgment resource, as well as (2) a word analogy and (3) a word intrusion test set. The use of evaluation resources is demonstrated in practice by presenting them with different language models built from varied corpora.

1 Introduction

In the spirit of the distributional hypothesis stating that semantically similar words appear in similar contexts (Harris, 1954), distributional language models of recent years have successfully been able to capture semantics properties of words given large corpora (e.g., Mikolov et al., 2013a; Pennington et al., 2014). However, there are only few resources for evaluating the accuracy or validity of language models, particularly for less-spoken languages, due to language dependence of such resources (Leviant and Reichart, 2015). Further, a single good resource may not be sufficient due to the complexity of semantics; performance in an intrinsic evaluation task may not predict performance in extrinsic downstream language technology applications (Chiu et al., 2016). Therefore, the evaluation of semantics should be based on a variety of tasks, estimating different semantic phenomena (Baroni et al., 2014).

With respect to language models, two distinct measures of semantic quality can be identified: validity and completeness (Lindland et al., 1994).

The latter is dependent on the underlying corpus because a language model can only represent linguistic units which have been present in its training data. While it is possible for some models to infer the meaning of novel input, the inference can be considered an additional training step of the model and thus an extension of the training corpus. Completeness is also likely to affect the validity of a model; given the distributional hypothesis (Harris, 1954), more encompassing knowledge about the possible contexts of words results in more accurate knowledge of their semantics. In this study, the lack of completeness is estimated only by presenting a rate of out-of-vocabulary (OOV) words for each separate evaluation resource, but not investigated further.

The aim of this research is to present scientist and practitioners working with Finnish tools to evaluate their language models with respect to semantics.[1] While most research compares the performance of models to that of humans, we also present effortlessly extensible tools requiring no human annotation. Finally, baseline results for the evaluation methods are reported, utilizing varied corpora and language model architectures.

2 Materials and Methods

2.1 Language models

The distributional language models used in this research are constructed using word2vec (Mikolov et al., 2013a), GloVe (Pennington et al., 2014) and fastText (Bojanowski et al., 2016) software. These model architectures have been used to produce vector representations of words, known as word embeddings, efficiently from large corpora, with the vectors yielding intuitively semantic properties (Mikolov et al., 2013b; Baroni et al., 2014). The word embeddings have been used in a vari-

---

[1] The evaluation resources are available online at github.com/venekoski/FinSemEvl.

Proceedings of the 21st Nordic Conference of Computational Linguistics, pages 231–236,
Gothenburg, Sweden, 23-24 May 2017. ©2017 Linköping University Electronic Press

ety of semantics-incorporating downstream applications such as sentiment analysis and text generation (see e.g., Brigadir et al., 2015; Karpathy and Fei-Fei, 2015; Bansal et al., 2014).

The models are constructed utilizing the default hyperparameters as set out by the authors of each model, except for the minimum word frequency which is set to 5 for each model. Both Continuous Bag of Words (CBOW) and Skip-gram (SG) architectures of word2vec and fastText are used. It should be noted that these parameters may not be optimal, particularly for Finnish (Venekoski et al., 2016), and tuning of the parameters would likely lead to better results.

2.2 Corpora and pre-processing

The language models are created based on four different publicly available Finnish corpora. These include the Suomi24 (Aller Media Oy, 2014) and Ylilauta (Ylilauta, 2011) corpora of social media discussions, as well as corpora derived from a Wikipedia dump (Wikimedia Foundation, nd) and all Finnish language Project Gutenberg texts (Project Gutenberg, nd). No pre-processing other than lowercasing of characters was conducted on the data. The descriptives of the corpora are reported in Table 1.

Corpus	Tokens	Unique tokens
Suomi24	2834M	31508K
Ylilauta	30M	524K
Wikipedia	79M	2747K
Gutenberg	72M	2034K

Table 1: Corpora and their sizes after tokenization.

2.3 Word similarity resource

Arguably, the standard for evaluating semantic accuracy of language models is using word similarity resources. These typically comprise of a set of word pairs, each having a human-rated similarity score. The human ratings are then correlated with similarity scores produced by a computational language model. Among the most utilized resources are WordSim-353 (Finkelstein et al., 2001), MEN (Bruni et al., 2012), and SimLex-999 (Hill et al., 2015). However, the resources differ in what they quantify; the instructions of WordSim-353 lead its respondents to rate association between words (Agirre et al., 2009), whereas the instructions of SimLex-999 guided the subjects to evaluate similarity between words specifically (Hill et al.,

2015). Notably, performance in SimLex-999 predicts the performance in downstream applications, unlike most intrinsic evaluation benchmarks (Chiu et al., 2016).

Similarity judgment resources cannot be used cross-lingually by translating a resource to another language and using the scores of the original resource to evaluate cross-language models (Leviant and Reichart, 2015; but see Agirre et al., 2016). Thus, in order to evaluate Finnish language models, a new similarity resource based on SimLex-999 (henceforth SL999) was constructed. Following the same instructions as in SL999, an online survey was conducted in which respondents were asked to rate the similarity of pairs of two words on a scale of 0 to 10, where 0 meant no similarity between the words while 10 meant that the words were synonymous. The survey consisted of 300 word pairs from SL999 which were translated to Finnish. The chosen words each had a single unambiguous sense in both Finnish and English, hence excluding homographic words. This was to ensure that the Finnish participants would rate words denoting senses most similar to their English counterparts, allowing cross-lingual comparisons. The translations were agreed upon by two fluent bilingual researchers. The inflectional form of the Finnish words was singular nominative for nouns and adjectives and first infinitive for verbs. Finally, the set was randomly reduced to 300 pairs to reduce survey fatigue of the respondents. The presentation order of word pairs was randomized for each respondent. The survey was conducted online and the respondents recruited through social media. Only native Finnish speakers were instructed to fill out the survey. To filter out outliers, the exclusion criterion of SL999 was followed: the respondents whose answers' average Spearman correlation with all other respondents' answers deviated from the mean of all such averages by more than one standard deviation were excluded. As a result, 4 out of 59 total respondents were excluded from the subsequent analyses. The resulting data set of similarity ratings for 300 Finnish word pairs as judged by 55 respondents will henceforth be called the FinnSim-300 (or FS300) data set.

To obtain a human performance benchmark, inter-annotator agreement was calculated as the average pairwise Spearman correlation between two human raters. The agreement was $\rho = .53$, and while lower than the agreement in SL999 (Hill et al., 2015), $\rho = .67$, it can be considered sufficiently high as inter-annotator agreements can be relatively low in similar ambiguous tasks (Gamon, 2004; Strapparava and Mihalcea, 2007). The lower agreement in the Finnish resource and related greater variance in individual responses can be partially attributed to the fact that respondents in SL999 rated word pairs on a smaller scale of $1 - 7$ (which the researches extrapolated to a $0 - 10$ scale). The standard deviations of respondent similarity ratings for individual items in SL999 ranged from .34 to 2.18 (Hill et al., 2015), scoring notably higher compared to a range of .13 to 3.35 in the current Finnish survey.

More recently, it has been argued that the average correlation of one human rater with the average of all the other raters is a fairer measure for evaluating computational models performance compared to inter-rater agreement (Mrkšić et al., 2016). This score, gold standard agreement, was $\rho = .72$ in FS300, which is also more in line with the score in SL999, $\rho = .78$.[2] We consider this value as a point of comparison for language model evaluation. Should the correlation between the similarity scores of a language model and the similarity judgment resource exceed this number, the model can be considered to perform at a human level.

2.4 Analogies

Analogies have previously been used as a method for evaluating the semantic reliability of language models (see e.g., Bojanowski et al., 2016; Sun et al., 2016). Alongside word2vec model, its authors released an English language analogy test set, consisting of approximately 20 000 syntactic and semantic test units, each following the analogy A is to B what C is to D (Mikolov et al., 2013a). In the test task, a well-performing model is expected to estimate the correct word D given vectors of words A, B and C, by estimating the most similar word vector to that obtained from the linear operation $\mathbf{w}_B + \mathbf{w}_C - \mathbf{w}_A$. The test is correct if the most similar word is exactly that which has been determined by the test set. If there were no vector representation for one of the words in the analogy, the analogy determined incorrect. The overall percentage of correct analogies indicates the extent in which a model is able to capture known semantic relations.

The words the original English test set are not directly applicable to other language models, if translated, due to culture-specific terminology (e.g. US newspapers and sports teams). Thus, a small Finnish analogy test was created, consisting of 1037 analogies. The relation types in the analogy set were in part taken from the Google analogy set (capital-country, country-currency, female-male), but extended with other relation types as well (antonymic adjectives, orthogonal directions, hockey team-city, cardinal-ordinal number).

The semantics of models are highly reliant on the conceptual knowledge that is exhibited in the data. The human authors of the underlying corpus may have distorted conceptual knowledge compared to the curated analogy test sets. For instance, an individual may think that the capital of Australia is Sydney and consequently produce utterances corresponding to this proposition. Thus, even if a model would be able to perfectly capture the conceptual information of said individual, the model would fail at an analogy task utilizing capital-country relations. Therefore, the analogy task is not only an evaluatory tool for the semantic validity of a language model but also for the conceptual validity of the corpus. If only the former evaluation is desired, effort should be put onto making the analogy test sets such that they contain unambiguous, uncontroversial, common knowledge factual relationships, where the to-be-guessed word (notated word D above) is the only correct alternative in the vocabulary.

2.5 Word intrusion

Word intrusion task (also known as *odd-one-out* or *oddity task*) is a traditional experimental paradigm in psycholinguistic research where the subject is instructed to choose a word which is semantically incompatible with rest of the words in a list (see e.g., Albert et al., 1975; Campbell and Sais, 1995). More recently, the paradigm has been used in machine learning literature to evaluate the semantic coherence of topic models (Chang et al., 2009). In this setting, a list of n words (we call this an intrusion set) is created, out of which $n - 1$ words are taken from one topic, constructed by the topic model, and one outlier word is taken from another topic. Human subjects are asked to point out the outlier word, and if they agree with the topic model partition, the model is considered coherent.

The aim here is to utilize the intrusion task but

Task	Corpus	OOV	*GloVe*	*word2vec*		*fastText*	
				CBOW	SG	CBOW	SG
Similarity judgments	Suomi24	0.00%	.2381	.2431	.3070	.3724	**.3788**
	Ylilauta	1.00%	.0823	.1689	.1876	**.2605**	.2379
	Wikipedia	0.67%	.1385	.1460	.1855	**.2780**	.2121
	Gutenberg	10.67%	.2312	.2583	.2953	**.3430**	.3323
Analogies	Suomi24	0.00%	.1861	.1302	.1948	.0366	**.1986**
	Ylilauta	23.14%	.0897	.0984	**.1485**	.0492	.0916
	Wikipedia	0.00%	**.4330**	.2507	.3655	.1543	.4098
	Gutenberg	40.12%	.0540	.1138	**.1340**	.0569	.0887
Word intrusion	Suomi24	52.09%	.3983	.7227	**.8297**	.6081	.8288
	Ylilauta	81.89%	.3449	.5846	**.7016**	.4805	.6944
	Wikipedia	51.17%	.5484	.8116	**.9207**	.6805	.8825
	Gutenberg	85.75%	.2938	.4272	.5329	.4620	**.5901**

Table 2: Performance of different language models in the three presented evaluation tasks. The scores of the best performing models for each corpus in each evaluation task are marked in bold.

turn attention away from evaluating coherence of topics and towards evaluating the language model itself. We conduct the same task but manually construct the intrusion sets from words which are known, a priori, to belong to specified topics. The topics used in this research comprised of lists of articles from Finnish language Wikipedia. In total, 16 lists were extracted, including lists of sports, illnesses, minerals, and professions, among others. The lists contained 4127 unique items in total. In order to evaluate the language model and not the underlying corpus, only words which had a vector representation in the language model under evaluation were included in the intrusion sets.

Following (Chang et al., 2009), the size of the intrusion set was set to 6 words, where 5 words are randomly sampled from word list A and one outlier word from list B. The intrusion task is conducted 10 000 times with each ordered pair of the given lists. This was done to increase the task's reliability by reducing effects arising from random sampling of words from variable-length lists. A models score is the overall percentage of correctly determined intruder words.

3 Results

To demonstrate the evaluation methods in effect, results on multiple distributional language models are presented in Table 2. Out of vocabulary rates are reported for each task given a corpus.[3] The Gutenberg corpus has the highest OOV rate in all tasks, suggesting that these evaluation sets function best with models built from contemporary corpora.

---

[3]OOV words were excluded from similarity and intrusion tasks but included and counted as errors in the analogy task.

While the performance of different models is varied between different tasks and corpora, some trends can be observed. The word2vec Skip-gram and fastText models appear to produce better results compared to GloVe and word2vec-CBOW models. Conceptual relations as measured by the analogy task are best captured from Wikipedia corpus, while the large social media corpus of Suomi24 achieves the best correspondence with human similarity judgments.

4 Conclusions

In this study, Finnish language resources for evaluating semantic accuracy of language models were presented. Such resources are necessary for optimizing language model construction and they give researchers quantifiable estimates for the extent in which models are able to capture meaning from data. The resources constructed include a similarity judgment resource FinnSim-300, an analogy test set, and a word intrusion test set. Future research is encouraged to expand and adapt the resources because corpus and domain-specific test sets are likely to be more appropriate for most evaluations. While the presented methods serve as a starting point for evaluating semantic accuracy, a thorough discussion on what aspects of semantics can be reliably quantified is needed. Good performance in evaluation tasks provides basis for the claim that computational models can indeed be valid and reliable models of semantics.

References

Eneko Agirre, Enrique Alfonseca, Keith Hall, Jana Kravalova, Marius Paşca, and Aitor Soroa. 2009. A study on similarity and relatedness using distributional and wordnet-based approaches. In *Proceedings of Human Language Technologies: The 2009 Annual Conference of the North American Chapter of the Association for Computational Linguistics*, pages 19–27. Association for Computational Linguistics.

Eneko Agirrea, Carmen Baneab, Daniel Cerd, Mona Diabe, Aitor Gonzalez-Agirrea, Rada Mihalceab, German Rigaua, Janyce Wiebef, and Basque Country Donostia. 2016. Semeval-2016 task 1: Semantic textual similarity, monolingual and cross-lingual evaluation. *Proceedings of SemEval*, pages 497–511.

Martin L Albert, Avinoam Reches, and Ruth Silverberg. 1975. Associative visual agnosia without alexia. *Neurology*, 25(4):322–326.

Aller Media Oy. 2014. The Suomi 24 Corpus. May 14th 2015 version, retrieved October 27, 2016 from http://urn.fi/urn:nbn:fi:lb-201412171.

Mohit Bansal, Kevin Gimpel, and Karen Livescu. 2014. Tailoring continuous word representations for dependency parsing. In *ACL (2)*, pages 809–815.

Marco Baroni, Georgiana Dinu, and Germán Kruszewski. 2014. Don't count, predict! A systematic comparison of context-counting vs. context-predicting semantic vectors. In *ACL (1)*, pages 238–247.

Piotr Bojanowski, Edouard Grave, Armand Joulin, and Tomas Mikolov. 2016. Enriching word vectors with subword information. *arXiv preprint arXiv:1607.04606*.

Igor Brigadir, Derek Greene, and Pádraig Cunningham. 2015. Analyzing discourse communities with distributional semantic models. In *Proceedings of the ACM Web Science Conference*, page 27. ACM.

Elia Bruni, Gemma Boleda, Marco Baroni, and Nam-Khanh Tran. 2012. Distributional semantics in technicolor. In *Proceedings of the 50th Annual Meeting of the Association for Computational Linguistics: Long Papers-Volume 1*, pages 136–145. Association for Computational Linguistics.

Ruth Campbell and Efisia Sais. 1995. Accelerated metalinguistic (phonological) awareness in bilingual children. *British Journal of Developmental Psychology*, 13(1):61–68.

Jonathan Chang, Sean Gerrish, Chong Wang, Jordan L Boyd-Graber, and David M Blei. 2009. Reading tea leaves: How humans interpret topic models. In *Advances in Neural Information Processing Systems 21 (NIPS)*, pages 288–296.

Billy Chiu, Anna Korhonen, and Sampo Pyysalo. 2016. Intrinsic evaluation of word vectors fails to predict extrinsic performance. In *Proceedings of the 1st Workshop on Evaluating Vector Space Representations for NLP*, pages 1–6. Association for Computational Linguistics.

Lev Finkelstein, Evgeniy Gabrilovich, Yossi Matias, Ehud Rivlin, Zach Solan, Gadi Wolfman, and Eytan Ruppin. 2001. Placing search in context: The concept revisited. In *Proceedings of the 10th international conference on World Wide Web*, pages 406–414. ACM.

Michael Gamon. 2004. Sentiment classification on customer feedback data: noisy data, large feature vectors, and the role of linguistic analysis. In *Proceedings of the 20th international conference on Computational Linguistics*, page 841. Association for Computational Linguistics.

Zellig S Harris. 1954. Distributional structure. *Word*, 10(2-3):146–162.

Felix Hill, Roi Reichart, and Anna Korhonen. 2015. SimLex-999: Evaluating semantic models with (genuine) similarity estimation. *Computational Linguistics*, 41(4):665–695.

Andrej Karpathy and Li Fei-Fei. 2015. Deep visual-semantic alignments for generating image descriptions. In *Proceedings of the IEEE Conference on Computer Vision and Pattern Recognition*, pages 3128–3137.

Ira Leviant and Roi Reichart. 2015. Separated by an un-common language: Towards judgment language informed vector space modeling. *CoRR*, abs/1508.00106.

Odd Ivar Lindland, Guttorm Sindre, and Arne Solvberg. 1994. Understanding quality in conceptual modeling. *IEEE software*, 11(2):42–49.

Tomas Mikolov, Kai Chen, Greg Corrado, and Jeffrey Dean. 2013a. Efficient estimation of word representations in vector space. *arXiv preprint arXiv:1301.3781*.

Tomas Mikolov, Ilya Sutskever, Kai Chen, Greg Corrado, and Jeffrey Dean. 2013b. Distributed representations of words and phrases and their compositionality. In *Advances in neural information processing systems*, pages 3111–3119.

Nikola Mrkšić, Diarmuid Ó Séaghdha, Blaise Thomson, Milica Gašić, Lina Rojas-Barahona, Pei-Hao Su, David Vandyke, Tsung-Hsien Wen, and Steve Young. 2016. Counter-fitting word vectors to linguistic constraints. In *Proceedings of NAACL-HLT*, pages 142–148. Association for Computational Linguistics.

Jeffrey Pennington, Richard Socher, and Christopher D. Manning. 2014. GloVe: Global vectors for word representation. In *Empirical Methods in Natural Language Processing (EMNLP)*, pages 1532–1543.

Project Gutenberg. n.d. Retrieved October 27, 2016 from www.gutenberg.org.

Carlo Strapparava and Rada Mihalcea. 2007. Semeval-2007 task 14: Affective text. In *Proceedings of the 4th International Workshop on Semantic Evaluations*, pages 70–74. Association for Computational Linguistics.

Fei Sun, Jiafeng Guo, Yanyan Lan, Jun Xu, and Xueqi Cheng. 2016. Semantic regularities in document representations. *arXiv preprint arXiv:1603.07603*.

Viljami Venekoski, Samir Puuska, and Jouko Vankka. 2016. Vector space representations of documents in classifying finnish social media texts. In *Proceesings of the 22nd International Conference on Information and Software Technologies, ICIST 2016*, pages 525–535. Springer.

Wikimedia Foundation. n.d. Wikipedia – the free encyclopedia. 2016-10-20 dump, retrieved October 27, 2016 from https://dumps.wikimedia.org/fiwiki/20161020/.

Ylilauta. 2011. Ylilauta Corpus. March 4 2015 version, retrieved October 27, 2016 from http://urn.fi/urn:nbn:fi:lb-2015031802.

Málrómur: A Manually Verified Corpus of Recorded Icelandic Speech

Steinþór Steingrímsson
The Árni Magnússon
Institute for
Icelandic Studies
steinst@hi.is

Jón Guðnason
Reykjavik University
jg@ru.is

Sigrún Helgadóttir
The Árni Magnússon
Institute for
Icelandic Studies
sigruhel@hi.is

Eiríkur Rögnvaldsson
Department
of Icelandic
University of Iceland
eirikur@hi.is

Abstract

This paper describes the Málrómur corpus, an open, manually verified, Icelandic speech corpus. The recordings were collected in 2011–2012 by Reykjavik University and the Icelandic Center for Language Technology in cooperation with Google. 152 hours of speech were recorded from 563 participants. The recordings were subsequently manually inspected by evaluators listening to all the segments, determining whether any given segment contains the utterance the participant was supposed to read, and nothing else. Out of 127,286 recorded segments 108,568 were approved and 18,718 deemed unsatisfactory.

1   Introduction

A common way to gather speech corpora for automatic speech recognition is to build a large list of sentences that are then read and recorded by a large number of people. Ideally, the sentence list provides a good coverage of the language structure and the number of people is large enough to capture the acoustic and phonetic variation present in the spoken language. Each recording in the corpus is accompanied by its text transcription and possibly additional metadata, such as the speaker's gender, age, or recording conditions. The recordings are then commonly used in a supervised learning algorithm to produce an acoustic model for automatic speech recognition systems.

The quality of the trained model depends both on the quality of the recordings, and on the correctness of their transcriptions. Errors in speech corpora will lead to degraded acoustic models. Verifying the correctness of the data in a speech corpus increases its quality.

Almannarómur, a free Icelandic speech corpus, was created in 2011–2012 (Guðnason et al.,

2012). The data were recorded in cooperation with Google, on Android G1 phones using Datahound (Hughes et al., 2010). The main aim of the project was to create a database of spoken sentences to aid development of automatic speech recognition for Icelandic. However, the database can be used for many other types of spoken language technologies.

We created and executed a procedure to verify the recordings in Almannarómur. It was evident that a proportion of the Almannarómur recordings was flawed. The most prominent errors occur when the participants read the prompts only in part, read them incorrectly or say something completely different. Recordings are also sometimes incomplete, starting too late or stopping too early. The purpose of our verification process was to create a subset of a raw speech corpus that is as close to being 100% correct as possible. This was done by manually checking and verifying all the recordings. Manual verification of speech recordings can be a tedious and time consuming task so we designed a simple workflow, which could be used both for verification by an individual and by a group, and requires very little instruction.

All the recordings, along with the results of the verification process and other relevant metadata, are published with a CC BY 4.0 license[1] on a website for Icelandic Language Technology (LT) resources[2], *Málföng* (Helgadóttir and Rögnvaldsson, 2013), under the name *Málrómur*.

2   Evaluating the Speech Corpus

The process starts by pre-processing the recordings. The recordings then enter a two stage verification process and finally the accuracy of the verification is evaluated.

---

[1] http://www.malfong.is
[2] https://creativecommons.org/

Proceedings of the 21st Nordic Conference of Computational Linguistics, pages 237–240,
Gothenburg, Sweden, 23-24 May 2017. ©2017 Linköping University Electronic Press

2.1 Pre-Processing the Data

Before the verification process starts, we created new sound files by automatically trimming long periods of silence at the beginning and end of the recordings. By this we achieve two objectives. 1) The manual verification process takes less time. The total duration of the untrimmed files is 151 hours, 55 minutes and 26 seconds. The total duration of the trimmed files is 90 hours, 16 minutes and 4 seconds. The duration of the trimmed files is thus only 59% of the original files' duration. 2) Recordings that are expected to contain no speech can be identified as being completely truncated in this process and removed from the working database for the verification.

To reduce bandwidth and loading times during data verification, the audio is transcoded into smaller files using a lossy codec.

2.2 Data Verification

In the verification process, the recordings are played back to an evaluator who then classifies them according to given criteria. For a recording to be verified as correct it has to be read correctly and clearly and have no additional speech before or after it. Vocal segregates (e.g. uh, um, ah, eh) are an exception, they are allowed when they occur before the prompt is read, if there is a clear pause in between. Background noise is also allowed if it is clearly lower than the read segment.

To make the process as simple as possible for the evaluators, a web-based system was implemented for these tasks, using PyBossa[3], a crowd-sourcing environment. Due to the decentralized nature of the setup, evaluators are not bound to a physical workplace and, furthermore, collaboration of many hired evaluators and/or volunteers is easily achievable. No training is required, the guidelines for the evaluators can be explained in less than five minutes.

We set the evaluation up as a two stage process, designed so that we could build up a database of verified recordings as fast as possible. In the first stage the trimmed recordings, as described in Section 2.1, are used. Most of the recordings are expected to be correct so we only give the evaluators two choices. If a recording meets the criteria described above it is to be accepted as correct. If not it should be rejected.

____
[3] http://pybossa.com

In the second stage, recordings that were rejected in stage one are categorized into five categories: 1) Unclear – unclear, inaudible and silent recordings. 2) Incomplete – recording begins or ends during the reading of the prompt. 3) Additional Speech – read correctly, but there is additional speech before or after. 4) Incorrectly Read – but clear and sensible. 5) Correct – truncated file is flawed or the recording was incorrectly marked as flawed in stage one.

As the data pre-processing can generate errors of type 2 – Incomplete, the non-trimmed audio is used for playback in the second stage.

The time spent on the verification was logged. The logs give insight into the workload of the process and make it possible to estimate the duration of future verifications.

The process allows for each recording to be checked multiple times by different evaluators, which would likely reduce verification errors. The process also makes it possible to crowdsource the evaluation process. Using the workload calculations from this project the cost of doing more than one pass of evaluation and the feasibility of trying to crowdsource the work can be estimated.

Four evaluators worked on verifying the speech data in stage one and two. Each recording was only checked once, by one evaluator. Four other evaluators then estimated the accuracy of the evaluation process by listening to a subset of 3000 recordings and classifying them. All the accuracy evaluators listened to all the 3000 files, so each of the 3000 files was checked four times. The accuracy evaluators listened to the original untrimmed recordings and the results were compared to the classification in stage one.

3 Results

Total files recorded were 127,286. Failed recordings were 5,401, thus 121,885 were pre-processed. Out of these, 2,795 were identified as silent by the truncating process. Therefore, 119,090 recorded segments were to be verified.

In stage one, four evaluators listened to the recordings. 100,020 recordings were accepted as correct, and 19,070 were rejected and sent to stage two (see Table 1). Total duration af the segments labelled as correct was 136 hours.

There are three types of utterances in the corpus. Single word utterances, multiword utterances and internet domain names. There were considerably fewer errors for single word utterances and domain names than for multiword utterances, as illustrated in Table 1.

Utterance type	Correct	Total	Correct (%)
Single Word	30,670	35,262	(86.98%)
Multiword	58,053	71,092	(81.66%)
Web Domain	11,297	12,736	(88.70%)
Total	100,020	119,090	(83.99%)

Table 1: Stage one results for different utterance types.

The results obtained by each of the evaluators range from 18.6% to 19.3% error rate. Taking into account that the evaluators did not listen to the same ratio of each of the three utterance categories (see Table 1), this range should not be surprising.

In stage two, two evaluators listened to the original untrimmed 19,070 recordings. The evaluators classified each of the recordings into one of five classes, as described in Section 2.2. In this round 8,548 recordings, or 45% of the recordings previously classified as incorrect, were classified as correct, giving a total of 10,522 incorrect recordings, classified by four types of error:

Class	Count	(%)
Unclear	1,381	(7.24%)
Incomplete	5,526	(28.98%)
Additional Speech	592	(3.10%)
Incorrectly Read	3,023	(15.85%)
Correct	8,548	(44.82%)
Total	19,070	(100.00%)

Table 2: Stage two results.

Average time spent on each recorded segment in stage one was 4.2 sec. In stage two, the two evaluators spent 7.1 sec on average verifying each segment. By multiplying that duration with the total number of recorded segments entering stage one, we can approximate the time saved by verifying the data in two stages to be in the vicinity of 58 hours, compared to using the method in stage two for all the recordings.

In order to evaluate the correctness of the verification process four new evaluators listened to 3000 recordings as described in section 2.2. Their results were compared to that of the verification process in stage one. Out of the 3000 recordings

1509 had previously been classified as correct and 1491 had been classified as incorrect. Accuracy evaluation is shown in table 3.

Evaluation	Stage One Correct	Stage One Incorrect
Correct	1,499	726
Incorrect	10	765
Agreement	99.34%	51.31%

Table 3: Evaluating accuracy of stage one verification.

The recordings classified as correct in the verification process were classified in the same way in 99.34% of the cases in the correctness evaluation. Recordings classified as incorrect were classified the same way 51.31% of the time by the correctness evaluators. The ratio of segments previously marked as incorrect, but which the correctness evaluators mark as correct is not far from the ratio in stage two of the verification process, as evident by comparing tables 2 and 3. This is expected as the same kind of data was being evaluated, in both cases the original, untrimmed recordings. The trimmed versions of the same recordings were rejected in stage one. This may indicate that in the pre-processing trimming phase the threshold for cutting silent segments was set too low. Further tweaking of the parameters might have resulted in better results.

4 Availability and Use

The final, verified corpus is published on the Icelandic LT website *Málföng* under a permissive license (CC BY 4.0) to promote research and development using this Icelandic language resource. The recordings are made available for download as recorded, in 16 kHz WAV-format, accompanied by all relevant metadata: duration of recording in file, environment conditions, gender of speaker, age of speaker, prompt text and class determined by the verification process described in this paper and listed in table 2.

5 Conclusion and Further Work

We have determined that out of the 121,885 speech segments that were successfully recorded in the Almannarómur project, 108,568 files, or 89%, were verified to be correct.

The accuracy evaluation shows that over 99% of recordings classified as correct in stage one were verified to be correct. Having a corpus that has such a low ratio of incorrect data will be of great benefit for users of speech corpora.

About 51% of the recordings classified as incorrect were verified as incorrect by the accuracy evaluators (see Table 3). This is in line with the results of stage two of the verification process, where about 55% of the recordings previously classified as incorrect in stage one were verified as such (see Table 2). The reason for this is that in stage one trimmed recordings were used for classification but in the accuracy evaluation and in stage two untrimmed recordings were used. It was important to use the untrimmed recordings for evaluating accuracy of stage one verification to see the accuracy of the data classification rather than just the accuracy of the four stage one evaluators.

We have shown that rather than verifying speech data in one stage with no pre-processing, manual verification of a speech corpus can be done faster by using a two stage verification process after pre-processing. The pre-processing includes trimming the files used for the first stage of verification and removing recordings identified as silent.

Gathering information about different types of errors is important, as analysis of errors in the incorrect data may allow to identify patterns the incorrect recordings exhibit. This can give feedback to adjust the prompt selection or recording setup to improve the correctness of further recordings.

One error class in stage two, type 3 errors – Additional Speech, could be processed further in a third stage. These rejected recordings include correct utterances but they are preceded and/or followed by unwanted speech. The recording could be cropped and the good part of the segment added to the correct recordings. This has not been done as a part of this project, but it would be worthwhile to estimate how much time is needed to crop the recordings in a third stage.

The *Málrómur* corpus is the largest of its kind for Icelandic and is already being used for training an Icelandic speech recognizer. It will also be used to develop tools helping corpus creators to automatically evaluate the correctness of new Icelandic speech data.

References

Jón Guðnason, Oddur Kjartansson, Jökull Jóhannsson, Elín Carstensdóttir, Hannes Högni Vilhjálmsson, Hrafn Loftsson, Sigrún Helgadóttir, Kristín M. Jóhannsdóttir, and Eiríkur Rögnvaldsson. 2012. Almannarómur: An Open Icelandic Speech Corpus. In *Proceedings of SLTU '12, 3rd Workshop on Spoken Languages Technologies for Under-Resourced Languages*, Cape Town, South Africa.

Sigrún Helgadóttir and Eiríkur Rögnvaldsson. 2013. Language Resources for Icelandic. In K. De Smedt, L. Borin, K. Lindén, B. Maegaard, E. Rögnvaldsson, and K. Vider, editors, *Proceedings of the Workshop on Nordic Language Research Infrastructure at NODALIDA 2013*, pages 60–76. NEALT Proceedings Series 20. Linköping Electronic Conference Proceedings, Linköping, Sweden.

Thad Hughes, Kaisuke Nakajima, Linne Ha, Atul Vasu, Pedro Moreno, and Mike LeBeau. 2010. Building Transcribed Speech Corpora Quickly and Cheaply for Many Languages. In *Proceedings of the 11th Annual Conference of the International Speech Communication Association (INTERSPEECH 2010)*, pages 1914–1917, Makuhari, Chiba, Japan.

The Effect of Translationese on Tuning for Statistical Machine Translation

Sara Stymne
Department of Linguistics and Philology
Uppsala University
`sara.stymne@lingfil.uu.se`

Abstract

We explore how the translation direction in the tuning set used for statistical machine translation affects the translation results. We explore this issue for three language pairs. While the results on different metrics are somewhat conflicting, using tuning data translated in the same direction as the translation systems tends to give the best length ratio and Meteor scores for all language pairs. This tendency is confirmed in a small human evaluation.

1 Introduction

Translationese is a term that is used to describe the special characteristics of translated texts, as opposed to originally authored tests (Gellerstam, 1986). Translations are different from original texts, which can be due both to influences from the source language and as a result of the translation process itself. For instance, texts that are translated tends to have shorter sentences and a lower type/token ratio than original texts, and explicitate information, for instance by using more cohesive markers than in original texts (Lembersky, 2013). Several studies have shown that it is possible to use text classification techniques to distinguish between original and translated texts with high accuracy (Baroni and Bernardini, 2006; Volansky et al., 2015), further supporting that there is a clear difference between original and translated texts. However, the domain of the text interacts to a high degree with translationese identification (Rabinovich and Wintner, 2015).

Translationese has been shown to have an effect in relation to the training of statistical machine translation (SMT) systems, where the best results are seen when the texts used for training the SMT system have been translated in the same direction as that of the SMT system. This has been shown both for the translation model (TM) (Kurokawa et al., 2009; Lembersky et al., 2012; Joelsson, 2016) and for the language model (LM) for which it is better to use translated than original texts (Lembersky et al., 2011). It works nearly as well to use predicted translationese as known translationese, both for the LM and TM (Twitto et al., 2015). It has also been noted that the original language of the test sentences influences the Bleu score of translations (Holmqvist et al., 2009).

Besides the data used for the LM and TM, another important text for SMT training is the data used for tuning. The tuning set is used for tuning, or optimizing, the log-linear feature weights of the models, such as TM, LM, and reordering models. It is small compared to the other training data, and usually contains a couple of thousands of sentences, as opposed to millions of sentences for the LM and TM. It is supposed to be representative of the test set. To the best of our knowledge the effect of translationese has not previously been studied with respect to the tuning set.

We investigate the effect of the translation direction in the tuning text. We explore this for translation between English on one side, and German, French, and Czech on the other side, for the news domain. There is a tendency that tuning in the same direction as the SMT system performs best, especially as measured by length ratio and Meteor.

2 Experimental setup

To facilitate presentation we will use the abbreviations O for original texts and T for translated texts, and the term *foreign* to represent either of the languages German, French, and Czech.

2.1 Data

We use data from the WMT shared tasks of News translation between 2008–2013 (Bojar et

Proceedings of the 21st Nordic Conference of Computational Linguistics, pages 241–246,
Gothenburg, Sweden, 23-24 May 2017. ©2017 Linköping University Electronic Press

al., 2013).[1] This data includes the 5 languages English, German, Spanish, French, and Czech. The test and tuning sets contains roughly an equal amount of segments, normally a sentence, originally written in each language. We collected all test and tuning data from 2008–2013, a total of 17093 segments, and split it based on the original language of each text. The lowest number of segments for any source language is 2825. To have balanced sets we randomly selected 1412 segments from each original language for the test and tuning sets, respectively. We also created a mixed test set with segments from all five original source languages. The mixed and from-English sets are parallel across the language pairs, whereas the from-*foreign* sets are different for each language.

For the test set we follow previous research, that have either used a test set translated in the same direction as the SMT system, which mimics a realistic translation scenario, where we normally have an original text we want to translate, or a mixed test set, which is a common situation in MT evaluation campaigns. For tuning we use tuning texts originally written in English and *foreign*. We also tune systems for all 5 original languages, and create a custom system for the mixed test set, where for each sentence we use the tuning weights that matches the original language of that sentence.

Table 2.1 shows the length ratio of the number of words between the *foreign* and English side of the tuning and test sets. For all languages there is a large ratio difference depending on the direction of translation. The *foreign* texts are always relatively longer when translated from English than compared to being originally authored and translated to English. The actual ratios are different between the language pairs, though, where French has more words than English, Czech has fewer words than English, and for German it depends on the translation direction. The translationese in this news corpus, though, counted in words, is always relatively longer than originally authored texts, which is not a tendency that has been stressed in previous research on translationese. The ratios for the test and tuning corpus are similar in all cases except for Czech→English.

---

[1]Until 2013 the WMT test and tuning sets were parallel between all languages in the workshop, allowing us to use a five-way parallel corpus. From 2014 texts are parallel only per language pair, with no texts authored in a third language. In addition the language pairs used partly changed from 2014.

Data set	Original	German	French	Czech
Tuning	*Foreign*	0.88	1.07	0.79
	English	1.03	1.16	0.92
Test	*Foreign*	0.90	1.09	0.85
	English	1.03	1.17	0.95
	Mixed	0.98	1.14	0.88

Table 1: Ratio of *foreign* to English words for sets with different original language.

2.2 SMT system

We use Moses (Koehn et al., 2007) to train standard phrase-based SMT systems. For German↔English we use word and POS-tag factors (Koehn and Hoang, 2007) and have LMs for both; for the other language pairs we only use words. KenLM (Heafield, 2011) was used to train a 5-gram word LM and SRILM (Stolcke, 2002) was used to train a 7-gram POS LM. Tagging was performed using Tree Tagger (Schmid, 1994). For training we used Europarl and News commentary, provided by WMT, with a total of over 2M segments for German and French and .77M for Czech. For English→German we used additional data: bilingual Common Crawl (1.5M) and monolingual News (83M).

For tuning we used MERT (Och, 2003) as implemented in Moses, optimized towards the Bleu metric (Papineni et al., 2002). For each tuning condition we ran tuning three times and show the mean result, in order to account for optimizer instability (Clark et al., 2011). For the manual analysis we use the system with the median Bleu score.

2.3 Evaluation

In much of the work on translationese, with the exception of Lembersky (2013), only Bleu (Papineni et al., 2002) has been used for evaluation. Bleu has its limitations though, and to give a somewhat more thorough evaluation we also show results on Meteor (Denkowski and Lavie, 2010) and TER (Snover et al., 2006). These metrics capture somewhat different aspects of MT quality. Bleu is mainly based on the precision of n-grams up to length 4, and thus rewards local fluency highly. Meteor is based on a weighted F-score on unigrams, with a matching step that consider word forms, stems, synonyms (for English), and paraphrases with different weights for content and function words, and a fragmentation score. It is thus less sensitive than Bleu to allowable linguistic variation. Meteor is also tuned for different target languages, to increase correlation with human evaluation scores. TER is an extension of the Levenshtein distance, with the addition of a shift operation to account for movement. Like Bleu, TER only considers exact word form matches. We also give the length ratio (LR), counted as the number of words, of the translation hypothesis relative to the reference text.

In addition we perform a small human evaluation on a sample of segments for German→English translation. For each setting, we randomly picked 100 segments of length 10–15 words. One annotator compared the output from two systems for overall quality. Using only short segments can introduce a bias, since they might not be representative for all segments (Stymne and Ahrenberg, 2012), but it has the trade-off of being much faster and more consistent.

3   Results

Table 2 shows the results on the O→T test set. The scores are obviously different for the different language pairs, which are due to both differences between the languages, differences in the use of training data and factors in the SMT systems, and for from-*foreign*, different test sets.

The differences between O→T and T→O are often large, with up to 1.5 Bleu points difference for English–German. This is quite notable since the actual models in the SMT systems are identical; the only difference is in the weights balancing the models and features of the SMT system. For all language pairs, except Czech–English, the length ratio for O→T tuning is around 1, which is desired, and much lower for T→O tuning. That this is not the case for Czech–English is most likely due to the fact that the length ratios in the O→T tuning and test sets were different. On the metrics, however, the scores are somewhat conflicting. In most cases Bleu and Meteor have the best scores for O→T tuning, whereas the scores for TER are the worst. For Czech–English the two systems have the same Bleu score, which probably is due to the long length ratio with O→T tuning. For French–English O→T tuning gives a better TER score than T→O tuning. This is an exception to the pattern, for which we do not yet have an explanation.

Table 3 shows the results on the mixed test set. For all language pairs, the pattern is the same on this test set as regards Meteor, which is higher for O→T tuning, and TER which is lower for O→T tuning. The length ratio is always low with T→O tuning. For O→T tuning, it is around 1 for from-English, but always high for from-*foreign*. Bleu is better on O→T than T→O tuning for four out of the six translation directions.

Table 3 also includes a custom system, where the tuning direction was chosen separately for each sentence based on its original language. We would expect this system to give the best results on this test set, since it is optimized for each language direction, but again the results are conflicting. It overall gives a good length ratio, though, and has the best or (near)-equal Bleu score to the O→T tuning. The TER score is always between that of T→O and O→T tuning. The Meteor score, however, is always lower for the custom system than for O→T tuning, which might indicate that there is some advantage with O→T tuning that shows up when using the flexible matching in Meteor.

To get some further insight we performed a small, thus quite limited, human evaluation for German→English. A comparison on the O→T test set, between O→T and T→O tuning is shown in Table 4. The O→T system is preferred more often than the T→O system, even though the segments were often of equal quality. The difference is significant at the 0.01-level, using a two-sided sign test. This gives at least some indication that O→T is indeed the preferred system, as Bleu, Meteor and the length ratio suggests in most cases. Table 5 shows a comparison between custom and O→T tuning on the mixed test set. In this case the translations are similar to an even larger extent, and we can find no difference between the systems. This might indicate that Bleu punishes the longer O→T system too harshly. In both cases there is no agreement between TER and the human evaluation.

Overall it seems that TER rewards very short translations; the shortest translation for each setting always has the best TER score. According to our, very limited, human evaluation, short translations should not be rewarded. On the other hand the longest system in each setting always has the best Meteor score, which is in contrast to Bleu, which generally prefers translations with a length ratio around 1. This is likely because Meteor takes recall into account, as opposed to Bleu, which is only based on precision and a brevity penalty. Long translations might be good, if they explici-

Tuning	English–German				English–French				English–Czech			
	Bleu↑	Meteor↑	TER↓	LR	Bleu↑	Meteor↑	TER↓	LR	Bleu↑	Meteor↑	TER↓	LR
O→T	**21.0**	**42.0**	61.4	**1.00**	**22.3**	**51.3**	57.6	**0.99**	**13.6**	**20.8**	70.0	**0.97**
T→O	19.5	39.3	**59.0**	0.89	21.8	50.4	**56.3**	0.94	12.5	19.7	**68.3**	0.88
	German–English				French–English				Czech–English			
O→T	**20.5**	**28.4**	62.4	**1.00**	**26.9**	**35.7**	**50.1**	**1.02**	**18.8**	**28.9**	66.2	1.06
T→O	19.8	27.8	**59.2**	0.90	25.8	33.9	51.0	0.95	**18.8**	28.1	**62.1**	**0.95**

Table 2: Metric scores and length ratio on the O→T test set.

Tuning	English–German				English–French				English–Czech			
	Bleu↑	Meteor↑	TER↓	LR	Bleu↑	Meteor↑	TER↓	LR	Bleu↑	Meteor↑	TER↓	LR
O→T	17.2	**38.1**	67.9	1.02	**20.4**	**49.7**	60.3	**0.99**	**13.0**	**20.6**	71.9	**1.00**
T→O	16.5	36.1	**64.3**	0.91	20.0	48.9	**59.1**	0.95	12.4	19.9	**69.5**	0.92
Custom	**17.7**	38.0	66.7	**1.00**	**20.4**	49.6	59.8	0.98	**13.0**	20.5	70.5	0.97
	German–English				French–English				Czech–English			
O→T	17.2	**28.1**	69.1	1.09	**18.6**	**31.3**	62.2	1.05	18.0	**28.9**	68.0	1.08
T→O	18.4	27.7	**63.3**	0.97	18.0	30.0	**60.9**	0.98	18.2	28.1	**63.9**	0.96
Custom	**18.5**	27.8	64.8	**1.01**	18.5	30.7	61.1	**1.02**	**18.6**	28.7	65.5	**1.02**

Table 3: Metric scores and length ratio on the mixed test set.

Equal	Equal quality	O→T better	T→O better
28	37	26	9

Table 4: Human comparison of O→T and T→O tuning for German-English O→T test set.

Equal	Equal quality	O→T better	Custom better
51	26	12	11

Table 5: Human comparison of O→T and custom tuning for German-English mixed test set.

cate information in a good way. We doubt, however, that this is what Meteor rewards, since it, like the other metrics, is based on matching towards one reference translation. We believe that a situation like this, when the lengths of the two systems to be compared are very different, is very difficult for automatic metrics to handle in a fair way.

4   Conclusion

In this paper we have investigated the effect of translationese on SMT tuning for three language pairs. We found that across language pairs, using tuning texts translated in the same original direction as the SMT system tended to give a better length ratio, Meteor score, and often a better Bleu score. However, the very short translations that were the result of tuning with a text translated in the opposite direction were preferred by the TER metric. We also explored a custom system, with tuning in the same direction as each test sentence, which overall performed on par with the system with tuning in the same direction. A small human evaluation confirmed that tuning in the same direction was preferable to the opposite direction, but performed on par with custom tuning.

As the study was relatively small we think there is a need for extending it to more language pairs, other domains than news, and other tuning algorithms than MERT. We also think it would be important to do a more large-scale human evaluation. Especially we want to find out if there are other differences than length ratio, based on tuning direction, which we could not find in this small study. We would also like to extend the study of translationese to other types of MT than SMT. Specifically, we want to focus on neural MT, which have given very good translation results recently, but for which no studies of the relation to translationese have been attempted.

For most SMT research the translation direction of neither test sets nor tuning sets have been taken into account. The data from the WMT workshops, for instance, contains data sets translated from many different languages or in both directions between a pair of languages. It is well-known that tuning sets should be representative of the type of text the SMT system should be used for, but this has mostly been considered for content or domain. This study shows that at least the length ratio of the tuning set, and possibly also the translation direction, is important. This study also indicates that automatic MT metrics may not be reliable for situations where the hypotheses have very different lengths and that different metrics favor different length ratios. However, this needs to be further explored in future work. The interactions with domain should also be further investigated.

Acknowledgments

This work was supported by the Swedish strategic research programme eSSENCE.

References

Marco Baroni and Silvia Bernardini. 2006. A new approach to the study of translationese: Machine-learning the difference between original and translated text. *Literary and Linguistic Computing*, 21(3):259–274.

Ondřej Bojar, Christian Buck, Chris Callison-Burch, Christian Federmann, Barry Haddow, Philipp Koehn, Christof Monz, Matt Post, Radu Soricut, and Lucia Specia. 2013. Findings of the 2013 Workshop on Statistical Machine Translation. In *Proceedings of the Eighth Workshop on Statistical Machine Translation*, pages 1–44, Sofia, Bulgaria.

Jonathan H. Clark, Chris Dyer, Alon Lavie, and Noah A. Smith. 2011. Better hypothesis testing for statistical machine translation: Controlling for optimizer instability. In *Proceedings of the 49th Annual Meeting of the ACL: Human Language Technologies*, pages 176–181, Portland, Oregon, USA.

Michael Denkowski and Alon Lavie. 2010. METEOR-NEXT and the METEOR paraphrase tables: Improved evaluation support for five target languages. In *Proceedings of the Joint Fifth Workshop on Statistical Machine Translation and MetricsMATR*, pages 339–342, Uppsala, Sweden.

Martin Gellerstam. 1986. Translationese in Swedish novels translated from English. In Lars Wollin and Hans Lindquist, editors, *Translation Studies in Scandinavia: Proceedings from The Scandinavian Symposium on Translation Theory II*, pages 88–95. CWK Gleerup, Lund, Sweden.

Kenneth Heafield. 2011. KenLM: Faster and smaller language model queries. In *Proceedings of the Sixth Workshop on Statistical Machine Translation*, pages 187–197, Edinburgh, Scotland.

Maria Holmqvist, Sara Stymne, Jody Foo, and Lars Ahrenberg. 2009. Improving alignment for SMT by reordering and augmenting the training corpus. In *Proceedings of the Fourth Workshop on Statistical Machine Translation*, pages 120–124, Athens, Greece.

Jakob Joelsson. 2016. Translationese and Swedish-English statistical machine translation. Bachelor thesis, Uppsala University.

Philipp Koehn and Hieu Hoang. 2007. Factored translation models. In *Proceedings of the 2007 Joint Conference on Empirical Methods in Natural Language Processing and Computational Natural Language Learning*, pages 868–876, Prague, Czech Republic.

Philipp Koehn, Hieu Hoang, Alexandra Birch, Chris Callison-Burch, Marcello Federico, Nicola Bertoldi, Brooke Cowan, Wade Shen, Christine Moran, Richard Zens, Chris Dyer, Ondrej Bojar, Alexandra Constantin, and Evan Herbst. 2007. Moses: Open source toolkit for statistical machine translation. In *Proceedings of the 45th Annual Meeting of the ACL, Demo and Poster Sessions*, pages 177–180, Prague, Czech Republic.

David Kurokawa, Cyril Goutte, and Pierre Isabelle. 2009. Automatic detection of translated text and its impact on machine translation. In *Proceedings of MT Summit XII*, pages 81–88, Ottawa, Canada.

Gennadi Lembersky, Noam Ordan, and Shuly Wintner. 2011. Language models for machine translation: Original vs. translated texts. In *Proceedings of the 2011 Conference on Empirical Methods in Natural Language Processing*, pages 363–374, Edinburgh, Scotland.

Gennadi Lembersky, Noam Ordan, and Shuly Wintner. 2012. Adapting translation models to translationese improves SMT. In *Proceedings of the 13th Conference of the EACL*, pages 255–265, Avignon, France.

Gennadi Lembersky. 2013. *The Effect of Translationese on Statistical Machine Translation*. Ph.D. thesis, University of Haifa, Israel.

Franz Josef Och. 2003. Minimum error rate training in statistical machine translation. In *Proceedings of the 42nd Annual Meeting of the ACL*, pages 160–167, Sapporo, Japan.

Kishore Papineni, Salim Roukos, Todd Ward, and Wei-Jing Zhu. 2002. BLEU: A method for automatic evaluation of machine translation. In *Proceedings of the 40th Annual Meeting of the ACL*, pages 311–318, Philadelphia, Pennsylvania, USA.

Ella Rabinovich and Shuly Wintner. 2015. Unsupervised identification of translationese. *Transactions of the Association for Computational Linguistics*, 3:419–432.

Helmut Schmid. 1994. Probabilistic part-of-speech tagging using decision trees. In *Proceedings of the International Conference on New Methods in Language Processing*, pages 44–49, Manchester, UK.

Matthew Snover, Bonnie Dorr, Richard Schwartz, Linnea Micciulla, and John Makhoul. 2006. A study of translation edit rate with targeted human notation. In *Proceedings of the 7th Conference of the Association for Machine Translation in the Americas*, pages 223–231, Cambridge, Massachusetts, USA.

Andreas Stolcke. 2002. SRILM – an extensible language modeling toolkit. In *Proceedings of the Seventh International Conference on Spoken Language Processing*, pages 901–904, Denver, Colorado, USA.

Sara Stymne and Lars Ahrenberg. 2012. On the practice of error analysis for machine translation evaluation. In *Proceedings of the 8th International Conference on Language Resources and Evaluation (LREC'12)*, Istanbul, Turkey.

Naama Twitto, Noam Ordan, and Shuly Wintner. 2015. Statistical machine translation with automatic identification of translationese. In *Proceedings of the Tenth Workshop on Statistical Machine Translation*, pages 47–57, Lisbon, Portugal.

Vered Volansky, Noam Ordan, and Shuly Wintner. 2015. On the features of translationese. *Digital Scholarship in the Humanities*, 30(1):98–118.

Multilingwis[2] – Explore Your Parallel Corpus

Johannes Graën, Dominique Sandoz, Martin Volk
Institute of Computational Linguistics
University of Zurich
{graen|volk}@cl.uzh.ch, dominique.sandoz@uzh.ch

Abstract

We present Multilingwis[2], a web based search engine for exploration of word-aligned parallel and multiparallel corpora. Our application extends the search facilities by Clematide et al. (2016) and is designed to be easily employable on any parallel corpus comprising universal part-of-speech tags, lemmas and word alignments.

In addition to corpus exploration, it has proven useful for the assessment of word alignment quality. Loading the results of different alignment methods on the same corpus as different corpora into Multilingwis[2] alleviates their comparison.

1 Introduction

In (ibid.), we introduced *Multilingwis* (Multilingual Word Information System), our approach for exploring translation variants of multi-word units in multiparallel corpora. It relies on a part-of-speech tagged and word-aligned parallel corpus as source material, a *PostgreSQL* database for efficient retrieval (see Graën, Clematide, et al. 2016) and a standard web server equipped with *PHP* for the user interface. Our corpus data comes from CoStEP (Graën, Batinic, et al. 2014), which is a cleaner version of the Europarl corpus (Koehn 2005), and comprises 240 million tokens in English, German, French, Italian, and Spanish.

We, subsequently, received several requests regarding the portability of our retrieval engine and search interface to other corpora. Our decision to decouple Multilingwis from the particular data structure that our corpus had grown into and to release a version that can easily be adopted to other corpora coincided with the introduction of

---

[2]This is the second version, not a footnote number.

a proximity search operator (see Bartunov and Sigaev 2016, pp. 14–23) into PostgreSQL's full text search engine (PostgreSQL Global Development Group 2017). This led to the redesign of Multilingwis' search engine to allow for more complex searches by combining our queries with a full text search vector index.

In this paper, we describe the preparatory steps to produce the required corpus data, the functionality of Multilingwis[2] and the background of our search engine.

2 Corpus Preparation

We discriminate between content and function words and define content words to be either adjectives, adverbs, nouns or verbs, which we tell apart by means of universal part-of-speech tags (Petrov et al. 2012). Any corpus to be used with Multilingwis[2] thus requires these tags. They can be obtained directly using a tagger that produces universal tags or indirectly by mapping the language-specific tagsets to the universal one.

In addition to tagging, lemmatization is required by Multilingwis to provide a lemma-based search. The new version of our search engine is also capable to perform searches on word forms, but the resulting translation variants are always conflated to lemma sequences.

For our own corpus, we use the *TreeTagger* (Schmid 1994) for both, tagging and lemmatization and apply a subsequent lemma disambiguation algorithm similar to the one described in (Volk et al. 2016). This step reduces the amount of ambiguous lemmas, i.e. those for which the TreeTagger had seen more than one lemma during training, but some lemmas remain ambiguous. While they will not match any regular search query, they might appear in the list of translation variants, though.

Alongside those annotations, word alignments (see Tiedemann 2011, ch. 5) are crucial for Multilingwis. Any translation variant is derived from

Proceedings of the 21st Nordic Conference of Computational Linguistics, pages 247–250,
Gothenburg, Sweden, 23-24 May 2017. ©2017 Linköping University Electronic Press

the list of tokens aligned with a particular search hit. Word alignment is usually preceded by sentence alignment as word alignment tools are typically not capable of aligning whole documents.[1] For our corpus data, we used *hunalign* (Varga et al. 2005) for sentence alignment, which can be provided with a dictionary for a particular language combination, or learn the dictionary from the parallel documents using a two-pass bootstrapping approach.

Word alignment tools such as *Giza++* (Och and Ney 2003) or *fast_align* (Dyer et al. 2013) produce unidirectional alignments which need to be symmetrized to obtain symmetric alignments. This requirement does not apply to the *Berkeley Aligner* (Liang et al. 2006) whose models are trained to produce symmetric alignments in the first place. Multilingwis expects word alignments to be symmetric. Independent of whether they are symmetric or not, union symmetrization is performed during corpus initialization, which has no effect on already symmetric alignments.

Additional attributes used by Multilingwis for visualization purposes are: white spaces that have been deleted during tokenization and any meta information related to a particular document in form of attribute value pairs. All this information is optional and will merely be visualized if available.

3 Functionality

Multilingwis' search strategy used to be simple: starting from a sequence of lemmas[2], all occurrences of those lemmas in the given order and with nothing in between them but (at most three) function words were selected and the translation variants calculated on this basis (see Clematide et al. 2016, sec. 3). We now extend the search to allow for any combination of search terms. The standard search mode conforms with what most search engines do: they find documents in which all of the given terms appear. In addition, a sequence of search terms enclosed in brackets is expected to occur consecutively without any intermediate token (phrasal search expressions).

For all searches, the user can choose whether the search is based on word forms or lemmas and if

function words should be ignored. Having chosen lemma search and to ignore function words, a search where all search terms are enclosed in brackets will yield multi-word units.[3] A combination of phrasal and non-phrasal search expressions facilitates the search of multi-word expressions with flexible and fixed parts, e.g. German [in Frage] stellen *'to question'* finds "Ich möchte das in Frage stellen." *'I would like to question it.'* as well as "Keiner stellt das in Frage." *"Nobody questions it."* in our corpus, whereas in Frage stellen (without the phrasal restriction) will also yield sentences such as "Diese Frage stellt sich in der Tat." *"This question arises as a matter of fact."*.

Placeholders in phrasal search expressions provide means to express variable positions in multi-word expressions such as "to keep one's head above water". The search query [keep * head above water] will match "They use drug dealing, theft, and small-scale crime as means of keeping their heads above water." and "We have been trying to keep our heads above water for years.".

In case meta information has been provided, the attributes can serve as a filter. Europarl comprises the debates of the European Parliament, where speakers typically use their native language. The information, which language has originally been used is available in 82 % of the speaker contributions and is of great value for linguist, as we have learned in various occasions where we presented Multilingwis. By providing the original language as meta information, we enable the user to limit their search to a particular source language.

The user interface allows to select the search language. If none has been selected, Multilingwis evaluates which languages comprise the search terms as word forms or lemmas (depending on the search mode) and picks the one with the highest frequency averaged over all results. In our corpus, the search con *'with'* and calma *'rest'* (together *'at rest'* in both languages) will prefer Spanish over Italian since 'con' is much more frequent in Spanish and 'calma' shows approximately the same frequency in both languages. The third-ranked option is the combination of preposition 'con' with adjective 'calmo', which comprises 'calma' as word form. While search is performed

---

[1]Shorter sentences provide less opportunities for wrong alignment. That is why we split sentences when we come across a colon or semicolon.

[2]The user was allowed to enter any sequence of word forms, which was transformed into a sequence of lemmas by a finite-state conversion mechanism built on the corpus data.

[3]That is the only search mode in the first version of Multilingwis.

using the first-ranked option, the user can explicitly select the search language, which will perform a search based on the top-ranked option in that language.

4 Search Engine

Searches are performed by a PostgreSQL database, which not only provides fast retrieval but also performs the aggregation of individual search hits to distributions of translation variants in all languages efficiently. The import of corpora into the database is done by means of a single tabular-separated input file (similar to the CoNLL format but extended with columns for all the information specified in section 2). Parting from that import data, Multilingwis reconstructs the hierarchical structure of the corpus (documents, sentences, tokens), replaces columns involved in search (word forms, lemmas, meta information) by foreign key relationships with numerical identifiers, calculates full text search vectors on word forms and lemmas for both search modes (all tokens or content words only), and extracts and symmetrizes word alignments.

The last but most important step in preparation of the database is to index all attributes that will be used in retrieval. We create an inverted index on each text search vector, so that the index can be queried for the occurrence of all search terms (in a particular positional configuration if required by phrasal search expressions). All other attributes are indexed by standard B-tree indices. For the word alignment relation, we use a composite index as described in (Graën, Clematide, et al. 2016).

At search time, one of the inverted indices is scanned according to the search configuration and the matching tokens account for the search hits. With these hits as basis, the word alignment index is used to retrieve the tokens aligned to each of source tokens. The sequence of lemmas of those aligned tokens constitute the translation variants that are subsequently counted separately per language and build the statistics of translation variants shown in the user interface. The order of the aligned tokens makes a difference, i.e. the same set of lemmas in different orders makes for different translation variants. This is to distinguish expression like "human rights violations" and "violations of human rights".

After searching, the list of hits and aligned tokens can be inspected. The results are ordered by common shortness, i.e. shorter sentences in all languages come first.[4] The user may filter the result list for individual sets of translation variants in all languages. If there is no corpus example agreeing with the intersection of those filters, an empty list is shown.

5 Conclusions

We present Multilingwis[2], an exploration tool for parallel corpora based on word-alignment. Unlike the first version of Multilingwis, search is not limited to lemmas, and function words are not ignored per se.

Our own search engine is equipped with three different corpora: a seven-language corpus extracted from CoStEP (Graën, Batinic, et al. 2014) covering English, German, Finnish, French, Italian, Polish, and Spanish, the Text+Berg corpus (Göhring and Volk 2011) and the Bulletin corpus (Volk et al. 2016), and can be accessed at `https://pub.cl.uzh.ch/purl/multilingwis2`.

We also provide the source code and an extended installation manual at the same place. We offer Multilingwis[2] to anyone interested in using it on their own corpus.

Acknowledgments

This research was supported by the Swiss National Science Foundation under grant 105215_146781/1 through the project "SPARCLING – Large-scale Annotation and Alignment of Parallel Corpora for the Investigation of Linguistic Variation".

---

[4]The more the sentences deviate in length, the more likely they will have alignment errors.

References

Bartunov, Oleg and Teodor Sigaev (2016). "FTS is DEAD ? – Long live FTS !" https : / / www . slideshare . net / ArthurZakirov1 / better - full - text - search - in - postgresql. Accessed March 12th, 2017.

Clematide, Simon, Johannes Graën, and Martin Volk (2016). "Multilingwis – A Multilingual Search Tool for Multi-Word Units in Multiparallel Corpora". In: *Computerised and Corpus-based Approaches to Phraseology: Monolingual and Multilingual Perspectives – Fraseología computacional y basada en corpus: perspectivas monolingües y multilingües.* Ed. by Gloria Corpas Pastor. Geneva: Tradulex, pp. 447–455.

Dyer, Chris, Victor Chahuneau, and Noah A. Smith (2013). "A Simple, Fast, and Effective Reparameterization of IBM Model 2". In: *Proceedings of the Conference of the North American Chapter of the Association for Computational Linguistics: Human Language Technologies*, pp. 644–649.

Göhring, Anne and Martin Volk (2011). "The Text+Berg Corpus An Alpine French-German Parallel Resource". In: *Traitement Automatique des Langues Naturelles*, p. 63.

Graën, Johannes, Dolores Batinic, and Martin Volk (2014). "Cleaning the Europarl Corpus for Linguistic Applications". In: *Proceedings of the Conference on Natural Language Processing.* (Hildesheim). Stiftung Universität Hildesheim, pp. 222–227.

Graën, Johannes, Simon Clematide, and Martin Volk (2016). "Efficient Exploration of Translation Variants in Large Multiparallel Corpora Using a Relational Database". In: *4th Workshop on Challenges in the Management of Large Corpora Workshop Programme.* Ed. by Piotr Bański, Marc Kupietz, Harald Lüngen, et al., pp. 20–23.

Koehn, Philipp (2005). "Europarl: A parallel corpus for statistical machine translation". In: *Machine Translation Summit.* (Phuket). Vol. 5, pp. 79–86.

Liang, Percy, Ben Taskar, and Dan Klein (2006). "Alignment by Agreement". In: *Proceedings of the main conference on Human Language Technology Conference of the North American Chapter of the Association of Computational Linguistics*, pp. 104–111.

Och, Franz Josef and Hermann Ney (2003). "A Systematic Comparison of Various Statistical Alignment Models". In: *Computational linguistics* 29.1, pp. 19–51.

Petrov, Slav, Dipanjan Das, and Ryan McDonald (2012). "A Universal Part-of-Speech Tagset". In: *Proceedings of the 8th International Conference on Language Resources and Evaluation.* Ed. by Nicoletta Calzolari et al. Istanbul: European Language Resources Association (ELRA).

PostgreSQL Global Development Group (2017). *PostgreSQL 9.6 Documentation – Chapter 12. Full Text Search.* https://www.postgresql. org/docs/9.6/static/textsearch.html. Accessed March 12th, 2017.

Schmid, Helmut (1994). "Probabilistic part-of-speech tagging using decision trees". In: *Proceedings of International Conference on New Methods in Natural Language Processing.* (Manchester). Vol. 12, pp. 44–49.

Tiedemann, Jörg (2011). *Bitext Alignment.* Vol. 4. Synthesis Lectures on Human Language Technologies 2. Morgan & Claypool.

Varga, Dániel, László Németh, Péter Halácsy, András Kornai, Viktor Trón, and Viktor Nagy (2005). "Parallel corpora for medium density languages". In: *Proceedings of the Recent Advances in Natural Language Processing.* (Borovets), pp. 590–596.

Volk, Martin, Chantal Amrhein, Noëmi Aepli, Mathias Müller, and Phillip Ströbel (2016). "Building a Parallel Corpus on the World's Oldest Banking Magazine". In: *Proceedings of the Conference on Natural Language Processing.* (Bochum).

A modernised version of the Glossa corpus search system

Anders Nøklestad[1]

anders.noklestad@iln.uio.no

Janne Bondi Johannessen[1,2]

jannebj@iln.uio.no

Joel Priestley[1]

joel.priestley@iln.uio.no

Kristin Hagen[1]

kristin.hagen@iln.uio.no

Michał Kosek[1]

michal.kosek@iln.uio.no

[1]The Text Laboratory, ILN, University of Oslo, P.O. Box 1102 Blindern, N-0317 Oslo, Norway

[2]MultiLing, University of Oslo, P.O. Box 1102 Blindern, N-0317 Oslo, Norway

Abstract

This paper presents and describes a modernised version of Glossa, a corpus search and results visualisation system with a user-friendly interface. The system is open source and can be easily installed on servers or even laptops for use with suitably prepared corpora. It handles parallel corpora as well as monolingual written and spoken corpora. For spoken corpora, the search results can be linked to audio/video, and spectrographic analysis and visualised geographical distributions can be provided. We will demonstrate the range of search options and result visualisations that Glossa provides.

1 Introduction

The paper presents and describes Glossa, a corpus search and results visualisation system. Glossa is a web application that allows a user to search multilingual (parallel) corpora as well as monolingual written and spoken corpora. It provides the user with advanced search options, but at the same time great care has been taken to make the interface as user-friendly as possible. The system supports login via eduGAIN as well as local accounts. Figure 1 shows the search interface of the Lexicographic Corpus of Norwegian Bokmål.

Glossa is open source and can be freely downloaded from GitHub. It can easily be installed on servers or even laptops for use with corpora that have been suitably prepared.

Figure 1: *Leksikografisk bokmålskorpus* (Lexicographic Corpus of Norwegian Bokmål). The metadata filtering options are located to the left, the linguistic search box is in the middle.

The version of Glossa presented in this paper is a modernised, reimplemented and improved version of the search system described in Johannessen et al. (2008). Glossa is part of the CLARINO infrastructure at the Text Laboratory, University of Oslo, and is financed by the CLARINO project. In the following months, all corpora in the Text Lab portfolio will be searchable in this new version. Already, important corpora like NoWaC, CANS, NORINT, ELENOR, and the Nordic Dialect Corpus are included.

Several alternative corpus interfaces are available, see e.g. Bick (2004), Hoffmann and Evert (2006), Meurer (2012) and Borin et. al (2012). What makes Glossa special compared to

Proceedings of the 21st Nordic Conference of Computational Linguistics, pages 251–254,
Gothenburg, Sweden, 23-24 May 2017. ©2017 Linköping University Electronic Press

other systems is its combination of user friendliness, especially with respect to approachability for non-technical users, ease of installation, and a unique set of search result visualisations that includes audio and video clips, spectrographic analysis and geographical map views.

2 Technical details

The server code in Glossa is written in Clojure, a modern dialect of Lisp that runs on the Java Virtual Machine. Likewise, the client/browser code is written in ClojureScript, a variant of Clojure that is compiled to JavaScript in order to run in the browser. Metadata pertaining to texts or speakers in a corpus is recorded in a MySQL database.

Running on the JVM enables Clojure to take advantage of the huge number of libraries available in the Java ecosystem. At the same time, Clojure syntax is extremely concise compared to that of Java, and its functional rather than imperative nature typically helps reduce bugs, especially when doing parallel processing like we do in Glossa.

Glossa is agnostic with respect to search engines, and different search engines may be used for different corpora within the same Glossa installation. Out of the box, Glossa comes with built-in support for the IMS Open Corpus Workbench (CWB, with the CQP search engine) as well as the Federated Content Search mechanism defined by the CLARIN infrastructure.

Glossa is able to take advantage of multiple CPU cores by automatically splitting a corpus into a number of parts corresponding to the number of cores on the machine. This leads to a significant reduction in search time, especially for heavy searches in large corpora. Search speeds will keep increasing as the number of cores grows, since Glossa automatically utilizes all cores.

For instance, when searching for a first person pronoun followed by a past tense verb in the 700 million words NoWaC corpus, a search directly in CWB (on a single core) returns 1,190,403 occurrences in 38 seconds (measured on the second run of the same query in order to allow CWB to take advantage of any result caching). The same search in Glossa, running on the same machine but taking advantage of all of its 8 cores, returns the same results in 12 seconds, i.e., about one third of the time. Furthermore, the first 8775 results are displayed within a couple of seconds, making the perceived search speed very high.

3 Querying with Glossa

A corpus user can query the corpus for linguistic features or non-linguistic features, or a combination. Glossa offers three different search interfaces, ranging from a simple Google-like search box for simple word or phrase queries, via an extended view that allows complex, grammatical queries, to a CQP query view that allows the user to specify the CQP query expression directly, potentially taking advantage of all the sophisticated options that the CQP search engine provides, see figure 1.

The most common linguistic queries involve specifying a token by given attributes: word, lemma, start or end of word, part of speech, morphological features, and sentence position. These queries can always be done in a user-friendly way.

In (1) we exemplify what a search using a search language of regular expressions would be like, in order to search for a plural noun starting with the letter sequence *dag*. In figure 2 we see the same query in *Extended Search* in Glossa. *Noun plural* is chosen from the box in figure 3. (Example 1 is translated by Glossa into regular expressions.)

(1) [word="dag.*" %c & ((pos="noun" & num="pl"))]

All searches are done using checkboxes, pull-down menus, or writing simple letters to make words or other strings. Lists of metadata categories are conveniently located to the left of the search results, allowing the results to be gradually filtered through successive selections of metadata values (see figure 4a).

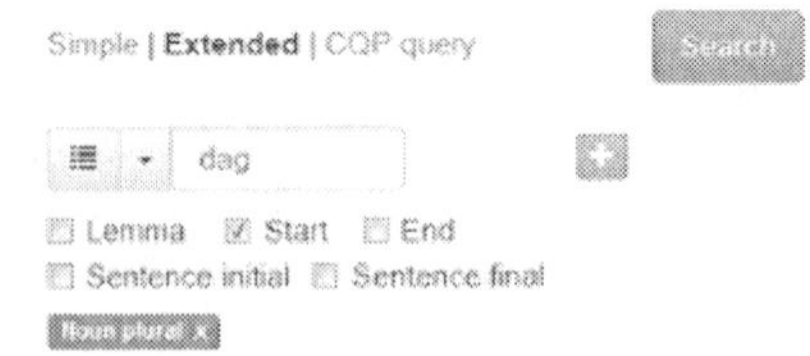

Figure 2: Extended Search in Glossa.

Figure 3: Choosing parts of speech in Glossa.

4 Result visualisations in Glossa

The default result visualisation is in the form of a concordance as in figure 5, but results can also be shown as frequencies as in figure 4b or as locations on a geographical map as in figure 6. The results can also be downloaded as Excel or CSV files.

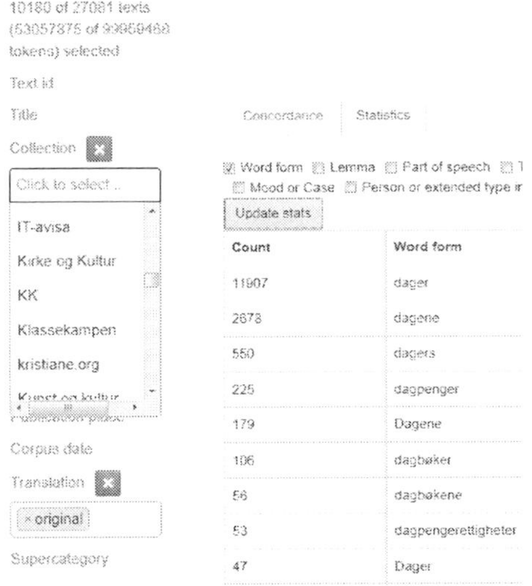

Figure 4: a) Filtering metadata in the left menu. b) Results shown as frequency list.

Figure 5: Results shown as concordance.

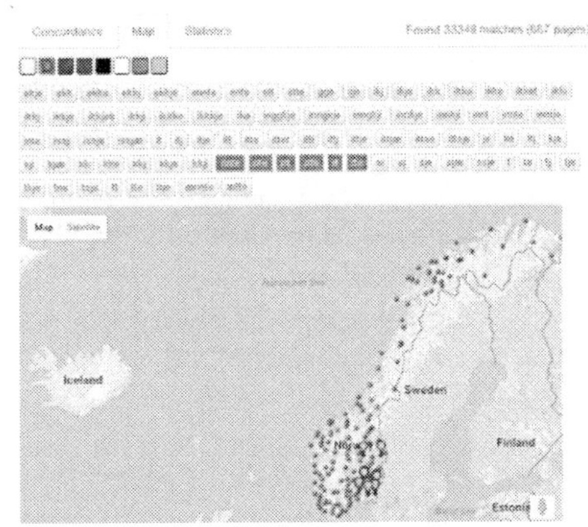

Figure 6: Geographical distribution of phonetic forms.

With spoken corpora, search results can be linked to audio and video files (figure 7), and spectrographic analysis of the sound can be displayed (figure 8).

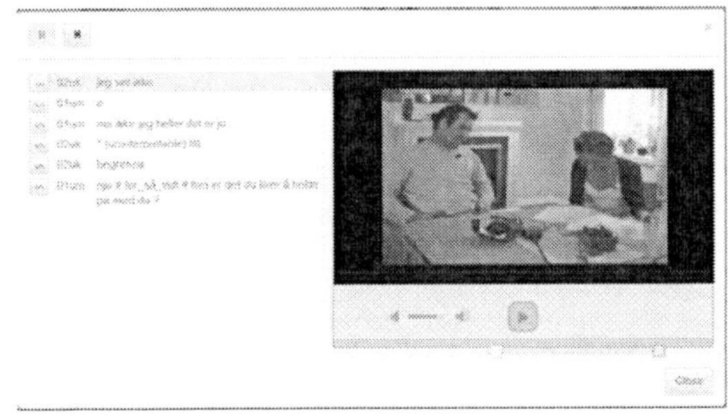

Figure 7: Video of search result with transcription.

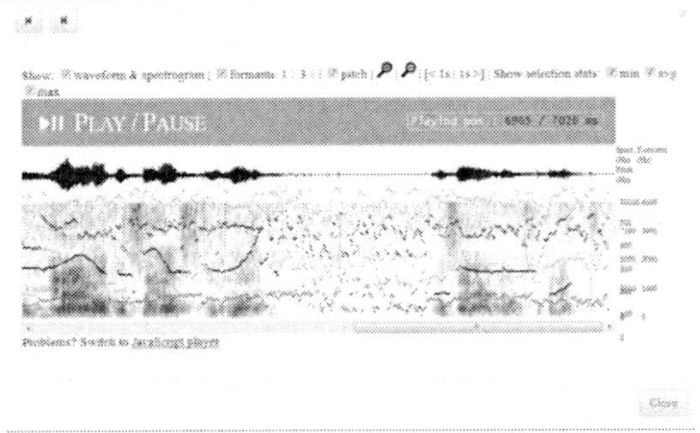

Figure 8: Spectrogram view of search result.

5 Future work

In the future we plan to implement search in syntactic annotations. We also plan to include more result views such as collocations, syntactic structures, and topic models.

References

Eckhard Bick. 2004. Corpuseye: Et Brugervenligt Webinterface for Grammatisk Opmærkede Korpora. Peter Widell and Mette Kunøe (eds). *Møde om Udforskningen af Dansk Sprog, Proceedings.* Denmark: Århus University. 46-57.

Lars Borin, Markus Forsberg and Johan Roxendal. 2012. Korp – the corpus infrastructure of Språkbanken. *Proceedings of LREC 2012.* Istanbul: ELRA, pages 474–478.

Sebastian Hoffmann and Evert, Stefan. 2006. Bncweb (cqp-edition): The Marriage of two Corpus Tools. S. Braun, K. Kohn, and J. Mukherjee (eds). *Corpus Technology and Language Pedagogy: New Resources, New Tools, New Methods, volume 3 of English Corpus Linguistics.* Frankfurt am Main: Peter Lang. 177 - 195.

Janne Bondi Johannessen, Lars Nygaard, Joel Priestley, Anders Nøklestad. 2008. Glossa: a Multilingual, Multimodal, Configurable User Interface. *Proceedings of the Sixth International Language Resources and Evaluation (LREC'08).* Paris: European Language Resources Association (ELRA).

Paul Meurer. 2012. Corpuscle – a new corpus management platform for annotated corpora. In: Gisle Andersen (ed.). *Exploring Newspaper Language: Using the Web to Create and Investigate a large corpus of modern Norwegian, Studies in Corpus Linguistics 49,* John Benjamins, 2012.

Web sites

CANS (Corpus of Norwegian-American Speech): http://tekstlab.uio.no/norskiamerika/english/index.html

CLARIN federated content search: https://www.clarin.eu/content/federated-content-search-clarin-fcs

CLARINO: http://clarin.b.uib.no/

Clojure: https://clojure.org/

ELENOR: http://www.hf.uio.no/ilos/studier/ressurser/elenor/index.html

Glossa on GitHub: https://github.com/textlab/cglossa

IMS Open Corpus Workbench: http://cwb.sourceforge.net/

Leksikografisk bokmålskorpus:https://tekstlab.uio.no/glossa2/?corpus=bokmal

MySql: https://www.mysql.com/

Nordic Dialect Corpus: http://www.tekstlab.uio.no/nota/scandiasyn/index.html

NORINT: http://www.hf.uio.no/iln/english/about/organization/text-laboratory/projects/norint/index.html

NoWaC (Norwegian Web as Corpus): http://www.hf.uio.no/iln/om/organisasjon/tekstlab/prosjekter/nowac/index.html

Dep_search: Efficient Search Tool for Large Dependency Parsebanks

Juhani Luotolahti[1,2]**, Jenna Kanerva**[1,2]**, and Filip Ginter**[1]
[1]Turku NLP Group
[2]University of Turku Graduate School (UTUGS)
University of Turku, Finland
`mjluot@utu.fi, jmnybl@utu.fi, figint@utu.fi`

Abstract

We present an updated and improved version of our syntactic analysis query toolkit, *dep_search*, geared towards morphologically rich languages and large parsebanks. The query language supports complex searches on dependency graphs, including for example boolean logic and nested queries. Improvements we present here include better data indexing, especially better database backend and document metadata support, API access and improved web user interface. All contributions are available under open licences.

1 Introduction

Huge text collections crawled from the Internet have become a popular resource for natural language processing and linguistic studies. Recently, massive corpora with automatically analyzed full syntactic structure became available for 45 languages (Ginter et al., 2017). To efficiently find and access specific types of sentences or syntactic structures from corpora with billions of tokens, powerful search systems are needed for both text and tree based queries, and combinations thereof.

The SETS dependency tree search tool (Luotolahti et al., 2015) is developed for efficient and scalable tree search in dependency treebanks and parsebanks, supporting complex searches on words, lemmas, detailed morphological analyses and dependency graphs. It is implemented using efficient data indexing and turning search expressions into compiled code.

In this paper we present the *Turku dep_search* tool, an improved version of SETS. In addition to changing the name, our main contributions are: 1) major speed-up and reduction of stored index size by changing backend from SQLite to Solr[1]

and LMDB[2]; 2) API access and improved web user interface; 3) supporting arbitrary sentence/-document metadata enabling for example sub-corpora and multilingual searches; 4) Universal Dependencies[3] treebanks and automatically analyzed UD parsebank data for 45 languages publicly available through dep_search API and online interface.

2 Query Language

The query language is in many ways inspired by languages used in existing tree query software such as TGrep (Rohde, 2004). The query language defines criteria for tokens and their relations in dependency graphs to be queried. It allows the user to specify graph structures in the syntactic trees, tokens by their properties, linear order of the tokens, and combinations thereof. Boolean logic is supported and queries can be combined and nested. The query itself is parsed into a tree structure, reflecting the nature of syntactic trees, and it is transformed into executable code with Cython[4]. The query parser is able to differentiate between token word forms and tags present in the queried corpora.

The query language is best presented by examples. Arguably the most simple query is querying for all tokens. This is achieved by the query _, underscore representing any token. To restrict the token by a word form or a tag the query is the word form itself, for example, to query the word *cat* the expression is `cat`. The lemma *cat* can be queried with the expression `L=cat`. Similarly to find tags, a query to find *nouns* is `NOUN`. Token queries can easily be combined using boolean operators. For example to search for a token with the lemma *cat* or *dog*, that is not in genitive case, one can query: `(L=cat | L=dog) & !Case=Gen`.

---

[1]`http://lucene.apache.org/solr/`
[2]`http://www.lmdb.tech/doc/`
[3]`http://universaldependencies.org/`
[4]`http://cython.org`

Proceedings of the 21st Nordic Conference of Computational Linguistics, pages 255–258,
Gothenburg, Sweden, 23-24 May 2017. ©2017 Linköping University Electronic Press

We can add dependency restrictions to our query to search for syntactic structures in the dependency graphs. A simple query like this, looks like `cat > _`, which finds tokens with word form *cat* with a dependent token. In a similar vein, we can search for a token with a typed dependent, for example to find the token *cat* with an *amod* dependent, query is: `cat >amod _`. The query for *cat* with two separate *amod* dependents query is `cat >amod _ >amod _` and to look for chains of *amod* dependencies from the token *cat*, one needs to use parenthesis in their query: `cat >amod (_ amod> _)`.

Boolean operators can be used with dependencies similarly as they can be used with the tokens. To negate a dependency relation, two options are offered: The query `cat !>amod _` looks for token *cat* without an *amod* dependent, where as the query `cat >!amod _` searches for the token *cat* with a dependent not the type of *amod*. Since all parts of the query support boolean logic, subtrees can be negated, for example querying `cat >amod !pretty` would find token *cat* if it has an *amod* dependent which is anything but the word *pretty*. Besides using negation, one can use OR operator to query dependency relations. For example, the query `cat >amod|>nmod _` finds *cat* with *amod* or *nmod* dependents.

The third class of query operators has to do with the sentence; linear order of the tokens and set operations on subqueries. To query for tokens next to each other in the sentence, query syntax is: `first . second`, query to search for tokens in a window is `cat <lin_2:3 NOUN`, which finds *cat* - tokens with a *noun* within two to three tokens from it. The operation can be limited to a particular direction by adding @R/@L - operator. The previous query limited to only tokens to the right is: `cat <lin_2:3@R NOUN`. The @R/@L -operator can also be applied to all dependency types. The universal quantifier operator (->) allows searching for sentences in which all tokens of certain type have a property. For example query: `(_ <nsubj _) -> (Person=3 <nsubj _)`, finds sentences in which all subjects are in third person. The plus operator allows us to find sentences with multiple properties, eg. to find sentences with both tokens *cat* and *dog*, where *dog* is a subject, query is: `(dog <nsubj _) + cat`. In addition to these, the size of the result can be set by adding `{len_set=limit}` after the query. For

Operator	Meaning
`<, >`	governed by, governs
`<@L, <@R`	governed by on the left, right
`>@L, >@R`	has dependent on the left, right
`.`	tokens are next to each other in linear order
`<lin_s:e`	tokens are in s:e distance from each other
`!, &, |`	negation, and, or
`+`	match if both sets not empty
`->`	universal quantification

Table 1: Query language operators.

example: `Clitic=Han {len_set=2}`.

3 Design

The search is executed in two main steps: 1) fetching candidate sentences from the indexed data, so that in a returned candidate sentence, all restrictions must be individually met, and 2) evaluating these candidates to check whether the configuration of the sentence fully matches the query. As the full configuration evaluation (part 2) stays mostly untouched compared to earlier version of the search tool, it is only briefly discussed here, and more detailed information can be found from Luotolahti et al. (2015).

For fast retrieval of candidate sentences, we use the Solr search engine to return a list of sentence ids, where a sentence has to match all query restrictions individually (for example, sentence has a specific word, morphological tag, and/or relation type), but no relations of these individual restrictions are evaluated at this point. For fast retrieval of candidate sentences, an index is build individually for all possible attributes (e.g. words, lemmas, morphological features and dependency relations). The actual sentence data is stored separately in a fast memory-mapped database, LMDB, where for each sentence the data is already stored in the binary form used when the full sentence configuration is evaluated. The sentences can be fetched from the LMDB using sentence ids given by the search engine.

Together with the different attribute indices, the search engine index can be used to store any necessary metadata related to sentences and documents and further restrict the search also on metadata level. Metadata can be used for example to restrict the search to a specific language, sub corpora or time span, naturally depending on the metadata available for a corpus in use. This way we can keep all data from different corpora and languages in one database, giving us also the possibility to search similar structures across languages.

Especially in the case of Universal Dependencies, cross-linguistically consistent treebank annotation, this gives a great opportunity to study similar structures across languages without compromising on speed or ability to limit the set of interesting languages.

After fetching the candidate sentences, their full configuration is evaluated against the actual search expression. The search expression is turned into a sequence of set operations, which can be compiled into native binary code. This compilation is done only once in the beginning of the search, taking typically less than a second. All sentences passing this step are then returned to the user.

4 Benchmarks

Generally, by changing the database backend we are able to gain in terms of speed and disk space. We are also able to remove two major bottleneck queries.

In the previous version of the search tool, one major bottleneck was queries involving rare lexical restrictions. When the SQLite backend was used, the data index needed to be divided into multiple small databases in order to keep retrieving fast. This however resulted slower queries when rare lexical items were queried because it was needed to iterate through many of these small databases with very few hits in each in order to find enough hits for the user. The new Solr backend is able to hold the whole data in one index, giving us a major speed-up when rare lexical items are searched.

Even bigger speed-up in the new version of dep_search is noticed when the query involves OR statements. Solr handles alternative restrictions much faster than SQLite is able to do, removing the most computationally heavy part of these queries.

In addition to faster queries, dep_search needs now much less disk space for the data index. In the index of 20M trees the disk usage is ∼45G, which is about half of the size compared to what the old version was using.

5 Web User Interface and API

In addition to the search tool, we also provide a graphical web interface, which can be set to talk to dep_search API, and render results in browser using Python Flask[5] library, Ajax and BRAT annota-

tion tool (Stenetorp et al., 2012). Dep_search API is accessed through http, and receives the query and the database name, and returns the matching trees as a response.

We maintain a public server for online searches at `http://bionlp-www.utu.fi/dep_search/`, where we have indexed all 70 Universal Dependencies v2.0 treebanks (Nivre et al., 2017), as well as automatically analyzed parsebank data for all the 45 languages present in UD parsebank collection. For each of these 45 languages, 1M sentences are made available in the dep_search web interface. Additionally, dep_search is used through its API to provide automatic content validation in the Universal Depedencies project,[6] automatically reindexed upon any update of a UD treebank development repository. In the past 6 weeks, the server processed over 11,000 requests — mostly related to the automated UD validation.

6 Conclusions

In this paper we presented the Turku dep_search dependency search tool with expressive query language developed to support queries involving rich morphological annotation and complex graph structures. The search tool is made scalable to parsebanks with billions of words using efficient data indexing to retrieve candidate sentences and generating algorithmic implementation of the actual search expression compiled into native binary code. Dep_search tool supports indexing varying sentence and document metadata making it possible e.g. to focus the search to a specific time span or a set of languages. Source code for the search backend and the web user interface is publicly available at `https://github.com/fginter/dep_search` and `https://github.com/fginter/dep_search_serve`, respectively.

Additionally, we provide a public, online search interface, where we host all Universal Dependencies version 2.0 treebanks, together with UD parsebank data for 45 different languages.

Acknowledgements

This work was supported by the Kone Foundation. Computational resources were provided by CSC – IT Center for Science.

---

[5] `http://flask.pocoo.org/`

[6] `http://universaldependencies.org/svalidation.html`

References

Filip Ginter, Jan Hajič, Juhani Luotolahti, Milan Straka, and Daniel Zeman. 2017. CoNLL 2017 shared task - automatically annotated raw texts and word embeddings. LINDAT/CLARIN digital library at the Institute of Formal and Applied Linguistics, Charles University in Prague.

Juhani Luotolahti, Jenna Kanerva, Sampo Pyysalo, and Filip Ginter. 2015. Sets: Scalable and efficient tree search in dependency graphs. In *Proceedings of the 2015 Conference of the North American Chapter of the Association for Computational Linguistics: Demonstrations*, pages 51–55. Association for Computational Linguistics.

Joakim Nivre, Željko Agić, Lars Ahrenberg, Maria Jesus Aranzabe, Masayuki Asahara, Aitziber Atutxa, Miguel Ballesteros, John Bauer, Kepa Bengoetxea, Riyaz Ahmad Bhat, Eckhard Bick, Cristina Bosco, Gosse Bouma, Sam Bowman, Marie Candito, Gülşen Cebirolu Eryiit, Giuseppe G. A. Celano, Fabricio Chalub, Jinho Choi, Çar Çöltekin, Miriam Connor, Elizabeth Davidson, Marie-Catherine de Marneffe, Valeria de Paiva, Arantza Diaz de Ilarraza, Kaja Dobrovoljc, Timothy Dozat, Kira Droganova, Puneet Dwivedi, Marhaba Eli, Tomaž Erjavec, Richárd Farkas, Jennifer Foster, Cláudia Freitas, Katarína Gajdošová, Daniel Galbraith, Marcos Garcia, Filip Ginter, Iakes Goenaga, Koldo Gojenola, Memduh Gökrmak, Yoav Goldberg, Xavier Gómez Guinovart, Berta Gonzáles Saavedra, Matias Grioni, Normunds Grūzītis, Bruno Guillaume, Nizar Habash, Jan Hajič, Linh Hà M, Dag Haug, Barbora Hladká, Petter Hohle, Radu Ion, Elena Irimia, Anders Johannsen, Fredrik Jørgensen, Hüner Kaşkara, Hiroshi Kanayama, Jenna Kanerva, Natalia Kotsyba, Simon Krek, Veronika Laippala, Phng Lê Hng, Alessandro Lenci, Nikola Ljubešić, Olga Lyashevskaya, Teresa Lynn, Aibek Makazhanov, Christopher Manning, Cătălina Mărănduc, David Mareček, Héctor Martínez Alonso, André Martins, Jan Mašek, Yuji Matsumoto, Ryan McDonald, Anna Missilä, Verginica Mititelu, Yusuke Miyao, Simonetta Montemagni, Amir More, Shunsuke Mori, Bohdan Moskalevskyi, Kadri Muischnek, Nina Mustafina, Kaili Müürisep, Lng Nguyn Th, Huyn Nguyn Th Minh, Vitaly Nikolaev, Hanna Nurmi, Stina Ojala, Petya Osenova, Lilja Øvrelid, Elena Pascual, Marco Passarotti, Cenel-Augusto Perez, Guy Perrier, Slav Petrov, Jussi Piitulainen, Barbara Plank, Martin Popel, Lauma Pretkalnia, Prokopis Prokopidis, Tiina Puolakainen, Sampo Pyysalo, Alexandre Rademaker, Loganathan Ramasamy, Livy Real, Laura Rituma, Rudolf Rosa, Shadi Saleh, Manuela Sanguinetti, Baiba Saulīte, Sebastian Schuster, Djamé Seddah, Wolfgang Seeker, Mojgan Seraji, Lena Shakurova, Mo Shen, Dmitry Sichinava, Natalia Silveira, Maria Simi, Radu Simionescu, Katalin Simkó, Mária Šimková, Kiril Simov, Aaron Smith, Alane Suhr, Umut Sulubacak, Zsolt Szántó, Dima Taji, Takaaki Tanaka, Reut Tsarfaty, Francis Tyers, Sumire Uematsu, Larraitz Uria, Gertjan van Noord, Viktor Varga, Veronika Vincze, Jonathan North Washington, Zdeněk Žabokrtský, Amir Zeldes, Daniel Zeman, and Hanzhi Zhu. 2017. Universal dependencies 2.0. LINDAT/CLARIN digital library at the Institute of Formal and Applied Linguistics, Charles University in Prague.

Douglas L. T. Rohde, 2004. *TGrep2 User Manual.* Available at http://tedlab.mit.edu/~dr/Tgrep2.

Pontus Stenetorp, Sampo Pyysalo, Goran Topić, Tomoko Ohta, Sophia Ananiadou, and Jun'ichi Tsujii. 2012. Brat: a web-based tool for nlp-assisted text annotation. In *Proceedings of the Demonstrations at the 13th Conference of the European Chapter of the Association for Computational Linguistics*, pages 102–107. Association for Computational Linguistics.

Proto-Indo-European Lexicon: The Generative Etymological Dictionary of Indo-European Languages

Jouna Pyysalo
Department of Modern Languages
University of Helsinki
`jouna.pyysalo@helsinki.fi`

Abstract

Proto-Indo-European Lexicon (PIE Lexicon) is the generative etymological dictionary of Indo-European languages. The reconstruction of Proto-Indo-European (PIE) is obtained by applying the comparative method, the output of which equals the Indo-European (IE) data. Due to this the Indo-European sound laws leading from PIE to IE, revised in Pyysalo 2013, can be coded using Finite-State Transducers (FST). For this purpose the *foma* finite-state compiler by Mans Hulden (2009) has been chosen in PIE Lexicon. At this point PIE Lexicon generates data of some 120 Indo-European languages with an accuracy rate of over 99% and is therefore the first dictionary in the world capable of generating (predicting) its data entries by means of digitized sound laws.

1 Introduction: The IE language family, PIE and the generation of the data

The Indo-European language family, with some three billion native speakers, is the largest in the world. The family comprises some six hundred languages including one hundred and fifty archaic, partly extinct ones, the oldest of which were attested more than three thousand years ago. The IE language family is divided into a dozen subgroups (e.g. Germanic, Italic, and Anatolian), each of which was given a specific character by the common vocabulary of the subgroup and the set of common sound changes distinguishing it from the other subgroups.

The comparative method of reconstruction is the gold standard in the postulation of the proto-language, PIE. The method is based on comparison of originally identical IE morphemes. The postulation of the proto-language is exclusively determined by the measurable features of the data. Consequently the reconstruction of a data segment is the equivalent of the data set it was inferred from. By coding the sound laws of each Indo-European language the words of the languages can be generated by sound law *(foma)* scripts detailing the changes applying to the languages.

In order to generate the data the most ancient Indo-European sound laws,[1] critically chosen and revised in Pyysalo 2013, have been formulated in the *foma* finite-state compiler and arranged chronologically.[2] By now also later sound laws have been added and the scripts have been implemented in PIE Lexicon at http://pielexicon.hum.helsinki.fi, generating the data in a manner explicated in this paper.

2 On the coding of sound laws and generation of data in PIE Lexicon

The digitization of the IE sound law system starts with the coding of the individual sound laws as the *foma* rules. These are then arranged in a chronological order into *foma* scripts of the languages.

2.1 Coding of the IE sound laws

The IE sound laws are of the implicational form PIE $*x \rightarrow$ IE$_z$ y ('the PIE sound $*x$ turns into sound y in the Indo-European language z').

---

1   For the core of the traditional Indo-European sound law system, see Collinge 1985, 1995, and 1999.

2   For a state-of-the-art formulation of the finite-state technology, see Beesley & Karttunen 2003.

Proceedings of the 21st Nordic Conference of Computational Linguistics, pages 259–262,
Gothenburg, Sweden, 23-24 May 2017. ©2017 Linköping University Electronic Press

In *foma* the equivalents of the IE sound laws are expressed together with the environments in which they are operational. In practice the *foma* rules assume the format *A -> B* ‖ *C _ D* ('*A* changes into *B* in environment *C_D*'). Corresponding to the principle of regularity of sound changes in comparative Indo-European linguistics, the *replacement* of *A* with *B* is *obligatory* in *foma*, i.e. it always occurs in all instances of the environment *C_D*.

For example, the revised Brugmann's law adds the glottal *H* to the environment: PIE **oHCV* → PIIr. *āCV* (Pyysalo 2013: 121-125). This is written in *foma* as:

o -> ā ‖ _ Glottal Consonant Vowel ;

Each *foma* rule coded is tested by the compiler and then placed in the *foma* (sound law) scripts.

2.2 Coding of the IE sound law *foma* scripts

After the digitization of the IE sound laws, each IE language is equipped with a *foma script* consisting of chronologically ordered *foma* rules. The data of PIE Lexicon has required all major archaic sound laws (i.e. ones applying to at least two subgroups) to be coded. The *foma* scripts of some 120 languages or dialects have already been implemented on the PIE Lexicon site, and are available in the control bar at the bottom of the site. E.g. the Hittite sound law script can be opened by first clicking *Select rule set*, then *Hitt.*, and finally *Show rules*, opening the file: http://pielexicon.hum.helsinki.fi/?showrule=24.

Once the *foma* rules have been arranged into scripts, the consistency of the rules is tested both internally (with regard to the other rules of the script) and externally (with regard to the portion of the data the script is capable of generating).

2.3 On the generation of the IE data in PIE Lexicon

By March 2017 PIE Lexicon consists of some 120 *foma* scripts and generates some 35000 phonemes, some 175 of which are erroneous, i.e. the general accuracy rate is 99,5%.

Since the choice of the material is random, the digitized glottal fricative theory (GFT) of Pyysalo 2013, now tested and digitally published in PIE Lexicon, is valid, i.e. sound and complete.

The remaining errors – shown in red in PIE Lexicon – represent open research problems, for which *foma* rules cannot be specified, because the sound laws remain unknown. The errors can divided into two subsets:

(a) The PIE accent/tone problem, not treated in Pyysalo 2013, accounts for almost half of the errors, making it the fundamental problem of Indo-European linguistics at this point.

(b) A dozen minor sound law problems related to individual subgroups, languages and/or dialects are also open or only partially solved. In order to solve these problems the project has opened a journal, *Proto-Indo-European Linguistics*, at http://pielinguistics.org.

2.4 On the explicit *foma* proof chains

PIE Lexicon has added a special feature to the basic version of *foma*, which makes the proof chains of the generation of the data explicit for the PIE Lexicon users and editors. Consequently the entire generation of data can be immediately verified. Clicking the reconstruction on the left side of the individual IE data entries reveals the respective *foma* proof chain, and all *foma* chains can be opened simultaneously by clicking the *Chains* button at the bottom of the site.

A proof chain explicitly detailing all sound laws applied and their mutual order in the generation is thus attached to every IE form. This makes the proofs fully explicit and to a degree confirms the PIE reconstructions serving as the starting point of the generation of the data.

3 Concluding observations, remarks, and an outline of the project's future development

The high success rate of PIE Lexicon in the automatic generation of the IE data shows that managing historical sound laws by applying finite-state transducers provides a rigorous formal calculus for mapping cognates from PIE to the daughter languages and automatically evaluating the consistency of such a system.

3.1 On the background of the successful generation of IE data

The success rate achieved in the generation of the Indo-European data is also explained by the following factors:

(a) In the comparative method the input (the PIE reconstruction) is not hypothetical, but a sum of the measurable features of the data and its comparison, hence the logical equivalent of the data. This in turn results in the respective success in its generation.

(b) The GFT comprises all correct sound law proposals, perfected if necessary, of two centuries of research in IE linguistics. Consequently, the sound law system stands on the shoulders of giants.

3.2 The coding of the IE language family tree

By the spring 2017 the coding of the ancient sound laws of the most archaic languages has been completed. Only late, unproblematic sound laws need be added when appearing in the new data to be published in PIE Lexicon.

Consequently the next, more abstract phase, the coding of the IE language family tree on the basis of the common sound laws, has already begun. For this purpose a *foma* rule bank, consisting of some 800 rules, has been coded. Instead of full sound law scripts the operating system uses the names of the rules which call the rules from the bank. This allows us to place the rules in an excel template in which identical rules are placed on the same row.

By means of this procedure the first IE language family tree based purely on the common sound laws is already being coded and will be published in PIE Lexicon once ready.

3.3 The coding of the decision method of Indo-European etymology

Once the main features of the IE language family tree have been coded, the preconditions for the digitization of the decision method of IE etymology have been created. This feature, originally outlined by August Schleicher (1852: iv-v)[3] has a counterpart in language technology. Once the sound law (*foma*) scripts are ready it is possible to run them in reverse direction, i.e. starting from the bottom ("apply up"). The technology already exists and once implemented it will generate all possible PIE prototypes of an

Indo-European word. The coding only requires the addition of tailored, language-family specific phonological constraints in order to eliminate potential infinite chains caused by historically lost phonemes.

Once the disjunctions of possible PIE prototypes of all IE words have been digitally generated it is not complicated to code an intersection function that seeks identical PIE prototypes between the disjunctions and proposes an etymology when there is an intersection of the disjunctions of two languages. If the identity is semantically feasible, the computer has found a PIE etymology.

After the coding of this feature it is in principle possible to test every etymology proposed during the history of Indo-European linguistics and to mechanically identify all potential etymologies, which in turn may reveal identities not noticed by the scholars, and thus revitalize the research.

3.4 Conclusion: Coding of the comparative method of reconstruction in Indo-European linguistics

Taken together the coding of the IE sound law system (§3.1), the IE language family tree (§3.2), and the decision method of IE etymology (§3.3) mean that the critical components of the comparative method of reconstruction itself have been digitized.

Once achieved, Operating System (OS) PIE Lexicon will be able to manage the comparative IE linguistics digitally for the first time in history. Thus in the 21st century, Indo-European linguistics will be in the frontline of digital humanities, equipped with a next-generation theory embedded in the methodic framework of natural sciences.

Credits

This paper summarizes a joint collaboration of Dr. Jouna Pyysalo (IE languages and their reconstruction), Prof. Mans Hulden (language technology and *foma*) and Mr. Fedu Kotiranta (web design and node.js), the coding of PIE Lexicon that started in the autumn 2014.

References

Kenneth E. Beesley & Lauri Karttunen. 2003. *Finite State Morphology*. Studies in computational

---

3   For a precise formulation of the decision method with a data example, see Pyysalo 2013: 475-476.

linguistics 3. Center for the Study of Language and Information, Stanford.

N. E. Collinge. 1985. *The Laws of Indo-European.* Benjamins, Amsterdam.

N. E. Collinge. 1995. Further Laws of Indo-European. In: *On Languages and Language: The Presidental Adresses of the 1991 Meeting of the Societas Linguistica Europaea. ed, Werner Winter.* BTrends in Linguistics. Studies and Monographs, 78. Mouton, Berlin: 27-52.

N. E. Collinge. 1999. The Laws of Indo-European: The State of Art. *Journal of Indo-European Studies*, 27:355-377.

Mans Hulden. 2009. *Finite-State Machine Construction Methods and Algorithms for Phonology and Morphology*, PhD Thesis. University of Arizona.

Jouna Pyysalo. 2013. *System PIE: The Primary Phoneme Inventory and Sound Law System for Proto-Indo-European.* Publications of the Institute for Asian and African Studies 15. Unigrafia Oy, Helsinki.

August Schleicher. 1852. *Die Formenlehre der kirchenslavischen Sprache, erklärend und vergleichend dargestellt.* H. B. König, Bonn.

Tilde MODEL - Multilingual Open Data for EU Languages

Roberts Rozis
Tilde
roberts.rozis@tilde.com

Raivis Skadiņš
Tilde
raivis.skadins@tilde.com

Abstract

This paper describes a Multilingual Open Data corpus for European languages that was built in scope of the MODEL project. We describe the approach chosen to select data sources, which data sources were used, how the source data was handled, what tools were used and what data was obtained in the result of the project. Obtained data quality is presented, and a summary of challenges and chosen solutions are described, too.

This paper may serve as a guide and reference in case someone might try to do something similar, as well as a guide to the new open data obtained.

1 Introduction

The European language technology community relies on public corpora such as the DGT-TM (Steinberger et al., 2012) and Europarl (Koehn, 2005) as a primary resource for developing machine translation (MT) and many other technologies for EU languages. DGT-TM is an invaluable asset, making it the most-viewed resource in the EU Open Data Portal. However, it is also very limited, covering only the legislative domain, therefore cannot lead to quality MT systems in other domains.

The lack of language resources is one of the biggest obstacles to the development of language technology in Europe. In an effort to overcome this obstacle, we have made a commitment to create new multilingual corpora for European languages – particularly the smaller languages that need them most – and make them openly available to researchers and developers.

As part of this initiative, we have identified and collected multilingual open data sets in multiple languages and several key domains. In addition, collected resources has been cleaned, aligned, and formatted using data-processing tools, thus rendering the corpora useable for developing new products and services.

At the end of the project (April, 2017), we plan to submit over 10M segments of multilingual open data for publication on the META-SHARE[1] repository, maintained by the Multilingual Europe Technology Alliance, and on the EU Open Data Portal[2]. These open data sets will be available to technology developers, researchers, localization companies, and machine translation providers. The corpora will provide a crucial resource for boosting the quality of MT engines, including the new breed of MT systems built with neural networks.

The activities have been undertaken as part of the ODINE Open Data Incubator for Europe[3], which aims to support the next generation of digital businesses and fast-track the development of new products and services.

2 Data Sources

In ODINE Tilde undertook to collect 10 million parallel segments of open parallel data from the Web.

The extensive approach would mean crawling hundreds of thousands of web sites in attempt to identify parallel content and trying to build a parallel corpus. The downside of this approach is immense crawling and computing requirements as well as our observation that only a small fraction of multilingual content is really parallel, mostly comparable or not really parallel at all. Going this way we would not fit in the time frame allocated (6 month) and would require intensive human work.

The intensive approach – first work on identifying sources and selecting web sites of public data containing large number of parallel texts. We chose this approach and selected domains, which have not been processed for at

---

[1] http://www.meta-share.org/
[2] https://data.europa.eu/euodp/en/data/
[3] https://opendataincubator.eu/

Proceedings of the 21st Nordic Conference of Computational Linguistics, pages 263–265,
Gothenburg, Sweden, 23-24 May 2017. ©2017 Linköping University Electronic Press

least for last 5 years. We ended up with the following data sources:

- RAPID – Press Releases database of European Commission[4] in all EU languages. The content of the press releases is translated precisely, which makes it interesting for being used as a source for parallel corpus.
- EMA – European Medicines Agency [5] documents - Descriptions of medicines and instructions of use of medicines as well as various medical conditions.
- Documents portal of European Economic and Social Committee[6]
- Web site of European Central Bank (ECB)[7]
- Web site of World Bank[8] – content on World Bank projects and activities in various regions of the world.

Corpora from EMA and ECB web sites have been collected before (Tiedemann, 2009), but a lot of new data have been published in these sites since that. Besides processing the mentioned major multilingual web sites, we also processed many small web sites to collect data in culture and travel domains; typical examples of such web sites are airbaltic.com, fold.lv, riga2014.org, umea2014.se, plzen2015.cz, wroclaw2016.pl, dss2016.eu etc.

In great degree, the data processing workflow is fixed and similar in top-level steps for any resource processed. When a data source candidate is selected, we crawl and download the data, convert it to a normalized format – plain text, and align the data resulting in data files usable for training MT systems – Moses format (parallel plain text files where file extension signifies the language of the file) and TMX format files. Each of these steps include many smaller steps and processes carried out depending on each and individual resource.

Crawling and downloading means exploring the structure how the data is held in the server and how we can reference each and individual page or file. Often this is a multi-step process where table of content pages must be crawled, or search by a list of keywords must be queried. Doing so we get a list of pages where the content can be found, or a starting page to that, or a list of files metadata. Only then we can get to the files or pages to download them into a local storage. Downloading

hundreds of thousands of files/pages must be done politely in order not to abuse the remote server.

Conversion to a normalized format means extraction of plain text from whichever format be it PDF or HTML, or DOC, DOCX, etc. It is critical to retain the original text flow and structure and sequence of paragraphs. Last step of conversion is segmentation – the text is split in segments, mostly sentences which are the smallest granularity of data.

Alignment takes place by passing a large number of data, mostly aligned files of plain text segments to the alignment tool. The aligner builds statistical model of matching data, and selects matching segments, which are saved to the output.

3   Challenges & Solutions

Content downloading. We use custom-built and tailored PERL/Python scripts for downloading each of the selected resources. We do so to ensure usage of all the metadata (file identification by content and language) available from the source to obtain aligned files by language in the input. There are processing risks in other steps. The smaller languages are not so well represented in terms of parallel data, they tend to be more complex and contain inflections leading to potential alignment errors. We want to minimize that risk in this step; it is part of the approach chosen.

Content normalization. We used LibreOffice on Linux to convert various **office file formats** to plain text.

Dealing with **PDF** format files is still the hard nut. In rare and specific cases like with files of EMA (files originating from Microsoft Word) using commercial tools (Adobe Acrobat) yield in a very smooth process and high conversion quality. However, when working with content originating from QarkXPress or Adobe layout tools, use of a mix of other tools (Skadiņš et al., 2014) is needed. It remains a challenge to deal with

- Damaged files – files which might open for view but would take forever to process
- Protected DOCs/PDFs – we just have to skip those.
- Scanned PDFs – since multiple tools were used, we did not learn how to identify and skip those.

---

[4] http://europa.eu/rapid/
[5] http://www.ema.europa.eu/ema/
[6] https://dm.eesc.europa.eu/
[7] http://www.ecb.europa.eu/
[8] http://web.worldbank.org/

Segmentation. Until MODEL project we used our in-house as well as third party tools for segmentation of content before alignment. In this project we adapted SRX segmentation rules and integrated them with a Segment Program[9].

To perform **alignment of segments** we use Microsoft Bilingual Sentence Aligner[10] (Moore, 2002). We had to split the content in smaller packages, otherwise the aligner would stop working due to lack of memory.

Parallel computing. We did use the cloud computing potential to speed up processing of parallel data for multiple language pairs. With the use of Amazon Web Services cloud, we could achieve the result in 3 weeks for a resource that would otherwise take a whole year in a serial processing manner.

4 Results

We processed web sites described above and obtained the following data (Table 1) in the output. Corpus contains multilingual entries, English, French and German segments aligned with segments in all other represented languages. We selected random subsets of data and manually evaluated alignment quality, depending on language pair only 2-8% of segments contained alignment issues (Table 2).

	Files	**Langu-ages**	**Aligned segments**
RAPID	401K	24	4 M
EMA	81K	22	6 M
EESC portal	660K	36	6 M
ECB, World Bank	103K	32	70 K
Culture and travel domain	est. 5K	15	est. < 1M

Table 1: Amount of aligned data

	de-en	en-lv	en-pl
RAPID	92	96	93
EMA	95	92	99
EESC portal	99	92	96

Table 2: Human QA results (% of correctly aligned segments)

5 Conclusions

Scattered and isolated, without care about reuse in MT from the side of data origin, there does exist parallel content out there in the internet, which can be found, collected, processed and used in training MT systems. We are proud about being able to share with MT community over 16M of parallel segments of Tilde MODEL corpus collected and processed during MODEL project. At the end of the project (April, 2017), we released the corpus as open data and published on the META-SHARE[11] repository and on the EU Open Data Portal.

Not all data crawled has been processed and aligned, we had to discard huge amounts of PDF files due to unsatisfactory text extraction tools available. This leaves room for future work.

Acknowledgments

Work has been done in project "Multilingual Open Data for EU Languages (MODEL)" under the project framework "Open Data INcubator for Europe (ODINE ID: 644683)".

References

Koehn, P. 2005. *Europarl: A Parallel Corpus for Statistical Machine Translation.* In Conference Proceedings: the tenth Machine Translation Summit. Phuket, Thailand: AAMT, pp. 79-86

Moore, R.C. 2002. Fast and Accurate Sentence Alignment of Bilingual Corpora. In *Proceedings of the 5th Conference of the Association for Machine Translation in the Americas on Machine Translation: From Research to Real Users.* London, UK: Springer-Verlag, pp. 135-144.

Skadiņš R., Tiedemann J., Rozis R., Deksne D. 2014. *Billions of Parallel Words for Free: Building and Using the EU Bookshop Corpus.* Proceedings of the 9th International Conference on Language Resources and Evaluation (LREC'14), pp. 1850–1855.

Steinberger, R., Eisele, A., Klocek, S., Pilos, S., & Schlüter, P. 2012. *DGT-TM: A freely Available Translation Memory in 22 Languages.* Proceedings of the 8th international conference on Language Resources and Evaluation (LREC'2012). Istanbul, Turkey, pp. 454-459.

Tiedemann, J. 2009. *News from OPUS - A Collection of Multilingual Parallel Corpora with Tools and Interfaces.* In N. Nicolov and K. Bontcheva and G. Angelova and R. Mitkov (eds.) Recent Advances in Natural Language Processing (vol V), pp. 237-248, John Benjamins, Amsterdam/Philadelphia

---

[9] https://github.com/loomchild/segment
[10] https://www.microsoft.com/en-us/download/details.aspx?id=52608

[11] http://metashare.tilde.com/repository/search/?q=Tilde+MODEL

Mainstreaming August Strindberg with Text Normalization

Adam Ek
Department of Linguistics
Stockholm University
adek2204@student.su.se

Sofia Knuutinen
Department of Linguistics
Stockholm University
irkn8107@student.su.se

Abstract

This article explores the application of text normalization methods based on Levenshtein distance and Statistical Machine Translation to the literary genre, specifically on the collected works of August Strindberg. The goal is to normalize archaic spellings to modern day spelling. The study finds evidence of success in text normalization, and explores some problems and improvements to the process of analysing mid-19th to early 20th century Swedish texts. This article is part of an ongoing project at Stockholm University which aims to create a corpus and web-friendly texts from Strindsberg's collected works.

1 Introduction

The purpose of the current study is to assert how well the Levenshtein and Statistical Machine Translation (SMT) methods developed by Eva Pettersson work on the 19th century texts of August Strindberg. This is done to see preliminary results on how well the normalization works on the text and in the future apply other Natural Language Processing (NLP) tools to the normalized data.

Normalizing historical text is a fairly new area in NLP, but it has a growing interest among researchers. The main interest has been in normalizing spelling and improving part of speech (POS) tagging. There is earlier research on normalizing historical spelling to modern spelling and to follow are a few examples on some. Rule-based approaches have been studied by Rayson et al. (2005), Baron and Rayson (2008) and Pettersson et al. (2012).

A rule-based study was done by Rayson et al. (2005) on 16th to 19th century English texts. This study resulted in a tool called VARD (VARiant

Detector). The VARD tool was compared to the results of modern spellcheckers (MS-Word and Aspell) that are not trained for historical data. The results showed that VARD was more accurate in normalizing historical text. This same tool was later developed even further by Baron and Rayson (2008). They implemented phonetic matching against a modern dictionary and candidate replacement rules for spelling variants within a text.

Pettersson et al. (2012) hand-crafted a small set of normalization rules based on 17th century court records and church texts to improve tagging and parsing of historical text. Their results showed that a small set of rules can work well in normalizing historical text and that it works for spellings even more archaic than their training data.

Pettersson et al. (2013b) researched a Levenshtein based approach which was tested on the same data as Pettersson et al. (2012) used. The Levenshtein approach uses a weighted distance measure for comparing the original word form to word forms listed in a modern corpus or dictionary. The accuracy baseline for the Levenshtein method turned out to become 77% and by adding an error handling cache, in the form of a manually normalized training corpus the results increased even more up to 86,9%.

Pettersson et al. (2013a) approached the normalization task as a form of translation. It resulted in a statistical machine translation (SMT) based approach. The translation was done based on characters and not on words as whole. The results showed that having even a small amount of training data works well and the SMT normalization showed an accuracy increase and reached a level of 86,1%.

This paper deals with spelling normalization of August Strindbergs books, which were written between 1869 and 1909. Strindbergs books are mainly written during the era of Late Mod-

Proceedings of the 21st Nordic Conference of Computational Linguistics, pages 266–270,
Gothenburg, Sweden, 23-24 May 2017. ©2017 Linköping University Electronic Press

ern Swedish. This means that they are a bit more modern than the data Pettersson et al. (2012) used when they began to research the different approaches to text normalization. There is even some shifts in spelling in the books since Strindbergs last books were written at the time when Contemporary Swedish was making its way forward. Strindberg is even considered as one of the authors who had a big influence on the changes of the Swedish language.

The approaches used are Levenshtein-based normalisation and SMT-based normalization which is two out of four possible approaches presented by Pettersson (2016a). It will concentrate on a qualitative analysis on both distinctive features of archaic Swedish and how well they are translated and on a few problematic areas in normalization picked from the data collected.

2 Method

2.1 Data

The data consists of August Strindbergs collected works,[1] of which 59 books have been parsed to XML and then into raw text format. The collected works consists of novels, short stories, poems and plays. The data used for testing is the chapters from each book excluding foreword, afterword, word clarifications, public reception. The data was preprocessed by removing all non-alphabetic characters and tokenizing the text with one token per line.

It is noteworthy that Strindberg uses *code-switching* frequently in the text, which are words that should not be considered as candidates for normalization. Chapters containing only french text has been removed manually and as many individual words as possible have been removed manually by identifying french spelling patterns.

The Swedish corpus, training and tuning data for both methods was provided by Eva Pettersson (Pettersson 2016b).[2] The corpus data (language model data) consists of 1166539 tokens, the training data consists of 28777 tokens and the tuning data of 2650 tokens. The data is from a different genre, court records and church documents, while Strindbergs works are mainly literary fiction. The data is also older (15th to 17th century) compared to the texts of Strindberg which were written from

1869 to 1909.[3] This results in that the training data is not fully optimized for the current task.

The modern language dictionary used for both methods is the SALDO dictionary (version 2) (Baron et al., 2008). The corpus of original spelling mapped to manually normalized word forms is compiled from the Gender and Work corpus of court records and church texts from 15th to 17th century. (Pettersson, 2016b)

2.2 Normalization

2.2.1 Levenshtein

The Levenshtein-based approach calculates the extended Levenshtein edit distance [4] between the original word and any token present in a modern language dictionary. It picks out the candidate(s) with the smallest distance and then proceeds to choose the best candidate out of several (given there are more than one candidate for the word). Perl was used to perform the Levenshtein-based normalization. The data used for this was a modern language dictionary, a corpus of original words mapped to manually normalized spelling, a corpus of modern language to choose the most frequent candidate in the case of more than one candidate, a file containing weights lower than 1 for commonly occurring edits observed in training data and a file containing the edit distance threshold value. All these, except for the input file, were provided in Pettersson's HistNorm package.

2.2.2 SMT

When using SMT, the task of text normalization is seen as a translation, where the translation is between spelling conventions rather than between different languages. This is achieved by using character-based translations, where the individual characters rather than words are treated as the lowest level entity, words are treated as middle level, and sentences as the top level. The SMT-based normalization was performed using Moses Statistical Machine Translation System,[5] GIZA++[6] and SRILM.[7]

---

[3]Strindberg wrote his later texts just as the Swedish spelling reform of 1906 took place. It is unclear if he decided to follow their directions.

[4]Extended edit distance uses both single character edits and additional operations such as double deletion and single-to-double substitution (Pettersson,2016a)

[5]http://www.statmt.org/moses/

[6]http://www.statmt.org/moses/giza/GIZA++.html

[7]http://www.speech.sri.com/projects/srilm/

---

[1]72 books in total provided by Litteraturbanken.

[2]http://stp.lingfil.uu.se/~evapet/histNorm/

The input data was tokenized, then each character in the word was separated with a whitespace to indicate that each character should be regarded as the lowest level entity, and newlines to indicate the end of a paragraph.

In a standard language model (LM) where words are considered words etc. a slightly lower n-gram order might be appropriate, but as the current data is based on characters rather than words the n-gram order is increased to capture longer words, and their spellings. Work on this has been done by Nakov and Tiedmann (2012), and their results pointed towards an order of 10 for character-based SMT.

Moses SMT was initialized with a language model of order 10, with standard smoothing (Good-Turing Discounting) and (Linear) interpolation created with SRILM then trained and tuned with the Minimum Error Rate Training (MERT) algorithm.

3   Results

The evaluation of Levenshtein and SMT is done with a quantitative analysis (Table 1) and two qualitative analyses (Table 2, Table 3).

The quantitative analysis of the normalization is illustrated in Table 1, where the total number of tokens and types normalized in the text is shown. The normalizations in Table 1 shows all normalizations that were made, regardless of their correctness.

Method	Data	Total	Norm.	%
LEV	Types	162841	54505	33,4
	Tokens	5941139	535956	9,2
SMT	Types	178292	40856	22,9
	Tokens	5939067	380577	6,4

Table 1: Data normalization percentages for Levenshtein (LEV) and SMT. Norm = Normalized.

It can be seen that a significant yet not particularly large amount of tokens were normalized, 6,4% (SMT) and 9,2% (Levenshtein), however the normalization rate for types is much higher for both methods, 22,9% (SMT) and 22,9% (Levenshtein).

The features examined in Table 2 is the following: *hv (hvad, hvilken), qv (qvinna/kvinna, qvantfysik/kvantfysik), dt (fasdt/fast, måladt/målat), fv (hufvud/huvud, öfver/över)*, archaic preteri-

tum conjucation of verbs ending with *-o* e.g. *gingo/gick, fingo/fick, voro/var*, these features were chosen based on their frequency and recognizability.

These words are only a subset of the totality of words with archaic Swedish spelling, changes such as $e \rightarrow \ddot{a}$ and less frequent archaic spelling conventions have been ignored.

Method	Correct	Incorrect	Accuracy
LEV	895	105	89,5%
SMT	818	182	81,8%

Table 2: Normalizations of Swedish words with archaic spelling. Correct = Archaic spelling normalized correctly, Incorrect = Archaic spelling normalized incorrectly, Accuracy = $\frac{\text{Correct}}{\text{Correct+Incorrect}}$.

In Table 2, 1000 words with archaic spelling was chosen randomly, the evaluations is then done by manually checking if the words with archaic spelling is normalized to the correct modern version of the words.

True positives (TP), false positives (FP) and false negatives (FN) were identified manually. Among the 1000 candidates surnames such as *Lindqvist* are normalized to *Lindkvist*, which is correct, but in modern Swedish the archaic spelling is still being used, so these cases have been removed from the evaluation in Table 2. Many cases of French and English words appear and have been marked as FP (False Positive), also compound words such as *sandtorrt* have been marked as FP, the archaic Swedish spelling *dt* occurs in *sandtorrt*, but it is formed as the the two words *sand* and *torrt* are concatenated, it is not an actual instance of archaic spelling.

At this stage the most interesting percentage is the relationship between correct and incorrect normalizations, i.e. $\frac{\text{Correct}}{\text{Correct+Incorrect}}$, this shows how well these methods perform on words with archaic spelling, which is 89,5% for Levenshtein and 81,8% for SMT.

These numbers show how the methods perform when only relevant data is selected by the methods, however the score for the successful selection rate among the selected elements (precision) is rather low for both methods, 8,2% for Levenshtein and 7,3% for SMT. This means that out of all the words selected by the methods, 8,2% and 7,3% have archaic spelling. In contrast to this, the selection rate for the words with archaic spelling (recall) is 95.3% for Levenshtein and 92.1% for SMT, which means that out of all the words with archaic spelling, 95,3% and 92,1% of them are caught. Table 3 shows the precision and recall on types in the dataset for both methods.

Method	Precision	Recall
LEV	8,2%	95,3%
SMT	7,3%	92,1%

Table 3: Precision $\frac{TP}{TP+FP}$ and recall $\frac{TP}{TP+FN}$ for Levenshtein and SMT based on the normalization of types.

It can be observed that both methods generally output similar result for correct and incorrect normalizations on archaic words, the same trend is seen in both precision and recall where the difference is not huge, 3.2% for recall and 0.9% for precision. An extensive and complete analysis of the errors in word selection has not been done at this point, but the observed phenomenas will be addressed below.

4   Discussion

From the normalization data it has been observed that a large portion of the incorrectly normalized words is compound words, e.g. *qvinnotårar* → *kvinnoårar* (SMT), *nordljuset* → *mordlust* (Levenshtein). As shown in the first example (SMT), the first part of the compound is normalized correctly, however the second compound part is incorrectly normalized with the removal of *t*, which makes this into an incorrect normalization.

The second example (Levenshtein) shows that the entire compound word may change form, both the first and the second compound.

Levenshtein does word to word mappings and normalizes compound words as two separate words while searching for candidates. SMT on the other hand regards each word as a collection of characters and does not differentiate between compounds words and normal words.

SMT removed one letter in the first example from the compound while Levenshtein regarded its compound as two separate entities which resulted in that the two words received normalizations separately which changed the meaning of both parts instead of just one. For the Levenshtein-based approach there should be some tuning around normalizing compound words. Compound

splitting can be a good thing but there could be some restrictions made to improve it.

The main issue for SMT is the different genres in the training data and the texts of August Strindberg. Common words with archaic Swedish spelling is caught, but also a few words that were not archaic but had archaic spelling features by accident were normalized, such as *sandtorrt* → *stort* (SMT). This phenomena is quite hard to solve during the normalization process, the best method would be a lexicon which consists of an updated vocabulary with a larger scope than the current one, this enables us to identify that *sandtorrt* is a compound word consisting of two modern Swedish words and not an instance of archaic Swedish spelling.

As noted many instances of *code-switching* appear in the text of Strindberg, and not all foreign words are caught in the preprocessing as these often appear randomly in the text. This lowers the representability of the test on total amount of types and tokens normalized by the methods, the accuracy is unaffected as the foreign words can be ruled out when manually checking the results.

The two problems, *code-switching* and *compound words* in conjunction is responsible for a large portion of the normalised words in both method, which as mentioned above distorts the actual number of relevant words that are normalized. Another issue is that the 5 features from Table 2 which were analyzed is not all of the words that were normalized correctly, or have archaic Swedish spelling, which means that another portion of the normalized texts is correct. Many features of archaic Swedish has been overlooked at the moment due to time limitations, as the data has to be validated by hand.

What remains to do is to Part-Of-Speech tag the text and evaluate the results of both the Levenshtein and SMT normalized versions, as well as the original texts. The suspicion is that the normalized versions will perform better than the original, but the question remains, if and how much the text normalization has done to improve the results.

Another use for POS-tagging is that the results of the POS-tagging may be an indicator of the overall performance for both SMT and Levenshtein. This can be seen from the fact that the meaning of an archaic spelled word should not be different from the modern day spelling of the word. And thus, if the POS-tag has changed it can be assumed that the word has been normalized incorrectly.[8] Some changes in the POS-tagging is wanted, for words with archaic spelling, but all other changes in the POS-tags should be regarded as incorrect, thus in performing POS-tagging all the false positive (FP) normalizations can be identified.

5   Conclusions

The accuracy of both the methods showed success, however both methods in conjunction with the training data results in a very low precision rate. Some solutions to this has been suggested, such as foreign word recognition (FWR), furthermore another data set for training that is more genre specific and closer to 19th century Swedish as well as specific methods to handle compound words better, for both Levenshtein and SMT.

In conclusion, the current methods work rather well when the input is Swedish words with archaic spelling, but for texts which contains words with modern Swedish spelling, a more complex system with additional components will be needed. This is seen clearly when comparing precision and recall of the two methods. Both methods pick up most of the instances of archaic spelling, but they also pick up a large amount of irrelevant data.

References

A. Baron and P. Rayson. 2008. *Vard2: A tool for dealing with spelling variation in historical corpora*, In Postgraduate Conference in Corpus Linguistics, Aston University, Birmingham, UK.

E. Pettersson, B. Megyesi and J. Nivre. 2012 *Rule-Based Normalisation of Historical Text   a Diachronic Study*, Proceedings of KONVENS 2012 (LThist 2012 workshop),   Vienna, September 21, 2012

E. Pettersson, B. Megyesi and J. Tiedemann. 2013 *An SMT Approach to Automatic Annotation of Historical Text*, Proceedings of the workshop on computational historical linguistics at NODALIDA 2013. NEALT Proceedings Series 18 / Linkping Electronic Conference Proceedings 87: 5469.

E. Pettersson, B. Megyesi and J. Nivre.   2013 *Normalisation of Historical Text Using Context-Sensitive Weighted Levenshtein Distance and Compound Splitting* , Proceedings of the 19th Nordic Conference of Computational Linguistics (NODALIDA 2013); Linkping Electronic Conference Proceedings 85: 163-179

E. Pettersson   2016 *Spelling Normalisation and Linguistic Analysis of Historical Text for Information Extraction*, Studia Linguistica Upsaliensia 17. 147 pp. Uppsala: Acta Universitatis Upsaliensis, Uppsala, Sweden.

E. Pettersson   2016 *User Manual for Normalisation of Noisy Input Data using HistNorm*, Department of Linguistics and Philology. Uppsala: Uppsala university, Uppsala, Sweden.

L. Borin, M. Forsberg and L. Lönngren.   2008 *Saldo 1.0 (svenskt associationslexikon version 2)*, Sprkbanken, Gothenburg: University of Gothenburg. Gothenburg, Sweden.

P. Rayson, D. Archer, and N. Smith. 2005. *VARD versus Word   A comparison of the UCREL variant detector and modern spell checkers on English historical corpora*, In Proceedings from the Corpus Linguistics Conference Series online e-journal, volume 1, Birmingham, UK.

P. Nakov, J. Tiedmann   2012. *Combining word-level and character-level models for machine translation between closely-related languages.*, In Proceedings of the 50th Annual Meeting of the Association for Computational Linguistics (Volume 2: Short Papers) pages 301-305. Jeju Island, Korea. Association for Computational Linguistics.

---

[8]This method works with the assumption that the original POS-tag is correct. A change of tags could also mean that the normalization is successful and an incorrectly tagged word now is tagged correctly.

Word vectors, reuse, and replicability:
Towards a community repository of large-text resources

Murhaf Fares, Andrey Kutuzov, Stephan Oepen, Erik Velldal

Language Technology Group
Department of Informatics, University of Oslo

{murhaff|andreku|oe|erikve}@ifi.uio.no

Abstract

This paper describes an emerging shared repository of large-text resources for creating word vectors, including pre-processed corpora and pre-trained vectors for a range of frameworks and configurations. This will facilitate reuse, rapid experimentation, and replicability of results.

1 Introduction

Word embeddings provide the starting point for much current work in NLP, not least because they often act as the input representations for neural network models. In addition to be being time-consuming to train, it can be difficult to compare results given the effects of different pre-processing choices and non-determinism in the training algorithms. This paper describes an initiative to create a shared repository of large-text resources for word vectors, including pre-processed corpora and pre-trained vector models for a range of frameworks and configurations.[1] This will facilitate rapid experimentation and replicability. The repository is available for public access at the following address:

```
http://vectors.nlpl.eu
```

To demonstrate the impact of different pre-processing choices and parameterizations, we provide indicative empirical results for a first set of embeddings made available in the repository (Section 3). Using an interactive web application, users are also able to explore and compare different pre-trained models on-line (Section 4).

2 Motivation and background

Over the last few years, the field of NLP at large has seen a huge revival of interest for distributional semantic representations in the form of word vectors

---

[1] Our repository in several respects complements and updates the collection of Wikipedia-derived corpora and pre-trained word embeddings published by Al-Rfou et al. (2013).

(Baroni et al., 2014). In particular, the use of dense vectors embedded in low-dimensional spaces, so-called *word embeddings*, have proved popular. As recent studies have shown that beyond their traditional use for encoding word-to-word semantic similarity, word vectors can also encode other relational or 'analogical' similarities that can be retrieved by simple vector arithmetic, these models have found many new use cases. More importantly, however, the interest in word embeddings coincides in several ways with the revived interest in neural network architectures: Word embeddings are now standardly used for providing the input layer for neural models in NLP, where their low dimensionality is key. Some of the most popular frameworks for training embeddings are also themselves based on neural nets, like the neural language models underlying the *word2vec*-like algorithms (Mikolov, Sutskever, et al., 2013).

These models are sometimes referred to as 'prediction-based', and contrasted with traditional 'count-based' models based on representing co-occurrence counts, as the vector values of these embeddings are optimized for predicting neighboring words. In practice, this distinction is not clear-cut, and a more useful distinction can be made between explicit representations, where each dimension of a high-dimensional and sparse vector directly corresponds to a contextual feature, and embeddings in the sense of dimensionality-reduced continuous representations. Of course, research on vectorial representations of distributional semantics dates back several decades, including dimensionality reduced variants like *Latent Semantic Analysis* (LSA) based on Singular Value Decomposition (Landauer & Dumais, 1997), *Probabilistic LSA* based on a version of the EM algorithm (Hofmann, 1999), *Random Indexing* based on random projections (Kanerva et al., 2000; Karlgren & Sahlgren, 2001; Widdows & Ferraro, 2009; Velldal, 2011), *Locality Sensitive Hashing* (LSH) (Ravichandran

Proceedings of the 21st Nordic Conference of Computational Linguistics, pages 271–276,
Gothenburg, Sweden, 23-24 May 2017. ©2017 Linköping University Electronic Press

et al., 2005; Durme & Lall, 2010), and others.

It it is important to note that although the practical examples, experimental results and discussion in this paper will be concerned with embeddings generated with neural skipgram models and *Global Vectors* (GloVe) (Pennington et al., 2014), most of the issues will apply to word vectors more generally. The repository itself is also intended to host word vectors across all paradigms.

Deep learning and neural network architectures are now increasingly replacing other modeling frameworks for a range of core different NLP tasks, ranging from tagging (Plank et al., 2016) and parsing (Dyer et al., 2015; Straka et al., 2015) to named entity recognition (Lample et al., 2016) and sentiment analysis (Socher et al., 2013; Kim, 2014). Word embeddings typically provide the standard input representations to these models, replacing traditional feature engineering. Training is usually done on large amounts of unlabeled text, and all stages involved in the data preparation can potentially affect the resulting embeddings; content extraction from mark-up, sentence segmentation, tokenization, normalization, and so on. Just as important, the process for generating embeddings in with the aforementioned algorithms is *non-deterministic*: For the same set of hyperparameters and the same input data, different embeddings can (and most probably will) be produced. In sum these factors pose serious challenges for replicability for any work relying on word embeddings (Hellrich & Hahn, 2016).

The availability of pre-trained models is important in this respect. It can ensure that the same embeddings are re-used across studies, so that effects of other factors can be isolated and tested. Pre-trained models are currently available for a range of different algorithms: *Continuous Skipgram, Continuous Bag-of-Words, GloVe, fastText* (Bojanowski et al., 2016) and others. However, even when comparing the results for different pre-trained embeddings for a given data set, it can still be hard to know whether an observed difference is due to the embedding algorithm or text pre-processing.

Moreover, the available choices for pre-trained vectors are very limited in terms of data sets and pre-processing. Typically only embeddings trained on full-forms are available. However, given the convenience of using pre-trained vectors – training your own can often take several days and be computationally demanding – many studies use embeddings not ideally suited for the particular task.

For many semantically oriented tasks for example, embeddings trained on PoS-disambiguated lemmas would make more sense than using full-forms.

Given the considerations above, we find it important to establish a shared repository where it is possible to share training data, pre-processing pipelines, and pre-trained embeddings. Whenever possible, the training texts should be made available with various levels of pre-processing (e.g., lemmatized and PoS-tagged). In cases where licensing does not permit this, standardized pipelines for pre-processing should still be shared. In addition, a selection of sets of pre-trained word vectors should be made available for a few different parameterizations across different modeling frameworks, trained on data with varying degrees of pre-processing.

This will facilitate reuse and rapid experimentation. Should you still need to train you own vectors, you can use a standardized pipeline for pre-processing the training data. Most importantly, such a repository will help to ensure the replicability of results.

3   On the effects of corpus preparation

Levy et al. (2015) show that careful optimization of hyperparameters is often a more important factor for performance than the choice of embedding algorithm itself. The explicit specification of these hyperparameters is therefore essential to achieving a nuanced comparison between different word embedding approaches as well as replicability – inasmuch as replicating word embeddings is possible. As discussed in Section 2, the space of parameters associated with text pre-processing prior to training is also an important factor. To the best of our knowledge, however, there has been little research on the effect of corpus preparation on the training and performance of word embeddings.

In addition to the choice of training corpus itself, e.g. Wikipedia or Gigaword (Parker et al., 2011), there are many pre-processing steps involved in creating word embeddings. These steps include, but are not limited to, defining the basic token unit (full-form vs. lemma vs. PoS-disambiguated lemma), stop-word removal, downcasing, number normalization, phrase identification, named entities recognition and more. Other pre-processing steps depend on the nature of the training corpus; for example in training embeddings on text extracted from Wikipedia, the actual training corpus depends on the content-extraction tools used to interpret Wiki markup. Moreover, in most cases the choice of the particular *tool* to use for steps like tokenization and sentence splitting will also make a difference. One of the important considerations we take in creating a shared repository of word embeddings is to spell out such choices.

A pilot study To empirically demonstrate the impact of text pre-processing on word embeddings, we here present a pilot experiment, presenting intrinsic evaluation of a suite of embeddings trained for different choices of training corpora and pre-processing.

We trained twelve word embedding models on texts extracted from the English Wikipedia dump from September 2016 (about 2 billion word tokens) and Gigaword Fifth Edition (about 4.8 billion word tokens). We extracted the content from Wikipedia using *WikiExtractor*.[2] Further, we sentence-split, tokenized, and lemmatized the text in Wikipedia and Gigaword using *Stanford CoreNLP Toolkit 3.6.0* (Manning et al., 2014). We also removed all stop-words using the stop list defined in *NLTK* (Bird et al., 2009). In terms of pre-processing, the models differ in whether they were trained on full-forms or lemmas. Additionally, the models differ in the training text: Wikipedia (words with frequency less than 80 were ignored), Gigaword (frequency threshold 100) and Wikipedia concatenated with Gigaword (frequency threshold 200). All the corpora were shuffled prior to training.

The combination of the token choices and the training corpora leads to six different configurations. To eliminate the possibility of the effect of text pre-processing being approach-specific, we trained embeddings using both GloVe (Pennington et al., 2014) and Continuous Skipgram (Mikolov, Chen, et al., 2013) with negative sampling (SGNS). In terms of hyperparameters, we aligned GloVe and SGNS hyperparameters as much as possible: in both approaches we set the dimensionality to 300 and the symmetric context window size to 5. The SGNS models were trained using the Gensim implementation (Řehůřek & Sojka, 2010), using identical seed for all models; the GloVe models were trained with the reference implementation published by the authors.

We then evaluated the resulting models on two standard test datasets: SimLex-999 semantic sim-

ilarity dataset (Hill et al., 2015) and the Google Analogies Dataset (Mikolov, Chen, et al., 2013). The former contains human judgments on which word pairs are more or less semantically similar than the others (for example '*sea*' and '*ocean*' are more similar than '*bread*' and '*cheese*'). The task for the model here is to generate similarity values most closely correlating with those in the dataset. We follow the standard approach of evaluating performance towards SimLex-999 by computing Spearman rank-order correlation coefficients (Spearman, 1904), comparing the judgments on word pair similarities according to a given embedding model and the gold data.

The Google Analogies Dataset contains question pairs with proportional analogies: $a : a* :: b : b*$. For example, '*Oslo*' is to '*Norway*' as '*Stockholm*' is to '*Sweden*'. The task for the model is, given the vectors $(a, a*, b)$, to generate a vector, for which the closest vector in the model is $b*$. As a rule, the models solve this using the *3CosAdd* approach (Levy & Goldberg, 2014): $b* = a* + b - a$.

Results for the Google analogies test are standardly reported for two distinct sets of analogies in the data: 5 sections of 'semantic' relations (8,869 in total) and 9 sections of 'syntactic' relations (10,675 in total). The semantic relations are similar to the example with the capitals, while the syntactic part features analogies like '*walk*' is to '*walks*' as '*run*' is to '*runs*'. Measuring the effect of choices like using lemmas or full-forms only makes sense for the semantic tests, so we will not focus on the morphological and derivational analogies in our experiments.[3]

Results and discussion Table 1 presents the results of evaluating our trained models on the benchmark datasets described above, showing how the results depend both on linguistic pre-processing and on the embeddings algorithm used. In Table 1, 'wiki', 'giga' and 'comb' denotes our 3 training corpora. The GloVe embeddings were trained with the default parameters except for the initial learning rate (0.02), number of iterations (100) and the window and vector size (cf. Section 3), 'SGNS' denotes Continuous Skipgram embeddings using

---

[3]It is worth noting that some of the sections standardly regarded as 'syntactic' could well be argued to contain semantic relationships, like the 'nationality–adjective' section, but for comparability of results we here adhere to the standard split, where the semantic part include the sections titled 'capital-common-countries', 'capital-world', 'currency', 'city-in-state', and 'family'.

Model	SimLex	Analogy
GloVe wiki lemmas	36.13	**83.08**
GloVe wiki forms	31.27	81.80
GloVe giga lemmas	37.74	73.37
GloVe giga forms	32.36	72.20
GloVe comb lemmas	39.96	78.90
GloVe comb forms	34.81	77.46
SGNS wiki lemmas	40.19	78.86
SGNS wiki forms	35.54	77.60
SGNS giga lemmas	41.90	67.47
SGNS giga forms	37.96	66.84
SGNS comb lemmas	**42.58**	72.62
SGNS comb forms	38.21	72.54

Table 1: Results for SimLex-999 and the semantic sections of the Google Analogies Dataset.

10 negative samples.

Analysis of the evaluation results shows several important issues. First, while our SGNS models perform slightly better for the semantic similarity task, our GloVe models are more efficient in the semantic analogy test. The latter observation is perhaps not so surprising given that analogical inference was one of the primary aims of its authors.

Second, we see that more data is not necessarily better. For the benchmarking against SimLex-999, we do see that more data consistently leads to higher scores. For the semantic analogies task, however, the Gigaword corpus consistently results in models performing worse than Wikipedia, despite the fact that it is 2.5 times larger. Combining Gigaword and Wikipedia still yields lower scores than for Wikipedia alone. Moreover, with an accuracy of 83.08 for the semantic analogies, the GloVe model trained on the lemmatized version of Wikipedia outperforms the GloVe model trained on 42 billion tokens of web data from the Common Crawl reported in (Pennington et al., 2014), which at an accuracy of 81.9 was the best result previously reported for this task.

Finally, for both the semantic analogy task and the similarity task, we observe that the models trained on the lemmatized corpora are consistently better than the full-form models. In the future we plan to also evaluate our models on more balanced analogy datasets like that of Gladkova et al. (2016).

4 Infrastructure: Embeddings on-line

To achieve our goals of increased re-use and replicability, we are providing a public repository of texts, tools, and ready-to-use embeddings in the context of the Nordic e-Infrastructure Collaboration[4] and with support from national supercomputing centers. A comprehensive collection of resources for English and Norwegian[5] is available for download as well as for direct access by supercomputer users, combined with emerging documentation on the complete process of their creation, 'getting started' guides for end users, as well as links to indicative empirical results using these models. We invite feedback by academic peers on the repository already in this early stage of implementation and will welcome contributions by others.

In ongoing work, we are extracting even larger text corpora from web-crawled data and collaborating with other Nordic research centers (notably the University of Turku) to provide resources for additional languages. As the underlying supercomputing infrastructure is in principle open to all (non-commercial) researchers in the Nordic region, we hope that this repository will grow and develop into a community-maintained resource that greatly reduces the technological barrier to using very large-scale word vectors. The exact procedures for community contributions have yet to be determined, but we anticipate a very lightweight governing scheme. We intend to 'snapshot' versions of the repository at least once a year and publish these releases through the Norwegian Data Archive, to ensure long-term accessibility and citability.

The repository also provides the *WebVectors* web-service featuring pre-trained vectors for English and Norwegian.[6] Serving as an interactive explorer for the models, it allows users to retrieve nearest semantic associates, calculate similarities, apply algebraic operations to word vectors and perform analogical inference. It also features visualizations for semantic relations between words in the underlying models. This web service is thoroughly described by Kutuzov & Kuzmenko (2017).

---

[4]`https://neic.nordforsk.org/`

[5]While intended to continually grow, in mid-2017 the repository already makes available the pre-trained English word embedding models produced by *word2vec*, *fastText* and *GloVe*. For these frameworks and for varying levels of text pre-processing, it contains models based on the Gigaword Corpus, the British National Corpus and an English Wikipedia dump from February 2017; we plan to regularly update the Wikipedia-derived corpora and models, and also evaluate alternative text extraction frameworks for Wiki markup, e.g. *Wikipedia Corpus Builder* by Solberg (2012). Additionally, there are corresponding models trained on the Norwegian News Corpus (Hofland, 2000).

[6]`http://vectors.nlpl.eu/explore/`
`embeddings/`

Acknowledgments

This initiative is part of the Nordic Language Processing Laboratory (`http://www.nlpl.eu`), an emerging distributed research environment supported by the Nordic e-Infrastructure Collaboration, the universities of Copenhagen, Helsinki, Oslo, Turku, and Uppsala, as well as the Finnish and Norwegian national e-infrastructure providers, CSC and Sigma2. We are grateful to all Nordic taxpayers.

References

Al-Rfou, R., Perozzi, B., & Skiena, S. (2013). Polyglot. Distributed word representations for multilingual NLP. In *Proceedings of the 17th Conference on Natural Language Learning* (p. 183–192). Sofia, Bulgaria.

Baroni, M., Dinu, G., & Kruszewski, G. (2014). Don't count, predict! A systematic comparison of context-counting vs. context-predicting semantic vectors. In *Proceedings of the 52nd Annual Meeting of the Association for Computational Linguistics (Volume 1: Long Papers)* (p. 238–247). Baltimore, Maryland: Association for Computational Linguistics.

Bird, S., Klein, E., & Loper, E. (2009). *Natural language processing with Python.* Beijing: O'Reilly.

Bojanowski, P., Grave, E., Joulin, A., & Mikolov, T. (2016). Enriching word vectors with subword information. *arXiv preprint arXiv:1607.04606.*

Durme, B. V., & Lall, A. (2010). Online generation of locality sensitive hash signatures. In *Proceedings of the 48th Meeting of the Association for Computational Linguistics* (p. 231–235). Uppsala, Sweden.

Dyer, C., Ballesteros, M., Ling, W., Matthews, A., & Smith, N. (2015). Transition-based dependency parsing with stack long short-term memory. In *Proceedings of the 53rd Meeting of the Association for Computational Linguistics and of the 7th International Joint Conference on Natural Language Processing.* Bejing, China.

Gladkova, A., Drozd, A., & Matsuoka, S. (2016). Analogy-based Detection of Morphological and Semantic Relations with Word Embeddings: What Works and What Doesn't. In *Proceedings of the NAACL Student Research Workshop* (p. 8–15). San Diego, California: Association for Computational Linguistics.

Hellrich, J., & Hahn, U. (2016). Bad Company—Neighborhoods in Neural Embedding Spaces Considered Harmful. In *Proceedings of COLING 2016, the 26th International Conference on Computational Linguistics: Technical Papers* (p. 2785–2796). Osaka, Japan: The COLING 2016 Organizing Committee.

Hill, F., Reichart, R., & Korhonen, A. (2015). SimLex-999: Evaluating Semantic Models With (Genuine) Similarity Estimation. *Computational Linguistics, 41*(4), 665–695.

Hofland, K. (2000). A self-expanding corpus based on newspapers on the Web. In *Proceedings of the Second International Conference on Language Resources and Evaluation (LREC-2000).*

Hofmann, T. (1999). Probabilistic latent semantic analysis. In *Proceedings of the fifteenth conference on uncertainty in artificial intelligence* (p. 289–296). Stockholm, Sweden.

Kanerva, P., Kristoferson, J., & Holst, A. (2000). Random indexing of text samples for latent semantic analysis. In *Proceedings of the 22nd annual conference of the cognitive science society* (p. 1036). PA, USA.

Karlgren, J., & Sahlgren, M. (2001). From words to understanding. In Y. Uesaka, P. Kanerva, & H. Asoh (Eds.), *Foundations of real-world intelligence* (p. 294–308). Stanford, CA, USA: CSLI Publications.

Kim, Y. (2014). Convolutional neural networks for sentence classification. In *Proceedings of the 2014 Conference on Empirical Methods in Natural Language Processing* (p. 1746–1751). Doha, Qatar.

Kutuzov, A., & Kuzmenko, E. (2017). Building Web-Interfaces for Vector Semantic Models with the WebVectors Toolkit. In *Proceedings of the Demonstrations at the 15th Conference of the European Chapter of the Association for Computational Linguistics.* Association for Computational Linguistics.

Lample, G., Ballesteros, M., Subramanian, S., Kawakami, K., & Dyer, C. (2016). Neural architectures for named entity recognition. In *Proceedings of the 2016 Meeting of the North American Chapter of the Association for Computational Linguistics and Human Language Technology Conference* (p. 260–270). San Diego, CA, USA.

Landauer, T. K., & Dumais, S. T. (1997). A solution to Plato's problem: The Latent Semantic Analysis theory of the acquisition, induction, and representation of knowledge. *Psychological Review*(104), 211–240.

Levy, O., & Goldberg, Y. (2014). Linguistic Regularities in Sparse and Explicit Word Representations. In *Proceedings of the Eighteenth Conference on Computational Natural Language Learning* (p. 171–180). Ann Arbor, Michigan: Association for Computational Linguistics.

Levy, O., Goldberg, Y., & Dagan, I. (2015). Improving Distributional Similarity with Lessons Learned from Word Embeddings. *Transactions of the Association of Computational Linguistics, 3*, 211–225.

Manning, C. D., Surdeanu, M., Bauer, J., Finkel, J., Bethard, S. J., & McClosky, D. (2014). The Stanford CoreNLP Natural Language Processing Toolkit. In *Association for Computational Linguistics (ACL) System Demonstrations* (p. 55–60).

Mikolov, T., Chen, K., Corrado, G., & Dean, J. (2013). Efficient Estimation of Word Representations in Vector Space.

arXiv preprint arXiv:1301.3781.

Mikolov, T., Sutskever, I., Chen, K., Corrado, G. S., & Dean, J. (2013). Distributed Representations of Words and Phrases and their Compositionality. *Advances in Neural Information Processing Systems 26*, 3111–3119.

Parker, R., Graff, D., Kong, J., Chen, K., & Maeda, K. (2011). *English Gigaword Fifth Edition LDC2011T07* (Tech. Rep.). Technical Report. Linguistic Data Consortium, Philadelphia.

Pennington, J., Socher, R., & Manning, C. (2014). GloVe: Global Vectors for Word Representation. In *Proceedings of the 2014 Conference on Empirical Methods in Natural Language Processing (EMNLP)* (p. 1532–1543). Doha, Qatar: Association for Computational Linguistics.

Plank, B., Søgaard, A., & Goldberg, Y. (2016). Multilingual part-of-speech tagging with bidirectional long short-term memory models and auxiliary loss. In *Proceedings of the 54th Meeting of the Association for Computational Linguistics*. Berlin, Germany.

Ravichandran, D., Pantel, P., & Hovy, E. (2005). Randomized algorithms and NLP: using locality sensitive hash function for high speed noun clustering. In *Proceedings of the 43rd Meeting of the Association for Computational Linguistics* (p. 622–629). Ann Arbor, MI, USA.

Řehůřek, R., & Sojka, P. (2010). Software Framework for Topic Modelling with Large Corpora. In *Proceedings of the LREC 2010 Workshop on New Challenges for NLP Frameworks* (pp. 45–50). Valletta, Malta: ELRA.

Socher, R., Perelygin, A., Wu, J., Chuang, J., Manning, C., Ng, A., & Potts, C. (2013). Recursive deep models for semantic compositionality over a sentiment treebank. In *Proceedings of the 2013 Conference on Empirical Methods in Natural Language Processing* (p. 1631–1642). Seattle, WA, USA.

Solberg, L. J. (2012). *A corpus builder for Wikipedia*. Unpublished master's thesis, University of Oslo, Norway.

Spearman, C. (1904). The Proof and Measurement of Association between Two Things. *The American Journal of Psychology*, *15*(1), 72–101.

Straka, M., Hajič, J., Straková, J., & Hajič jr., J. (2015). Parsing universal dependency treebanks using neural networks and search-based oracle. In *Proceedings of the 14th International Workshop on Treebanks and Linguistic Theories.* Warsaw, Poland.

Velldal, E. (2011). Random indexing re-hashed. In *Proceedings of the 18th Nordic Conference of Computational Linguistics* (p. 224–229). Riga, Latvia.

Widdows, D., & Ferraro, K. (2009). Semantic vectors: a scalable open source package and online technology management application. In *Proceedings of the 6th International Conference on Language Resources and Evaluation.* Marrakech, Morocco.

Improving Optical Character Recognition of Finnish Historical Newspapers with a Combination of Fraktur & Antiqua Models and Image Preprocessing

Mika Koistinen
National Library of Finland
The Centre for Preservation
and Digitisation
mika.koistinen@helsinki.fi

Kimmo Kettunen
National Library of Finland
The Centre for Preservation
and Digitisation
kimmo.kettunen@helsinki.fi

Tuula Pääkkönen
National Library of Finland
The Centre for Preservation
and Digitisation
tuula.pääkkönen@helsinki.fi

Abstract

In this paper we describe a method for improving the optical character recognition (OCR) toolkit Tesseract for Finnish historical documents. First we create a model for Finnish Fraktur fonts. Second we test Tesseract with the created Fraktur model and Antiqua model on single images and combinations of images with different image preprocessing methods. Against commercial ABBYY FineReader toolkit our method achieves 27.48% (FineReader 7 or 8) and 9.16% (FineReader 11) improvement on word level.

Keywords: Optical Character Recognition, OCR Quality, Digital Image Processing, Binarization, Noise Removal, Tesseract, Finnish, Historical Documents

1 Introduction

These days newspapers are published in digital format (born digital). However, historical documents were born before the digital age and need to be scanned first and then extracted as text from the images by using optical character recognition (OCR). Currently the National Library of Finland (NLF) has over 10 million scanned historical newspaper and journal pages and there is need to improve the OCR quality, because it affects the usability and information retrieval accuracy for individual users, researchers and companies at the Digi newspaper collection.[1]

NLF's current document collection is discussed more in detail in Kettunen et al. (2016). Usually OCR quality of a historical document collection is many times on the level of 70-80% word accuracy. Tanner et al. (2009) estimated that OCR quality of the British 19th century newspaper collection

has 78% word accuracy. According to Järvelin et al. (2015) improved OCR quality would improve the usability and information retrieval results for the Digi collection. Evershed and Fitch (2014) show that over 10% point OCR word accuracy improvement could improve the search recall by over 9% point on OCRed historical English documents. According to Lopresti (2009) better OCR quality would improve the possiblities to utilize other text analysis methods for example sentence boundary detection, tokenization, and part-of-speech tagging. Also other methods such as named entity recognition, topic modeling and machine translation could benefit from better quality input data.

There are many existing commercial and open source OCR tools available. Open source tools are attractive choices, because they are free and open for improvement. For example Tesseract[2] is an open source OCR engine, that is combined with Leptonica image library processing. It has models for over 100 languages. Some of the open source OCR tools e.g. Tesseract, Cuneiform, and OCRopus are discussed more in detail in (Smitha et al., 2016; Smith, 2007). From commercial tools ABBYY FineReader is one of the most known ones.

In our work, we develop a Tesseract Finnish Fraktur model using an existing German Fraktur model[3] as a starting point. We compare the resulting model with the commercial ABBYY FineReader toolkit. Previously, OCR quality of Tesseract and ABBYY FineReader has been compared by Heliński et al. (2012) on Polish historical documents. In their experiments, Tesseract outperformed FineReader on good quality pages containing Fraktur fonts, while FineReader performed better on Antiqua fonts and bad quality pages.

In addition to developing a new Finnish Fraktur model we study the effect of various preprocess-

---

[1] digi.kansalliskirjasto.fi

[2] https://code.google.com/p/tesseract-ocr/
[3] https://github.com/paalberti/tesseract-dan-fraktur

Proceedings of the 21st Nordic Conference of Computational Linguistics, pages 277–283,
Gothenburg, Sweden, 23-24 May 2017. ©2017 Linköping University Electronic Press

ing methods employed to improve the image quality on final OCR accuracy. Previously these kind of methods have shown to yield improvements in the image and/or OCR quality in several works (Smitha et al., 2016; Ganchimeg, 2015; El Harraj and Raissouni, 2015; Wolf et al., 2002; Sauvola and Pietikäinen, 1999).

The rest of the paper is organized as follows. In Section 2, we discuss challenges and methods related to scanned newspaper image quality improvement and Tesseract model teaching. The developed method and its evaluation are then discussed in Sections 3 and 4, respectively. Finally, we present conclusion on the work in section 5.

2 Challenges

OCRing of Finnish historical documents is difficult mainly because of the varying quality newspaper images and lack of model for Finnish Fraktur. Also the speed of the OCR algorithm is important, when there is need for OCRing a collection containing millions of documents. Scanned historical document images have noise such as scratches, tears, ink spreading, low contrast, low brightness, and skewing etc. Smitha et al. (2016) present that document image quality can be improved by binarization, noise removal, deskewing, and foreground detection. Image processing methods are briefly explained next as a background for improving the scanned image quality.

2.1 Improving the image quality by image processing methods

Digital images can be processed either by sliding a rectangular window through image to modify it's pixel values inside the window (local) or the whole image can be processed at once (global).

Binarization is image processing method that turns grayscale image pixels into binary image. The pixels in image are transferred to either black (0) or white (255) by a threshold value. Binarization methods according to Segzin and Sankur (2004) are based on histogram shape-based methods, clustering-based methods such as Otsu (1979), entropy-based, object atribute-based, spatial methods and local methods such as Niblack (1986); Sauvola and Pietikäinen (1999). Tesseract toolkit uses Otsu's algorithm for binarization as a default, which is not always the best method for degraded documents.

Wolf et al. (2002) developed image binarization

algorithm with much better recall and slightly better precision. The method is based on Niblack and Sauvola algorithms. Niblack's algorithm is using rectangular window that is slided through the image. It's center pixel threshold (T) is calculated by using the mean (m) and variance (s) of the values inside the window.

$$T = m + k * s, \tag{1}$$

where k is constant set to 0.2. This method unfortunately usually creates noise to areas where there is no text. To avoid noise Sauvola's method included hypothesis on gray values of text and background pixels, thus modifying the formula into

$$T = m * (1 - k * (1 - \frac{s}{R})), \tag{2}$$

where R is the dynamics of standard deviation that is set to 128. However this hypothesis does not hold in every image documents such as variable contrast degraded documents. Therefore the formula was changed to normalize the contrast and mean gray level of the image.

$$T = m - k * (1 - \frac{s}{R}) * (m - M)), \tag{3}$$

where R is the maximum standard deviation from all of the windows. M is the minimum graylevel of the image.

Smoothing or blurring is a method to attenuate the most frequent image pixels. It is typically used to reduce image noise. Gonzales and Woods (2002) (p. 119-125) presents smoothing windows (Figure 1),

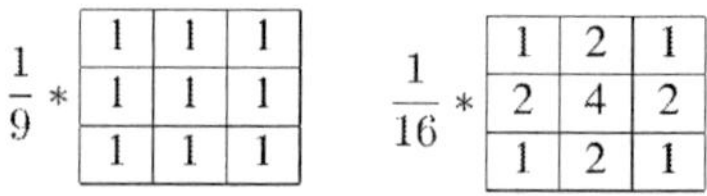

Figure 1: Smoothing windows

where the former is the average of gray levels and latter is the weighted average approach (window is rough approximation of a Gaussian function). These windows can be slided through image and the output is smoothed image. Ganchimeg (2015) presents history of document preprocessing methods noise removal and binarization. These methods can be based on thresholding, fuzzy methods, histograms, morphology, genetic algorithms, and marginal noise removal. The filtering techniques Gaussian, Sharpen, and Mean are compared, and it is noted that Gaussian blur is best for creating clear and smooth images. Droettboom (2003) mentions problem with broken and touching characters in recognizing older documents, and proposes broken character connection algorithm using k-nearest neighbours, which is able to find and join 91% of the broken characters. Original, blurred and some binarization methods for four different images can be seen below in Figure 2.

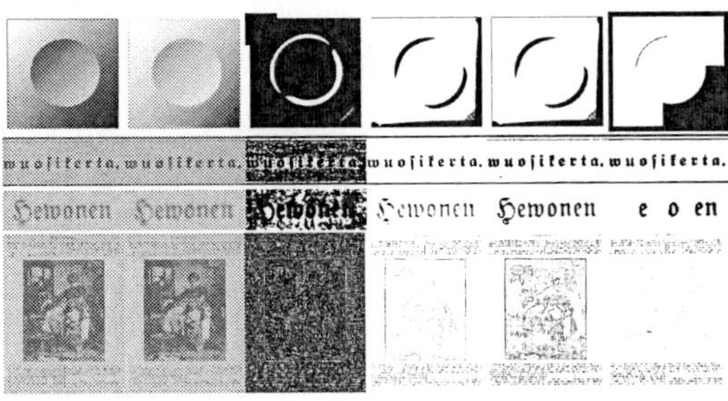

Figure 2: a) Grayscale(left) , b) Gaussian blur c) Niblack, d) Sauvola e) WolfJolion, f) Howe 3[67].

Image histogram presents image grayscale values(x) between 0-255 and frequencies(y) for all of the image pixels, where value 0 is black and 255 is white. It is a common way to visualize the image contents. According to Krutsch and Tenorio (2011) histogram equalization methods are Histogram expansion, Local area histogram equalization, Cumulative Histogram Equalization, Par Sectioning and Odd Sectioning. These methods try to improve the dynamic range of the image. High dynamic range means same as high contrast. Typically images with low contrast are visually very dull, grayish.

Linear normalization is also called contrast stretching or histogram expansion. Below in Equation 4, a linear transformation function is shown. This function is utilized to map the original images pixel values for broader range.

$$y = y_{max} * \frac{x - x_{min}}{x_{max} - x_{min}} \qquad (4)$$

Histogram equalization is another more advanced method for enchancing image contrast. It differs from linear transformation by using statistical probability distributions instead of linear functions. Image pixel probability density function (PDF) and cumulative density function (CDF)

are utilized to to calculate new image gray levels. However, global methods had problems with varying intensities inside the image. Thus an Adaptive Histogram Equalization (AHE) was developed. It partitions the image usually to 8 x 8 windows. For each of these image windows sub-histogram is used to equalize each window separately, but still AHE created problematic artifacts inside regions that contained noise, but no text.

Pizer et al. (1990) developed Contrast Limited Adaptive Histogram Equalization (CLAHE) that was limiting the error in the AHE. CLAHE uses the slope of transform function. It clips the top part of histogram (by predefined clip limit value) before calculating the CDF for each of the images in sliding window (see figure 3). The clipping reduces the over-amplification AHE had. Result image depends from window size and clip limit, and are selected by the user.

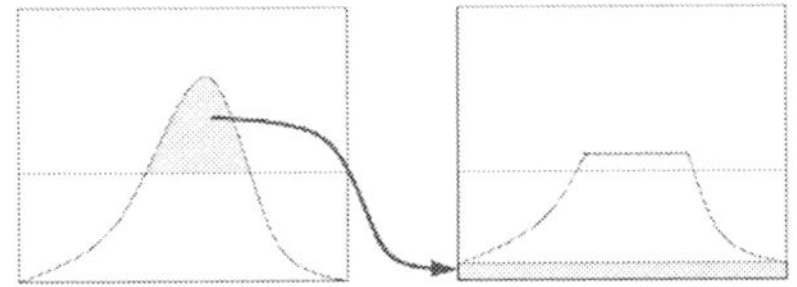

Figure 3: CLAHE histogram clipping from Stanhope (2016)

Below in Figure 4 results of contrast improvement methods are shown. CLAHE histogram has clearly equalized more than the linear normalized image.

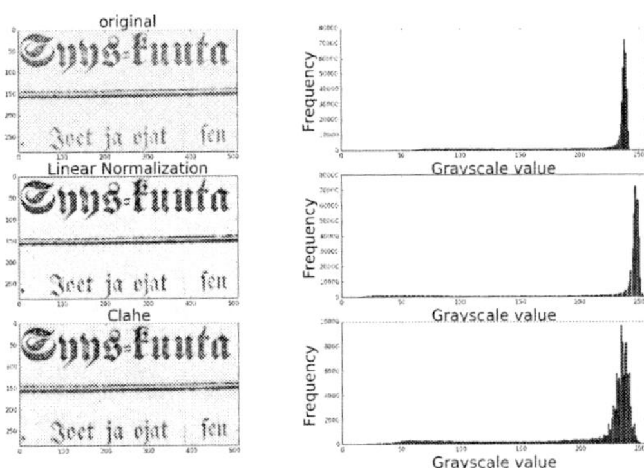

Figure 4: Original, Linear Normalized and Contrast Limited Adaptive Histogram Equalized image and their histograms

Skewing can also be a problem and it can be solved by skew detection and deskewing. According to Parashar and Sogi (2012) common methods for skew detection are Hough transform, projection profile and principal component analysis. Skew can be single or multiple. In multiple skew multiple parts of the document are skewed in different angle, and in single skew the image has been skewed only to one angle. We are dealing with multiple skew documents. More information about deskewing can be found from (Smith, 1995; Makkar and Singh, 2012). Our method does not use deskewing so far, but it could be included to possibly improve the accuracy.

Multiple other image processing methods exist, too. Image processing methods are widely researched for the use of historical document processing. For example annual International Conference on Document Analysis and Recognition DIBCO competition offers new methods for historical document image processing (Pratikakis et al., 2013; Ntirogiannis et al., 2014; Howe, 2013).

3 Method

We created a model for Finnish Fraktur character recognition for Tesseract. After that we run Tesseract OCR with different image preprocessing methods and chose the best one, by comparing the average confidence measure documents have. We used the hOCR-format[8], which is an open standard for presenting OCR results and it has confidence value for each word given by the used OCR tool. The average of Tesseract's word confidences in a document is used in this method.

Creation of Finnish Fraktur model was started by using German Fraktur model as a baseline. The Fraktur model was iteratively improved. The characters that had most errors were improved in training data boxes (letters and two letter combinations). Then Tesseract is run 1 to N times with the developed Finnish Fraktur model and already existing Finnish Antiqua model[9] in dual model mode, where it selects best choice from Fraktur and Antiqua results.

The images passed into Tesseract OCR on each run are either no processing, or processed by some image processing methods. In case of 1 run that run is selected as a final document, and in case of 2-N runs, the final resulting document is selected by the highest document confidence measure value. Our proposed solution for preprocessing and OCRing using the obtained Finnish Fraktur model can be seen below in Figure 5. Tesseract has build in Otsu's binarization so actually no processing means running the Otsu's algorithm before OCR. Otsu is also run inside Tesseract before OCR for all other methods.

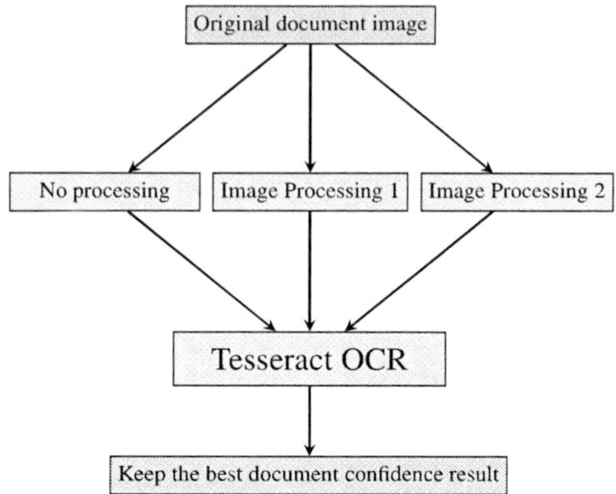

Figure 5: Proposed OCR method

4 Experiments

4.1 Data

For training the Finnish Fraktur model we used 72 images. The images contained 34 newspaper page images from our newspaper collection, and 38 synthetically created images with one column texts with various Finnish Fraktur fonts. The documents were manually boxed by using a box editor[10]. Training data contained 184,852 characters and two character combinations. Testing data was a proofread set of 462 scanned newspaper pages. It contained 530,579 word tokens, 4,175,710 characters. 434 pages were Fraktur, and the rest partly Fraktur and/or Antiqua pages.

4.2 Accuracy measure

As accuracy measures we use word error rate (WER) and character accuracy rate (CER)[11]. They are defined below in Equations 5 and 6.

$$CER = \frac{i + s + d}{n} \qquad (5)$$

<hr>

[8] https://kba.github.io/hocr-spec/1.2/

[9] https://github.com/tesseract-ocr/langdata/tree/master/fin

[10] https://github.com/zdenop/qt-box-editor

[11] http://www.digitisation.eu/training/succeed-training-materials/ocr-evaluation/ocrevaluation/measuring-ocr-quality/computing-error-rates/

where n is the total number of characters in reference text, i is the minimal number of insertions, s is substitutions and d is deletions on character level to obtain the reference text.

$$WER = \frac{i_w + s_w + d_w}{n_w} \qquad (6)$$

where n_w is the total number of words in reference text, i_w is the minimal number of insertions, s_w is substitutions and d_w is deletions on word level to obtain the reference text. Smaller WER and CER means better quality for words and characters. For the WER results Impact centre's accuracy evaluation tool developed by Carrasco (2014) was utilized in this research. The Fraktur model CER results were compared by utilizing the Information Science Research Institute's OCR accuracy tool developed by Rice and Nartker (1996).

4.3 Results

WER results for the different runs of our method can be seen below in Table 1. Result of ABBYY FineReader 11 and 7 or 8 are shown as a baseline, our method with different image processing methods and an Oracle are given as comparison. In our method, Tesseract was run with two models (Fraktur and Antiqua), where Tesseract selects the better one as a result. Oracle is the best result of the combined 2-4 images based on the resulting WER.

Method	Result	Oracle
ABBYY FineReader 11	20.94	N/A
ABBYY FineReader 7 or 8	26.23	N/A
Tesseract (fi_frak_mk41+fin)		
original (otsu)	23.32	N/A
gaussian blur	24.24	N/A
sauvola	39.49	N/A
wolf	**22.67**	N/A
clahe	29.19	N/A
l.norm	23.36	N/A
clahe+wolf	32.67	N/A
l.norm+wolf	22.76	N/A
Combined 2		
l.norm+wolf,clahe+wolf	20.30	19.42
clahe+wolf,orig	20.40	19.30
clahe+wolf,blur	20.58	19.44
clahe+wolf,wolf	**19.98**	**19.19**
Combined 3		
clahe+wolf,wolf,blur	19.58	**17.53**
l.norm+wolf, clahe+wolf,blur	19.68	17.57
l.norm+wolf, clahe,orig	19.69	17.99
l.norm, clahe+wolf,wolf	**19.14**	17.69
Combined 4		
l.norm, clahe+wolf,orig,blur	19.11	17.61
l.norm, clahe+wolf,orig,wolf	19.32	**16.94**
l.norm+wolf, clahe+wolf,orig,blur	19.41	**16.94**
l.norm+wolf, clahe+wolf,orig,wolf	**19.02**	17.50

Table 1: WER results, the best of each 1-4 runs on bold (smaller is better)

CER results for the Fraktur model for original images can be seen below in Figure 3 and 4. The figures present the most frequent character errors, and their correctness percentage for the Fraktur model, respectively.

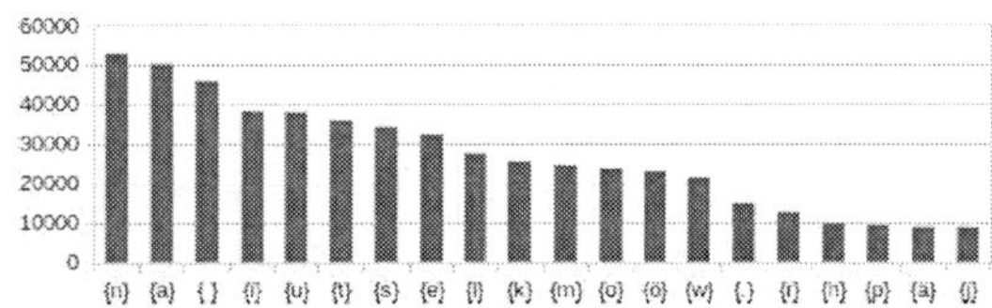

Figure 6: Most frequent character errors

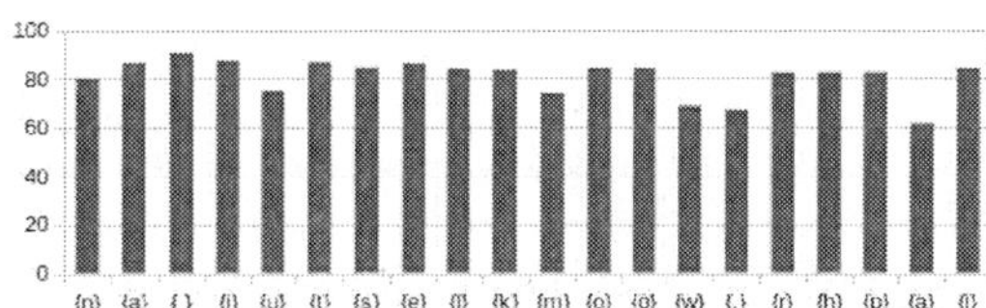

Figure 7: Correctness percentage

4.4 Execution times

Tesseract was run on IT Centre for Science (CSC)[12] machines on 8 core Intel 2.6GHz CPU, 2GB RAM, in Red Hat Enterprise Linux 7 (64-bit) virtual environment, in 8 document batches by GNU parallel, developed by Tange (2011). ABBYY FineReader 11 was run on 1 core Intel 2.6GHz CPU, 4GB RAM, in Windows Server (32-bit) virtual environment. Decoding speeds for the Tesseract and ABBYY FineReader were 722,323 tokens/hour and 30,626 tokens/hour, respectively. Re-OCRing millions of pages is feasible using multiple CSC machines in parallel.

---

[12]https://www.csc.fi

5   Conclusions

We have described a method for improving the Tesseract OCR toolkit for Finnish historical documents. In the tests Tesseract was run in dual model mode using created Finnish Fraktur model and Finnish Antiqua model, and selecting the best document by its confidence value with different 2-4 image combinations. This method has clearly outperformed the ABBYY FineReader results.

The best method was achieved by combining four methods (Linear Normalization + WolfJolion, Contrast Limited Adaptive Histogram Equalization+WolfJolion, original image and WolfJolion), which improves the word level quality of OCR by 1.91 percentage points (which is 9.16%) against the best result on FineReader 11 and by 7.21 percentage points (which is 27.48%) against the FineReader 7 and 8. It is great that FineReader 11 results have clearly improved from an earlier FineReader results. However, our current whole collection have been run only on FineReader 7 and 8, and the FineReader 11 is not feasible to be run for the whole collection due to the current licencing policy. Therefore, our method would correct about 84.6 million words (27.48%) more in the current 1.06 million Finnish newpaper page collection (containing Finnish language). However, it can still be improved. The method is 2.08 percentage points from the optimal Oracle result (16.94).

The character accuracy results for Fraktur model show that characters u, m and w have under 80 percent correctness. These letters are overlapping with letters such as n and i. It seems, however, that if accuracy for one of them is increased accuracy of others will decrease. Possibly also letter ä could be improved, though is has similar overlapping with letters a and å. From 20 most frequent errors only five are under 80% correct. Still, the Fraktur model could be developed more, possibly to recognize also bold letters.

Tesseract's document confidence value can be used to find the weak quality documents for further processing. However, it is not a perfect measure when comparing and/or combining other model results together. The confidence measure could possibly be improved by integrating it with a morphological tool, that checks words after OCR, and then weights the confidence measure for each word. The image quality is one of the most important factors in the recognition accuracy, so further research with image processing algorithms should continue. In addition to utilizing the confidence measure value, methods to determine noise level in the image could possibly be utilized to choose only bad quality images for further preprocessing.

Acknowledgments

This research was supported by European Regional Development Fund (ERDF), University of Helsinki, Mikkeli University Consortium and the City of Mikkeli. (Project Digitalia)

References

R. C. Carrasco. 2014. An open-source OCR evaluation tool. In *DATeCH '14 Proceedings of the First International Conference on Digital Access to Textual Cultural Heritage*, pages 179–184.

M. Droettboom. 2003. Correcting broken characters in the recognition of historical documents. In *JCDL 03 Proceedings of the 3rd ACM/IEEE-CS joint conference on Digital libraries*, pages 364–366.

A. El Harraj and N. Raissouni. 2015. Ocr accuracy improvement on document images through a novel preprocessing approach. In *Signal & Image Processing : An International Journal (SIPIJ)*, volume 6, pages 114–133.

J. Evershed and K. Fitch. 2014. Correcting Noisy OCR: Context beats Confusion (2014). In *DATeCH '14 Proceedings of the First International Conference on Digital Access to Textual Cultural Heritage*, pages 45–51.

G. Ganchimeg. 2015. History document image background noise and removal methods. In *International Journal of Knowledge Content Development & Technology*, volume 5, pages 11–24.

R. C. Gonzales and R. E. Woods. 2002. *Digital Image Processing*. Prentice-Hall.

M. Heliński, M. Kmieciak, and T. Parkoła. 2012. Report on the comparison of Tesseract and ABBYY FineReader OCR engines. Technical report, Poznań Supercomputing and networking center, Poland.

N. Howe. 2013. Document Binarization with Automatic Parameter Tuning. In *Journal International Journal on Document Analysis and Recognition*, volume 16, pages 247–258.

A. Järvelin, H. Keskustalo, E. Sormunen, M. Saastamoinen, and K. Kettunen. 2015. Information retrieval from historical newspaper collections in highly inflectional languages: A query expansion approach. In *Journal of the Association for Information Science and Technology*, volume 67.

K. Kettunen, T. Pääkkönen, and M. Koistinen. 2016. Between diachrony and synchrony: evaluation of lexical quality of a digitized historical Finnish newspaper collection with morphological analyzers. In *Baltic HLT 2016*, volume 289, pages 122–129.

R. Krutsch and D. Tenorio. 2011. Histogram Equalization, Application Note. Technical report.

D. Lopresti. 2009. Optical character recognition errors and their effects on natural language processing. In *International Journal on Document Analysis and Recognition*, volume 12, pages 141–151.

N. Makkar and S Singh. 2012. A Brief tour to various Skew Detection and Correction Techniques. In *International Journal for Science and Emerging Technologies with Latest Trend*, volume 4, pages 54–58.

W. Niblack. 1986. *An Introduction to Image Processing*, volume SMC-9. Prentice-Hall, Eaglewood Cliffs, NJ.

K. Ntirogiannis, B. Gatos, and I. Pratikakis. 2014. ICFHR2014 Competition on Handwritten Document Image Binarization (H-DIBCO 2014). In *2014 14th International Conference on Frontiers in Handwriting Recognition*, pages 809–813.

N. Otsu. 1979. A Threshold Selection Method from Gray-Level Histograms. In *IEEE Transactions on Systems, Man and Cybernetics*, volume SMC-9, pages 62–66.

S. Parashar and S. Sogi. 2012. Finding skewness and deskewing scanned document. 3(4):1619–1924.

S. M. Pizer, R. E. Johnston, J. P. Ericksen, B. C. Yankaskas, and K. E. Muller. 1990. Contrast Limited Histogram Equalization Speed and Effectiveness.

I. Pratikakis, B. Gatos, and K. Ntirogiannis. 2013. ICDAR 2013 Document Image Binarization Contest (DIBCO 2013). In *2013 12th International Conference on Document Analysis and Recognition*, pages 1471–1476.

S. V. Rice and T. A. Nartker. 1996. The ISRI Analytic Tools for OCR Evaluation Version 5.1. Technical report, Information Science Research Institute (ISRI).

J. Sauvola and M. Pietikäinen. 1999. Adaptive Document Image Binarization. In *The Journal of the Pattern recognition society*, volume 33, pages 225–236.

M. Segzin and B. Sankur. 2004. Survey over image thresholding techniques and quantitative performance evaluation.

R. Smith. 1995. A Simple and Efficient Skew Detection Algorithm via Text Row Algorithm. In *Proceedings 3rd ICDAR'95, IEEE (1995)*, pages 1145–1148.

R. Smith. 2007. An Overview of the Tesseract OCR Engine. In *Proc. Ninth Int. Conference on Document Analysis and Recognition (ICDAR), IEEE (1995)*, pages 629–633.

M. L. Smitha, P. J. Antony, and D. N. Sachin. 2016. Document Image Analysis Using Imagemagick and Tesseract-ocr. In *International Advanced Research Journal in Science, Engineering and Technology (IARJSET)*, volume 3, pages 108–112.

T. Stanhope. 2016. Applications of Low-Cost Computer Vision for Agricultural Implement Feedback and Control.

O. Tange. 2011. GNU Parallel - The Command-Line Power Tool. In *The USENIX Magazine*, pages 42–47.

S. Tanner, T. Muñoz, and P. Hemy Ros. 2009. Measuring Mass Text Digitization Quality and Usefulness. Lessons Learned from Assessing the OCR Accuracy of the British Library's 19th Century Online Newspaper Archive. 15(7/8).

C. Wolf, J. Jolion, and F. Chassaing. 2002. Text Localization, Enhancement and Binarization in Multimedia Documents. In *Proceedings of the International Conference on Pattern Recognition (ICPR)*, volume 4, pages 1037–1040. Quebec City, Canada.

Redefining Context Windows for Word Embedding Models:
An Experimental Study

Pierre Lison
Norwegian Computing Center
Oslo, Norway
plison@nr.no

Andrei Kutuzov
Language Technology Group
University of Oslo
andreku@ifi.uio.no

Abstract

Distributional semantic models learn vector representations of words through the *contexts* they occur in. Although the choice of context (which often takes the form of a sliding window) has a direct influence on the resulting embeddings, the exact role of this model component is still not fully understood. This paper presents a systematic analysis of context windows based on a set of four distinct hyper-parameters. We train continuous Skip-Gram models on two English-language corpora for various combinations of these hyper-parameters, and evaluate them on both lexical similarity and analogy tasks. Notable experimental results are the positive impact of cross-sentential contexts and the surprisingly good performance of right-context windows.

1 Introduction

Distributional semantic models represent words through real-valued vectors of fixed dimensions, based on the distributional properties of these words observed in large corpora. Recent approaches such as prediction-based models (Mikolov et al., 2013b) and *GloVe* (Pennington et al., 2014) have shown that it is possible to estimate dense, low-dimensional vectors (often called *embeddings*) able to capture various functional or topical relations between words. These embeddings are used in a wide range of NLP tasks, including part-of-speech tagging, syntactic parsing, named entity recognition and semantic role labelling; see (Collobert et al., 2011; Lin et al., 2015; Zhou and Xu, 2015; Lample et al., 2016), among others.

As recently shown by (Levy et al., 2015), the empirical variations between embedding models are largely due to differences in hyper-parameters (many of which are tied to the underlying definition of context) rather than differences in the embedding algorithms themselves. In this paper, we further develop their findings with a comprehensive analysis of the role played by context window parameters when learning word embeddings. Four specific aspects are investigated:

1. The *maximum size* of the context window;

2. The *weighting scheme* of context words according to their distance to the focus word;

3. The relative *position* of the context window (symmetric, left or right side);

4. The treatment of *linguistic boundaries* such as end-of-sentence markers.

The next section 2 provides a brief overview on word embeddings and context windows. Section 3 describes the experimental setup used to evaluate the influence of these four aspects. Finally, Section 4 presents and discusses the results.

2 Background

The works of (Bengio et al., 2003) and (Mikolov et al., 2013b) introduced a paradigm-shift for distributional semantic models with new prediction-based algorithms outperforming the existing count-based approaches (Baroni et al., 2014). The *word2vec* models from (Mikolov et al., 2013b), comprising the Continuous Skip-gram and the Continuous Bag-of-Words algorithms, are now a standard part of many NLP pipelines.

Despite their differences, all types of distributional semantic models require the definition of a context for each word observed in a given corpus. Given a set of (word, context) pairs extracted from the corpus, vector representations of words can be derived through various estimation methods, such as predicting words given their contexts

Proceedings of the 21st Nordic Conference of Computational Linguistics, pages 284–288,
Gothenburg, Sweden, 23-24 May 2017. ©2017 Linköping University Electronic Press

(CBOW), predicting the contexts from the words (Skip-Gram), or factorizing the log of their co-occurrence matrix (*GloVe*). In all of these approaches, the choice of context is a crucial factor that directly affects the resulting vector representations. The most common method for defining this context is to rely on a *window* centered around the word to estimate (often called the *focus word*)[1]. The context window thus determines which contextual neighbours are taken into account when estimating the vector representations.

The most prominent hyper-parameter associated to the context window is the maximum window size (i.e. the maximum distance between the focus word and its contextual neighbours). This parameter is the easiest one to adjust using existing software, which is why it is comparatively well studied. Larger windows are known to induce embeddings that are more 'topical' or 'associative', improving their performance on analogy test sets, while smaller windows induce more 'functional' and 'synonymic' models, leading to better performance on similarity test sets (Goldberg, 2016).

However, the context window is also affected by other, less obvious hyper-parameters. Inside a given window, words that are closer to the focus word should be given more weights than more distant ones. To this end, CBOW and Continuous Skip-gram rely on a dynamic window mechanism where the actual size of the context window is sampled uniformly from 1 to L, where L is the maximum window size. This mechanism is equivalent to sampling each context word w_j with a probability that decreases linearly with the distance $|j - i|$ to the focus word w_i:

$$P(w_j|w_i) = \sum_{window=1}^{L} P(w_j|w_i, window)P(window)$$
$$= \frac{1}{L}(L - |j - i| + 1)$$

where *window* is the actual window size (from 1 to L) sampled by the algorithm. Similarly, the co-occurrence statistics used by *GloVe* rely on harmonic series where words at distance d from the focus word are assigned a weight $\frac{1}{d}$. For example, with the window size 3, the context word at the position 2 will be sampled with the probability of $2/3$ in *word2vec* and the probability of $1/2$ in *GloVe*.

Another implicit hyper-parameter is the symmetric nature of the context window. The *word2vec* and *GloVe* models pay equivalent attention to the words to the left and to the right of the focus word. However, the relative importance of left or right contexts may in principle depend on the linguistic properties of the corpus language, in particular its word ordering constraints.

Finally, although distributional semantic models do not themselves enforce any theoretical limit on the boundaries of context windows, word embeddings are in practice often estimated on a sentence by sentence basis, thus constraining the context windows to stop at sentence boundaries. However, to the best of our knowledge, there is no systematic evaluation of how this sentence-boundary constraint affects the resulting embeddings.

3 Experimental setup

To evaluate how context windows affect the embeddings, we trained Continuous Skip-gram with Negative Sampling (SGNS) embeddings for various configurations of hyper-parameters, whose values are detailed in Table 1. In particular, the "weighting scheme" encodes how the context words should be weighted according to their distance with the focus word. This hyper-parameter is given two possible values: a linear weighting scheme corresponding to the default *word2vec* weights, or an alternative scheme using the squared root of the distance.

Hyper-parameter	Possible values
Max. window size	$\{1, 2, 5, 10\}$
Weighting scheme	$\{\frac{L-d+1}{L}, \frac{L-\sqrt{d}+1}{L}\}$
Window position	$\{$left, right, symmetric$\}$
Cross-sentential	$\{$yes, no$\}$
Stop words removal	$\{$yes, no$\}$

Table 1: Range of possible hyper-parameter values evaluated in the experiment.

The embeddings were trained on two English-language corpora: Gigaword v5 (Parker et al., 2011), a large newswire corpus of approx. 4 billion word tokens, and the English version of OpenSubtitles (Lison and Tiedemann, 2016), a large repository of movie and TV subtitles, of approx. 700 million word tokens. The two corpora correspond to distinct linguistic genres, Gigaword being a corpus of news documents (average sentence length

---

[1]Other types of context have been proposed, such as dependency-based contexts (Levy and Goldberg, 2014) or multilingual contexts (Upadhyay et al., 2016), but these are outside the scope of the present paper.

21.7 tokens) while OpenSubtitles is a conversational corpus (average sentence length 7.3 tokens). OpenSubtitles notably contains a large number of non-sentential utterances, which are utterances lacking an overt predicate and depend on the surrounding dialogue context for their interpretation (Fernández, 2006). The corpora were lemmatized and POS-tagged with the Stanford CoreNLP (Manning et al., 2014) and each token was replaced with its lemma and POS tag. Two versions of the corpora were used for the evaluation: one raw version with all tokens, and one filtered version after removal of stop words and punctuation.

The word embeddings were trained with 300-dimensional vectors, 10 negative samples per word and 5 iterations. Very rare words (less than 100 occurrences in Gigaword, less than 10 in OpenSubtitles) were filtered out. The models were then evaluated using two standard test workflows: Spearman correlation against SimLex-999 semantic similarity dataset (Hill et al., 2015) and accuracy on the semantic sections of the Google Analogies Dataset (Mikolov et al., 2013a).

4   Results

All in all, we trained 96 models on Gigaword (GW) and 96 models on OpenSubtitles (OS)[2]. Figure 1 illustrates the results for the SGNS embeddings on lexical similarity and analogy tasks using various types of context windows. The main findings from the experiments are as follows.

Window size

As expected for a lexical similarity task (Schütze and Pedersen, 1993), narrow context windows perform best with the SimLex999 dataset, which contains pairs of semantically similar words (not just related). For the analogy task, larger context windows are usually beneficial, but not always: the word embeddings trained on OpenSubtitles perform best with the window size of 10, while the best results on the analogy task for Gigaword are obtained with the window size of 2.

Window position

Table 2 shows how the position of the context window influences the average model performance. Note that symmetric windows of, for instance, 10 are in fact 2 times larger than the 'left' or 'right'

---

²Encompassing different values of window size, weighting scheme, window position, cross-sentential boundaries and stop-words removal ($4 \times 2 \times 3 \times 2 \times 2 = 96$).

Window position	SimLex999	Analogies
OS left	0.40	0.35
OS right	0.43	0.35
OS symmetric	0.43	**0.45**
GW left	0.43	0.64
GW right	0.44	0.65
GW symmetric	0.45	**0.68**

Table 2: Average performance across all models depending on the window position.

windows of the same size, as they consider 10 words both to the left and to the right of the focus word. This is most likely why symmetric windows consistently outperform 'single-sided' ones on the analogy task, as they are able to include twice as much contextual input.

However, the average performance on the semantic similarity task (as indicated by the Spearman correlation with the SimLex999 test set) does not exhibit the same trend. 'Left' windows are indeed worse than symmetric ones, but 'right' windows are on par with the symmetric windows for OpenSubtitles and only one percent point behind them for Gigaword. It means that in many cases (at least with English texts) taking into account only n context words to the right of the focus word is sufficient to achieve the same performance with SimLex999 as by using a model which additionally considers n words to the left, and thus requires significantly more training time.

Cross-sentential contexts

The utility of cross-sentential contexts depends on several covariates, most importantly the type of corpus and the nature of the evaluation task. For similarity tasks, cross-sentential contexts do not seem useful, and can even be detrimental for large window sizes. However, for analogy tasks, cross-sentential contexts lead to improved results thanks to the increased window it provides. This is especially pronounced for corpora with short sentences such as OpenSubtitles (see Table 3).

Weighting scheme

Our experimental results show that none of the two evaluated weighting schemes (with weights that decrease respectively linearly or with the square-root of the distance) gives a consistent advantage averaged across all models. However, the squared weighting scheme is substantially slower (as it

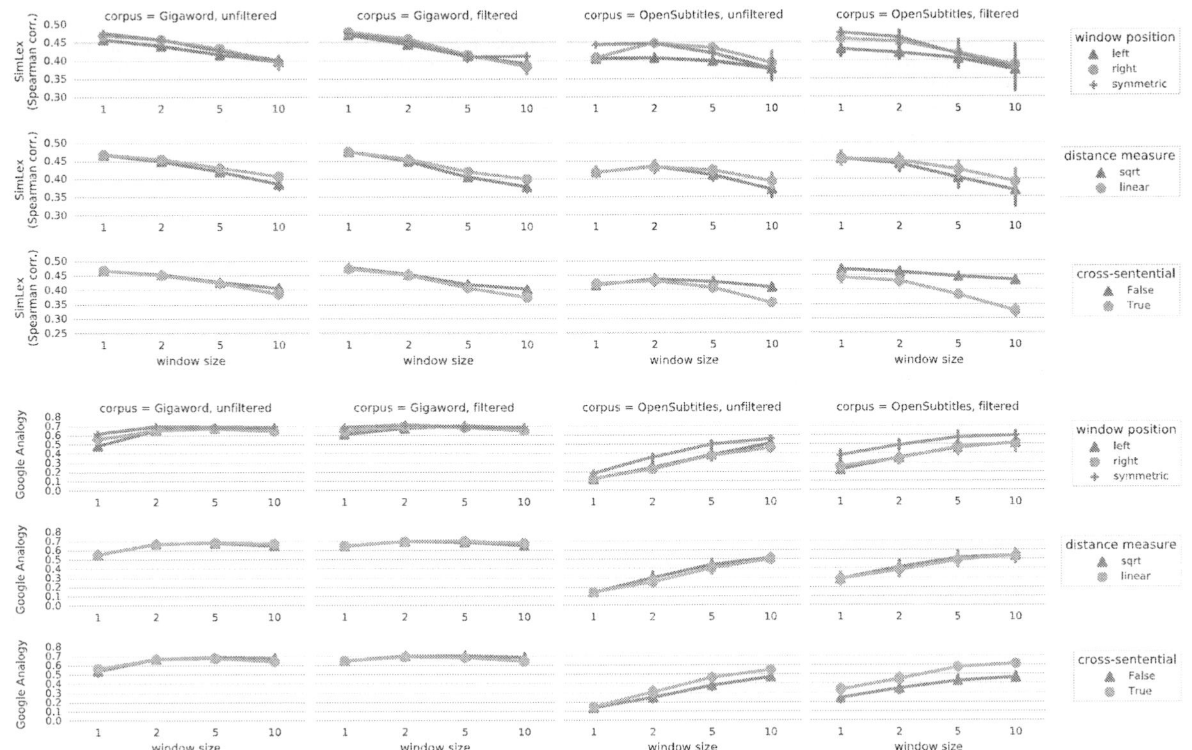

Figure 1: Results for the SGNS word embeddings trained with various types of context windows.

Cross-sentential	SimLex999	Analogies
OS False	**0.44**	0.34
OS True	0.40	**0.43**
GW False	0.44	0.66
GW True	0.44	0.65

Table 3: Average performance across all models with and without cross-sentential contexts.

Stop words removal	SimLex999	Analogies
OS no removal	0.41	0.34
OS with removal	0.42	**0.43**
GW no removal	0.44	0.64
GW with removal	0.44	**0.68**

Table 4: Average performance across all models depending on the removal of stop words.

increases the number of context words to consider for each focus word), decreasing the training speed about 25% with window size 5. Thus, the original linear weighting scheme proposed in (Mikolov et al., 2013b) should be preferred.

Stop words removal

As shown in Table 4, the removal of stop words does not really influence the average model performance for the semantic similarity task. The analogy task, however, benefits substantially from this filtering, for both corpora. Although not shown in the table, filtering stop words also significantly decreases the size of the corpus, thereby reducing the total time needed to train the word embeddings.

5 Conclusion

Our experiments demonstrate the importance of choosing the right type of context window when learning word embedding models. The two most prominent findings are (1) the positive role of cross-sentential contexts and (2) the fact that, at least for English corpora, right-side contexts seem to be more important than left-side contexts for similarity tasks, and achieve a performance comparable to that of symmetric windows.

In the future, we wish to extend this study to the CBOW algorithm, to other weighting schemes (such as the harmonic series employed by *GloVe*), and to non-English corpora.

References

Marco Baroni, Georgiana Dinu, and Germán Kruszewski. 2014. Don't count, predict! a systematic comparison of context-counting vs. context-predicting semantic vectors. In *Proceedings of the 52nd Annual Meeting of the Association for Computational Linguistics (Volume 1: Long Papers)*, pages 238–247. Association for Computational Linguistics.

Yoshua Bengio, Rejean Ducharme, and Pascal Vincent. 2003. A neural probabilistic language model. *Journal of Machine Learning Research*, 3:1137–1155.

Ronan Collobert, Jason Weston, Léon Bottou, Michael Karlen, Koray Kavukcuoglu, and Pavel Kuksa. 2011. Natural language processing (almost) from scratch. *Journal of Machine Learning Research*, 12(Aug):2493–2537.

Raquel Fernández. 2006. *Non-Sentential Utterances in Dialogue: Classification, Resolution and Use.* Ph.D. thesis, King's College London.

Yoav Goldberg. 2016. A primer on neural network models for natural language processing. *Journal of Artificial Intelligence Research*, 57:345–420.

Felix Hill, Roi Reichart, and Anna Korhonen. 2015. Simlex-999: Evaluating semantic models with (genuine) similarity estimation. *Computational Linguistics*, 41(4):665–695.

Guillaume Lample, Miguel Ballesteros, Sandeep Subramanian, Kazuya Kawakami, and Chris Dyer. 2016. Neural architectures for named entity recognition. In *Proceedings of the 2016 Conference of the North American Chapter of the Association for Computational Linguistics: Human Language Technologies*, pages 260–270, San Diego, California, June. Association for Computational Linguistics.

Omer Levy and Yoav Goldberg. 2014. Dependency-based word embeddings. In *Proceedings of the 52nd Annual Meeting of the Association for Computational Linguistics, ACL 2014*, pages 302–308.

Omer Levy, Yoav Goldberg, and Ido Dagan. 2015. Improving distributional similarity with lessons learned from word embeddings. *Transactions of the Association for Computational Linguistics*, 3:211–225.

Chu-Cheng Lin, Waleed Ammar, Chris Dyer, and Lori Levin. 2015. Unsupervised pos induction with word embeddings. In *Proceedings of the 2015 Conference of the North American Chapter of the Association for Computational Linguistics: Human Language Technologies*, pages 1311–1316, Denver, Colorado, May–June. Association for Computational Linguistics.

P. Lison and J. Tiedemann. 2016. Opensubtitles2016: Extracting large parallel corpora from movie and TV subtitles. In *Proceedings of the 10th International Conference on Language Resources and Evaluation (LREC 2016)*, pages 923–929.

Christopher D. Manning, Mihai Surdeanu, John Bauer, Jenny Finkel, Steven J. Bethard, and David McClosky. 2014. The Stanford CoreNLP natural language processing toolkit. In *Association for Computational Linguistics (ACL) System Demonstrations*, pages 55–60.

Tomas Mikolov, Kai Chen, Greg Corrado, and Jeffrey Dean. 2013a. Efficient estimation of word representations in vector space. *arXiv preprint arXiv:1301.3781*.

Tomas Mikolov, Ilya Sutskever, Kai Chen, Greg S Corrado, and Jeff Dean. 2013b. Distributed representations of words and phrases and their compositionality. In C. J. C. Burges, L. Bottou, M. Welling, Z. Ghahramani, and K. Q. Weinberger, editors, *Advances in Neural Information Processing Systems 26*, pages 3111–3119. Curran Associates, Inc.

Robert Parker, David Graff, Junbo Kong, Ke Chen, and Kazuaki Maeda. 2011. English gigaword fifth edition, June. LDC2011T07.

Jeffrey Pennington, Richard Socher, and Christopher D. Manning. 2014. GloVe: Global vectors for word representation. In *Empirical Methods in Natural Language Processing (EMNLP)*, pages 1532–1543.

Hinrich Schütze and Jan Pedersen. 1993. A vector model for syntagmatic and paradigmatic relatedness. In *Proceedings of the 9th Annual Conference of the UW Centre for the New OED and Text Research*, pages 104–113.

Shyam Upadhyay, Manaal Faruqui, Chris Dyer, and Dan Roth. 2016. Cross-lingual models of word embeddings: An empirical comparison. In *Proc. of ACL*.

Jie Zhou and Wei Xu. 2015. End-to-end learning of semantic role labeling using recurrent neural networks. In *Proceedings of the 53rd Annual Meeting of the Association for Computational Linguistics and the 7th International Joint Conference on Natural Language Processing (Volume 1: Long Papers)*, pages 1127–1137, Beijing, China, July. Association for Computational Linguistics.

The Effect of Excluding Out of Domain Training Data from Supervised Named-Entity Recognition

Adam Persson
Department of Linguistics
Stockholm University
SE-106 91 Stockholm
adam@ling.su.se

Abstract

Supervised named-entity recognition (NER) systems perform better on text that is similar to its training data. Despite this, systems are often trained with as much data as possible, ignoring its relevance. This study explores if NER can be improved by excluding out of domain training data. A maximum entropy model is developed and evaluated twice with each domain in Stockholm-Umeå Corpus (SUC), once with all data and once with only in-domain data. For some domains, excluding out of domain training data improves tagging, but over the entire corpus it has a negative effect of less than two percentage points (both for strict and fuzzy matching).

1 Introduction

In named-entity recognition, the aim is to annotate all occurrences of explicit names, like John (person) and General Motors (organization) in a text, using some defined set of name tags. Machine learning algorithms can be trained to perform this task. However, names manifest themselves quite differently in different domains. It is challenging to create systems that perform well out of domain (Ciaramita & Altun, 2005).

In many cases, NER systems are trained with a balanced corpus to provide as much data as possible. However, this generates a very general model that perhaps is not the best possible for any one domain. This study aims to find out is such a model could be outperformed by removing all out of domain training data. This is done using a basic maximum entropy model (Berger et. al, 1996). There are of course other, more up to date methods for NER, for example various types of neural networks, such as the state of the art systems

presented by Lample et al. (2016). However, the maximum entropy model is sufficient for this study as the subject of interest is the effect of excluding out of domain data, not the machine learning algorithm itself.

The results of this study have previously been presented in Persson (2016).

2 Data

Stockholm-Umeå Corpus (Källgren, 2006) is a balanced Swedish corpus, divided into nine top-level domains: reportage, editorials, reviews, skills/trades/hobbies, popular lore, biographies/essays, miscellaneous, learned/scientific, and imaginative prose. These domains differ substantially in scope and size, ranging from 17 to 127 documents per domain, each document consisting of approximately 2000 words. The distribution is inspired by The Brown Corpus (Francis & Kucera, 1964), but in SUC, imaginary prose is apparently considered a top-level domain, making it the largest one. In The Brown Corpus, imaginary prose is a section consisting of six top-level domains.

In addition to SUC, the system created for this study also takes advantage of two custom made gazetteers. One includes 1800 common Swedish person names, equal parts boys' names, girls' names, and surnames. The other one is made up of location names, including names of every Swedish town, municipality, county, and province, as well as all countries, capitals, continents, and US states. This was decided to be the very lowest level of gazetteers that any Swedish NER-system should implement.

3 System architecture

The system is implemented in Python 3.4.2 with SciKit-Learn (Pedregosa et al., 2011) 0.17.1's logistic regression (maximum entropy) model with

Proceedings of the 21st Nordic Conference of Computational Linguistics, pages 289–292,
Gothenburg, Sweden, 23-24 May 2017. ©2017 Linköping University Electronic Press

default settings, and the tagging was performed with greedy search.

Following Salomonsson et al. (2012) and Östling (2013), the SUC name tags are remapped into a more coarse-grained tag set of person, location, organization and other. On top of these name tags, the system also implements BILOU-tags (Ratinov & Roth, 2009), giving one tag to each token based on its position in a name. Multi-token names can consist of beginning (B), inside (I) and last (L), while single-token names are tagged as unit-length (U). All non-name tokens are tagged as outside (O).

The label of each observed token is a concatenation of name tag and BILOU-tag, while its features consists of the following:

- The label of the previous token.

- Word forms (3 features). 1: current token, 2: previous + current tokens, 3: current + following tokens.

  Word forms are used exactly as they appear in the text. Lemmatization or case-insensitivity is not used.

- POS-tags (2 features). 1: current token, 2: previous + following tokens.

- Matching of gazetteers (2 features). 1: person names, 2: location names.

  The gazetteer matching is done on the token level. To be able to match names in the genitive case, tokens that end with ''s'' are compared twice, first with the ''s'' included, and then with it removed. The same token can be matched with both gazetteers (for example Sofia, capital of Bulgaria and the corresponding girls' name).

- Pattern of capitalisation (2 features). 1: current token, 2: previous token.

  The pattern of capitalisation have five possible values: no capitalisation (xxx), full capitalisation (XXX), normal capitalisation (Xxx), sentence-initial capitalisation (. Xxx), capitalisation following dash (- Xxx), and other capitalisation (xXx, xXX, xxX).

As POS-tags are used as features, the trained system cannot be applied to raw text. It must be used as a part of a pipeline, where the text is already tokenised and POS-tagged.

These features were selected intuitively as they are some of the most common features to be used in NER-systems. Some basic testing was done during the constuction of the system, but there was no real process of structured feature selection.

4 Experiment design

To measure the effect of excluding out of domain training data, two balanced 10-fold cross-validations are carried out for each domain. The 500 documents of SUC are sorted alphanumerically with respect to their name (they are named after domain), and every tenth in-domain document is used for testing, beginning with the k'th document for each fold k. In the first cross-validation, all remaining documents in the corpus are used for training, while in the second cross-validation, only the remaining in-domain documents are used.

When the system is comparing its tagging to the gold standard for evaluation, any given name can only be part of one match, which can either be a partial match or a full match. The results of all ten folds are summed and an F1-value is calculated for the whole cross-validation.

Results are presented both for strict and fuzzy matching. Fuzzy matching accepts all names that have at least one token correctly tagged, while strict matching demands the tagging of a name to be identical to the gold standard.

In this study, the system uses SUC's gold standard POS-tagging instead of using a separate POS-tagger to prepare the test data.

5 Results

The overall result (summing all domains) shows that the in-domain training data perform slightly worse than the mixed training data. The decrease in F1-score is 1.9 percentage points for strict matching (see table 1) and 1.3 percentage points for fuzzy matching (see table 2).

There are some domains (editorial, miscellaneous) and name classes (person, institution) which are, in total, improved by excluding out of domain training data in the total count, but none of them show improvement in more than half of its domain-class combinations.

Training, tagging, and evaluating the system ninety times (10-fold cross-validation for each of the nine domains) with a 2.4 GHz Intel Xeon E5645 processor took 41 minutes using only in-

	Person	Place	Institution	Other	TOTAL
Reportage (44)	**79.3 - 78.3**	72.8 - 74.8	41.4 - 41.5	12.6 - 20.0	64.8 - 67.1
Editorial (17)	**71.4 - 70.4**	64.3 - 70.0	**66.1 - 57.6**	0.0 - 25.6	**65.3 - 64.3**
Reviews (27)	81.4 - 82.5	61.9 - 64.1	5.9 - 23.3	11.5 - 17.3	66.7 - 67.5
Skills/trades/hobbies (58)	**75.2 - 69.7**	60.6 - 68.0	46.0 - 46.7	13.2 - 20.8	56.3 - 59.9
Popular lore (48)	70.3 - 78.5	74.6 - 78.0	14.8 - 32.3	31.4 - 34.3	64.0 - 69.5
Biographies/essays (26)	78.1 - 84.3	68.3 -69.8	0.0 - 34.3	8.0 - 25.0	67.9 - 72.4
Miscellaneous (70)	**75.2 - 52.3**	78.6 - 81.4	**41.9 - 38.2**	37.9 - 40.3	**63.2 - 60.8**
Learned/scientific (83)	61.5 - 67.4	67.3 - 69.6	10.1 - 27.0	17.0 - 23.7	52.6 - 57.8
Imaginative prose (127)	68.1 - 86.6	74.4 - 74.7	0.0 - 16.5	**54.0 - 52.9**	80.3 - 80.9
TOTAL (500)	**78.5 - 78.3**	71.3 - 73.9	**39.4 - 39.0**	23.7 - 29.4	65.7 - 67.6

Table 1: Strict matching results. F1-values are presented in pairs of in-domain training data (left) and mixed training data (right). Cases where in-domain training data gets the better result are highlighted.

	Person	Place	Institution	Other	TOTAL
Reportage (44)	**84.4 - 83.3**	74.3 - 76.8	**49.3 - 48.5**	18.5 - 26.9	69.5 - 71.6
Editorial (17)	82.0 - 82.8	64.3 - 71.4	**70.8 - 61.9**	2.9 - 30.2	70.8 - 71.0
Reviews (27)	86.4 - 89.1	63.1 - 66.0	7.8 - 30.8	25.2 - 27.5	72.1 - 73.8
Skills/trades/hobbies (58)	**81.9 - 74.3**	66.5 - 70.1	49.9 - 50.9	19.2 - 27.3	61.9 - 63.9
Popular lore (48)	75.5 - 82.9	77.9 - 81.4	16.8 - 40.2	36.3 - 41.9	68.1 - 74.0
Biographies/essays (26)	84.5 - 86.5	69.0 - 72.8	0.0 - 38.7	9.6 - 28.9	72.8 - 75.1
Miscellaneous (70)	**85.6 - 56.1**	80.3 - 83.0	**55.3 - 48.2**	37.9 - 44.0	**69.7 - 65.1**
Learned/scientific (83)	68.7 - 72.0	67.7 - 70.3	12.6 - 35.7	23.5 - 29.8	57.4 - 62.0
Imaginative prose (127)	91.1 - 91.9	76.2 - 76.6	0.0 - 19.9	55.8 - 57.7	84.5 - 84.8
TOTAL (500)	**84.3 - 83.1**	73.4 - 75.8	**46.2 - 45.8**	29.3 - 35.7	70.7 - 72.0

Table 2: Fuzzy matching results. F1-values are presented in pairs of in-domain training data (left) and mixed training data (right). Cases where in-domain training data gets the better result are highlighted.

domain training data. Performing the same task with all available training data took 11 hours and 16 minutes.

6 Summary and future work

This paper describes a maximum entropy system which carries out a named-entity recognition task with different sets of training data. The purpose is to find out whether an NER-task can be improved by removing all out of domain training data for each fold in a cross-validation. Results are quite varied. Some domains and name classes show improvement, but most do not. The total count shows a worsening of less than two percentage points in both strict and fuzzy matching.

As this is a relatively small (and inconsistent) loss in performance, but a very big saving in training data size, the idea to focus more on relevance than quantity in training data should not be dismissed yet.

Future work should include normalisation of training data size, as the domains in SUC are of drastically different size. Many different training data sizes should be tested to see if there are critical points where in-domain data and mixed data stop getting better results with bigger data sets. Perhaps better results can be reached with a certain ratio of in- and out of domain training data.

On the assumption that there is a way to achieve better results by excluding (some of the) out of domain training data, an NER-system might benefit from having different models trained for different domains, and using a text-classifier to choose the appropriate model before tagging texts of unknown domain.

References

Berger, A. L., Pietra, V. J. D. & Pietra, S. A. D. 1996. *A maximum entropy approach to natural language processing.* Computational linguistics, 22(1), 39-71.

Ciaramita, M. & Altun, Y. 2005. *Named-entity recognition in novel domains with external lexical knowledge.* In Proceedings of the NIPS Workshop on Advances in Structured Learning for Text and Speech Processing.

Francis, W. N. & H. Kučera. 1964. *Manual of Information to accompany A Standard Corpus of Present-Day Edited American English, for use with Digital Computers.* Providence, Rhode Island: Department of Linguistics, Brown University. Revised 1971. Revised and amplified 1979.

Källgren, G. 2006. *Documentation of the Stockholm-Umeå Corpus.* Manual of the Stockholm Umeå Corpus version 2.0. Sofia Gustafson-Capková and Britt Hartmann (red). Stockholm University: Department of Linguistics.

Lample, G., Ballesteros, M., Subramanian, S., Kawakami, K. & Dyer, C. 2016. *Neural Architectures for Named Entity Recognition.* In Proceedings of NAACL-HLT, 260-270.

Pedregosa, F., Varoquaux, G., Gramfort, A., Michel, V., Thirion, B., Grisel, O., Blondel, M., Prettenhofer, P., Weiss, R., Dubourg, V., Vanderplas, J., Passos, A., Cournapeau, D., Brucher, M. & Perrot, M. (2011). Scikit-learn: Machine learning in Python. The Journal of Machine Learning Research, 12, 2825-2830.

Persson, A. 2016. Övervakad namntaggning med domänspecifik träningsdata. (Bachelor thesis, Stockholm University, Stockholm, Sweden) Retrieved from http://www.diva-portal.org/smash/get/diva2:934145/FULLTEXT01.pdf

Ratinov, L., & Roth, D. 2009. *Design challenges and misconceptions in named entity recognition.* Proceedings of the Thirteenth Conference on Computational Natural Language Learning, 147-155. Association for Computational Linguistics.

Salomonsson, A., Marinov, S. & Nugues, P. 2012. *Identification of entities in swedish.* SLTC 2012, 63.

Sjöbergh, J. 2003. *Combining POS-taggers for improved accuracy on Swedish text.* Proceedings of NoDaLiDa, 2003.

Östling, R. 2013. *Stagger: An open-source part of speech tagger for Swedish.* Northern European Journal of Language Technology (NEJLT), 3, 1-18.

Quote Extraction and Attribution from Norwegian Newspapers

Andrew Salway, Paul Meurer, Knut Hofland and Øystein Reigem
Language and Language Technology Group
Uni Research, Bergen, Norway
`firstname.lastname@uni.no`

Abstract

We present ongoing work that, for the first time, seeks to extract and attribute politicians' quotations from Norwegian Bokmål newspapers. Our method – using a statistical dependency parser, a few regular expressions and a look-up table – gives modest recall (a best of .570) but very high precision (.978) and attribution accuracy (.987) for a restricted set of speaker names. We suggest that this is already sufficient to support some kinds of important social science research, but also identify ways in which performance could be improved.

1 Introduction

Social science researchers are increasingly incorporating automatic text analysis techniques into their research methods in order to exploit large corpora, such as newspaper articles, social media posts and political speeches. To date, it has mostly been bag-of-words techniques, such as topic modelling, that have been used and, as such, the text is normally the basic unit of analysis (Grimmer and Stewart, 2013).

For further progress, there is a need to be able to recognize other units of analysis within texts, such as quotations attributed to their speakers in newspaper articles. The ways in which news media select and present the reported speech of politicians is important for the functioning of democratic societies. Given a data set comprising who is reported to have said what, and when, social science researchers could study the opinions of political leaders on key issues and how they relate to those of the electorate (representative democracy), and how different newspapers present the views of different politicians (media coverage and framing). This data would also be relevant for citizens and journalists to keep track of what a politician has said about a certain issue and how this changes over time. Our aim is to develop a method to generate such data sets from Norwegian Bokmål newspapers.

Quote extraction and attribution have been well studied for English-language newspapers (Krestel et al., 2008; O'Keefe et al., 2012; Pareti et al., 2013). That research highlighted how the ways in which quotes are presented, and hence the challenges for extraction and attribution, vary quite markedly between different varieties of English and even different newspapers. Hence it makes sense for us to look for a Norwegian-specific solution. Also, in contrast to previous work, our focus on generating data sets for social science researchers leads us to prioritize very high precision, at the cost of recall if necessary, so long as there is no systematic bias in how recall fails (Section 5 says more on this).

This paper presents ongoing work to extract and attribute politicians' quotes from Norwegian Bokmål newspaper stories. Section 2 gives a more precise task definition and describes the creation of a testing set of newspaper stories in which quotations are annotated. Section 3 describes the method for extraction and attribution that we have implemented so far. Section 4 presents an evaluation and discusses remaining challenges, and Section 5 makes some tentative conclusions.

2 Task Definition and Testing Set

Following O'Keefe et al. (2012), we define quote extraction to be the task of identifying continuous spans of direct speech – an instance of a speaker's words being presented exactly as they were spoken, and of indirect speech – an instance of a speaker's words being reported, but

Proceedings of the 21st Nordic Conference of Computational Linguistics, pages 293–297,
Gothenburg, Sweden, 23-24 May 2017. ©2017 Linköping University Electronic Press

not as direct speech. The span of a quote may go across sentence and paragraph boundaries. In cases in which direct quotes are embedded within indirect quotes, we take the whole span of the indirect quote, with embedded direct quotes, to be one quote. Quote attribution is then the task of associating text spans with speakers.

Direct speech is marked with pairs of quotations marks, and, in Bokmål newspapers at least, more commonly with a preceding long dash which leaves the end of the quote less explicitly marked. For English-language newspapers, O'Keefe et al. (2012) reported over 99% accuracy for extracting direct quotes by searching for text between quotation marks. Such a straightforward solution is not possible for Bokmål newspapers, in part because of the dashed quotes, and also because we observed the frequent use of quotation marks around non-speech text spans, especially to highlight words and terms, and also for film and book titles.

Determining which text spans should be considered as indirect reported speech is somewhat problematic. Indirect speech implies that the writer is, to some extent, filtering and/or interpreting the spoken words. However, judging how much filtering and interpreting can happen before it is no longer reported speech can be hard. On the one hand, it may be defined in syntactic terms, e.g. a change from a first person to a third person pronoun used to refer to the speaker, and a change from absolute to relative tense, but these criteria do not cover all cases. On the other hand, although it may be harder, it also may be more appropriate to define indirect speech in semantic or pragmatic terms, e.g. according to different categories of verbs, or the attitude that the writer is perceived to express towards the proposition. These criteria leave fuzzy boundaries, for example between a clear case of indirect reported speech such as *'Person X said that Proposition'* and something like *'Person X thinks that Proposition'*: in the latter, it is hard to know how much the writer has interpreted the spoken words. See Pareti et al. (2013), and references therein, for a comprehensive treatment of these issues.

To create annotated material for evaluation purposes, two of the authors were responsible for annotating quotes in a sample of Bokmål newspaper texts. They first worked independently on different parts of the material, and then inspected, discussed and jointly edited each other's annotations. Although the aim was to create a gold standard, at this stage in our work we are not yet confident about a few cases of indirect speech, for reasons mentioned above.

Quote attribution requires resolution of pronouns and other nominal references. In our work to date, with a focus on social science applications, we have simplified this situation by defining a closed set of speakers comprising 99 Norwegian politicians, subjectively selected for their prominence from lists of governments over the past 20 years. This made it feasible for our method to include a manually compiled look-up table with gender information and alternative forms of full names (which may vary over time, e.g. after marriage). We have not yet attempted to resolve nominal references such as *'the trade minister'*, which are time-sensitive, but these are annotated in the test set and hence have a negative impact on recall in evaluation (this challenge is discussed in Section 4).

The sample of Bokmål texts was taken from a Norwegian monitor corpus of newspaper texts – Aviskorpus (Andersen and Hofland, 2012). Having retrieved all texts which contained a politician name, a speech verb and a nearby quotation mark, we selected every 220th text for the sample. For this, a list of 64 speech verbs was compiled from a data-driven analysis of the co-texts of politicians' names in newspaper articles, and extended with synonyms. It should be noted that it appeared that a very few verbs account for the vast majority of reported speech, i.e. *'si'* (*'to say'*), *'mene'* (*'to think'*) and *'kalle'* (*'to call'*).

After manually removing articles in which the mentioned politicians were not speakers this gave 162 texts from 10 newspapers for 2001-2016; most appeared to be regular news stories of 600 words or less. A total of 1031 quotes were annotated comprising 690 instances of direct speech and 341 of indirect speech. This ratio is different from the 50:50 estimated for English-language newspapers (Pareti et al. 2013). We also note that the majority of direct quotes – 630 out of 690 – appear with a preceding dash, rather than in a pair of quotation marks.

3   Method

The main idea is to take the subject and the complement of speech verbs as speaker and reported speech respectively. Two extensions to improve recall were conceived, in part from our initial corpus-based investigations into how quotations are expressed, and in part from analysis of the annotated data (Section 2), which was later used for evaluation. Thus, there may be potential for a kind of "overfitting", but the extensions comprise a few simple heuristics which we believe are generally applicable.

For each text that contains the full version of a politician's name, each sentence is analyzed by a statistical dependency parser for Norwegian Bokmål that was developed, in other ongoing work, using the Stanford Neural Network parser framework (Chen and Manning, 2014). It was trained with a dependency treebank that was derived from the INESS NorGramBank gold standard treebank, i.e. the subset of manually disambiguated and checked parses (Dyvik et al., 2016). The word embeddings were trained on 1.58 billion tokens from news, parliamentary and popular science texts.

If an inflected form of a speech verb is detected, then its grammatical subject and complement are extracted. Only speech verbs that subcategorize for a sentence complement were considered; a list was formed through a search for verbs allowing a sentence complement in the NorGram grammar lexicon. In practice, this meant that the vast majority of detected instances were for the verbs *'si'* (*'to say'*) and *'mene'* (*'to think'*). The subject is taken to be the speaker and the complement is taken to be the reported speech. We do not explicitly distinguish direct and indirect speech, but note that complements with a complementizer are mostly indirect speech.

In the simplest case the subject is one of the politicians' full names. In the case that it is a surname, or another variant of their name, then the full name is looked up, and if the full name is mentioned somewhere in the current story then this is taken to be the speaker. If the subject is a third person singular pronoun (*'han'*, *'hun'*) then the pronoun is resolved to the most recent politician's name if it has the correct gender.

The prevalence of dashed quotes requires an extension to the core method. Sometimes these are contained within a single sentence that starts with a long dash, followed by direct speech, followed by a speech verb and speaker. However, there are also cases where the direct speech continues over several sentences: only the first sentence starts with a dash, and the verb and speaker come only in the final sentence. Thus, in those cases where the complement comes before the speech verb, we use a simple regular expression to check whether the current sentence, or any preceding sentence in the paragraph, starts with a dash. If so, then the text span from the dash to the end of the complement is taken to be the quote.

This extension to deal with dashed quotes was refined to deal with dialogs such as when a journalist is interviewing a politician. Here dashed quotes typically follow each other with alternate quotes coming from the politician but the politician may only be mentioned with a speech verb near the final quote. So, once a dashed quote is found we look backwards for a sequence of dashed quotes in which alternating quotes end with a question mark, and then attribute every other quote to the politician who is attributed to the final quote.

A second extension was implemented to deal with some of the cases in which the parser failed to find either the subject or the complement of a speech verb. Each sentence is tested for a simple pattern comprising a comma followed by a speech verb and a personal pronoun or a politician's name within three tokens to the right. If this pattern matches, then the text span from the start of the sentence to the comma is taken to be a quote.

4 Evaluation

The quote extraction performance of the core method, and of the two extensions, was evaluated on the basis of the testing set (Section 2) with measures of recall and precision. Here recall is the proportion of the quotes in the testing set that were extracted by the method; either wholly or at least partially. Precision is the proportion of the extracted quotes that were actually quotes according to the testing set; either wholly, or at least partially.

The results for quote extraction are presented in Table 1, with a best recall of .570 and a best precision of .978. The need for the extension to deal with dashed quotes that go over multiple sentences is highlighted by the increase from .246 to .409 for recall of whole quotes, whilst there is little change in the value for recall of at least partially extracted quotes (.503 to .509). Adding one pattern to capture quotes that were missed by the parser gives a useful increase in recall (.409 to .469, for whole quotes), at the expense of some precision (.974 to .951).

The performance for quote attribution was measured as attribution accuracy, i.e. the proportion of the extracted actual quotes that were attributed to the correct speaker. For 'parse + dashed quotes', 519 out of 526 quotes were correctly attributed, giving an accuracy of 0.989.

It is not surprising that attribution accuracy is very high because a quote will only be extracted if one of the politician's names is found as its subject, or as the resolution of a pronoun.

Method	Recall whole *(partial)*	Precision whole *(partial)*
Parse only	254/1031 = **.246** *519/1031 = .503*	518/531 = **.976** *519/531 = .977*
Parse + dashed quotes	422/1031 = **.409** *525/1031 = .509*	523/537 = **.974** *525/537 = .978*
P. + d.q. + simple pattern	484/1031 = **.469** *588/1031 = .570*	583/613 = **.951** *588/613 = .959*

Table 1: Evaluation of quote extraction.

Consideration of the quotes that were not recalled suggests several ways in which the method could be extended. It seems the most common problem is the occurrence of nominal references such as *'handelsministeren'* (*'the trade minister'*) in subject position. It would be expensive to create a knowledge-base of which politician held which role at which time. Our next step will be to evaluate a simple look around method, similar to how we resolve pronouns and to the baseline method described by O'Keefe et al. (2012). Beyond that, we may look to connect nominal references and politicians with evidence from the text, e.g. introductions like *'the trade minister, NAME ... '*.

Recall could also be improved by capturing more ways in which quotes are signaled. Firstly, we may extend the method to look for more kinds of constructions such as: (i) extrapositions in which a quote is split around the verb phrase, e.g. *'[Q part 1] sa Politician at [Q part 2]'* (*'[Q part 1] said Politician [Q part 2]'*); (ii) particle verbs, e.g., *'legge til'* (*'to add'*); and, (iii) other constructions that can take sentential complements, e.g. *'ifølge'* (*'according to'*).

Of course, however many constructions are added, the performance of the parser will still be a limit on extraction and attribution results. For example, we think that problems with the parsing of co-ordination could be significant for explaining the difference between partial recall (.509) and whole recall (.409). The parser has a labeled attachment score of about 89% which, although it is quite close to the state-of-art, means that 1 in 10 attachments will be incorrect. More could be done to catch the cases where parsing fails, i.e. by using more regular expressions to match known patterns, although a fall in precision would be expected. If recall was to be prioritized over precision, or quotes for an unrestricted set of speakers were needed, then the use of machine learning with a large set of diverse features should also be considered. However, even then the best recall achieved in the literature (for English) is 0.54 (P=0.66) for whole quotes and 0.74 (P=0.79) for at least partial quotes (Pareti et al., 2013).

5   Conclusions

This paper initiated work on quote extraction and attribution from Norwegian Bokmål newspapers, with the aim of creating data sets to support social science research in areas such as democratic representation, media coverage and media framing. The creation of a testing set of annotated quotations may be seen as a step towards a gold standard to be used as the basis for future work, but tricky issues remain around the definition and annotation of indirect quotes.

Our method for extraction and attribution addresses some of the characteristics of Bokmål quotations (more direct speech and the common use of dash quotes). We have identified ways to improve on our method, particularly for recall, but it can be argued that the levels of recall, precision and attribution accuracy that were achieved already may be sufficient for some social science research.

Having high levels of precision and attribution accuracy means that researchers can trust that almost all of the extracted text spans are quotes and that they are attributed to the correct politician. It seems likely that very high precision would be a prerequisite for using the data in social science research, unless it was to be checked manually; note, we estimate many 10,000's quotes for 99 politicians in Aviskorpus. Conversely, it seems to us that a modest recall value (c. 0.5) would be acceptable if the set of quotes is considered to be a good sample, i.e. if there is no bias towards particular newspapers or politicians when the method fails to extract quotes. Whilst we cannot see any way in which the method is biased towards certain politicians (so long as the data in the look-up table is accurate), it is possible that the idiosyncratic style of some newspapers could have an impact, and this must be investigated.

Acknowledgments

We thank the anonymous reviewers for their insightful and constructive input.

References

Gisle Andersen and Knut Hofland. 2012. Building a large corpus based on newspapers from the web. In: Gisle Andersen (ed.), *Exploring Newspaper Language: Using the web to create and investigate a large corpus of modern Norwegian*: 1-30. John Benjamins.

Danqi Chen and Christopher Manning. 2014. A Fast and Accurate Dependency Parser Using Neural Networks. *Procs. 2014 Conference on Empirical Methods in Natural Language Processing*: 740-750.

Helge Dyvik, Paul Meurer, Victoria Rosén, Koenraad De Smedt, Petter Haugereid, Gyri Smørdal Losnegaard, Gunn Inger Lyse, and Martha Thunes. 2016. NorGramBank: A 'Deep' Treebank for Norwegian. *Procs. 10th International Conference on Language Resources and Evaluation, LREC 2016*: 3555-3562.

Justin Grimmer and Brandon M. Stewart. 2013. Text as Data: The Promise and Pitfalls of Automatic Content Analysis Methods for Political Texts. *Political Analysis*, 21(3): 267-297.

Ralf Krestel, Sabine Bergler, and René Witte. 2008. Minding the Source: Automatic Tagging of Reported Speech in Newspaper Articles. *Procs. 6th International Language Resources and Evaluation Conference, LREC 2008*.

Tim O'Keefe, Silvia Pareti, James R. Curran, Irena Koprinska, and Matthew Honnibal. 2012. A Sequence Labelling Approach to Quote Attribution. *Procs. 2012 Joint Conference on Empirical Methods in Natural Language Processing and Computational Natural Language Learning*: 790-799.

Silvia Pareti, Tim O'Keefe, Ioannis Konstas, James R. Curran, and Irena Koprinska. 2013. Automatically Detecting and Attributing Indirect Quotations. *Procs. 2013 Conference on Empirical Methods in Natural Language Processing*: 989-999.

Wordnet extension via word embeddings:
Experiments on the Norwegian Wordnet

Heidi Sand and **Erik Velldal** and **Lilja Øvrelid**
University of Oslo
Department of Informatics
{heidispe,erikve,liljao}@ifi.uio.no

Abstract

This paper describes the process of automatically adding synsets and hypernymy relations to an existing wordnet based on word embeddings computed for POS-tagged lemmas in a large news corpus, achieving exact match attachment accuracy of over 80%. The reported experiments are based on the Norwegian Wordnet, but the method is language independent and also applicable to other wordnets. Moreover, this study also represents the first documented experiments of the Norwegian Wordnet.

1 Introduction

This paper documents experiments with an unsupervised method for extending a wordnet with new words and automatically identifying the appropriate hypernymy relations. Using word embeddings trained on a large corpus of news text (~330 million tokens), candidate hypernyms for a given target word are identified by computing nearest neighbors lists towards the wordnet and retrieving the ancestors of the neighbors. The candidate hypernyms are then scored according to a combination of distributional similarity and distance in the wordnet graph. While the particular experimental results reported here are for the Norwegian Wordnet (NWN), and using vectors estimated on POS tagged lemmas of the Norwegian news corpus, the methodology is generally applicable and not specific to neither the language nor the particular language resources used.

2 Background

Due to the coverage limitations of manually constructed semantic resources, several approaches have attempted to enrich various taxonomies with new relations and concepts. The general approach is to attempt to insert missing concepts into a taxonomy based on distributional evidence. In their probabilistic formulation, Snow et al. (2006) maximize the conditional probability of hyponym-hypernym relations based on observed lexico-syntactic patterns in a corpus. Jurgens and Pilehvar (2015) extend the existing WordNet taxonomy using an additional resource, Wiktionary, to extract sense data based on information (morphology/lexical overlap) in the term glosses.

The work which is most directly relevant to our study is that of Yamada et al. (2009). They extend an automatically generated Wikipedia-taxonomy by inserting new terms based on various similarity measures calculated from additional web documents. As the approach described in the current paper will abstractly adapt the approach of Yamada et al. (2009), we will devote some space to elaborate how the algorithm works, glossing over details that does not pertain to our setting. The insertion mechanism works as follows: For a given target word w we first find the k similar words that are already present in the hierarchy, according to some distributional similarity measure sim and with the constraint that the similarity is greater than some cutoff m. Secondly the hypernyms of each of these k similar words are assigned scores, based on a combination of the similarity measure and a depth penalty d. The latter is a function of the distance r in the hierarchy between the neighbor and the hypernym, as the hypernym candidates also include ancestor nodes beyond the immediate parents. Finally, the hypernym $h_\uparrow$ with the highest score will be selected for attaching w.

The function used for scoring hypernym candidates is defined as follows (paraphrased here according to the notation of the current paper):

$$score(h_\uparrow) = \sum_{h_\downarrow \in desc(h_\uparrow) \cap ksim(w)} d^{r(h_\uparrow, h_\downarrow)-1} \times sim(w, h_\downarrow) \qquad (1)$$

Proceedings of the 21st Nordic Conference of Computational Linguistics, pages 298–302,
Gothenburg, Sweden, 23-24 May 2017. ©2017 Linköping University Electronic Press

$ksim(w)$ picks out the k nearest neighbors of the target word w according to the distributional similarity measure sim, with the constraint that the similarity is greater than a cutoff m. The function $desc(h_\uparrow)$ picks out the descendants (hyponyms) of the candidate hypernym $h_\uparrow$. The term $d^{r(h_\uparrow,h_\downarrow)-1}$ is the depth penalty where the parameter d can have a value between 0 and 1, $r(n_\uparrow,n_\downarrow)$ is the difference in hierarchy depth between $h_\uparrow$ and $h_\downarrow$.

For sim, two distributional similarity measures are tested by Yamada et al. (2009), based on respectively 1) raw verb-noun dependencies and 2) clustering of verb-noun dependencies. Yamada et al. (2009) also apply a baseline approach, selecting the hypernym of the most similar hyponym (baseline approach 1), which essentially is the same as specifying $k=1$ when computing the nearest neighbors in the approach outlined above. Manually evaluating a random sample of 200 of the highest scoring insertions, Yamada et al. (2009) report an attachment accuracy of up to 91.0% among the top 10,000, and 74.5% among the top 100,000, when using the clustering based similarity – a result which substantially improves over the baseline (yielding scores of ~55%).

Although Yamada et al. (2009) work with a semantic taxonomy based on the Wikipedia structure, the scoring function in Equation 1 which forms the pivot of the approach is general enough to be adopted for other settings as well. Notably, no assumptions are made about the particular similarity function instantiating $sim(w_i, w_j)$. In the work reported in the current paper we experiment with instead using a similarity function based on word embeddings computed from a large unannotated corpus, and apply this for extending NWN.

3   The Norwegian Wordnet

The Norwegian Wordnet (NWN) was created by translation from the Danish Wordnet (DanNet) (Pedersen et al., 2009). DanNet encodes both relations found in Princeton Wordnet (Fellbaum, 1998) and EuroWordNet (Vossen, 1998), some of which are also employed in NWN. There are no prior publications documenting NWN, and the current study provides the first reported experiments on this resource. Before commencing our experiments it was therefore necessary to pre-process NWN in order to (i) correct errors in the format and/or the structure of NWN, and (ii) remove named entities and multiword expres-

POS	Lemmas	Synsets	Senses	Monos.	Polys.
Noun	38,440	43,112	48,865	31,957	6,483
Verb	2,816	4,967	5,580	1,612	1,204
Adj	2,877	3,179	3,571	2,413	464
Total	44,133	51,258	58,016	35,982	8,151

Table 1: Number of lemmas, synsets, senses and monosemous/polysemous words for nouns, verbs and adjectives in NWN.

sions. The resulting wordnet is summarized in Table 1, showing the number of lemmas, synsets and monosemous/polysemous terms broken down by their part-of-speech (nouns, adjectives and verbs). The modified NWN, which forms the basis for our experiments, is made freely available.[1]

4   Word embeddings for tagged lemmas

This section describes how we generate the semantic context vectors representing both unseen target words and the words already present in the existing wordnet synsets. These vectors form the basis of our distributional similarity measure, used both for computing nearest neighbors within NWN for unclassified target words and for scoring candidate hypernyms according to Equation 1 (where the similarity function will correspond to the cosine of word vectors). Our semantic vectors are given as word2vec-based word embeddings (Mikolov et al., 2013a; Mikolov et al., 2013b) estimated on the Norwegian Newspaper Corpus[2]. This is a corpus of Norwegian newspaper texts from the time period 1998–2014. We used approximately 25% of this corpus (due to some technical issues), which amounts to 331,752,921 tokens and 3,014,704 types.

Rather than estimating word embeddings from raw text, we use POS-tagged lemmas in order to have embeddings that more closely correspond to the word representations found in NWN. In order to extract lemmas and their parts of speech, we pre-processed the data using the Oslo-Bergen Tagger[3] (Johannessen et al., 2012), a rule-based POS-tagger for Norwegian which also performs tokenization and lemmatization. The tagger was accessed through the Language Analysis Portal (LAP[4]) which provides a graphical web interface

---

[1] https://github.com/heisand/NWN
[2] http://www.nb.no/sprakbanken/repositorium
[3] http://www.tekstlab.uio.no/obt-ny
[4] https://lap.hpc.uio.no

to a wide range of language technology tools (Lapponi et al., 2013).

Word2vec implements two model types: continuous bag-of-words (CBOW) and skip-gram. These differ in the prediction task they are trained to solve: prediction of target words given context words (CBOW) or the inverse, prediction of context words given target words (skip-gram). We used the word2vec implementation provided in the free python library *gensim* (Řehůřek and Sojka, 2010), using the default parameters to train skip-gram models. The defaults are a minimum of 5 occurrences in the corpus for the lemmas and an embedding dimension of size 100. Five iterations over the corpus was made.

5 The attachment process

In this section we detail the steps involved in classifying a new word w in the wordnet hierarchy.

5.1 Selecting nearest neighbors

The first step in the process is to compute the list of k nearest neighbors of w according to the distributional similarity $sim(w, w')$, a measure which in our case corresponds to the cosine of word embeddings described in Section 4. Candidate neighbors are words that are *(a)* already defined in NWN, *(b)* have a hypernym in NWN, *(c)* have the same part of speech as the target and *(d)* occur in the news corpus with a sufficient frequency to have a word embedding in the model described in Section 4. In addition we discard any neighbors that have a similarity less than some specified threshold m. As described in Section 6 we tune both k and m empirically.

5.2 Selecting candidate hypernyms

Hypernymy is a relation between *synsets* representing word senses, which means that the process of selecting candidate hypernyms for scoring has the following steps: First we *(a)* identify the list of k nearest neighbors for a given target word w, and then *(b)* for each neighbor word retrieve all synsets that encode a sense for that word, before we finally *(c)* retrieve all hypernym synsets, including all ancestor nodes, for those synsets.

Each candidate hypernym synset $h_\uparrow$ will in turn be assigned a score according to Equation 1. The synset with the highest score is finally chosen as the hypernym synset for the target word to be attached in NWN. Note that a given target word will only be assigned a single hypernym.

5.3 Evaluation

There are several ways one could choose to evaluate the quality of the words that are automatically inserted into the hierarchy. For example, Yamada et al. (2009) chose to manually evaluate a random sample of 200 unseen words, while Jurgens and Pilehvar (2015) treat the words already encoded in the hierarchy as gold data and then try to re-attach these. We here follow the latter approach. However, while Jurgens and Pilehvar (2015) restrict their evaluation to monosemous words, we also include polysemous words in order to make the evaluation more realistic.

For evaluation and tuning we split the wordnet into a development set and a test set, with 1388 target words in each. Potential targets only comprise words that have a hypernym encoded (which, in fact, are not that many, as NWN is relatively flat) and occur in the news corpus sufficiently often (≥ 5) to be represented by a word embedding.

We evaluate hypernym selection according to both *accuracy* and *attachment*. While accuracy reflects the percentage of target words added that were correctly placed under the right hypernym, the attachment score is the percentage of target words that actually were inserted into NWN. A candidate target word might end up not getting attached if it has no neighbors fulfilling the requirements described in Section 5.1.

Computing accuracy based only on exactly correct insertions is rather strict. Intuitively, a hypernymy relation can be right or wrong with varying degrees. We therefore also include a *soft accuracy* measure that aims to take account of this by counting how many hyponym or hypernym edges that separates a lemma from its correct position. Each edge will weight the count by a factor of 0.5, partly based on the accuracy measure of Jurgens and Pilehvar (2015), who, instead of weighting the score, only measures accuracy as the number of edges away that a lemma is placed from its original position. We defined the formula for *soft accuracy* as:

$$\frac{count(correct) + \sum_0^{count(misplaced)} 1 * 0.5^{edges}}{count(attached)} \quad (2)$$

6 Experiments and results

The parameters that need to be empirically tuned are: the depth penalty d, the number of k nearest

≥Freq.	Dev. set	#Words	Att.	Acc.	Soft
5	1388	1337	96.33	55.80	63.25
100	854	840	98.36	61.67	68.08
500	461	448	97.18	62.50	68.89
1000	316	304	96.20	64.47	70.85

Table 2: Accuracy restricted to target words with a frequency higher than some given threshold. #Words shows the number of attached words.

≥Hyp. score	#Words	Att.	Acc.	Soft
0.2	1337	96.33	55.80	63.25
1.0	1185	85.38	59.41	66.85
1.8	958	69.02	65.66	73.20
2.6	720	51.87	72.92	80.16
3.4	505	36.38	78.22	85.00
4.6	239	17.22	83.26	89.33

Table 3: Accuracy restricted to hypernyms with a score higher than some given threshold, computed over the 1388 words in the development set. #Words shows the number of attached words, e.g. 1337 is 96.33% of 1388.

neighbors to consider, and the minimum threshold m for the similarity of neighbors towards the target. After an initial round of experiments that determined the approximate appropriate range of values for these parameters, we performed an exhaustive grid search for the best parameter combination among the following values:

$k \in [1,12]$ in increments of 1.

$m \in [0.5,0.9]$ in increments of 0.05.

$d \in [0.05,0.5]$ in increments of 0.05.

Optimizing for attachment accuracy, the best parameter configuration after tuning on the development set was found to be k=6, m=0.5, and d=0.05, yielding an accuracy of 55.80% and a degree of attachment of 96.33%.

As one might expect that the embeddings are more reliable for high-frequent words than for low-frequent words, we also computed the dev-set accuracy relative to frequency of occurrence in the corpus used for estimating the embeddings. The results are shown in Table 2. We indeed see that the accuracy goes up when enforcing a higher frequency cutoff, reaching 64.47% when setting the cutoff to 1000, though per definition this means sacrificing coverage.

We also evaluated the effect of only inserting words that had hypernyms with a score higher than a given cutoff, which again naturally leads to a lower degree of attachment. Table 3 shows the accuracies over the development set when enforcing different cutoffs, showing an increased accuracy. We see that the best performance is when the cutoff on the hypernym score is set to 4.6, with a corresponding attachment accuracy of 83.26%.

Held-out results Applying the model configuration (without cutoffs) to the held-out test words of NWN yields an attachment of 95.97% and an accuracy of 59.91% (soft acc. = 66.04%). We see that there is a slight increase in the accuracy

for the insertions performed with the word embeddings when moving from the development data to the held-out data. As a baseline approach we also tried attaching each target word to the hypernym of its 1-nearest-neighbor. (When there are several candidate hypernyms available, we simply pick the first candidate in the retrieved list.) Yielding an accuracy of 47.61%, it is clear that we improve substantially over the baseline when instead performing insertion using the scoring function.

Applying the scoring function to the test set using the cutoff with the highest accuracy from Table 3, yields an accuracy of 84.96% (soft = 90.38%), though at the cost of a lower attachment rate (16.28%).

7 Summary and further work

This paper has demonstrated the feasibility of using word embeddings for automatically extending a wordnet with new words and assigning hypernym relations to them. When scoring candidate hypernyms we adopt the scoring function of Yamada et al. (2009) and show that this yields high accuracy even-though we apply it with a different type of taxonomic hierarchy and different types of distributional similarity measures. We compute distributional similarity based on word embeddings estimated from the Norwegian news corpus, using this as our basis for automatically attaching new words into hypernym relations in the Norwegian Wordnet, with exact-match accuracies of over 80%. For immediate follow-up work we plan to let the parameter tuning be optimized towards a combination of attachment and accuracy, rather than just accuracy alone.

References

Christiane Fellbaum, editor. 1998. *WordNet: An Electronic Lexical Database*. MIT Press, Cambridge, MA.

Janne Bondi Johannessen, Kristin Hagen, André Lynum, and Anders Nøklestad. 2012. Obt+stat: A combined rule-based and statistical tagger. In Gisle Andersen, editor, *Exploring Newspaper Language: Using the web to create and investigate a large corpus of modern Norwegian*. John Benjamins, Amsterdam, The Netherlands.

David Jurgens and Mohammad Taher Pilehvar. 2015. Reserating the awesometastic: An automatic extension of the wordnet taxonomy for novel terms. In *Proceedings of the 2015 Conference of the North American Chapter of the Association for Computational Linguistics Human Language Technologies (NAACL HLT 2015)*.

Emanuele Lapponi, Erik Velldal, Nikolay Aleksandrov Vazov, and Stephan Oepen. 2013. HPC-ready language analysis for human beings. In *Proceedings of the 19th Nordic Conference of Computational Linguistics (NODALIDA 2013)*.

Tomas Mikolov, Kai Chen, Gregory S. Corrado, and Jeffrey Dean. 2013a. Efficient estimation of word representations in vector space. In *Proceedings of the International Conference on Learning Representations (ICLR)*.

Tomas Mikolov, Ilya Sutskever, Kai Chen, Gregory S. Corrado, and Jeffrey Dean. 2013b. Distributed representations of words and phrases and their compositionality. *Advances in Neural Information Processing Systems*.

Bolette Sandford Pedersen, Sanni Nimb, Jørg Asmussen, Nicolai Hartvig Srensen, Lars Trap-Jensen, and Henrik Lorentzen. 2009. DanNet: the challenge of compiling a WordNet for Danish by reusing a monolingual dictionary. *Language Resources and Evaluation*, 43:269–299.

Radim Řehůřek and Petr Sojka. 2010. Software Framework for Topic Modelling with Large Corpora. In *Proceedings of the LREC 2010 Workshop on New Challenges for NLP Frameworks*.

Rion Snow, Daniel Jurafsky, and Andrew Y. Ng. 2006. Semantic taxonomy induction from heterogenous evidence. In *Proceedings of the 21st International Conference on Computational Linguistics and the 44th Annual Meeting of the Association for Computational Linguistics*.

Piek Vossen, editor. 1998. *EuroWordNet: A Multilingual Database with Lexical Semantic Networks*. Kluwer, Dordrecht, The Netherlands.

Ichiro Yamada, Kentaro Torisawa, Jun'ichi Kazama, Kow Kuroda, Masaki Murata, Stijn De Saeger, Francis Bond, and Asuka Sumida. 2009. Hypernym discovery based on distributional similarity and hierarchical structures. In *Proceedings of the 2009 Conference on Empirical Methods in Natural Language Processing*.

Universal Dependencies for Swedish Sign Language

Robert Östling, Carl Börstell, Moa Gärdenfors, Mats Wirén
Department of Linguistics
Stockholm University
{robert,calle,moa.gardenfors,mats.wiren}@ling.su.se

Abstract

We describe the first effort to annotate a signed language with syntactic dependency structure: the Swedish Sign Language portion of the Universal Dependencies treebanks. The visual modality presents some unique challenges in analysis and annotation, such as the possibility of both hands articulating separate signs simultaneously, which has implications for the concept of *projectivity* in dependency grammars. Our data is sourced from the Swedish Sign Language Corpus, and if used in conjunction these resources contain very richly annotated data: dependency structure and parts of speech, video recordings, signer metadata, and since the whole material is also translated into Swedish the corpus is also a parallel text.

1 Introduction

The Universal Dependencies (UD) project (Nivre et al., 2016b) has produced a language-independent but extensible standard for morphological and syntactic annotation using a formalism based on dependency grammar. This standard has been used to create the Universal Dependencies treebanks (Nivre et al., 2016a), which in its latest release at the time of writing (version 1.4) contains 64 treebanks in 47 languages—one of which is Swedish Sign Language (SSL, ISO 639-3: SWL), the topic of this article.

There are very few sign languages for which there are corpora. Most of the available sign language corpora feature only simple sign segmentation and annotations, often also with some type of translation into a spoken language (either as written translations or as spoken voice-overs). Sign language corpora with more extensive syntactic annotation is limited to Australian Sign Language, which contains some basic syntactic segmentation and annotation (Johnston, 2014). Apart from this, smaller parts of the corpora of Finnish Sign Language (Jantunen et al., 2016) and Polish Sign Language (Rutkowski and Łozińska, 2016), have had some syntactic segmentation and analysis, and another such project is under way on British Sign Language.[1]

To the best of our knowledge, we present the first dependency annotation and parsing experiments with sign language data. This brings us one step closer to the goal of bridging the gap in availability between written, spoken and sign language natural language processing tools.

2 Universal Dependencies

The Universal Dependencies project aims to provide uniform morphological and syntactic (in the form of dependency trees) annotations across languages (Nivre et al., 2016b).[2] Built on a language-universal common core of 17 parts of speech and 40 dependency relations, there are also language-specific guidelines which interpret and when necessary extend those in the context of a given language.

3 Swedish Sign Language

Swedish Sign Language (SSL) is the main sign language of the Swedish Deaf community.[3] It is estimated to be used by at least 10,000 as one of their primary languages, and is the only sign language to be recognized in Swedish law, giving it a special status alongside the official minor-

---

[1]http://www.bslcorpusproject.org/projects/
bsl-syntax-project/

[2]Note that our work predates version 2 of the UD guidelines, and is based on the first version.

[3]Capital D "Deaf" is generally used to refer to the language community as a cultural and linguistic group, rather than 'deaf' as a medical label.

Proceedings of the 21st Nordic Conference of Computational Linguistics, pages 303–308,
Gothenburg, Sweden, 23-24 May 2017. ©2017 Linköping University Electronic Press

ity languages (Ahlgren and Bergman, 2006; Parkvall, 2015). The history of SSL goes back at least 200 years, to the inauguration of the first Deaf school in Sweden, and has also influenced the two sign languages of Finland (i.e. Finnish Sign Language and Finland-Swedish Sign Language) with which SSL can be said to be related (Bergman and Engberg-Pedersen, 2010).

4   Data source

The SSL Corpus Project ran during the years 2009–2011 with the intention to establish the first systematically designed and publicly available corpus of SSL, resulting in the SSL Corpus (SSLC). Approximately 24 hours of video data of pairs of signers conversing was recorded, comprising 42 signers of different age, gender, and geographical background, spanning 300 individual video files (Mesch, 2012). The translation and annotation work is still on-going, with new releases being made available online as the work moves forward. The last official release of the SSLC includes just under 7 hours of video data (Mesch et al., 2012) along with annotation files containing 53,625 sign tokens across 6,197 sign types (Mesch, 2016).

The corpus is annotated using the ELAN software (Wittenburg et al., 2006), and the annotation files are distributed in the corresponding XML-based `.eaf` format. Each annotation file contains tiers on which annotations are aligned with the video file, both video and annotation tiers being visible in the ELAN interface (see Figure 1). The SSLC annotation files currently include tiers for sign glosses, and others for Swedish translations. Sign glosses are written word labels that represent signs with approximate meanings (e.g. PRO1 for a first person pronoun). The sign gloss annotation tiers are thus segmented for lexical items (i.e. individual signs), and come in pairs for each signer—each tier representing one of the signer's hands (one tier for the so-called *dominant hand*, and another for the *non-dominant hand*) (Mesch and Wallin, 2015).[4] Sign glosses also contain a part-of-speech (PoS) tag which have been derived from manually correcting the output of a semi-automatic method for cross-lingual PoS tagging (Östling et al., 2015). The translation tier is segmented into longer chunks, representing stretches

---

[4]The dominant hand is defined as the hand preferred by a signer when signing a one-handed sign.

of discourse that can be represented by an idiomatic Swedish translation. However, the translation segmentations do not represent clausal boundaries in either SSL or Swedish (Börstell et al., 2014). More recently, a portion of the SSLC was segmented into clausal units and annotated for basic syntactic roles (Börstell et al., 2016), which led to the current UD annotation work. Figure 1 shows the basic view of the SSLC videos and annotations in the ELAN software, with tiers for sign glosses and translations on the video timeline.

5   Annotation procedure and principles for SSL

For practical purposes, annotation was performed by extending the ELAN files of our source material from the SSLC project (see Figure 2 for an example). These annotations were automatically converted to the CoNLL-U format used by Universal Dependencies.

The annotation of UD based syntactic structure started by coming up with a procedure for annotating a signed language using ELAN. Signed language is more simultaneous than spoken language, particularly in the use of paired parallel articulators in form of the signer's two hands (Vermeerbergen et al., 2007). We handle this by allowing signs from both hands into the same tree structure, which leads to well-formed trees consistent with the dependency grammar formalism's single-head, connectedness and acyclicity constraints. These trees can however have some unusual properties compared to spoken languages. For the purpose of conforming to the CoNLL-U data format, which requires an ordered sequence of tokens, we sort signs by their chronological order. The chronological order spans both sign tiers per signer, and is defined as the onset time of each sign annotation. In the case of two signs on each hand tier (i.e. dominant vs. non-dominant hand) having identical onsets, favor is given to signs articulated by the signer's dominant hand. This working definition is by no means the only reasonable linearization, which means that the notion of projectivity to some extent loses its meaning. A tree can be considered projective or non-projective depending on how the ordering of simultaneously articulated signs is defined—assuming one wants to impose such an ordering in the first place.

Because the source material contains no segmentation above the sign level, we decided to use

Figure 1: Screenshot of an SSLC file in ELAN. This is the material we base our dependency annotations on, and the annotator can easily view the source video recording.

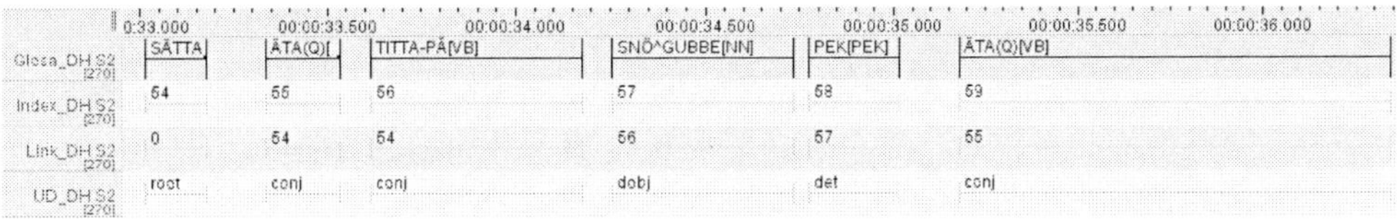

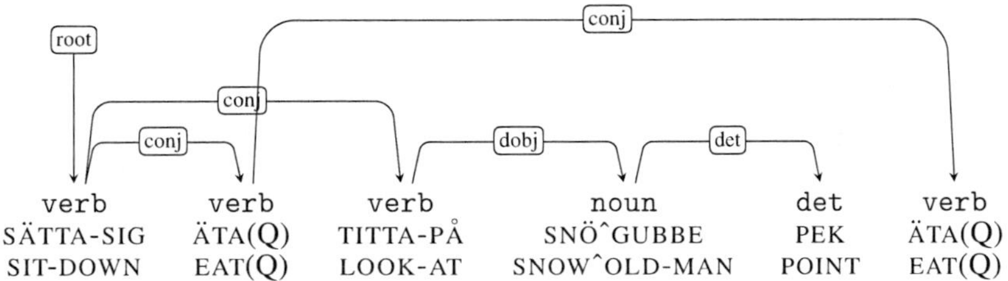

Figure 2: Screenshot zooming into the UD annotation tiers and sign–dependency linking for the utterance from Figure 1. This is the interface used by the annotator.

root	conj	conj	dobj	det	conj
verb	verb	verb	noun	det	verb
SÄTTA-SIG	ÄTA(Q)	TITTA-PÅ	SNÖ^GUBBE	PEK	ÄTA(Q)
SIT-DOWN	EAT(Q)	LOOK-AT	SNOW^OLD-MAN	POINT	EAT(Q)

'He is sitting there eating looking out at the snowman.'

Figure 3: The example from Figure 1 and Figure 2 with dependency annotations visualized. The (Q) suffix on the ÄTA(Q) gloss indicates which of the multiple signs for 'eat' in SSL is used in this case.

305

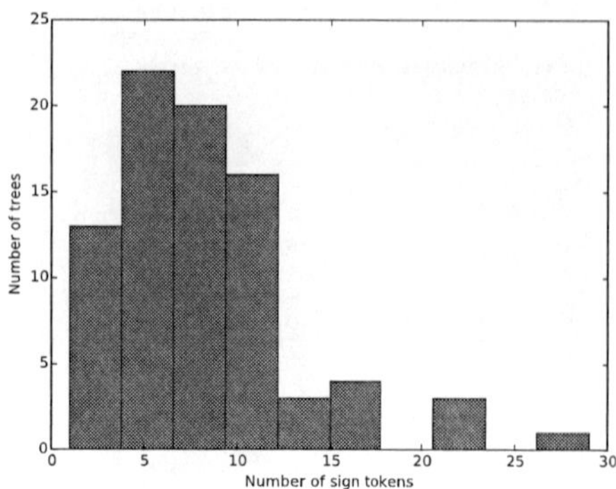

Figure 4: Distribution of tree sizes for the Swedish Sign Language Universal Dependencies treebank.

a bottom-up annotation procedure where subtrees were connected until we could find no more suitable mergers. In other words, the segmentation is entirely based on syntactic structure. The resulting fully connected trees were then used as "sentences" in the CoNLL-U format.

One peculiar feature of many sign languages is the repetition of verbs, sometimes referred to as *verb sandwiches*, in which one verb occurs in the middle of a sentence and also repeated at the end (Bergman and Dahl, 1994). Such a construction is found in Figure 3, in which the verb EAT appears in two places. Whereas verb chains (i.e. multiple verbs in one clause) were treated as coordinated elements linked to the `root` verb using the label `conj`, we decided to treat repeated verbs differently by labeling the repeated verb as a coordinated element linked to its first occurrence (see Figure 3).

6 Treebank statistics

The SSL treebank released in version 1.4 of the UD treebanks contains 82 trees with a total of 672 sign tokens (mean 8.2, median 7). The distribution of tree sizes (in tokens) is shown in Figure 4, as described in Section 5 these were produced in a bottom-up fashion and reflect our judgment of the largest sensible syntactic segmentation of the material. As could be expected from a corpus of spontaneous conversation, there is a large number of small trees. For comparison, the only spoken language (Slovenian) treebank has mean 9.1 and median 6, while the written Swedish treebank has mean 14.3 and median 13 sentence length, not counting punctuation.

7 Dependency parsing

Given that this is the first sign language UD treebank, we decided to perform some dependency parsing experiments to establish baseline results. We use the parser of Straka et al. (2015), part of the UDpipe toolkit (Straka et al., 2016), for our experiments. The training (334 tokens), development (48 tokens) and test (290 tokens) split from UD treebanks 1.4 was used. A hundred iterations of random hyperparameter search was performed for each of their parser models (projective, partially non-projective and fully non-projective), and the model with highest development set accuracy was chosen. Unsurprisingly given the small amount of training data, we found the most constrained projective model performed best, in spite of the data containing non-projective trees (see Figure 3). Development set attachment score was 60 and 56 (unlabeled and labeled, respectively) while the corresponding test set scores were 36 and 28. The discrepancy can be partly attributed to the much shorter mean sentence length of the development set: 6.0 vs 10.4 for the test set. Such low scores are not yet useful for practical tasks, but we emphasize that our primary goal in this work is to explore the possibility of UD annotation for a sign language. Our annotation project is ongoing, and we intend to further expand the SSL part in future UD treebanks releases.

8 Conclusions and future work

In releasing the Universal Dependencies treebank of Swedish Sign Language (SSL), the first such resource for a signed language, we hope to enable new computational research into sign language syntax. We have shown that even though some theoretical and practical issues exist when applying UD principles to a sign language, it is possible to come up with a reasonable annotation scheme. In the long run, we hope this will stimulate the development of Natural Language Processing (NLP) tools capable of processing sign languages. Finally, because we have both parallel data in Swedish and language-independent syntactic annotations, we also believe this resource could prove particularly useful in cross-lingual NLP.

Acknowledgments

Part of this work has been supported by an infrastructure grant from the Swedish Research Council (SWE-CLARIN, project 821-2013-2003).

References

Inger Ahlgren and Brita Bergman. 2006. Det svenska teckenspråket. In *Teckenspråk och teckenspråkiga: Kunskaps- och forskningsöversikt (SOU 2006:29)*, pages 11–70. Statens offentliga utredningar.

Brita Bergman and Östen Dahl. 1994. Ideophones in sign language? The place of reduplication in the tense-aspect system of Swedish Sign Language. In Carl Bache, Hans Basbøll, and Carl-Erik Lindberg, editors, *Tense, Aspect and Action. Empirical and Theoretical Contributions to Language Typology*, pages 397–422. Mouton de Gruyter.

Brita Bergman and Elisabeth Engberg-Pedersen. 2010. Transmission of sign languages in the Nordic countries. In Diane Brentari, editor, *Sign languages: A Cambridge language survey*, chapter 4, pages 74–94. Cambridge University Press, New York, NY.

Carl Börstell, Johanna Mesch, and Lars Wallin. 2014. Segmenting the Swedish Sign Language Corpus: On the possibilities of using visual cues as a basis for syntactic segmentation. In Onno Crasborn, Eleni Efthimiou, Evita Fotinea, Thomas Hanke, Jette Kristoffersen, and Johanna Mesch, editors, *Proceedings of the 6th Workshop on the Representation and Processing of Sign Languages: Beyond the Manual Channel*, pages 7–10, Paris. European Language Resources Association (ELRA).

Carl Börstell, Mats Wirén, Johanna Mesch, and Moa Gärdenfors. 2016. Towards an annotation of syntactic structure in Swedish Sign Language. In Eleni Efthimiou, Stavroula-Evita Fotinea, Thomas Hanke, Julie Hochgesang, Jette Kristoffersen, and Johanna Mesch, editors, *Proceedings of the 7th Workshop on the Representation and Processing of Sign Languages: Corpus Mining*, pages 19–24, Paris. European Language Resources Association (ELRA).

Tommi Jantunen, Outi Pippuri, Tuija Wainio, Anna Puupponen, and Jorma Laaksonen. 2016. Annotated video corpus of FinSL with Kinect and computer-vision data. In Eleni Efthimiou, Stavroula-Evita Fotinea, Thomas Hanke, Julie Hochgesang, Jette Kristoffersen, and Johanna Mesch, editors, *Proceedings of the 7th Workshop on the Representation and Processing of Sign Languages: Corpus Mining*, pages 93–100, Paris. European Language Resources Association (ELRA).

Trevor Johnston. 2014. The reluctant oracle: Adding value to, and extracting of value from, a signed language corpus through strategic annotations. *Corpora*, 9(2):155–189.

Johanna Mesch and Lars Wallin. 2015. Gloss annotations in the Swedish Sign Language Corpus. *International Journal of Corpus Linguistics*, 20(1):103–121.

Johanna Mesch, Lars Wallin, Anna-Lena Nilsson, and Brita Bergman. 2012. Dataset. Swedish Sign Language Corpus project 2009–2011 (version 1).

Johanna Mesch. 2012. Swedish Sign Language Corpus. *Deaf Studies Digital Journal*, 3.

Johanna Mesch. 2016. Annotated files for the Swedish Sign Language Corpus. Version 4.

Joakim Nivre, Željko Agić, Lars Ahrenberg, Maria Jesus Aranzabe, Masayuki Asahara, Aitziber Atutxa, Miguel Ballesteros, John Bauer, Kepa Bengoetxea, Yevgeni Berzak, Riyaz Ahmad Bhat, Eckhard Bick, Carl Börstell, Cristina Bosco, Gosse Bouma, Sam Bowman, Gülşen Cebirolu Eryiit, Giuseppe G. A. Celano, Fabricio Chalub, Çar Çöltekin, Miriam Connor, Elizabeth Davidson, Marie-Catherine de Marneffe, Arantza Diaz de Ilarraza, Kaja Dobrovoljc, Timothy Dozat, Kira Droganova, Puneet Dwivedi, Marhaba Eli, Tomaž Erjavec, Richárd Farkas, Jennifer Foster, Claudia Freitas, Katarína Gajdošová, Daniel Galbraith, Marcos Garcia, Moa Gärdenfors, Sebastian Garza, Filip Ginter, Iakes Goenaga, Koldo Gojenola, Memduh Gökrmak, Yoav Goldberg, Xavier Gómez Guinovart, Berta Gonzáles Saavedra, Matias Grioni, Normunds Grūzītis, Bruno Guillaume, Jan Hajič, Linh Hà M, Dag Haug, Barbora Hladká, Radu Ion, Elena Irimia, Anders Johannsen, Fredrik Jørgensen, Hüner Kaşkara, Hiroshi Kanayama, Jenna Kanerva, Boris Katz, Jessica Kenney, Natalia Kotsyba, Simon Krek, Veronika Laippala, Lucia Lam, Phng Lê Hng, Alessandro Lenci, Nikola Ljubešić, Olga Lyashevskaya, Teresa Lynn, Aibek Makazhanov, Christopher Manning, Cătălina Mărănduc, David Mareček, Héctor Martínez Alonso, André Martins, Jan Mašek, Yuji Matsumoto, Ryan McDonald, Anna Missilä, Verginica Mititelu, Yusuke Miyao, Simonetta Montemagni, Keiko Sophie Mori, Shunsuke Mori, Bohdan Moskalevskyi, Kadri Muischnek, Nina Mustafina, Kaili Müürisep, Lng Nguyn Th, Huyn Nguyn Th Minh, Vitaly Nikolaev, Hanna Nurmi, Petya Osenova, Robert Östling, Lilja Øvrelid, Valeria Paiva, Elena Pascual, Marco Passarotti, Cenel-Augusto Perez, Slav Petrov, Jussi Piitulainen, Barbara Plank, Martin Popel, Lauma Pretkalnia, Prokopis Prokopidis, Tiina Puolakainen, Sampo Pyysalo, Alexandre Rademaker, Loganathan Ramasamy, Livy Real, Laura Rituma, Rudolf Rosa, Shadi Saleh, Baiba Saulīte, Sebastian Schuster, Wolfgang Seeker, Mojgan Seraji, Lena Shakurova, Mo Shen, Natalia Silveira, Maria Simi, Radu Simionescu, Katalin Simkó, Mária Šimková, Kiril Simov, Aaron Smith, Carolyn Spadine, Alane Suhr, Umut Sulubacak, Zsolt Szántó, Takaaki Tanaka, Reut Tsarfaty, Francis Tyers, Sumire Uematsu, Larraitz Uria, Gertjan van Noord, Viktor Varga, Veronika Vincze, Lars Wallin, Jing Xian Wang, Jonathan North Washington, Mats Wirén, Zdeněk Žabokrtský, Amir Zeldes, Daniel Zeman, and Hanzhi Zhu. 2016a. Universal dependencies 1.4. LINDAT/CLARIN digital library at the Institute of Formal and Applied Linguistics, Charles University in Prague.

Joakim Nivre, Marie-Catherine de Marneffe, Filip Ginter, Yoav Goldberg, Jan Hajic, Christopher D. Manning, Ryan McDonald, Slav Petrov, Sampo Pyysalo, Natalia Silveira, Reut Tsarfaty, and Daniel Zeman. 2016b. Universal dependencies v1: A multilingual treebank collection. In Nicoletta Calzolari (Conference Chair), Khalid Choukri, Thierry Declerck, Sara Goggi, Marko Grobelnik, Bente Maegaard, Joseph Mariani, Helene Mazo, Asuncion Moreno, Jan Odijk, and Stelios Piperidis, editors, *Proceedings of the Tenth International Conference on Language Resources and Evaluation (LREC 2016)*, Paris, France, may. European Language Resources Association (ELRA).

Robert Östling, Carl Börstell, and Lars Wallin. 2015. Enriching the Swedish Sign Language Corpus with part of speech tags using joint Bayesian word alignment and annotation transfer. In Beata Megyesi, editor, *Proceedings of the 20th Nordic Conference on Computational Linguistics (NODALIDA 2015), NEALT Proceedings Series 23*, pages 263–268, Vilnius. ACL Anthology.

Mikael Parkvall. 2015. *Sveriges språk i siffror: vilka språk talas och av hur många?* Språkrådet.

Paweł Rutkowski and Sylwia Łozińska. 2016. Argument linearization in a three-dimensional grammar: A typological perspective on word order in Polish Sign Language (PJM). *Journal of Universal Language*, 17(1):109–134.

Milan Straka, Jan Hajič, Jana Straková, and Jan Hajič jr. 2015. Parsing universal dependency treebanks using neural networks and search-based oracle. In *Proceedings of Fourteenth International Workshop on Treebanks and Linguistic Theories (TLT 14)*, December.

Milan Straka, Jan Hajič, and Straková Jana. 2016. UD-Pipe: trainable pipeline for processing CoNLL-U files performing tokenization, morphological analysis, pos tagging and parsing. In *Proceedings of the Tenth International Conference on Language Resources and Evaluation (LREC'16)*, Paris, France, May. European Language Resources Association (ELRA).

Myriam Vermeerbergen, Lorraine Leeson, and Onno Crasborn, editors. 2007. *Simultaneity in signed languages: Form and function.* John Benjamins, Amsterdam/Philadelphia, PA.

Peter Wittenburg, Hennie Brugman, Albert Russel, Alex Klassmann, and Han Sloetjes. 2006. ELAN: A professional framework for multimodality research. In *Proceedings of the 5th International Conference on Language Resources and Evaluation (LREC 2006)*, pages 1556–1559.

Services for Text Simplification and Analysis

Johan Falkenjack, Evelina Rennes, Daniel Fahlborg, Vida Johansson, Arne Jönsson
Linköping University and RISE SICS East AB
Linköping, Sweden
johan.falkenjack@liu.se, evelina.rennes@liu.se, arne.jonsson@liu.se

Abstract

We present a language technology service for web editors' work on making texts easier to understand, including tools for text complexity analysis, text simplification and text summarization. We also present a text analysis service focusing on measures of text complexity.

1 Introduction

Our research on digital inclusion has resulted in a variety of tools for making texts easier to understand, including an automatic text summarizer (Smith and Jönsson, 2011a; Smith and Jönsson, 2011b), syntactic (Rennes and Jönsson, 2015) and lexical (Keskisärkkä and Jönsson, 2013; Johansson and Rennes, 2016) simplification, and a number of measures of text complexity (Falkenjack et al., 2013; Falkenjack and Jönsson, 2014). In the project TECST[1] (Text Complexity and Simplification Toolkit) we developed a web service that integrated all these tools and made them easily available for producers of easy-to-read texts. The service can also be used by end users, i.e. anyone wanting to make a text easier to comprehend. Similar systems exist for other languages, such as Spanish (Saggion et al., 2015), Brazilian Portuguese (Scarton et al., 2010) and English (Lee et al., 2016).

The set of text complexity measures provided by the TECST service is limited to a subset of features that is meant to be easily understandable by non-linguists. The complete set of features has instead been made available in the separate service SCREAM[2]. All services presented in this paper can also be accessed through the SAPIS REST API (Fahlborg and Rennes, 2016). In what follows we will first present the features included in SCREAM and continue with the tools included in TECST.

2 Text analysis

All tools in TECST use Stagger (Östling, 2013) for tagging and MaltParser (Nivre et al., 2007) for parsing. We have also implemented support for the OpenNLP part-of-speech tagger (Morton et al., 2005) and older versions of MaltParser.

3 SCREAM – Text complexity features

SCREAM currently comprises 117 features.

3.1 Shallow features

Shallow text features are features that can be extracted after tokenization by simply counting words and characters. They include:

MWLC Mean word length calculated as the average number of characters per word.

MWLS Mean word length calculated as the average number of syllables per word. The number of syllables is approximated by counting the number of vowels.

MSL Mean sentence length calculated as the average number of words per sentence.

3.2 Lexical features

Our lexical features are based on categorical word frequencies extracted after lemmatization and calculated using the basic Swedish vocabulary SweVoc (Heimann Mühlenbock, 2013). SweVoc is somewhat comparable to the list used in the classic Dale-Chall formula for English (Dale and Chall, 1949). Though developed for similar purposes, special sub-categories have been added (of which three are specifically considered). The following frequencies are calculated:

---

[1]http://www.ida.liu.se/projects/scream/
webapp/

[2]http://www.ida.liu.se/projects/scream/
webapp/analysis/index.html

Proceedings of the 21st Nordic Conference of Computational Linguistics, pages 309–313,
Gothenburg, Sweden, 23-24 May 2017. ©2017 Linköping University Electronic Press

SweVocC SweVoc lemmas fundamental for communication (category C).

SweVocD SweVoc lemmas for everyday use (category D).

SweVocH SweVoc other highly frequent lemmas (category H).

SweVocT Unique, per lemma, SweVoc words (all categories, including some not mentioned above) per sentence.

3.3 Morpho-syntactic features

The morpho-syntactic features concern a morphology based analysis of text. The analysis relies on previously part-of-speech annotated text, which is investigated with regard to the following features:

UnigramPOS Unigram probabilities for 26 different parts-of-speech tags in the document, i.e. the ratio of each part-of-speech, on a per token basis, as individual attributes. Such a unigram language model based on part-of-speech, and similar metrics, has shown to be a relevant feature for readability assessment for English (Heilman et al., 2007; Petersen, 2007; Dell'Orletta et al., 2011). The tag set used is collected from the Stockholm-Umeå Corpus (Ejerhed et al., 2006).

RatioContent The ratio of content words (nouns, verbs, adjectives and adverbs), on a per token basis, in the text. Such a metric has been used by for instance Alusio et al. (2010).

3.4 Syntactic features

These features are estimable after syntactic parsing of the text. The dependency based features consist of:

ADDD The average dependency distance in the document on a per dependent basis. A longer average dependency distance could indicate a more complex text (Liu, 2008).

ADDS The average dependency distance in the document on a per sentence basis. A longer average total dependency distance per sentence could indicate a more complex text (Liu, 2008).

RD The ratio of right dependencies to total number of dependencies in the document. A high ratio of right dependencies could indicate a more complex text.

SD The average sentence depth. Sentences with deeper dependency trees could be indicative of a more complex text in the same way as phrase grammar trees have been shown to be (Petersen and Ostendorf, 2009).

Dependency type tag ratio Unigram probabilities for the dependency type tags resulting from the dependency parsing, on a per token basis, as individual parameters. This is viewed as a single feature but is represented by 63 parameters. These parameters make up a unigram language model and is comparable to the phrase type rate based on phrase grammar parsing used in earlier research (Nenkova et al., 2010).

VR The ratio of sentences with a verbal root, that is, the ratio of sentences where the root word is a verb to the total number of sentences (Dell'Orletta et al., 2011).

AVA The average arity of verbs in the document, calculated as the average number of dependants per verb (Dell'Orletta et al., 2011).

UVA The ratio of verbs with an arity of 0-7 as distinct features (Dell'Orletta et al., 2011). This is viewed as a single feature but is represented by 8 parameters.

TPC The average number of tokens per clause in the document. This is related to the shallow feature average number of tokens per sentence.

PreM The average number of nominal pre-modifiers per sentence.

PostM The average number of nominal post-modifiers per sentence.

PC The average number of prepositional complements per sentence in the document.

TokensPerClause The average number of tokens per clause in the document. This is related to the shallow feature average number of tokens per sentence.

PreModifiers The average number of nominal pre-modifiers per sentence.

PostModifiers The average number of nominal post-modifiers per sentence.

PrepComp The average number of prepositional complements per sentence in the document.

3.5 Text quality metrics

The three most used traditional text quality metrics used to measure readability for Swedish are:

LIX Läsbarhetsindex, readability index. Ratio of words longer than 6 characters coupled with average sentence length.

OVIX Ordvariationsindex, word variation index, which is essentially a reformulation of type-token ratio less sensitive to text length.

NR Nominal ratio, the ratio of nominal word, used to measure formality of text rather than readability, however, this is traditionally assumed to correlate to readability.

4 TeCST

TeCST consists of a subset of the features from SCREAM, the text simplifier STILLETT, and the text summarizer FRIENDLYREADER.

4.1 STILLETT

STILLETT is a rule-based tool for automatic text simplification in Swedish. StilLett was originally developed as an extension of CogFlux (Rybing et al., 2010) that included a set of text rewriting operations (Decker, 2003). The first version of STILLETT (Rennes and Jönsson, 2015) was extended to support additional rules; rewriting from passive to active tense, quotation inversion, rearrangement to straight word order, and sentence split. Due to the inefficiency of phrase based parsers, a new version of STILLETT was developed, now relying on dependencies, providing faster simplification. We are currently working on methods for the automatic extraction of simplification operations based on an aligned corpus of simplified and regular texts (Rennes and Jönsson, 2016; Albertsson et al., 2016). The automatically harvested rules will eventually be included in addition to the existing rule sets.

4.2 FRIENDLYREADER

FRIENDLYREADER (Smith and Jönsson, 2011a; Smith and Jönsson, 2011b) is the automatic text summarizer used in TeCST that extracts the most important sentences in a text based on distributional semantics. It uses a word space model, in this case Random Indexing (RI) (Hassel, 2007; Hassel, 2011) with pre-trained word vectors. Furthermore, to handle long sentences with many words, the mean document vector is subtracted from each of the sentence's word vectors before summarizing the vectors (Higgins and Burstein, 2007). FRIENDLYREADER does not directly use a vector distance metric to select sentences, instead it uses the Weighted PageRank algorithm to rank the sentences (Chatterjee and Mohan, 2007). In this case each vertex depicts a unit of text and the edges between the units represent a connection between the corresponding text units, c.f. TextRank (Mihalcea, 2004). Thus, the importance of a vertex within a graph considers global information from the entire graph, not only the local context of the vertices, as ranks are recursively computed so that the rank of a vertex depends on all the vertices' ranks.

5 SAPIS

SAPIS[3] (StilLett SCREAM API Service) is a back-end solution providing the calculation of text complexity features (SCREAM) and the application of simplification operations (STILLETT) on a remote server. SAPIS is able to present simplification feedback on a sentence level by identifying sentences where any of the rules in STILLETT is applicable. A textual feedback is returned for each sentence that matches any of the patterns given in the simplification rule sets.

SAPIS also provides simple access to part-of-speech tagging and dependency parsing.

6 Conclusions

We have presented a service that integrates a variety of tools aiming to make texts easier to understand. Current work focuses on corpus collection for STILLETT, and interaction design to improve usability and make the measures of text complexity easier to interpret.

Acknowledgments

This research is financed by Internetfonden, Vinnova and SweClarin.

References

Sarah Albertsson, Evelina Rennes, and Arne Jönsson. 2016. Similarity-based alignment of monolingual

---

[3]http://www.ida.liu.se/projects/stillett/
Publications/SAPIS_User_Manual.pdf

corpora for text simplification. In *Coling 2016 Workshop on Computational Linguistics for Linguistic Complexity (CL4LC), Osaka, Japan.*

Sandra Alusio, Lucia Specia, Caroline Gasperin, and Carolina Scarton. 2010. Readability assessment for text simplification. In *Proceedings of the NAACL HLT 2010 Fifth Workshop on Innovative Use of NLP for Building Educational Applications*, pages 1–9.

Nilhadri Chatterjee and Shiwali Mohan. 2007. Extraction-Based Single-Document Summarization Using Random Indexing. In *Proceedings of the 19th IEEE international Conference on Tools with Artificial intelligence – (ICTAI 2007)*, pages 448–455.

Edgar Dale and Jeanne S. Chall. 1949. The concept of readability. *Elementary English*, 26(23).

Anna Decker. 2003. Towards automatic grammatical simplification of swedish text. Master's thesis, Stockholm University.

Felice Dell'Orletta, Simonetta Montemagni, and Giulia Venturi. 2011. READ-IT: Assessing Readability of Italian Texts with a View to Text Simplification. In *Proceedings of the 2nd Workshop on Speech and Language Processing for Assistive Technologies*, pages 73–83, July.

Eva Ejerhed, Gunnel Källgren, and Benny Brodda. 2006. Stockholm Umeå Corpus version 2.0.

Daniel Fahlborg and Evelina Rennes. 2016. Introducing SAPIS - an API service for text analysis and simplification. In *The second national Swe-Clarin workshop: Research collaborations for the digital age, Umeå, Sweden.*

Johan Falkenjack and Arne Jönsson. 2014. Classifying easy-to-read texts without parsing. In *The 3rd Workshop on Predicting and Improving Text Readability for Target Reader Populations (PITR 2014), Göteborg, Sweden.*

Johan Falkenjack, Katarina Heimann Mühlenbock, and Arne Jönsson. 2013. Features indicating readability in Swedish text. In *Proceedings of the 19th Nordic Conference of Computational Linguistics (NoDaLiDa-2013), Oslo, Norway*, NEALT Proceedings Series 16.

Martin Hassel. 2007. *Resource Lean and Portable Automatic Text Summarization.* Ph.D. thesis, ISRN-KTH/CSC/A–07/09-SE, KTH, Sweden.

Martin Hassel. 2011. Java Random Indexing toolkit, January 2011. http://www.csc.kth.se/~xmartin/java/.

Michael J. Heilman, Kevyn Collins-Thompson, Jamie Callan, and Maxine Eskenazi. 2007. Combining Lexical and Grammatical Features to Improve Readability Measures for First and Second Language Texts. In *Proceedings of NAACL HLT 2007*, pages 460–467.

Katarina Heimann Mühlenbock. 2013. *I see what you mean. Assessing readability for specific target groups.* Dissertation, Språkbanken, Dept of Swedish, University of Gothenburg.

Derrick Higgins and Jill Burstein. 2007. Sentence similarity measures for essay coherence. In *Proceedings of the 7th International Workshop on Computational Semantics (IWCS), Tilburg, The Netherlands.*

Vida Johansson and Evelina Rennes. 2016. Automatic extraction of synonyms from an easy-to-read corpus. In *Proceedings of the Sixth Swedish Language Technology Conference (SLTC-16), Umeå, Sweden.*

Robin Keskisärkkä and Arne Jönsson. 2013. Investigations of Synonym Replacement for Swedish. *Northern European Journal of Language Technology*, 3(3):41–59.

John Lee, Wenlong Zhao, and Wenxiu Xie. 2016. A customizable editor for text simplification. In *Proceedings of COLING, Osaka, Japan.*

Haitao Liu. 2008. Dependency distance as a metric of language comprehension difficulty. *Journal of Cognitive Science*, 9(2):169–191.

Rada Mihalcea. 2004. Graph-based ranking algorithms for sentence extraction, applied to text summarization. In *Proceedings of the ACL 2004 on Interactive poster and demonstration sessions*, ACLdemo '04, Morristown, NJ, USA. Association for Computational Linguistics.

Thomas Morton, Joern Kottmann, Jason Baldridge, and Gann Bierner. 2005. Opennlp: A java-based nlp toolkit.

Ani Nenkova, Jieun Chae, Annie Louis, and Emily Pitler. 2010. Structural Features for Predicting the Linguistic Quality of Text Applications to Machine Translation, Automatic Summarization and Human–Authored Text. In E. Krahmer and M. Theune, editors, *Empirical Methods in NLG*, pages 222–241. Springer-Verlag.

Joakim Nivre, Johan Hall, Jens Nilsson, Atanas Chanev, Gülşen Eryigit, Sandra Kübler, Svetoslav Marinov, and Erwin Marsi. 2007. MaltParser: A language-independent system for data-driven dependency parsing. *Natural Language Engineering*, 13(2):95–135.

Robert Östling. 2013. Stagger: an open-source part of speech tagger for swedish. *Northen European Journal of Language Technology*, 3.

Sarah Petersen and Mari Ostendorf. 2009. A machine learning approach toreading level assessment. *Computer Speech and Language*, 23:89–106.

Sarah Petersen. 2007. *Natural language processing tools for reading level assessment and text simplification for bilingual education.* Ph.D. thesis, University of Washington, Seattle, WA.

Evelina Rennes and Arne Jönsson. 2015. A tool for automatic simplification of swedish texts,. In *Proceedings of the 20th Nordic Conference of Computational Linguistics (NoDaLiDa-2015), Vilnius, Lithuania,*.

Evelina Rennes and Arne Jönsson. 2016. Towards a corpus of easy to read authority web texts. In *Proceedings of the Sixth Swedish Language Technology Conference (SLTC-16), Umeå, Sweden.*

Jonas Rybing, Christian Smith, and Annika Silvervarg. 2010. Towards a Rule Based System for Automatic Simplification of Texts. In *Swedish Language Technology Conference, SLTC, Linköping, Sweden.*

Horacio Saggion, Sanja Stajner, Stefan Bott, Simon Mille, Luz Rello, and Biljana Drndarevic. 2015. Making it simplext: Implementation and evaluation of a text simplification system for spanish. *ACM Transactions on Accessible Computing*, 6(4).

Carolina Scarton, Matheus de Oliveira, Arnaldo Candido, Jr., Caroline Gasperin, and Sandra Maria Aluísio. 2010. Simplifica: A tool for authoring simplified texts in brazilian portuguese guided by readability assessments. In *Proceedings of the NAACL HLT 2010 Demonstration Session*, HLT-DEMO '10, pages 41–44, Stroudsburg, PA, USA. Association for Computational Linguistics.

Christian Smith and Arne Jönsson. 2011a. Automatic Summarization As Means Of Simplifying Texts, An Evaluation For Swedish. In *Proceedings of the 18th Nordic Conference of Computational Linguistics (NoDaLiDa-2010), Riga, Latvia.*

Christian Smith and Arne Jönsson. 2011b. Enhancing extraction based summarization with outside word space. In *Proceedings of the 5th International Joint Conference on Natural Language Processing, Chiang Mai, Thailand.*

Exploring Properties of Intralingual and Interlingual Association Measures Visually

Johannes Graën, Christof Bless
Institute of Computational Linguistics
University of Zurich
`graen@cl.uzh.ch, christof.bless@uzh.ch`

Abstract

We present an interactive interface to explore the properties of intralingual and interlingual association measures. In conjunction, they can be employed for phraseme identification in word-aligned parallel corpora.

The customizable component we built to visualize individual results is capable of showing part-of-speech tags, syntactic dependency relations and word alignments next to the tokens of two corresponding sentences.

1 Introduction

In corpus linguistics, statistical association measures are used to empirically identify words that attract each other, i.e. that appear together in a corpus significantly more often than pure change would let us expect. Several association measures have been proposed and motivated in different ways (for an overview see Evert 2004, 2008). What they have in common is that they provide a scale that allows for ordering: from high association to no measurable association to negative association.[1]

Association measures can not only be applied to monolingual corpora, where they help identifying collocations, but also to interlingual relations, in our case word alignments in parallel corpora. In (Graën 2017), we exploit the fact that while some words in parallel texts are regular translations of each other, others are forced by idiomatic constraints. To find these constraints and thus identify phrasemes, we combine intralingual association measures on syntactical relations with interlingual association measures on word alignments.

This paper describes the necessary steps to prepare our corpus, which association measures we defined and how the results can visually be explored through our graphical interface.

2 Corpus Preparation

We extracted parallel texts from the *Corrected & Structured Europarl Corpus (CoStEP)* (Graën et al. 2014), which is a cleaner version of the *Europarl* corpus (Koehn 2005).

For tagging and lemmatization, we used the *TreeTagger* (Schmid 1994) with the language models available from the TreeTagger's web page. To increase tagging accuracy for words unknown to the language model, we extended the tagging lexicons, especially the German one, with lemmas and part-of-speech tags for frequent words. In addition, we used the word alignment information between all the languages (see below) to disambiguate lemmas for those tokens where the Tree-Tagger provided multiple lemmatization options. This approach is similar to the one described by Volk et al. (2016).

On the sentence segments identified (about 1.7 million per language), we performed pairwise sentence alignment with *hunalign* (Varga et al. 2005) and based on that word alignment with the *Berkeley Aligner* (Liang et al. 2006).[2] To increase alignment accuracy, we not only calculated the alignments on the word form of all tokens, but also on the lemmas of content words.[3] For the latter, we mapped the tagsets of the individual languages to the universal tagset defined by Petrov et al. (2012)

---

[1] It is worth mentioning that some association measures do not differentiate between high positive and high negative associations. Our application only uses those that make this difference.

[2] The Berkeley Aligner employs a symmetrically trained alignment model, whereas other word alignment tools such as *Giza++* (Och and Ney 2003) or *fastalign* (Dyer et al. 2013) require an additional symmetrization step for obtaining symmetrical alignments. Symmetric alignment in the first place is to be preferred over symmetrization of two asymmetric alignments (cf. Tiedemann 2011).

[3] Here, we used the word form instead if no lemma was provided.

Proceedings of the 21st Nordic Conference of Computational Linguistics, pages 314–317,
Gothenburg, Sweden, 23-24 May 2017. ©2017 Linköping University Electronic Press

and defined content words to be those tokens that are tagged as either nouns, verbs, adjectives or adverbs.

We used the *MaltParser* (Nivre et al. 2006) to derive syntactical dependency relations in German, English and Italian. As there was no pre-trained model available for Italian, we built one based on the *Italian Stanford Dependency Treebank (ISDT)*.[4] Each parser model uses particular language-specific dependency relations. Universal dependency relations (McDonald et al. 2013) could facilitate the definition of syntactic relations. For our purpose however (see next section), it suffices to identify the direct object relationship of verbs. Moreover, at the time we prepared the corpus, there were no ready-to-use universal dependency parsers available for the languages required. Mapping language-specific parser models to universal dependency relations is not as straightforward as mapping individual tagsets to universal part-of-speech tags (cf. Marneffe et al. 2014).

3 Interlingual Association Measures

We aim at identifying phrasemes, i.e. highly idiomatic multi-word units. In (Graën 2017), we employ the example of support verb constructions consisting of a verb and its direct object, where the verb "supports" the semantics of the expression leaving aside its own. A *walk*, for instance, cannot literally be *taken* or *given* (Spanish: *dar un paseo*, literally *'give a walk'*). Supporting verbs often show a "light" character, hence the alias light verb construction.

Following the example of support verb constructions, we regard all verbs with aligned direct objects in parallel sentences as candidates. There are four relations that can be evaluated: Besides the intralinguistic association measure on the verb and its direct object in each language, we can also measure the association of both verbs and both objects by using the same association measures on the interlinguistic relation of word alignment. While an intralinguistic association measure makes a statement about the relative frequency of two words appearing in a particular constellation in a monolingual corpus, an interlinguistic association measures makes a statement about the relative frequency of two words being aligned in a parallel corpus.[5]

In the – frequent – case that the supporting verbs are otherwise not common translations of each other, i.e. they show little attraction apart from the constellation we are looking at, the interlinguistic association measure of the aligned verbs yields a comparably low score. We exploit this fact and rank all candidates in such a way that for a high rank this verb alignment score is required to be low while all other scores are required to be high.

4 Visual Exploration

Different properties of the well-known association scores make them suited for different tasks and different levels of cooccurrence (Evert 2008, cps. 3–5). It is less clear though, what the characteristics of association on word alignment are. We, therefore, implemented an interface (depicted in Fig. 1) to explore the results of different association measures applied to particular patterns, which are described by syntactic relations and attributes.

This pattern is searched in the corpus, results are aggregated using the lemmas of all tokens and sorted by frequency of such lemma combinations.[6] The user can change the sort criterion to any of the following association measures: t-score, z-score, mutual information (MI), observed/expected ratio (O/E) and O^2/E. Both lemmas can be filtered using regular expressions.

When the user select a combination from the resulting list, the distribution of aligned lemma combinations of all available languages[7] is shown. The same association measures can be employed for sorting.

To explore the individual examples, we set up a visualization that displays the sentence and its aligned counterparts on top of each other. The user can navigate through all the sentences that include the selected linguistic constellation (source and target lemma combinations).

Two kinds of relations can be switched on and off: syntactic dependency relations between the words in both languages and the word alignments. In addition, universal part-of-speech tags are shown if requested. The tokens belonging to one of the lemma combinations are highlighted by

---

[4]http://medialab.di.unipi.it/wiki/ISDT

[5]When calculating association measures, we only take lemmas into account to reduce variation and get more reliable values.

[6]We do this for English, German and Italian as source languages and store the precalculated association measures in a database.

[7]Our corpus comprises alignments between English, Finnish, French, German, Italian, Polish and Spanish.

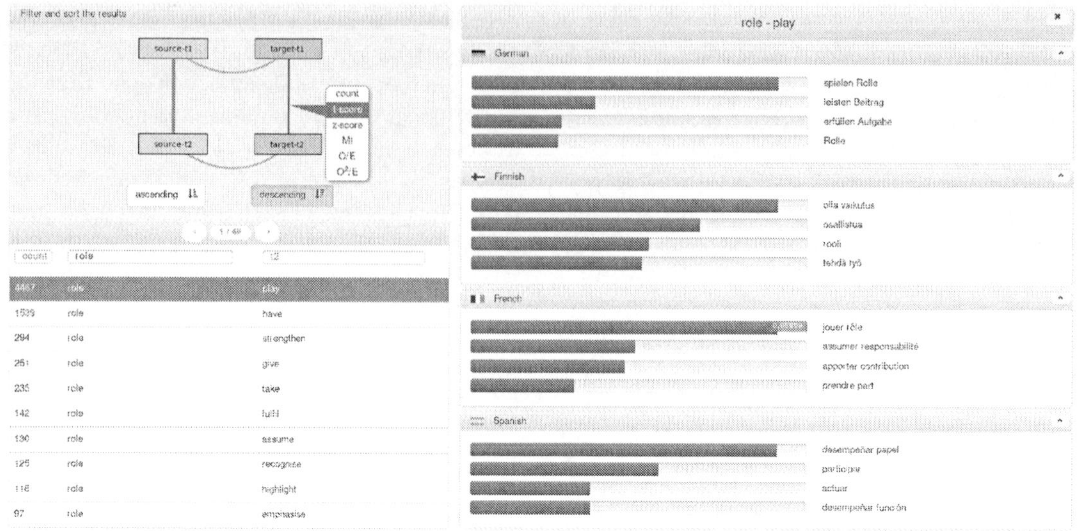

Figure 1: The support verb construction "play a role" and its translation into four other languages. Results in the target languages are sorted using t-score as association measure.

default. The attributes of all other tokens can be made visible interactively or switched on permanently. Integrating all this information on one page facilitates tracing differences in the usage of a particular linguistic schema.[8]

The graphical display is designed to be customizable and reusable. Its output can not only be used interactively, it also serves for printing as the graphics is rendered in Scalable Vector Graphics (SVG) format. Furthermore, the user can adjust the spacing between individual tokens and the gap between both sentences, and reposition dependency labels to achieve the best visual appearance.

5 Conclusions

We built an interface for exploration of different types of association measures. Intralingual association measures are widely used to assess the attraction of pairs of words in a corpus. Interlingual association measures do essentially the same but on word-alignments between corresponding sentences in two languages.

Our interface is an approach to visually explore the properties of different association measures. Results of a particular pattern applied to a source language and the aligned patterns in different target languages can be sorted according to a selection of association measures. Unlike the approach described in (Graën 2017), we do not (yet) provide the option of a weighted combined score.

The interface described here is available for exploring at: http://pub.cl.uzh.ch/purl/visual_association_measures. We also provide the source code of the visualization component there.

Acknowledgments

This research was supported by the Swiss National Science Foundation under grant 105215_146781/1 through the project "SPARCLING – Large-scale Annotation and Alignment of Parallel Corpora for the Investigation of Linguistic Variation".

---

[8]It also helps to detect recurring tagging, parsing or alignment errors.

References

Dyer, Chris, Victor Chahuneau, and Noah A. Smith (2013). "A Simple, Fast, and Effective Reparameterization of IBM Model 2". In: *Proceedings of the Conference of the North American Chapter of the Association for Computational Linguistics: Human Language Technologies*, pp. 644–649.

Evert, Stefan (2004). "The Statistics of Word Cooccurrences: Word Pairs and Collocations". PhD thesis. Universität Stuttgart.

– (2008). "Corpora and collocations". In: *Corpus linguistics: An international handbook* 2. Ed. by A. Lüdeling and M. Kytö, pp. 1212–1248.

Graën, Johannes (2017). "Identifying Phrasemes via Interlingual Association Measures". In: *Lexemkombinationen und typisierte Rede im mehrsprachigen Kontext*. Ed. by Christine Konecny et al. Tübingen: Stauffenburg Linguistik.

Graën, Johannes, Dolores Batinic, and Martin Volk (2014). "Cleaning the Europarl Corpus for Linguistic Applications". In: *Proceedings of the Conference on Natural Language Processing*. (Hildesheim). Stiftung Universität Hildesheim, pp. 222–227.

Koehn, Philipp (2005). "Europarl: A parallel corpus for statistical machine translation". In: *Machine Translation Summit*. (Phuket). Vol. 5, pp. 79–86.

Liang, Percy, Ben Taskar, and Dan Klein (2006). "Alignment by Agreement". In: *Proceedings of the main conference on Human Language Technology Conference of the North American Chapter of the Association of Computational Linguistics*, pp. 104–111.

Marneffe, Marie-Catherine de, Timothy Dozat, Natalia Silveira, Katri Haverinen, Filip Ginter, Joakim Nivre, and Christopher D. Manning (2014). "Universal Stanford Dependencies: A cross-linguistic typology". In: *Proceedings of the Ninth International Conference on Language Resources and Evaluation*. Ed. by Nicoletta Calzolari et al. Vol. 14. European Language Resources Association (ELRA), pp. 4585–4592.

McDonald, Ryan T., Joakim Nivre, Yvonne Quirmbach-Brundage, Yoav Goldberg, Dipanjan Das, Kuzman Ganchev, Keith B. Hall, Slav Petrov, Hao Zhang, Oscar Täckström, Claudia Bedini, Núria Bertomeu Castelló, and Jungmee Lee (2013). "Universal Dependency Annotation for Multilingual Parsing". In: *Proceedings of the 51st Annual Meeting of the Association for Computational Linguistics*. 2, pp. 92–97.

Nivre, Joakim, Johan Hall, and Jens Nilsson (2006). "Maltparser: A data-driven parser-generator for dependency parsing". In: *Proceedings of the 5th International Conference on Language Resources and Evaluation*. Vol. 6, pp. 2216–2219.

Och, Franz Josef and Hermann Ney (2003). "A Systematic Comparison of Various Statistical Alignment Models". In: *Computational linguistics* 29.1, pp. 19–51.

Petrov, Slav, Dipanjan Das, and Ryan McDonald (2012). "A Universal Part-of-Speech Tagset". In: *Proceedings of the 8th International Conference on Language Resources and Evaluation*. Ed. by Nicoletta Calzolari et al. Istanbul: European Language Resources Association (ELRA).

Schmid, Helmut (1994). "Probabilistic part-of-speech tagging using decision trees". In: *Proceedings of International Conference on New Methods in Natural Language Processing*. (Manchester). Vol. 12, pp. 44–49.

Tiedemann, Jörg (2011). *Bitext Alignment*. Vol. 4. Synthesis Lectures on Human Language Technologies 2. Morgan & Claypool.

Varga, Dániel, László Németh, Péter Halácsy, András Kornai, Viktor Trón, and Viktor Nagy (2005). "Parallel corpora for medium density languages". In: *Proceedings of the Recent Advances in Natural Language Processing*. (Borovets), pp. 590–596.

Volk, Martin, Chantal Amrhein, Noëmi Aepli, Mathias Müller, and Phillip Ströbel (2016). "Building a Parallel Corpus on the World's Oldest Banking Magazine". In: *Proceedings of the Conference on Natural Language Processing*. (Bochum).

TALERUM - learning Danish by doing Danish

Peter Juel Henrichsen
Danish Center for Applied Speech Technology
`pjh.msc@cbs.dk`

Abstract

Talerum is an interactive L2 learning environment, here presented publicly for the first time. Talerum is designed for use in Danish language classes throughout the vast and sparsely populated West-Nordic area. In a town-like setting (resembling Copenhagen) the pupil navigates among shops (foods, clothes, tools), a cafe, a school and, importantly, a home base where the game opens and the pupil is welcomed as an exchange student. Through elaborate dialogues with the game characters, the pupil discovers and pursues a *secret mission*. Talerum thus uses elements of game-logic, informal dialogue, and relatively deep semantic analysis to get and keep the attention of the language student of generation IT.

1 Background

Talerum is the last corner stone in the suite of language training tools developed and user-tested by the working group FRASAR. The entire suite is hosted by Iceland University at

`https://taleboblen.hi.is`

Established in 2012, the Frasar group (Nordic computational linguists and didacticians) reaches out to language teachers and pupils in the vast West-Nordic area (Greenland, Iceland, the Faroese Islands) where Danish is taught as a second/third language. The Frasar tools support the productive aspects of language learning, especially informal Danish as used in everyday situations (smalltalk, friends' conversations, greetings, shopping, ...). The tools are browser-based and combine gaming elements, example dialogues (with recordings by native Danes), spoken language exercises (acoustic analysis of pupils' pronunciation), songs, jokes, puzzles and interactivity to stimulate language awareness and prepare the pupil to meet the Danes. See Lihong (2013) and Chik (2014) for perspectives on gaming as a strategy for L2 teaching wrt. individual and social learning.

2 Talerum

At NODALIDA-17 we will demonstrate Talerum, perhaps the most ambitious Frasar tool. Talerum offers a free-style exploration of a virtual suburb with shops, a cafe, a school, and a home base. Pupils enter the game with little or no formal preparation. The intended, but untold, plan is for the pupil to first explore the game universe aimlessly, then uncover a hidden mission, and finally work systematically on solving her task to earn a reward of points and praise. Each step requires (and rewards) concise and relevant Danish-language productions in numerous dialogues with the game characters. While most of the Frasar tools aim at language correctness, Talerum allows the pupil to *do* things with language: present themselves to a stranger, obtain information through dialogue, negotiate with a shop attendant, and even smalltalk. Contrary to most CALL tools (Johnson 2005, Godwin-Jones 2014, Chun 2016) Talerum combines shallow syntax analysis (not penalizing syntax errors) with fairly deep semantic evaluation. See Berns (2012) and Chik (2014) for relevant discussion. Also we admit to being inspired by the classical Larry Laffer game.

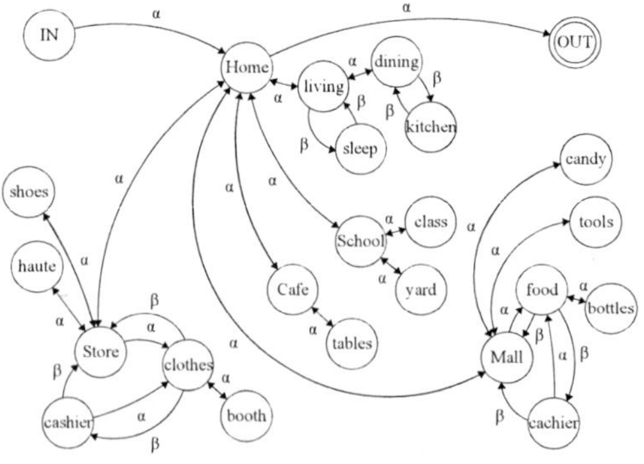

Figure 1. Talerum scenes and gates. All sessions begin and end at the family home (state "Home"). α-gates are always open, β-gates depend on the pupil's current game status.

Proceedings of the 21st Nordic Conference of Computational Linguistics, pages 318–321,
Gothenburg, Sweden, 23-24 May 2017. ©2017 Linköping University Electronic Press

2.1 Interaction modalities

Pupil clicks a gate button. **System** responds by changing the scene (e.g. "Prøverum" in fig.2).

Pupil initiates or continues a dialogue with one of the Talerum characters, e.g. an opener "Dav, jeg hedder Thor", *hello I'm Thor,* or a specific query "har du et par sorte cowboybukser i small?", *do you have pair of black jeans size S?* **System** returns a Danish phrase in response.

Pupil clicks on a former phrase. **System** responds by playing back the phrase in speech synthesis (prosody of Danish vernacular: high speech rate, falling contour, phonetic reductions).

Pupil clicks a help button. **System** responds by supplying context-relevant information, either language assistance (specific Danish terms or phrases, with translations in the pupil's L1) or game-related advice (usually 'indirect', e.g. "I Danmark betaler næsten alle med dankort", *Most Danes pay their bills with the dankort,* a hint to the user to search for and collect a paycard.

2.2 Environments, scenes and gates

Talerum has five main environments, viz. a home base, a school, a café, a department store, and a food court (see fig. 1, Home, School, Cafe, Store, Mall, respectively). The environments serve as hubs, each connecting a sub-system of scenes (lowercased in the graph). Some scenes are static, others dynamic. Static scenes only allow entry and exit (they serve to widen the navigation space and add a little suburb realism, liked by our child testers). Passage through static scenes does not contribute to the game mission and is neither rewarded nor punished wrt. performance evaluation. Dynamic scenes, in contrast, involve dialogue potentially promoting the mission.

The most elaborate interaction takes place in the home environment (living room, sleeping room, kitchen), the food market, and the clothing shop SuperChik (fig. 2). The latter is a second-hand store for fashion items (becoming ever more popular in Copenhagen), the pupil taking the role as a customer enquiring about particular items specifying her wishes and negotiating quality and price. She may even change her mind or ask broader questions not relating to clothing. The system's replies are generated by a range of strategies including canned lines ("Hvad skulle det være?"), phrase

templates ("Vi fører desværre ikke *X*"), and genuinely compositional constructions (introduced below). On the user side, Talerum's spelling control is strict, syntax control relaxed.

As illustrated in fig.2, the three most recent turns remain visible. The line "Dig før: <u>en blå kjole</u>" (*You before: <u>a blue dress</u>*) quotes the pupil (and also links to the TTS playback). The next line is the attendant's turn (here describing a particular dress). The third line "Din tur: ja tak, den tager jeg" (*Your turn: OK, I'll take it*) has just been entered by the pupil, but not sent yet. Pressing "Sig det!" at this point will have the effect of a classical speech act. The attendant will acknowledge the sale transferring the commodity to the pupil's basket, while the gate panel (right side) will change accordingly replacing gate "Megazin" (building exit) by a new gate "Kassen" (*Cashier,* fig.3).

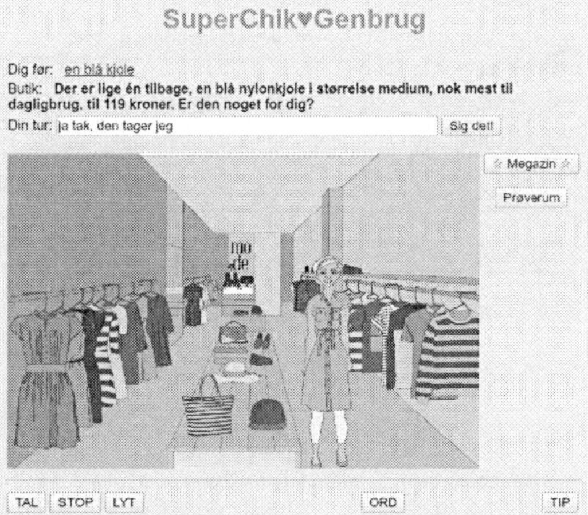

Figure 2. SuperChik, a second-hand clothing shop in the Department Store environment.

Figure 3. The cachier's desk. Access to this scene requires an item in the pupil's shopping basket. Exit from this scene to the Department Store's main hall requires a successful payment.

2.3 Talerum dialogue - an example

Pupil:- Dav, jeg vil gerne se på et par støvler.
[hello, I'd like to see some boots]

Clerk:- Vi fører desværre ikke fodtøj. Var der andet, du kunne tænke dig?
[I'm sorry, but we don't have footware; anything else?]

Pupil:- Så vil jeg gerne have nogle bukser.
[then I'd like to look at some trousers]

Clerk:- Ja tak. Vi har mange forskellige slags, var der noget bestemt du kunne tænke dig?
[we have several kinds, anything in particular you'd like?]

Pupil:- Gerne hvide, og helst af ren bomuld
[white is best, and of pure cotton if possible]

Clerk:- Hvad med den her, en lækker hvid buks i bomuld til 149 kroner. Noget for dig?
[what about this, a nice pair of white jeans size M, at 149]

Pupil:- kan jeg prøve den på?
[can I try them on?]

Clerk:- ja, prøverummet er lige her ved siden af
[certainly, the booth is right next to us]

Pupil:- [kommer tilbage] De er lidt for store
[they're somewhat large]

Clerk:- Her er en skøn bomuldsbuks i small, nok mest til dagligbrug, til 89 kroner. Var det noget?
[what about this lovely cotton, size S, at 89, you like it?]

Pupil:- ja tak, den tager jeg.
[yes please, I'll take them]

Clerk:- mange tak. Du kan betale i Kassen.
[thank you very much, please proceed to the cachier]

2.4 Semantic evaluation

Dialogues in the Home environment follow a predefined sequence of stages where each production may or may not allow a step forward.

In contrast, dialogues in the shops are user-driven, and responses are generated with inference-based methods. The derived discourse-information is accumulated (until the pupil leaves the scene) enabling the use of pronominal anaphor, stepwise clarification of wishes and offers, re-negotiation, and even intermediate off-topic enquiries.

The response generator takes as input (*i*) the pupil's latest production (normalized by filtering out function words etc.), (*ii*) a stack of propositions representing the preceding discourse (may contain contradicting information after re-negotiation, such as "size medium" *and* "larger than medium", giving priority to the most-recent), (*iii*) the set of all entities (goods), (*iv*) a no-go list of entities already rejected or sold, (*v*) a focus entity (only defined if a particular entity is being negotiated). The resulting type-logical expression is mapped to a Danish phrase reflecting its type: a yes/no-question (e.g. "Kan du lide denne her?", *do you like this one?*), a material question ("Hvad kunne du ellers tænke dig?", *what else would you like?*), a statement ("Vi har ikke flere kjoler i den farve", *we have no more dresses in that color*), or a simple boolean (e.g. "Ja tak", *yes please,* or "Nej, desværre", *no we don't*).

The inference system is written in Prolog, the language-specific and www-related parts in Perl, Python and Linux-shell. Client-side code is html5 (including css and JavaScript). The overall architecture is module-based, so most functional modifications require local changes only, such as commodity types and properties, scenes&gates, dialogues, characters, and more. Portation of the entire Talerum to a new language locale only requires rewriting a single module (the phrase database used by the response generator) and replacing the lexicon file (word forms *cum* PoS). More technological details are to be published soon. Do ask us at NODALIDA.

2.5 The challenge

We have tested Talerum with children during the construction phase. Most like shopping around randomly and trying their hand with Danish dialogue for a while. However, after a while they loose interest, so we added a secret challenge. Through dialogue with your roomy (called *Emil* for boy users, *Ida* for girls, same age as the pupil) and family members you learn the details of your task, eventually sending you to town to obtain something (e.g. a present) making someone relieved or surprised. Completing the task will earn you a seasoned appreciation (depending on your time score and efficiency).

3 Concluding remarks

Talerum is currently being tested in folkeskoler and gymnasier in Kalaallit Nunaat, Ísland and Føroyar (pupils 11-14Y). The results (metadata and performance data) will be released in late 2017 and might be interesting for comparative studies. We already know from earlier work (Henrichsen 2015A&B, forthcom.) that Icelandic and Greenlandic pupil groups differ markedly wrt. proficiency, motivatedness, and linguistic challenges faced with the Danish language.

Talerum (ver. 2.0) will be released soon for classroom use. For practical info contact FRASAR's founder and chair Auður Hauksdóttir.

References

Anke Berns, A Gonzalez-Pardo. D. Camacho. 2012. Game-like Language Learning in Virtual 3D Environments. 2012. *Journal of Computers and Education.* 60(1):210-220.

Alice Chik. 2014. Digital Gaming and Language Learning: Autonomy and Community. *Journal of Language Learning and Technology.* 18(2): 85-100

Dorothy Chun, R. Kern, B. Smith. 2016. Technology in Language Use, Language Teaching, and Language Learning. *The Modern Language Journal.* 100(S1):64-80.

Robert Godwin-Jones. 2014. Games in Language Learning: Opportunities and Challenges. *Jorunal of Language Learning and Technology.* 18(2): 9-19.

Peter Juel Henrichsen. 2015A. *Talebob – an Interactive Speech Trainer for Danish.* NODALIDA 2015.

Peter Juel Henrichsen. 2015B. *Taking the Danish Speech Trainer from CALL to ICALL.* NLP4CALL (workshop at NODALIDA 2015).

W. Lewis Johnson, Hannes Vilhjalmsson, and Stacy Marsella. 2005. *Serious Games for Language Learning: How Much Game, How Much AI?* C.-K. Looi et al. (Eds.) IOS Press.

Cao Lihong. 2013. Development and Prospect of Online Language Learning, *Journal of Xiangnan University.* 13(03)

Cross-Lingual Syntax:
Relating Grammatical Framework with Universal Dependencies

Aarne Ranta
University of Gothenburg
aarne@chalmers.se

Prasanth Kolachina
University of Gothenburg
prasanth.kolachina@gu.se

Thomas Hallgren
University of Gothenburg
hallgren@chalmers.se

Abstract

GF (Grammatical Framework) and UD (Universal Dependencies) are two different approaches using shared syntactic descriptions for multiple languages. GF is a categorial grammar approach using abstract syntax trees and hand-written grammars, which define both generation and parsing. UD is a dependency approach driven by annotated treebanks and statistical parsers. In closer study, the grammatical descriptions in these two approaches have turned out to be very similar, so that it is possible to map between them, to the benefit of both. The demo presents a recent addition to the GF web demo, which enables the construction and visualization of UD trees in 32 languages. The demo exploits another new functionality, also usable as a command-line tool, which converts dependency trees in the CoNLL format to high-resolution LATEXand SVG graphics.

1 Introduction

GF (Grammatical Framework, (Ranta, 2011) and UD (Universal Dependencies, (Nivre et al., 2016)) are two attempts to use shared syntactic descriptions for multiple languages. In GF, this is achieved by using **abstract syntax trees**, similar to the internal representations used in compilers and to Curry's tectogrammatical formulas (Curry, 1961). The trees can be converted to strings in different languages by **linearization functions**, similar to pretty-printing rules in compilers and to Curry's phenogrammatical rules. Linearization rules are reversible to parsers (Ljunglöf, 2004).

In UD, the shared descriptions are dependency labels, part of speech tags and morphological features used in dependency trees. The words in the leaves of UD trees are language-specific, and each language can extend the core descriptions to have a set of its own tags and labels. The relation between trees and strings is not defined by grammar rules, but by constructing a set of example trees — a treebank. From a treebank, a parser is typically built using statistical methods (Nivre, 2006).

The abstract syntax trees of GF can be automatically converted to UD trees (Kolachina and Ranta, 2016), by utilizing the shared abstract syntax of GF to allow simultaneous generation of UD trees in many languages. The proposed demo shows tools that use this conversion. An example is shown in Figure 3, whose contents are produced by these tools. The configurations used are defined for the GF Resource Grammar Library (GF-RGL) (Ranta, 2009), which currently contains 32 languages. An inverse conversion from UD to GF is work in progress (Ranta and Kolachina, 2017) and can also be shown in the demo.

All grammars, configurations, and software are available from the GF homepage. [1]

2 Command-line functionalities

The richest set of functionalities is available in the GF shell (the program launched by the command gf). Figure 1 shows a part of the help entry for these functionalities.

The -conll2latex option can be independently interesting for dependency parser community. It is the only tool known to us that converts CoNLL to standard LATEXcode (lines, ovals, etc) with no extra packages required. The same code base also produces SVG graphics from CoNLL.

3 UD trees in the incremental parser interface

This functionality is the easiest one to test, since it does not require any software to be installed, other

---

[1] www.grammaticalframework.org

Proceedings of the 21st Nordic Conference of Computational Linguistics, pages 322–325,
Gothenburg, Sweden, 23-24 May 2017. ©2017 Linköping University Electronic Press

```
options:
 -v                show extra information
 -conll2latex      convert conll to latex

flags:
 -file             configuration file for labels, format per line 'fun label*'
 -output           output format of graph source (dot, latex, conll)
 -view             program to open the resulting file

examples:
  gr | vd -view=open -output=latex                      --generate tree, show on Mac
  gr -number=1000 | vd -file=dep.labels -output=conll   --generate random treebank
  rf -file=ex.conll | vd -conll2latex | wf -file=ex.tex --convert conll file to latex
```

Figure 1: The usage of GF shell command vd = visualize_dependency.

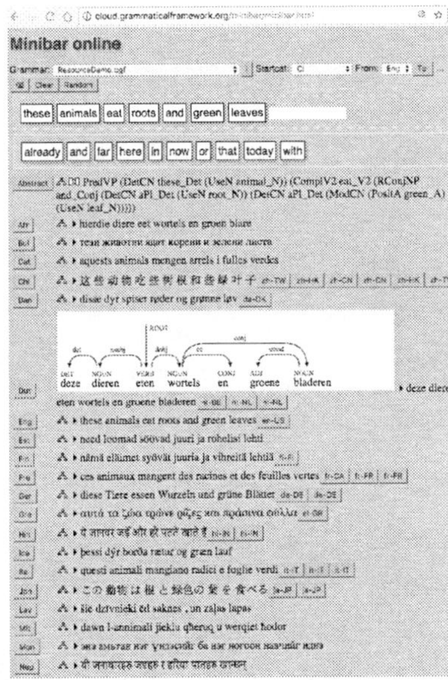

Figure 2: Dependency tree in the "minibar" incremental parser interface. Clicking the tree symbol for each language shows the UD tree. A second click shows the phrase structure tree. (The choice of words in this purely syntax-based generation can be wrong: e.g. the verb "eat" when used for animals should in German be *fressen'*.)

than a web browser. It builds on GF's web-based tool set (Ranta et al., 2010). It is accessible via the GF Cloud[2]. The currently supported grammar option is "ResourceDemo"; see Figure 2.

4 UD trees in the PGF web service

For grammars that have been equipped with a UD label configuration file, UD trees can be requested

from the PGF web service. An example request:

```
http://cloud.grammaticalframework.
org/grammars/ResourceDemo.pgf?command=
deptree&format=svg&to=ResourceDemoEng&
tree=...
```

The GF web demo Minibar allows users to select a grammar, construct grammatical sentences in one language and see translations to the other languages supported by the grammar. UD trees can be displayed next to the translations by clicking on a tree icon (Figure 2).

5 Annotating Configurations

The example in Figures 2 and 3 is produced by the following abstract syntax configurations included in an annotation file:

```
PredVP    nsubj head
DetCN     det head
ComplV2   head dobj
RConjNP   cc head conj
ModCN     head amod
```

A configuration consists of an abstract syntax function together with a list of labels, one for each argument of the function. An extended notion of these configurations is described in (Kolachina and Ranta, 2016). The basic algorithm is a top-down tree-transducer that deterministically maps each argument of a function in the abstract syntax tree to its UD label, generating a connected dependency tree. We refer the reader to Kolachina and Ranta (2016) for more details.

---

[2]http://cloud.grammaticalframework.org/minibar/minibar.html

323

Figure 3: An abstract syntax tree and UD trees in 14 languages. The abstract syntax tree is shown in the middle. The languages corresponding to the UD trees from top-left: Thai, Sindhi, Nepali, French, Icelandic, English, Italian, Bulgarian, Latvian, Japanese, Maltese, Finnish, Greek, Polish. The gf2ud function uses language-independent configurations specified on the abstract syntax to simultaneously generate UD trees for all the languages. Here, we use png dump of the high-resolution originals, due to difficulties in rendering all the fonts in LaTeX.

References

Haskell B. Curry. 1961. Some Logical Aspects of Grammatical Structure. In *Structure of Language and its Mathematical Aspects: Proceedings of the Twelfth Symposium in Applied Mathematics*, pages 56–68. American Mathematical Society.

Prasanth Kolachina and Aarne Ranta. 2016. From Abstract Syntax to Universal Dependencies. *Linguistic Issues in Language Technology*, 13(2).

Peter Ljunglöf. 2004. *The Expressivity and Complexity of Grammatical Framework*. Ph.D. thesis, Department of Computing Science, Chalmers University of Technology and University of Gothenburg.

Joakim Nivre, Marie-Catherine de Marneffe, Filip Ginter, Yoav Goldberg, Jan Hajic, Christopher D. Manning, Ryan McDonald, Slav Petrov, Sampo Pyysalo, Natalia Silveira, Reut Tsarfaty, and Daniel Zeman. 2016. Universal Dependencies v1: A Multilingual Treebank Collection. In *Proceedings of the Tenth International Conference on Language Resources and Evaluation (LREC 2016)*, Paris, France, May. European Language Resources Association (ELRA).

Joakim Nivre. 2006. *Inductive Dependency Parsing*. Springer.

Aarne Ranta and Prasanth Kolachina. 2017. From Universal Dependencies to Abstract Syntax. In *NoDaLiDa Workshop on Universal Dependencies (UDW 2017) (to appear)*, Gothenburg, Sweden.

Aarne Ranta, Krasimir Angelov, and Thomas Hallgren. 2010. Tools for Multilingual Grammar-Based Translation on the Web. In *Proceedings of the ACL 2010 System Demonstrations*, pages 66–71, Uppsala, Sweden, July. Association for Computational Linguistics.

Aarne Ranta. 2009. The GF Resource Grammar Library. *Linguistic Issues in Language Technology*, 2(2).

Aarne Ranta. 2011. *Grammatical Framework: Programming with Multilingual Grammars*. CSLI Publications, Stanford.

Exploring Treebanks with INESS Search

Victoria Rosén
University of Bergen
victoria@uib.no

Helge Dyvik
University of Bergen
helge.dyvik@uib.no

Paul Meurer
Uni Research
paul.meurer@uni.no

Koenraad De Smedt
University of Bergen
desmedt@uib.no

Abstract

We demonstrate the current state of INESS, the *Infrastructure for the Exploration of Syntax and Semantics*. INESS is making treebanks more accessible to the R&D community. Recent work includes the hosting of more treebanks, now covering more than fifty languages. Special attention is paid to NorGramBank, a large treebank for Norwegian, and to the inclusion of the Universal Dependency treebanks, all of which are interactively searchable with INESS Search.

1 Introduction

The richly structured information in treebanks requires powerful, user friendly tools for their exploration. We demonstrate the current state of INESS, the *Infrastructure for the Exploration of Syntax and Semantics* (Rosén et al., 2012a; Meurer et al., 2013). The project implementing and operating this infrastructure is carried out by the University of Bergen (Norway) and Uni Computing (a division of Uni Research, also in Bergen), and is funded by the Research Council of Norway and the University of Bergen (2010–2017).

INESS is aimed at providing access to treebanks to the R&D community in language technology and the language sciences. It is is developed and operated in Norway, and has been integrated in CLARINO, the Norwegian part of CLARIN. One of the project's main activities is the implementation and operation of a comprehensive open treebanking environment for building, hosting and exploring treebanks. The other main activity is the development of a large parsebank for Norwegian.

INESS offers comprehensive services for the construction, management and exploration of treebanks. A modern web browser is sufficient as a client platform for accessing, searching and downloading treebanks, and also for the annotation of LFG-based parsebanks, including computer-aided manual disambiguation, text cleanup and handling of unknown words (Rosén et al., 2009; Rosén et al., 2012b; Rosén et al., 2016). These functions are supported by cataloguing, resource management and visualization (Meurer et al., 2016).

INESS has become a valuable service for research groups who have developed or want to develop treebanks, but who cannot or do not want to invest in their own suite of web services for treebanking. Among the larger treebanks developed by others and made available through INESS are the Icelandic Parsed Historical Corpus (IcePaHC, 73,014 sentences) (Wallenberg et al., 2011), the German Tiger treebank (50,472 sentences with dependency annotation, 9,221 with LFG annotation) (Brants et al., 2002) and the dependency part of the Bulgarian BulTreeBank (11,900 sentences) (Simov and Osenova, 2004).

The remainder of this paper provides search examples in recently added treebanks. In Section 2 we present NorGramBank and illustrate search in LFG treebanks. Search in the UD treebanks is illustrated in Section 3.

2 NorGramBank

NorGramBank (Dyvik et al., 2016) is a large treebank constructed by parsing Norwegian text with a wide coverage grammar and lexicon (NorGram) based on the Lexical-Functional Grammar (LFG) formalism (Bresnan, 2001). Approximately 350,000 words of parsed text have been manually disambiguated and checked using computer-generated discriminants. Through stochastic disambiguation the corpus has been extended to about 50 M word tokens. A grammar coverage test was performed on 500 random sentences, of which 78.4% received gold analyses and 6.8% received analyses with only a single local error (Dyvik et al., 2016).

INESS Search is is a querying system for tree-

Proceedings of the 21st Nordic Conference of Computational Linguistics, pages 326–329,
Gothenburg, Sweden, 23-24 May 2017. ©2017 Linköping University Electronic Press

banks in a variety of formats (Meurer, 2012). It handles search in constituency, dependency and HPSG treebanks as well as in LFG treebanks. The core of INESS Search is a reimplementation of TIGERSearch in Common Lisp and contains numerous extensions and improvements. INESS Search supports almost full first-order predicate logic (existential and universal quantification; negation; quantifier scope can be specified), with the exception of universal quantification over disjunctions (Meurer, 2012, for further details on the query language and the implementation). Partial structures that match variables in queries are highlighted in the interface.

The query language contains some operators that are specific for searching in LFG structures. Among them are the projection operator (to query for c- to f-structure projections), the path operator (to search for f-structure paths satisfying a regular expression over f-structure attributes), the c-command and the extended head operator.

The rich information in NorGramBank allows highly detailed queries. As an example, consider the task — of interest to lexicographers, for example — to study the set of nouns modified by a given adjective, with frequencies. The syntactic expression of such modification may take several forms: attributive position (*a successful result*), simple predicative (*the result wasn't very successful*), object predicative (*they considered the result highly successful*), predicative in a relative clause (*it is difficult to get a result which is completely successful*), etc. Across all these varieties the noun and the adjective always share the value of the feature GEND (gender) by reentrancy in the f-structure representations. This can be exploited in a query like (1), searching for nouns modified in various syntactic ways by *vellykket* 'successful'.

(1) #x_ >PRED 'vellykket' & #x_ >ATYPE & #x_ >GEND #g_ & #y_ >GEND #g_ & #y_ >(NTYPE NSEM) & #y_ >PRED #p

The query says that there exists an f-structure #x_ which has 'vellykket' as the value of the attribute PRED (predicate), has a value for ATYPE (i.e., it is an adjective), and has the value #g_ for GEND. Furthermore there exists an f-structure #y_ which also has #g_ as the value of GEND, has a value for the path (NTYPE NSEM) (i.e., it is a noun), and has the value #p for PRED. The absence of an underscore in the variable name #p signals that its values should be listed in the output, which makes it possible to sort the hits by the predicate values of the modified nouns. This gives the output shown in Table 1, showing the top of the list of 355 nouns found, with frequencies. Clicking on one of the lines in the table brings up a display of the sentences found for that word combination.

Count	#p: value
24	forsøk
23	prosjekt
18	operasjon
15	resultat
14	behandling
12	kveld
10	1
10	landing
9	menneske
9	eksperiment
8	aksjon

Table 1: Top of the list of nouns modified by *vellykket* 'successful'

Figure 1 shows the analysis of a sentence from the search output with the values of the search variables from the query expression highlighted in red: *Ekspedisjonen ble ansett som vellykket* 'The expedition was considered (as) successful'. The example illustrates how the query expression, based on a shared GEND value, finds examples where the modification relation between adjective and noun is mediated by complex syntactic constructions involving object predicatives, passive, control, etc.

3 The UD treebanks

The Universal Dependencies (UD) project is developing cross-linguistically consistent treebank annotation for many languages.[1] The number of UD treebanks has been increasing dramatically. We have imported and indexed all publicly available UD treebanks (up to v2.0), in order to make them searchable with INESS.

Since all treebanks in this large collection follow the same general annotation principles, they are good targets for showing the capability of INESS Search to search across many treebanks at the same time. For instance, an earlier pilot study (De Smedt et al., 2015) illustrated the use of INESS Search to get a quick indication of the correctness and consistency of annotation across all the UD version 1.1 treebanks.

---

[1] http://universaldependencies.org

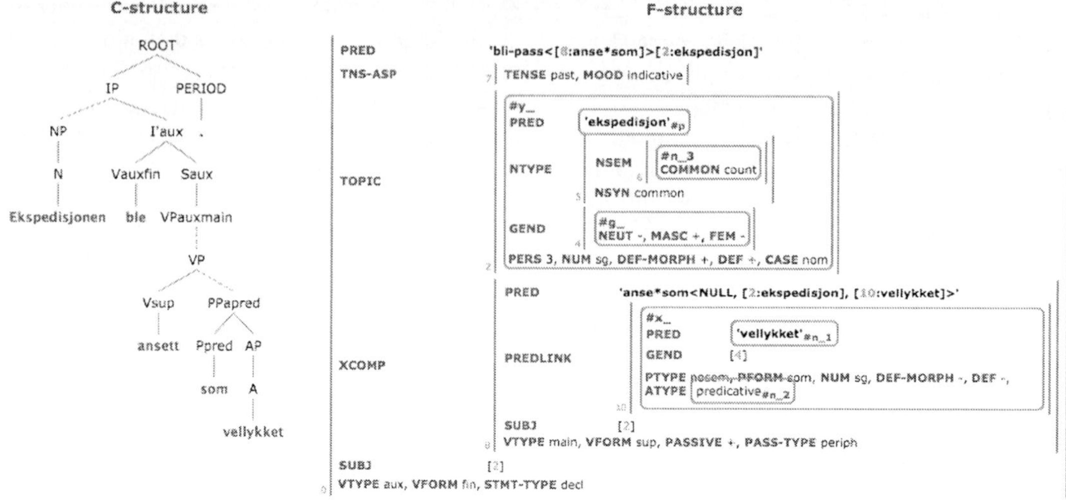

Figure 1: The analysis of a retrieved sentence with the values of the search variables highlighted in red

According to the UD guidelines version 2 on the UD website, the *fixed* dependency relation is one of the three relations for multiword expressions (MWEs). The *fixed* label is to be used for certain fixed grammaticized expressions without any internal structure, but the guidelines do not make it entirely clear whether such expressions must consist of only adjacent words. If one is interested in finding out whether this relation is actually used for annotating non-adjacent words, query (2) can be used to search for binary *fixed* relations that are non-adjacent.

```
(2)  #x >fixed #y & !(#y . #x) & !(#x .
     #y) & !(#x >fixed #z & #z != #y) ::
     lang
```

Query (2) says that there is a node #x which dominates a node #y through a *fixed* relation. Furthermore, it is not the case (the exclamation point is the negation operator) that #y immediately precedes #x, and it is not the case that #x immediately precedes #y. It is also not the case that #x has a *fixed* relation to a node #z which is not equal to #y.

The result in Table 2 shows the top search results obtained by (2) from the UD v1.3 treebanks for German, Italian, Spanish and Swedish, and also illustrates that the global variable lang (for language) can add useful information from the metadata. Figure 2 shows an example of a non-adjacent *fixed* relation in Swedish. The search variables are added in red, making it easy to spot them when inspecting a large dependency structure.

Count	#y: *word*	#x: *word*	globals: *lang*
63	que	de	por
40	ل	ب	ara
23	da	tako	slv
23	sedan	för	swe
22	من	ب	ara
21	quod	quod	lat
19	من	على	ara
19	toe	tot	nld
18	إلى	ب	ara
17	الى	ب	ara
16	menos	a	spa
14	في	ب	ara
13	satunya	satu	ind
12	que	tudo	por
12	ker	zato	slv
11	quod	ita	lat
9	hari	sehari	ind
9	ある	必要	jpn

Table 2: Top search results for nonadjacent *fixed* relations obtained by query (2)

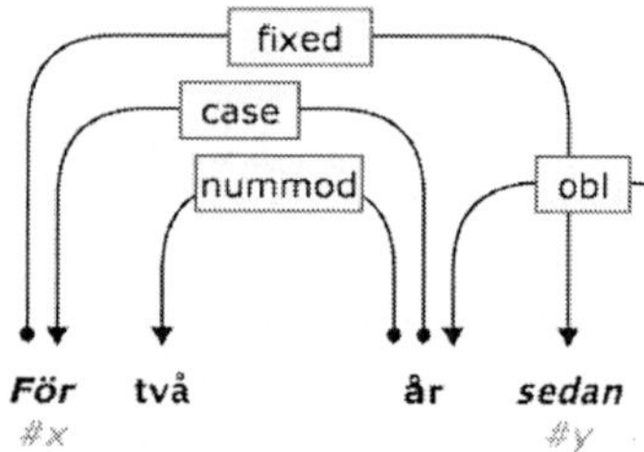

Figure 2: The analysis of a retrieved *fixed* relation with the search variables in red

References

Sabine Brants, Stefanie Dipper, Silvia Hansen, Wolfgang Lezius, and George Smith. 2002. The TIGER treebank. In *Proceedings of the 1st Workshop on Treebanks and Linguistic Theories*, pages 24–41.

Joan Bresnan. 2001. *Lexical-Functional Syntax*. Blackwell, Malden, MA.

Koenraad De Smedt, Victoria Rosén, and Paul Meurer. 2015. Studying consistency in UD treebanks with INESS-Search. In Markus Dickinson, Erhard Hinrichs, Agnieszka Patejuk, and Adam Przepiórkowski, editors, *Proceedings of the Fourteenth Workshop on Treebanks and Linguistic Theories (TLT14)*, pages 258–267, Warsaw, Poland. Institute of Computer Science, Polish Academy of Sciences.

Helge Dyvik, Paul Meurer, Victoria Rosén, Koenraad De Smedt, Petter Haugereid, Gyri Smørdal Losnegaard, Gunn Inger Lyse, and Martha Thunes. 2016. NorGramBank: A 'Deep' Treebank for Norwegian. In Nicoletta Calzolari, Khalid Choukri, Thierry Declerck, Marko Grobelnik, Bente Maegaard, Joseph Mariani, Asunción Moreno, Jan Odijk, and Stelios Piperidis, editors, *Proceedings of the Tenth International Conference on Language Resources and Evaluation (LREC'16)*, pages 3555–3562, Portorož, Slovenia. ELRA.

Paul Meurer, Helge Dyvik, Victoria Rosén, Koenraad De Smedt, Gunn Inger Lyse, Gyri Smørdal Losnegaard, and Martha Thunes. 2013. The INESS treebanking infrastructure. In Stephan Oepen, Kristin Hagen, and Janne Bondi Johannessen, editors, *Proceedings of the 19th Nordic Conference of Computational Linguistics (NODALIDA 2013), May 22–24, 2013, Oslo University, Norway. NEALT Proceedings Series 16*, number 85 in Linköping Electronic Conference Proceedings, pages 453–458. Linköping University Electronic Press.

Paul Meurer, Victoria Rosén, and Koenraad De Smedt. 2016. Interactive visualizations in the INESS treebanking infrastructure. In Annette Hautli-Janisz and Verena Lyding, editors, *Proceedings of the LREC'16 workshop VisLR II: Visualization as Added Value in the Development, Use and Evaluation of Language Resources*, pages 1–7. ELRA.

Paul Meurer. 2012. INESS-Search: A search system for LFG (and other) treebanks. In Miriam Butt and Tracy Holloway King, editors, *Proceedings of the LFG '12 Conference*, LFG Online Proceedings, pages 404–421, Stanford, CA. CSLI Publications.

Victoria Rosén, Paul Meurer, and Koenraad De Smedt. 2009. LFG Parsebanker: A toolkit for building and searching a treebank as a parsed corpus. In Frank Van Eynde, Anette Frank, Gertjan van Noord, and Koenraad De Smedt, editors, *Proceedings of the Seventh International Workshop on Treebanks and Linguistic Theories (TLT7)*, pages 127–133, Utrecht. LOT.

Victoria Rosén, Koenraad De Smedt, Paul Meurer, and Helge Dyvik. 2012a. An open infrastructure for advanced treebanking. In Jan Hajič, Koenraad De Smedt, Marko Tadić, and António Branco, editors, *META-RESEARCH Workshop on Advanced Treebanking at LREC2012*, pages 22–29, Istanbul, Turkey.

Victoria Rosén, Paul Meurer, Gyri Smørdal Losnegaard, Gunn Inger Lyse, Koenraad De Smedt, Martha Thunes, and Helge Dyvik. 2012b. An integrated web-based treebank annotation system. In Iris Hendrickx, Sandra Kübler, and Kiril Simov, editors, *Proceedings of the Eleventh International Workshop on Treebanks and Linguistic Theories (TLT11)*, pages 157–167, Lisbon, Portugal. Edições Colibri.

Victoria Rosén, Martha Thunes, Petter Haugereid, Gyri Smørdal Losnegaard, Helge Dyvik, Paul Meurer, Gunn Inger Lyse, and Koenraad De Smedt. 2016. The enrichment of lexical resources through incremental parsebanking. *Language Resources and Evaluation*, 50(2):291–319.

Kiril Simov and Petya Osenova. 2004. BulTreeBank Stylebook. BulTreeBank Project Technical Report 5, Bulgarian Academy of Sciences.

Joel Wallenberg, Anton Karl Ingason, Einar Freyr Sigurðsson, and Eiríkur Rögnvaldsson. 2011. Icelandic Parsed Historical Corpus (IcePaHC) version 0.9.

A System for Identifying and Exploring Text Repetition in Large Historical Document Corpora

Aleksi Vesanto,[1] Asko Nivala,[2,3] Tapio Salakoski,[1] Hannu Salmi,[2] and Filip Ginter[1]

[1]Turku NLP Group, Department of FT
[2]Cultural History
[3]Turku Institute for Advanced Studies
University of Turku, Finland
`first.last@utu.fi`

Abstract

We present a software for retrieving and exploring duplicated text passages in low quality OCR historical text corpora. The system combines NCBI BLAST, a software created for comparing and aligning biological sequences, with the Solr search and indexing engine, providing a web interface to easily query and browse the clusters of duplicated texts. We demonstrate the system on a corpus of scanned and OCR-recognized Finnish newspapers and journals from years 1771 to 1910.

1 Introduction

The task of finding repeated passages from old newspapers and magazines is relevant to the historians who study the spread of news in time and space. The underlying corpora – in our case scanned and OCR-transcribed newspapers and journals, some over 200 years old – pose a number of technical challenges. Firstly, the size of the corpora is large, in the millions of pages range. And, more importantly, the text produced using OCR is often of poor quality – sometimes nearly unreadable as shown in Figures 1 and 2. This makes the corpora inaccessible to commonly used fast methods such as Passim (Smith et al., 2014) which rely on identifying seed overlaps that are several full words in length, a rare occurrence in our data whose error rate has been estimated to 25-30% in terms of words, depending on period of print (Kettunen et al., 2016).

In this demo, we present a system for identifying text repetitions and forming their clusters using BLAST (Altschul et al., 1990), a software developed to compare and align biological sequences. To browse and search these clusters, we index them using Solr, an open-source search engine, and provide a web interface that is capable of searching and visualizing these repeated text clusters and their associated metadata.

We demonstrate the software and its web interface on a corpus of OCR scanned old Finnish newspapers and journals from years 1771 to 1910, around 3 million pages in total.

2 Software Architecture

2.1 Data Preprocessing and Indexing

NCBI BLAST is built for fuzzy-aligning protein and nucleotide sequences and querying massive sequence databases. As such, it seems an ideal tool for the task, but the assumption of working with biological data is ubiquitous throughout the BLAST codebase, and it cannot be easily used for matching arbitrary alphabets. Therefore, to apply BLAST in our setting, we need to first encode our whole corpus into protein sequences composed of an alphabet of 23 amino acids. As we are limited by the number of distinct amino acids, we can only map the 23 most common lowercase letters in our corpus to distinct amino acids. We then lowercase our corpus and replace all characters using this mapping. Characters that do not have an equivalent in our mapping are discarded – and naturally restored later. This encoding also simultaneously works as a preprocessing method, as the documents have a lot of noise in them in the form of arbitrary characters and spaces. These characters are not among the 23 most common letters, so they are discarded in the encoding process. Interestingly, although space is the most used character in the corpus, we found that discarding spaces nevertheless makes the BLAST query process more than twice as fast and the hits we find are also slightly longer. Once encoded into protein sequences, the documents are indexed using BLAST for a subsequent fast retrieval.

Proceedings of the 21st Nordic Conference of Computational Linguistics, pages 330–333,
Gothenburg, Sweden, 23-24 May 2017. ©2017 Linköping University Electronic Press

cru— i._,i,1 il and malfilly to ligiht mndcr C;, balncr ;as;!iit't fin, the worHd, :,:i(tli (tc\'i; ;il a tio conltiiiie
CihrlC' tiilif'ul ifolli't—'aind flrvant iitc(/.ii lilc's encl. Anlleil. T7jeJZa/nl/ t/h P/ri/?/1J9', iC J—eing now,
dearly hbel ed bhrc— i. i hrci, that this (Chi/i! by Balp— ;lli re.negncirate, ;land grafted into hile l:;,dy of Chritlt
's Chillreh, let iiS ix e thankls unto Alnight y (,odl :or thcle bellneits

crucified, and mlanfully to fight undler hi; banne! aigm~nit fin, the vorldJ, and the devil ; an—d to continuoe Chrift's fa~
ithfal foldlier and ferviant unto his life's end., Amlen. Theni jh~all the Pries3 fay, S E EilN~ G now. dearlyr belovedi
breihren, ththis hi is by Baptifmrgneaean rftdit the bodly of Chrifi~s Chuirch, let us give tha~nks unto Almlighlty God
fat theiie benefits

Figure 1: A hit pair from a run with ECCO dataset. (OCR-scanned books from 18th century)

Multa t\ä@tä fyNlkÄÐsiii kchtalostu ,ct , Äbouil Äsi,3 wic!lä ticiun't>t ,mitää>«, »vaalii luiftti iloista M,m<iä
Tshiragauissa, Âl'elä fi:föf3>i'öi että uiUfatfpäim —uhkaisiloui i Hviarat, miinto fu^tiaani 'fatifefi— fuffotai» lÄÐuja
THi roinin, puutarhassa ja, ipici'ilitsi hwi'tt<iiöii fmmiamcrk^iUi ja anoo» »imilyMla,

Mutta tästä synkästä kohtalosta ei Äbbul Äsib »ielä tiennyt mitään, vaan »ietti iloista elämää TshiraganiSsa. Sekä sis»Stä «tt
ä ulkoapäin uhkasivat «aarat. mutta sulttaani katseli lukkotaisteluja Tfhiiaaanin puutarhassa ja palkitsi voittajan
lunnicnnerleillä ja arÂř vonimityksillä.

Figure 2: A hit pair from Finnish newspapers.

2.2 Clustering

Every document in the corpus, 3 million pages in our case, is subsequently matched by BLAST against the entire indexed collection – i.e. all pairwise comparisons are calculated. The matching document pairs contain the starting and ending offsets from each document, which we use to connect and combine pairs that share a text passage with a sufficient overlap. Because the matching is fuzzy and the texts are very noisy, if the same text passage is reused in a number of documents, each of the identified document pairs will mark a slightly different beginning and end of the passage. For instance, if a passage from a document A is reused in documents B and C, the offsets in A will be slightly different between the A-B and A-C pairs. To deal with the problem, we calculate consensus indexes that combine all passages in one document from individual document pairs that are close to each other – in our example the two passages in A from the A-B and A-C pairs. We do this by averaging the starting and ending indexes of passages that overlap by at least 80%, obtaining consensus passages.

After identifying all the distinct consensus passages for each document, we create a graph with the consensus passages in individual documents as nodes, and edges between corresponding passage pairs. Subsequently, we extract all connected components from the graph, providing us with an initial estimate of clusters of documents that share a passage. The identification of passage clusters through connected components in the graph can be seen as a high recall method. A stray edge – not uncommon in the noisy data – may connect two otherwise disjoint clusters together. To deal with this, we separate these clusters using community detection. To this end, we apply the Louvain method (Blondel et al., 2008) which identifies communities within the connected components of the graph and we subdivide those connected components that have several distinct, highly-connected communities (subcomponents). This removes the likely stray edges that were connecting them. After this subdivision, we obtain the final clusters and the nodes within them are the repeated text passages we seek.

2.3 Finnish newspapers

We applied our system to old OCR-scanned Finnish newspapers and journals from years 1771 to 1910, around 3 million pages in total. We found nearly 8 million passage clusters containing around 49 million repeating passages. We only considered hits that are 300 characters or longer, as the shorter hits would either be too fractioned to be useful or they are just boilerplate text. The most computationally intensive part of the process is running the BLAST queries, which took 150,000 CPU-core hours. Clearly, a dataset of this size requires an access to a cluster computer, which is not surprising given the complexity involved in fuzzy-matching 3 million pages of text against each other. This computationally intensive step however only needs to be performed once and its results can be reused at a later point.

3 Web User Interface

For the user interface, we index our data with Solr. More specifically, we index the data as nested doc-

Figure 3: A screenshot showing the user interface.

uments, where the parent document is the cluster and child documents are the hits within that cluster. Solr is capable of querying the data very efficiently, easily allowing for a swift, real-time search. Solr has built-in support for Apache Velocity Template Engine and out of the box it provides a simple browse page where one can browse the query results. Using this template engine, we implement an easy-to-use interface suitable to the nature of the data.

A screenshot of a result page is shown in Figure 3. At the top, a search field allows a free text search. Below is a field for direct search by cluster number. This will result in all hits that belong to that cluster as well as other information about the cluster, such as average length of hits, number of hits and the year of its first occurrence. On the right, we see a small snippet of the results. For every matching hit we can see the name of the original file, date when that issue was published, the name of the newspaper or journal, URL for viewing the original scanned document online, cluster number and the text itself with the query hits highlighted. Clicking the cluster number link shows all hits, i.e. occurrences of the same repeated text passage, within the cluster. Finally on the left we have a facet view, currently giving an overview of hits from a specific magazine. The rich query language employed by Solr gives us the capability of performing fuzzy and proximity search, which is especially useful in our case of low-quality OCR-recognized documents.

As one would expect from a mature search engine like Solr, querying this large collection of repeated text clusters is effortless and real-time. For instance, querying for *kissa*, the Finnish word for *a cat*, found over 23,000 results, returning the first page of 10 results in 38ms.

4   Conclusions

The ability to identify text repetition in large historical corpora is of great importance to historians, and the problem of fuzzy match in large text collections is of a broader interest in corpus research and NLP in general. We have presented a fully implemented and currently deployed software and web interface to identify repeated text passages in large corpora of poor OCR quality, and present them through a simple web interface. We have shown that the BLAST algorithm works efficiently in identifying regions of similarity in historical text corpora, even in cases where the quality of OCR is extremely low, for instance where the original text has been printed with Gothic typeset (*Fraktur*), or with poor paper and ink quality. The development of new tools for text reuse detection is essential for further enhancement of the use of scanned historical documents, and work with noisy corpora in general.

Acknowledgments

The work was supported by the research consortium *Computational History and the Transformation of Public Discourse in Finland, 1640-1910*, funded by the Academy of Finland. Computational resources were provided by CSC — IT Centre for Science, Espoo, Finland.

References

Stephen F. Altschul, Warren Gish, Webb Miller, Eugene W. Myers, and David J. Lipman. 1990. Basic local alignment search tool. *Journal of Molecular Biology*, 215(3):403–410, Oct.

Vincent D Blondel, Jean-Loup Guillaume, Renaud Lambiotte, and Etienne Lefebvre. 2008. Fast unfolding of communities in large networks. *Journal of Statistical Mechanics: Theory and Experiment*, 2008(10):P10008.

Kimmo Kettunen, Tuula Pääkkönen, and Mika Koistinen. 2016. Between diachrony and synchrony: Evaluation of lexical quality of a digitized historical finnish newspaper and journal collection with morphological analyzers. In *Baltic HLT*.

David A. Smith, Ryan Cordell, Elizabeth Maddock Dillon, Nick Stramp, and John Wilkerson. 2014. Detecting and modeling local text reuse. In *Proceedings of the 14th ACM/IEEE-CS Joint Conference on Digital Libraries*, JCDL '14, pages 183–192, Piscataway, NJ, USA. IEEE Press.

Author Index

Association for Computational Linguistics
209 N. Eighth Street
Stroudsburg, Pennsylvania 18360

ISBN 978-1-5108-4170-3